The Path of Flames

The Path of Flames: Understanding and Responding to Fatal Wildfires is an edited volume covering the complexities of response and recovery issues relative to catastrophic wildfires.

As wildfires become more frequent throughout the world—and the loss of life greater, especially among residents trapped in the path of the flames—it is essential that agencies in fire-prone areas understand the complexity of the response as it relates to finding and identifying the remains of those who perished. While covering wildfire dynamics, risks for vulnerable populations, and the emergency response to wildfires, this book focuses largely on the recovery of human remains within the context of the overall response to mass disasters resulting from wildfires. As such, search protocols, staffing needs, pre-event coordination and organization, and logistical support are addressed. The scientific basis for understanding how fire will affect human remains—as well as how the level of destruction can be interpreted—is also addressed.

Recognizing the multidisciplinary nature of the field, this volume covers forensic issues relating to the recovery of remains, forensic anthropology, DNA analysis, forensic odontology, and forensic pathology. The book also includes contributions from international wildfire response professionals looking at global best practices in wildfire response and human remains recovery. Specifically, several chapters cover the lessons learned from the devastating Camp Fire of 2018 in California that led to the deaths of 85 people. The Camp Fire burned nearly 19,000 structures and was ultimately the most destructive—and deadly—in California's history.

The Path of Flames is a one-of-a-kind reference that serves as a valuable resource for professionals working in the areas of emergency services, search and rescue, law enforcement, fire service, disaster planning and response, victim recovery and identification, and mass disaster and mass fatality response.

Ashley Kendell, PhD, is Associate Professor and Forensic Anthropologist at California State University, Chico (Chico State). She is also a POST-certified instructor who teaches forensic anthropology and archaeology through the Institute of Criminal Investigation. Prior to beginning her position at Chico State, she was a visiting professor at the University of Montana and a forensic anthropologist for the State of Montana. While completing her doctorate at Michigan State University, she worked as a medicolegal death investigator and was a registry diplomate of the American Board of Medicolegal Death Investigators for five years.

Alison Galloway, PhD, D-ABFA, is a board-certified forensic anthropologist and Professor Emerita from University of California, Santa Cruz. She has worked on wildfire recovery including the Camp, Almeda, and Caldor Fires and taught for 12 years with a fatal fire investigation course. She has edited books on human evolution, blunt force trauma, and forensic anthropology and the US judicial system.

Colleen Milligan, PhD, D-ABFA, is Professor and Chair of Anthropology at California State University, Chico (Chico State). She is a board-certified forensic anthropologist and co-director of the Human Identification Lab at Chico State. The Human Identification Lab regularly provides forensic anthropological analysis, recovery services, and mass disaster/mass fatality response services for law enforcement throughout California. Prior to her position at Chico State, she was a fellow with the Department of Homeland Security.

The Path of Flames
Understanding and Responding to Fatal Wildfires

Edited by
Ashley Kendell, Alison Galloway,
and Colleen Milligan

CRC Press
Taylor & Francis Group
Boca Raton London New York

CRC Press is an imprint of the
Taylor & Francis Group, an **informa** business

Designed cover image: TBC

First edition published 2024
by CRC Press
6000 Broken Sound Parkway NW, Suite 300, Boca Raton, FL 33487–2742

and by CRC Press
4 Park Square, Milton Park, Abingdon, Oxon, OX14 4RN

CRC Press is an imprint of Taylor & Francis Group, LLC

Library of Congress Cataloging-in-Publication Data
Names: Kendell, Ashley E., editor. | Galloway, Alison, 1953– editor. | Milligan, Colleen F., editor.
Title: The path of flames : understanding and responding to fatal wildfires / edited by Ashley Kendell, Alison Galloway and Colleen Milligan.
Description: Boca Raton, FL : CRC Press, 2024. | Includes bibliographical references and index.
Identifiers: LCCN 2023018404 (print) | LCCN 2023018405 (ebook) | ISBN 9780367750534 (hardback) | ISBN 9780367766719 (paperback) | ISBN 9781003168010 (ebook)
Subjects: LCSH: Wildfires—Prevention and control. | Emergency management. | Rescue work. | Wildfire fighters. | First responders. | Fires—Casualties.
Classification: LCC SD421 .P24 2024 (print) | LCC SD421 (ebook) | DDC 634.9/618—dc23/eng/20230720
LC record available at https://lccn.loc.gov/2023018404
LC ebook record available at https://lccn.loc.gov/2023018405

ISBN: 9780367750534 (hbk)
ISBN: 9780367766719 (pbk)
ISBN: 9781003168010 (ebk)

DOI: 10.4324/9781003168010

Typeset in Sabon
by Apex CoVantage, LLC

Contents

Foreword

We've all had those moments in our life. Those "How did I get here?" moments that seem to sneak up unannounced. Those moments that are such a bizarre break from "business as usual" they make us question exactly which poor life decisions caused us to arrive here. I remember walking in to my first public meeting for search and rescue and mumbling something about how I like to hike and wanted to help. Some years later, there I was – standing in the wreckage of a house decimated by fire, getting an anatomy lesson from forensic anthropologist Dr. Colleen Milligan as we looked down at the charred remains of the homeowner. I was having one of those moments.

A few days prior, residents of Chico, California stepped outside to witness a large plume of smoke rising from the town of Paradise in what would soon be known as the Camp Fire. By 2018, fighting fire in the WUI was not new for CalFire, nor evacuations for Butte County Sheriff's Office and their Search & Rescue team. However, the speed at which the Camp Fire moved and the magnitude of destruction challenged nearly every aspect of response and recovery efforts. The experience of those on scene tells a harrowing story. If 9/11 is seen as the key turning point in emergency management for manmade disasters, the Camp Fire will be seen as a key turning point for emergency management of wildfire and a wakeup call for those of us who live in rural areas.

RESPONSE

If you've never been behind the fire line, it's hard to describe and even harder to comprehend. Reality is upside-down. While everything might be explained by physics, it seems like the laws of nature no longer apply. The normal color of homes and commercial buildings is replaced with the angry glow of fire as the path of flames take the shape of the former structure, wrapping around whatever studs or structural beams are the last to stand their ground before collapse. Healthy trees burn like newspaper. Meanwhile, everything else is black and white. This includes the midday sky which is black as night when the sun is blocked by smoke.

The experience isn't just visual. Its sensory overload. Large fires approach with a low rumbling sound. Some describe it as a freight train, others as a jet engine. All agree it is ominous. This is replaced by deafening loud snapping and popping noises once the fire gets closer. Think about the sound of the last campfire you sat around roasting smores. Except instead of the relaxing sound of little twigs crackling as the fire boils the moisture out of them, the volume is turned up to eleven as a million twigs, large branches, and entire trees explode or fall to the ground.

The radiant heat from the burning vegetation can be felt from hundreds of feet away. Footage at Camp Fire from Butte County S.A.R. showed propane tanks exploding from that same radiant heat which was literally boiling the liquid gas inside the tanks. These weren't the little five- or ten-pound tanks used for your summer grille out. Rural areas lack access to city gas lines and rely instead on large 500- to 2000-gallon propane "pigs" that explode with enough force to shatter glass and shake emergency vehicles.

Eventually, the flames move downwind from your location or are put out. The ground cools. And recovery efforts begin.

RECOVERY

Emergency management has become increasingly complex. The days are gone where your local volunteer fire department is also your local ambulance crew and your local law enforcement unit who are also your postmaster, dentist, and plumber. To adapt to the complex disasters we face, and the technology used for them, first responders and emergency management teams have had to specialize. This allows for the highest qualified resources to support the varied tasks required to manage a disaster. For structure fire, flood, storm, building collapse, and nearly every bad thing you can think of, the processes and procedures follow a well-known script within the Incident Command System. But that system is challenged when a wildfire of never-before-seen size decimates a rural area.

The Camp Fire recovery was one of the largest non-combat search and rescue missions in modern history. It required a wide range of resources to work together. Urban Search & Rescue Task Forces were needed to assess structure damage, the National Guard for communications and logistics, forensic anthropologists for victim identification, and hundreds of civilian volunteer wilderness Search & Rescue teams to cover the vast wildland urban interface (WUI) around the homes. Coordinating this effort was not without its challenges.

MITIGATION

With all the attention given to the response and recovery of major disasters, it's easy to forget that some of the most important work is often done in times of peace and quiet by those who will never wear a badge or flame resistant nomex suit. Public officials and government agencies have the power to reduce the severity of fire through the planning and funding of mitigation projects. This saves lives.

The general public understands very little about fire suppression. We like to see large planes flying overhead, and the dramatic pictures of the pink fire retardant drops make for great social media posts. But more large air tankers are not going to save the day. Funding projects to create massive fuel breaks give firefighters a chance to make a stand against fast moving fires. Enacting policies that make it easy for residents to clear their own properties and create defensible space buy emergency responders time to get to residential areas before it is too late.

It's not just preparing the areas around one's property that will increase survivability.

PREPAREDNESS

Everyone who lives in the WUI understands the risk. We're constantly reminded to have emergency supplies in our "go bag" packed, important documents uploaded to the cloud, the evacuation routes scouted in advance, and to create our neighborhood emergency buddy system. Our municipalities can be doing the same on a larger scale. Identifying "vulnerable populations" on the map by zip code, district, or neighborhood works fine when you are applying for grants. In an emerging disaster, local emergency operations centers need more detailed information. They need to know where every single group home, care facility, and even individual household with a disabled person is located, and have a plan to get them out of harm's way. Following the Camp Fire, there were stories of nurses and care worker stacking their elderly patients like cord wood in the back of their personal vehicles to run from the fire. Kudos to the care workers for improvising and saving lives. But we can do better.

There are several lies in the age-old tale of "the hero's journey." From documentaries to classic works of fiction like Lord of the Rings, the tale follows a predictable path as the hero leaves home, goes on an adventure in the name of doing good, and returns as a better person. Yet our own real world heroes are not so lucky. Rural fire departments, facing declines in funding, are reducing hours of service or closing their stations. This puts a strain on nearby small town fire departments who have to expand their areas of service. Law enforcement agencies have vacancies to fill as deputies are lured away by big city salaries. Search and rescue teams have seen a massive increase in deployments as more urbanites are drawn to outdoor recreation. Across the board, our real world heroes are underfunded, underappreciated, and exhausted. We need a plan to better support them.

At the Camp Fire, more than one elected official or leader in a uniform with stripes and chevrons told me, "We're writing the book," in reference to our improvised response and recovery efforts at that event. The text in your hands right now represents the first pass at that book. Please don't take it lightly. I and many first responders are relying on its implementation as key to the third part of our own hero's journey – the safe return home.

Scott Beesley is a Certified Financial Planner® who volunteers as Chair of Nevada County Coalition of Firewise Communities, Grass Valley California Disaster Airlift Response Team Operations Director, and is a wilderness first responder for his local search and rescue team. He is a graduate student in the M.S. in Data Analytics & Policy program at Johns Hopkins University completing his capstone project in disaster management policy analysis. He lives on 20 acres in the woods with his wife Lindy and rescue dog Hayduke. Their go bags are packed.

Contributors

Deirdre Amaro, MD, is a board-certified forensic pathologist and Assistant Professor in the Department of Pathology and Anatomical Sciences at the University of Missouri School of Medicine.

Eric Bartelink is a board-certified forensic anthropologist and Professor of Anthropology at California State University, Chico. He is the co-director of the Human Identification Laboratory and assists agencies in California with forensic scene recovery and casework. He has co-authored and co-edited books in forensic anthropology and biological anthropology, and his research focuses on applications of stable isotope analysis, trauma analysis, and the study of burned remains.

Scott Beesley is a Certified Financial Planner® who volunteers as the chair of Nevada County Coalition of Firewise Communities and director of Grass Valley California Disaster Airlift Response Team Operations, and he is a wilderness first responder for Nevada County Sheriff's Search and Rescue. He is a grad student in the MS in data analytics and policy program at Johns Hopkins University completing his capstone project in disaster management policy analysis.

David R. Bibby has been a member of Amador County Search and Rescue for seven years. During this time, he has typically been a "ground pounder," but he has also done ATV, communications, overhead, and tracking and worked as a flanker for the K9 units. He received the SARTECH II certification in 2018. During his employment with Operating Engineers #3 JATC, he was the safety training instructor. He was a certified instructor in OSHA 10 and 30, HAZMAT, and first aid. During this time, he also received training in the National Incident Management System, ICS for Single Resources and Initial Action Incident, and ICS for Confined Spaces and Fall Protection. As a member of Amador SAR, he worked on the Camp Fire in 2018.

Lt. Joshua Brazzi began his law enforcement career in Glenn County working as a correctional deputy, a patrol deputy, and then a narcotics agent with a multi-jurisdictional narcotics task force. While working for Butte County, Lieutenant Brazzi worked patrol as a deputy and supervised the Designated Area Deputy Team as a sergeant, the Felony Investigations Unit as a sergeant, and the SWAT Team as a SWAT team leader. Currently, he oversees the Operations Division (patrol, dispatch, SWAT, EOD, K9). He has been assigned to numerous emergencies, including the Oroville Dam Spillway incident, the Camp Fire, the Bear Fire (North Complex Fire), and the Dixie Fire, while working in the Operations Division of the Emergency Management Team.

Jacquelyn Chase is Professor Emerita of Geography and Planning at California State University, Chico. She has studied land use planning and community organization in the wildland-urban interface in Butte County. She has been researching the displacement of people by the Camp Fire and is investigating the rebuild process in Paradise, California.

Stephen Collins has worked for the Butte County Sheriff's Office (BCSO) for 26 years. He was responsible for the search and recovery operations during the Camp Fire. He served as the emergency manager from 2019 to 2022 for BCSO. He has also been the incident commander for the North Complex Fire in 2020 and provided support to Plumas County during the Dixie Fire in 2021. He has presented the wildfire response lessons learned to the San Diego Sheriff's Department in 2022. He has taught Critical Incident and Terrorism Awareness at Butte College Law Enforcement Academies.

Damon P. Coppola is a systems engineer and disaster risk management specialist with over 25 years of experience assisting clients in the public, non-profit, and private sectors. Mr. Coppola has supported the development of an extensive array of national and global disaster risk management policy, programs, and guidance currently in place, including the National Disaster Recovery Framework and the Sendai Framework for Disaster Risk Reduction. He has worked directly with national governments in all regions of the world, including to conduct response and recovery assessments of some of the most devastating disaster events.

The late **John D. DeHaan**, PhD, FABC, CFI, FSSDip, FIFireE, passed away on May 7, 2022, shortly after completing this chapter. John began his career in 1970 as a criminalist, ultimately becoming the program manager for the California Criminalistics Institute in Sacramento. In 1998, he set up his own company, Fire-Ex Forensics Inc., providing consulting advice in criminal and civil cases and bringing his expertise and systematic and methodical approach in fire- and explosion-related forensic science to a new arena. He authored *Forensic Fire Scene Investigation* and the newer editions of *Kirk's Fire Investigation*, as well as many journal articles detailing correct procedures and debunking common myths in fire investigation.

Tim Enright is a certified fire investigator with the International Association of Arson Investigators. He has worked for 34 years in the fire service and spent almost 27 years at the City of Stockton Fire Department (CA), where he was the full-time fire investigator from 2005 until he retired in 2017. During his career, he investigated structure fires, vehicle fires, and wildland fire incidents. Tim has taught fire investigation classes to include wildland origin and cause determination, fatal fire investigation, and vehicle and structure fire investigation. Tim continues to teach and work in the industry after retirement.

Gillian Fowler, PhD, is a forensic anthropologist and Senior Lecturer at the University of Lincoln. She has acted as an expert in forensic anthropology for UK police forces in investigations of missing persons, suspicious deaths, murder, clandestine grave search, and location and recovery for 12 years. She has extensive international experience working in the human rights field, including six years working as the forensic identification coordinator and a forensic anthropology expert for the Guatemalan Forensic Anthropology Foundation (FAFG), providing reports that have been submitted as evidence in genocide and crimes against humanity trials in Guatemala.

Kim Gin is a skilled medicolegal death investigator with over 24 years of experience in the field and served as the coroner for nine years. She worked on mass identification for wildfire victims and managed the morgue operations during the Camp Fire in 2018. She also worked on mass identification of the Santa Barbara Dive Boat fire victims in 2019. She teaches mass fatality management classes and has taught criminal justice classes for 14 years.

Tim Gocha is the associate director of the Forensic Anthropology Center at Texas State University. Prior to this appointment, he was a forensic anthropologist in southern Nevada. He has assisted with victim recovery and/or identification from several mass fatality events including the deadliest hot air balloon crash in US history, the deadliest mass shooting in US history, the deadliest wildfire in California history, and the ongoing humanitarian crisis of migrant deaths along the US-Mexico border.

Jason Hadjuk began his career in emergency services in 1990 as a State of California lifeguard. He was hired as a firefighter/paramedic with the City of Santa Cruz, where he worked his way through the ranks and retired as the fire chief in 2021. He served in multiple operational and management positions within the fire service at both the local and state level. He was the incident commander for the type 3 management team brought in to assist with the CZU Fire before transitioning to a type 1 team.

Lt. Jason Hail began his career in law enforcement with the Butte County Sheriff's in 1996, working in a multitude of assignments. Always passionate about in-depth investigation, his career path led to specializing in crime scene investigation, digital forensics, investigation on drug-endangered children, death investigation, and other major crimes. Lieutenant Hail has spent more than a decade working as a detective sergeant in major crimes, managing evidence staff. In 2019, he was promoted to be the chief deputy coroner for Butte County. In 2021, he was honored to be a part of the California POST committee putting on the first ever Detective Training Symposium for Investigators in the State of California.

Carla Halford retired as a fire captain with CAL FIRE Academy after 30 years of service. Since then, she is able to devote more time to working with canines in a number of arenas. As a seven-year member of Amador Search and Rescue, she works with her mission-ready area K9 Jax. For the past five years, she has also been a member of the California Rescue Dog Association (CARDA).

Casey Hegel is aluma of California State University, Chico. Her thesis focused on a spatial analysis of the fatalities from the Camp Fire. She has assisted with wildfire recoveries, including the Camp Fire. She has a geospatial certificate, an MA in anthropology from Chico State, and a BA in anthropology from Humboldt State University.

Chelsey Juarez is Associate Professor in Biological Anthropology at California State University Fresno and the director of the Fresno State Forensic Anthropology Laboratory. She has worked on wildfire recovery, including the 2020 Creek Fire, and analyzed over

30 cases of burned human remains from fatal fire deaths across multiple states. She is a co-author of the FADAMA database and has co-authored several publications on trauma, fire classification, isotope analysis of provenance, and methods accuracy in forensic anthropology.

Carolyn G. La Jeunesse is a field traumatologist, thanatologist, veterinarian, compassion fatigue educator, spiritual director, and crisis and medical communications specialist. She contributes both biomedical and behavioral health expertise in crises and on domestic and international disaster and humanitarian assistance efforts around the world, including in post-conflict Liberia; on multinational initiatives in Oceania, Latin America, the Caribbean, and Africa; and during the Camp Fire, the SR 530 landslide, and the COVID-19 pandemic. She is a 2014–2015 alumna Congressional Science and Technology Policy fellow where she worked primarily on the 2014–2015 West Africa Ebola epidemic response. She is the founder and principal consultant for La Jeune Consulting.

Gaille MacKinnon has been Consultant in Forensic Anthropology and Archaeology since 1998 and is currently the only dually accredited senior reporting forensic anthropologist and archaeologist in the United Kingdom. She has worked for an extensive number of United Kingdom police forces, the Special Investigation Branch of the Royal Military Police, and three forensic science service providers on cases of terrorist incidents, disaster victim identification, murder, suspicious and unexplained deaths, child abduction, historic child abuse, slavery and servitude, missing persons, and clandestine grave search, location, and recovery.

Jason Martin is a Cal Fire Incident Management Team 4 plans chief. He has worked as a type 1 plans chief on incidents such as the Camp, Thomas, Boles, and the Soberanes Fires, developing techniques to mitigate incidents using the incident command system while leveraging emergent technologies to better coordinate resources. He has been part of the development team for long-term planning frameworks, such as the Statewide Tree Mortality Response Plan, Oroville Dam Flood Contingency Framework, and the Montecito Flood Debris Flow Response Framework. Jason has been a type 1 incident management teams member for the past 15 years.

Samuel Mijal holds a bachelor of science in anthropology from Arizona State University. He has worked on wildfire recovery, including the Camp Fire.

Brad Milliken is a former officer and search and rescue team leader of the United States Coast Guard. He has spent the past decade supporting planning and information management activities in federal and international emergency and disaster management in various leadership roles at the National Guard Bureau, Pacific Disaster Center, White House Operations Center, and Global Support and Development, where he is currently the director of operations and plans for the organization's humanitarian vessel.

Tom Oldag is retired from the California Department of Forestry and Fire Protection (CAL FIRE). He was a full-time fire investigator from 2000 to 2015 when he retired. He investigated wildland, structure, and vehicle fires during his career and worked on investigation teams relating to fire deaths of firefighters and civilians. He taught various fire investigation classes, including a fatal fire investigation course for ten years, as well as wildland fire origin and cause determination. He continues to teach fire investigation classes to this day.

Nader Oweis is a law enforcement professional with over 28 years of experience. Nader began his career in 1994 as a police officer and quickly rose through the ranks to chief of police. Nader has served as chief of police for over 12 years with two police departments and was assigned as incident commander during numerous large-scale incidents throughout his career. Since 2005, he has brought his expertise and approach to assist the California Commission on Peace Officer Standards in developing training videos and guidelines for handling major events and other major law enforcement functions.

Marin A. Pilloud is Associate Professor at the University of Nevada, Reno. Prior to this appointment, she was a forensic anthropologist with the Defense POW/MIA Accounting Agency. She is a board-certified forensic anthropologist and a registered professional archaeologist. She has numerous publications on forensic anthropology, including an edited volume and a book.

Elayne Pope is a forensic anthropologist with a research specialty of how the human body burns and burn pattern analysis of soft tissues, bones, and teeth. Dr. Pope is a forensic consultant for fatal fire casework, national and international lecturer, and researcher at Fatal Fire Forensics (www.burnedbone.com). She is an instructor and field researcher with the San Luis Obispo Fire Investigation Strike Team (SLO FIST) Fatal Fire Death Investigation Course for fire investigators, law enforcement, and coroners/CSI, which recreates fatal fire scenes involving human cadavers in structures, vehicles, outdoor settings, confined spaces, and wildfire settings (www.slofist.org). She worked as the forensic anthropologist and autopsy supervisor for six years at the Tidewater Office of the Chief Medical Examiner in Norfolk, Virginia.

David Russell, CAL FIRE Incident Management Team 4. Dave has served on incident management teams for 13 years prior to his retirement in 2022. Dave served as the incident commander of Team 4 on numerous incidents but specifically the North Complex, Camp, Thomas, and Mendocino Redwood Complex. As the incident commander, his duty was to develop new strategies to include multiple governmental agencies and nongovernmental organizations into the firefighting organization. An example would be urban search, rescue, recovery and damage inspection. Dave is part of the Advanced All Hazard Incident Management and Complex Incident Management Cadre.

Richard F. Selden founded ANDE in 2004 with a vision to move DNA analysis from sophisticated laboratories to the field, where it could have daily impact on forensic human identification in military, mass casualty, law enforcement, and homeland security applications. He received his BA degree from Harvard College, MA and PhD degrees in genetics from the Harvard Graduate School of Arts and Sciences, and MD from Harvard Medical School. He trained as a pediatrician at the Massachusetts General Hospital. Dr. Selden is an author on 48 scientific publications and an inventor on 51 US patents.

Jake Smith graduated from California State University Chico and began his career with the Butte County Probation Department in 2006 working with adult and juvenile offenders. Sergeant Smith then worked as a patrol officer, a detective, and a patrol sergeant for Paradise Police Department before joining Butte County Sheriff's Office, where he is currently sergeant. In addition to patrol and investigations, He has held collateral duties as a crime scene investigator, a field training officer, a crisis negotiator, a tactical communications instructor, and a court security supervisor.

Eugene Tan leads the development of Rapid DNA systems for forensic identification, disaster victim identification, and biothreat detection. He is responsible for the design, building, testing, and optimization of the optical, mechanical, and electrical systems of Rapid DNA instruments; microfluidic design and testing; and development and optimization of chip manufacturing processes. He is also responsible for the development of data processing and expert system algorithms. Dr. Tan was the program manager and chief system architect for the joint DoD/DHS/FBI ANDE Rapid DNA program. He is an inventor on 27 US patents on technology for Rapid DNA analysis.

Rosemary Turingan Witkowski is an integral player in the development, validation, and commercialization of the ANDE Rapid DNA analysis system—an FBI-approved technology for use in human forensic identification. Her technical expertise on sample type processing has led to the identification of the 2018 California Camp Fire remains and also in the resolution of numerous criminal and investigative cases (including sexual assault evidence) by law enforcement agencies across the country. She is first author and co-author of several publications and co-inventor of a number of US patents.

P. Willey is a board-certified forensic anthropologist and Professor Emeritus at Chico State. He lives in fire-prone Northern California, where he has worked on wildfire search and recoveries including the 2015 Valley, 2018 Camp, 2021 Caldor, and 2022 McKinney Fires. In addition to wildfire fieldwork, he has performed laboratory assessments of burned remains from the 2014 Interstate 5 FedEx bus crash and the 2018 Carr Fire. Topics of his books include skeletal remains from a prehistoric massacre, Battle of the Little Bighorn, Lewis and Clark's infectious legacy, and a 19th-century San Francisco anatomical waste pit.

Kyle Wilson began his career in law enforcement in 2007 as a deputy sheriff/coroner. In 2015, he was assigned as an assistant search and rescue coordinator and assumed the role of coordinator in 2022. Throughout his career, he has participated in several fire-related body recoveries and responded with search and rescue to the Camp Fire in 2018 to assist in the recovery effort.

James D. Wood has been an active forensic odontologist for over 25 years. His work has been extensive including the Wine Country Fires (2017), Hurricane Katrina, and the World Trade Center. He is currently a California state assemblymember representing the Second District.

Gavriil Xanthopoulos holds a BSc degree in forestry from the Aristotelian University of Thessaloniki, Greece, and MSc and PhD degrees in forestry with specialization in forest fire science from the University of Montana, USA. He has been active in European forest fire research for more than 30 years. He has extensive experience in forest fire management training and post-graduate university teaching and has produced numerous scientific publications. Throughout his career, he has focused on horizontal integration of scientific knowledge in the field and transfer to the operational world. He currently serves as research director and is head of the Forest Fire Laboratory at the Institute of Mediterranean Forest Ecosystems of the Hellenic Agricultural Organization (Dimitra).

Lauren Zephro is a forensic anthropologist based in central California. Lauren is currently the forensic services director for the Santa Cruz County Sheriff's Office, where she oversees crime scene investigation and the forensic laboratory. Her research interests and publications are primarily focused on skeletal trauma, secular change, method and theory in forensic anthropology, and burned bone.

SECTION I

Overview of Wildfires and Wildfire Fatalities

The first three chapters of this volume provide an overview of the wildfire situation across the globe, with a focus on the West Coast of the United States. The world is facing increasing extremes of weather conditions due to climatic shifts, and with these changes come a heightened risk of wildfires. Because of the spread of residential areas into wilderness, the possibility of fatalities with these fires is high. How communities assemble and deploy resources to deal simultaneously with the recovery of human remains, the containment and control of the fire, and the physical recovery of the communities will be tested.

The introductory chapter lays out the issue of wildfire, how it is defined, and the factors that lead to the increased frequency. The text explains the definition of "disaster" and how and when wildfires fall into this category. The prime areas for catastrophic landscape fires have been identified in the Mediterranean region, Australia, and North America where the wildland-urban interface places inhabited areas squarely in the path of the flames. The result is a cost in financial terms of expenses, losses, and deferred costs but most importantly in human lives.

The second chapter provides an overview of fire behavior, particularly with regards to wildfires. It explains the conditions in which wildfires are initiated, spread, and move across the landscape. An understanding of this information is critical in the assessment of the risk for communities at the interface of the wilderness and, ever more frequently, suburban communities that have thought they were immune from such disasters.

The third chapter looks at the international scene in terms of where and when fatal wildfires have occurred. It separates the deaths of firefighters and civilians and examines how and why these deaths may occur for different reasons. While deaths of firefighters have gradually lessened over the years, there has been a contrasting increase in civilian deaths.

DOI: 10.4324/9781003168010-1

CHAPTER 1

Wildfires

Introduction, Impact, Policy, and Planning

Megafires are becoming more common, more widespread, longer lasting, and increasingly destructive. Unfortunately, a small number of these fires may spread so rapidly that evacuation of residents, tourists, and workers in an area cannot be completed before the arrival of the fire front or spotting fires. This volume is specifically designed to help those who are planning for or facing a mass casualty wildfire. Such raging infernos are often associated with wilderness areas but are, with increasing frequency, destroying areas that interface or intermix with wildlands and suburban and even urban areas. The inclusion of multiple fatalities significantly increases the complexity of the response by (1) requiring the location, removal, and identification of burned remains, (2) increasing the number and types of crews involved in the aftermath of a fire, (3) significantly increasing public pressure and scrutiny of the response, (4) often leaving local communities heavily hit by the repercussions of the loss, and (5) leaving local agencies to deal with massive requests for information about possible missing persons in a time when those missing but still alive are not easy to locate or may not wish to be located.

The principles laid out in this volume are applicable to the location, recovery, and identification of fire victims utilizing a multidisciplinary approach that recognizes that the recovery operations are part of a much larger effort to deal with the emergency. The complexity of the overall response and the massive need for outside resources dictate that this is not a situation that can be addressed only as the need arises.

Mass disasters receive significant attention in the media and in public planning but often defy full preparation due to the scale, unpredictability, and diversity of causes. Mass disasters are defined by both the catastrophic nature of the event and also by the impact upon the human population. The US Federal Emergency Management Agency defines "disaster" as follows (US FEMA, 2021):

> *An occurrence of a natural catastrophe, technological accident, or human caused event that has resulted in severe property damage, deaths, and/or multiple injuries. As used in this Guide, a "large-scale disaster" is one that exceeds the response capability of the local jurisdiction and requires State, and potentially Federal, involvement. As used in the Stafford Act, a "major disaster" is "any natural catastrophe . . . or, regardless of cause, any fire, flood, or explosion, in any part of the United States, which in the determination of the President causes damage of sufficient severity and magnitude to warrant major disaster assistance under [the] Act to supplement the efforts and available resources or*

DOI: 10.4324/9781003168010-2

> *States, local governments, and disaster relief organizations in alleviating the damage, loss, hardship, or suffering caused thereby."*

Many natural events can be large-scale but do little to impact the human population. For example, fires in remote areas with a low population base that have sufficient time to evacuate are often not seen as mass disasters since the impact on human lives and economy are minimal. However, a similar or smaller fire in the wildland-urban interface (WUI) or suburban area can be devastating.

1.1 INTERNATIONAL FACTORS

Wildfires are measured by the number of fires ignited and acreage burned. Also considered are the cost of response, impact on human life, and total economic impact to the region (structural loss, loss of income, loss of revenue, infrastructure replacement, etc.). Many of these costs are difficult to ascertain, particularly in wildfires due to the widespread destruction, the complexity of the recovery process, and the uncertainty of comparing what should have happened versus what has happened. However, what is certain is that the impact to both lives and the economy has been substantial and appears to be increasing.

Internationally, concern centers on the changes in climate and the impact on wildfires, bushfires, and shrubland fires. Predictive models globally forecast increasing temperatures that would normally drive an increase in wildfires (Rocca et al., 2014). However, localized modeling shows a much more complex picture with variations in precipitation, wind speed, and seasonal drought influencing the probability of fires. In addition, there are issues of ignition sources, topography, and fuel load that must be taken into account. For example, many areas of the world suffer from the same temperature and precipitation changes but discontinuity in fuel lowers the potential for major fires.

Already three swaths of the globe have seen increasing incidents of large wildfires. These are the Mediterranean region of Europe, North America (Canada and USA), and Australia. Fires in these areas have resulted in loss of vegetation, wildlife, homes, infrastructure, and most importantly, lives. Already these have forced countries, and the regional governments within them, to increase the fire suppression budgets and begin considering alternate means of fire management, including prescribed burns, use of suppression fire, and accommodation for traditional methods of burning.

1.1.1 The Mediterranean Region

In the Mediterranean area, fires are already a major concern in the Iberian peninsula, France, Italy, Greece, and the Mediterranean islands (Corsica, Sardinia, Sicily). Reviews of the current predictive models coalesce around an increase in fire danger throughout the 21st century as both fuel dryness and fuel continuity increase (Dupuy et al., 2020). The models cannot account for all factors, such as effects of fire suppression and socioeconomic factors, but do highlight the probability that, without significant changes in fire management, southern Europe will experience drastic increases in burned area, possibly as high as 15–25% increases per decade.

This situation is exacerbated by the number of fires started due to arson (Ganteaume & Jappoit, 2013) and agricultural burning. Arson-caused fires are often larger and rooted in long-standing and complex land conflicts, such as trying to return forest land to grazing or hunting or in land disputes over development rights. Unlike much of northern Europe, agricultural use of fire in the region is traditional but is complicated by both changes in fuel dryness and in fuel continuity. Abandonment of many rural areas has allowed fuel loads to drastically increase so that any escaped fire becomes less easy to manage. Fewer full-time residents in rural communities also mean there are less people available who would otherwise be involved in managing such burns.

In assessing the future for the Mediterranean region, similar issues begin to emerge. One central Mediterranean simulation, examining three periods (1981–2010, 2011–2040, and 2041–2070), and a fine-grained spatial scale showed that there would be an increase in temperatures for the entire area accompanied by a decrease in relative humidity and rainfall (Lozano et al., 2017).

Portugal has already been hit by deadly fires in 2003, 2007, and 2017 (Turco et al., 2019). While a review of 1980 through 2017 did not show decadal changes, it clearly shows that burned area correlates to high temperatures and low soil moisture levels. Looking forward, the country is likely to see an increase in burned area during the peak fire months of July and August but also see changes in the pre–"fire season" that allows for fuel accumulation and dehydration (Pereira et al., 2013). The boreal and temperate climate areas will be the most affected, and there will also be considerable inter-annual variability. It is also of note that the worst 2017 fires both occurred outside of the traditional fire season (Turco et al., 2019). This suggests that worsening conditions will be coupled with an extended fire season.

Simulation studies on the Italian peninsula and associated islands show similar responses, again graded by the local environments. For example, while future wind conditions are not expected to be a problem in northern Italy, wind speeds should increase in the already vulnerable areas of Sardinia, Sicily, South Italy, and Corsica (Lozano et al., 2017). These are the same areas where dry, very dry, or extremely dry moisture days are also anticipated in the future. The major factor to consider in future fire risk, according to this study, is not wind but fuel moisture content. Significant reduction in fuel loads through forest management seemed the best strategy.

While more northern areas, such as southern France, are currently less affected by large wildfires, it is anticipated that, with the current trajectory of climate change, fires will encroach into these areas as well (Ganteaume & Jappoit, 2013). The Fire Weather Index (FWI), which is based on moisture codes for vegetation types along with fire behavior data, is expected to be higher in France by 7% per decade for the rest of this century (Dupuy et al., 2020). If we discount fuel continuity changes, the burned area could likely increase by 15–25% per decade for most of southern Europe.

On the islands of Corsica and Sardinia, fires are often attributable to either arson or negligence associated with agricultural burns (Ager et al., 2014). Susceptible landscapes include the forests and shrublands, but also agricultural lands. Fires often start near roads, but these are also the ones that are the easiest to suppress. In contrast, those starting away from roads require much more significant resources to control as response times are delayed. The best predictor based on recent history of fires is FWI. When the FWI is 60, the chance of a large fire increases eightfold over an FWI of 30. Climate change that will increase temperatures and lower precipitation will push the FWI higher in future decades.

In Greece, drought already has been linked to an increase in the number of fires and in area burned (Dimitrakopoulos et al., 2011; Kalabokidis et al., 2015). In the southern and central regions of the country, these increases are tied to the summer drought, while elsewhere both winter and summer precipitation is responsible (Dimitrakopoulos et al., 2011). In the tip of the country, projected increases in fires and burned areas endanger not only homes and businesses but also major cultural heritage sites (Kalabokidis et al., 2015). Future predictions again show complexity as local terrain will produce differences in temperature and precipitation. However, in areas already badly affected, particularly in southern Greece, landscape fires are likely to be on the increase.

1.1.2 North America

Modeling effects of climate change on wildfire frequency and intensity has a long history in Canada (Flannigan & Van Wagner, 1991). Wildfires currently consume about 2 million hectares of forest annually in Canada, and this pattern is influenced by both climate change and fire suppression strategies (Gralewicz et al., 2012; Wotton et al., 2017). The fire season is becoming more severe, with increased fire occurrence and greater area burned. With increased fire suppression, there has been an accumulation of fuel, increasing the intensity of the fires, especially crown fires. Canadian fires occur most often in the vast coniferous forests where they are important to the evolutionary history of certain conifers and are often not suppressed. Fire reduces the coniferous forest amount in the short term, but since conifers often need fire for regeneration, they will regenerate. Regeneration takes a mean of 20 years, but times vary. In addition, climate change is bringing some more moisture in some times of the year, increasing fuel production only to then have moisture lost to evapotranspiration during the dry season.

There is a high occurrence of crown fires in Canada due to low conifer crown moisture (Gralewicz et al., 2012). Broadleaf and mixed wood areas damaged by fire may transform into non-treed or non-vegetation-dominated areas. Wildfires also increase fragmentation by increasing the number of coniferous forest patches and decreasing patch size and percentage of forest cover. When forest patch numbers increase, leaving areas with less fuel between patches, large wildfires decline. Low forest patch number and larger patch size enable fire propagation over large areas.

Canada has already adapted many modern practices of fire management that are under discussion elsewhere (Tymstra et al., 2020). Because much of the forested land has low population, fires are often monitored or receive a modified response rather than a direct response geared toward suppression. Fires in remote areas are allowed to burn until they self-extinguish, creating discontinuity in the forest patches and inhibiting future burns. Modified responses determine the maximum allowable perimeter and ensure that burns do not overwhelm those lines. Again, increased forest patchiness acts as an inhibitor of future fires.

In the United States, predictions are for increased temperatures across the country (Liu et al., 2013; Rocca et al., 2014). While the western US is currently bearing the brunt of the wildfire activity, it is likely that this activity will expand eastward (Rocca et al., 2014). Other models suggest that the West will continue to see high wildfire activity due to drastic drops in winter precipitation (Liu et al., 2013). The entire country is likely to see lower summer and fall precipitation, particularly in the West and southeastern US. Drought indices should increase in the Southwest, Rocky Mountains, and northern Great Plains. Overall, fire activity should increase in the Southwest, Rocky Mountain regions, northern Great Plains, Southeast, and Pacific coast, with fire season also increasing in the South.

The Pacific Northwest is already experiencing climate change with higher temperatures, lower snowpack, more rain-dominated than snow-dominated land, decreased mountain rain/snow, and lower summer streamflow (Halofsky et al., 2018). Projections show temperature increases of 0.5–5.2°C and increased wildfires by 2100. With climate change, vegetation shifts may also occur, leading to declines in some old-growth forests. Douglas fir may expand as it is better suited to drought and is more fire resistant. Fire risk will also tend to increase due to the frequency of ignition, often by human activity, and east wind events will increase the spread and intensity of fire. However, other simulations suggest that the picture is complicated and the area may see changes in humidity and wind that will offset the higher temperatures (Liu et al., 2013). If that is the case, this part of the country may maintain at close to current, but already severe, levels.

Models of the south-central regions of the US also show the complexity of local variation (Stambaugh et al., 2018). Mean temperature increases are relatively consistent across the areas. While the greatest decreases in mean annual precipitation may be expected along the coast, the greatest increases in fire probability come in the western New Mexico high country. Much of the difference is explained by the availability of fuel and how dry that fuel will be. More vulnerable areas already suffer from lower precipitation and fuel moisture levels, so the relative drop is more catastrophic.

1.1.3 Australia

The third major area for increased wildfire risk is Australia, an area that has seen devastating recent bushfires with multiple fatalities in 2009 and in 2019–20. The conservation aspect is an additional complication in Australia since, with more than 800 endemic species of eucalypts, fire is a necessity (Lucas et al., 2007). Australian vegetation relies on fire for regeneration.

Climate change and weather conditions have quadrupled the risk of bushfires compared to 1900 levels, an increase that is projected to continue through the current century (van Oldenborgh et al., 2021). In addition, annual fluctuations can be disastrous. For example, in 2019, the dry conditions were enhanced by the positive excursion of the Indian Ocean Dipole and a strong negative anomaly of the Southern Annular Mode. These contributed to an overall precipitation deficit. Overall, the most devastating changes are likely in northern New South Wales where extreme fire danger could increase by 10–300% (Lucas et al., 2007).

In addition, climate change will affect the availability of days suitable for prescribed burns (Di Virgillio et al., 2020; Lucas et al., 2007). However, this will be offset by an increase in available winter days in some scenarios. Overall, there are projections of substantial increases in fire danger indices, particularly in southeastern Australia, longer burn seasons, and more intense fires.

1.2 THE HISTORY OF WILDFIRES IN THE WESTERN US IN THE 20TH/21ST CENTURY

Within North America, the western states, particularly California, have borne much of the brunt of climate change and public land management as it relates to wildfires. The top 12 states ranked by percentage of federal land are all in the west. California, already a large and very populous state, houses 45.8% of its land in federal hands. Added to that is an additional 3% of state-owned land so that, in total, about half of the state is publicly owned. Much of this land is wildland where management to mitigate fire hazard is subject to political and financial tides.

A review of the history of wildfires in the United States shows that until about the year 2000, annual acres burned in the US only occasionally topped 4 million (National Fire Information Center, 2021), with most years burning about 2 million acres or less (Figure 1.1). However, since 2000, the acres burned has increased dramatically, with most years exceeding 4 million and some years extending to 10 million acres.

Interestingly, the number of fires has not changed noticeably. The number of fires appear to have jumped in the early 1980s but have remained relatively level since that time. This supports the contention that it is not the frequency of ignitions but that those ignitions are more likely to produce massive fires.

The "fire season" that had traditionally lasted a few months, often July through September, is now beginning earlier and lasting longer. Even winter wildfires are becoming more frequent.

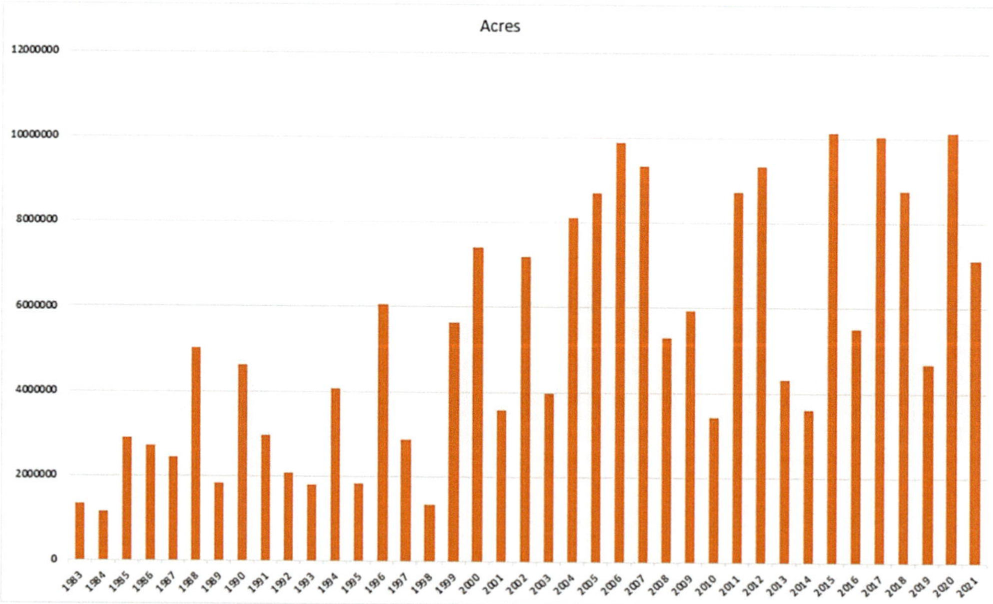

FIGURE 1.1 Acres burned in the US from 1983 to 2021.

Source: NFIC (2021)

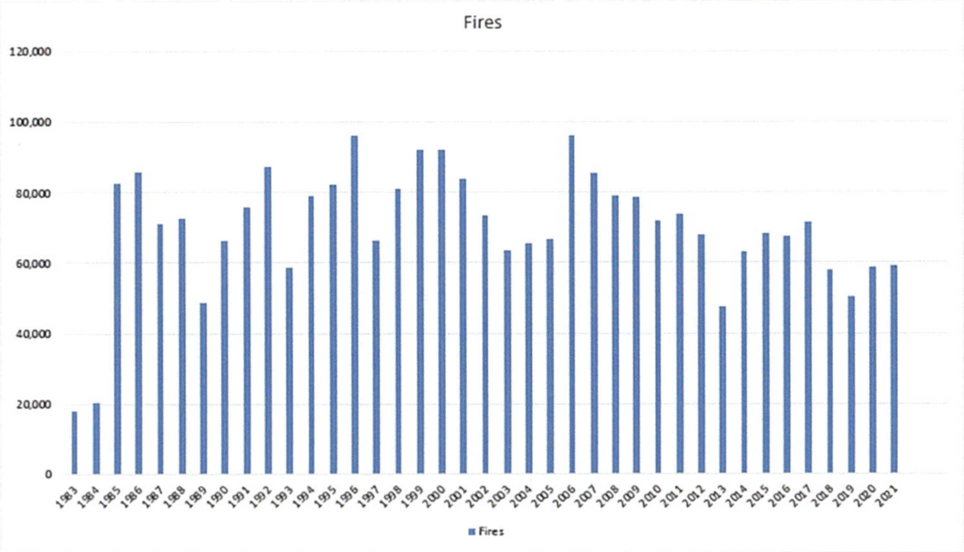

FIGURE 1.2 Number of fires in the US from 1983 to 2021.

Source: NFIC (2021)

1.2.1 Deadly Wildfires in California

California is no stranger to fatal wildfires. Table 1.1 lists the top 20 deadliest wildfires. What is remarkable is the diversity of acreage to deaths as well as the span of time covered. Many of the Southern Californian deaths are due to fires in chamise, sage, and sumac, while those in Northern California occur in mixed forests that lean toward conifers in some areas.

The earliest fires tended to result in deaths of those fighting the fires, often due to the lack of detailed knowledge of fire behavior in wildland settings. The oldest of these is the Griffith Park Fire that occurred in 1933, during the height of the Depression. At that time, men were hired to clear brush from Griffith Park. When a small fire started in debris, the men switched to firefighting mode but lacked any training. As seen throughout the world, fire behavior tends to concentrate the fire intensity in canyon settings and, in this case, it did just that—jumping a hasty fire line and killing 27 men at the scene with another two dying of injuries in hospital. Similarly, in the Hauser Creek Fire in 1943, US Marines and US Forest Service workers were fighting a fire when fire behavior changed as it approached a gully, trapping many men (US Marine Corps, n.d.). Some appeared to have ignored orders, or did not hear them, and attempted to outrun the fire. In total, 11 died, with many more suffering severe burns.

The 1953 Rattlesnake Fire, resulting in 15 deaths (one US Forest Service and 14 New Tribes Mission firefighters), also involved changing wind direction and firefighters stationed in a canyon setting. In this case, the men were finishing dinner, thinking containment was imminent, when the fire rushed down the canyon, engulfing the group. In 1955, five members of the LA County Probation Forestry Camp Crew, along with a fire captain who was attempting to rescue them, were killed in the Hacienda Fire. Again,

TABLE 1.1 The 20 Deadliest California Wildfires in Order of Fatalities

Fire	County	Date	Acres Burned	Deaths
Camp	Butte	2018	153,336	85
Griffith Park	Los Angeles	1933	47	29
Tunnel (Oakland Hills)	Alameda	1991	1600	25
Tubbs	Napa, Sonoma	2017	36,807	22
Rattlesnake	Glenn	1953	1340	15
Cedar	San Diego	2003	273,246	15
North Complex	Plumas, Butte	2020	318,935	15
Loop	Los Angeles	1966	2028	12
Hauser Creek	San Diego	1943	13415	11
Inaja	San Diego	1956	43904	11
Iron Alps Complex	Trinity	2008	105,855	10
Redwood Valley Complex	Mendocino	2017	36,523	9
Canyon	Los Angeles	1968	22,197	8
Harris	San Diego	2007	90,440	8
Carr	Shasta, Trinity	2018	229,651	8
Hacienda	Los Angeles	1955	1150	6
Decker	Riverside	1959	1425	6
Old	San Bernadino	2003	91281	6
Atlas	Napa, Solano	2017	51,624	6
LNU Complex	Colusa, Lake, Napa, Sonoma, Solano, Yolo	2020	363,220	6
Laguna	San Diego	1970	175,425	5
Esperanza	Riverside	2006	40,200	5

Source: CAL FIRE (2021)

changing wind direction and a steep slope resulted in an alteration in the fire front. A year later, 11 were killed in San Diego County, when the area suffered from drought and experienced the infamous Santa Ana winds that form an intermittent offshore flow in fall months. Three US Forest Service workers, a probation officer, and seven inmates of an honor camp died when the Inaja Fire suddenly rushed uphill, trapping the men at the base of a 15-foot bluff (US Forest Service, 1957). The 1959 Decker Fire followed a few weeks after another fire in the vicinity where firefighters had already noted the problem of dramatic wind shifts during the day (Lee, n.d.; US Forest Service, 1960). While attempting to set backfires, the crews were killed as the downslope winds died and the fire suddenly rushed upslope, trapping them against a bluff on the road.

By the mid-1960s, some of the lessons delivered by the earlier deadly fires were learned by the firefighting crews, but there were still fatal incidents. In 1966, the Loop Fire killed 12 El Cariso hotshots who were attempting to cut a fire line in a chimney canyon (National Wildfire Coordinating Group, 2021). Spotting resulted in fires on their flank, trapping them in an area with extensive fuels. Poor communication methods prevented the crew being warned of the danger, although it was seen and recognized by other crews in the area. Two years later, in 1968, eight firefighters from the Los Angeles County Fire Department died in the Canyon Fire (Countryman et al., 1969). Working under prevailing Santa Ana winds, the crew became trapped while working on steep terrain. The winds and high fuel load contributed to the production of a fire whirl that pushed intense heat ahead of the flames.

Although no longer on the list of the top 20 deadliest California wildfires, the 1970 Laguna Fire (Alderdice, n.d.; Gabbert, 2009; US Forest Service, n.d.) is a notable recent example of civilian death. This fire devastated over 30 miles of land within 24 hours, from Mount Laguna to El Cajon and Spring Valley. It occurred in a year of drought and high winds, often called the "year of the big wind." Dispatch of crews to the fire was delayed due to mop-up activities on an earlier fire and a belief that the Santa Ana winds would decrease, thereby limiting the spread of the fire. Instead, the winds doubled in intensity and the fire spread quickly, prompting civilian evacuations. Because of the multiple agencies involved, there was considerable confusion and miscommunication as well as problems deploying aerial support due to the wind conditions. The problems that arose with this fire, as well as lessons learned from the fires in the 1960s, prompted a reassessment of firefighting coordination leading, eventually, to the Incident Management System (IMS) for Southern California and eventually the national IMS system.

Over 20 years passed before another fire made it into the top 20 deadly fires in California, but this one, started as a reignited brushfire along Tunnel Road in the Oakland Hills, quickly moved into a wildland interface community with limited egress (US Fire Administration, 1991). From there it crossed two major freeway systems and moved into the Oakland Hills residential community, another area with many narrow and very twisty roads. Almost all the deaths, of which there were 25, occurred within a half-hour span of time in the area immediately west of the point of origin. Firefighters and civilians alike were trapped in the area due to collisions on the roads or falling power lines blocking the streets. In the end, 23 civilians died along with one firefighter and one police officer. The dead ranged in age from 18 to 85 years, many of whom were unable to evacuate due to disabilities or blocked exits. Though a small fire in terms of acreage burned, the impact of this fire on the understanding of urban vulnerability was powerful.

Beginning in 2003, there has been a dramatic increase in the frequency of multiple fatality wildfires. Eleven of the top 20 deadly wildfires have occurred since 2000. The Cedar Fire occurred during a period of strong Santa Ana winds, sweeping through Wildcat Canyon and Moreno Valley toward the urban outskirts of San Diego (Bowman, 2004). Fourteen civilians and one firefighter died, mostly from the area of Wildcat Canyon, north of Lakeside (Mutch, 2007). Many of the dead were found in their vehicles, having attempted to flee the area. In 2007, the San Diego area was again hit by a devastating wildfire in the form of the Harris Fire and 16 other significant Southern California fires that occurred in the same red-flag-warning time span. The Harris Fire crossed into northern Mexico and hit the eastern portions of San Diego County. Seventeen people died in the series of fires, including eight in the Harris Fire alone. This number included four undocumented people that were killed near the border. After-action reports highlight the complexity of having to constantly move resources to mitigate potential disasters while dealing with approximately 900,000 people displaced by this widespread series of simultaneous fires. The following year, 2008, saw another major fire but this time in the northern reaches of the state. The Iron/Alps Complex Fires resulted from the amalgamation of multiple, separate fires, as well as spot fires from the original sources. Of the ten reported deaths, nine were due to a helicopter crash carrying a fire crew. The tenth victim was also a firefighter.

The final seven deadliest fires all occurred between 2017 and 2020. The Redwood Valley, Atlas, and Tubbs Fires all killed multiple people on October 8, 2017. All were due to electrical problems including downed power lines in windy conditions. In total, 37 people died in these three fires, with 22 of these in the Tubbs Fire. Across the state, a total of 47 died, 45 of whom were civilians. The following year saw the Carr Fire in July, in which eight died, and then the Camp Fire in November, which killed 85 civilians caught as the fire swept toward the west driven by morning winds. While 2019 was relatively quiet, 2020 returned with massive wildfires triggered by thunderstorms in August that produced multiple, massive fires across the state. Two of these, the North Complex Fire and the LNU Lightning Complex, killed 21 people.

Much of the discussion about wildfires in the western United States changed with the Camp Fire. This fire, while not the worst in terms of land burned, destruction, or even lives lost, is certainly the worst in recent memory. However, the West Coast of the United States and other areas of the world (further discussed here) have been heavily hit since then, giving little chance for agencies to regroup and attempt to try alternate strategies.

What is frightening is that the 2018 fire season, which produced the Camp Fire, was actually below normal for the number of reported wildfires. According to the National Interagency Fire Center (NIFC), the number of wildfires reported in 2018 was only 84% of the ten-year average, with 58,083 reported wildfires nationally. However, the number of acres burned was above normal at 132 percent of the ten-year average with the Great Basin Area leading the nation with almost 2.1 million acres burned (NICC, 2018: 7).

The "relatively quiet" 2019 fire season resulted in 4.7 million acres burned from 50,477 wildfires (National Fire Information Center, 2021). In 2020 there were an estimated 58,950 wildfires in the United States, burning approximately 10.1 million acres. One of the hardest hit states, California experienced six of the top 20 largest wildfires in state history, leading to record damage, including 4.3 million acres burned, 10,500 structures destroyed, and 33 lives lost (Insurance Information Institute, 2021). However, the fires also extended into Oregon with additional lives lost. Of all of the states, California ranked number one in both the number of fires and the number of acres burned in wildfires in the year 2020, with 10,431 fires on record and 4,092,151 acres burned (National Fire Information Center, 2021).

Many of the fires in 2020 were caused by lightning strikes in a single storm front resulting in multiple fires that amalgamated into large fire complexes. With over 11,000 lightning strikes within a three-day period, fires were started in over 375 locations in California. As a result, four large complex fires developed: the August Complex Fire (1,032K acres), the LNU Fire (363K acres), the SCU Fire (396K acres), the SZU Fire (85K acres), and the SQF Fire (174K acres). Of these the August Complex ranks as the largest wildfire in California, but four other fires in the same month rank in the top 20 largest California wildfires.

It was primarily in the last several years of wildfire response, in particular since 2017, that the anthropology teams began to work in more prominent roles, handling much of the recovery process and coordinating on-scene training for search and rescue teams. As it became apparent that these fires were likely to be "the new norm," resiliency in the aftermath became critical—how to recover and repopulate an area quickly included how to locate and remove those whose lives were lost.

1.3 COST OF FIRE SUPPRESSION, EVACUATION, AND RECOVERY

While we have focused on the cost in human lives, it is also important to understand that the financial, economic, and emotional toll of wildfires is tremendous (Girnius et al., 2008). There are the short-term costs of evacuation and suppression/containment. There are longer-term goals in recovery, rebuilding, and relocating. There are far longer impacts to health from the stress of the event and the effects of contaminants in the environment. The latter includes pollution of water supplies, heightened risk of infrastructure failure due to surface erosion, and the detrimental effects of poor air quality for wide swaths of land around the globe. Residents of the wildland-urban interface, in particular, also need to invest heavily in home-hardening, and they also live with the constant uncertainty of wildfire occurrence for months due to the extended fire season.

Wildfire risk is assessed according to three primary factors: distribution of vegetative fuel, steepness of slope, and degree of access or firefighting equipment. As of September 2019, when western states were ranked according to the wildfire risk to properties, California was ranked number one with 2,019,800 properties at risk of wildfire destruction. In 2019, the top ten states with high to extreme wildfire risk to

TABLE 1.2 Ten Costliest Wildfires in the US through 2021
This amount includes losses by private insurers and government-sponsored programs. Note that all the listed fires occurred in California. Ranking is based on 2021 values, which are adjusted for inflation by Aon using the US Consumer Price Index.

			Estimated Insured Loss (in $ Million)	
Rank	**Year**	**Name**	**Dollars When It Occurred**	**In 2021 Dollars**
1	2018	Camp Fire	10,000	10,750
2	2017	Tubbs Fire	8700	9560
3	2018	Woolsey Fire	4200	4520
4	1991	Oakland Hills Fire (Tunnel)	1700	3350
5	2017	Atlas Fire	3000	3300
6	2020	Glass Fire	2950	3070
7	2020	CZU Lightning Complex Fire	2500	2600
8	2017	Thomas Fire	2250	2470
9	2020	LNU Lightning Complex Fire	2250	2340
10	2007	Witch Fire	1600	2080

properties were as follows: California, Texas, Colorado, Arizona, Idaho, Washington, Oklahoma, Oregon, Montana, and Utah (ranked according to the estimated number of total properties at risk to wildfire damage) (Verisk Wildfire Risk Analytic using data from FireLine).

Suppression costs alone have become astronomical. Between 1985 and 1999, federal suppression costs in the US were generally, with a couple of exceptional years, below a half billion dollars annually (US National Interagency Fire Center, 2021). After 1999, costs tended to run at $1–1.5 billion per year until about 2012 when costs were more likely to be around or over $2 billion annually. In 2020, for example, federal costs were $2,274,000,000. The State of California spent over $1 billion in fiscal year 2020/21 on emergency fire suppression.

The Camp Fire was the deadliest and costliest in California recorded history, with $16.5 billion in losses including $12.5 in insured losses (Insurance Institute for Business and Home Safety, 2021). The year 2020 was also a bad year, with $5–9 billion in losses. Improvements to the California fire hazard severity zone maps (FHSZ) and expansion of the wildfire building code could strengthen the resilience.

In addition to the immediate damage to forests, the environmental impact is long-lasting and requires significant investment. Two large components are the hazards associated with significant and widespread smoke, often concentrated in areas far from the fire, and the surface damage that facilitates erosion with the return of rains in the winter months.

1.3.1 Future Response to Climate Change

Current climate models have difficulty with the extremes in that they tend to overestimate variability and underestimate the observed trends (van Oldenborgh et al., 2021). This pattern results in an underestimation of the change due to anthropogenic climate change. While it also tends to highlight annual variability, this feature often is dismissed as a "possibility" rather than a deadly reality in terms of spatial planning (Norman et al., 2014) and vegetation management.

It is increasingly imperative that we develop better approaches to fire management in order to avoid or lessen the frequency and intensity of fires. Much will rely on developing integrated fire management strategies that are tailored to each region. The key is the reduction of the dry fuel load available combined with public education of fire dangers and best preparations and responses on the part of residents. Training of fire specialists (Molina et al., 2010) who can predict wildfire behavior and determine how best to protect lives and property will be needed.

It is said that fire is "a bad master but a good servant," and we must lean more heavily on the service aspect of fire (Silva et al., 2010). Not every fire needs suppression, and as Canada has shown, monitoring of some fires is the appropriate action (Tymstra et al., 2020). In other cases, when fires threaten the wildland-urban interface, evacuation may be appropriate. The Australian example has shown that "stay and defend" works with a major caveat—that the property must already be defensible, that there be adequate resources and equipment, and that those staying play an active role in defense (Crompton et al., 2010). Whatever the strategy, given the probable future of climate change, how we plan fire management must involve financial investment, careful and long-term planning, and public education and empowerment.

1.4 THIS VOLUME: IMPORTANCE OF INTERDISCIPLINARY PLANNING AND RESPONSES

Planning for mass disasters will vary by region. One of the first steps is an understanding of the regional hazards—dams that might break, fires, flash floods, earthquakes, hurricanes, tsunamis, tornadoes, and so on. Most of the attention for planning usually focuses on the most expected hazard, but there should be sufficient flexibility so that plans can be adapted when an unexpected hazard surfaces.

While some of this planning can be done based on available educational information, much of the learning has been "on the job." The editors of this volume have been part of the search/recovery teams on numerous wildfires. The California State University at Chico (Chico State) has been the first line of response on the 2010 San Bruno Pipeline explosion where a natural gas line exploded and ignited a fire that destroyed 38 homes, killing eight residents. They also responded to the Orland I-5 bus crash in which a truck collided with a bus carrying students on a college tour, resulting in ten fatalities. Then, beginning in 2015, Chico State anthropologists worked on a series of wildfires including the 2015 Valley Fire, the 2017 Mendocino Complex Fire, the 2017 Yuba County Fire, the 2018 Carr Fire and Camp Fire, the 2020 North Complex/Bear Fire, the 2021 Caldor Fire, and the 2022 McKinney Fire. In addition, one editor also worked on the 2020 Almeda Fire in Oregon. With this level of intensity of involvement, we have seen the role of recovery teams in wildfires change over time, and we have also adapted our recovery techniques for the unique circumstances of wildfire work.

This volume contributes to the discussion of how to approach wildfire fatality recovery in a number of ways. We look to provide a basic information packet for those who are planning for the possibility of a deadly wildfire by discussing the various aspects of the initial response. When a fire is rapid and many people are missing, the agencies charged with the response will be not only scrambling but also under intense public scrutiny. Having a framework for what the response entails, from fire to law enforcement, to incident command, to investigation of the fire's origin, allows the leadership to provide a balanced and informed picture of what is occurring.

Second, we want to specifically address the recovery of human remains in the field. While there is a sense of urgency in retrieving remains, careful preparation and deployment of trained and competent staff is essential to avoid distressing and embarrassing situations later. We explore how to deploy search and rescue teams and how to organize and deploy recovery teams. We also address what to expect in terms of field conditions of the remains and where they are most likely located.

Third, we discuss the post-recovery analysis that must be arranged. Identification of the remains may be presumed based on location, but there are significant hazards in not requiring a positive identification if possible. However, such an identification requires a multidisciplinary approach, including pathologists, odontologists, anthropologists, and DNA specialists. Such teams require planning, networks, and support—the groundwork for which should be planned well before the need arises.

Finally, we conclude with some after-care comments and some overall observations on who among us is the most vulnerable. The editors have all had extensive experience in wildfires and fire deaths. Furthermore, we all live in fire-prone areas and have been subject to evacuations and red flag warnings. As anthropologists in the field, we see how the victims faced death—fleeing in fear, facing the inevitable, or cowering in a space they hoped would be safe but was not. For us, discussing these impacts and the lessons we have learned from our work is essential to protect the welfare of others in future fire events and also to care for those first and last responders who must handle matters when fatalities occur.

REFERENCES

Ager, A., Preisler, H., Arca, B., Spano, D., & Salis, M. (2014). Wildfire risk estimation in the Mediterranean area. *Environmetrics*, *25*, 384–396.

Alderdice, J. (n.d.). *Laguna Fire of 1970*.

Bowman, J. (2004). *Cedar Fire 2003 after action report*.

CAL FIRE. (2021). *Top 20 deadliest California wildfires*. www.fire.ca.gov/media/lbfd0m2f/top20_deadliest.pdf

Countryman, C., McCutchan, M., & Ryan, B. (1969). *Fire weather and fire behavior at the 1968 Canyon Fire*. https://www.fs.usda.gov/psw/publications/documents/psw_rp055/psw_rp055.pdf

Crompton, R., McAneney, K., Chen, K., Pielke, R., & Haynes, K. (2010). Influence of location, population, and climate on building damage and fatalities due to Australian bushfire: 1925–2009. *Weather, Climate, and Society*, *2*, 300–310.

Dimitrakopoulos, A., Vlahou, M., Anagnostopoulou, C., & Mitsopoulos, I. (2011). Impact of drought on wildland fires in Greece: Implications of climatic change? *Climatic Change*, *109*, 331–347.

Di Virgillio, G., Evans, J., Clarke, H., Sharples, J., Hirsch, A., & Hart, M. (2020). Climate change significantly alters future wildfire mitigation opportunities in southeastern Australia. *Geophysical Research Letters*, *47*.

Dupuy, J., Fargeon, H., Martin-St Paul, N., Pimont, F., Ruffault, J., Guijarro, M., Hernando, C., Madrigal, J., & Fernandes, P. (2020). Climate change impact on future wildfire danger and activity in southern Europe: A review. *Annals of Forest Science*, *77*, 35.

Flannigan, M., & Van Wagner, C. (1991). Climate change and wildfire in Canada. *Canadian Journal of Forest Research*, *21*, 66–72.

Gabbert, B. (2009). *Laguna Fire, September 26, 1970*. Wildfire Today.

Ganteaume, A., & Jappoit, M. (2013). What causes large fires in southern France? *Forest Ecology and Management*, *294*, 76–85.

Girnius, T., Hauteniemi, T., & Stransky, S. (2008). California wildfire: How large can the losses be? *AirCurrents*, 1–4.

Gralewicz, N., Nelson, T., & Wulder, M. (2012). Factors influencing national scale wildfire susceptibility in Canada. *Forest Ecology and Management*, *265*, 20–29.

Halofsky, J., Conklin, D., Donato, D., Halofsky, J., & Kim, J. (2018). Climate change, wildfire, and vegetation shifts in a high-inertia forest landscape: Western Washington, U.S.A. *PLoS One*, *13*(12), e02090490. https://doi.org/10.1371/journal.pone.0209490

Insurance Information Institute. (2021). *Facts + statistics: Wildfires*. www.iii.org/fact-statistic/facts-statistics-wildfires

Insurance Institute for Business and Home Safety. (2021). *California wildfire public policy: Mapping the wildfire hazard*. https://ibhs.org/wp-content/uploads/member_docs/IBHS_Wildfire-Mapping-and-Building-Codes_2021.pdf

Kalabokidis, K., Palaiologou, P., Geraspopoulos, E., Giannakopoulos, C., Kostopoulou, E., & Zerefos, C. (2015). Effect of climate change projections on forest fire behavior and values-at-risk in southwestern Greece. *Forests*, *6*, 2214–2240.

Lee, J. (n.d.). *The dynamics of a catastrophy—the Decker Wildland Fire of 1959*. https://sbfiresafecouncil.org/wp-content/uploads/2020/05/Decker_Fire_Lee-report.pdf

Liu, Y., Goodrick, S., & Stanturf, J. (2013). Future U.S. wildfire potential trends projected using a dynamically downscaled climate change scenario. *Forest Ecology and Management*, *294*, 120–135.

Lozano, O., Salis, M., Ager, A., Arca, B., Alcasena, F., Monteiro, A., Finney, M., Del Giudice, L., Scoccimarro, E., & Spano, D. (2017). Assessing climate change impacts on wildfire exposure in Mediterranean areas. *Risk Analysis*, *37*(10), 1898–1916.

Lucas, C., Hennessy, K., Mills, G., & Bathols, J. (2007). *Bushfire weather in southeast Australia: Recent trends and projected climate change impacts*. Consultancy Report prepared for the Climate Institute of Australia (pp. 1–80). Bushfire CRC and Australian Bureau of Meteorology.

Molina, D., Castellnou, M., Garcia-Marco, D., & Salgueiro, A. (2010). Improving fire management success through fire behavior specialists. In J. Silva, F. Rego, P. Fernandes, & E. Rigolot (Eds.), *Towards integrated fire management—outcomes of the European project fire paradox* (pp. 105–119). European Forest Institute.

Mutch, R. (2007). *FACES: The story of the victims of southern California's 2003 fire siege* (pp. 1–104). Wildland Fire Lessons Learned Center. https://nsjfire.org/wp-content/uploads/2014/04/Faces-20031.pdf

National Fire Information Center. (2021). *Statistics*. www.nifc.gov/fire-information/statistics

National Interagency Coordination Center. (2018). *Wildland fire summary and statistics annual report*. www.predictiveservices.nifc.gov/intelligence/2018_statssumm/annual_report_2018.pdf

National Wildfire Coordinating Group. (2021). *Loop Fire (California)—November 1, 1966*. 6 Minutes for Safety. www.nwcg.gov/committee/6mfs/loop-fire

Norman, B., Weir, J., Sullivan, K., & Lavis, J. (2014). *Planning and bushfire risk in a changing climate* (pp. 1–78). Bushfire Cooperative Research Center. www.bushfirecrc.com/sites/default/files/urban_and_regional_planning.pdf

Pereira, M., Calado, T., DaCamara, C., & Calheiros, T. (2013). Effects of regional climate change on rural fire in Portugal. *Climate Research*, *57*, 187–200.

Rocca, M., Miniat, C., & Mitchell, R. (2014). Introduction to the regional assessments: Climate change, wildfire, and forest ecosystem services in the USA. *Forest Ecology and Management*, *327*, 265–268.

Silva, J., Rego, F., Fernandes, P., & Ricolet, E. (2010). Introducing the fire paradox. In J. Silva, F. Rego, P. Fernandes, & E. Rigolot (Eds.), *Towards integrated fire management—outcomes of the European project fire paradox* (pp. 3–6). European Forest Institute.

Stambaugh, M., Guyette, R., Stroh, E., Struckhoff, M., & Whittier, J. (2018). Future of southcentral US wildfire probability due to climate change. *Climate Change*, *147*, 617–631.

Turco, M., Jerez, S., Augusto, S., Tarin-Carrasco, P., Ratola, N., Jimenez-Guerrero, P., & Trigo, R. (2019). Climate drivers of the 2017 devastating fires in Portugal. *Scientific Reports*, *9*.

Tymstra, C., Stocks, B., Cai, X., & Flannigan, M. (2020). Wildfire management in Canada: Review, challenges and opportunities. *Progress in Disaster Science, 5*.

US FEMA. (2021). *Glossary of terms*. www.fema.gov/pdf/plan/glo.pdf

US Fire Administration. (1991). *The East Bay Hills Fire, Oakland-Berkeley, California*. USFA Technical Report Series 060.

US Forest Service. (1957). *The Inaja Forest Fire disaster, Cleveland National Forest, California*. USDA.

US Forest Service. (1960). *Decker Fire August 8, 1959; Southern California; Five fatalities*. 06-05-S230-HO [typewritten report].

US Forest Service. (n.d.). *Regional fire analysis: Laguna Fire, September 26, 1970, Cleveland National Forest* [undated typewritten report].

US Marine Corps. (n.d.). *Report of casualties and injuries of U.S. Marine Corps men on Hauser Creek Fire, Cleveland National Forest, October 2, 1943* [undated typewritten report].

US National Interagency Fire Center. (2021). *Federal firefighting costs (suppression only)*. www.nifc.gov/fire-information/statistics/suppression-costs

van Oldenborgh, G., Krikken, F., Lewis, S., Leach, N., Lehner, F., Saunders, K., van Weele, M., Haustein, K., Wallom, D., Sparrow, S., Arrighi, J., Singh, R., van Aalst, M., Philip, S., Vautard, R., & Otto, F. (2021). Attribution of the Australian bushfire risk to anthropogenic climate change. *Natural Hazards and Earth System Sciences, 21*, 941–960.

Wotton, B., Flannigan, M., & Marshall, G. (2017). Potential climate change impacts on fire intensity and key wildfire suppression thresholds in Canada. *Environmental Research Letters, 12*.

CHAPTER 2

Fatal Wildland Fires

John D. DeHaan

2.1 INTRODUCTION: RECONSTRUCTION AND MODELING

With all the variables of wildland fires (fuels, terrain, winds, humidity, temperature, etc.), it is not surprising that reconstruction and modeling are not as easily accomplished as in a structure fire. In a wildland fire, there is typically an identifiable fuel load, consisting of trees, brush, and other vegetation, but what is actually burning can vary widely during the fire. Was it the ground-level fuels, mid-height fuels, or the canopy overhead that promoted the fire spread? What were their pre-fire conditions—wet, moist, or severely dry? What were the wind conditions—including the meteorological winds and fire-induced winds—and how did they vary? How did those conditions change during the fire? What was the topography of the location—open flat ground, hillside, steep and narrow valley? How did all these factors affect the intensity and speed of movement of the fire?

In contrast, in a structural fire, the remains of unburned fuel packages allow the recreation of the major fuels present, their location and their content as relatively fixed elements. Similarly, the location and condition of ventilation openings (doors, windows, even HVAC vents) can be established from their remains or witness observations (were they closed, open, or broken during the fire?). All of these factors allow for a reasonably accurate reconstruction of the initiation and spread of a fire within the confines of the structure.

In the wildfire context of this text, we are faced with recreating the nature of heat from a fire (both radiant, convective, and direct flame contact) with human remains and the intensity and duration of that exposure. This ability to understand and recreate is important for three circumstances: (1) when looking at a landscape at risk for wildfire to see how to best reduce that risk, (2) when a wildfire has emerged and plans must be developed quickly to control and contain the blaze, and (3) when there are fatalities to understand how and why the victims died. To recreate or model a wildfire, we must try to anticipate the movement of a fire front in a wildfire situation or predict how a potential fire would move through a landscape in order to reduce risk. In order to do that, it is important to have a solid understanding of fire behavior and dynamics, the factors that affect that behavior, and the significant limitations we face when working with wildfire. In this chapter, we begin with a discussion of fuels and ignition sources in wildfires, then turn to the development and spread of such fires and the effect of weather, and conclude with discussions of modeling issues around wildland fires and the problems associated with the wildland-urban interface (WUI).

DOI: 10.4324/9781003168010-3

2.2 FUELS

Fuels in wildland fires can range from light, thin-stemmed grasses, weeds, and ground litter (often considered *flashy* fuels for their ease of ignition and rapid flame spread), to intermediate, mid-range brush, shrubs, and saplings under 6 feet in height, to the canopy of leaves, needles, and branches, considered the *canopy* or *crown* of mature trees, that can be up to 200 feet in height. These fuel loads will vary by the types of native vegetation, the time interval between burn episodes, rainfall or drought conditions (moisture availability), and human manipulation of the landscape. Fuel categories in wildland fires are presented in Table 2.1.

Fuels are "rated" by the diameter of the main stalk or trunk as that determines how quickly they respond to changes in atmospheric humidity. Small cross-section fuels, such as grasses, twigs, and pine/fir needles, and ends are considered 1-to-10-minute (or <1-hour) fuels; branches, saplings, brush are 1-to-10-hour fuels; heavy branches and tree trunks are rated 10-to-100-hour fuels (DeHaan & Icove, 2012, p. 332). Dead stumps or boles of mature trees are sometimes considered 1,000-hour fuels. Once ignited, such fuel packages can burn for days or weeks and, therefore, form a source for reignition.

Light fuels such as grasses with a high surface-to-mass ratio will ignite readily when dry and allow the spread of fire by rapid "flashing" across the tops of the stalks or by slow, creeping, smoldering spread along the ground fuels. In semi-arid regions, brush (sometimes generically termed "chaparral") protects its living cells from death by water evaporation (dehydration) by developing a high oil, grease, or wax content in the wood (Johnson, 1992, p. 39). This oil content protects the plant from a hot, dry environment, allowing the cells to maintain a normal moisture level. Eucalypts, sage, and chamise are typical such varieties. The oils and greases in this brush, however, provide an excellent fuel for a fire. A fire in this type of fuel causes the oils and greases to evaporate by radiant heat, creating clouds of flammable vapors that can support awesome, ferocious fire spread as they explode in flames.

TABLE 2.1 Fuel Categories in Wildfires

Category	Example
Duff	Decomposed organic litter (humus) on the base soil
Ground or surface litter	Dropped leaves and branches Needles and twigs
Ladder fuels	Intermediate-height grasses Shrubs (less than 2 meters (6 feet) in height) Seedlings Small trees Lower branches Loose bark
Crown	Canopy of foliage leaves, needles, and fine twigs more than 2 meters aboveground
Slash	Branches and foliage left as heavy ground cover after logging operations

Source: Rothermel (1983, pp. 10–12)

The canopy of leaves and needles of mature trees offer a significant fuel load that is considered to be "porous" as it consists of a lot of thin fuels with significant amounts of air mixed in. These thin fuels can dehydrate quickly due to high atmospheric temperatures and by the radiant heat of an oncoming fire, allowing them to burn very quickly with short duration. Trees growing in close proximity to each other allow for rapid direct flame spread through the canopy. Fires reach the canopy through the presence of extensive *ladder* fuels (between 2 and 6 feet in height) that permit rapid growth of the fire from ground level fuels (grasses) to the fuel-rich canopy. Native peoples in many parts of the world were keenly aware of this danger and reportedly burned off low-growing grasses and shrubs to prevent too many crown fires, which would have endangered the mature trees (Johnson, 1992, pp. 4–6).

Leaf and needle litter and dried ground cover (mosses and duff—the partially decomposed vegetation that covers the mineral base) support low-energy fires. These fires tend to burn fairly slowly (depending on the fuel moisture) but can smolder and then ignite to flame if wind speed increases. The typical duration of such fires is short and their temperatures moderate (less than 500°C). The speed with which the flames advance is controlled largely by the ambient wind (atmospheric, slope-induced, or other). The ground litter may accumulate moisture from contact with the ground, and such mulch will reduce the flammability and flame advance speed.

Heat from typical wildland fires is measured in radiant heat (in kW or MW) per linear meter of fire front. Van Wagner (Van Wagner, 1983) has classified fires in boreal forests as ranging in frontal intensity as

- <10 kW/m from smoldering fire in the organic ground litter,
- 100–800 kW/m in a backfire,
- 200–15,000 kW/m on a surface advancing fire, and
- 8,000–30,000 kW/m for crown fires with a single front (Johnson, 1992, p. 45).

The intensity of these fires show how they may impact structures that are in the proximity even when there is no direct contact. The radiant heat flux from fully developed crown fires can ignite nearby wood structures from considerable distances. They have been measured to produce incident radiant heat fluxes of 40–150 kW/m^2 at distances of 10 meters (33 feet) from experimental fires in stands of 10-meter-tall jack pine/black spruce trees (Cohen, 2004; Stocks et al., 2004). This radiant heat range should be compared to the 20–50 kW/m^2 found in well-ventilated room fires that are capable of igniting furniture and most other common fuel loads as they approach full-room involvement, with room temperatures of 500–1,000°C.

The temperatures reached in wildland fires are dependent on the fuels involved and the ventilation (wind) conditions and are reflected in the height of the flames from the forest floor. Flames one meter (3 feet) in height can reach temperatures of 800°C (1,472°F). Under extreme conditions (10,000 kW/m on the advancing flame front), the flames would be expected to be some 50 feet in height and flame temperatures on the order of 1,200°C (2,192°F) (Gabbert, 2011).

2.3 IGNITION SOURCES

Because of the ease with which many forest or grassland fuels can be ignited, many types of ignition sources have to be considered from small mechanical (friction) sparks to lightning strikes. Electrical power transmission lines (from residential overhead services to interstate networks) have become a major source of fires particularly in today's extensive dry wildland conditions. Un-extinguished camping fires, agricultural clearance, trash fires, and intentional (controlled) grass/brush clearance have caused major fires. Use of machinery—tractors, mowers, harvesters, or even trucks and passenger vehicles—with malfunctioning brakes, bearings, exhaust systems or dragging metal components or tow-chains have been witnessed to be competent ignition sources. Arson fires are not a common source but do occur, particularly in some parts of the world. Discarded smoking materials are, of course, always a consideration. Establishing the ignition source of each fire is the responsibility of the responding fire or law enforcement authorities. Those processes will be discussed in detail in later chapters of this text.

2.4 WILDLAND FIRE DEVELOPMENT AND SPREAD

The growth of a wildfire is dependent on many factors that are rarely considered in structure fires. They are as follows:

- *Topography*: The slope of the ground will determine initial direction and speed of spread of the fire.
- *Aspect*: Fuels on south-facing slopes in the Northern Hemisphere are often exposed to more sun than those on north-facing slopes and are therefore more likely to be drier and able to support larger, faster-moving fires.
- *Terrain*: Flat expanses or surfaces are variable with valleys and defiles of rock or soil (non-combustible) and can draw fires upward (compared to rocky bluffs or cliffs, which divert the fire's flow).
- *Fuels*: These are variable, from short grasses to brush (undergrowth) to saplings to tree canopy. Vegetation fuels may be limited, stunted, or completely blocked by geological features. This is particularly true of grasses and shrubs, which are denied water by the exposure.

A fire ignited in a fuel array on flat ground with no wind creates a vertical column of hot gases, combustion products, and flames. This is a turbulent column, losing temperature and buoyancy as it mixes with the surrounding air and loses heat by radiation and irregular mixing (as seen in Figure 2.1), unlike that of a candle flame which is laminar—maintaining a core of hot, luminous combustion products with slow mixing. With a uniform layer of fuel, it leaves a circular pattern on the substrate below as seen in Figure 2.2. The heat from the lowest portion of the flame plume (periphery) may heat the adjacent fuel bed and spread the fire out from the fire, but most of the spread to the fuel bed, or the supporting (combustible) layer, will be by direct contact with flames or coals. As a result, horizontal growth of the char pattern will be limited. Air movement around the column will begin at the base of the fire by entrainment (drawing air into the flame plume) and upward by buoyancy.

Exterior fires are most likely accompanied by some form of air movement, even if it is minimal. The presence of any slope to the supporting surface can trigger upslope spread of the fire. For example, air heated by even a modest grass fire will promote upslope spread to the fire. The introduction of air movement can be from atmospheric effects (high-/low-pressure zones). It can also result from diurnal winds caused by daytime solar heating and nighttime cooling. These are typically upslope on sunny days and downslope after sunset. In some areas, there are also foehn winds when warm, dry winds flowing across mountain ridges can produce very strong downslope winds on the leeward side, particularly when funneled into valleys or passes. These are referred to as Diablo, Santa Ana, or Chinook winds in some areas. They are particularly dangerous on hot days in late summer or fall when the fuels are most ignitable due to desiccation. All winds can cause movement of a fire across a slope, or down a slope when its normal direction would be upslope as the hot gases from the fire move upward. The weather in the area of origin of a wildland fire (and at the apparent time of detection) is particularly critical to documentation.

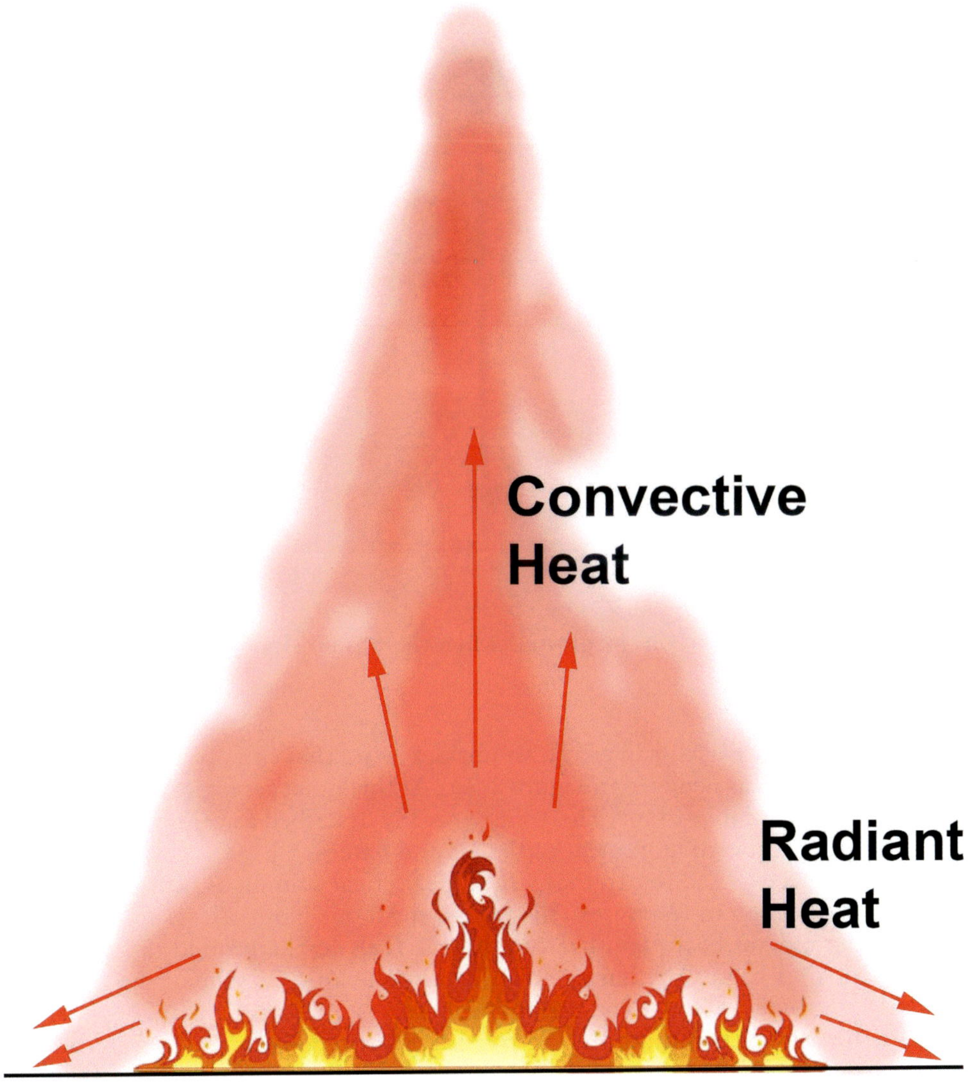

FIGURE 2.1 Wildfire on flat ground with no wind.

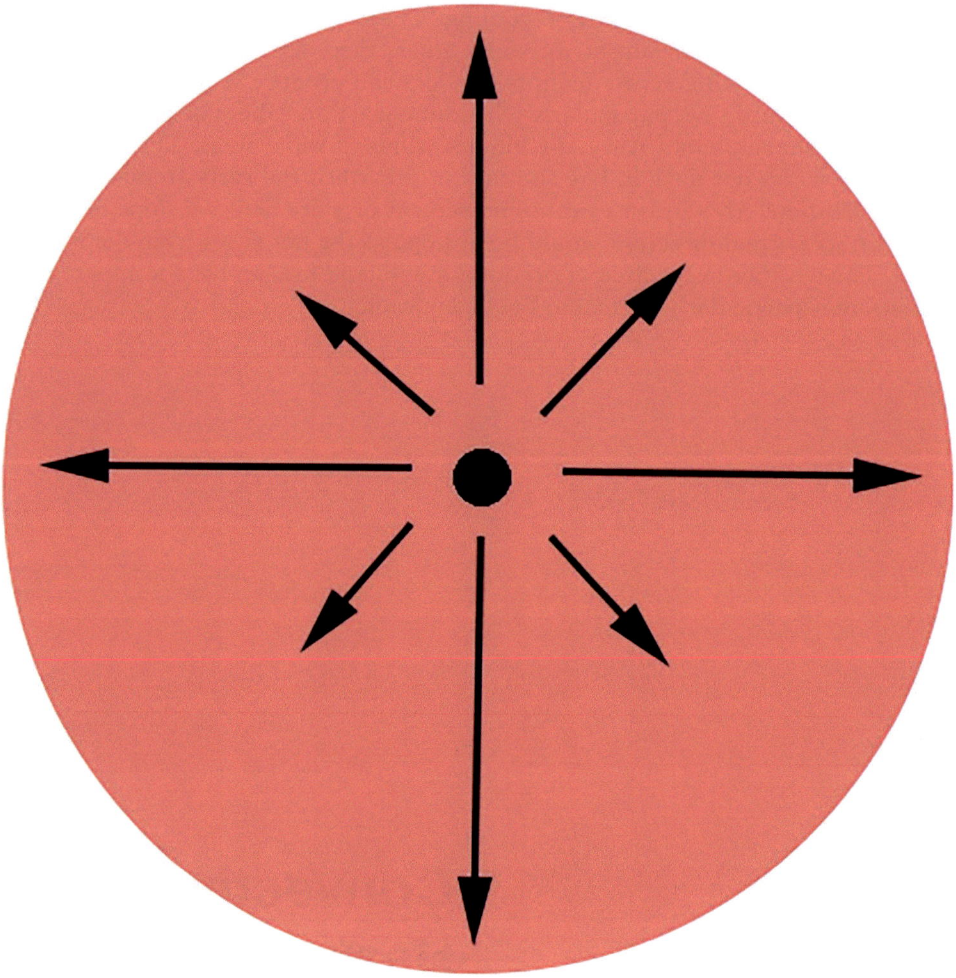

FIGURE 2.2 Burn pattern on the ground when there is no slope and no wind.

Ignition of the fire itself can create an upslope wind that can produce extension of the fire up the slope, as depicted in Figure 2.3A. At this time, geological features of the surroundings become important. These are generally described as valleys or defiles and can accelerate the upward movement of the air and flames.

When a fire is exposed to external wind, the vertical column of heated gases leans in the wind's direction in response. This pushes the flame plume closer to the ground, increasing the radiant heat exposure of adjacent fuels to the ground (as depicted in Figure 2.3B). This causes the burn pattern to assume an oval shape. The higher the wind speed, the more extended the pattern becomes (as in Figure 2.3C). These patterns give rise to descriptive names for the fire pattern. The predominant direction of spread is designated the *head*. The sides of the elongated burn pattern are called the *flanks* and the slowest growing edge is called the *foot* or *heel* of the fire pattern. These are denoted in Figure 2.4.

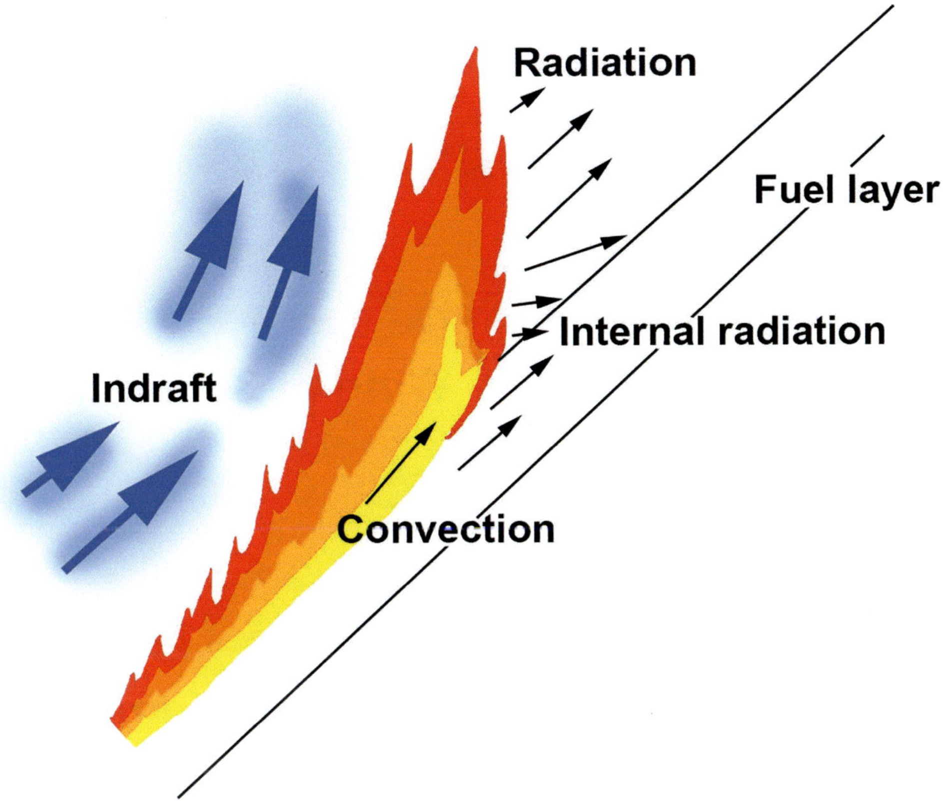

FIGURE 2.3A Upslope fire.

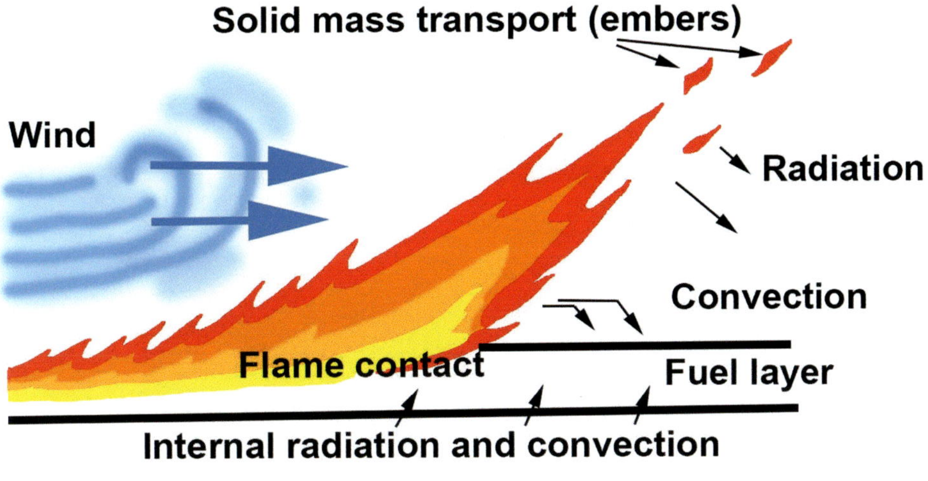

FIGURE 2.3B Wind-driven fire.

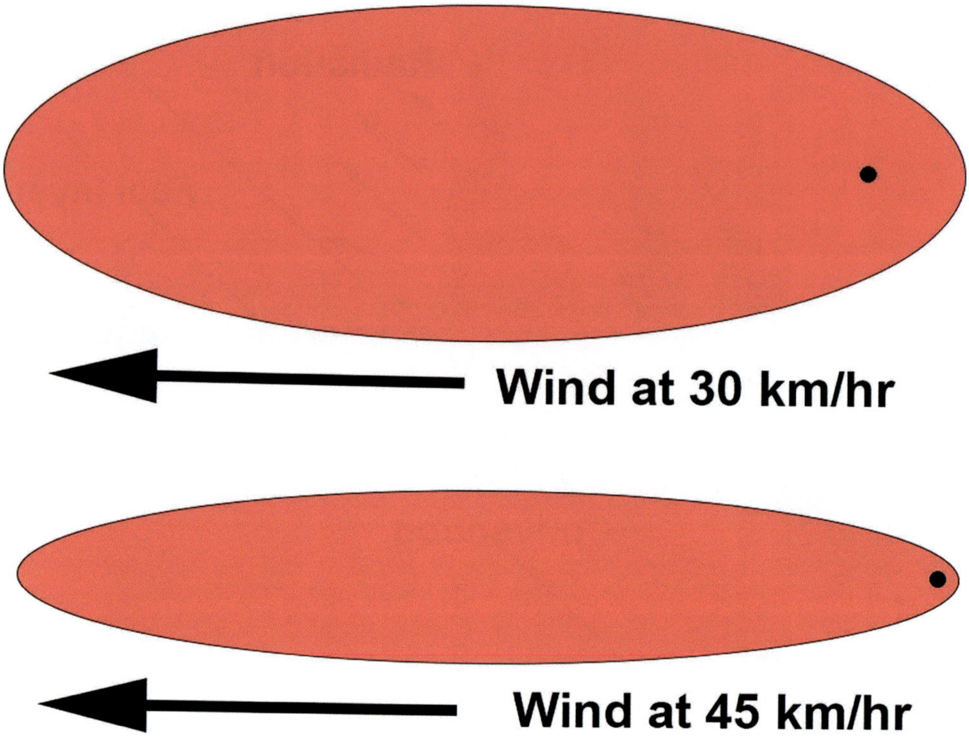

FIGURE 2.3C Effect of wind on ground fuel burn pattern of different speeds with ignition source indicated by the black dot.

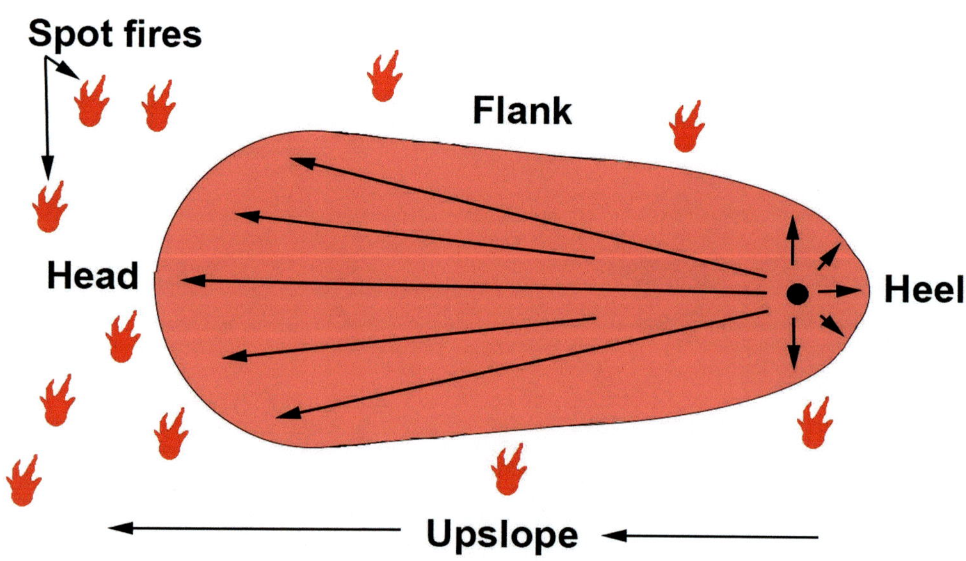

FIGURE 2.4 Typical wildland fire pattern development.

The speed with which a wildfire can travel depends on the winds developed, the terrain it is moving across, and the nature of the fuel materials involved. Light fuels (<1 hour) have been estimated to exhibit maximum forward speeds of 15–20 km/hr (9–12.5 mph) (Shaw, 2022). The larger the diameter of the fuels (the main fuel is heavy timber), in general the slower the progression will be.

The stronger the wind, the higher the chances of hot embers or burning brands (burning leaves, twigs, small branches, and ground fuels) escaping the flame plume and falling away from the main fire to create small, separate *spot fires* to be noted and documented during the early inspection. In severe fire conditions, massive curtains of embers and brands can be the major source of fire spread, sometimes reaching half a mile or more in front of the main body of fire.

With very large fires, an external wind can initiate a spiral motion to the rising fire plume. This rotating mass of flame usually stays in place above the hottest part of the fire, usually referred to as a *fire whirl.* In some rare cases, a very large spinning plume can actually detach from the burning forest or structure and move into unburned fuels as a separate fire labeled a *fire tornado.*

2.4.1 Weather Data

Pre-fire weather conditions can have a very large effect on the ignition and progression of a wildfire. From a recent rain or heavy dew, accumulated moisture must be driven off before the vegetation target fuel can be dried out and heated to the point of ignition. Periods of high temperatures and low humidity will make any exposed vegetation easier to ignite. This is the cause of much larger acreage of wildland fire losses in the US and many other countries as climate change is decreasing annual rainfalls and increasing periods of increased ambient temperatures. The US Environmental Protection Agency (EPA) reported that the average number of wildfires in the US has been steadily dropping since 2006 with an average of about 70,000 reported fires per year. The annual acreage burned, however, has been rising steadily since 1995 and now frequently ranges from 8 to 10 million acres per year (US Environmental Protection Agency, n.d.).

Today, there are numerous sources of weather data (for both pre-fire conditions and fire progression analysis) even for remote areas accessible by digital sources. These can provide accurate information about possible origins even for historical events. This author has used the Weather Underground website for data on both structural and wildland fires. Advice on field-portable weather stations or equipment will be discussed in the chapter on scene investigation.

2.5 MODELING OF WILDLAND FIRES

Because of the number of factors that shape the development and spread of wildland fires, accurately modeling such fires has proven to be very difficult. The earliest modeling was reported by Rothermel in 1972 (Rothermel, 1972, 1983).

These interpretative tools began as algebraic equations of flame height, heat transfer, and radiative heat loss that can be done with a pocket calculator with scientific functions to model fires within structures. They have been codified in software packages such as FPETools (developed at National Institute of Standards and Technology

[NIST]) and Fire Dynamics Tools (FDT) developed at NIST and are usable on a personal computer or laptop. During the 1980s and 1990s, a series of computer programs were developed to predict specific fire behaviors, such as smoke and fire travel, sprinkler activation, or safe evacuation times. These were in turn developed into programs, called zone models, that would predict the development of general room fire processes, like the growth of the hot gas layer in the room given heat release rates of major fuel packages and the transition to flashover (where all fuels exposed in the room ignite and burn as fast as ventilation permits). The most advanced room fire models today are considered computational fluid dynamics (CFD) models because they divide the room or building into numerous small volumes and calculate heat transfer and fluid flows into and out of each small volume. The most widely known one is FDS—the Fire Dynamics Simulator, developed at NIST and revised periodically (McGrattan et al., 2020).

Since 1999, two wildfire computer modeling programs, BEHAVE and FARSITE, have been widely used (Andrews & Bevins, 1999; Finney & Andrews, 1999). They have been modified and improved over recent years, with BEHAVE Plus and FARSITE 4 being the most recent versions. Modeling of large-scale wildland fires has proven to be challenging when attempts were made to predict fire progression in complex exposures with variations in weather or topography (Mell et al., 2007; Sullivan, 2009). NIST reported that several programs currently in development and use for forecasting fire progression on a regional scale include Bluesky (a smoke transport model by NIST), Firefly (University of Maryland), FireMap (UC San Diego and LAFD), and Prometheus (Canadian Interagency Forest Fire Centre) (McDermott et al., 2019).

FARSITE 4 was incorporated into a recent product called FlamMap (developed by US Forest Service Rocky Mountain Research Station and Alturas Solutions of Missoula Montana). It was employed in the Markley Fire (part of the LNU Lightning Complex Fire, August 14–18, 2020). It is a fire mapping and analysis system capable of dealing with large, complex geological landscape contours. It is limited in dealing with weather, fuel moisture, and temperature variations. However, it has proved useful in specific situations. When the remains of a homicide victim were found in the burned area (some two weeks after the fire passed through the location), it was found that its predictions of the direction of the fire growth across complex terrain did not match the actual growth pattern of the fire as it burned itself out. This information was critical in establishing the time of ignition near the body. Refinement of this model and others in use continues to improve their accuracy.

2.6 WUI FIRES

The development of fully developed crown fires and high winds pose the threat of wildland-urban interface (WUI) fires. The US Forest Service estimates more than 35,000 structures were destroyed by wildfires in the last ten years, and some 70,000 communities and 44 million homes are at risk from WUI incidents (US Forest Service, 2022). The risks are many to both residential and commercial properties. Hot embers and flaming brands can ignite wood shingle roofs and siding, wood exterior decks (and new wood fiber/polymer composite features), and leaf-filled gutters and enter the structure through roof and attic vents to ignite interior fuels. Brands can also readily ignite dry, decorative ground cover (dry grass or chipped/shredded bark). Large exterior fires can cause windows to shatter and gravel and tar composite shingles to melt and ignite. As residential development continues in wildland areas, the annual losses mount across the US.

For many years, multi-lane highways were considered to be reliable "fire breaks" that wildland fires could not cross. Notable exceptions, such as the Oakland Hills Fire in 1991 and, more recently, the 2017 Tubbs Fire in Santa Rosa, California, proved wildfires could cross wide freeways and destroy city neighborhoods when supported by strong winds. City fire departments are capable of controlling and extinguishing most structural fires but cannot stop the development of WUI fires where entire neighborhoods are on fire at the same time. With continuing effects of climate change killing large swaths of forests, it has become a problem many cities face.

There has been significant progress recently in addressing these risks through a variety of means. Community-wide wildfire protection plans are strongly suggested (Evans et al., 2004; Mell et al., 2009). Civil engineers are now coming to serve in a fire prevention role. Landowners are encouraged to remove large trees considered too close to residences and modify landscaping to minimize the chances of blown embers or brands from igniting potential fuels, such as dry grass and ground cover close to the structure. Clearing defensible space around residential and commercial properties includes removal of wood and leaf piles, lawn furniture, propane-tank barbecues, discarded cardboard waste and freight pallets. Radiant heat from the crown fire of a single large tree can ignite wood structures many feet away. Prescriptive "controlled burn" fires have been used in many areas to reduce the size of community threats by producing a defensible space around the community (US Forest Service, 2022).

Building codes are slowly being revised to prevent the construction of residences and outbuildings too close to one another or too close to high-risk wildland areas. Non-combustible structural finishes, such as metal roofs, metal vents over roof openings, and brick or stucco wall finishes, should be strongly urged in fire-susceptible areas. Masonry barrier walls have been used to surround housing developments in high-fire-risk areas. Emergency evacuation plans are being developed to better advise residents of the risks of major fires. City planners have to ensure that streets in fire-susceptible areas are wide enough for emergency vehicles to enter and residents to escape and are laid out to permit speedy evacuation along multiple routes. A new professional field is being developed called fire-resilient community design, which considers all of the elements involved in minimizing fire dangers and losses of both life and property. The need for this was evident in the deaths of so many people while trying to escape firestorms in rural areas served by only one or two roads (such as the Camp Fire in Paradise, California, in 2018).

REFERENCES

Andrews, P., & Bevins, C. (1999). BEHAVE Fire modeling system: Redesign and expansion. *Fire Management Notes*, *59*, 16–19.

Cohen, J. (2004). Relating flame radiation to home ignition using modeling and experimental crown fire. *Canadian Journal of Forest Research*, *34*, 1616–1626.

DeHaan, J., & Icove, D. (2012). *Kirk's Fire investigation* (7th ed.) Pearson Health Science.

Evans, D., Rehm, R., & Baker, E. (2004). Physics-based modeling of community fire. *Interflam*, *2004*, 1065–1076.

Finney, M., & Andrews, P. (1999). FARSITE: A program for fire growth simulation. *Fire Management Notes*, *59*, 13–15.

Gabbert, B. (2011). *At what temperature does a forest fire burn?* Wildfire Today.

Johnson, E. (1992). *Fire and vegetation dynamics*. Cambridge University Press.

McDermott, R., Bryner, N., & Heintz, J. (2019). *Large outdoor modeling (LOFM) workshop summary report*. Special Publication (NIST SP). National Institute of Standards and Technology. https://doi.org/10.6028/NIST.SP.1245

McGrattan, K., Hostikka, S., Floyd, J., McDermott, R., & Vanella, M. (2020). *Fire dynamics simulator (version 5). Technical reference guide, Volume 1: Mathematical modeling*. National Institute of Standards and Technology Special Publication.

Mell, W., Jenkins, M., Gould, J., & Cheney, P. (2007). A physics-based approach to modeling grassland fires. *International Journal of Wildland Fire*, *16*(1), 1–22.

Mell, W., Manzello, S., Maranghides, A., Butry, D., & Rehm, R. (2009). The wildland-urban interface fire problem. *International Journal of Wildland Fire*, *19*, 238–251.

Rothermel, R. (1983). *How to predict the spread and intensity of forest and range fires*. Gen. Tech. Rep. INT-143 (pp. 1–161). U.S. Department of Agriculture, Forest Service, Intermountain Forest and Range Experiment Station. www.fs.usda.gov/rm/pubs_int/int_gtr143.pdf

Rothermel, R. C. (1972). *A mathematical model for predicting fire spread in wildland fuels* (Research Paper INT-115). U.S. Department of Agriculture, Forest Service.

Shaw, E. (2022). *How fast can forest fires spread?* https://sciencing.com/three-examples-environmental-disturbances-biomes-11864.html

Stocks, B., Alexander, M., Wooton, M., Stefner, C., Flannigan, M., Taylor, S., Lavoie, N., Mason, J., Hartley, G., Maffey, M., Dalrymple, G., Blake, T., & Cruz, M. (2004). Crown fire behavior in a northern jack pine-black spruce forest. *Canadian Journal of Forest Research*, *34*, 1548–1560.

Sullivan, A. (2009). Wildland surface fire spread modelling 1997–2007.3: Simulation and mathematical analogue models. *International Journal of Wildland Fire*, *18*, 387–403.

US Environmental Protection Agency. (n.d.). *Climate change indicators: Wildfires 2021*. www.epa.cov/climate/indicators/climate-change-indicators-wildfires

US Forest Service. (2022). *Fire adapted communities*. www.fs.usda.gov/managing-land/fire/fac

Van Wagner, C. (1983). Fire behavior in northern conifer forests and shrublands. In R. Wein & D. MacLean (Eds.), *The role of northern circumpolar ecosystems* (pp. 65–80). John Wiley and Sons.

CHAPTER 3

An International Perspective on Fatal Wildfires

Gavriil Xanthopoulos and Alison Galloway

3.1 INTRODUCTION

Fatalities due to vegetation fires are not uncommon around the world. They are caused in various ways, and all of them are worth studying in order to prevent future deaths. Statistics show that wildfires may indirectly increase the probability of health problems and cause numerous fatalities due to smoke exposure (Reid et al., 2016), but here our concern is the fatalities caused directly by exposure to wildfires at the fire scene or as a direct outcome of such exposure. The discussion of wildfire fatalities is centered on both firefighter and civilian deaths. These deaths have many common characteristics but also certain significant differences. Examining the global picture and highlighting some of the most striking events help us develop a better understanding of where they happen and the conditions that lead to accidents.

The elements that are of interest, in addition to the distinction of firefighter versus civilian deaths, include the following:

- Coincidental loss of one or two persons versus a mass fatality
- Weather and fuel conditions
- Fire behavior conditions under which the accident occurred
- Location of where the accident happened (in open space, in a vehicle or in a building)
- Access conditions
- Time available for the victims to react
- In case of a building, the way it was built and if it was prepared for a fire
- The sex and age of the victims
- The response of the victims
- The preparation of the victims (PPE, clothing, tools)

As a rule, especially in mass fatalities, all these may vary by each individual. Furthermore, it is rare to find reliable data on all these elements. In this chapter, first we present a number of serious accidents, including both firefighter and civilian deaths, and briefly highlight the contributing factors. Then we examine some of the studies that have analyzed fire fatalities data around the world. These form the basis for a discussion

DOI: 10.4324/9781003168010-4

that 40aims at highlighting the most important commonalities and differences, leading to some interesting conclusions.

Before presenting these cases, however, we need to point out that in many countries, fires affecting tall forests and other forest lands, classified as forests by national legislation or according to international standards, are only a portion of the fires that burn vegetation across the various natural landscapes. In some areas, low bush, shrubs, and grasses can produce devastating fires with both ecological and sociopolitical consequences. There are many names for referring to all these fires, such as forest fires, wildfires, brushfires, bushfires, and grass fires. Since fires burning on all types and sizes of vegetated lands can potentially cause fatalities, in this section we call them "landscape fires." This term includes all natural and cultural fires, as well as fires in developed peri-urban landscapes, where homes, other structures, and even industrial installations are mixed or border with vegetation, as long as the fire is mainly carried by vegetation. There is also a cross-cutting category that may include any of the types of fire and is described through the term "megafire." This term, coined in the 2000s (The Brookings Institution, 2005), refers to "those fires that exhibit fire behaviour characteristics that exceed all efforts at control, regardless of the type, kind, or number of firefighting assets that are brought to bear." They are usually "extreme wildfire events (EWE)" (Tedim et al., 2018), being impressive, destructive, and sometimes fatal. The overall size of a megafire, however, may not reflect the deadliness of its nature, which depends more on fire rate of spread and intensity of the flames, often within a local area or even within a particular part of a fire.

3.2 LANDSCAPE FIRE FATALITIES AROUND THE GLOBE

The focus in this chapter is on fatalities caused by exposure to hot flame gasses, smoke, and/or radiant heat. However, it must be remembered that only a portion of deaths during a wildfire fit within this category. Fatalities are often caused indirectly by working on fire suppression, such as falling trees, vehicle and aerial firefighting accidents, or health problems, such as heart attack due to stress. This expanded group of deaths are not included in our selection of fire death examples. We begin by looking separately at firefighter deaths and then at civilian deaths.

3.3 FIREFIGHTER FATALITIES IN LANDSCAPE FIRES AROUND THE WORLD

As fire crews are placed on the frontlines of a fire, it is expected that they are at high risk (Dickman, 2018; Mangan, 2007). Through time, there have been numerous accidents involving firefighters on the fire line. Those involving one or two individuals are often the result of coincidence. The actual cause varies from lack of information (e.g., low visibility) to poor judgment (e.g., heroic stance against the odds) and from a mechanical failure (e.g., a water pump failure, a driving accident, a firetruck failure, or a blown-up tire) to a sudden health problem (e.g., a strained ankle or a heart attack) later masked by the fire damage and is often hard to determine with certainty. However, accidents involving a larger number of firefighters often have received deeper investigation, as they are of higher interest and can contribute more to understanding the conditions under which they happened, looking for commonalities that will lead to safer firefighting guidelines in the future.

Most of the well documented and analyzed cases with multiple firefighter fatalities can be found in the United States. For example, the Griffith Park Fire killed at least 29 volunteer firefighters in 1933 (Glendale News Press, 1993). Better documentation exists on the Mann Gulch Fire of August 5, 1949, which killed 16 firefighters (Rothermel, 1993) and became the spark for making safety of firefighters a priority for the USDA Forest Service. In addition to a good description of the event, numerous scientific publications have debated the errors that were made, including organizational shortcomings. In 2010, the crew of Edward Pulaski near Wallace, Idaho, became entrapped by the Great Fire of 2010, on August 20th. Realizing that he and his 45-man crew were doomed if they stayed where they were, Pulaski led his men to safety in an abandoned prospector's mine. He did not allow anyone to leave the tunnel, threatening to shoot him with his pistol; he lost only five of his men (https://en.wikipedia.org/wiki/Ed_Pulaski). However, firefighter deaths continued with the tragic loss of 19 "hotshot" firefighters in the 2013 Yarnell Hill Fire in Arizona (Yarnell Hill Fire Serious Accident Investigation Team, 2013; Dickman, 2018).

In other countries, major forest fire disasters are almost always reported in the mass media, but detailed investigation and scientific analysis are sometimes weak or missing. However, it is always important to make use of whatever information is available in order to remember and learn as much as possible and ultimately to compare cases with the well documented examples from the USA. The latter are not presented here but are considered in the discussion. Here, we refer to some of the most important and interesting cases with multiple firefighter fatalities outside of the USA, mentioning a few key points about each of them that help to illustrate the reasons for the disaster.

- 1949. The fire that caused the highest number of firefighter fatalities in Europe was a 50,000-hectare fire in the Landes region of Southwest France. It burned near the Atlantic coast between Bordeaux and Arcachon, under dry and hot weather conditions, in a non-Mediterranean area, mostly covered with maritime pine (*Pinus pinaster*) forest. On August 20, the fire, responding to a change in wind direction and strong gusts, flared up to produce flames of 100 meters or more, overwhelming, in less than an hour, the poorly equipped (by current standards) firefighters who were trying to suppress it. Eighty-two firefighters, volunteers, and soldiers lost their lives.
- 1971. On April 4, near Kure, western Honshu, Japan, a fire, started by construction workers to clear weeds, got out of control when a strong wind moved through the area. Eighteen of the firefighters who tried to control it were trapped in the blaze and lost their lives.
- 1975. The largest forest fire in Germany happened between August 8 and 17 on the Lüneburger heath in Lower Saxony, in the north of the country. It followed a long period of drought with hot summer weather and dried-out coniferous forests, where there existed a lot of storm-damaged wood left in the wake of Hurricane Quimburga on November 13, 1972. About 15,000 firefighters and 3,800 fire engines from across Germany fought the fire, which probably had a behavior beyond the level for which they were prepared. In one case, near a village called Meinersen, a sudden wind direction change created flames of 20 meters that cut off a Volunteer Fire Service fire truck, killing five firefighters.

- 1987. The Black Dragon Fire, also known as the 1987 Daxing'anling Wildfire, started on May 6 near the border of China with the Soviet Union and continued burning for almost a month, finally burning one million hectares in both countries. China sent about 60,000 troops to fight the fire, but they were poorly equipped, mostly with fire beaters (sticks with large flaps used to swat out the flames). Burning in drought-stricken conifer forests under high winds, the fire took the characteristics of a firestorm. It caused many fatalities, with reports varying between 191 and 211 people, most of them on May 7 and 8. More than 250 people were injured.
- 1994. Twenty-five volunteer firefighters died in a rangeland fire on the coast of northeastern Patagonia (Dentoni et al., 2001). The rangeland caught fire and the firefighters were dispatched to what was thought to be a manageable blaze. A sudden change in wind direction triggered by a sea breeze coupled with the energy produced by the fire transformed a flank of the fire into the fire front. The fire surrounded the fire crews, and no one survived.
- 1998. One volunteer and three professional firefighters died during the Mt. Hymettus Fire on July 22, 1998, only a few hundred meters from Athens (Xanthopoulos, 2007). They stopped their fire engine at the U-point of a road in a canyon with the fire below them, preparing to fight. However, the fire suddenly picked up speed and swept up the canyon spreading perpendicular to the prevailing wind direction. They were surprised, and rather than stay with the fire engine, they tried to outrun the fire uphill in the canyon, but they were overrun. The engine, which was full of water, suffered only minor damages.
- 2005. A landscape fire showing eruptive behavior killed 11 firefighters in Guadalajara, Spain (Viegas & Caballero, 2009). They were attempting to hold the advance of the flames to a ridge, thereby protecting a local village. However, the flames got into a large pine stand and developed into a fire eruption. This change prompted most of the firefighters to flee along the ridge in smaller vehicles above the waterline for the slope. They were overcome when there was a second fire eruption that swept over them. A 12th firefighter, who remained with the heavy fire engine, in an area with less vegetation, survived.
- 2006. Six firefighters lost their lives in Famalicão da Serra in Portugal (Viegas et al., 2009). They were protecting a pine plantation stand in a canyon when there was a massive fire eruption resulting in a crown fire. As they raced along the road across the waterline of the canyon, the fire erupted again. One took refuge along the road while the others tried to outrun the flames uphill. Their bodies were found scattered among the terraces above the road.
- 2007. Kornati Fire in Croatia resulted in the deaths of 12 professional and volunteer firefighters in a small canyon with a relatively low fuel load near Sipnate Bay on Kornat Island (Stipanicev & Viegas, 2009; Viegas et al., 2008). Landed by helicopter on the top of a hill, they initially set out toward a water reservoir that had been placed there earlier. They could not see the approaching flames come over the ridge until they were well on their way across the canyon. At that point they decided to retreat but did not realize the fire had also come across the southern mouth of the canyon. The steep slopes created a fire eruption along the waterline that outpaced their ability to climb back up the steep, boulder-strewn slope, and all but one perished. The sole survivor ran back through the flames and into burned ground.

- 2007. In Greece, three firefighters perished at the fire of Doxaro on the island of Crete when a brushfire they were fighting in a canyon picked up speed following the passage of a heavy firefighting helicopter above them. They tried to escape running up the canyon with the fire behind them but in vain. A fourth firefighter survived taking refuge behind rocks, but he was seriously injured. Three more firefighters died that year, together with 21 civilians, at an accident near the village of Artemida in Peloponnese, which is described in the following civilian fatalities section (Xanthopoulos et al., 2009b).
- 2012. On January 1, 2012, in the Carahue area of the La Araucanía region, in the south of Chile, seven firefighters lost their lives fighting an arson fire in the lands of a private company. Strong winds were blamed as the cause of the disaster by a surviving firefighter. In the aftermath, there were accusations of delayed initial attack to keep the fire small and of inadequate training of the firefighters who had been contracted by the private company.
- 2014. On October 18, 2014, in Guachipas, Salta, Argentina, four young firefighters were trapped by a forest fire and lost their lives. They were sent to fight a fire that, according to a video recorded 44 minutes before their death, was much more intense than what they could handle. There was no planning; they received no information about what the fire was doing, and there were no foreseen escape routes.
- 2019. On March 31, a lightning-caused forest fire in Muli County, Liangshan Yi Autonomous Prefecture, Sichuan Province, China, burning at an elevation of 3,800 meters, killed 27 firefighters and four local helpers. A change in wind direction caused a huge fireball, trapping them.
- 2020. Eighteen firefighters and a farm worker acting as their guide were killed on March 31, battling a fire in rugged terrain, at an elevation of 4,000 meters, in Muli County, Liangshan Yi Autonomous Prefecture, Sichuan Province, China. The fire was burning Yunnan pine (*Pinus yunnanensis*) and shrubs. The group became trapped due to a sudden change in wind direction. Ultimately, the fire resulted in the deaths of 31 people after burning for nine days (Li et al., 2021).

3.4 CIVILIAN FATALITIES IN LANDSCAPE FIRES AROUND THE WORLD

Civilian deaths may vary more regarding the conditions, as they have not purposefully put themselves in the vicinity of the fire. People are largely fleeing the fire or have been sheltering in their homes, either passively or as a last survival strategy after actively defending the house.

- 1936. One of the worst fire accidents ever occurred on August 3, 1936, at an industrial community named Kursha-2, in the Central Meshchyora, Ryazan Oblast, Russia. It was a community built for the exploitation of the local forests. It was destroyed completely by a crown fire that took the characteristics of a firestorm on that day. Evacuation by rail was delayed due to bad decisions, and when it was attempted, the train was trapped at a burning bridge. Nearly all the people on the train and those who had remained at the locomotive depot, unable to get on the train, died. In total there were 1,200 fatalities.

- 1983. More than 180 bushfires occurred in southeastern Australia on February 16, 1983, under severe drought conditions. They were fanned by winds that reached 110 km/hr. Most importantly, these winds were associated with the passage of a cold front that brought a sudden change in wind direction surprising people and firefighters as the flanks of fires with long perimeters became kilometers-wide fire fronts in a matter of minutes. The fires caused 47 fatalities in Victoria (14 firefighters) and 28 in South Australia (three firefighters).
- 1993. In a very dry year, on July 30, on the island of Ikaria, Greece, a fire that broke out under very strong wind, burning Calabrian pine (*Pinus brutia*) forest and agricultural fields, spread quickly in the area of the main town of the island Agios Kyrikos. Thirteen people lost their lives, mainly due to delayed evacuation. On one occasion, five people perished when they tried to flee in their car. After an apparent collision, these people were caught by smoke and flames as they were trying to leave their damaged car.
- 2000. Eleven people died near the Greek-Albanian border in 2000, in a fire season characterized by extreme drought. The fire had been burning for several days before winds increased and the fire front crossed the border into Greece, near the village of Haraugi. There, it spread up a wide valley, covering a distance of 17 km in four hours. Many were evacuated by the authorities, but some were caught by the flames as they left or stayed to defend their homes. All 11 individuals who died were older than 67 years of age suggesting that either mobility or health issues may have played a role in their circumstances (Xanthopoulos, 2007).
- 2007. In the extreme 2007 fire season in Greece, a total of 84 people lost their lives due to forest fires. Twenty four of the fatalities occurred in an accident near the village of Artemida in Ilia, Peloponnese (Xanthopoulos et al., 2009a, 2009b). During a very dry year with a series of heat waves, August 24 brought high winds, while relative humidity dropped below 20% in midday, exacerbating an already dangerous situation. A fire, started by a backyard stove, jumped into vegetation and spread, fed by the dry grasses in the olive groves. Spotting allowed the fire front to expand extremely rapidly. The people of the village of Makistos, which was hit first, mostly fled to nearby Artemida with the fire behind them. Together with the people of Artemida, they moved as a convoy of private cars toward the town of Zaharo. On the way, they met an incoming firetruck with three seasonal firefighters who turned around to escort the convoy. In a matter of minutes, however, the fire cut off their route and also their possibility to turn back, trapping them in a shallow ravine and surrounding them completely. The fire moved so quickly that the firefighters were unable to deploy their equipment. Some chose to drive through the flames and survived, but a total of 24 people, including the firefighters, lost their lives, either in their cars or trying to outrun the flames. A group of cars that were delayed by a few minutes in leaving Artemida, realized that the road would be cut off by the flames. They chose a different route, to the village of Smerna, and survived. There were no fatalities among those who stayed in Makistos and Artemida. In Artemida, only 17 of the 70 houses, which are mostly of stone or brick construction, burned.
- 2009. For the two weeks prior to the disastrous "Black Saturday," the southeastern area of Australia had experienced a massive and severe heat wave, resulting in a significant increase in heat-related deaths (Cordner et al., 2011; Teague et al., 2010a). On February 7, 2009, this heat was accompanied by extreme wind conditions with erratic gusts exceeding 144 km/hr (90 mph), causing spot

fires up to 20–40 kilometers away. About 400 separate fires resulted, the deadliest of which was the Kilmore East Fire, originating with fallen powerlines. Origin could not be determined for all the fires, although arson was confirmed or strongly suspected in a number of fires. In all the fires, over 2,000 homes were destroyed, along with 61 businesses. As recovery began, it was found that 173 people lost their lives in the fire complex, 119 of them by the Kilmore East Fire. Nine died in hospital of their injuries, while 163 bodies were recovered in the aftermath and remains of one individual were never found (Cordner et al., 2011; Haynes et al., 2020; Leditschke et al., 2011; Teague et al., 2010b, 2010a). The bodies included 17 minors, most of whom died with parents or another adult. Adults were often late in evacuating or had chosen to stay and defend their properties. Of special interest was the Murrindindi Fire, which, following a change in wind direction, swept through the unsuspecting tourist town of Marysville, killing 40 people and injuring 73, as they were not able to shelter in their homes. All but 14 of the houses of the town were destroyed.

- 2010. An accidental fire that started on December 2, 2010, in the Mediterranean forests of Mount Carmel, northern Israel became the deadliest landscape fire in Israel's history. The contributing circumstances included a prolonged period of hot, dry weather and high winds. Forty-four people lost their lives in this fire, 36 of whom were Israel Prison Service cadets. This latter group was on a bus en route to a prison with orders to evacuate the prisoners. The bus was trapped by the fire and probably a tree falling across the narrow road to the prison. The fire also cut off the possibility of retreat. The cadets left the bus trying to escape on foot, but they were not able to make it. The dead included the chief of Haifa's police, two other police officers whose car was also trapped, and three firefighters.
- 2017. In total, 500,000 hectares burned in 2017 in Portugal with the loss of more than 120 lives. Following an intense heat wave, a series of four fires on June 17, 2017, swept across central Portugal in the Pedrógão Grande region, probably originating from dry lightning (Tedim et al., 2018). Over the next week, 45,000 hectares were burned. Warning systems were inadequate or delayed. The prevailing wind was not strong, but the heavy and dry fuels resulted in a convection plume dominated fire (Rothermel, 1991) which created strong, erratic, and unpredictable downdrafts, rapidly expanding the fire fronts. Sixty-six people were confirmed to have died including one firefighter. Most of them were trapped in their vehicles trying to evacuate. Four died at home when their mobility limitations prevented their timely escape. Thirty-one people died in or around their vehicles.
- More extreme fires came between the 13th and 18th of October 2017 in the Central Region of Portugal as a result of very strong winds associated with the passage of Hurricane Ophelia along the Atlantic coast. Seven of the fires grew very large exhibiting two different fire behavior patterns. Wind near the coast, under the influence of Hurricane Ophelia, caused winds and plumes to be driven inland. The combination of fuel aridity and high and erratic winds resulted in unprecedented peak fire growth rates (Castellnou et al., 2018). The fires resulted in the deaths of 53 people, 51 of whom were civilians (Viegas, 2019). Deaths were scattered between five of the more than 500 fire events at the time. The fatalities most often occurred as people attempted to flee, but 17 of them died in their homes. In many cases, the homes of people who died as they were fleeing, remained unharmed.
- 2018. A forest fire in Northeast Attica in Greece caused 102 fatalities as it burned through forests and urbanized areas (Lekkas et al., 2018;

FIGURE 3.1 The cliff over the sea at Mati where 24 people were trapped by the flames, unable to escape (upper image); Silver Point at the beach at Mati where people were trapped and were forced into the sea (middle image); and the road to Silver Beach at the point where more than 60 cars were jammed, leaving people to abandon the vehicles and run 100 meters to Silver Beach to get into the sea (lower image).

Source: All photos by G. Xanthoupoulos

Xanthopoulos & Athanasiou, 2019). This area consisted largely of pine forest in which were nestled homes along with coastal communities, the hardest hit was Mati (Figure 3.1). Vegetation corridors within the settlement area provided routes for the fire to the coast. As people fled, they were often trapped on narrow roads that became impassable due to abandoned cars or they were actually forced into the sea, where some of them drowned. Survivors often had to wait in the sea for hours until they could be rescued by boat. Firefighting response had been delayed as most resources had been dispatched to an earlier landscape fire that threatened homes and an oil refinery, in West Attica.

- 2019–2020. Between October 2019 and February 2020, in a fire season characterized by extreme fire danger due to drought, a long series of very intense fires stressed the firefighting forces to the maximum and burned an estimated 18,736,070 ha, mostly in the Northern Territory and in New South Wales (NSW). Thirty-four people lost their lives in this fire season that became known as the Black Summer. NSW suffered 26 deaths with other fatalities occurring in Victoria and South Australia. The NSW deaths included 19 community members, three Rural Fire Service volunteers (who were involved in fire-related vehicle accidents), and three American aviators (who died in a crash) (*New South Wales Rural Fire Service*, 2020). Of the civilian deaths, most occurred in or near the structures they had stayed to defend or in vehicles attempting to escape the fire.

3.5 A STATISTICAL LOOK AT THESE ACCIDENTS

The fatal fires presented thus far do not represent an exhaustive list. Nevertheless, they include some of the most characteristic cases in various parts of the world, other than the USA. Without a claim for statistical validity, listing them in a table (Tables 3.1 and 3.2) and presenting the results in graphical form (Figures 3.2 and 3.3) does reveal certain patterns and allows some comparisons. The tables indicate the presence or not of certain factors that are thought to usually contribute to such accidents. The value of 1 indicates that the factor contributed to the disaster. It should be mentioned that this binary decision has been based on best judgment according to the often-scarce information that is available.

The meaning of the short name of the factors in Tables 3.1 and 3.2 is as follows:

Factor Short Name	Meaning of the Factor
Drought	Extreme conditions (drought, high temperature, very dry fuels)
Wind	Very strong wind
Change	Abrupt fire behavior change due to topography or wind shift
Spotting	Spotting
Flashy	Fine "flashy" fuels
Awareness	Lack of situation awareness
Escape	Poor or blocked escape routes
Late	Late evacuation decision
Ill-prepared	Inadequately prepared people/poorly equipped firefighters

TABLE 3.1 Fourteen Important Fatal Wildfires around the World Involving Deaths of Firefighters and the Factors that Contributed to Each Accident

			Factors									
Year	**Fire**	**Fatalities**	**Drought**	**Wind**	**Change**	**Spotting**	**Flashy**	**Awareness**	**Escape**	**Late**	**Ill-prepared**	**Total**
1949	Landes	82	1	1	1	0	0	0	0	0	1	4
1971	Kure	18	0	1	0	0	1	0	0	0	0	2
1975	Lüneburger heath	5	1	0	1	0	0	0	0	0	1	3
1987	Daxing'anling	211	1	1	0	0	0	0	0	0	1	3
1994	NE Patagonia	25	0	0	1	1	0	0	0	0	0	2
1998	Mt. Hymettus	4	0	0	1	0	0	0	0	0	1	2
2005	Guadalajara	11	0	1	1	1	0	1	0	0	0	4
2006	Famalicão da Serra	6	1	0	1	1	0	1	0	0	0	4
2007	Kornati	12	0	1	1	0	1	1	0	0	0	4
2007	Doxaro	3	0	0	1	0	1	1	0	0	0	3
2012	Carahue	7	0	1	0	0	0	1	0	0	1	3
2014	Guachipas	4	0	1	0	0	0	1	1	0	1	4
2019	Muli	31	0	0	1	0	0	0	0	0	0	1
2020	Muli	19	0	0	1	0	0	0	0	0	0	1
	Total	438	4	7	10	3	3	6	1	0	6	

TABLE 3.2 Twelve Important Fatal Wildfires around the World Where the Victims Were Mainly Civilians and the Factors That Contributed to the Accident

			Factors									
Year	**Fire**	**Fatalities**	**Drought**	**Wind**	**Change**	**Spotting**	**Flashy**	**Awareness**	**Escape**	**Late**	**Ill-prepared**	**Total**
1936	Kursha-2	1200	0	1	0	0	0	0	0	1	1	3
1983	SE Australia	75	1	1	1	0	0	0	0	0	0	3
1993	Ikaria	13	1	1	0	0	0	0	1	1	1	5
2000	Haraugi	11	1	1	1	0	0	0	0	1	1	5
2007	Artemida	24	1	1	0	1	1	0	1	0	1	6
2009	Kilmore East	119	1	1	1	1	0	0	0	0	0	4
2009	Marysville	40	1	1	1	0	0	0	1	0	1	5
2010	Mount Carmel	44	1	1	0	1	0	1	1	0	0	5
2017	Pedrógão Grande	66	1	0	1	1	0	1	1	0	1	6
2017	Central Portugal	53	1	1	1	1	0	1	0	0	1	6
2018	NE Attica	102	0	1	0	0	0	1	1	1	1	5
2020	South Australia	34	1	1	0	1	0	0	0	1	0	4
	Total	**1,781**	**10**	**11**	**6**	**6**	**1**	**4**	**6**	**5**	**8**	

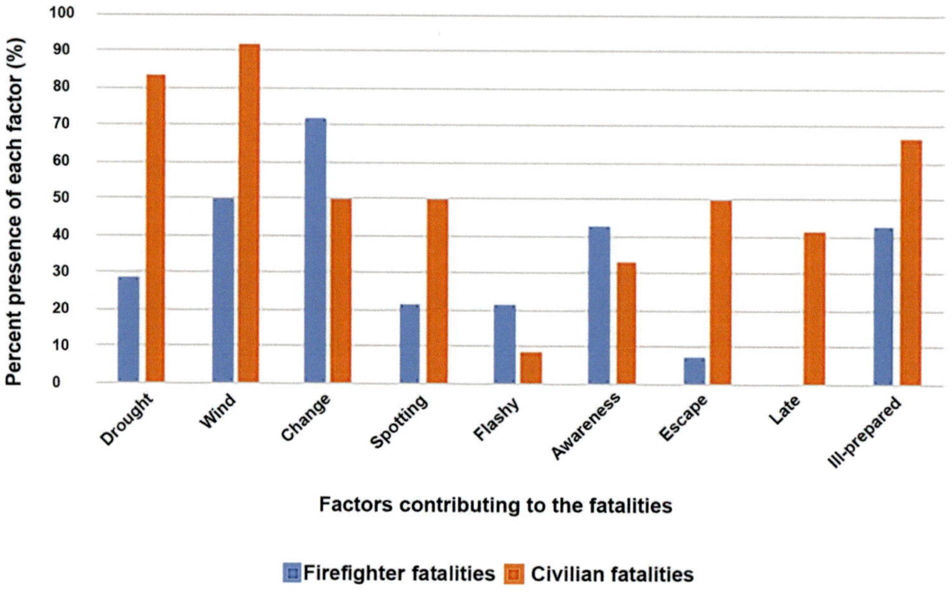

FIGURE 3.2 Percentage of the presence of each of the contributing factors to the fire death of firefighters and civilians.

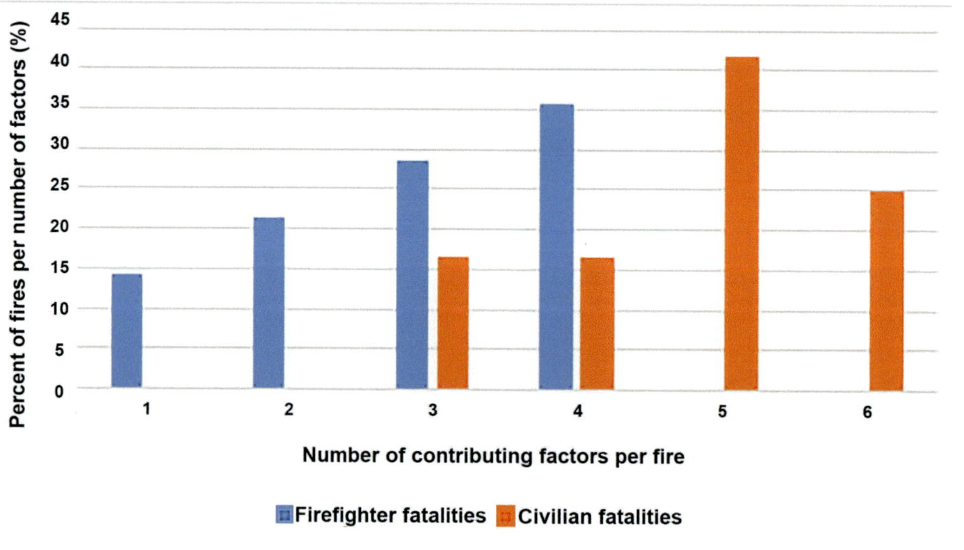

FIGURE 3.3 Percentage of fires influenced by a particular number of contributing factors in each of the two fatality categories.

Figure 3.2 presents a comparison of the presence of each of the major contributing factors in the fires with firefighter fatalities (blue) versus the presence of these factors in the fires with citizen fatalities (orange). The presence is expressed as a percent of the total in each of the two categories to allow comparisons because the absolute number of fires was different (14 versus 12 fires). For example, the factor "drought" was present in four of the 14 fires in the firefighter fatality category (29% of the fires) and in 10 of the 12 fires in the civilian fatality category (83% of the fires).

A total of nine factors were identified as potentially linked with fatal wildfires, but these factors do not need to be acting simultaneously for fatalities to happen. As shown in the rightmost column of Tables 3.1 and 3.2, each fire was affected by a different number of factors. The number ranged between one and four factors acting simultaneously in fires with firefighter fatalities and between three and six factors in fires with civilian fatalities. Figure 3.3 presents these results graphically, in percentage form, illustrating the difference between the two categories of fires. For example, there were four firefighter fatality fires (of the total of 14) with three contributing factors identified, which amounts to a percentage of 29%, while there were two civilian fatality fires with this number of factors (of the total of 12) or 17% of the total.

3.6 DISCUSSION

The fire fatalities presented thus far are some of the most notable, excluding accidents in the USA. They have not been picked with any specific bias, and although the list is far from complete, a number of observations can be made based on the tables and figures presented.

Regarding firefighter fatalities, the most important factor contributing to fatalities is a change of the conditions, mainly regarding wind direction and topography, which results in abrupt fire behavior change for which they are not prepared (71%). Furthermore, in 50% of the fires there was very strong wind. Lack of awareness of what the fire is doing is also quite common (43%), while in another 43% of these fires the firefighters were either poorly equipped or poorly trained and coordinated, at least by modern standards.

Civilian fatalities are mostly linked to very strong wind (92%) and drought conditions (83%), which result in high-intensity, fast-moving fires, leaving little time for warning and response. Poor preparation and information on how to react, capacity to stay safely in place, etc. is a contributing factor in 67% of the fires. Poor escape routes or routes blocked by the fire were a factor in 50% of the fires. Fire behavior change or contribution of heavy spotting to entrapment were present in 50% of the fires. Also, in 42% of the fires, the decision to evacuate was delayed, while in 33% the people were poorly aware of the level of danger and/or what the fire was doing.

Figure 3.2 shows that as firefighters generally know about the fire they are trying to suppress, their fatalities are mostly affected by a smaller number of factors (one to four). As a rule, the main culprit are unexpected fire behavior changes combined with one or two additional factors. On the other hand, the deaths of civilians are linked to an interplay of many factors (three to six) occurring simultaneously, usually covering both aspects: intense and unexpected fire behavior on one side, combined with poor response of the civilians on the other.

Overall, in studying fire fatalities, it becomes evident that risk assessment by both firefighters and civilians in the face of very intense fire often fails to capture the intensity or unpredictability of the fire front. There are issues with wildland-urban interface, how and where we build homes that also link to the road networks that could allow egress from more remote areas. Preparation for "red flag" days, when high temperatures, low humidity, and high winds combine to make conditions particularly difficult, is often limited, at a time when people should already be on the brink of leaving and firefighting strength should be maximized. There are also local differences, many of which are tied to the changing socioeconomic landscape that allows or exacerbates the problem of rural abandonment, reduced forest management, and increased reliance on fire suppression.

With both firefighters and civilians, assessment of risk appears to be an issue in the response to wildfires. Regarding fire suppression, poor risk assessment may lead to dispatching of inadequate resources, escape of the fire, and hence a much more dangerous situation. This was clearly a factor in the Patagonian Fire of 1994.

Among fire managers, decisions are filtered through complex social, political, institutional, and psychological factors (Thompson, 2014). There is the need for realistically assessing the value of the resources threatened by a fire (Dickman, 2018). In some cases, a fire is in an area that could be allowed to burn, as was pointed out for the Kornati Fire (Stipanicev & Viegas, 2009; DX Viegas et al., 2008). A more difficult question for fire management is whether to put lives at risk to try to protect structures that are inherently indefensible. Sometimes, a fire is aggressively fought, at the risk of firefighters' lives, when the area was already designated for prescribed burning. Complete elimination of the risk to firefighters lives and safety, while a laudable goal, is probably not feasible in the immediate future (Dickman, 2018), but balancing that risk to realistic outcomes should be done. The Black Dragon Fire of 1987, which spread both in China and in the Soviet Union, provides an excellent case study. In the Soviet Union, the fire was allowed to burn as there was no serious risk to precious timber reserves. In China, where important timber resources were threatened, it was fought very aggressively but mainly with poorly equipped troops. As a result, there were 211 fatalities and 266 people were injured while huge financial damage was not averted (https://en.wikipedia.org/wiki/1987_Black_Dragon_fire).

For civilians, surveys after a wildfire showed that many people had plans of how they would respond in the face of a wildfire. However, these plans were often poorly developed in terms of timing and overall preparation. For those who planned to evacuate early, many waited for warning or evacuation warnings that did not arrive. In the 2009 Victoria fires, only 2% of householders evacuated the day before, despite high-fire-danger warnings (McLennan et al., 2013). Follow-up studies showed that there was a disparity between bush and suburban dwellers (Whittaker & Handmer, 2010). The former was generally aware of their risks and of the fire danger rating system, while the latter did not consider themselves affected by bushfires. There was also a great deal of variation in the fire plans of those at risk, although two-thirds had some plans. No matter the plans, in actuality, there was a significant difference between the plans and the actual responses. The majority of people, while intending to leave early, did not, and among those who stayed to defend their property, a third later tried to evacuate. In the 2009 Australian bushfires, a number of the dead showed no indication that they were aware that there was even a fire danger at all (McLennan et al., 2013).

In planning the possible responses, determinants are often linked to (1) perception of risk, (2) knowing possible mitigation options, (3) accepting responsibility, (4) expectation that mitigation will be effective, and (5) prioritizing costs of mitigation (McLennan et al., 2013). Other factors may be age and gender of householder, attachment to the place, and informal community networks. Attachment to the property is often a deciding factor in staying and defending, while concern for family members may lead to plans for evacuation.

For those who plan to stay and defend their homes, there are other issues (Handmer & Tibbits, 2005; Haynes et al., 2008, 2010; McLennan et al., 2013; Wilkinson & Eriksen, 2015). Many have fire plans, but the quality of those plans is highly variable. Many do not have any contingency plans and the plans in place rely on availability of water and power. Adequate defense of even a normal wildfire would require a large water supply, generators, and dedicated firefighting equipment. As most extreme fire conditions come during the driest months of the year, water supplies are frequently extremely low. In the megafires we are experiencing, it is estimated that the intense front may take an hour to pass through so adequate water and stamina are essential for those defending their homes.

Preparation to stay and defend often is postponed until the threat of fire is imminent. Instead, preparations need to be underway well beforehand (Penman et al., 2013). Residents need to have adequate personal protection equipment for each person staying, including goggles, gloves, helmets, dust masks, and low flammable clothing (cotton, wool, denim). A wet woolen blanket can provide some cover for each resident against radiant heat and flames. House equipment can include sprinklers that can dampen surfaces. A diesel pump is needed to maintain the water supply when the fire front is passing through. Gas and electric pumps will not last due to flammability or loss of power. House gutters need to be free of leaves and debris. To fight embers and firebrands that land around the house, a conservative estimate is 10,000 liters (2,600 gallons) of water should be available. Hoses need to be strategically placed and ready with water around the house, with enough replacement hoses at hand should those melt. Rakes, spades, buckets, and wet mops can address small fires from embers and firebrands. Preparing the grounds includes work on landscaping, maintenance and dealing with heavy fuels. Plantings and dry lawns that provide fuel need to be removed from around the house. Susceptible structures, such as wooden fences, outbuildings, and wood piles, are of concern. Even a simple step of removing a flammable doormat can also reduce risk. Obviously, these are not things that can be done at the last minute.

Most of those who stay and plan to defend are anticipating the scale of fire that they have seen in past decades. Such fires are low-intensity and may not spread into the crowns of trees. However, recent fires in some areas have been far more intense, driven by extremely abundant dry fuel, high winds, and high temperatures. This combination is deadly in that it also increases the risk of fire spotting in which the embers blown upward by the flow of heated air from the fire can land well ahead of the fire front, starting new fires. The arrival of the fire front, therefore, comes much faster than anticipated. This feature is well known to firefighters (Butler, 1976b) but is often outside of the experience of civilians.

Many who delayed evacuation or who changed their minds after attempting to stay and defend will take to the roads at a time when there is intense traffic congestion, limited visibility, and fire along the roads producing radiant heat that may be almost unbearable. All too often, there are vehicle accidents that further hinder egress from the area. Many who die are still in their vehicles, while some will leave and attempt to outrun the fire. There is not a consistent pattern as in some cases virtually all deaths occur while trying to flee (vehicle or on foot) (Diakakis et al., 2016; Haynes et al., 2008, 2010; Molina Terren et al., 2019), while in others there is a mix of those who died in their homes or while fleeing (*The Camp Fire Public Report: A Summary of the Camp Fire Investigation*, 2020).

Unfortunately, many people take a "wait and see" attitude about whether to stay or leave. Many have a "fallback" plan in which children, other dependents, pets, and valuables are loaded into a vehicle in case the decision to stay becomes nonviable (Haynes et al., 2008). These late decisions to evacuate cause delays, increasing the risk that the roads will no longer be passable should they try to evacuate. One factor that has been identified in the decision-making is a huge reliance on physical triggers, such as smoke, sight of flames, or arrival of burning embers (Haynes et al., 2008; McCaffrey et al., 2018; McLennan et al., 2013; Prior & Paton, 2008). There is less reliance on official evacuation warnings, although social cues (neighbors leaving) do play a role. As seen in the 2009 Australian bushfires, official notifications may be delayed or absent (McLennan et al., 2013). The reasons for the delayed notification are plentiful—difficulty in understanding the magnitude of a fast-moving fire from a distant command post, the delays inevitable in a complex bureaucracy, loss of power and communication lines within the fire zone, loss of cell towers in remote areas, and basic awareness.

Risk assessment must also include those whose ability to flee may be diminished by mobility or comprehension issues. Analyses of many fires note that the elderly are over-represented among the dead (Diakakis et al., 2016), and in some cases others have died trying to assist those who are mobility-impaired (Xanthopoulos, 2007). In the Haraugi Fire of 2000 in Greece, all 11 victims were over 67 years old (Xanthopoulos, 2007). Of course, many fires seem not to end in larger numbers of elderly dying, probably as many will evacuate in a timely manner (Haynes et al., 2008, 2010, 2020; Haynes & Tibbits, 2007). Instead, deaths are higher in later middle-aged individuals. Children also show spikes in the fatalities associated with specific fires, usually as they were affected by the decisions made by their adult caretakers.

3.6.1 Issues in the Wildland-Urban Interface (WUI)

Civilian wildfire fatalities as a rule happen either close to the victim's residence or when they are on the road, usually trying to escape. In the former case, the culprit are usually areas described under the term wildland-urban interface, or WUI. The term originated in the USA and refers to areas where urban settlements encroach into or border forested sites. When this happens in wildfire-prone environments, it increases the potential for wildfire-caused disasters as such areas are hard to protect in case of fire (Butler, 1976a, 1976b, Xanthopoulos et al., 2012). Development of such areas is increasing dramatically worldwide (Moritz et al., 2014). In the western US, WUI has seen 60% expansion since 1970 and about 70% in private ownership, mostly in areas at high fire risk. Australia has seen expansion of WUI in a variety of ecozones. In the Mediterranean, the greatest areas of burning coincide with high population areas. Risk perception and homeowner preparedness and response is uneven.

The WUI has evolved over time due to (1) expansion of the urbanized areas into previously uninhabited or under-inhabited wildlands, (2) development of vacation homes or second homes in wildland areas, and (3) abandonment or reduced activity on agricultural lands, allowing then to revert more to wildlands reaching traditional villages (Xanthopoulos et al., 2012). Four spatial arrangements are noted: (1) classic interface where urban sprawl meets wildland, (2) intermix where clusters of homes are developed within wildland or agricultural areas, (3) isolated interface where individual structures are scattered in wildland, and (4) occluded interface where there are isolated instances of wildland within urban areas, often from greenbelts or parks or because the land is unsuitable for development.

Across the globe, factors within the wildland also affect the impact of fire, including the topography, the type and density of vegetation, location, size and design of structures, maintenance of structures and surrounding areas, adequacy of the road system, and the firefighting infrastructure (Xanthopoulos et al., 2012). The strongest influence is due to the flammability of structures. While wood construction is prevalent in countries, such as the USA, Canada, and Australia, fire-resistant materials are mainly used in the WUI areas of the Mediterranean. Whereas wooden homes can become fuel for intense fires impinging on them, facilitating the spread through communities, the generally fire-resistant structures in the Mediterranean region delay fire spread in WUI there and even stop it altogether when home density is high. The contrast is quite sharp and necessitates a different response by the authorities and the people. With examples of whole vulnerable settlements or neighborhoods of cities having been almost wiped out (e.g., Panorama Fire in San Bernadino, California, USA, November 20, 1985; Oakland Hills Fire, California, October 19, 1991; Marysville, Victoria, Australia, February 7, 2009; Fort McMurray, Alberta, Canada, May 3, 2016; Camp Fire, California, USA, November 8, 2018), and with extreme behavior fires becoming more common, the authorities propose or enforce early evacuation of the citizens in the countries with flammable structures. More specifically, in Australia, where fire authorities once advised communities to "prepare, stay and defend, or leave early," after the experience with the fires of 2009, the message changed to "prepare, act, and survive," following the fire danger prediction. This message emphasizes the importance of evacuation, but the need to adequately prepare property for bushfire by clearing vegetation to ensure a building is defensible is still clearly recognized (Xanthopoulos et al. 2012). In the same line, in the USA and Canada, where building construction is also based on wooden frame, fire preparedness has focused on evacuation and some efforts toward ignition reduction. There are two widespread public education programs on fire preparedness (FireSmart in Canada and Firewise in the US). There is a system of fire warnings in both countries that restricts use of public and sometimes private lands. Possibly due to the recent arrival of some residents to the WUI, there may be an expectation that firefighters are able to suppress any fire in their area. However, the spate of recent destructive wildfires throughout the western US and Canada has demonstrated that this is far from reality.

In the Mediterranean region, well-built homes in WUIs are generally safe, but there are often neighborhoods or settlements with homes of poorer construction, with the damages reflecting this difference (Xanthopoulos, 2008). Until recently, the relatively safer homes in the Mediterranean region created a sense of security. However, the massive fatalities in Greece (2007), Portugal (2017), and Greece (2018) instigated second thoughts, in spite of the fact that most of the victims were exposed to the flames away from their homes. The need for better preparation of the people, recognized for a long time in the USA, Canada, and Australia, became evident in the Mediterranean countries as well.

While those living in high-fire-risk areas understand there is a risk, they often fail to act appropriately. They do little to "hardshell" their structures, removing places where embers can ignite the structure. Even structures that appear to be non-combustible, such as most homes in Greece, may suffer from weaknesses. For example, the tar paper used under roof tiles and the stacks of firewood next to the house were sufficient to allow ignition of the structure (Xanthopoulos et al., 2003, 2012). As a rule, most people do not understand the principle that "a house is as vulnerable as its weakest element," and this should be a major issue in the efforts to educate the public.

As wildland and rural areas have become a prime target for second homes and vacation spots, part-time residents are less likely to devote time to maintenance of the property in terms of lowering the fuel load. Many seem unaware that the area comes with fire risks (Diakakis et al., 2016), and this is something that should be conveyed to them, optimally before making the decision to move to a WUI. Such an effort would currently be very timely, as the trend of moving to a WUI has accelerated with the COVID-19 pandemic that forces many people to work from home. They realize that, as long as internet access is stable, they can reside far from the place of employment. Consequently, many are moving away from urban areas and into the WUI yet not fully understanding the physical work involved in maintaining remote properties.

3.6.2 A Holistic View of the Reasons behind Fire Disasters

The second part of the 20th century saw the problem of wildfire disasters increasing sharply, with the trend continuing until today. The occurrence of fatalities is also unexpectedly high, in spite of improvements in transportation capacity (cars, roads) and communications, the modern methods of fire danger prediction and fire detection, the development of extremely effective firefighting resources, and so on. Figures 3.1 and 3.2 provide some clues about the main categories of factors leading to this: worse fire behavior, poor response of firefighters and civilians at the time of the fire, and inadequate preparation of firefighters, civilians, and their homes.

Fire behavior is the result of weather, fuels, and topography. Assuming that the latter does not change, except when people spread their homes and activities to steep topography, the emphasis should be on the first two. Research findings in the last two decades have demonstrated clearly that climate change affects the frequency and intensity of adverse weather conditions, including the onset and duration of droughts, very low air relative humidity, and extremely strong wind. Global circulation patterns and changes in atmospheric profiles are still under investigation, regarding their influence. Furthermore, there are indications that the fire seasons are elongated, increasing the duration of high fire risk each year.

The influence of forest fuels on fire behavior is also more than obvious. Fuel loading, depth arrangement, and horizontal and vertical continuity, in addition to the physical and chemical properties of fuel particles, act to increase or decrease the type of fire (ground, surface, or crown), the flame length, the rate of spread, and even the conditions that may make a fire stop. Fuels change with time, from hours to days, months, or years, as a result of the life cycle of living vegetation and of the influence of the weather conditions on dead biomass. Management of the landscape, be it forest or agricultural, affects all these fuel properties in various ways. The activities of man, from large reforestation efforts that may create homogeneous, densely vegetated landscapes to creation of firebreaks and fuel breaks intended to break this continuity, can play a crucial role on how a fire spreads. Agricultural fields within forest lands, intensely grazed areas by ruminants, and even burned areas created by small wildfires or through prescribed burning by fire managers all contribute to the development of a landscape mosaic that does not favor the development of large intense wildfires. On the other hand, as vegetation grows with time, total exclusion of fire inevitably leads to fuel accumulation in a matter of a few years or decades. Intensive forest management can delay this accumulation but at a relatively high cost. Fire suppression may seem to be effective for a few years but in the long-term it leads to biomass accumulation and fuel continuity, as it reduces the number and extent of fire scars that serve as opportunistic fire breaks in subsequent fires. When adverse weather acts on such fuels the stage is set for disaster, often in the form of megafires.

Megafires are explosive, very large, intense fires that exceed all efforts at control until firefighters get a favorable change in weather or a break in fuels (Williams et al., 2011). This phenomenon, where the short-term success in fire suppression leads in the long-term to more intense and devastating wildfires, has been called the fire paradox and has been identified, documented, and explained in international scientific literature quite well (Rego et al., 2010; Calkin et al., 2014; Arévalo and Naranjo-Cigala, 2018). However, in many countries, complete fire suppression is still practiced and is further strengthened with additional firefighting forces after each fire disaster, in a typical application of the metaphor of the firefighting trap: trying to suppress the symptom rather than understanding and addressing the factors that cause the problem (Xanthopoulos et al., 2020). Furthermore, disproportionate emphasis on fire suppression, not only leads to the fire paradox but, often, also deprives funds from fire prevention and forest management, adding further to fuel accumulation and intense fire behavior.

On the side of firefighters, weaknesses that may lead to increased chance for accidents often originate in poor training and inadequate equipment. However, there can be other factors involved, such as erroneous dispatching decisions, poor awareness (poor information availability [e.g., about the weather], no local lookouts, communication breakdown, etc.), poor knowledge of the landscape, fighting fire in conditions with which they are not familiar, and of course, erroneous decisions on the fire line (e.g., trying direct frontal attack on fires beyond their capacity, fighting a fire in dangerous topography, or not ensuring escape routes). Sometimes, decisions made at a central level, without understanding the local conditions, result in major firefighting disasters (e.g., Landes and Daxing'anling Fires).

Regarding civilians, there are two major factors that lead to disasters. Both spring from ignorance about forest fires or from underestimation of the threat, starting from the period before the fires. Especially for people living in WUI areas, such a shortcoming is unforgivable, but it may only be partly their fault. Lack of organized education of the public effort by the authorities, who should also apply serious risk analysis, planning, and guidance (Calkin et al., 2014), is a very serious weakness. Informed people are more likely to take care of the property, something they usually do not have time to do when the fire approaches their doorstep. Furthermore, being aware of the risk that wildfires pose in WUI areas they are more likely to have a response plan ready and to follow it in a timely manner. Knowledge about the entrapment risk that wildfires may pose is also important even for those not living in a WUI. In the Mediterranean region, for example, there are many examples of tourist fatalities when they found themselves in an environment they did not know, facing fires with which they were not familiar and having poor knowledge of the landscape, escape routes, safety areas, and so on (e.g., Lloret de Mar fire in Girona, Spain, on August 7, 1979, with 21 holidaymaker fatalities, or the deaths of five people, tourists, and hotel owners trying to lead them to safety, on August 24, 2007, in Oitylo, Peloponnese, Greece).

All these justify the assertion of Moreira et al. (2020) that a paradigm change is needed since current fire suppression methods focused wildfire management policies are destined to fail, at least in Mediterranean-type regions. The new paradigm they propose is that "policy effectiveness should not be primarily measured as a function of area burned (as it usually is), but rather as a function of avoided socio-ecological damage and loss."

3.7 CONCLUSIONS

The fatal fires presented and discussed here have revealed the major factors that lead to fatalities. Some of the key points include the following:

- The need for keeping fuels under control rather than focusing only on firefighting; the need to maintain fire-resilient landscapes, which in turn requires support and empowerment of rural populations
- The need for well-organized and trained firefighters, backed by high-quality decision-making
- The importance of maintaining a good balance between prevention and suppression
- The importance of informing the public regarding the risk forest fires may pose for their life and their property
- The need for well-planned and prepared WUI areas regarding both the layout and the reduced vulnerability of structures and the preparation of the people.

3.7.1 The Future

Climate change (see Chapter 1), expanding wildland-urban interface, and problems with forest management have set the stage for a potential increase in megafires. It raises the question as to whether our current approach of fire suppression and repeated loss of property is sustainable. Many are calling for a much larger role of prescribed burning, including a return to indigenous fire management to lower the fuel loads. Others are addressing the issues of further encroachment by residential areas into wildlands.

We are beginning to see major shifts in how we think about wildfires and bushfires. Prevention, particularly utilizing prescribed burns to reduce fuel loads, is increasing. Wildfire management is bound to change as more managers and politicians gradually realize that "wildfires are inevitable, but the destruction of homes, ecosystems, and lives is not" (Calkin et al., 2014).

REFERENCES

Arévalo, J. R., & Naranjo-Cigala, A. (2018). Wildfire impact and the "fire paradox" in a natural and endemic pine forest stand and shrubland. *Fire*, *1*(3), 44.

The Brookings Institution. (2005). *The mega-fire phenomenon: Toward a more effective management model. A concept paper* (pp. 1–19). www.bushfirecrc.com/sites/default/files/managed/resource/mega-fire_concept_paper_september_20_2005.pdf

Butler, C. (1976a). The urban/wildland fire interface: Part I. Abstract. *Fire Prevention Notes*, *10*, 1–7.

Butler, C. (1976b). The urban/wildland fire interface: Part II: Two disciplines in fire research. *Fire Prevention Notes*, *10*, 8–14.

Calkin, D. E., Cohen, J. D., Finney, M. A., & Thompson, M. P. (2014). How risk management can prevent future wildfire disasters in the wildland-urban interface. *Proceedings of the National Academy of Sciences*, *111*(2), 746–751.

The Camp Fire Public Report: A Summary of the Camp Fire investigation. (2020). Butte County District Attorney. https://htv-prod-media.s3.amazonaws.com/files/pge-the-camp-fire-public-report-1592448040.pdf

Castellnou, M., Guiomar, N., Rego, F., & Fernandes, P. M. (2018). Fire growth patterns in the 2017 mega fire episode of October 15, central Portugal. *Advances in Forest Fire Research*, 447–453.

Cordner, S., Woodford, N., & Bassed, R. (2011). Forensic aspects of the 2009 Victorian bushfires disaster. *Forensic Science International*, *205*, 2–7.

Dentoni, M., Defossé, G., Labraga, J., & del Valle, H. (2001). Atmospheric and fuel conditions related to the Puerto Madryn Fire of 21 January 1994. *Meteorological Applications*, *8*, 361–370.

Diakakis, M., Xanthopoulos, G., & Gregos, L. (2016). Analysis of forest fire fatalities in Greece: 1977–2013. *International Journal of Wildland Fire*, *25*, 797–809.

Dickman, K. (2018). What we learned from the Yarnell Hill Fire deaths. *Outside*, 1–7.

Glendale News Press. (1993). *The fire of '33.* https://lafire.com/famous_fires/1933-1003_GriffithParkFire/1933-1003_GriffithParkFire.htm

Handmer, J., & Tibbits, A. (2005). Is staying at home the safest option during bushfires? Historical evidence for an Australian approach. *Environmental Hazards*, *6*, 81–91.

Haynes, K., Handmer, J., McAneney, J., Tibbits, A., & Coates, L. (2010). Australian bushfire fatalities 1900–2008: Exploring trends in relation to the. *Environmental Science & Policy*, *13*, 185–194.

Haynes, K., Short, K., Xanthopoulos, G., Viegas, D., Ribeiro, L., & Blanchi, R. (2020). Wildfires and WUI fire fatalities. In *Encyclopedia of wildfires and wildland-urban interface* (pp. 1–16). www.fs.usda.gov/rm/pubs_journals/2020/rmrs_2020_haynes_k001.pdf

Haynes, K., & Tibbits, A. (2007). *Trends in Australian bushfire fataltes over the last 100 years*. Bushfire CRC.

Haynes, K., Tibbits, A., Coates, L., Ganewatta, G., Handmer, J., & McAneney, J. (2008). *100 years of Australian civilian bushfire fatalities: Exploring the trends in relation to the "stay or go policy"*. Bushfire CRC.

Leditschke, J., Collett, S., & Ellen, R. (2011). Mortuary operations in the aftermath of the 2009 Victorian bushfires. *Forensic Science International*, *205*, 8–14.

Lekkas, E., Carydis, P., Mavroulis, S., Diakakis, M., Andreadakis, E., Gogou, M., Spyrou, N.-I., Athanassiou, M., Kapourani, E., Vassilakis, E., Kotsi, E., Speis, P.-D., Delakouridis, J., Millios, D., Katsetsladou, K.-N., Kagouvardos, K., Kotroni, V., Giannaros, T., Dafix, S., . . . Parcharidis, I. (2018). The July 2018 Attica (Central Greece) wildfires. *Newsletter of Environmental, Disaster and Crises Management Strategies*, *8*, 48.

Li, Q., Cui, J., Jiang, W., Jiao, Q., Gong, L., Zhang, J., & Shen, X. (2021). Monitoring of the Fire in Muli County on March 28, 2020, based on high temporal-spatial resolution remote sensing techniques. *Natural Hazards Research*, *1*(1), 20–31.

Mangan, R. (2007). *Wildland firefighter fatalities in the United States: 1990–2006 (PMS 841)*. National Wildfire Coordination Group (.gov) https://www.nwcg.gov/sites/default/files/publications/pms841-hist.pdf

McCaffrey, S., Wilson, R., & Konar, A. (2018). Should I stay or should I go now? Or should I wait and see? Influences on wildfire evacuation decisions. *Risk Analysis*, *38*(7), 1390–1404.

McLennan, J., Elliott, G., Omodei, M., & Whittaker, J. (2013). Householders' safety-related decisions, plans, actions and outcomes during the 7 February 2009 Victorian (Australia) wildfires. *Fire Safety Journal*, *61*, 175–184.

Molina Terren, D., Xanthopoulos, G., Diakakis, M., & Ribeiro, L. (2019). Analysis of forest fire fatalities in Southern Europe: Spain, Portugal, Greece and Sardinia (Italy). *International Journal of Wildland Fire*, *28*(2), 85–98.

Moreira, F., Ascoli, D., Safford, H., Adams, M. A., Moreno, J. M., Pereira, J. M.C., Catry, F. X., Armesto, J., Bond, W., González, M. E., Curt, T., Koutsias, N., McCaw, L., Price, O., Pausas, J. G., Rigolot, E., Stephens, S., Tavsanoglu, C., Vallejo, V. R., Van Wilgen, B. W., Xanthopoulos, G., & Fernandes, P. M. (2020). Wildfire management in Mediterranean-type regions: Paradigm change needed. *Environmental Research Letters*, *15*(1), 011001.

Moritz, M., Batllori, E., Bradstock, R., Gill, A., Handmer, J., Hessberg, P., Leonard, J., McCaffrey, S., Odion, D., Schoennagel, T., & Syphard, A. (2014). Learning to coexist with wildfire. *Nature*, *515*, 58–66.

Penman, T., Eriksen, C., Blanchi, R., Chladil, M., Gill, A., Haynes, K., Leonard, J., McLennan, J., & Bradstock, R. (2013). Defining adequate means of residents to prepare property for protection from wildfire. *International Journal of Disaster Risk Reduction*, *6*, 67–77.

Prior, T., & Paton, D. (2008). Understanding the context: The value of community engagement in bushfire risk communication and education. Observations following the East Coast Tasmania bushfires of December 2006. *Australiasian Journal of Disaster and Trauma Studies*, *14*.

Rego, F. C., Silva, J. S., Fernandes, P., & Rigolot, E. (2010). Solving the fire paradox. Regulating the wildfire problem by the wise use of fire. In *Towards integrated fire management. Outcomes of the European Project fire paradox* (pp. 219–228). European Forest Institute Research Report 23.

Reid, C., Brauer, M., Johnston, F., Jerrett, M., Balmes, J., & Elliott, C. (2016). Critical review of health impacts of wildfire smoke exposure. *Environmental Health Perspectives*, *124*(9), 1334–1343.

Rothermel, R. C. (1991). *Predicting behavior and size of crown fires in the Northern Rocky Mountains* (Vol. 438). US Department of Agriculture, Forest Service, Intermountain Forest and Range Experiment Station.

Rothermel, R. C. (1993). *Mann Gulch fire: A race that couldn't be won* (General Technical Reports, INT-299, 10 p., 299). US Department of Agriculture, Forest Service, Intermountain Research Station.

Stipanicev, D., & Viegas, D. (2009). The accident of Kornati (Croatia) 2007. In D. X. Viegas (Ed.), *Recent forest fire related accidents in Europe* (pp. 26–53). Institute for Environment and Sustainability.

Teague, B., McLeod, R., & Pascoe, S. (2010a). *Final report summary.* 2009 Victorian Bushfires Royal Commission. https://apo.org.au/node/22187

Teague, B., McLeod, R., & Pascoe, S. (2010b). The lessons learnt. In *The fires and fire-related deaths* (pp. 334–340). http://royalcommission.vic.gov.au/Finaldocuments/volume-1/PF/VBRC_Vol1_Introduction_PF.pdf

Tedim, F., Leone, V., Amraoui, M., Bouillon, C., Coughlan, M., Delogu, G., Fernandes, P., Ferreira, C., McCaffrey, S., McGee, T., Parente, J., Paton, D., Pereira, M., Ribeiro, L., Viegas, D., & Xanthopoulos, G. (2018). Defining extreme wildfire events: Difficulties, challenges, and impacts. *Fire, 1*(9), 1–28.

Thompson, M. (2014). Social, institutional, and psychological factors affecting wildfire incident decision making. *Society and Natural Resources, 27*, 636–644.

New South Wales Rural Fire Service (2020). Unprecedented season breaks all records. *Bushfire Bulletin, 42*(1), 2–3, https://issuu.com/nswrfs/docs/rfs1121_bushfire_bulletin_vol_42_no1

Viegas, D., & Caballero, D. (2009). The accident of Guadalajara (Spain) 2005. In D. X. Viegas (Ed.), *Recent forest fire related accidents in Europe* (pp. 10–17). Institute for Environment and Sustainability.

Viegas, D., Pita, L., Rossa, C., & Ribiero, L. (2009). Accident of Famalicão da Serra (Portugal) 2006. In D. X. Viegas (Ed.), *Recent forest fire related accidents in Europe* (pp. 18–25). Institute for Environment and Sustainability.

Viegas, D. X., Stipanicev, D., Ribeiro, L., Pita, L., & Rossa, C. (2008). The Kornati fire accident—eruptive fire in relatively low fuel load herbaceous fuel conditions. *WIT Transactions on Ecology and the Environment, 119*, 365–375.

Whittaker, J., & Handmer, J. (2010). Community bushfire safety: A review of post-Black Saturday research. *Australian Journal of Emergency Management, 25*(4), 7–13.

Wilkinson, C., & Eriksen, C. (2015). Fire, water and everyday life: Bushfire and household defence in a changing climate. *Fire Safety Journal, 78*, 102–110.

Williams, J., Albright, D., Hoffmann, A. A., Eritsov, A., Moore, P. F., Mendes De Morais, J. C., Leonard, M., San Miguel-Ayanz, J., Xanthopoulos, G., & Van Lierop, P. (2011). Findings and implications from a coarse-scale global assessment of recent selected mega-fires. In *Proceedings "FAO at the Vth International Wildland Fire Conference"* (pp. 27–40), 9–13 May, Sun City (Working Paper FM/27/E, Rome, FAO, 168 p).

Xanthopoulos, G. (2007). Forest fire related deaths in Greece: Confirming what we already know. *Wildfire 2007: IV International Wildland Fire Conference*, 12.

Xanthopoulos, G. (2008). Parallel lines. *Wildfire, 17*(1), 8–20.

Xanthopoulos, G. (2015). Forest fires in Greece: Past, present and future. In A. Gonçalves & A. Vieira (Eds.), *Wildland fires: A worldwide reality* (pp. 141–151). NOVA Science.

Xanthopoulos, G., & Athanasiou, M. (2019). Attica region, Greece July 2018. *Wildfire, 28*(2), 18–21.

Xanthopoulos, G., Bushey, C., Arnol, C., & Caballero, D. (2012). Characteristics of wildland-urban interface areas in Mediterranean Europe, North America and Australia and the differences between them. In *First International Conference in Safety and Crisis Management in the Construction, Tourism and SME Sectors* (pp. 702–734).

Xanthopoulos, G., Labris, C., and Golfinos, C. (2003). The June 4, 2001 fire in the wildland-urbaninterface areas of Northern Attica: evolution, firefighting problems and damages. In *Proceedings of the International Workshop on Forest Fires in the Wildland-Urban Interface and Rural Areas in Europe: an integral planning and management challenge*, 19–28. Athens, Greece.

Xanthopoulos, G., Leone, V., & Delogu, G. M. (2020). The suppression model fragilities: The "firefighting trap." In *Extreme wildfire events and disasters* ed by F. Tedim, V. Leone, and TK McGee (pp. 135–153). Amsterdam: Elsevier.

Xanthopoulos, G., Viegas, D., & Caballero, D. (2009a). The fatal fire entrapment of Artemida (Greece) 2007. In D. X. Viegas (Ed.), *Recent forest fire related accidents in Europe* (pp. 65–75). Institute for Environment and Sustainability.

Xanthopoulos, G., Viegas, D., & Caballero, D. (2009b). The fire entrapment of Artemida (Greece) 2007. In D. X. Viegas (Ed.), *Recent forest fire related accidents in Europe* (pp. 65–75). JRC-IES.

Yarnell Hill Fire Serious Accident Investigation Team. (2013). *Yarnell Hill Fire, 2013: Serious accident investigation report.* www.documentcloud.org/documents/800042-yarnell-hill-serious-accident-investigation-report

SECTION II

Wildfire Management Response

This section looks at how wildfire response is organized, whether or not it involves fatalities, and how it should be adapted when there is suspected loss of life. Disaster management is typically handled through an incident command center in which there is a unified command of the operation. Actual leadership may change during the course of the work as the mission shifts in response to the varying needs, resources, and accomplishments. Internationally, there are added challenges with working through the incident command as either teams are composed of multinational groups or the disaster itself has transcended national boundaries.

Wildfire response obviously begins with the attempts by the fire service to manage and contain the fire. Fire suppression efforts may be limited in the face of a wildfire. Simultaneously, law enforcement must manage the evacuation procedures and shortly thereafter begin to deal with the question of missing persons. Resources must be pulled from neighboring areas and balanced against competing needs. Much of this work falls to levels of government above the local authorities, even though their immediate response is imperative.

In Chapter 4, the authors discuss the role of the incident command center and how a unified command is structured. In a fire, the unified command also involves transitions of power from fire to law enforcement to recovery operations (transportation, utilities, etc.). As events change, it is very possible that the authority levels will fluctuate and waver. Within this structure, fatal wildfires can be best addressed by inclusion of a senior anthropologist in the dispatch of recovery teams to sites with identified or possible human remains.

Chapter 5 examines how disaster management is addressed outside of the United States. Drawing upon a variety of natural mass disasters, such as hurricanes, tornadoes, and earthquakes, the authors show how coordinated multidisciplinary efforts can be most effective. Understanding the various structures by which emergency response is organized internationally allows better linkages to be established and some political minefields avoided.

While the fire teams focus on limiting the progress of the fire, particularly looking to protect lives and, secondarily, property, law enforcement is heavily involved in evacuations and identifying those who may be missing (Chapter 6). The former activity is complicated by the often-limited means of egress, particularly when roads become

DOI: 10.4324/9781003168010-5

blocked by disabled vehicles. The latter is a huge task, made more difficult by a transient or isolated population. Often law enforcement is faced with massive numbers of potential victims, the vast majority have scattered upon evacuation.

Chapter 7 is written by CAL FIRE and outlines how their teams are organized for the most efficient and effective response to a wildfire. In the immediate circumstances, suppression efforts are often limited due to the terrain and relative inaccessibility. Air support is recognized as "support" with ground crews, including bulldozer operations, being necessary to cut containment lines while the aircraft slow the progress of the fire. Mop-up activities are also extended and necessary.

Fire investigation starts as soon as personnel can safely access the region of origin (Chapter 8). Typically, this is simultaneous with the fire containment/control efforts, evacuations, and initiation of recovery. In the Camp Fire, investigators were on scene by noon of the day of the fire. Careful examination of the area of origin, documentation of the remaining evidence, analysis of smoke and burn patterns, and interpretation of fire behavior over the terrain are critical for accurate interpretations of fire behavior.

CHAPTER 4

Incident Command System

Resolving a Clash of Cultures

Nader Oweis and Jason Hadjuk

Working within the management of an incident, such as a wildfire, can at times be a clash of cultures—differences in values, language, problem-solving strategies, experience, expectations, organizational structure, social norms, and other elements of professional behavior. In the context of a mass disaster, particularly one where there are suspected fatalities, resolving these issues quickly and effectively is critical. For this reason, a standardized and commonly adopted structure has been developed in the United States, known as the Incident Command System (ICS). This system is designed to quickly bring order to the confusion that can occur in the immediate aftermath of a disaster.

The ICS was developed in 1968 by fire chiefs in Southern California but was not broadly implemented. A series of wildfires in California in the 1970s devastated broad sections of Southern California, killing many and causing millions of dollars in property damage. Because they occurred in areas that not only included an intermix of wildlands and residences but also abutted major urban areas, the response involved a large number of agencies. Later studies of the response found that gaps in the response existed not because of lack of resources but because of management weaknesses (Stumpf, 1999). These issues included lack of clarity in command, poor communication, lack of systematic planning, lack of efficient delegation pathways, and lack of integration of interagency efforts. In 1972 the Firefighting Resources of Southern California Organized for Potential Emergencies (FIRESCOPE) adopted the ICS model under the term Field Command Operations System. The system spread throughout the country and by 2004 the Department of Homeland Security adopted ICS under the National Incident Management System (NIMS). The federal government also mandated that ICS must be utilized by agencies to receive federal funding.

This chapter reviews the incident command structure and how it is implemented. The text also uses examples from the CZU Fire in 2020 in the Santa Cruz Mountains within the highly complex wildland-urban interface to show how and why the ICS and, frequently, a unified command, also utilizing the ICS, is often essential in mounting an effective and coordinated response among multiple agencies and different jurisdictions.

DOI: 10.4324/9781003168010-6

4.1 INCIDENT COMMAND SYSTEM: STRUCTURE AND RESPONSIBILITY

An ICS or unified command is designed to accomplish clear lines of authority, effective communication, and a means to effectively delegate responsibilities. In addition to meeting the goals and objectives of the mission, which change throughout the incident, the incident command or unified command is supposed to bring about a leadership structure where multiple agencies and disciplines cooperate and coordinate a response. With this, there must be defined roles and responsibilities, increased communication, collaborative decision-making, and a mechanism to reduce conflict and pressure associated with developing priorities, objectives, and incident response plans to manage an incident. ICS is also a method of bringing multiple voices to the table so that the leadership can understand the full complexity of the situation and the potential ramifications of certain choices.

In most small situations, the ICS works relatively smoothly as it builds on pre-existing relationships between agencies. Members of the leadership in the various agencies have learned to rely on the judgment of the leaders of parallel groups or have developed ways to work together. Often in a larger disaster, such as wildfire, however, the range of agencies involved increases dramatically and we cannot assume that any, much less good, prior relationships exist. The advantage of the system is that, regardless of the familiarity between players, people can step into clearly defined and understood roles.

ICS is a documented method to establish accountability and lines of authority (US FEMA, 2018). ICS is initially established within an agency. In that case, its predetermined offices and people move quickly into those roles. However, in complex situations, it is common that ICS be established within various realms, such as firefighting and law enforcement, but the complexity of the event often necessitates the merging of these agencies into a unified command. In practice, there are nuances that must be recognized.

The ICS is designed to be implemented quickly, on the scene, and without specificity for any particular type of situation. It has established functions that must be covered with the personnel adjusting in number based on the complexity and scale of the incident. The lead of these functions is incident command itself, and reporting to this role are the functions of operations, planning, logistics, and finance/administration. The *command* function will assess the situation and, with input from others, develop the goal, objectives, and priorities of the mission. The command function is supported by public information, safety, and liaison positions. *Operations* is responsible for executing the tactical approaches that have been developed, including assignments and organization of the resources. *Planning* is responsible for the preparation and documentation of the incident action plan. This function also includes the collection and evaluation of information on the incident and the available resources. *Logistics* looks at what resources are available, when additional resources may be added if necessary, and how these can be deployed. Finally, *finance/administration* monitors the incident costs, records times, and conducts an analysis of costs so that these can be addressed in an orderly manner as the incident is closed. For very simple incidents, these functions can be combined into one or more individuals and expanded as needed.

ICS works well because it avoids duplication of effort and "trust" can be based in the system rather than entirely on personal relationships. This trust works because of the training required of all personnel who move into the ICS functions. People are trained not only for the function but also by the level of complexity, graded as types (1–5) with most complex situations requiring a type 1 level of training. This system allows personnel to move into geographic regions in which they have never worked and still be able to assume a role within the ICS.

The first step with any incident command is to establish who is in charge and why they are in charge. The command position may, in small incidents, take on the additional functions, but this position is always present. Equally important as to who is in charge is to understand what they are in charge of and for how long? These seem like straightforward questions but actually underly much of the tension that can be generated in the ICS. At times, there may be a titular head, such as an elected sheriff with less specific training, particularly when the area is large and complex or the agency head lacks the necessary training and experience. The *de facto* head will be their subordinate but be the primary decision-maker at the scene and serve as the incident command. The titular head, however, deserves the respect of their position. Why a certain person is in charge also may vary by the evolving situation, especially under a unified command. For example, with a wildfire, fire agencies may have the lead in the initial response with law enforcement taking on the evacuation role. However, as the fire front is contained or moves into more remote areas, then law enforcement may need to take the lead as the search and recovery operations and other protection efforts become more critical. The smoothness of the transition from one lead to the next often rides on the prior working relationships between agencies and their confidence in each other.

One of the primary duties of the ICS is to set the shared vision of the mission. In wildfire situations, this is first and foremost the prevention of deaths of both civilians and firefighters. A secondary consideration is the loss of property, followed by environmental concerns. From the shared vision, which is constant, the leadership can set the more immediate priorities and objectives—which can change as the situation evolves. Once these are set, the team works to develop a range of options for how to handle the various aspects of the situation. Selection of tactics will depend on what resources are available and how they can be deployed. Confirmation of a decision through a cross-check with the broad leadership team allows all to be on the same page and to surface any critical concerns.

Obtaining and allocating the appropriate resource is a primary responsibility of the ICS leadership. Local agencies bring to the table what they have through local and statewide mutual aid agreements and programs. In the ideal situation, there is a focus on the common goal so that if one agency has unused resources, they can be lent to another agency. For example, if a police department has three officers who can be deployed outside of their normal jurisdiction, they may be able to assist in patrols or road closures in other areas. It may also be that once a task is assigned through the ICS, the local agencies who now bear responsibility will need to coordinate how to actually accomplish that duty. For example, if highway patrol and a local police agency have been assigned to work road closures within a certain area, together they will work out exactly which agency will work which road.

This "team" and "shared vision" approach will only work well if the involved agencies are willing to listen to the voices of allied agencies and if the liaisons for those agencies are willing to speak up with both concerns about possible ramifications and about other options that may not have been considered. How this is done requires balance. One needs to have a voice but becoming insistent on only one approach will lead to that voice being sidelined. Often other competing needs must be prioritized.

The input of these groups is not only facilitated but documented in the ICS. This process is managed through two avenues, one being cooperators' meetings and the other being the duties of the liaison officer. Cooperators' meetings are, in a large incident such as a wildfire, held daily and bring together all the ancillary groups that are involved in not only the immediate response but also the steps that are necessary to work through the recovery effort. The information from this meeting is documented and then becomes part of the next planning meeting. The liaison officer will conduct outreach to non-frontline groups whose efforts may be critical. Because conversations fade from memory, all such information should be documented.

One of the advantages of a unified command is that it can greatly reduce the chaos that can form in the immediate aftermath of an event. With separate ICS operating, there can be significant communication issues, even as basic as no consistency on the use of radio channels. Conflicting information coming into separate ICS can result in inactivity in critical areas and even decisions that counteract those of another agency. Confusion can result from not having a shared understanding of the objectives, which is a primary goal of the IC operation. The element of unfamiliarity between agencies will add significantly more stress to working collaboratively because of the lack of understanding of the processes or individuals upon which a unified command would be able to draw.

It is important not to overlook the contributions of local agencies and affiliated organizations. Often, they may have solutions to unanticipated problems or understand local issues or communities better. These groups are quite varied but include local community representatives (cities, towns, colleges, universities, etc.); aid groups, such as the Red Cross and Salvation Army; utility companies, such as electrical power corporations, water authorities, and internet providers; and the regional or state roads and transportation groups, which must ensure that passage back into the area is secure. It may well be that these groups may raise safety concerns of which the IC would otherwise be unaware.

These groups also may be critical in the support of the frontline forces. They are often a good source of food and water, usually centered at the staging areas. However, arrangements must also be made to get food and water distributed throughout the zone, including for groups who might not have their own supply network, such as recovery teams. Also, arrangements need to be made to provide some breaks to front line staff.

Core to success of the incident are strong problem-solving skills within the leadership team. Often, inaction can be fatal so lengthy decision-making because leadership is insecure should be avoided. The team needs to be able to reduce the issues down to clear goals, assess what resources they have at hand (being open to unconventional contributions), and get the right resources to the problem at the right time.

IC is often faced with very difficult decisions, particularly in wildfire situations. The intensity and speed of a fire front may mean that property considerations have to be set aside in order to prevent loss of life. As conditions in a wildfire change constantly, the decisions that may be appropriate on one day may be ill-advised the next due to wind changes or differences in the terrain along the fire front. For this reason, increasingly the decision has been made to conduct early evacuations in the fire zones. This process largely removes the highest priority for the mission, the preservation of life, allowing fire crews to focus on saving property and the environment.

Communication is critical, both communication coming into the IC and that going from the IC to the agencies and to the public. Since IC centers are usually remote from the event so that they do not have to be moved if the incident area expands, leadership may not have a true sense of the situation. Communication back to the leadership is critical so that they will understand what is feasible and where certain tactics may endanger the people close to the front. They also must be aware of the possible shifts in circumstances predicted in the near future. For example, weather and fire behavior modeling analysts are now commonly included in the ICS for wildfires. Unfortunately, it is also apparent that more research needs to be conducted on how fire behavior can be predicted in the higher-intensity and larger burns we are seeing more recently.

Clear communication is also essential on the outward side. Once a decision is made, leadership needs to give clear and precise direction. The communication should underscore the constant goal, and the tactics and expectations of the next phase of the response, with clear delegation of actions to the various sectors.

One concern in working, particularly with press releases in a wildfire situation, is to ensure that the outward communication to the public reflects the decision—for example, when evacuations are ordered or lifted, exactly what areas are involved, when will it occur, and what is the process for enacting it. If the public simply hears that orders are affecting one city, they will make assumptions about surrounding areas that may interfere with the overall response.

Because decisions often appear arbitrary from outside the inner circle, communications should also include some evidence of the reasoning behind them. Simply citing that some action is considered "best practice" is insufficient. Instead, why certain decisions are being made must be laid out concisely so they will appear well-considered rather than "off the cuff."

In wildfires, evacuation orders and warnings may come quickly, and people do not have much time. Unfortunately, they also do not anticipate that they will be away from their homes for a long time. However, many evacuations, even from areas that were spared from the fire, will continue for weeks as mop-up operations need clear access to the burned areas beyond the evacuated zone. There is often a rise in tension as residents want to return home, even for a quick visit—often to care for pets or livestock that could not be evacuated, to retrieve additional medications, or to simply check to see if their property has been affected. To the last point, real-time online surveys by those assessing the damage have provided some answers. Communications should also be upfront that the vast majority of properties affected by fire will have been completely destroyed.

Politics are an inevitable part of human interactions, and the ICS is no exception. However, the politics can be overcome. The focus needs to be on who the key people are, then egos have to be relinquished for the good of the team. Part of the politics of leadership is often an instinctive need to keep all activities within the group of people with whom the leadership is comfortable working. However, in the wildfire situation, inserting non-first-responders into an incident may be the best means to achieve the mission. This may mean that someone needs to mentor these groups as to how to be effective team members or establish multidisciplinary teams. For example, in fatal wildfires, teams of anthropologists were matched with sheriff's coroner personnel and local officers. The coroner groups are responsible for documentation and issuing body numbers, while the local officers can get people in and out of areas where normal access may be difficult, and often they know the situation at a residence where a fatality is suspected.

ANTHROPOLOGIST IN THE IC

The Incident Command System (ICS) lies with the local jurisdiction. In the Camp Fire, regardless of the area from which mutual aid was drawn, this authority lay with Butte County. While the mission to protect lives and property in the face of fire is constant, the immediate goals and objectives will vary throughout the incident that triggered its formation. In a situation such as a wildfire, initial focus is on the control of the forward movement of the fire (fire ICS) and evacuation of those living in its projected path (law enforcement ICS). As incidents develop, there is often the need for a unified command, linking the various agency's IC structures.

In the Camp Fire, two separate commands (CAL FIRE and Butte Co. Sheriff's Office) operated for approximately two weeks. As the efforts to contain the fire relaxed and more and more fire crews were diverted to assist with the search for victims, communication between different agency ICS operations became more complex. The problem was exacerbated by the physical separation of the locations of the ICS centers. In subsequent fires, such as the 2020 Bear Fire, where search activities for victims were again required, the transition was more rapid and smooth.

In the early hours of the Camp Fire, Butte County Sheriff's Office reached out to Chico State University anthropologists as "added resources" who could be brought in to assist with the search for those missing and presumed dead in the wake of the fire. The discussions centered around how many anthropologists could be mustered, what equipment they could bring with them, and what support would be needed for their work. This early inquiry was based upon years of working to establish a solid relationship with the county, so they had familiarity with the Chico State anthropologists and their expertise in scene recoveries.

As the first few days of recovery progressed, it became quickly apparent that the search and rescue (SAR) teams needed to be diverted toward looking at residential structures due to the rapidly mounting missing persons list. It also became evident that law enforcement was not in a good position to make decisions about the identification of human remains in such a complex site, nor could they effectively deploy the recovery teams of anthropologists. In the re-evaluation of the ICS operation, the greater presence of an anthropologist allowed for more efficient and effective coordination of the effort.

As the operations of the search ICS progressed, the anthropologist worked on radio with County Dispatch to coordinate identification and recovery teams (see Chapter 12). SAR personnel used GPS to map their search patterns (see Chapter 11) and that information was fed into GIS software by SAR command stations, generating a set of maps that was utilized by ICS. The anthropologist could, therefore, coordinate the deployment of the nearest identification or recovery teams to a report of "human remains" by the SAR groups in the field. Based on the report of the findings and cell phone photos, it was also possible to determine the size of the team needed.

The advantage of having the anthropologist in ICS was that this placed the anthropologist in a line of authority so that this person could make decisions about recovery that carried weight across all other agencies. This means that the local authority who runs the ICS must have confidence in the ability of the anthropologist to make decisions that benefit the mission and understand the role (and budgets) of the agency.

As communications between the different groups evolved during the Camp Fire, the role of the anthropologist also changed. As recovery progressed, the ICS-based anthropologist became responsible for calculating the rate of recovery. Initially, this was simply how many remains had been found and retrieved. As the process progressed, the anthropologist also provided information on how many searches resulted in the discovery of human remains, broken down as to whether these were searches targeted at suspected locations for missing persons or non-targeted searches. Information on the most efficient methods also became apparent as the anthropologist compiled what strategies tended to generate the highest number of false alerts to remains.

Because the anthropologist was in the command center, they were able to hear all the dispatch calls and, because all teams were equipped with nano tracking systems, simultaneously track the location of all the teams via the monitors. This position also facilitated a good assessment of the efficiency of resource utilization.

As the Camp Fire search continued, additional factors came to bear on the work. About two weeks after the fire, rains finally came to the area, producing a significant risk of mudslides in the denuded forests. The California Office of Emergency Services (CalOES) established a series of sensors and monitors on the hillsides to predict the danger of a slide. These data were fed directly to the ICS center and used with the locational data for the various teams. The anthropologist could then include this information in the dispatch of the recovery teams, allowing them to avoid areas with potential danger. Other factors that can arise include reignition of the fire, problems with looting, and in the Camp Fire, an officer-involved shooting in the middle of the evacuation area. Because the anthropology recovery teams often operate outside of the agency communication lines, there is the risk that they will be unaware of these types of dangers without the link in the IC center.

The ICS-based anthropologist was in communication with the anthropology team based in the morgue. This connection allowed for information on incomplete recoveries to be linked back to the field teams. The finding of commingled remains at the morgue also allowed for the resolution of a missing person's case, allowing teams to move to other locations.

Each evening the anthropologist developed the strategy for the following day's recovery efforts. This task required staying in the center after all the recovery teams finished for the day and working with other personnel in the ICS to make sure data collection was complete for the day. At that time, the law enforcement teams who worked on the missing persons list would update the list based on those located (dead or alive). Together, they then worked on who still needed to be located and what would be the highest priority search and possible recoveries for the following day. The anthropologist provided the final tally of the recoveries to the Sheriff's Office before each evening press conference.

The anthropologist also played a role in the overall ICS decision-making process. Because so many agencies sent groups to assist in the search and recovery efforts, the issue of varying command structures was recurring. For example, some SAR teams wanted to establish their own ICS centers and determine their own search protocols. This desire was problematic as it often involved methods that were not appropriate to a complex fire scene, such as extensive raking in all properties searched. While potentially helpful in other scene contexts, raking through debris on a fire scene is a tactic that the anthropologists have found to be ineffective and, when remains are present, potentially extremely destructive. Inconsistencies within the various agencies in how remains were flagged and how to recognize remains complicated the situation. When problems with consistency of search protocol arose in the field, the anthropologist was able to engage in discussion across all agencies, with ICS support, about best practices in the field.

As the number of recoveries began to slow, the anthropologist worked with the ICS to transition from a full deployment to one where the teams would still be available but would no longer be in the field on a continuous basis.

The role of the anthropologist in ICS is one that requires a person who is willing and able to fulfill the delicate role of integrating effectively in a pre-existing command structure. Such a person should have prior training in mass fatality management, understand the mutual aid command structure, and have a good working relationship with the local authority. In the Camp Fire, the anthropologist tasked with the ICS station had an extensive background in mass fatality management and had worked with the US Department of Homeland Security. Courses are available online in mass fatality management for those who need to prepare for this eventuality.

Above all, the anthropologist's role requires diplomacy and communication. Our role is to make the teams more efficient and more effective, and this means that we need to see ourselves as embedded in a common mission. It is also a mission in which our authority is derived from the agency in command and not simply through possession of an advanced degree, a strong research profile, or even years of experience.

Efficient and effective ICS operations require preparation and training. It works most smoothly if it has been rehearsed beforehand. The leadership needs to shift quickly and seamlessly into the unified IC structure and find ways to smooth the junctions between agencies. This process can be greatly augmented by having a pattern of joint training so that trust and comfort can be developed well before any incident arises. Even when joint training between specific groups is not possible, other joint training exercises will help people recognize where different internal work patterns, communication styles, and behaviors based on experience can affect coordination and cooperation. With that knowledge, people are less suspicious of differences with other groups and more willing to include the different perspectives.

Relationships and proper and current training are key to success and must be cultivated in anticipation of an incident. That cannot be over-emphasized. Outreach to outside organizations, bringing them into training events, and having periodic meetings to plan for eventual joint operations is highly beneficial. Ancillary and associated groups should also be trained in the ICS structure and procedures so they know how they are integrated, where they can avoid duplicating effort, and where their input is critical.

4.1.1 Case Study: The CZU Lightning Complex Fire Event

In the early hours of August 16, 2020, a massive storm swept through Northern California with lightning strikes causing a multitude of fires. In the Santa Cruz Mountains, including both Santa Cruz and San Mateo counties, there were over 300 strikes, which, combined with years of dangerous drought conditions, resulted in a number of fires. These fires quickly amalgamated into the CZU Lightning Complex Fire, named for the state fire district in which it occurred. This complex of fires burned for about two days, but then a change in wind direction caused rapid expansion of the fire front, threatening local urbanized areas.

The speed and intensity of the fire was frightening. Overnight, the fires consumed 40,000 acres. This phenomenon, being seen more frequently in modern wildfires, is due to a number of factors. Many areas of the Santa Cruz Mountains have not seen a significant burn in a hundred years. Rainfall was low, so the fuel load present was not only thick but dry. Fuel mitigation projects were also far too small to substantially affect the fire, which, like most wildfires, moves not only along the front but also by spotting.

Air support was only effective in very specific situations, many of which did not occur in the CZU Complex Fire. Because much of the fire occurred in redwood canopy forest, fire retardant was unable to penetrate below the canopy to slow the fire in the undergrowth. Wind conditions were also variable so that sea breezes hitting the mountain range could produce winds higher than tolerable for the air support. Also smoke produced by the fire tended to then settle in the valleys when wind conditions eased, making the targets invisible and safety a significant factor.

In total, 86,509 acres (63,754 acres in Santa Cruz County and 22,755 acres in San Mateo County) were consumed, 1,490 buildings destroyed (1,431 structures in Santa Cruz County of which 911 were single family homes), and one person was found dead. Over 77,000 people were evacuated (70,000 in Santa Cruz County), including those living on the University of California, Santa Cruz campus. Because of the rural nature of much of this area, evacuation decisions also entailed moving a large number of pets and livestock (horses, goats, llamas, alpaca, pigs, chickens, etc.). Historic state parks, including Big Basin Redwoods, California's oldest state park, were significantly affected with the loss of many of the buildings, including the visitors' center. The cost of the fire reached over $68 million.

Full containment was not accomplished until September 22 (37 days later). Full control was not declared until four months after the fire. However, smoldering fires within the redwoods were still found into the following year.

4.2 UNIFIED COMMAND IN THE CZU FIRE

A unified command, led by CAL FIRE and the Santa Cruz County Sheriff's Department, was established at the beginning of the fire. Other agencies, such as local fire departments, city police departments, and university police, were also incorporated under this command. From the outset, it was clear who were lead agencies, so the contributing agencies did not need to set up their own incident command post. What they did do was to set up an Emergency Operations Center to coordinate their own response—what resources did they have, how could they manage shifts, what issues did they need to bring to the central incident command, and so on.

As in most such situations, information was difficult to decipher and there was some confusion, as is normal in such situations, but leadership worked to quickly smooth the path to the shared vision. They realized that having a common direction of priorities was essential. For many agencies and other groups such as non-profit organizations, this was the first time their representatives had experienced a unified command structure. It took time for them to realize that their voice needed to be heard at the table. Often their involvement with the local communities can point out issues that would escape attention without their input. Such organizations may know of people living "off the grid" or those with mobility or cognitive disabilities that may require additional help. Some may have gained the trust of groups that would shun direction from governmental agencies.

As the fire progressed, many areas lost infrastructure, including communication, electric power, internet, water, and other critical utilities. The need for mutual aid increased, and resources were pulled from outside the immediate area. This contribution was complicated by the wide array of fire complexes active at the same time in the state, all produced by the storm front and associated lightning strikes. While greatly appreciated, some agencies arriving from outside the area took time to understand the shared vision. For example, the middle of a wildfire is probably not the best time to be making arrests for running an illegal marijuana growing facility.

The complexity of the fire did require a number of difficult decisions. Often evacuations were ordered well ahead of a visible fire threat but were needed to facilitate access should conditions shift. Experience has shown that fire fronts can turn quickly and move rapidly given a change in wind directions, something particularly common along the coast. Moving fire crews into areas while simultaneously trying to evacuate could spell disaster. While in previous decades there was great reluctance to displace residents with evacuations, experience has shown that, in the long run, early mandatory evacuation is highly beneficial. Where fire crews are trying to operate in non-evacuated areas, residents tended to expect individual support to protect their properties, while fire crews needed to direct their resources to broader containment efforts. These efforts were largely on developing primary and secondary containment lines that needed to be widened and, in some places, cut and on slowing the fire front with air support. Fire lines require the use of large bulldozers, trucked into the area. Since many of these rural roads were narrow, bringing in the trucks along with larger fire engines made the roads impassable for other vehicles, such as evacuees.

As an example of how even a smaller agency can be involved, one can look at the University of California, Santa Cruz (UCSC). The UCSC campus was minimally inhabited due to the timing of the fire in the late summer but still had around 2,000 residents. Due to the fire, the campus did lose power—a significant problem for a research university with both IT and cold storage needs. Even as the fire started, the EOC was developing plans to both evacuate and to recover.

The campus sent a police sergeant to the incident command center to be the regular liaison for the campus for the first 27 days. After that point, there was a shift to recovery and demobilization of the various teams. The chief of police for the campus was at the Scotts Valley–based unified incident command center twice daily. The first meeting was to work out the finalized assignments for the day and note any new information or factors and then, later in the day, was a debrief of the day's events and a discussion of the tactics for the next day. These decisions could involve needed road closures, evacuation warnings or orders, where to move those evacuated, and the like.

However, the university campus had resources that might have been overlooked had it not been for the involvement of the chief of police in the daily briefings. For example, discussions in the incident command center raised the issue of lack of lighting to work in a specific remote area—a problem that was solved by moving in the athletic field lighting from the campus. In a more powerful response, the campus took on the ballrooms and kitchens at the local amusement area, the Santa Cruz Boardwalk, in order to house the displaced campus staff and faculty. Because dining staff were among those displaced, the Boardwalk kitchens were used to provide food for the evacuees. However, realizing that this service could be applied more broadly, the dining staff began to supply meals for others, eventually making 6,000 meals per day.

Within the incident command structure, there is room for local decision-making. For example, on the campus, residents were concerned about getting medication or caring for pets that had been left on what they initially thought was a short evacuation. In some suburban areas, residents were allowed to return for "short" visits, but this proved fairly hard to control and distinguishing authorized visits from looters was problematic. On the campus, parking staff, who were affiliated with the police department, were deployed to handle such issues, leaving police officers free to patrol.

4.3 CONCLUDING COMMENTS

The ICS is a robust system of emergency management. Like all such systems, it works best when participants bring their full efforts to the table. From our experience, beyond being comfortable with the command structure and trained in the role that is to be played, we have found that certain behaviors are particularly helpful. One of the most important of these behaviors is building relationships within the ICS. Getting to know the possible contributions of team members and solidifying the shared vision as a common mission is essential. Typically, this process should be done before emergency management is critically needed and occurs in regular meetings and training sessions. It also needs to occur during the event of a disaster.

Let the command know what you and your team can bring to the table—in the form of resources, experience, and perspective. In many cases, the resources may be obvious, such as vehicles and personnel. However, there are often resources within the community that local agencies may know but are not well understood beyond those areas—for example, ideal staging areas or sources of water. Prior experience with specific areas and communities may be critical for how a response is planned or how an evacuation is managed.

Participants should be invested in both the strategy for the immediate response and the long-term recovery. A tactic that may yield a win in the short term may have longer-term detrimental effects that may not be visible to someone outside of the community. In wildfires, the recovery and repopulation of areas is a lengthy and stressful process and should not be extended needlessly.

Participating agencies need to clarify roles and boundaries. While the ICS lays out the roles, there are many finer distinctions and details that must be considered. Taking the time to quickly review which agency is responsible for what specific tasks goes a long way to improve overall function.

Like all group interactions, the ICS is subject to team and power dynamics. Leadership must be aware and willing to intervene if and when these dynamics interfere with the optimal performance of the command. This action must be handled diplomatically as often the teams most vociferous are those who also have the best local knowledge. Leadership needs to be able to provide clear direction and lay out their decisions concisely. Emotions and egos have little role in the ICS in the face of an emergency. This means that all team members need to understand the importance of their own contributions and those of others. This is no time or place for making assumptions about others or holding onto prejudices.

Because people are coming to the situation with different experiences and modes of operation, they will, naturally, have different views on best practice.

- People may have different views on best practice: know how best to work together.
- Do not underestimate the value of listening.

REFERENCES

Stumpf, J. 1999. Incident command system: the history and need. Internet J Rescue Disaster Med. 2(1): 6.

US Federal Emergency Management Agency. 2018. ICS review document (extracted from—E/L/G 0300 intermediate incident command system for expanding incidents. ICS 300. https://training.fema.gov/emiweb/is/icsresource/assets/ics%20review%20document.pdf

CHAPTER 5

Incident Command (IC) Role in Coordination (Logistics and Politics)—International Perspective

Damon P. Coppola and Brad Milliken

5.1 INTRODUCTION

When the scope and scale of a disaster grows to such an extent that an international response is initiated, the capacity of national disaster risk management systems and structures may be strained or even exceeded. In wildfires, this could occur when the wildfire overwhelms the resource capacity for the local, regional, and national agencies and additional international resources are procured or when the fire itself crosses one or more international borders, requiring a coordinated effort to contain the flames. For the national, subnational, and local government agencies and offices, managing an influx of atypical international stakeholders and resources and navigating command, control, and coordination (CCC) can overwhelm even the most seasoned professionals. For the intergovernmental and regional organizations (IGOs), international financial institutions (IFIs), foreign governments, international nongovernmental organizations (NGOs), and businesses that may be present during disaster response, a lack of familiarity and potential conflicts with local laws and CCC structures presents additional challenges. Past events suggest that while confusion is to be expected in any large-scale response, chaos is not a foregone conclusion. By implementing adequate protocols, authorities, and structures, building relationships, and conducting training, disaster-impacted countries can quickly establish an effective, consistent international response.

5.2 COMMAND, CONTROL, AND COORDINATION DEFINED

Disaster response effectiveness and efficiency hinge on the establishment of *command*, *control*, and *coordination*. While these terms are related and occasionally used interchangeably in colloquial language, in practice there are several key distinctions between them. In the international disaster management context, where a diverse

DOI: 10.4324/9781003168010-7

range of operational systems and cultures may converge, understanding such distinctions is critical. The commonalities and relationships that exist among domestic organizations—as a result of shared cultural and social norms, common expectations, collaboration on planning and capacity development, and familiarity with existing laws, systems, and frameworks—are what enables effective implementation of CCC in domestic events. As the number of disparate organizations increases, a frequent occurrence in the international disaster management context, commonalities and preexisting relationships diminish even among similarly categorized organizations (e.g., national search and rescue organizations) and especially where foreign responding organizations are concerned. While many differences may be superficial or perhaps simply frustrating, such as with language or terminology, other challenges like contrasting chains of command and longstanding political partialities can be insurmountable if ignored.

For the purpose of understanding challenges present during international disaster response, consider the following definitions (Coppola, 2021).

5.2.1 Command

In the simplest terms, *command* (defined here as a noun) refers to the authority to make someone do something. The "someone" could be an individual, a team, or an organization engaged in support of disaster response. In reference to an emergency or disaster incident, command authority is often triggered by the occurrence of events or conditions and linked to defined response requirements. Leaders in emergency and disaster response situations are not chosen at random but are instead identified as leadership through the formal recognition of their command. Command authority is established through law, policy, plans, procedures, or any formal recognition of leadership responsibility. Given the potential for confusion and chaos, it is critical that each task required during the response to a major disaster—whether flood, earthquake, wildfire, or otherwise—has someone identified to direct the appropriate personnel, agencies, or organizations. Such direction carries little weight in the absence of established legal or regulatory command authority.

5.2.2 Control

Whereas command establishes the authority granted to the individuals or agencies in charge, *control* represents what and whom they oversee. In general use, control is closely linked to command in that it refers to the power to direct or manipulate. However, rather than representing an established authority itself, control represents the extent of where and how that authority may be applied. In disaster management, control defines the limits of the command authority. Control can apply to individuals, agencies, organizations, or teams just as easily as it can be applied to physical areas, operations, or even specific tasks. The physical, legal, and policy boundaries that define the extent of a command's control indicate there are limits to that which may fall under the command authority of the emergency manager or management organization during the response to a disaster.

5.2.3 Coordination

Coordination refers to the mechanisms used to ensure an incident is handled in such a manner that all incident response requirements are met. Most simply stated, it is the cohesion of all disparate agencies and individuals working to bring about response and recovery of an incident. As disaster events grow in scope and scale, the ability of command and control mechanisms to address all response and recovery requirements decreases, given these functions simply outline the boundaries of authority and jurisdictions. With an increase in stakeholders, especially those which are not typically involved in day-to-day emergency operations, the authority of the agency or individual responsible for incident management may become increasingly diluted. In the absence of such authorities, there is increasing risk that operations and associated tasks will progress in an unorganized or counterproductive manner. These tasks include (1) acquiring the systems, tools, and procedures by which key information may be obtained and exchanged, (2) matching the required resources and staff to the response needs of the affected area, (3) maintaining the standards of care, and (4) developing a common understanding of response and recovery goals that may be achieved.

Through command, control, and coordination, effective response and recovery operations require the direction of specific operational tasks, the acquisition and coordination of necessary resources, staff, and equipment, the delivery of those resources to incident sites, and the sharing of information about the incident with the public. While multiple agencies or individuals might be able to perform each of these tasks independently, the absence of a cohesive and orchestrated effort may contribute to confusion, inefficiencies, redundancies, or omissions of required tasks—a scenario that can be catastrophic during a wildfire. Through command, control, and coordination systems, the complexity associated with sorting through these tasks and answering questions of where each task is to be performed, when it is to be performed, and for how long, among others, is minimized (US Federal Emergency Management Agency, n.d.).

There is universal recognition that command, control, and coordination need to be established for the effective management of emergencies and disasters. This does not mean that formalized systems or structures are always in place; in fact, the opposite is more often true. Decades of advocacy and intense policy-driven incentives were required to make the Incident Command System (ICS), a ubiquitous component of emergency and disaster response in the United States. For many countries, there is much more work to do before any similar claims can be made. There are no international standards or universal structures for command, control, or coordination, and so where systems are in place, so will there be idiosyncratic features—even within the same country.

Incident command and control systems are considered tactical-level tools because they formalize and guide the process for completing required tasks. These systems apply common rules and authorities in accordance with established organizational structures and hierarchies of responsibility and accountability. They are enabled by policies that establish authorities and reporting relationships (often through purposeful and proactive incident action planning) while ensuring enough flexibility exists to function effectively in incidents of differing scope and scale. The underlying assumption of all incident command and control systems is that although each incident may be somewhat different from a tactical perspective, the overall management approach still necessitates the same major functions regardless of incident-specific details (e.g., the Incident Command System is structured according to five functions: command, logistics, operations, finance, and planning).

Coordination systems are likewise established to increase the efficiency of response and recovery efforts, but the focus of coordination is establishing mechanisms that enhance multi-stakeholder cooperation. In doing so, they seek to ensure that the resources of these unaffiliated and oftentimes disparate stakeholders are organized in a manner that is cost-effective, equitable, informed, and synchronized. Through coordination mechanisms, agencies can more easily determine whether their efforts are duplicative or whether any geographic or demographic coverage gaps exist. Finally, effective coordination systems can enable participating agencies and organizations to act as a singular response force through the pooling of people, effort, equipment, resources, and capabilities. Unlike command and control systems, coordination systems do not generally require any formal association between participants; rather, a willingness must be established among all participating agencies to accept the decisions and actions of the coordinating body.

In a perfect scenario, an effective incident management system would establish the following:

- Clear command authority
- Common terminology among all responders
- The ability for those in command to communicate requirements to those who would perform the necessary actions
- The ability for responders to communicate with each other
- A common understanding of response requirements
- Knowledge of and access to necessary supplies, staff, equipment, and resources
- Ample staff trained in the necessary skills required to manage response requirements
- Established agreements between response partners and stakeholders
- Established systems to track and reimburse expenses
- A clear channel for communication between disaster management decision-makers, response partners and stakeholders, and the public

5.3 CCC SYSTEMS IN THE INTERNATIONAL CONTEXT

On the international stage, the difficulty of establishing many aspects of command and control increases, particularly when the capacity of a single country or several countries in a region are exceeded such that response assistance must be requested from the greater international community (US Federal Emergency Management Agency, n.d.). Coordination in these international incidents becomes especially difficult when the host country government is unable to perform coordination or responding agencies do not wish to adhere to coordination mechanisms set up by the host government.

Disaster-affected national governments strive to maintain operational command, control, and coordination even in the most devastating disasters. This is a nation's sovereign right under international law, even when that country requests the support of the United Nations, a regional organization, or a bilateral partner. The responding foreign and/or international responding organizations, however, may not understand, agree with, or otherwise elect not to operate under the command and control of the host country government—and in the most extreme cases, they may actively pursue their own objectives outside the avenues of official coordination systems. Such disconnects threaten to cause (and in many cases result in) extensive bilateral or multilateral discord (such as occurred in the early days of the response to Cyclone Nargis in Myanmar, when foreign nations wishing to provide response support were prevented from entering the country).

Other reasons that coordination is especially difficult in the case of international disasters include the following:

- The host country government is unable to perform coordination.
- Responding agencies do not wish to adhere to coordination mechanisms set up by the host government.
- There is no functioning host country government in place.

In situations where effective coordination is not established by the host country government, such efforts will typically be assumed by or through a special coordinating body. In countries where the United Nations has a significant presence, the United Nations Office for the Coordination of Humanitarian Affairs (UNOCHA) will likely fill this role. Because almost every country is a member of the United Nations, UNOCHA's parent organization, there exists a relationship which is pre-existing and thus can be capitalized on to bring order to chaos among otherwise unaffiliated stakeholders. Moreover, the UN provides a buffer between donor governments and the host government, thereby decreasing the likelihood that (among other things) the following will happen:

- A host government is concerned that a foreign government's staff might be commanding operations within their sovereign borders.
- A donor government is concerned that the host government might misuse or misappropriate donated goods.
- Humanitarian assistance is distributed in an inequitable manner based upon social or cultural biases or preferences.
- There is a lack of common operating picture among responding agencies and organizations.

As with domestic incidents, international coordination systems commonly utilize the *command post* at the field level and an *emergency operations center* (EOC). Participation in an EOC serves to foster consensus building and problem solving in support of operations and typically provides the following:

- The collection and centralization of assessment and intelligence information
- Incident prioritization
- Reporting
- Priorities and strategy development
- Resource and logistics management
- Interagency coordination
- Executive decision-making support

While international NGOs and private entities active during disasters are oftentimes under no obligation to operate within official command and/or coordination structures, foreign governments are party to an accepted framework of international law that dictates bilateral relations. Agencies from one country's government cannot simply enter a foreign jurisdiction uninvited and begin operating independent of official incident management, as that is akin to a territorial invasion. At the same time, a donor government needs to assess its own ability to provide effective support according to the degree to which an impacted government is

1. capable of directing operations,
2. maintaining a safe and secure working environment,
3. maintaining effective situational awareness, and
4. directing assistance in such a way as to ensure it is fair and equitable.

Recipient governments must understand that, in the absence of any of these four factors, there may be an attempt on the part of donor governments to work outside or parallel to the established command structure. In the event that a donor government is permitted to (or is otherwise successful in their efforts to) operate independently of the national government, or even in place of it, the affected government faces a crisis of credibility. Such a crisis exceeds the simple loss of situational command and control. In fact, even a partial transfer or loss of control has resulted in perceptions of incompetence or negligence on the part of the affected population and other participating donor nations. Ultimately, the political impact of such scenarios is highly damaging.

The 2010 earthquake in Haiti, in response to which the United States military assumed operational control of the Toussaint L'Ouverture Airport, provides an example of a situation where response was challenged by a perception of the host country's loss of command, control, or coordination. Immediately following the transfer of operational control of this particular key facility, several other donor nations immediately accused the Haitian government of "playing favorites," and French response officials went as far as to call the airport a "US annex" (Carroll & Nasaw, 2010). Ultimately, this weakened the standing of Haiti's government both in the short term with regards to impressions of their situational control and ultimately (and with irreparable consequences) in the longer term as evidenced by the election that followed.

Of related concern is the risk that donor government response staff find themselves unfamiliar with local response structures, policies, practices, terminology, and equipment. For instance, any responders from a country that does not use the Incident Command System (ICS) that deploys overseas to a disaster-impacted country where ICS is used cannot be expected to be aware of, let alone be trained in, that system. Responders are also likely to be unfamiliar with the structure of local systems of response if the impacted country to which they deploy has a very different government structure in place or if emergency management leadership structures differ significantly. Differences in governance structures between federal and socialist systems, for instance, can have profound impacts on how incidents are managed. The same is true between centralized and decentralized government systems.

Response standards, including those related to privacy, ethics, medical safety, and responder safety, among others, must be locally appropriate. It would be incumbent upon both donor and recipient governments to ensure that alignment between the two occurs with regards to these factors and standards. In the response to Hurricane Katrina in 2005, the government of Singapore was successful in providing integrated support through the provision of four Chinook heavy-lift rotary-winged aircraft. The assets and their operators were already stationed in Texas with the Air National Guard and had become very familiar with US command, control, and coordination procedures through months of joint training and exercises that preceded the incident. The United States government accepted this offer, and each aircraft was commanded by a US military officer assigned to ride along on the missions conducted.

It should be understood, however, that the same level of comfort would not likely exist in most situations. Speaking to the potential challenges of international coordination for disaster response, the United Nations Office for the Coordination of Humanitarian Affairs states the following in the United Nations Disaster Assessment and Coordination (UNAC) Field Handbook:

> *Coordination efforts will need to acknowledge the legitimacy of competing authorities and humanitarian advocacy will become a strong focus. Thus, one may need to develop and maintain effective relationships not only with the State but also with the antagonists, political opposition and in some situations, non-state actors.*
>
> (United Nations Office for the Coordination of Humanitarian Affairs (UNOCHA), 2018)

5.4 THE CLUSTER SYSTEM

(See the Bahamas case study.)

In 2006, the United Nations Office for the Coordination of Humanitarian Affairs' Inter-Agency Standing Committee implemented the use of a global cluster system, whereby global "cluster leaders" are responsible for predetermined functional areas irrespective of any particular event (see Table 5.1). With the explicit purpose of limiting ad hoc responses to humanitarian crises, the cluster approach to managing disasters is meant to eliminate confusion and barriers that might deteriorate the ability for international organizations to coordinate their efforts. Predictability lies at the center of the cluster system. For example, a nutrition cluster operating in response to a tsunami in

TABLE 5.1 Functional Groups by Cluster and Global Cluster Lead Agencies

Cluster	Global Cluster Lead Agency
Camp Coordination and Camp Management	International Organization for Migration/United Nations Refugee Agency (UNHCR)
Early Recovery	United Nations Development Programme
Education	UNICEF and Save the Children
Emergency Telecommunications	World Food Programme (WFP)
Food and Security	WFP and Food/Agriculture Organization
Health	World Health Organization
Logistics	WFP
Nutrition	UNICEF
Protection	UNHCR
Shelter	International Federation of the Red Cross and Red Crescent Societies/UNHCR
Water Sanitation and Hygiene (WASH)	UNICEF

Southeast Asia should operate in an organizationally similar way to a nutrition cluster supporting the response to a hurricane in Central America (UNOCHA Inter-Agency Standing Committee (IASC), 2006).

The cluster approach to humanitarian crises, as implemented by the international disaster management community, serves as a coordination-system-in-a-box that may be implemented in support or in lieu of an effective coordination mechanism during disaster response. The cluster approach provides the structure for coordination and, to a degree, control but maintains no provisions to establish command authority within itself. Essentially, the successful implementation of the cluster approach to international disaster coordination requires approval from whichever governing body maintains command authority.

For countries and authorities that maintain their own response coordination structures and mechanisms that do not closely resemble the cluster approach, integration of the cluster approach (and the structure that it brings) sometimes represents a difficult decision. It requires relinquishing aspects of command authority that allow the international response community to implement the cluster approach as it was designed. In practice, it is common for aspects of the cluster approach to integrate into crises with significant international response participation without fully activating the entire cluster system. In the 2019 response to Tropical Cyclone Idai in Mozambique, the World Food Programme, as the food security cluster lead, coordinated the efforts of 12 supporting international agencies engaged in activities relating to short- and long-term food security. The reach and resources brought forth into the response through the food security cluster mechanism filled a necessary gap that existing coordination mechanisms in Mozambique were unlikely to fill.

During the same response, the capabilities, resources, and coordination efforts of local private and public telecommunications organizations were operating successfully within the established coordination mechanisms of the local government. In this case, the emergency telecommunications cluster was mobilized for the sole purpose of directing international effort into the local government's existing coordination mechanisms. It is likely that shifting command authority of the telecommunication sector's response to the emergency telecommunications cluster in this scenario would have done more harm than good by introducing more confusion to a system that was already operating effectively (United Nations Office for the Coordination of Humanitarian Affairs (UNOCHA), 2019).

While the cluster approach to managing international disaster management and humanitarian crisis efforts represents a predictable coordination structure that can be implemented in virtually any scenario, it is rarely viewed by stakeholders as an "all or nothing" option. Instead, individual clusters are typically used to fill existing gaps that arise in existing domestic command, control, and coordination systems. Assessing the situation and identifying such gaps requires the involvement of all parties and a willingness to be honest, objective, and diplomatic in the high-stress and time-constrained early stages of disaster response decision-making.

INTEGRATION OF FOREIGN RESPONDERS INTO OFFICIAL COMMAND, CONTROL, AND COORDINATION STRUCTURES—THE CASE OF THE BAHAMAS FOLLOWING HURRICANE DORIAN

When Hurricane Dorian struck the Bahamas in 2019, the country's National Emergency Management Agency (NEMA) successfully integrated international governmental and nongovernmental response organizations into their command structure. NEMA's response framework is based on a system of emergency support functions that align organizational efforts, including those of relevant stakeholder agencies, into 14 distinct areas of support (National Emergency Management Agency (NEMA), 2018). The system provides structure for foreign, private sector, and nongovernmental responding organizations. For example, support from an international telecommunications NGO might fall under the communications emergency support function (ESF), which is led by the Royal Bahamas Police Force.

For international organizations familiar with ESF-based coordination mechanisms, minimal stakeholder education and training was required prior to their integration into the ongoing response in the Bahamas. The United States uses a similar construct at the national level through the National Response Framework (NRF), and many state and local emergency management departments have applied the same in their management frameworks. In the response to Hurricane Dorian, any organization familiar with response in the US—namely, the NRF—was immediately familiar with the system in place in the Bahamas. US government agencies and international NGOs trained on the NRF already maintained a working understanding of the command and coordination structures and were thus quickly incorporated.

There were, however, a number of international organizations that were unfamiliar with or unaware of the Bahamas' ESF construct outlined in the National Disaster Plan and Instruction for Emergency Situations (the Bahamian equivalent to the US NRF). This led to many of these organizations attempting to organize themselves in accordance with the United Nations' cluster system (another function-based approach to coordination) in parallel to the national government's construct. For instance, under this alternate system, the World Food Programme assumed the lead agency role for emergency telecommunications and, therefore, led coordination during disaster response for those organizations participating.

Although the existence of disparate coordination systems initially led to response inefficiencies, these were ultimately rectified. In the event's initial days, for instance, communications ESF coordination efforts were primarily conducted in person at the National Emergency Operations Centre using email and the messaging platform WhatsApp. International response stakeholders unfamiliar with or unaware of the communications ESF, including responding entities participating in the cluster system, used the cluster system's IT infrastructure and mechanisms to initiate coordination. This platform was initially seen as having filled a coordination gap, but for several days, these two systems operated in parallel and largely unaware of the other. This ultimately led to increased confusion and redundancy. Of particular note is that the parallel ESF and cluster organizations each maintained independent 3W rosters, which tracked the "who, what, and where" of ongoing response efforts.

Once the duplicative efforts were identified, consolidated, and resolved, communications and coordination improved significantly. As the response operations became more organized, the international community of governmental and nongovernmental organizations capitalized on opportunities to integrate into the ESF structure. The fact remains, however, that the initial confusion and lack of cohesion that existed during the first wave of response was not without impact.

5.5 CHALLENGES PRESENT IN INTERNATIONAL COMMAND, CONTROL, AND COORDINATION

There are a number of unique challenges that make command, control, and coordination in the international context much more complex than in domestic national or local disaster events.

5.5.1 Involvement of Foreign Militaries in Domestic Relief, Response, and Recovery Operations

Many countries have established strict regulations to guide the use of military, paramilitary, or defense forces in the course of disaster response and recovery, while others have based their response around maximizing such resources. In the international context, where significant assistance is often provided via military support, issues of command, control, and coordination can be problematic for military organizations. The hierarchical structure and organization of most military chain of commands prohibit their staff or resources from falling within a foreign chain of command, except for instances where an agreement between militaries is already in place. As such, the establishment of effective bilateral coordination for military support is of paramount importance.

As an example of effective international coordination of military support, the use of military and paramilitary police forces for international disaster response operations in the Caribbean Community (CARICOM) is guided by agreements between the 18 member countries and outlined in the Regional Disaster Support Doctrine. This doctrine maintains the explicit purpose to outline the command and coordination mechanisms for humanitarian assistance in direct support to civil authorities of CARICOM member nations (Caribbean Disaster Emergency Management Agency (CDEMA), 2016). Under the CARICOM Regional Response Mechanism, the executive director of the Caribbean Disaster Emergency Management Agency (CDEMA) may designate a senior official to the role of special coordinator. This special coordinator is responsible for overseeing the international coalition of military and paramilitary forces for disaster response.

Command authority of the special coordinator is established via Article XXI of the CDEMA Agreement (which all member states have signed). Control in this context extends to whichever military and paramilitary forces are identified to support the response to a specific disaster. The special coordinator's role is to facilitate support and liaise between those forces and the nation impacted by a disaster, taking lead on identifying and implementing appropriate coordination mechanisms. Depending on the need of an impacted nation, CDEMA and the special coordinator can bring a variety of capabilities into a response to include operational support, disaster assessment, and search and rescue teams to augment existing national capacities.

The successful coordination of international military forces in the Caribbean is the result of a comprehensive multinational agreement and decades of extensive training, continued buy-in from participating member nations, and opportunities which put the Regional Response Mechanism into action. These opportunities spur secondary opportunities to gather routine feedback which allows CARICOM to make improvements to the coordination mechanisms themselves. Under a special coordinator, questions regarding multinational command across a body of international military and paramilitary forces are proactively and routinely addressed, significantly reducing the opportunity for confusion and conflict.

The capabilities of military forces, particularly regarding international logistics, training, mobility, and personnel, make them ideal partners for civil authorities engaged in disaster response. The successful integration of military forces into an international coordination scheme requires a proactive approach which establishes command and coordination mechanisms before a disaster occurs. When the proactive establishment of command and coordination mechanisms does not occur, a capable military partner may not be authorized to support the response to a disaster in a way that maximizes their capabilities or impact.

5.5.2 Image of "Weakness" among the Public or by the International Community

Disasters are highly political events, whether at the domestic or international scale. In fact, disasters are among the *most* political events because leaders establish their power on their ability to effectively lead during times of crisis. For this reason, some leaders hesitate to accept international assistance under the assumption that acceptance of foreign assistance may result in public impressions that the affected government is unable to manage the needs of its people. The mere act of declaring an international disaster is, after all, an admission of exceeded capabilities, and a clear indication of vulnerability.

Governments may be acutely concerned with "saving face," with key policy-makers believing that the refusal of assistance or to share information may help to downplay the disaster and give the illusion of adequate capability. For this reason, it is believed that the government of China traditionally kept tight control over information pertaining to disaster fatalities. This practice, which did not cease until September 2005, made the assessment of disaster magnitude almost impossible for outside response agencies (a factor which became a source of debate during the COVID-19 pandemic) (Coleman, 2020). Rejection of this nature is the result of a national government believing the situation is manageable even though it is not. This can result in a subsequent reversed course of action when such an assumption is found to be inaccurate as dictated by events.

In this context, where a government or government entity identified by policy or regulatory framework as the command authority does not recognize a disaster situation or respond appropriately, the construct of command can become a hindrance to the successful coordination of response effort. While aspects of risk communication from leadership, particularly political leadership, will assuredly maintain elements of posturing and demonstrating a sense of control during a crisis, such efforts may actively hinder the successful coordination of an ongoing response if left unchecked by the international community of stakeholders.

5.5.3 Protection of State Sovereignty

Perhaps the most oft-cited reason that foreign aid is refused, at least in the initial hours of a disaster, is confusion relating to customs and visa regulations. To ensure the proper flow of people and products in and out of a country, governments establish customs and visa frameworks that are based upon agreements with foreign governments.

Typically, these systems are designed to operate in a controlled, non-disaster environment, and they depend upon bureaucratic processes that have developed over time. In times of disaster, during the initial hours and days when life-saving and life-sustaining resources are most needed, these same systems can pose immediate and insurmountable roadblocks to both donor and recipient governments. Following the 2007 magnitude 8.0 earthquake in Peru, many bilateral offers of assistance were offered and accepted. However, strict customs and visa regulations held up responders, vehicles, equipment, and other supplies. Following the 2011 magnitude 9.0 earthquake in Japan, search and rescue teams from the United States and Switzerland were held up needlessly because strict regulations dictating the import of animals into Japan held up the release of the highly trained dogs upon which the teams depend. In September 2010, the secretary general of the World Customs Organization, Kunio Mikuriya, and director of the United Nations Office for the Coordination of Humanitarian Affairs, Rashid Khalikov, signed a memorandum of understanding (MoU) to support and encourage UN member states to apply simplified customs procedures to speed up the delivery of international humanitarian assistance. Many regional efforts have been established, or are currently being debated, to develop regional mutual assistance constructs that simplify customs and immigration issues in the special circumstances that a disaster presents. However, the fact that these delays continue today are a testament to the difficulty of establishing mechanisms with sufficient scope and flexibility.

5.6 GLOBAL EXAMPLES OF INCIDENT COMMAND AND COORDINATION SYSTEMS

While the ICS is the most widely used system in the United States, the United Kingdom, Brazil, and parts of Canada, for instance, other countries use alternative systems to manage incident command, control, and management. These systems may be based in part on the ICS, considering its historical significance as one of the earliest established systems, or they may have little in common. Like all emergency management capacities throughout the world, systems evolve according to what works best in light of the political, economic, and social influences that exist.

5.6.1 The Incident Command System (ICS)

The most widely utilized incident command and control system is the Incident Command System, or ICS as it is most commonly referred. The ICS was developed in the United States in the 1970s when multiple wildfire incidents involving large-scale response efforts from a number of different fire suppression resources resulted in less-than-optimal outcomes, including preventable losses of life and property. It was recognized that a key to the success of any national incident management system is the existence of a subcomponent system through which incident command and control is standardized. In the United States, it is the ICS that fulfills this role.

The ICS was created out of recognition that widespread duplication of efforts, a lack of coordination, and problematic communication hindered response efforts. The ICS was developed to provide a definitive determination of who is in charge of the overall response effort.

Its main purpose is to allow for the establishment of a set of planning and management systems that help the various agencies that respond to disasters to work together in a coordinated and systematic approach. The step-by-step process is ultimately what enables the numerous responding agencies to most effectively combine and utilize their resources and personnel to respond to those in need.

ICS is effective because it provides for effective operations in the three distinct incident types (in terms of the number of jurisdictions affected by the disaster, and the number of jurisdictions responding):

1. Single jurisdiction and/or single agency
2. Single jurisdiction with multiple agency support
3. Multi-jurisdictional and/or multi-agency support.

The organizational structure of the ICS is also adaptable to a wide variety of emergencies of any hazard origin, which include natural, technological, or intentional, or a combination of hazards from one or more of these categories. In that sense, it is truly all-hazards. The ICS is so important to the success of response and recovery efforts of all sizes because it allows its users to adopt an integrated organizational structure to match the complexities and demands of single or multiple incidents without being hindered by jurisdictional boundaries.

In the United States, the federal government (as a requirement under HSPD-5) has developed and mandated the national adoption of the National Incident Management System (NIMS), an outgrowth of the ICS that allows for increased inter-organizational coordination that is not necessarily addressed under standard ICS structures. NIMS is technically a more comprehensive incident management system than the ICS because it goes beyond the field-level incident command and control and addresses all phases of emergency management, as well as all stakeholders (including the NGO and private sectors). NIMS adoption is a requirement for many Federal grant programs, so most local and state emergency management agencies have adopted the system. However, its use is optional among all other organizations, including many non-traditional emergency management stakeholders like hospitals and schools, for example, so the degree to which it has been adopted and understood by these organizations remains undetermined.

NIMS is heavily based upon the ICS, which is one of three integral components of the system. Another component is the Multi-agency Coordination System (MACS), a widely applied incident coordination system that operated independently from but often concurrently with ICS in large-scale US incidents.

The ICS offered responding agencies a number of key functions that made their job more effective. They include the following:

1. A common use of terminology
2. Integrated communications
3. A unified command structure
4. Management of resources
5. Incident action planning

The ICS is also scalable, which is key to its incorporation by agencies of all sizes and in their response to events of all magnitudes.

5.6.2 The Coordinated Incident Management System (CIMS) (New Zealand)

CIMS is an incident management system developed and adopted by the New Zealand emergency services and other agencies as a basis for operational response. The government of New Zealand supported the development of CIMS to ensure coordination among the different response agencies in that country in order to ensure consistent and effective response and recovery efforts.

CIMS originated in the 1990s during a time when the New Zealand Fire Service Commission was advocating for an interagency incident management system for emergency service providers. This proposal developed into CIMS, which is based on international incident management systems developed in the United States (ICS) and Australia (AIIMS—see the next section).

Several different New Zealand governmental agencies were involved in the system's development, including the National Rural Fire Authority, the National Police, St. Johns Ambulance, the Department of Conservation (similar to the US Department of the Interior), and the Ministry of Emergency Management and Civil Defense.

The foundation of CIMS is the building of "teamwork in emergency management" through the following:

1. Sharing common terminology
2. Using a modular organizational structure
3. Integrating communications
4. Using common incident action plans
5. Ensuring manageable spans of control
6. Sharing resources

Under CIMS, coordination is based on four core elements:

1. Control
2. Planning and intelligence
3. Operations
4. Logistics

CIMS dictates that the control of multiple agencies operating within a common incident (horizontally across agencies) is exercised by the senior first responder but is transferred on the basis of which agency has primacy for the incident type (for example, police for law enforcement purposes).

CIMS is a standard, all-hazards system. During any major national emergency or disaster, of any hazard type, national operations are conducted in accordance with the four CIMS core elements. All participating agencies (including the Ministry of Civil Defense and Emergency Management [CDEM—the New Zealand national-level emergency management agency] and all local authorities) use CIMS as the basis for their response procedures. CIMS standardizes terminology and procedures among these agencies, which might otherwise not communicate or integrate well. Agencies may use their own systems on a routine basis, but they plan for an effective interface between their CIMS functions and those of other agencies involving incident "controllers" from different agencies.

The New Zealand system uses the term *control* rather than *command* in order to distance it from a military connotation, as many military incident management systems (as well as the military culture in general) use the term command to describe management authority.

5.7 THE AUSTRALASIAN INTER-SERVICE INCIDENT MANAGEMENT SYSTEM (AIIMS) (AUSTRALIA)

AIIMS was first introduced by the Australian fire authorities in the mid-1980s but has since been adopted by the various Australian state emergency services and a number of other public safety organizations. Like ICS and CIMS, AIIMS was developed to enable the integration of activities and resources from multiple agencies in response to any emergency incident.

AIIMS has been adopted by all of the Australian fire and land management agencies and the Australian Council of State Emergency Services. A number of other public safety agencies and non-emergency services have adopted AIIMS and are in the process of implementing the system within their organizations. AIIMS provides a common incident management framework, which can be applied to any size incident as it is designed to be flexible and grow or shrink with incident size and complexity.

Like NIMS, AIIMS provides a single management structure that facilitates the coordination of all resources, from one or several organizations, to work cooperatively and cohesively in resolving an incident. Its application is intended to achieve the following:

1. Minimize the impact on the community and environment
2. Provide for the welfare of people involved in controlling the incident
3. Effectively and efficiently control the incident
4. Provide a safe working environment

AIIMS is based on three key principles:

1. Management by objectives
2. Functional management (including control, planning, operations, and logistics)
3. Span of control

5.7.1 The British Columbia Emergency Response Management System (BCERMS) (British Columbia, Canada)

While the Canadian national government uses the ICS system, the Canadian province of British Columbia emergency management structure has developed and adopted an incident management system called BCERMS, which provides the framework for response standardization among all responding organizations and agencies. This is very similar to a system called SEMS (Standardized Emergency Management System), which was developed by the State of California to supplement ICS in terms of the incident coordination function.

BCERMS has also adapted the ICS framework such that it better meets the specific needs of British Columbia. BCERMS operates under the concepts of organizational unity and hierarchy of command. Organizational unity means that every individual within a BCERMS organization has a designated supervisor.

Hierarchy or chain of command means an orderly line of authority within the ranks of the organization with lower levels subordinate to and connected to higher levels. BCERMS operates according to four incident response levels. These levels each represent the successive increases in incident scope and jurisdiction:

1. Site level
2. Site support level
3. Provincial regional coordination level
4. Provincial central coordination level

Like ICS, BCERMS uses the following *incident management functions*:

1. Command or management
2. Operations
3. Planning
4. Logistics
5. Finance/administration

5.7.2 Disaster Response Command System (Sistem Komando Penanganan Darurat Bencana—SKPDB) (Indonesia)

Incident command and coordination in Indonesia have changed considerably in recent years as a result of an ongoing effort to revamp the country's national emergency management capabilities. A new system of incident command and coordination has been developed in alignment as dictated in the country's new National Disaster Response Framework (NDRF), which was released in 2018.

Incident command in Indonesia is established using a newly released Disaster Response Command System (Sistem Komando Penanganan Darurat Bencana—SKPDB). Under this new system, a standard construct for incident command is established from the local to national level. At the national level, BNPB Regulation 3/2016 mandates the use of the ICS and is considered the basis of the NIMS SKPDB Management Support Annex. This regulation details the roles and responsibilities within the incident command construct at all government levels and among all components.

Incident coordination is guided by incident management systems established through release of a new National Disaster Response Framework (NDRF) in 2018. This framework, authorized by the country's national disaster law (Law 24/2007), is closely linked to the SKPDB. The two systems work together to establish more closely synchronized command and control constructs, as based on prevailing statutory authority. It is likewise structurally similar to the UN cluster system, which helps to increase coordination effectiveness in the event that UNOCHA involvement occurs.

Through the SKPDB, plans and procedures delineate leadership and coordination for disaster and emergency support functional areas, such as search and rescue, public health, and shelter. The NDRF utilizes a system of disaster response task forces (DRTFs) to delineate the leadership and coordination arrangements that guide seven distinct emergency management functions. These include search and rescue, displacement and protection, health, logistics, public works and utilities, education, and early recovery.

To facilitate interagency coordination, there are several standard procedures and other tools in place including interagency agreements, mechanisms to request assistance and mission assign national-level agencies, reporting requirements, and mechanisms for interagency reimbursement. This is also facilitated through operation of the NDRF system of DRTFs. Each task force that is activated in a disaster event by BNPB or by the president is led by a ministry or agency that coordinates all other partner organizations and agencies, including those that are nongovernmental and/or international. Once activated, a national DRTF may in turn assign staff at the regional and incident levels to support response in the disaster impacted areas.

Data, a centerpiece of coordination constructs, is freely shared between each level of government within Indonesia during disasters, but also with NGO and other partners and with the public. Data sharing is guided by the NDRF and by the provisions of the SKPDB (namely, sectoral coordination meetings). Sectoral coordination meetings are intended to enable sharing between governmental and nongovernmental stakeholders and between different administrative levels of government.

5.8 CONCLUSION

While much of this chapter draws from examples involving hurricanes, typhoons, and earthquakes, the same principles apply for wildfires. In anticipation of climate change inducing more precarious conditions for the rapid and massive spread of fires, fire-prone areas should plan for the possibility of needing aid from beyond their national borders. Understanding the differing systems and how these have worked effectively by focusing on command, control, and coordination will help sidestep many of the potential pitfalls at a time when effective and efficient response is critical. Understanding the impediments of politics, regulations, and concerns about state sovereignty will also help mitigate the barriers of accessing needed assistance in a timely manner.

REFERENCES

Caribbean Disaster Emergency Management Agency (CDEMA). (2016). *The regional response mechanism* (pp. 1–32). www.cdema.org/RRM_Booklet_Final_PDF_version.pdf

Carroll, R., & Nasaw, D. (2010, January 17). US accused of annexing airport as squabbling hinders aid effort in Haite. *The Guardian*. www.theguardian.com/world/2010/jan/17/us-accused-aid-effort-haiti

Coleman, J. (2020, November 30). Leaked documents show china mishandled early COVID-19 pandemic. *The Hill*. https://thehill.com/policy/international/528055-leaked-documents-show-china-mishandled-early-covid-19-pandemic-report/

Coppola, D. (2021). *Introduction to international disaster management* (4th ed.). Butterworth-Heinemann (Elsevier).

National Emergency Management Agency (NEMA). (2018). *The commonwealth of the Bahamas national disaster plan & instructions for emergency situations 2018–2020.*

United Nations Office for the Coordination of Humanitarian Affairs (UNOCHA). (2018). *United Nations Disaster Assessment and Coordination (UNDAC) field handbook.* www.unocha.org/sites/dms/Documents/UNDAC%20handbook%20-%20English.pdf

United Nations Office for the Coordination of Humanitarian Affairs (UNOCHA). (2019). *Humanitarian response plan: Mozambique.* https://reliefweb.int/report/mozambique/2018-2019-mozambique-humanitarian-response-plan-revised-following-cyclones-idai

UNOCHA Inter-Agency Standing Committee (IASC). (2006). *Guidance note on using the cluster approach to strengthen humanitarian response.* https://www.humanitarianresponse.info/en/coordination/clusters/document/iasc-guidance-note-using-cluster-approach-strengthen-humanitarian

US Federal Emergency Management Agency. (n.d.). *Comparative emergency management: Command, control, coordination, and disaster declarations review material.*

CHAPTER 6

Law Enforcement Response to Wildfire

Joshua Brazzi, Stephen Collins, Jason Hail, and Jake Smith

In the case of wildfires, law enforcement plays a critical role in evacuating residents and workers from the endangered areas, providing security within the evacuated areas, and in tracing the "missing" persons for whom no contact has been made with family and/or friends. Because of the enormity of this role, preparation is critical. This chapter outlines the response from law enforcement, focusing on the Camp Fire but also incorporating lessons from subsequent wildfires and experience on mutual aid. Discussion is divided between (1) the efforts needed in the area of the fire and surrounding communities and (2) the identification of those missing, location of antemortem information, and resolution of those who survived but are unaccounted for. We conclude with the lessons learned and what the future may hold for those who face the devastation of a wildfire.

6.1 LAW ENFORCEMENT INCIDENT RESPONSE TO WILDFIRE

Law enforcement response to a wildfire occurs over an extended period of time, from the initial notification of a problem to the return of evacuated residents. Due to the duration of the event, the roles played by various agencies change and flexibility is critical. It is also essential to not only know what steps will come next but to simultaneously be planning for the transition well ahead of the actual event.

6.1.1 Phase 1: In the Face of Fire

Wildfires often arrive quickly and with incredible intensity, resulting in utter chaos. In areas such as the California Sierra foothills, evacuations are complicated by narrow, winding, and heavily wooded roads, higher numbers of older and/or disabled residents, and many seasonal or itinerant workers, many of whom may be employed in illicit activity. The speed is such that, in large counties, much of the area is relatively unaware of the scale of the disaster as it unfolds. Such was definitely the case with the 2018 Camp Fire. In all such situations, the top priority was to save lives. Preservation of property falls to a more distant second in the face of saving people.

DOI: 10.4324/9781003168010-8

As word of a wildfire reaches the dispatch center and command posts, the first focus will be on evacuation of people, making sure that people can leave and exit routes are clear. Second, focus will shift to getting resources into place. Typically, basic information is needed in order to begin this work such as where the fire currently is located, what direction is it moving, and what lies in its path. Once that is known, then law enforcement can dispatch units to work on the evacuation procedures.

Much of this initial work falls to patrol teams but in rural areas patrolled by sheriff's offices or small towns with an equally small police department, these teams are few in number and often patrol a wide area. Nevertheless, they would be the ones obtaining information from CAL FIRE (California Department of Forestry and Fire Protection) about the direction and intensity of the fire. This information designates areas to be evacuated immediately, a task that falls to the local law enforcement.

As soon as they can, additional units would be added through mutual aid, if they can successfully reach the areas given the outflow of evacuees and the fire conditions. These requests first go locally and only after that to the outlying region and the state. In the Camp Fire, the first outreach involved Chico Police Department and Oroville Police Department, but these resources were quickly drained. Mutual aid often also arrives ill-prepared for the fire/post-fire environmental conditions. Street shoes were inappropriate, and the residual heat often caused melting of the soles. The higher altitude coupled with the dense smoke cover meant that the fire zone could become quite cold, but incoming personnel may have not expected such a change. Even patrol cars suffered heat damage from the fires along with scrapes and dents in trying to maneuver between the various hazards in dense smoke. Centralized pools of supplies are also helpful. For the 2020 Bear Fire, the sheriff's office had to buy power tools to get through gates and into vehicles to check for remains or for people who might be injured. There may also be a need for specialized equipment, such as drones, or similar technology that may require qualified personnel to operate them.

Communication is often a challenge as different agencies may be utilizing different radio bands or have different communication capabilities. Incompatibility of communication systems can be overcome with agreed frequencies for communication or supplementing with stocked equipment. If these resources are insufficient, it may be necessary to pair mutual aid officers with local officers.

With many mutual aid personnel working in the area, unfamiliarity with the locale, as well as visibility issues, can be problematic. For example, emergency calls are common as those who initially refused to leave realize their peril. In the Camp Fire, one mutual aid unit had only just arrived at the incident command center when they had to be dispatched to rescue people. This involved driving at high speed, in smoke with downed trees and power lines, no reliable communication, and no power for traffic lights. While successful, it was harrowing for both the unit dispatched and those who had to send them.

One of the items to note is that in the chaos of initial response, it is difficult to keep tabs on who has come, how many units are present, where they are located, and what else is available. This was particularly apparent in the Camp Fire, with its extremely quick arrival. A significant difference was noted in the subsequent North Complex Fire in 2020 where there was more notice and resources could be tracked better during the evacuation process. In that later fire, law enforcement could be dispatched to assigned areas. Some deputies were sent to high points to get visuals on the fire and asked to send information back to the Butte County Sheriff's Office, a practice learned from

CAL FIRE. This provided situational awareness of the location, as well as speed and scale of the fire. Evacuations were conducted five miles over the county line initially, with an evacuation warning preceding the order. In the end, the radius was 16 miles from the county line.

The Butte County Sheriff's Office uses a number of different platforms to send out emergency alerts to the public. Because there is not any one alerting platform that works in every situation, it is recommended that individuals have multiple forms of receiving alerts during emergencies. Potential platforms include the CodeRed and Integrated Public Alert and Warning System (IPAWS). CodeRed allows for text, voice message, email, and the CodeRed App. IPAWS does text, voice message, TV, and radio. Alerts are also sent through Facebook and Twitter, General Mobile Radio Service (GMRS) and Amateur (HAM) radio channels, and the Community Advisory Radio Systems (CARS). Messages can be broadcast in multiple languages to maximize reach. As an example, in Butte County, messages can be sent in English, Spanish and Hmong, depending on the platform. Cell phone warnings are not always effective. For example, in the Bear Fire, people using Wi-Fi-dependent phones did not receive calls. If cell towers are lost, the cell service will be severely limited. In mountainous areas, cell coverage is usually spotty even before a disaster, so we need to develop other ways of warning people. A public map (www.buttecounty.net/sheriffcoroner) has been created, which shows all evacuation zones in the county and is updated during an emergency to show the status of each zone. People can search for their zone by inputting their address. The public often rely on a variety of cell phone apps, such as Watch Duty and Zonehaven, to inform them of wildfire evacuations and law enforcement links to these should be utilized.

There are also inherently issues associated with each of the systems outlined earlier. If the telecommunications system is functioning and there is cell phone reception in the area, then CodeRed and IPAWS can reach the most people; however, due to topography and population density, the systems can experience complications. The GMRS works well, provided there is GMRS radio reception in the impacted area and people have their GMRS radio turned on. The GMRS radios are not dependent on the power grid or internet connectivity as they can operate on batteries and on the vehicle's cigarette lighter port. The Community Advisory Radio System (CARS) can also be effective, provided people tune their radio to the local community AM channel. Currently, there are only two functioning CARS in Butte County. The online zone map will show the most current status of zones, and people can search by address to determine which zone the address is in and the status of that zone.

Because distributed messages may still not reach everyone, law enforcement also goes door to door making notifications while sounding a Hi-Lo evacuation siren and will use their loudspeakers when appropriate. This process is time-consuming but often allows for identification of properties where the residents are refusing to evacuate. Many people will wait for a formal evacuation order before leaving and that order may come too late, or the agency may be unable to distribute it once it is made due to breakdowns in the communication networks. People who do not know about a fire will not have a chance to escape. It is better to have the residents leave needlessly rather than people not getting a chance to escape. While people cannot be forced to leave, it is helpful to note these addresses as these locations may need to be checked later either for a late evacuation or possible recovery.

Butte County automatically produces calls for service in the Sheriff's Office Dispatch for people who require assistance during evacuations and who are registered in the Special Needs Awareness Program (SNAP). This allows improved accountability for those individuals, and the Alert FM system enables the county to send emergency messages to specialized receivers in homes. In the North Complex Fire, which was more slow-moving, the SNAP list provided names of those people with health or mobility issues. Those names were immediately assigned to deputies at the start of evacuations. This list had been available during the Camp Fire but, in that instance, due to the speed of the fire, all individuals were potential victims.

The evacuation process is complex, and in the case of the Camp Fire, the evacuation process took about 24 hours to complete for the core affected areas of Paradise and Magalia. This process can be shorter or longer, depending on the scale of the fire. It is also subject to change. For example, in the Camp Fire, the winds shifted after passing through Paradise and placed the Berry Creek area in danger. Evacuations were therefore shifted to the new area. In the 2020 Santa Cruz Mountain fires, it was decided to evacuate large suburban areas along the southern border in anticipation of an expansion of the fire and also to provide uninterrupted access for emergency services. In that case, over 60,000 people were displaced in waves.

6.1.2 Phase 2: Beginning of Recovery

As the evacuations wind down, the law enforcement agency is establishing its incident command post. Potential locations should be identified throughout the county in anticipation of such events, and the location must provide adequate space for vehicles and other needed infrastructure. The path of the fire and the level of destruction are, however, an issue as often the previously identified locations are no longer suitable. For Butte County Sheriff's Office after the Camp Fire, this was somewhat easier in that the agency had already experienced a major evacuation due to failure of a spillway on the Oroville Dam. Following that event, they had put in place an incident management team. However, in the initial period of the Camp Fire, evacuations required "all hands on deck," so the incident management team took a little longer to get into place.

Incident command was well-established by the second phase of the fire response in the 2018 Camp Fire (see Chapters 4 and 5). This center included daily command staff meetings to discuss what tasks still needed to be done, what resources were needed, and what needed to be planned ahead. Round table discussion occurred daily and assessed the available resources, the logistics of obtaining those resources, and what support they would need. Requesting resources and then not using them is disheartening for all involved and should be avoided if at all possible. People with experience should be involved in the discussion, as they are best at communicating what resources are needed and how they should be requested.

The recovery process needs attention from the very beginning of the incident and thus attention must persist throughout the duration of the process. The emergency manager must look at the broad-view thinking about how to move to the next stage of the process, which is the full recovery and repopulation. The planning should always be anticipating the next step and have its eye on several steps ahead. Ideally, planning for repopulation is underway even while the evacuation is being completed. For the Camp Fire, Butte County worked with other agencies to come up with a strategy for recovery response drawing upon communal experience, as well as outreach to subject matter experts. This began with a resources list and plan for the response for what was initially thought to be a fire with 400–500 victims.

By this phase, law enforcement personnel have usually been significantly augmented by mutual aid from other areas. For instance, within 24 hours into the Camp Fire, over 200 officers had been added from mutual aid. While the additional personnel are greatly needed and appreciated, there are also issues with a large influx of people unfamiliar with the area. Often they simply do not know where to go, especially when street names and other indicators have been obscured or lost. Many remote areas have a lot of unknown hazards after a fire but also many dead-end roads or roads blocked by fallen trees or abandoned vehicles. In the Butte County fires, it was found that pairing officers with US Fish and Game or US Forest Service personnel who knew the area worked well.

While it is almost always possible to get additional personnel into the field, many things must be considered, including how and what will they be fed, what equipment will they need, where will they sleep when all hotels have been taken for evacuated citizens, whether there are restroom facilities in the field, and what decontamination facilities can be mounted given the number of personnel. These functions also need to be coordinated with the fire crews who are still mopping up hot spots and dealing with hazards, the power companies and communications workers trying to repair the infrastructure that benefit the law enforcement teams, and the transportation workers who rebuild and inspect roads and bridges.

It is also important to be transparent in communications with the public. Frequent communications, such as morning and evening briefings, are helpful in reducing anxiety. These times allow for explanation as to why people are not allowed to return to their homes within the evacuation zone. While they may want a date, it is detrimental to give a date that cannot be met. The information released to the media should also be disseminated through the law enforcement personnel so that there is no disconnect between broadcasts through the media and by people in the field (e.g., at roadblocks). Many incident commands now utilize social media to speak directly to the public, and this allows for some control over the material.

After the evacuation of people, there are often pets and livestock left. Most counties have both emergency preparations to house small and large animals and also evacuation teams that will return to the area to retrieve and transport out animals. In the Camp Fire, such work was done by the North Valley Animal Disaster Group (NVADG), which already had a strong working relationship with the Butte County Sheriff's Office. Groups such as this have registered lists of volunteers who will either transport animals out or provide food and water to animals that need to shelter in place. A decision during the Camp Fire was made relatively early that all animal rescue volunteers would be coordinated through NVADG.

One issue with animal rescue efforts during the Camp Fire was that a large number of people volunteered to help outside of the established agency. Some were from similar agencies in neighboring counties, but others were well-intentioned volunteers without experience or connections. Such volunteers cannot be allowed into the secured area. Unfortunately, passions can run very high, and one group whose help was turned down immediately went on social media to complain that animals were being neglected. Eventually, even NVADG was overwhelmed and had to decline additional help as they were able to sustain their work with the available qualified resources.

In the Camp Fire, the numbers of people reported as missing kept increasing, and there was the expectation among the search and rescue groups (see Chapter 11) that bodies would be widely distributed. Search and rescue (SAR) operations were coordinated through the Butte County Sheriff's Office. In the Camp Fire, the Butte County sheriff insisted that all properties be searched prior to the return of residents. Some areas are difficult to plot due to the destruction, but county planning agencies may have maps of these areas with address or unit numbers. This required the concerted work of many SAR teams mobilized from across the state and even beyond. Some of the SAR teams were specifically trained in urban search and rescue (USAR), and they were helpful due to the large number of buildings. However, some USAR groups tended to only focus on building interiors or tried to search an entire property. With the subsequent Bear Fire, the USAR teams were better prepared and did perimeter searches, which has proven to be the most efficient process for wildfire recovery (see Chapter 11 and 12). Nevertheless, daily adjustments in search strategy were common, depending upon the specific communities, the resources, and the types of terrain.

In the immediate wake of the Camp Fire, it was evident that many remains would have been incinerated. Anthropologists were among the first responders requested (see Chapter 12). At first it was assumed that the work of the missing persons unit (discussed further here) would direct the locations for the anthropologist teams, but this did not prove effective due to the large number of missing people. Anthropologist/deputy teams were then deployed to respond to locations where remains were found to determine if they were human or animal. Leads were also given to field teams to follow up on missing persons reports. Law enforcement continued to serve as valuable resources to support recovery work as law enforcement and coroner's units were embedded into the recovery teams. Members of coroner's units were integrated into these teams, less for recovery and more for consistency in the documentation of the death, assignment of a case number and ensuring appropriate transportation from the scene. This integrated approach needed adjusting through the recovery period at the Camp Fire, but by the time of the North Complex Fire two years later, the integration was much smoother. Under the new protocols devised after the Camp Fire, leads were funneled to the field from the missing persons unit, which was tasked with targeting locations as high priority. Field teams of coroners' investigators and anthropologists were dispatched to specific locations where the missing person was last seen. In larger fires, this approach may require division of the area into separate zones.

As the need for emergency evacuations diminishes, law enforcement efforts divert to providing security for the area. The area to be patrolled should be divided into fairly small sections so that units can patrol these fairly easily. In the Camp Fire, the shift to a greater focus on security occurred by the third to fourth day after the fire. Establishing a secure network around and in the fire area is important for a number of reasons. There may be people who want to return to see what is left or gather animals or valuables from their property. In Butte County, it was noted that people who had evacuated were understanding of the situation at least for a couple of weeks. Looters often arrive fairly early after a fire, targeting those homes that are still standing. This invasion of fire-ravaged areas is so intense that special methods such as the use of night-vision goggles are needed to monitor homes. There are also people who had refused to leave but may now be in danger or need evacuation as they may be without power, water, food, medications, or communications.

6.1.3 Phase 3: Repopulation

As soon as an area is evacuated, the public typically begins seeking information about the status of their home and asking when repopulation can occur. During any evacuation, there will be people who do not understand why they are not allowed back on their property once the fire front has passed. Most do not understand the extent of the devastation or the hazards that still exist in the area. There is critical infrastructure, such as powerlines, guardrails, and bridges that must be repaired and inspected for integrity prior to the public's return. Managing all of the demands brought forth by the emergency is challenging; however, it is important to be sensitive to the public's situation and, where feasible, provide information. Law enforcement must also accept that they will never be able to make everyone happy.

Decisions on which areas and when to repopulate are made by coordination between all the agencies (law enforcement, fire, public works, transportation) involved in the emergency, including the utility companies (electric and gas lines, telephone/mobile providers, internet providers, propane distributors) and any stakeholders such as US Forest Service, Bureau of Land Management, and the like. When all the entities agree that an area (or portion thereof) is safe for repopulation, a date and time for repopulation is scheduled and preparations are made for public messaging to advise the citizens. The lead group is continually looking ahead as to when and what areas can be opened and collaborating with the agencies/entities that need to make the area safe. It is a complicated process and areas are only approved when all entities are in agreement that the area is safe for the public to return to. Safety is given highest priority with all other factors being considered. Ultimately the final decision is made by the sheriff of the county having jurisdiction, if there are any political or public pressures.

Repopulation is typically done in phases with those areas evacuated but untouched by the fire occurring before those areas in the fire zone. Once safety issues are addressed, escorted returns can be made before the actual repopulation is allowed. However, there may be significant reasons that full repopulation is delayed. Water contamination and danger from landslides are large factors to be considered.

Many people really just want to know what is left. Fortunately, fire damage assessment teams can be dispatched quickly into fire areas to document damaged or destroyed buildings. Often, the majority of homes are destroyed while those listed as "damaged" may have suffered only minor changes, such as cracked windows or warped siding. Online websites listing homes by untouched, partial damage or destroyed help let people know the status of their homes and allow them to move forward with some of the necessary paperwork without needing to return to the evacuated zone.

6.2 ISSUE OF OVERLAPPING MULTIPLE INCIDENTS

One cannot predict when multiple incidents co-occur, but law enforcement must be able to react quickly and effectively. The Camp Fire provided an excellent example of this situation. Several days after the fire had passed through the area, law enforcement was involved in assisting with body recovery, along with security of the area. A report came in that a car associated with someone suspected in a double homicide had been seen in Concow, one of the communities within the fire zone. There was a male sleeping in the driver's seat, believed to be a suspect in the homicides. The individual had also violated parole. Because of the man's reputation, the SWAT team was sent along with all available officers, including many assigned to other duties in the fire zone. The male decided to flee and then became involved in a police shooting that resulted in his death, along with that of a police canine and his own pet dog.

Not only was this an added complication to an already taxed system, but a police shooting mandates a specific set of protocols. Officers needed to be sent home and could not return until a full debrief was done and they were cleared for return to duty. Since a large portion of the people involved in the incident were also members of the incident command, this produced yet another wrinkle. At the time they left to deal with the suspect, there were people in the field awaiting orders or resources. In addition, other command members had to form the investigation team required after a law enforcement involved shooting, so they were also unavailable for a period of time. Mutual aid officers involved in the shooting also had to be cleared by their home agencies. Since the command post members could not return, the people awaiting direction were left dangling, while others got drafted into the roles and tried to regroup.

The lesson learned from this is not to think about who goes, for often there is little choice, but rather who are their designated secondaries that can quickly step into a role. While, in the Camp Fire, law enforcement had prepared for the shift from a daytime to a nighttime command team, they had not anticipated the need for a secondary designee within a shift.

Later in the Camp Fire recovery process, weather changes raised another issue that frequently follows wildfires, the possibility of mudslides. At the incident command center, the California Office of Emergency Services provided a large mudslide map showing mudslide danger zones based on sensors distributed in slide-prone areas. It became critical to see where evacuees were returning and ensure that search and recovery teams did not cross into these zones. By this time, the sheriff deputies were already performing escort services for residents returning to properties within the secured area, and some areas had already been repopulated. While there was no shortage of officers, the rains were extremely heavy and produced flooding along with the danger of mudslides. Flooding was so intense that it crossed the freeway south of the county seat of Oroville and threatened a nearby town. Reports started to come in of cars being swept away. Most of the dangerous areas were along one road in a steep canyon, Honey Run Road.

The issue of mudslides raised a number of questions. Leadership needed to decide how to shut down roads while still maintaining security on the fire area. Could people be re-evacuated when they had only just returned, often with their livestock? Were there vehicles powerful enough to get through on poor roads and across muddy areas? Eventually, National Guard trucks were commandeered to assist with evacuations and rescues. This second evacuation lasted about eight hours before the areas could be repopulated again.

6.3 TRACKING FOR MISSING/UNACCOUNTED-FOR PERSONS

Often at the beginning of a disaster involving residential areas, such as Paradise, Magalia, and Concow in the Camp Fire, there is a period of intense confusion as to who is missing and which of those people are thought to be dead. There will be a few credible reports, such as neighbors knowing that someone did not leave or victims calling for assistance that could not arrive in time. However, many of the missing persons reports are calls from family or friends who are worried about someone known or thought to live in the area and from whom they have had no contact.

Because of both the destruction and abandonment of facilities due to a fire, 911 calls first come into the local police or law enforcement agency but are typically then diverted to a county or regional center as agencies within the fire path must evacuate. In the Camp Fire, these calls came initially into Paradise but were then diverted to the Butte County Sheriff's Office. As the volume exceeded the capacity of the dispatchers, calls had to be diverted further, first to Chico PD and then to other agencies. Each agency tended to initially record this information in their own format, and consequently, it was difficult to amass all of the inquiries as to missing persons. The volume of calls was astonishing, and for those in charge of tracking the missing, there was the sense of starting with their heads already underwater only to find out that more and more was coming over them.

It is also important to remember that, at least in the Camp Fire, it was initially feared that the dead may well exceed a thousand people. The volume of calls regarding people who were thought to be missing supported this belief. Many of the calls were vague, such as "Grandma is missing from Paradise." Often three or four calls came in for the same person—or calls came in for the same person under various names, such as Robert Smith, Bobby Smith, or "Skip" Smith. For much of the initial time, there was barely enough personnel to take the messages of people inquiring after the missing.

Initial screening involved trying to find out if the home had been destroyed, but this information was less helpful as about 90–95% of homes were lost. In parallel, they were also using the shelter roll calls to strike off names of people who had made it to the designated locations. However, these lists usually only had first and last names and did not list addresses of origin. Many relief agencies were extremely hesitant to share even this information with law enforcement due to fears that it would be used to arrest or deport people who had warrants or were known to be undocumented. It took substantial time to reassure that the sheriff's office was only interested in the well-being of individuals. Because these particular communities often housed extended families, names were often less than helpful—more than one family member could have the same or similar names. Even the Safe and Well website was less than helpful as some families were reporting as "found" those who were later determined to be among the dead.

After trying to derive an accurate count with constant interruptions for updates, the detectives were forced to set aside a day just to work on organizing the approach. They quickly realized that they needed to devise a systematic approach, especially as the agency could only devote two detectives to the task. They needed to determine a format in which to lay out the information on their computers and do so quickly. Five days after the Camp Fire, detectives wiped the slate clean and began again, scrapping the old, bad data.

Just as that was happening, they were able to get help from Sonoma County, which had already gone through the "chaotic" phase during previous wildfires with fatalities and generated a reliable spreadsheet with which to profile those reported missing (Table 6.1). Interestingly, the Sonoma format closely paralleled the revised system that Butte had devised and so adoption was quickly implemented. However, it still took about three weeks before the Missing Persons Task Force would be able to work smoothly.

TABLE 6.1 Antemortem Data Collected from Missing Persons Reports

Identification number for missing person (MP)
Status
Last name of MP
First name of MP
Date of birth of MP
Age of MP
Gender of MP
Address of MP
Street of MP
City of MP
Phone number of MP
Cell phone number of MP
Reporting person's first name
Reporting person's last name
Relationship to MP
Reporting person's phone number
Source
Incident number
Assigned to
Case number

Notes: include details of status (located by other family members, self-reported, etc.) and identifying features (tattoos, surgical implants, dental characteristics, etc.).

Overall, the new format worked extremely well. The new master list was used for inputting, comparing, and storing information. Rather than call a person "missing," they were designated as "unaccounted for." Each such person was assigned a unique number. As additional "missing" people were found that duplicated the "unaccounted for" individuals, the duplicates were folded into the new format number. Analysts from nearby Placer County helped deconflict the data, especially dealing with the conflicts based on the agency who first received the calls.

Along with the spreadsheet, checklists were also developed. The checklist prioritized individuals based on the likelihood of finding them. The status of each person on the list needed to be verified. If they were found to be alive, they were checked off the list. Their home address was checked against the growing list of damage information. Information was collected on whether or not the person was probably at home at the time of the fire, whether they had transportation, and whether that vehicle was located.

This system was beneficial to the body recovery teams. In one instance, a family member was insistent that their relative had died in the fire and was demanding that the entire structure be screened, a lengthy and laborious process, despite the anthropologists having already done a thorough search of the building. A quick call to the "missing persons" detectives showed that the relative had already been found alive and well.

Once developed, this format for data comparison has been tested in the subsequent North Complex Fire in 2020. It virtually eliminated that initial period of chaos. Almost immediately, as the size of the fire was being estimated, law enforcement was also calculating the number of people unaccounted for. This fire was smaller, and the flow of reports about missing individuals was significantly less. However, the data collection forms and procedures were the same and already in place.

By the time that the missing persons tasks from the Camp Fire were terminated as a separate effort in January 2019, the total of those unaccounted for had been reduced to three. These three were not suspected of having died in the fire, but no sighting had been made of them. The detectives continued to pursue these leads as part of their normal duties. One was found walking down the road months later by one of the detectives while returning from a domestic violence call. Apparently, she had been "laying low" as she thought she had an arrest warrant. Initially, she provided a false name but then admitted to being the person. A second person from the list was arrested on a warrant in another part of the state, having had a long history with law enforcement. The final one had not actually been seen for two years prior to the Camp Fire, and this case remains under investigation.

6.4 LESSONS LEARNED

Every event shows us something new—we need to be aware of new things. The events of the Camp Fire utilized lessons learned from the evacuations during a prior dam failure. The lessons from the Camp Fire produced changes that were put into action for the 2020 fire season. The following are some of the most significant points.

One of the most immediate lessons was the need for a robust and effective evacuation plan. Many jurisdictions have a plan, but it is largely a cookie-cutter one. These plans often fail in the face of a real evacuation when there are many other factors—massive traffic moving away from the fire front, blocked roads, poor visibility, and so on. These plans need to be re-examined and then tested by "throwing curveballs" at them to see where the weaknesses lie. Without that, there is the assumption that everything is well in hand. However, when the existing plans are tested, it is important to be open-minded and solicit honest feedback about the deficits. This is a time when placing ego ahead of planning can be costly.

Prior knowledge of those individuals who may need additional assistance in the event of a disaster is extremely helpful. Butte County's Special Needs Awareness Program (SNAP) list significantly aided in the Bear Fire. Modifications had to be developed based on some specific communities where the percentages of those with special needs may be greater than expected.

In general, egos can be detrimental to coordination in a mass disaster response (see Chapter 4). Often units can have conflicting priorities as well as a contentious history. Sometimes these egos can be handled by the over-arching agency in charge of response. Sometimes the leading agency just needs to give a directive. However, it is also important to listen to all groups involved in the response rather than jumping to a quick conclusion as there may be merit in what may appear superficially as a trivial conflict.

Often those leading various components of the response may bring new ideas and suggestions to the table. For example, after the rains, the anthropology teams suggested switching from dry screening to wet screening for the recovery of remains. In such a case, the lead agency will need to know what resources are needed to implement the suggestion as that agency will be responsible for facilitating resources and response. There is no play book, so sometimes going with the best guess of what will work is the only option. If something is not working well, leadership needs to be willing to make changes. However, in all cases, taking at least a short amount of time to step back and look at the broader picture is critical.

Sufficient relevant training is the biggest weakness in disaster preparation. Training is often an issue for law enforcement in general. There is a fairly substantial list of things for which formal training is required, and adherence to that list is good. However, things like incident management are not on the required list, so responsibility for providing that training falls to the department. Many smaller agencies, such as rural and small-town sheriff and police departments, have constrained budgets and prioritize training to what are seen as the most common issues. Incident management tends to focus on strategy and paperwork and tends not to be an appealing topic for additional training to those who would step into management roles. Small agencies also have a more difficult time balancing training with the need for officers to be on patrol or fulfilling other duties.

The adoption of the Incident Command System (ICS) (see Chapter 4) has become more widespread, and large incidents such as wildfires tend to require a large number of personnel to organize and maintain. However, emergency management training is often not department-wide. In actual situations, people should be added to teams so they can gain experience. Departments must consciously look to have secondaries in place to assist and learn. This experience can provide another source of training when time, budgets, and turnover preclude formal courses.

Incident management teams learn in the face of repeated disasters. The 2017 dam spillway failure evacuations helped with the formation of a team in the 2018 Camp Fire. With the North Complex Fire in 2020, the team responded right away, and they were able to designate responsibilities on the first day. This allowed the response to the Bear Fire to be much smoother than for the Camp Fire.

The missing persons unit needs to be mobilized very early, allowing all the information to be organized and consolidated in one place. Dispatchers must have a system ready to record the calls, solicit relevant information, and prioritize these calls to the detectives. A separate reporting hotline for missing persons is an effective means of deflecting the impact on dispatch. Staff at this hotline need to know what information to collect, how to extract the needed information from callers who may have reservations about reporting, and how to track the data. Strict limitations are needed on the ability to edit the spreadsheet so that nothing is lost without full verification.

Clearing names of those reported missing who have actually survived requires a robust clearance system. Sufficient people with a strong investigative background will be needed to staff this unit so that there is not the continuous need to integrate new people with a variety of skill levels. Such people also know the importance of documenting the investigation at every step of the process so steps do not get repeated, and conclusions can be substantiated based on the records. When there are transient residences in the area, such as hostels, mobile home parks, or boarding facilities within the jurisdiction, it is helpful to have prior contact with the manager as the residents of these parks may be more difficult to trace once they evacuate.

While it sounds obvious, having a clear and consistent way in which to establish when people can be removed from the missing/unaccounted-for list is important.

A caller may wish to report someone as missing, but they may not have been in regular contact with them before the fire. Expect that vague calls may occur, such as "I am calling about someone that I went to high school with in 1970, and I think this person lived up there." A good question to ask is if the suspected missing person would normally contact the caller in an emergency. There may be people who have reasonable justifications for not being found, such as outstanding warrants, victims of abusive situations who have fled to the area, involvement in illegal activity such as marijuana cultivation, or being undocumented. Expect to get calls from people with restraining orders against the person being reported or from people who are owed money by the suspected missing person. For obvious reasons, such information should not be released to the caller.

Open lines of communication must be established early, preferably before an event, with those nongovernmental organizations (NGOs) that would likely be involved in the response. For example, the Red Cross may embed their teams in the response effort. Without this coordination, such agencies may be reluctant to share resources and help with the important task of locating those reported missing. Yet many people may turn to these organizations for assistance rather than the government-provided services, especially if they are wary of being tracked by government agencies. Hospitals and shelters should be within this network as well.

It is also important to think about the more peripheral impacts. Residents will be without their mail for an extended period of time so have the US Post Office ready to provide change of address forms. USPS must also know that many homes in the destroyed area will have to be accommodated by general delivery for a period of weeks.

Another lesson learned was to be careful what is asked of people. When a road needed to be cleared of fallen trees, several officers got chain saws and did the work. In hindsight, from a liability standpoint, this was problematic as they had no formal training. On the other hand, many people living in rural areas routinely use chain saws for property maintenance.

Peer support has proven critical in these incidents. People are working incredibly long hours day after day and may be unwilling to take a break. It is important to integrate counselors or chaplains to help people process emotions and stress. Building scheduled breaks into the staffing plans is important. This lesson was passed along by Solano County when they assisted in the Camp Fire Missing Persons Task Force. They required people to take regularly scheduled breaks throughout the day. Long-term responses like wildfires can and do lead to mental fatigue (see Chapter 22).

One consideration that should be incorporated into planning is that many members of the law enforcement and first responder community have themselves been evacuated and their homes may have been lost. Often these officers and staff will continue to work their assignments without complaint, but there are issues with fatigue and distraction that can affect performance. In the Camp Fire, the intensity of the work meant that it took about four days before these officers and staff could be sent to deal with their families, making sure that the sheltering was suitable and just trying to cope with the extent of their own loss. Once realized, the sheriff's office put in place a practice of calling each patrol officer to check on their well-being and arrange for them to take some time off the job for themselves and their families. Planning to relieve such personnel as soon as possible would be appropriate.

Additional outside support may also be advisable. In the Camp Fire, chaplains were brought on board early to intermingle with the teams. This can help, but many of the first responders may be heavily focused on what they can do. However, this type of work can have serious consequences (see Chapter 22), and Butte County still has two counselors available to help their personnel handle the stress from the Camp Fire.

In the end, much comes down to having the right people, at the right spots, at the right time. Having people who are willing to think outside the box and come up with solutions, then giving them trust and leeway makes the overall response work. Emergency response on this scale needs to be a team effort, and everyone has to be playing on the same side, or else failure is inevitable.

6.5 CONCLUSIONS

Dealing with the aftermath of a wildfire is taxing on law enforcement, who must deal with the evacuation of occupants of the area in front of the fire front, provide security to the area to allow for recovery, and identify the dead and missing. While we can hope that the development of a robust early warning network can prevent the type of catastrophic fire that occurred in Butte County, we also need to be prepared when that does not happen.

Training in emergency response and emergency management are important investments for agencies in fire-prone areas. In addition, sufficient supplies of emergency equipment and personal protective equipment suitable for use in fire zones are important. Finally, establishing networks of those types of agencies and personnel that will be needed before the need arises has proven instrumental in mounting a rapid and effective response.

Finally, the lengthy ordeal of responding to a wildfire from initial call to repopulation of the area takes a toll on those involved. Debriefs and other types of discussions serve to both help those who have worked through this situation and to disseminate information on best tactics and practices to others who may face this in the future.

CHAPTER 7

Organization of the Fire Response

Establishing Priorities and the Future of Wildfire Management

David Russell and Jason Martin

The response to a wildfire requires the coordination of many agencies, activating established avenues of communication and response, tracking and compensating for the utilization of resources, and allowing for the flexibility necessary to adapt emergency management practices to the local circumstances and communities. Unfortunately, California has had extensive experience with large-scale wildfires, providing ample opportunity to learn what makes a response successful and where the needed flow of information and resources can be impeded. In any wildfire response, operations need to be streamlined and highly coordinated in an effort to avoid complications so that the focus remains on the preservation of life and containment of the fire. Leading this effort is the California Department of Forestry and Fire Protection, commonly known as CAL FIRE.

7.1 EMERGENCY MANAGEMENT AND WILDFIRES

Wildfires, because of the scale, intensity, speed, and danger to life and property, require coordinated response. The response begins at the time of dispatch when crews assess the scale of the fire on the ground, utilizing the Incident Command System (ICS). This is a well-established management concept where the ICS sets out the division of labor within the management system.

7.1.1 Incident Command System in Wildfires

The concept of an Incident Command System (ICS) derives from California firefighting efforts, beginning in the 1950s when there were many large fires in southern parts of the state. In response, fire chiefs converged to design a system that was modeled on a military structure. It was formalized in the 1970s and is now the primary means of

DOI: 10.4324/9781003168010-9

designing and coordinating emergency response efforts. Since then, a national response framework and then the National Incident Management System (NIMS) and Standard Emergency Management System (SEMS) were established.

An ICS is a way to organize and provide a span of control over division of labor, define responsibilities, and disseminate information and directives. While ICS is responsible for meeting objectives that are typically determined very early on in the incident planning, the system itself requires flexibility and must be adaptable to unique situations. Establishing clear pathways to establish command, provide accountability, and eliminate conflicts at a time when a speedy response is critical. Additionally, ICS also determines how each unit fits into the fire response and defines unit tasks and responsibilities. While ICS establishes unit responsibilities, it is also designed to allow for input from each unit involved so that major perspectives or lines of thought will not be missed. The ICS provides a common terminology for use by all units so that there is no murkiness in understanding due to ambiguity in terms. Many of the management strategies employed by the ICS are derived from business models.

The major players in the ICS structure operate at different levels with the incident commander (IC) at the top of that hierarchy. Below the IC are the safety officer, public information officer, and liaison officer. Below that is the general staff, which has its own divisions of planning, operations, logistics, and finance. In California, the ICS has proved to be a scalable model so that it can be quickly adapted depending on the size of the incident. For example, with small wildfires that can be handled with the resources in the immediate area, such as a 2019 fire in Tehama County, where 1,200 people were dispatched to deal with the fire, a basic command and general staff organization was used. However, with the 2018 Camp Fire with 5,500 people involved, the command and general staff organization was augmented by the use of deputies, as well as officers and section chiefs, to manage the amount of work generated.

The ICS information flow generally begins with a strategy meeting to determine the objectives of the mission. Management objectives tend to be policy driven and are established by the agency administrator. Overall, management objectives provide for firefighter and civilian safety by utilizing the risk management process. The agency with jurisdictional authority develops the management objectives (with the Camp Fire, this was CAL FIRE). While the objectives are generated fairly quickly so that action can begin as soon as possible, it may take several meetings to finalize the operational response plan. Once the management objectives are set, a meeting of general staff will work on the tactics that are needed to meet the objectives. In addition to the general administratively derived message, there may also be incident-specific messages. For example, when Team 4 was involved in the 2020 North Complex Fire in Butte County, a strategy was implemented to not focus on the Camp Fire in any of their public comments. This strategy acknowledged the public's emotional recovery from the Camp Fire was not yet complete and the possibility of a repeat occurrence in the same area was very sensitive.

While the federal government utilizes a two-tier IC system, California ICS has three tiers. The tier-level indicates the complexity and size of the incident. Type 3 requires only basic organization and is useful for smaller incidents, and type 1 requires the most members and is utilized for large and complex incidents. Complexity can refer to the size of the geographic area, the difficulty of the terrain, the number of fires (often there are multiple fires in the same area that may coalesce), and/or the number of people involved in the mission. The Northern California Camp Fire was a type 1 incident due to the geographic scale and complexity of the event. In California, larger departments, such as the Los Angeles Fire Department, may internally have a dedicated type 3 team. This model allows them to handle more complex incidents within circumscribed geographic areas, such as larger fires or earthquake damage. In fact, multiple IC type 3 teams may work within a larger agency. These teams acquire a lot of experience and knowledge over time and often can work larger incidents. While some departments have designated type 3 teams, this is not the case with higher tier levels. There are several reasons for this. For example, it is difficult to get type 1 certification and training and many type 3 teams simply cannot take the time and effort to acquire the necessary certifications to qualify for type 1 level.

7.1.2 Incident Management Teams

An incident management teams (IMTs) is composed of federal, state, and local agency team members who are assigned to manage large-scale emergencies throughout the state. Within each IMT there are 54 discrete roles which are assigned during the initial response. The assigned roles, however, are fluid and may be adapted as the situation evolves. Another example of this fluidity occurs when the incident is particularly complex, and additional personnel are added to some of the preassigned categories. For example, more people may be added to address planning issues, such as integrating the various streams of data. Safety may also need more support as the incident may produce a range of hazardous conditions. In this sense, the IMT adds depth to any local agency by including people from other jurisdictions who already know what role they play.

One of the first responsibilities of the IMT is establishing a facility out of which operations can be run. General staff also obtain information to plan meeting schedules, establish how to mitigate the fire, and determine what resources are needed in terms of personnel and equipment. Other essential responsibilities are getting the command trailers in place and connected to power, establishing lines of communication, and getting food and housing for the teams. The IMT is also responsible for the reconciliation and tracking of the various people and resources coming into the zone for aid.

CAL FIRE has six IMTs designated to fight major incidents. As an example of member composition, CAL FIRE Team 4 has members drawn from throughout the state—from Siskiyou to San Diego Counties. Typically, each team will have a commander from the north and deputy from the south or vice versa. That means that at least a portion of the team can get to the incident quickly. For example, Team 4 was deployed to a large fire in Orange County, and by the time the Northern California IC arrived, part of the team including the deputy was already on the ground.

Each team is on-call for seven days, at which point the duties will rotate to the next team. Once a team is deployed, they will stay in place for the duration of the incident, typically between a week to a month. All six CAL FIRE teams work on a six-week rotation for the calendar year, with each team having a "cover week" during which time they will be deployed if there is an incident. The decision to request a team is based on the complexity of the fire and a request from the unit chief to the region chief for approval.

7.1.3 Unified Command

In large or more complex incidents, unified command coordinates the efforts of multiple agencies. Typically, each agency has its jurisdictional authority, but the efforts must be coordinated. For example, CAL FIRE is not responsible for evacuations in the face of a wildfire. This responsibility lies with the local sheriff's office or police department. However, in the face of a fast-moving fire, both agencies will be involved and cannot work independent of each other. So, if, as in the Camp Fire, CAL FIRE needs to assess what needs to be done to mitigate the fire, what the fuel loads are ahead of the fire, and what the dangers are in the burned areas, they coordinate with the sheriff's office who is responsible for evacuations and road closures. With the Camp Fire, public works were also needed to ensure water systems were functional in order to supply the fire crews with firefighting water. In the unified command planning meetings (when the objectives are being formed), all agencies have to have a voice about what they are expected to do, what resources they need to do that, and from where those resources come. Coordinated efforts across multiple agencies is key. For the Camp Fire evacuations, it was not only a problem of getting people out of the area safely but also knowing where they should go and how they could be supported with shelter, food, and clothing, while the fire services were fighting and containing the fire and law enforcement were securing the area. The objectives of the mission under unified command involve intertwining the objectives of multiple agencies. Once mission unified command objectives have been established, they are not static but continue to evolve through time as the fire moves, the incident escalates, or priorities change.

In the 2020 North Complex Fire, unified command was implemented and zoning was established within the massive area involved and the mission divided between two IMTs. Based on the intensity of the fire and the local conditions (population density, terrain, etc.), there were slight differences in the objectives. Where the zones merged, coordination was needed to align the tactics and allow people to cross over the zone lines, if needed. As many agencies have experience working collaboratively, establishing a unified command is typically a smooth process.

7.2 COOPERATIVE EFFORT IN WILDFIRE MANAGEMENT AND CONTAINMENT

The cooperative effort in fighting, controlling, and containing a fire depends on the level of resources available to deploy. In the case of a wildfire, the local agency will be quickly overwhelmed, and so other factors come into play in gauging how much and where resources will be dispatched. These factors include the amount and type of mutual aid, determining the weight of the response and the role of each cooperating agency.

7.2.1 Mutual Aid

Mutual aid is based on the unwritten agreement between agencies for the exchange of resources. This agreement usually involves neighboring jurisdictions so that when one agency runs out of resources it can ask for personnel or equipment from the neighbor, if needed. There is no expectation of payment for this work. Rather, it is done with the expectation that this contribution will be reciprocated in the future. There is a time limit to this agreement since the loss of personnel and equipment can place the contributing agency in jeopardy. Usually, the agreement is that after 12 hours, there needs to either be some form of payment or the personnel/equipment must be returned.

There are two major CA agreements, and often both agreements are utilized at once. The first agreement is the California Cooperative Wildland Fire Management and Stafford Act Response Agreement (CFMA), which is between CAL FIRE and a number of federal agencies (US Forest Service, Bureau of Land Management, Bureau of Indian Affairs, and US Fish and Wildlife). The CFMA's primary mission is to manage wildland, and it allows resources to be shared and coordinated across a designated region. The CFMA also allows for wildland resources to be mobilized quickly across a region. The second agreement is the California Fire Assistance Agreement (CFAA) and is between wildland fire agencies and local fire departments. These pre-standing agreements outline how long resources can be shared between the agencies. The agreements also guarantee that agencies will be compensated for resources or personnel. Because local districts also need to sustain their ongoing commitments to the community the agreements also guarantee that any units sent to a major event will be backfilled. This has particular relevance in rural areas of California where the local agency may largely be composed of volunteer firefighters with the support of CAL FIRE and local professional firefighting units. When an incident occurs, the closest available units are deployed.

7.2.2 Weight of Response

The weight of response refers to the availability of resources for a single incident and the need to balance the necessary resources while simultaneously balancing the potential resource needs if a second incident arises. In the best-case scenario, firefighters will have everything they want to help fight and contain the incident. This is rarely the case for several reasons, including presence of competing incidents, distance from the incident, effectiveness of the resources, and geographic and environmental impediments, such as terrain or visibility. More often, there are competing emergency incidents happening simultaneously and resources are spread thin. Local fire agencies also need to be able to handle the small fires, traffic accidents, medical emergencies and other incidents that are the normal activity in their community.

In California, regional coordination centers in Redding and Riverside manage the weight of response, monitoring what is available, how many resources can be contributed, and how much needs to be held back. For the Camp Fire, almost everything that was needed was sent within a short timeframe. The Camp Fire, however, was somewhat unusual in that it was a large fire occurring late in the fire season (November). In contrast, in the 2020 fire season, there were simply too many fires occurring throughout the West Coast to allocate maximum resources to any one fire. Decisions had to be made about how to prioritize the incidents. Fires in areas with few properties and residential areas were lower priority, so resources could be diverted to areas where population density was higher or there were other considerations, including high-value properties such as medical centers.

As highlighted earlier, objectives are adapted to what you have on hand rather than what you would like to have in the response. Considerations for the weight of response include the number of personnel available, time of year, type of environment (e.g., grassland fires are easier to contain and require fewer personnel), and number of simultaneous incidents.

The weight of response can change the timing of some of the objectives. This does not mean that the objectives are abandoned, but there may not be enough available resources to meet the objective in the short term. The objective stands but it will be reached over a longer time span. It is also necessary to coordinate between incidents so resources can be moved from one to another as the objectives of the prioritized incident are met.

7.2.3 Role of Cooperators and Cooperating Agencies

Outside the scope of the official incident command structure are a number of other very important players. In the incident, the liaison's role is to communicate with cooperating and assisting agencies that do not fit within unified command. Agencies that fall outside of unified command include private companies, either those with a specific support role or one that supplies either personnel or equipment for the mission. While it is not legal to include private agencies in the unified command it is important to understand each agency's perspective, including what they can contribute to the incident and what resources they would need to achieve the stated objectives. In some cases, the role of these cooperating entities are preplanned for responses within a stated region.

During a major incident, there is a cooperators' meeting in which there would be a time to raise concerns, such as a lack of water, power, or functioning cell towers, etc. The Liaison Officer needs to take the information from the cooperators meeting back to the Incident or Unified Incident Commanders to recognize each cooperator's priorities and how to implement these priorities, if appropriate, within the incident objectives in the interest of public safety. For example, there could be meetings with the power company over safety and recovery efforts with downed power lines and burned equipment. Private firefighters may be another component of the cooperators. Do they have the jurisdictional responsibility to permit them to be included? This meeting will also provide a time for the outside groups to state what problems they are having and what issues they need the IMT to address.

During the Camp Fire, where the expectation for fatalities was understood relatively soon after the fire front began to hit inhabited areas, the anthropologists were part of the initial cooperators meeting. As the recovery efforts developed, they became more integral as part of the search and rescue teams.

7.2.4 Emergency Operation Centers (EOCs)

Emergency operation centers (EOCs) are designed to support the communities and the membership of the region. A liaison officer is assigned from the IMT to ensure the coordinated effort of the EOC and IMT are aligned. The EOC must be aware of the planning and implementation decisions of the IMT so support can be coordinated. The EOC staff are usually organized by city or county and have pre-established, assigned roles.

As incidents escalate, the EOC must take on the responsibility of handling the effects of the incident. One common consequence is the flow of refugees from the fire-stricken area. The EOC must implement plans for providing food and shelter for the people who have evacuated—and often their pets and livestock. In California, CAL

FIRE must communicate with the EOC about what to expect given the fire behavior and the need to evacuate an increasingly larger area.

With the Camp Fire, there was a Butte County EOC for the recovery effort. This was necessary because of the need for coordination with the unified command. The EOC was dealing with the public, the difficulty of evacuating families, those seeking to find missing people, and those wanting to get back to their homes once the immediate fire danger had passed. Because the EOC is often stationed by local staff, the command may have information that is not common knowledge for unified command—such as unique communities within the region or specific properties where high-value material may be present. Agencies that provide donations or solicit and collect donations need to be assessed. Questions considered include: is it a legitimate organization and how do we work them into the system?

7.2.4.1 Strategy and Planning

The strategy for fighting a wildfire is developed by the various agencies involved, based on all the information that has been gathered. This information includes the knowledge of the threat to lives and property, what resources are available, logistics concerns (e.g.,

TABLE 7.1 One Typical 24-Hour Cycle in a Wildfire Response

Time	Description
0530	Incident summary review
0600	Incident summary submittal
0600	Pre-operations briefing with line supervision to review objectives and instructions for next 24-hour period
0700	Operational briefing for all line personnel
1000	Cooperators' meeting (all stakeholders, such as timber companies, ranchers, utility companies, and local entities)
1400–1500	Operation section makes resource requests and line work assignments for the following operational period
1500	Input from field observers to update and "ground-truth" the operations maps
1600–1700	Tactics meeting confirming information from the resource request and that safety and logistics units can support the plan
1730	Resource request orders are placed through interagency resource ordering capability (IROC)
1800	Planning meeting to review of upcoming operational period plan, presentation of current status of the incident, expected weather, fire behavior, and safety concerns or mitigation and to show support of the plan from the command, general staff, and our cooperators
1900	Operations confirms the resources for the following operational period, matching the request to what is available and resolving any resource conflicts
2100	Incident action plan (IAP) components are due from each component of the command and general staff to build the IAP
2100–2400	IAP is built including line and work assignments, communications, safety, weather, fire behavior, special messages, and maps
2400	IAP sent to printer service

whether they can support the personnel and equipment; accessibility to the fire, including issues regarding terrain and the road network), information on the fire behavior, the presence or absence of fuel loads in the likely path of travel, and financial concerns.

Development of strategy and tactics depends on the strength of the line supervision in the field. All information on the fire behavior needs to be verified from the field—known as ground-truthing. Line supervisors need to evaluate the fire with the knowledge of the standard production rates (i.e., how much of a fire break can be cut by hand crews per hour), the terrain with which they have to contend, what resources they have at hand and what would they like to have, and how successful they can be given the available resources. There are also safety and effectiveness concerns. For example, hand crews can cut a break if the flames are relatively low (less than about four feet), but beyond that, a bulldozer would need to be used. However, bulldozers are limited by the steepness of the terrain.

It is in this planning and strategy phase that the dissemination of information is essential. At this point, the focus is much less about the immediate fire situation and more on what is the big picture—how fast will the fire grow and in what directions, where will be the greatest impact in terms of loss of life or property, and how can we deploy resources to mitigate the effects of the fire in a timely manner. It also has to be determined what would be a reasonable timeline to accomplish the mission objectives.

An evaluation of the tactical decisions may be held multiple times a day in a complex fire. These discussions will look at where containment lines should be placed, what types of specialized equipment should be used and the feasibility of placing the equipment, and what types of values (lives and property) are at risk. This information must be integrated into the predictive models developed by the incident meteorologist, who will assess upcoming weather patterns, and the fire behavior analyst.

The operations section utilizes the tactics meeting to state what they need to be successful. For example, would additional bulldozers help in construction of fire breaks, how could they be obtained, how do they get to the fire break area, and what are safety issues with the cutting of the break? Would air support be useful at that time, and if possible, can the pilots safely fly given the smoke conditions and can they see their targets? Where will water be obtained to recharge units transporting water to the fire? The planning section of general staff must then try to obtain those resources against the need for them at other competing incidents. The finance unit also needs to track the work so that when there is cost sharing, the appropriate agencies and personnel can be compensated. If there is cost-share, how do we track the work so that people and agencies can be compensated?

Aircraft is one option for augmenting fire mitigation, but fire suppression cannot be accomplished with air tankers and helicopters alone. Primarily air support fulfills two functions: (1) it may make an area safer for ground crews to enter or (2) it may slow the spread of a fire front so that ground crews have the needed time to establish a fire break.

7.2.5 Evacuations

In the initial phases of the development of strategies and plans, much of the focus in a wildfire is on the evacuation process. This includes planning how evacuation routes will be secured so that people can leave. While the responsibility for evacuation lies with law enforcement, they cannot do that if roads are blocked due to fire or wrecked or burned vehicles. For example, with the Camp Fire, there were only two major roads leaving town and most of the exiting traffic left by one route that heads directly west ahead of the flames. Due to the pace of the fire and the level of smoke, crashes and engine failure were inevitable and roadways became blocked, trapping some and also preventing emergency personnel from gaining access.

Coordination is of the upmost importance in a unified command organization. By adding a sheriff office or police department to unified command, the agency with the jurisdiction and authority to remove people from their residences is integral to the planning and implementation. EOC also needs to be included as they are responsible for the accommodation of the refugees. EOC is also the unit responsible for the dissemination of the evacuation information by such programs as NIXEL, Code Red, reverse-911, and so on.

It is also important that there be a safe zone around the fire so that fire and other emergency responders do not need to deal with other traffic issues. This may mean that evacuations will be implemented well past potential fire danger. This process does add a security risk that will need to be mitigated by law enforcement to prevent residents from returning early or looters taking advantage of the evacuation.

7.2.6 Containment

In most situations, a fast and sizable response early after ignition of a fire in a wildland area means that the possibility of a larger incident is prevented. It is for this reason that there is quick mobilization of available resources when fires are first spotted and air support may be dispatched, especially if the fire is near populated areas. However, in many weather conditions where there are high temperatures, strong winds, and low humidity, the fire has already grown to many acres before it is reported. The situation is compounded by the rural and isolated nature of much of the area in which wildfires begin. Fire crews will be delayed simply in getting close to the fire. Once established, suppression of a wildfire is often not possible, and fire crews and the organizational structure must quickly shift to issues of containment and control.

Containment of the fire becomes a major early focus in the planning process, usually simultaneous with assisting evacuations. Operations section chiefs are asked to prioritize for the first 24 hours. They need to assess what could be accomplished if every means of firefighting were available. Then adjustments must be made based on effectiveness, given the actual conditions, accessibility of resources and competing needs. Air support may not be appropriate at certain times when smoke obscures the targets or when the density of smoke makes flying dangerous as planes and helicopters must fly close to the ground to drop their loads. At this height, the turbulence of the air currents makes the degree of lift less predictable and hence more dangerous. Despite the public's expectation that air support will be involved immediately, this is often not possible.

At times, during a fast-moving fire the fire front is too large, moving too quickly or the fuel load is too massive to be suppressed. During this time, the strategy must shift from immediate containment to preservation of life and property. Local agencies often have good knowledge of either established fire breaks that can be expanded or open areas that can be utilized. Fire breaks will take time to prepare and strengthen, even with pre-existing breaks. The intensity of a wildfire and the propensity for them to spot (blow embers ahead of the fire front that will ignite new fires) means that breaks that had previously been sufficient are now proving inadequate. Wildfires can and do jump large roadways such as freeways, as well as rivers and other natural breaks. This means that sufficient time will be required to strengthen the break and decide how to deploy fire crews to address spotting issues.

On top of these decisions, the operations section must also be ready for conditions to shift so that the efforts will be effective. For example, if winds shift suddenly, a fire with a relatively narrow front can turn to the side and the whole pathway of the fire will become a new and much larger front. Life, safety, and property are always the basic guiding principles.

In the Camp Fire, it quickly became apparent that the fire could not be stopped close to its ignition source by the community of Pulga. Therefore, the objective for the first 36 hours was life protection for residents and responders. As that mission was being implemented, the operations section was looking at the next 72 hours to determine where, given the terrain and various fuel loads, containment efforts could be successful and where an anchor point could be established. A containment line often needs to be far ahead of the fire. Then tactics must be decided—will this line be formed with cutting and clearing or will backfires be appropriate. Based on the decision, resources to implement this process must be secured, located, and dispatched. For the Camp Fire, many of the lines were well to the west of the fire and bordering the open grasslands and freeway system that cut in a north-south direction.

While this containment line represents the outer limits of the fire, if fire behavior, weather conditions, or resource availability changes so that the spread slows, it may be possible to move closer and begin suppression activities. This is done with the understanding that there is a backup plan—a far better situation than trying to fight the fire, losing and not having an outer containment line. If there are few properties of value, it may be that the fire is simply allowed to burn to the containment line so that firefighting resources can focus on parts of the fire front where lives or valuable property is threatened.

During operations, the suspicion of multiple fatalities does not directly affect the firefighting components of the response. However, it does place an extra burden on the planning stages and also on the need for public communications. As the lead agency is typically at the county or federal level, CAL FIRE will participate in the regular press conferences to provide updates on the progress to containment. This participation allows for clear presentation of the activities being conducted and ensures that misinformation is minimized.

7.3 RECOVERY AND COMPLETION

Recovery efforts also require planning and preparation. Normal recovery includes extinguishing hot spots, often found in tree roots or structural foundations where embers can be sustained long after the surface flames have ceased. Hazards, such as trees that may fall or are still burning internally, must also be handled. While the number of resources deployed during this phase is substantially less, it is still an essential part of the response to prevent rekindling of the fire. Deeper in the fire zone, hot spots are usually allowed to self-extinguish as they pose little risk of reigniting a fire without surrounding fuel available.

Mop-up activities will be focused primarily on the perimeter areas, depending on the size of the fire and the areas at risk. For example, the decision may be that all hot spots within two or three hundred feet from the edge of the containment area will be inspected for 100% clearance. Beyond that point, decisions would be made based on the threat to specific properties or need for additional personnel (power repair crews, recovery teams, etc.). Typically, in a large wildfire, focus is on the perimeter while a fire within a residential area such as parkland or a greenbelt would require complete coverage of the area.

Another aspect of the completion process on a fire is the fire suppression repair. This involves mitigations to control erosion damage that may have an impact on infrastructure or other natural features. It also includes the repair of gates and fencing that may have been damaged due to the need for fire crews to access the fire front. Damage from bulldozers may also need to be addressed. For this reason, the final 100% containment of the fire may be delayed as crews finish these points.

When there are a large number of fatalities associated with the fire, the recovery process may include additional responsibilities for the fire crews. The Camp Fire was a new experience for most of the fire administration in that there was a continued presence of fire crews in the body recovery phase. In subsequent fires, this aspect has been integrated into the planning process. Fire crews were essential for the recovery process in order to clear structures (removal of the roof or pulling back of fallen walls) and in providing supplies such as water to the recovery crews for wet screening. In addition, coordination of some repair activities, particularly with power and communication company crews, may be delayed in order to secure areas for body recovery.

7.3.1 Damage Inspections

Damage inspection is a twofold process in which fire services play an important role. When people have been evacuated, they soon want to know when they can go back and what is left. However, the area is often extremely dangerous with downed power lines, trees still burning and weakened by the fire, exploding propane tanks, exposed septic systems, etc. Therefore, it is often inappropriate to allow civilians to return immediately despite intense public and political pressure to do so. The fire service can begin to provide some information flow with their damage inspection programs.

Initially, damage inspection is coordinated with EOC and a "windshield survey" is conducted. This process involves people driving through the area and assessing for either specific (structure by structure) or estimated damage. For example, the Camp Fire was known to cover a very large area, and initial reports said that 95% of Paradise was gone. Then the estimated population affected can be combined with the windshield survey and the known census data. These data are then used for multiple purposes. It informs the law enforcement agencies of the scale of the search and rescue/recovery efforts that will be needed. This information also helps trigger the FEMA disaster relief funds from the federal government. FEMA can then start processing checks for immediate needs to people who have been evacuated, well before the specific information on the financial impact of property destruction is known on an individual basis.

After the initial windshield survey, there is a more specific assessment of each home and outbuilding. Those buildings that have suffered more than 50% damage are often considered irretrievable. If the county cannot do the inspections, then CAL FIRE provides the information.

In addition to the damage to private structures, there are also public buildings and infrastructure that needs to be cleared, repaired, or replaced. Guard rails with wooden supports often have been destroyed and need to be replaced. Rural bridges may have been damaged or destroyed. Many of these areas need to be made safe prior to the return of residents—either repaired or cordoned off.

Messaging about damage inspections can be problematic. In the 2017–18 Thomas Fire in Southern California, the national news said the community was wiped out while reports from CAL FIRE initially said that only 200 structures were involved. That contradiction was apparent as people were watching news shots showing the fire sweeping through the communities. The eventual tally was over 1,000 structures lost.

Larger agencies have their own teams do their own damage inspections without assistance from CAL FIRE. Many smaller counties do not have specific damage inspection teams. CAL FIRE will supply the information for smaller agencies, and there are now technologies to allow sharing of information not only between agencies but also with the public. This dissemination of information has helped ease anxiety for the evacuated families. Counties may also tell CAL FIRE about properties with which they are not familiar as rural areas often have very isolated properties or those that are "off the grid."

The recovery process requires a lot of meetings to coordinate efforts, but the efforts of fire services are gradually lessened as recovery is initiated. CAL FIRE does not have jurisdictional authority over most of these processes and this responsibility falls to the California Governor's Office of Emergency Services (Cal OES). CAL FIRE does, however, provide the initial information on damage and also may allow flights over the fire zone to assess damage. Because of the need for air support (manned or unmanned) during the fire, such flights are monitored by the fire service.

7.3.1.1 Use of Technology

Technology for fire management is ever evolving. Much of the development has been in the area of modeling. Models are used to predict fire spread based on local topography with no fire suppression activity. Fire behavior analysis is utilized to better predict how a fire will progress, when it will accelerate or slow, how it will move across an uneven terrain, and how it will change given changes in fuel load quality, quality, and dryness. Seven-day weather forecast is run, along with daily weather, and work with the dedicated incident meteorologist will focus on how changing winds or humidity can affect the fire. Also needing to be integrated is the change brought about by the fire itself in both drying nearby matter but also producing a thick layer of smoke that will cause temperatures under the layer to drop sharply. This analysis allows the fire service to know where to best position containment efforts.

Planning is conducted on both a daily and weekly basis. The daily plans look at what can be done immediately to mitigate the fire situation and what needs to be done for evacuations, expansion of the evacuation areas, and suppression/containment. The seven days is needed in wildfires to see where the ultimate lines of containment should be placed.

Unmanned aerial reconnaissance is becoming increasingly important. Drones will fly over the fire to see how it is burning through rate of spread, makeup of vegetation (brush, timber, grass, etc.), and whether it is fuel-driven (heat enough to burn no matter what) or not. Drone coverage is often supplemented by ground observation if there are questionable areas. For example, the fire may be more intense in areas than can be estimated from the air.

Drones are now utilized, and properly equipped unmanned aerial vehicles (UAV) allow the fire service to see through the fire and provide real time feedback to the line crews. This way the fire service can understand the rate of spread and know if the fire will impact a specific location, such as a community or road within a specific period of time. This knowledge allows them to move resources to protect the location or retreat if necessary. A large advantage of the UAV is that there are no time restrictions on flying time. In contrast, manned aircraft are hugely beneficial, but there are strict limitations on how long and how often pilots may fly. UAVs can also be flown high enough so that they are above the air support needed for fire suppression and help pinpoint additional hot zones.

A final technological advancement that is changing fire management strategies is the use of an early detection camera network that allows for recognition of fires earlier in their ignition stage. This network began to be deployed in 2017–18. These cameras give an accurate portrayal of the fire. For example, in the 2020 Zogg Fire in Shasta County, California, the camera system showed that, at the time it was initially reported, the fire was already at 100 acres so that there was no hope of suppression. Instead, fire crews immediately began to work toward containment. In fact, planning began before there were even crews on the ground. The cameras are also essential as a validation of a report. All information has to be validated, and this often requires dispatch of a fire crew. With the camera system, the validation can be accomplished earlier than getting crews to the scene or even to a place where they can see the fire. This ability helps weed out incorrect reports, prioritize fighting in small fires that are still suppressible, and begin the location of available resources for a larger incident.

7.3.1.2 Changing Fire Environments

No matter what the theoretical background on the impact of climate change, it is undoubtedly true that it is becoming harder to predict fire behavior. Current models no longer work and the management plans for the landscape were developed 30–40 years ago. Fire agencies clearly recognize that the fire environment is changing and doing so at a rapid pace. There has been an increase in the number and extent of the major fire incidents. Much of this is linked to the increasing incidence of drought and how that affects the production of fuel loads and the dryness of those loads. As a result, fires tend to burn hot and fast and also produce spotting whereby embers from the fire are blown ahead of the fire and ignite other fires. Agencies are now using models to predict the potential of a specific fire to spot based on fuel load, dryness, and wind. Such models affect how the fire can and should be fought. This is especially true when we know fires may be approaching areas where the fuel load is extremely high.

Fires are now burning more intensely than in the past so that the models developed earlier are no longer working. For example, typically, timber areas were more protected due to moisture levels and the absence of ground fuels. However, now timber is burning very readily and at a rapid pace. As a result, we are not seeing fire checks working the same way as they had in the past, so much so that they are no longer as effective in the mitigation of the fire.

The other aspect is the management of fire-prone areas. In the more distant past, controlled burns by ranchers and indigenous populations were very effective in reducing the fuel load. These burns were typically relatively small in scale, cleared the understory and fallen matter and could be conducted under conditions that limited the speed of spread. However, starting in the mid-20th century the culture of Smokey Bear depicted any type of wildland fire as needing suppression. As a consequence, the fuel load in wildlands has increased dramatically. Much of this fuel load has a "dead and down" component to it.

It is clear that we need to return to a system for reducing the understory fuel load in forested areas and to also limit the amount of dead vegetation in bushland and chaparral. This can be done by either mechanically chipping the matter or by controlled burns. However, many agencies, as well as private landowners, are extremely nervous about controlled burns for liability issues. Mechanical processing is effective in smaller areas but is labor-intensive for the great swaths of land covered by forests, bush, and mixed vegetation. It is also banned in some fire-prone areas over concern that the fire will get into the chipped matter, making fires harder to extinguish.

Burn piles are another means of coping with excess downed vegetation. However, burn pile usage is heavily regulated by air quality standards as well as for the risk of wildfire ignition. Now smoke management is beginning to categorize and document the effects from large wildfires and balancing that against the risk of allowing greater use of burn piles to clear vegetation. In the long term, it may be safer to have smaller burns (piles or controlled areas) than to see the devastating air quality consequences of an unchecked wildfire.

The expansion of the wildland-urban interface (WUI) has also changed the complexity of the fire situation. More people moving into the WUI has been a more recent change and will likely intensify as more people retire and move to these areas and more people are able to work from home. Before, if there was a wildland fire, it did not impact many people and in many cases could be allowed to self-extinguish in many areas. Now, fires are more likely to impact people, so evacuation becomes a priority and some means of firefighting is no longer feasible due to the risk to those who are trying to escape the flames.

Public education is going to take several years to make changes in fire management and public behavior. The first step is to change the public perspective on burning and their responsibilities of stewarding the land. It is likely that this will also require public support of fuel load reduction efforts in the form of reasonable policies to permit reduction, assistance in conducting it, and also enforcement for those who allow a dangerous accumulation to accrue. Many see residing in a WUI area as "getting away" from the responsibilities of city life, but rural living also comes with another set of responsibilities including maintaining a fire safe environment.

7.3.1.3 Future of Wildland Fire Prevention and Management

Much effort is now being placed on the further development of predictive modeling to reflect the changing fire environment. As there is greater tree mortality and greater accumulation of dead trees and branches, beneath the crowns and on the ground, current models need to be adjusted. However, currently the models must utilize educated guesses as to the extent of tree mortality and the dead fuel load. Satellite imagery may be one way to estimate the fuel potential within the forests to better predict how fire behavior will occur in various locations and when red-flag conditions need to be invoked based on potential for fire. At the moment, these satellite-produced data are used but are not integrated into the models. Therefore, there is not a lot of consistency. Fire services do see the need, and the typical pattern is to test the incorporation of these data in the field before combining it with the normal practice.

While various technologies can help once a fire occurs, the main future focus will probably be on fuel reduction. In the last couple of years, there has been a much higher emphasis on developing shaded fuel breaks or conducting controlled burns. However, implementation of these measures can be slowed drastically in the face of regulatory restrictions. For example, getting the necessary environmental and cultural resource (archaeological) clearance to conduct a controlled burn can take six months. Speeding this process would help in forest management.

There also has to be help for private landowners in reducing the fuel load on their lands. Often air quality restrictions aimed at limiting smoke pollution from burning undergrowth either in situ or in a burn pile prevents landowners from burning in the quantity needed to reduce fire risk. However, air quality studies following wildfires are drawing attention to the health risks of allowing fuel loads to accumulate to the point that fire in those areas cannot be controlled.

Finally, public education and policy changes can better target those areas where risk is higher. For example, roadside burns through easements for roads may reduce ignitions from vehicles.

CHAPTER 8

Fire Investigation Overview

Tom Oldag and Tim Enright

Fire investigation is a specialized area of forensic practice that incorporates understandings of fire behavior (Table 8.1), fire ignition source identification, and fire suppression effects to determine how, when, and where a fire originated, why it moved in the manner it did, and ultimately, who (if anyone) is allegedly responsible. A full discussion of fire investigation is beyond the scope of this chapter and other references are available (Icove and Haynes 2017, International Association of Arson Investigators 2018, Lentini 2018, Konefal and Nordskog 2019). In this chapter, an overview of fire investigation is presented, how that applies to wildfire investigation and the importance of anticipating this aspect in wildfire preparation.

A fire investigation, also known as an origin and cause (O&C) investigation, is a complete unbiased story of the events that lead to the cause of the fire. Without a doubt, fires are destructive and investigating fires is a dirty and dangerous task. There are many hidden, as well as obvious, dangers while conducting the investigation. Some of the dangers include the ash, smoldering by-products, sharp unseen objects, hidden burrowing fire, structural collapse, and falling trees, to name a few. With the associated dangers, investigators should not be investigating fires alone.

Conducting a fire investigation requires a systematic approach that should be done consistently and methodically from one fire to the next, no matter how small or large the fire is. During the investigation, investigators will find facts as to the origin and cause of the fire. Some believe all fires must have a cause. The truth be told, all fires have a cause, though sometimes determining the cause is not possible. Pressure, however, may be put on the investigator to find the cause to satisfy the legal question of blame as well as public interest. Sometimes this pressure is unfair and unrealistic. The inability to determine a cause is usually, but may not always, be a lack of training, education, and or experience on the part of the investigator but very well may speak to the level of destruction and the possibility of other causes that cannot be excluded due to the destruction of items in the fire. Determining the single cause of ignition of a fire may prove particularly difficult when multiple ignition sources are available. Multiple ignition sources, which are unable to be ruled down to one ignition source, or the lack of a most probable ignition source will leave the cause of the fire undetermined.

Even if the exact ignition cause cannot be determined, the investigator should be able to isolate the origin area. The origin area may be a large area or may be more localized and specific to one feature. The ability to narrow the fire's origin down to a relatively small area requires a thorough understanding of fire science, fire dynamics,

DOI: 10.4324/9781003168010-10

TABLE 8.1 Common Terminology Used in Fire Investigations

Fire-Related Definitions	
Fire	A rapid oxidation process, which is a chemical reaction resulting in the evolution of light and heat in varying intensities
Entrainment	The process of air or gasses being drawn into a fire, plume, or jet
Fire Plume	The column of hot gasses, flames, and smoke rising above a fire
Flashover	A transition phase in the development of a compartment fire in which surfaces exposed to thermal radiation reach ignition temperature more or less simultaneously and fire spreads rapidly throughout the space, resulting in full room involvement or total involvement of the compartment or enclosed space

and fire pattern analysis and, depending on the fire scene involved, may include many other skills that the investigator may need assistance performing.

To do this, the investigator follows the fire effects and fire patterns backward, narrowing the origin area down to a manageable size. For example, if the fire scene is a block in size, the investigator narrows the origin area down to a room and contents, or if the fire is 1,000 acres, the investigator narrows it down to an acre or two initially. This will be done by interviews, cell phone photos or videos, fire patterns, initial dispatch notes, or any other evidence available.

The Agency Having Jurisdiction (AHJ) will determine when a fire investigation will begin. Some jurisdictions or states have policies or laws that require a fire investigation for every fire. However, other jurisdictions evaluate the scale of the damage, size of the fire, loss of life, evidence of arson, or solvability requirements before an investigation will be started.

Many of the jurisdictions that require a fire report for every fire may have an engine company officer who has little, or no, investigative knowledge or experience conduct the investigation. The need to have all fires investigated competently by individuals whose training and experience allow for a thorough, science-based assessment is important because that is the only way to discover various fire-cause trends. The trends can be due to a faulty appliance, tool, or part that is defective and needs to be recalled. Serial arsonists also create trends by creating patterns based on when, where, and how they light fires. If the fire scene was not previously investigated, the investigator cannot return to resume an investigation after the area was cleaned up.

8.1 THE FUNDAMENTALS OF THE INVESTIGATIVE PROCESS

Conducting a fire investigation, as with any other investigation, requires the investigator to be open-minded and honest, to be a finder of the facts, and to act with the highest level of integrity. There have been past investigations where fire investigators falsified and lied about the facts during the investigation that brought shame and discredited the profession. In some cases, innocent people were convicted of crimes and others had to pay large amounts in civil penalties along with attorney fees for the investigators' lies. When investigators come across something they do not know or understand, they need to research it or get another opinion from someone who does understand what they are seeing. The investigator also needs to know when the evidence does not support a definitive conclusion and be willing to state that the origin or the cause of the fire is undetermined and why.

The fire investigation process utilizes the scientific method when determining possible areas of origin and possible ignition sources. The scientific method used by fire investigators is conducted using the following steps as outlined in *NFPA 921*, 2017 version:

Recognize the Need. First, one should determine that a problem exists. In this case, a fire or explosion has occurred, and the cause should be determined and listed so that future, similar incidents can be prevented.

Define the Problem. Having determined that a problem exists, the investigator or analyst should define the manner in which the problem can be solved. In this case, a proper origin and cause investigation should be conducted. This is done by an examination of the scene and by a combination of other data collection methods, such as the review of previously conducted investigations of the incident, the interviewing of witnesses or other knowledgeable persons, and the results of scientific testing.

Collect Data. Facts about the fire incident are now collected by observation, experiment, or other direct data gathering means. The data collected is called empirical data because it is based on observation or experience and is capable of being verified or known to be true.

Analyze the Data. The scientific method requires that all data collected be analyzed. This is an essential step that must take place before the formation of the final hypothesis. Identification, gathering, and cataloging of data does not equate to data analysis. Analysis of the data is based on the knowledge, training, experience, and expertise of the individual doing the analysis. If the investigator lacks expertise to properly attribute meaning to a piece of data, then assistance should be sought. Understanding the meaning of the data will enable the investigator to form hypotheses based on the evidence, rather than on speculation.

Develop a Hypothesis (Inductive Reasoning). Based on the data analysis, the investigator produces a hypothesis, or hypotheses, to explain the phenomena, whether it be the nature of fire patterns, fire spread, identification of the origin, the ignition sequence, the fire cause, or the causes of damage or responsibility for the fire or explosion incident. This process is referred to as inductive reasoning. These hypotheses should be based solely on the empirical data that the investigator has collected through observation and then developed into explanations for the event, which are based upon the investigator's knowledge, training, experience, and expertise.

Test the Hypothesis (Deductive Reasoning). The investigator does not have a valid or reliable conclusion unless the hypothesis can stand the test of careful and serious challenge. Testing of the hypothesis is done by the principle of deductive reasoning, in which the investigator compares the hypothesis to all known facts as well as the body of scientific knowledge associated with the phenomena relevant to the specific incident. Testing of a hypothesis should be designed to disprove, or refute, the hypothesis. This may also be referred to as falsification of the hypothesis. Working to disprove a hypothesis is an attempt to find all the data or reasons why the hypothesis is not supported or not true, rather than simply finding and relying on data that support the hypothesis or why the hypothesis is true. This method of testing the hypothesis can prevent "confirmation bias," which can occur when the hypothesis or conclusion relies only on supporting data. A hypothesis can be tested physically by conducting experiments, analytically by applying accepted scientific principles, or by referring to scientific research. When relying on the research of others, the investigator or analyst must ensure that the conditions, circumstances, and variables of the research and those of the hypothesis are sufficiently similar. Whenever the investigator relies on research as a means of hypothesis testing, references to the research relied upon should be acknowledged and cited. If the hypothesis is refuted or not supported, it should be discarded and alternate hypotheses should be developed and tested. This may require the collection of new data or the reanalysis of existing data. The testing process needs to be continued until all feasible hypotheses have been tested and one is determined to be uniquely consistent with the facts and with the principles of science. If no hypothesis can withstand an examination by deductive reasoning, the issue should be considered undetermined. Any hypothesis that is incapable of being tested either physically or analytically, is an invalid hypothesis. A hypothesis developed based on the absence of data is an example of a hypothesis that is incapable of being tested. The inability to refute a hypothesis does not mean that the hypothesis is true.

Select Final Hypothesis. The final step in applying the scientific method is to select the final hypothesis. Once the hypothesis has been tested, the investigator should review the entire process to ensure that all credible data are accounted for and all feasible alternate hypotheses have been considered and eliminated. When using the scientific method, the failure to consider alternate hypotheses is a serious error. A critical question to be answered is, "Are there any other hypotheses that are consistent with the data?" The investigator should document the facts that support the final hypothesis to the exclusion of all other reasonable hypotheses.

Using the scientific method enhances acceptance in the scientific community because conclusions are based on a methodical approach. Ultimately, the fire investigator after forming a probable ignition scenario opinion as to the cause of the fire needs to explain their findings of the investigation in a report. They will then potentially need to explain their findings to a judge and jury.

Fire investigations can be simple and straightforward or very complex. Sometimes, new investigators can become overwhelmed with an investigation because of the complexity. A simple way to look at a fire investigation is to compare it to your favorite pizza recipe. Your favorite pizza recipe contains known ingredients. Without those ingredients, your favorite recipe would not be complete. When your pizza is done, it can be sliced up into pieces. For the pizza to be whole or complete, it must contain all the pieces and ingredients. A completed investigation consists of unknown ingredients, which are known as the facts. It is the job of the investigator to gather all the facts and put them together in a report, thus making the complete pizza. When all the facts are discovered and documented, the report is complete. Without all the facts (ingredients), the report (the pizza) would not be complete and would leave a bad taste in your mouth.

The job of a fire investigator begins well before the fire. It is the job of the fire investigator to train themselves first and then educate others. This education is directed toward other investigators, fire personnel, law enforcement, coroners, attorneys, and ultimately, judges or juries. The fire investigator must educate fire crews and get them to have scene awareness. Fire is destructive, but so are the fire suppression efforts. Water used during suppression efforts destroys, moves objects and causes structural collapse, reconfiguring the evidence of the fire's origin and cause. Unfortunately, fire victims are usually not found until the fire is extinguished, which causes more issues as to the recovery process of the victims. One example is that water added to calcified bones can shatter the fragile remains and wash the bones away from the location of death. Personnel who respond to fires need to be educated about the effects of fire on fuel packages, to include deceased persons (see Chapter 10).

Some people become investigators because they think it will be an easier assignment to conduct investigations than running calls on a fire engine. Being an investigator, however, requires dedication, curiosity, and an investigative mind. It is more than a full-time job, and there are a lot more responsibilities when it comes to your training and education. Learning fire behavior while being a firefighter whether in training or suppressing fires is one thing. Understanding fire behavior and being able to articulate what occurred after the event is quite another.

There are various trainings from basic to advanced fire investigation classes for the various types of fires the investigator will likely encounter. These courses include work on structure, vehicle, and wildland fires. Additionally, the investigator will need to attend classes on electrical fires, building construction, fire dynamics, building codes, photography, and so on. A fire investigator should never stop going to trainings or expanding their knowledge base.

When an individual decides to be a fire investigator, most begin by getting on the job training. Most fire investigators will come from a firefighter background and so have experience with aspects of fire behavior as it pertains to how to suppress it most effectively. Part of investigating a fire is understanding how a fire ignites, spreads, and gains intensity and what fire suppression activities were used while extinguishing the fire, whether it is a structure, wildland, or vehicle fire. By having a background in fighting or suppressing fires, the investigator should be able to understand how various factors affect a fire. Specialized training builds on these aspects.

Once the investigator has prepared themselves through training and education, the next step is to get experience investigating fires, preferably with a properly trained fire investigator. This field training allows the new investigator to gain perspective and confidence and learn additional information on how fire patterns should be interpreted.

In addition to preparation through education and training, there are also the daily preparations that are required. Toolkits in terms of sample retrieval and testing equipment should be operable at all times (see the next section for toolkit specifics). Battery-operated equipment needs to be charged. Renewable supplies need to be replenished, and expiration dates on any components should be monitored. Items that need to be checked for calibration should be monitored with a calibration schedule.

It is important to realize that while working a fire scene and collecting evidence, the investigator does not want to cross-contaminate evidence because of dirty tools. Tools used in collecting samples must be changed out with new or cleaned/decontaminated tools prior to collecting any samples. The best way to show the integrity of cleaned or new tools is to photograph steps you take with each collection.

Being prepared also involves knowing who to contact in the event you need to phone a friend (a trusted and respected fire investigator, a peer, or a mentor). Investigators must have the capacity to recognize when they are in over their head with the investigation and ask for assistance or get another opinion. Unfortunately, sometimes an investigator's ego or pride can get in the way of asking for assistance.

A fire can erupt around the face and head of a person who is smoking while on oxygen. In this situation, the oxygen hose is equivalent to a fast-burning flaming fuse as the oxygen-rich atmosphere near the hose expedites the burning of the plastic hose. If the victim's room is closed and there is no air flow, you may only have the bed partially consumed by fire with the remains of a victim in a hole because of the wicking process from the body. The fire started very aggressively because of the oxygen from the tank, but due to the lack of oxygen in the room, the fire quickly became a low-intensity smoldering fire. If there is no one else at home at the time of this fire, the fire may self-extinguish to the bed area.

The tip, or cherry, of a cigarette can burn around 1,200 degrees Fahrenheit. However, a glowing cigarette will not ignite gasoline fumes. A burning cigarette exposed to normal atmospheric levels of oxygen, if put in the vapors of gasoline, will not ignite the vapors (please do not try this at home). It takes an electrical arc, spark, or flame to ignite the gasoline fumes. Having a person state that they dropped a lit cigarette into a gasoline puddle would require you to test that hypothesis as a possible cause. Using your training, education, and experience as well as research into cigarettes' potential to ignite gasoline vapors, you could rule this ignition source as not probable in the context of the statement made earlier. The investigator would then need to continue to collect more data and develop new hypotheses to include other cigarette ignition possibilities until they come to a probable ignition scenario (if possible).

Investigations are sometimes steered by what is seen or perceived rather than the evidence or facts. For example, the investigator may see powerlines over the top of the origin of a fire, a quarter-acre fire containing a deceased person next to an idling, partially burned tractor, or a wintertime room and contents fire with a deceased person near a light. Each of these fires needs to be investigated completely without bias. Initial questions to consider might be as follows:

Were the powerlines energized at the time of the contact?
Did the limbs or powerlines show any sign of electrical arcing or damage?
Could an idling diesel tractor ignite the vegetation?
What was the cause of death for the victim?
Was the heater turned on in the house?
Was the light turned on at the time of the fire or even plugged in?
What other ignition sources were found in the origin area.?

It is essential to look for the evidence with an open mind. If one jumps to conclusions, it is likely that one tends to only collect evidence that can be used to support that conclusion. Understanding the role of the fire investigator as an expert witness is, therefore, an essential aspect of the preparation.

8.2 TOOLS AND EQUIPMENT

The tools and equipment used for fire investigations go from basic to more advanced that may require extra training. Shovels, rakes, cans, tape measures, sifters, magnifying glasses, various cans, bags both plastic and paper, cameras, tape recorders, and various hand tools and saws are all among the basic equipment needed. Protective equipment for the investigator is also essential, given the hazards that often occur in fire scenes. Inventory lists can be found in various investigation books. *NFPA 921* (2017 edition), Chapter 15, Sections 4.2 and 4.3, has a list of recommended protective safety equipment and a list of tools and equipment. What some agencies carry will ultimately depend on the agency's policy or the investigators' needs given their knowledge of the types of fires they face.

8.3 THE FIRE INVESTIGATION TEAM

Fires are often large, complex, and hazardous scenes. Various fire types, such as structure, wildland, and vehicle, all have their own subcategories (for example, structural fires include agricultural buildings, single-family homes, multi-family structures, industrial buildings, and high-rises). Each subcategory can add additional complicating factors to consider in terms of fuel loads and the pattern of spread. Even though the cause categories are the same, there is a lot to know, and no investigator can do it alone. That is the basis for the team approach in investigations.

A team effort should be employed while conducting the investigation. This is not only for the investigator's safety but also for the integrity of the case. Multiple investigators aid the investigations with various levels of experience and skills as will be discussed later. Other skilled personnel used in investigating fires are local law enforcement, various engineers (structural, electrical, mechanical, etc.), crime scene technicians, registered professional foresters (RPFs), chemists, and anthropologists. Skilled personnel in the use of photogrammetry and 3D modeling are also useful. Above all, the prosecuting authority should be involved in the investigation whenever it has been determined that a crime has been committed as they will be the ones who will need to pursue this in the courts.

There are no hard-set rules as to the number of investigators used for an investigation. The AHJ will oversee the investigation, and they are usually responsible for the report. A wise investigator will know whom to call from their network of fire investigators whom they trust and respect when there is a need for additional help. The AHJ will determine how much money will also be spent on the investigation. Sadly, for criminal investigations, the threshold for how much money will be spent on the investigation may come down to the solvability of the case. Due to budgets and lack of personnel, many agencies will only pursue a case that meets their solvability factors. Since civil suits target financial recovery of losses suffered, civil cases spend a lot more money on the investigation by hiring more subject matter experts. The United States Department of Justice Bureau of Alcohol Tobacco and Firearms (ATF) may assist agencies with criminal investigations based on their criteria like fire size (dollar or damage loss) and complexity. A single ATF investigator may assist, or a national response team of investigators may come and conduct the investigation.

8.4 STARTING THE INVESTIGATION

The investigation starts with the request for a fire investigator at the scene. This step can be automatic with the fire dispatch or may have other factors within a jurisdiction's policy, which further defines when a fire investigator is called. There may be observations by the fire suppression crew that raise suspicions or law enforcement may request an investigation.

Arriving at the scene gives the investigator an idea of what they are dealing with and the magnitude of the investigation. Often while responding to a scene, radio traffic or a phone call can give the investigator a general sense of what is involved, but this is through a filter of another person's perspective. At the scene of the fire, investigators can observe and evaluate the fire directly: if the fire is still burning, what are the actions of the firefighters? At first, the scope of work can quickly become overwhelming. It is essential to take the time to start with development of a plan of action rather than jumping into action immediately.

Investigators are responsible for knowing what policies and procedures their agency has in place for incidents. Most agencies will have some standard operating procedures to follow. However, in many cases these procedures are relatively unspecific as they must be adapted for a wide variety of situations. Therefore, the investigator must know how to follow the policy while also adapting to the immediate circumstances.

Initial scene photo documentation needs to occur as soon as possible after arrival. The initial photos document how the fire looked when the investigator first arrived and the context in which the fire is placed. Photos should show the overall location, the overall level of damage, and any other structures or features that may be important later.

The incident commander can usually provide a good synopsis of the event—how it appeared at first contact and what actions were taken. It is important to identify potential witnesses, and if it is not possible to talk to them at that time, then get contact information. It may be that there are surveillance cameras in the area that can provide information on the time of ignition and even the cause.

8.5 FIREFIGHTING EFFORTS THAT AFFECT THE INVESTIGATION

The basic strategy in putting the fire out comes down to putting the "wet stuff on the red stuff"—water on the fire. Firefighters accomplish this in two basic ways. One way is by conducting an interior attack, and the other is a defensive attack. In an interior attack, firefighters enter the building and find the base of the fire and suppress it. Unlike how movies portray the inside of a burning building, in real life there is no visibility because of the smoke. As firefighters move toward the fire, they drag hoses with them, and things get knocked around. Additionally, spraying water at 80–100 psi, a normal pressure for fire hoses, moves things around the scene, items fall off walls, sheet rock falls off the ceiling, and so on. In a defensive attack, also known as "surround and drown," means no one goes into the building and a large amount of water is applied from the outside of the building. This is usually done because entry into the building is unsafe. Most of the time, when a decision is made to do a defensive attack, the building has been deemed a loss and the goal is to protect surrounding properties.

Mainly after an interior attack, firefighters enter the building after the fire is knocked down, and they conduct a salvage and overhaul. Firefighters remove things from the inside of the building and oftentimes carry or throw things outside. If the fire investigator did not educate the fire crews, the contents of the structure, including the cause, may have been taken outside.

Another example to look at or note is how the firefighters accessed the fire—for example, whether the firefighters access the fire by breaking open a door or cutting a fence to get to a fire along a roadside. Later, the door will need to be checked to see if the door was locked or unlocked. The fence must be checked to see if it was cut where the fire along the road started.

8.6 SCENE EXAMINATION/EXCAVATION

This is a labor-intensive process. During this step investigators will methodically plan and physically investigate the fire, using a systematic approach. When determined safe to do so, investigators access the fire scene usually starting on the perimeter getting an overall look and keeping an eye out for possible evidence and begin fire pattern analysis to determine the fire's progression and work their way back to the origin area.

There is also considerable work that must be done outside of the actual scene. Investigators will be identifying and gathering evidence or potential evidence such as dispatch logs, run sheets, identifying 911 callers, and identifying safe work areas.

8.7 FIRE EFFECTS/BURN PATTERNS

The common understanding of evidence is that it is an artifact that can be collected and analyzed in a laboratory. While fire investigation does include collection of samples for presence of accelerants or electrical wiring for further examination in a laboratory setting, much of the evidence utilized in fire investigation is more ephemeral. Observation and documentation of fire behavior indicators at the scene is critical. Indicators are visible or measurable artifacts that are left behind by the fire (Table 8.2). The direction of a fire's spread is imprinted on partially burned fuels and noncombustible objects. These visual fire effects may include differential damage, char patterns, discoloration, carbon staining, shape, location, and condition of residual unburned fuel. Analysis of the directional pattern shown by multiple indicators in a specific area will identify the path of fire spread through this site.

The only way to become proficient at reading fire patterns is time, experience, and training. Evidentiary items found in the burn area will oftentimes change form by becoming smaller, distorted, and discolored, but it is not to say they are not there. An example of this may be fires associated with children playing. Oftentimes, when children are playing with fire and using a lighter, they may light small fires and put

TABLE 8.2 Terminology for Common Indicators of Fire Behavior Pattern

Common Indicators	Definition
Fire Effects	The observable or measurable changes in or on a material as a result of a fire.
Fire Patterns	The visible or measurable physical changes, or identifiable shapes, formed by a fire effect or group of fire effects.
V-Shaped Patterns	Wildfire V-shaped patterns are horizontal ground-surface burn patterns generated by the fire spread. When viewed from above, they are generally shaped like the letter V. These are not to be confused with the traditional plume generated vertical V patterns associated with structure fires. These V-shaped patterns are affected by wind direction and/or the slope on which the fuel is located. As the fire spreads in the direction of the wind or up a slope, the widening legs of the V are created. The width of the pattern increases as the fire advances from the area of ignition. The origin of the heat source that created the pattern often is found at or near the base or most narrow point of the pattern.
Staining and Sooting	Staining is caused by hot gases, resins, and oils condensing on the surface of objects. This occurs most commonly with non-combustible objects, such as metal cans, glass bottles, or rocks. Stains will appear on the side of the object exposed to the flames. These yellow to dark brown stains will often feel tacky to the touch and may be covered with a thin layer of white ash. Closely related to staining is sooting. Carbon soot is caused by incomplete combustion and the natural fatty oil content in some vegetation. Carbon soot is typically more heavily deposited on the side facing the approaching fire.
Degree of Damage	The degree of damage to a fuel is an indication of the fire's intensity, duration, and direction. Leaves, branches, and limbs will show greater damage on the side from which the fire approached.
Angle of Char	Angle of char indicators are divided into two groups based on the types of fuels they occur in. Angle of char can occur in pole-type fuels (tree trunks, utility poles, fence posts, etc.) or in the foliage crowns of brush- or timber-type fuels.
Exposed and Protected Fuels	A non-combustible object or the fuel itself shields the unexposed side of a fuel from heat damage. Fuels will be unburned or exhibit less damage on the side shielded from the advancing fire. Look for charring, staining, white ash, and clean burn lines on exposed sides of fuels and non-combustible objects. Compare and contrast to the opposing sides of objects. Lift or remove objects to detect the exposed and protected fuels. Objects resting on top of ground and surface fuels will protect the fuels on the unexposed side

them out. If a fire escapes their control, they may often panic and drop the lighter. The lighter may burn, melt, or rupture, but the metal roller, small spring, flint, and other small metal pieces will be left behind. Using fire effect and fire pattern indicators will get the investigator back to the origin area, but having knowledge as to the components of various ignition sources like a lighter will assist the investigator in locating and confirming the ignition source.

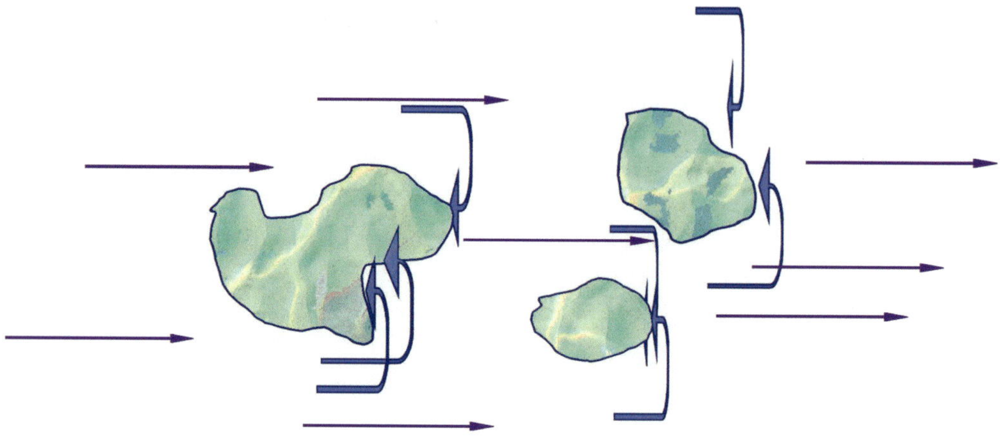

FIGURE 8.1 Eddies (blue arrows) from air currents (purple arrows) form on the backside of a solid object (mottled shapes) just like eddies form in a stream behind large rocks.

As the individual fire effects are accumulating, a fire pattern emerges. Correctly reading and interpreting these indicators is a learned skill. It is important that the investigator understands fire patterns and the various effects of fire progression. For example, as tall grass burns during a low-intensity fire, the grass burns from the bottom up. As the base of the grass stem is burned away, the grass usually falls backward into the fire. As that occurs, the top of the grass may be left intact and unburnt, depending on the moisture content in the grass stems. The top of the grass will point back toward the direction the fire came from. If the fire was burning intensely through the same grass area, the top of the grass stems will ignite first causing them to burn from the top down. As this occurs, most of the tops of the grass will be burned and laid down in the same direction as the fire traveled. This fire pattern interpretation is used to methodically work back toward the ignition area.

Another example of the physical nature of fire is that heat rises. An easy way to visualize how a fire burns is describing how water flows. It is obvious that heat rises upward and that water flows downhill. As air is heated, it becomes more buoyant than the surrounding unheated air. As the column of heated air is forced through an opening like a door or even a narrow canyon, its speed increases. Water does the same thing. As water is channeled downstream, its speed increases as it is forced through a narrow opening. On both occasions, as the air or water goes through the narrow opening into a larger area, there is a circling pattern (low-pressure area) on the downwind or downstream side; this circling is called an eddy. Burn indicators will show a distinct change in the direction the fire took after going through the narrowing area.

8.7.1 Documentation

Every part of the scene needs to be documented as your chances to come back to get something you missed is unlikely. Fire scenes degrade relatively quickly when exposed to the environment, and there may be reasons that clean-up efforts are accelerated for public safety. It may also simply be a lack of time that limits return visits. Once the initial scene is released, there will be a court order or consent from the owner or tenant to return for follow-up investigation.

Evidence will be found in and out of the origin area. All the evidence will need to be marked, labeled, photographed, and later collected. Prior to the collection of evidence, it should be examined by a subject matter expert in the position in which it was found—for example, have an electrical engineer look at electrical wiring or various components, a registered professional forester (RPF) look at damaged trees, an explosive expert and structural engineer look at a building that suffered from some sort of an explosion, and so on.

Additionally, it is vital to photograph the fire scene and get accurate measurements. When and how to accomplish these tasks should be discussed among the team so that work on one area or item does not produce collateral damage that impacts the ability to observe or collect other evidence. Personnel with specific skills in photography, videography, drone photography, diagramming, mapping, evidence recovery, and so on should be used. Scales should be included where possible. Such images are often crucial if this is deemed a criminal or civil matter and court presentation becomes necessary.

8.8 THE REPORT

Once the fire scene has been processed and documented with notes, photos, sketches, interviews, and all that data collected, the next step is to formalize the documentation of the investigation with the production of a report. The report should cover how the services of the investigation team was requested, who composed the team and what their various responsibilities were, what the overall appearance of the scene was, how the investigation proceeded, what evidence was located, what the interpretations of that evidence were, and how the interpretation was supported by the evidence.

There are various writing styles from simple to complex that may include the use of large, complicated words. Reports should be written for a more general audience, particularly if there is any suggestion of criminal charges or civil suits that may result from the findings. These reports will form the basis of a prosecution or a plaintiff's claim and must withstand the scrutiny of fire investigators hired by the defense or defendant's attorney. Keeping a report simple and factual is best; tell the story. A TV show from the 1960s called *Dragnet* sums up a fire investigation—"just the facts."

Part of the investigation process should be to have the investigation undergo an administrative, technical, and peer review. Having the review process begin during the initial investigation will only cause the investigation to be better and more competent. The idea is to have an investigation that is true and done with integrity while remaining void of any bias. The following are those three different reviews explained.

Administrative Review. An administrative review is one typically carried out within an organization to ensure that the investigator's work product meets the organization's quality assurance requirements. An administrative reviewer will determine whether all the steps outlined in an organization's procedure manual, or required by agency policy, have been followed and whether all the appropriate documentation is present in the file, and may check for typographical or grammatical errors.

Technical Review. A technical review can have multiple facets. If a technical reviewer has been asked to critique all aspects of the investigator's work product, then the technical reviewer should be qualified and familiar with all aspects of proper fire investigation and should, at a minimum, have access to all the documentation available to the investigator whose work is being reviewed.

Peer Review. Peer review is a formal procedure generally employed in prepublication review of scientific or technical documents and screening of grant applications by research sponsoring agencies. Peer review carries with it connotations of both independence and objectivity. Peer reviewers should not have any interest in the outcome of the review. The author does not select the reviewers, and reviews are often conducted anonymously. In forensic science, peer review also now refers to an outside technical review in which files are sent to a qualified expert outside the agency who will evaluate the methodologies used, the interpretation, and the clarity of the report.

8.8.1 Wildfire Investigations as It Relates to Origin and Cause

Wildfire investigation follows the same steps of initial observations, examination and excavation, documentation, and report production as any other fire investigation. Fire scenes can be a small spot or a large area encompassing thousands of acres. Like any other investigation, work in this area of origin should begin as soon as it is safe to do so and access to the area can be secured.

As an example, with the Camp Fire, the fire investigation was already underway by noon of the day of initiation, while evacuations were still underway in nearby communities (Butte County District Attorney 2020). The area was pinpointed based on initial reports of fire and observations of the first fire crews to approach the area. Investigatory teams were in place and were able to secure the location ahead of the arrival of utility crews who were also dispatched to the area.

Wildland fires can originate from several ignition sources. Common ignition sources for wildland fires are campfires, children playing with fire, debris burning, equipment, arson, lightning, miscellaneous (shooting, fireworks, spontaneous combustion, smoking, electrical, railroad, and vehicles). However, it is important to investigate with an open mind. For example, within known wildland causes are instances where a homicide was committed and the perpetrator sought to hide the victim by burning the crime scene and remains, which then spread to the surrounding area producing a wildfire. In a case like that, the cause would be arson. Depending on the local or state laws, when someone accidentally starts a fire, it may be considered a negligently caused fire but still carry a degree of arson because of the reckless behavior that led to the fire. Depending on the time of year, fireworks can contribute to the cause of fires. Other sources have included gender reveal parties, driving on rims due to a flat tire, dragging something metallic behind a vehicle, reflection from triple-pane windows, and extension cords that are used as permanent wiring lying on the ground for weeks or months and getting damaged or overheated. In addition, there are often fires in the footprint of other larger wildfires because of hot embers or tree roots smoldering then igniting a house on fire. There have also been times, though rare, where persons commit arson by intentionally burning down their structure or vehicle after a large damaging wildfire in order to collect the insurance money.

Whether investigating a wildfire or a structure fire, investigators use similar indicators. For example, with a wildland fire, rocks may be present which could present direction of travel indicators. We could compare one rock that was on the grass and another that was sitting on a desk in the house. As fire burned toward either rock, the heat and smoke would hit the side of the rock facing the fire first (Figure 8.1). On this side, soot would be deposited on the rock. In the wildfire situation, material like grass and other small matter on the ground would have protection from the initial flames, so portions of the rock covered by these materials would not have soot deposited on the surface. The back side of the wildfire rock would be somewhat protected from the flame and soot, and it would have less soot stuck to it. The rock on the desk would likewise protect the desk and items next to the rock if the room did not flash over. If you were to pick the rock up, there would be a sharper burned line on the side of the rock from which the fire came as compared to the side away from the fire. Of course, in a structure fire that reaches flashover and where destruction is more complete, the interpretation becomes more difficult. The investigator needs to walk around the scene evaluating and using the fire effect or fire pattern as a single point, potentially showing the direction of the fire.

For wildland fire that starts along a road, the investigator needs to look at how and where the firefighters accessed the fire. On flat ground without a breeze, a fire will burn equally in all directions. If the fire started next to the roadside, the fire would burn away from the road, which would act as a barrier. If a breeze or wind is blowing across and perpendicular to the road, the cause of the fire may be found in the middle of the black where fire crews accessed the fire. While doing this, they may drive over and obliterate the cause of the fire.

Lightning strikes are a frequent cause of fires and often ignite multiple fires. These individual fires may coalesce into a larger wildfire complex. For example, the August 2020 fires in Napa, Lake, and Sonoma Counties, classed as the LNU Lightning Complex, had about 60 different fires that merged into a massive fire scene. Weather data including information on lightning strikes are important in reconstructing the origin and cause in these cases.

Every year power lines cause fires throughout the United States. There are two types of power lines. Transmission lines carry large amounts of energy (voltage) over great distances, while distribution lines carry less voltage for commercial and residential users. The Camp Fire was caused by a failure in the transmission lines (Butte County District Attorney 2020). When investigating a wildland fire caused by an electrical issue, it is important to confirm the location of the electrical arc that caused fire, but it is also important to determine what caused the arc or spark. For the Camp Fire, the arc was produced when the line touched the tower to which it was attached. However, the line was able to touch the tower because a connector that suspended the line above the ground failed, releasing the line.

Electrical lines are also called conductors. There are various reasons that conductors arc and spark: bird strikes, such as geese, turkeys, hawks, owls, and eagles, hitting them; tree branches striking them; and mylar balloons entangling in them. All these issues can create electrical arcs and sparks, but a fire may not ignite at that location. Often, a fuse may blow on a transformer, or a safety device that is meant to prevent electrical surges from traveling throughout an electrical grid may function and the fire may start there. Another phenomenon, called leakage, occurs when dirt covers the insulator, or the insulator is damaged and the electricity crosses over or through the insulator to the power pole. The top of the power pole, over time, may catch fire. Of course, there is also the human factor to be considered as well. Careless people may shoot electrical equipment and cause fires and damage to the equipment.

Oftentimes, in a wildfire, the fire investigation does not overlap significantly with the recovery and investigation of the fatalities. Due to the progression of the fire, the wildfire fatalities will oftentimes be found well within the perimeter of the fire, frequently in areas that were affected early in the blaze before adequate time for evacuation. The fire investigation, therefore, does not overlap in location, but the significance of the work escalates due to the criminal and civil implications of these deaths.

8.9 CONCLUSIONS

In conclusion, a fire investigation report is the author's report, and it reflects their perception, expertise, and knowledge. It is important to the integrity of the investigation that the investigator maintain an open mind. Fire investigators must be finders of the facts because investigations are fact-based and should not be driven by opinions, egos, or emotions.

Fire investigations are where the investigator can state their opinion as to the origin and cause of the fire based on their relative education, training, and experience while using the known facts of the case. The author is a potential expert witness and, as such, must own the report and be prepared to articulate the facts as stated in the report. Their reputation is at stake and potentially someone's freedom. The document should reflect the care and dedication they have brought to the investigation.

For those anticipating wildfire events and planning for the aftermath, it is important to remember that fire investigation will have long-term consequences in the recovery process. Therefore, it must be done with care and with appropriately trained personnel, and it must be initiated as soon as possible. This activity requires preparation and investment well ahead of any event.

Once an event has occurred, it is imperative that fire investigation begin immediately. To delay response can allow for destruction of evidence, both intentional and unintentional. When fatalities are involved, there are not only legal issues but also public interest and scrutiny. A well-planned and well-executed fire investigation will bring resolution to many questions and allow for mitigation of future events.

REFERENCES

Butte County District Attorney. (2020) The Camp Fire Public Report: A Summary of the Camp Fire Investigation. www.buttecounty.net/Portals/30/CFReport/PGE-THE-CAMP-FIRE-PUBLIC-REPORT.pdf?ver=2020-06-15-190515-977

Icove, D. and Haynes, G. (2017) *Kirk's Fire Investigation* (Brady Fire). 8th Edition. London: Pearson.

International Association of Arson Investigators. (2018) *Fire Investigator: Principles and Practice to NFPA 921 and 1033*. 5th Edition. Burlington, MA: Jones and Bartlett Learning.

Konefal, J. and Nordskog, E. (2019) Fire Death Scene Investigation: A Field Guide for Homicide, Coroner and Arson Investigators. ArsonProfiler.com

Lentini, J.J. (2018) *Scientific Protocols for Fire Investigation*. 3rd Edition. Boca Raton, FL: CRC Press.

National Fire Protection Association. (2017) *NFPA 921: Guide for Fire and Explosions Investigations*. Quincy, MA: NPRA.

SECTION III

Mass Fatality Response

Section 3 focuses on the methods utilized in mass fatality wildfire response using lessons learned from past California wildfires. Each of the chapters presents a unique perspective on the advance preparations necessary for an efficient and effective response, along with guidelines and suggestions for future events. All chapters in this section discuss the importance of open lines of communication within the mutual aid model and the importance of understanding the impact of fire on human remains and the local environment. This information should be used to inform search protocols and deployment strategies.

Section 3 opens with Chapter 9, which presents an overview of the literature pertaining to human behavior in response to fire. Data is drawn from building evacuation research along with US wildfires and Australian bushfires. The chapter delves into the concepts of risk perception and risk vulnerability and how these concepts impact human decision-making in the face of fire notifications. The authors also discuss how the engineering of buildings can allow for safe evacuation in an emergency. Chapter 9 presents data on victim location within a residence using data from the Camp Fire. The authors suggest that knowing the most likely areas where people have died can reduce search time and prevent damage to already fragile osseous material.

Chapter 10 discusses the importance of having realistic expectations and an understanding of how fire impacts human remains prior to the recovery of wildfire victims. The chapter opens with an overview of how thermal trauma affects human remains and how soft tissues and osseous material will react in response to extreme heat. The authors provide detailed descriptions of the typical appearance of fire victims and describe how body location can be used to inform search strategy. The authors suggest that a greater understanding of how bodies burn and the typical appearance of burn victims allows for greater refinement of search protocols and may help to reduce the number of false-positive finds following a mass fatality wildfire event.

Chapter 11 provides a detailed discussion of the role and responsibilities of SAR/USAR teams in wildfire response. The chapter opens by providing an overview of the various types of SAR teams in California, along with a discussion of each team's function. The chapter then transitions into a detailed discussion of mutual aid, defined as the voluntary sharing of personnel and resources when an agency cannot sufficiently deploy its own resources to respond to an unusual occurrence. The three types of

DOI: 10.4324/9781003168010-11

mutual aid that are called upon in response to a wildfire are law enforcement, coroners/mass fatality, and SAR teams. It is imperative that all agencies called upon for mutual aid must work together seamlessly and have open lines of communication. The authors present an overview of the roles and responsibilities of search and rescue, how SAR teams fit within the mutual aid sphere, and how teams can be efficiently deployed and supported in wildfire recovery. The authors propose that mutual aid responders be trained in wildfire response, including annual in-depth training, as well as just-in-time training provided at the time of the response. Chapter 11 closes with lessons learned from recent wildfires.

Chapter 12 discusses the variability of recovery operations and the need for flexibility in wildfire response from an anthropological perspective. Each of the chapter's authors were involved in the 21-day recovery efforts following the Camp Fire. In the case of large-scale fires, variability can occur in the number of missing persons, the environmental conditions that first responders will be presented with and the size of the recovery area (ranging from several homes to entire towns). Using the 2018 California Camp Fire as an example, the authors discuss the best possible recovery techniques, what are their limitations, and how they are deployed.

Chapter 13 discusses how to be ready for deployment and what training and equipment are needed. The writing also covers what the needs for staffing are and what deployment expectations are during the recruitment process. Providing solid and realistic information to those who may be deployed is essential. The chapter also outlines a few of the bureaucratic hurdles that must be confronted before teams are deployed into the field. The chapter goes on to explain what supplies are needed in a response and how anthropologists can assist with training other responders, including SAR and USAR teams.

CHAPTER 9

Human Behavior in Fire as Evidenced by Wildfire Fatalities

Alison Galloway and Casey Hegel

Spatial analyses in mass disaster fatalities focus on where individuals are when they die within the geographic landscape (see Chapters 20 and 21). However, in search and recovery efforts, it is equally important to know where to look when examining a specific address where a missing person is thought to have died. This process can be grounded in a knowledge of human behavior in the face of wildfires and structural fires, fire survival education, and human actions in the face of impending destruction.

In wildfires, many victims are trapped at their homes when the fire front arrives before they can flee. This may simply be a matter of insufficient time, insufficient or ambiguous warning, mobility issues (including lack of a vehicle in which to leave), or refusal to evacuate/very late evacuation. Therefore, it is important to understand how people react in these times. Most information on escape behavior in fires comes from survivors reflecting on what decisions they made. However, information on the decisions made by those who died in the fire can be gleaned from data collected about their antemortem circumstances and the location and position of the body within the fire debris. Combining this information with what we know about the decision-making process in the face of fire from survivors' accounts, as well as experimental data, will provide some insight into what may have happened in the wildfire fatalities.

On a practical level, knowing the most likely areas where people have died can reduce search time and prevent damage to already fragile osseous material. It is important to know when and where it is necessary to make entry into a structure as opposed to a perimeter search. This chapter first examines what is known about human behavior in fires and secondly looks at what we can tell from the remains themselves. The discussion ties these threads of information together in terms of recommendations for the search and recovery process.

9.1 HUMAN BEHAVIOR IN THE FACE OF FIRE

An individual's response to a hazardous event is based on their own perceptions of risk (Smith, 2013). The science of risk assessment and an individual's perception of their own risk often does not align. There is a natural inclination to revert to an expectation of normal conditions in the face of disaster, known as normalcy bias, or they assume

DOI: 10.4324/9781003168010-12

that there will be a favorable outcome, known as optimism bias (Kuligowski, 2013). Therefore, people delay taking defensive action until the physical, social, or informational cues become overwhelming. Even when some environmental cues are significant, there will still be those who wait for an "official" evacuation order.

Research has repeatedly shown that panic, a term that is only loosely defined, is relatively uncommon in the fire situation, and most people engage in a decision-making process incorporating multiple lines of evidence (Kuligowski, 2016; Paulsen, 1984; Sime, 1983, 1995). Attribution of panic, where self-preservation surmounts all other concerns, is often invoked after the fact and serves to lay blame on the victims themselves. Similarly, the concept of disaster shock has been raised in which people are rendered incapable of taking any action (Kuligowski, 2016). However, there is little evidence that people take no action in the face of danger from fire.

Given that people often delay their actions in the face of fire, awaiting some confirmation that an emergency situation exists, it is apparent that they then embark on some form of action in which to pursue safety for themselves and their loved ones. Often this does not involve reasoning out the "best" option but rather taking the first possible action that looks like it might work (Kuligowski, 2013). This is a process known as "satisficing" and may partly explain what appear to be "irrational" actions attributed to panic.

Individuals who are older, have a disability, and are of lower-economic status have all been found to be more vulnerable during disaster events, possibly because their options for action may be fewer, yet they are still susceptible to the same biases just noted. Older individuals are more at risk and vulnerable during a fire as they are more likely to need assistance to evacuate (Fahey et al., 2016). The assistance that might be needed can range from sensory to mobility disabilities to a decline in mental acuity that could affect their understanding of the risk in an emergency (Howle, 2019). Older adults have the highest prevalence of multiple chronic conditions, including physical and cognitive disabilities and sensory impairments. These conditions can limit their ability to do the activities of daily living, much less cope with an impending disaster (Al-Rousan et al., 2014). Older adults can also be more socially isolated, this can result in them not receiving information or warnings about an event or being able to ask for help, often making them invisible to rescue teams (Al-Rousan et al., 2014). Many older adults are also vulnerable due to living in poverty, associated with a lower fire preparedness and a higher fire risk.

Areas with higher fire deaths were found to have a higher percentage of people who have a disability (Ahrens, 2019). This correlation may be due to the lower property values in these areas, making them affordable on a fixed or limited income. Like many elderly, those with disabilities may require additional assistance with evacuation, which will vary depending on the type of disability (Howle, 2019). This can range from physical assistance to evacuate to simply providing information about the event in a form accessible to those with communication impairments. Individuals with a disability might have a slower response time or might not be able to safely evacuate on their own (Bethel et al., 2011). Like all people, those with disabilities will also take time to come to terms with the emergency situation.

Higher fire risk is also associated with individuals who are of lower-economic status (Lehna et al., 2016) for the same reason noted earlier. As with disabilities, areas with higher fire death rates were also found to have a higher percentage of people whose income fell below the poverty line (Ahrens, 2019). Lower socioeconomic status has also been associated with unsafe conditions that can contribute to a higher fatality risk (Hannon & Shai, 2003). These risks may include older construction that does not provide sufficient fire protection, housing that is in need of repair and that has more vulnerabilities to ignition.

Knowing that those who are elderly or disabled or who are on lower income are already at a disadvantage means that these groups are the most likely to be unable to evade a fire. However, all people will make decision—even if that is to stay in one place. In the wildfire, people also are contending with smoke, extreme heat, and a lack of information as to where safety might lie. When conducting a search, knowing how people might have made those decision may assist in the location of remains. However, searchers are hindered by a massive transformation of the landscape with burned structures, loss of vegetation cover, and loss of obstacles, such as fences and retaining walls that may have affected egress during the fire itself.

Much of the research on human behavior in fire focuses on two areas of work: (1) the engineering of buildings to allow for safe evacuation in an emergency and (2) when and why people evacuate from fires, drawing from data on North American and Australian bushfires. From these areas of research, we can extrapolate to the situation of those who perished in a wildfire. For many of these people, there would have been no readily identifiable place left to which to escape once the fire front arrived. Some people resort to immersing themselves in swimming pools or ponds, but the fire consumption of oxygen as well as the intense heat may still be fatal. While remaining in a house that has already caught fire seems ill-advised, there is often little choice when the exterior of the house is a sea of flames and intolerable heat.

9.1.1 Evacuation Research in Structural Fires

The time between the start of a fire and full evacuation of an indoor space can be divided into several phases: the time between ignition and the first cues that are available to occupants that there is a fire, then the pre-movement time between perception of a cue and actually starting to leave, and the actual exit time (Graham & Roberts, 2000). To that one can add the point at which the conditions within the building become untenable, blocking possible exits, producing fatal toxic gases and intense heat, and eventually causing the death of any remaining occupants (Kobes et al., 2010).

Research on human behavior in the face of structure fires focuses primarily on the phase between when the first warning of disaster reaches the occupants and when they decide to begin evacuation (Kobes et al., 2010; Kuligowski, 2013, 2016; Proulx, 2003; Sime, 1992). The first event is the recognition of the threat itself and whether or not it presents a risk to the occupant. The second is the actual response, such as which exit people chose and with whom they exit. People go through a behavioral or decision-making process in which they perceive certain cues, interpret them, assess the risk, and then decide what to do. Variations in cue perception and how they interpret the cues and reach a decision all alter the outcome. Even in a relatively simple setting, such as a fire in a large lecture hall, about two-thirds of the time between alarm and full evacuation was spent in people trying to decide what to do. Without specific instructions, it is likely that this period is lengthened.

People depend on signals from others as much as they do the outward signs of fire (Kobes et al., 2010; Kuligowski, 2009, 2013; Kuligowski, 2016). During a building fire, occupants perceive social or physical cues and also assess other conditions (uncertainty, information overload, time pressure, and personal experience). With the available cues, they must then try to decide if this is a serious threat or a false alarm and how dangerous their situation is. Then they must decide what action, if any, to take. Finally, they must perform that action. For much of this information and decision-making, these cues come from the other occupants more than the environment. This collaborative process is known as milling and keynoting (Kuligowski, 2016).

Those with prior experience of fires or some type of training about fires and those having access to social cues (understanding language, having contact with family and friends) increases perception of risk and stimulates action sooner (Kuligowski, 2009). Those who are closer to the event and can see it tend to perceive it more. Perception is increased if there are clear cues such as flames, sounds of fire or screaming, or specific warnings. In contrast, there are many factors that tend to lower perception of risk. When there is too much information from many sources, people tend to spend time trying to reconcile this information, and consequently it will lower their perception of immediate risk. Those who are habituated to an environment, are older, or recognize themselves as having a disability tend to have a lower perception of risk. Those who are anxious/stressed are under time pressure with others or have just awoken tend to have decreased perception. In fires, cue perception can also be decreased by the fire itself and the dense smoke that often accompanies fire.

If other family members or friends are in the building, there is a reluctance on the part of those able to flee to actually to leave (Kuligowski, 2009, 2016; Sime, 1983). Instead, they will often head toward the last known location of those other parties. People often appear to only worry about waiting to reform the group prior to escape when it involves reconnecting with family members. Groups formed of non-family members do not appear to cause people to search for missing or separated members prior to evacuation. Prior building fires also show that people who have successfully escaped may return in order to save family members or others.

People will seek to help those who may be infirm or disabled. However, as noted earlier, preparation for the possibility of fire is often lower with those who have elderly or disabled persons within the household (Yang et al., 2006). People will also spend more time in a dangerous zone in order to guide out those who may need assistance. This guidance may involve holding their hands to lead or steer them out or even carrying people outside.

Somewhat bizarrely, people are also inclined to feel compelled to finish the task they were doing before leaving (Graham & Roberts, 2000; Proulx, 2003; Ramachandran, 1990). This behavior is often seen in evacuation from large public buildings where shoppers will continue to browse or attempt to make purchases or where diners will continue their meals despite alarms and even staff warnings. Essentially, people have assessed their situation and, often due to insufficient information, fallen back on their belief that the warnings are false or that the threat is not serious enough to warrant their action.

Familiarity with exit routes can be a major factor in large building fires (Ramachandran, 1990). People gravitate toward the exits that they have used previously rather than the closest ones and often perceive these as shorter or at least more easily navigated. However, while this is not a factor in home fires, people may forget that there are windows or other exits by which they can escape. Unfortunately, in a wildfire, there is no good place from which to escape once the fire front is near to the victim.

In summary, in building fires, people often delay their actions to evacuation until the signals (environmental, social, or informational) are clear. Without information, with ambiguous information, or with too much information, they tend to delay. When they do start to leave, they are often doing so with loved ones, assisting with their escape at the cost of speed on their own behalf.

9.1.2 Wildfire Evacuation Behavior

The ways in which individuals respond to a wildfire threat is often influenced by the policies of where they are located. In Australia, there is no forced evacuation, whereas the policies and recommendations in the US involve evacuation, usually in the form of mandatory evacuation in the case of a wildfire threat (McLennan et al., 2019). Unfortunately, data on wildfire deaths and what people do in the immediate face of a wildfire is limited for the US, there are some general conclusions of how people react to voluntary versus mandatory evacuation based on survey data prior to and after fire events. In the US, even in the face of a mandatory evacuation order or a voluntary evacuation warning, it is likely that there will be individuals that choose to stay to try to protect their property (McLennan et al., 2019). Not relying on social cues or official communications, some feel compelled to assess the risks themselves and will delay leaving, often until flames are within sight. Some individuals might return to their property prior to the fire arriving.

Actions taken by residents threatened by wildfire range from waiting to assess risk and then deciding to stay or evacuate, planning for evacuation but waiting for an official evacuation or authority figure to tell them to leave, leaving prior to mandatory evacuation orders, or choosing to stay for the purpose of trying to defend their property (Kuligowski, 2020). Some individuals are not at their residence at the time of the fire, or choose to do other activities, such as assisting firefighters, and may try to return once the fire threat to their home is imminent.

Communication of information during disaster events, such as a wildfire, is vital, as an individual's perception of risk is partially reliant on timely and accurate information of the event as it is occurring (Toledo et al., 2018). Decisions made by residents vary based on whether evacuation is voluntary or mandatory. Official evacuation orders are more likely to result in evacuation rather than announcements that evacuation is recommended or that a voluntary evacuation process is in place (Toledo et al., 2018). With voluntary evacuation, leaving tends to be delayed as individuals then have to make decisions on how and when they want to evacuate, as well as personally assess what their fire risk is. Delayed evacuation can also be caused by fear and high levels of anxiety during a wildfire event and lack of preparation. One of the recommendations to prepare for wildfire events and evacuations is to have a plan and a bag already packed (McLennan et al., 2019).

Perception of risk often affects how people end up reacting and exhibiting certain behaviors during a disaster (Hilhorst & Bankoff, 2004). Perception of risk is also influenced by past experiences; individuals are more likely to perform mitigation efforts for future fire events if they have past experiences with fire events (Smith, 2013). Higher rates of evacuation have been linked to past experiences of evacuation, having a prior plan for evacuation, or living in houses that offer weak protection from a fire (Toledo et al., 2018). It is also more likely when evacuations are more complex as when there is livestock to be moved, requiring multiple trips. Decisions and behaviors during disaster events are complex; this is discussed further in the discussion section of this chapter through some examples from the Camp Fire and other fires.

The choice to stay or evacuate during a fire event is influenced by the source of information (McLennan et al., 2019). As with a building fire, during a wildfire, cues signal and influence whether one chooses to evacuate or stay. These cues can be both social and/or environmental. An example of a social cue is other people, such as neighbors, choosing to evacuate, whereas an environmental cue would be visually seeing smoke or flames or being able to smell the fire. Decision to evacuate is suggested to also be influenced by other household members and dynamics. There is a likelihood of evacuation if all members of the household are present at the time of the event or if there is the presence of children or elderly in a household (Toledo et al., 2018). The presence of pets was found to either not influence the likelihood to evacuate or decreases the likelihood of evacuating (Toledo et al., 2018).

Much of the research on wildfire/bushfire evacuation decision-making comes from Australia. The Australian bushfires, many of which have resulted in multiple fatalities, have plagued the southeastern portion of the continent but have also yielded information on how people respond to the threat. Australia has long had a "stay and defend or leave early" policy with regards to the bushfires (Haynes et al., 2008). From early fires, it was known that those who stayed and defended their property survived better than those who tried to evacuate late. This advice came under question with the 2009 Victoria fires that claimed 173 lives (Blanchi et al., 2014). It was then replaced by a "prepare, act, and survive" guideline, which highlighted the benefits of early evacuation.

A review of 674 civilian deaths from 1901 to 2011 due to wildfire showed that men were disproportionately represented in the pre-1965 period (82.2%) as opposed to the more recent period (56.1%) (Blanchi et al., 2014). Deaths within structures were about equally male and female, but those outside a residence or in a vehicle were weighted heavily toward males (75% and 70%, respectively). Deaths outside a structure tended to occur when the fire index was lower, suggesting that they were actively fighting to defend their property when they were overcome. As the fire index was heightened, meaning the fires were often faster and more intense, more deaths occurred as people tried to shelter from the horrendous fire front. The number of deaths inside structures have increased dramatically to 44% in the most recent period compared to only 7.1% between 1901 and 1964. Interestingly, of those dying within the house and where some room information was available, 37% died in a room with reduced outside visibility compared to 29% in a room with a view to the outside. Similar results were found in a review of Australian bushfire deaths from 1900 to 2006 which found that males were most often killed while defending property while women tended to die during late evacuation (Haynes & Tibbits, 2007). Children were usually killed while evacuating, often with a parent.

In looking at deaths within the 2009 Victoria bushfires, the ferocity of the fire front was grossly underestimated by the population (Handmer et al., 2010). Consequently, people did not evacuate early and then were forced to take refuge. Bathrooms and bunkers were used but offered little protection from the flames or the toxic gasses generated by the fire.

Evidence from both areas, Australia and North America, suggest that people grossly underestimate the speed and intensity of modern wildfires. They will often delay evacuation or try to defend their property until being forced to seek shelter as the fire front nears. In many ways, at that point they are facing similar situations as those trapped in buildings—having to find any workable option as opposed to the best possible option for survival.

9.2 CAMP FIRE OBSERVATIONS: ROOM LOCATION WITH HIGHEST RECOVERY RATES

Based on the Camp Fire and other wildfire data, Hayes and colleagues mapped out the location within the house where bodies were recovered (Hayes et al., 2020) (Figure 9.1). Almost three-quarters were found within their residences. Of the remainder, some were found outside, usually close to the house or even under a vehicle. The rest were killed in their vehicles trying to flee before the fire front swept over them.

If we refine this to look at the location of the bodies within homes, there are significant differences between rooms (Figure 9.2). Of these, the bathroom yielded the highest frequency and is the most likely place to search. This is followed by the bedrooms, often with people still either on their beds or nearby. The third most frequent location

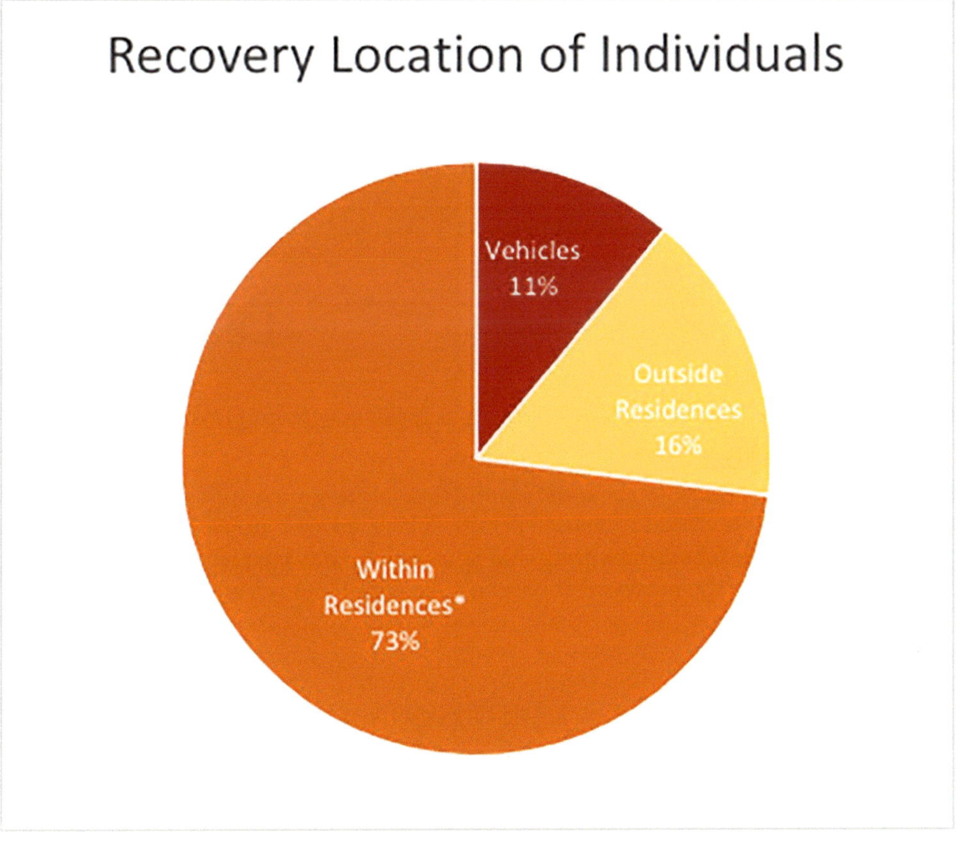

FIGURE 9.1 Location of bodies found at the Camp Fire.

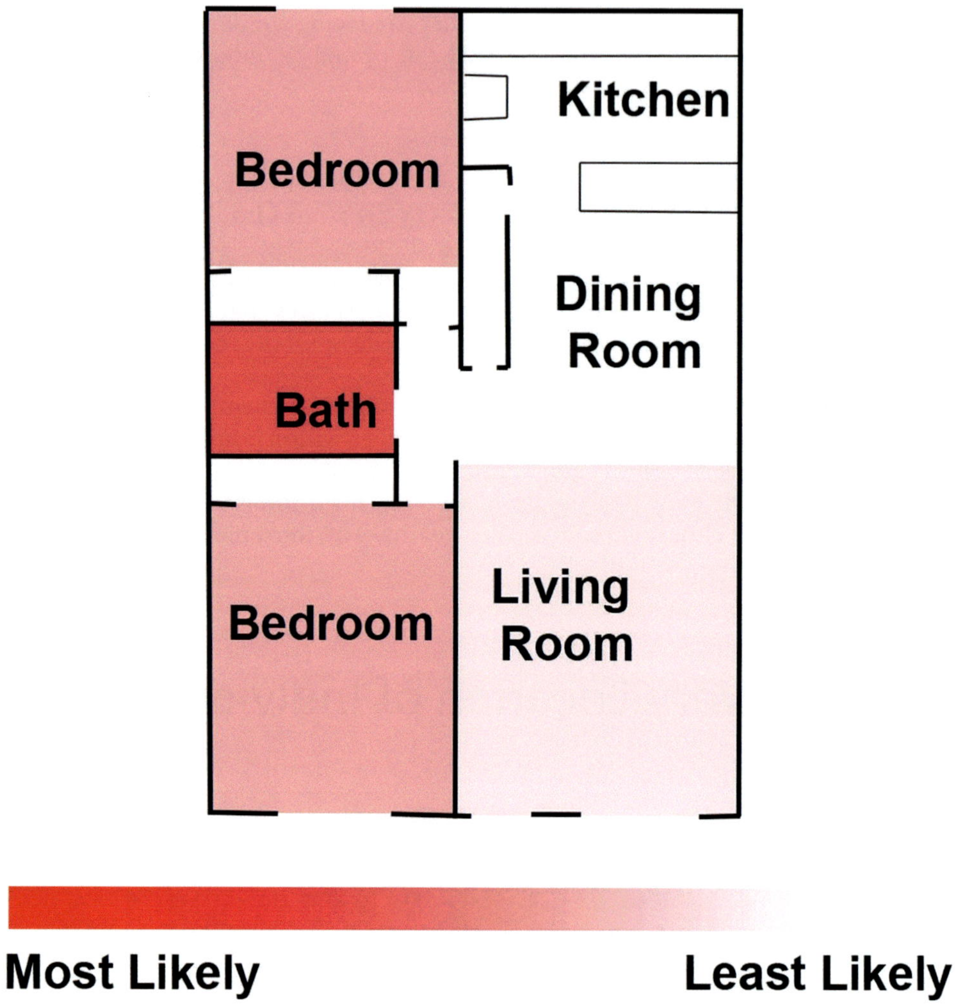

FIGURE 9.2 Priority for search areas within a residence (from Hayes et al., 2020).

is the living room, often with the individuals found sitting on a sofa or chair, indicated by the presence of the metal internal springs. The area of a house where victims are rarely found is the kitchen; however, this is a region that frequently garners interest from searchers due to the presence of osseous material from refrigerators, freezers, and so on.

9.3 DISCUSSION

Studies of human behavior in the fire context focus frequently on the time it takes for people to understand that there is a major threat and then make the decision as to their response. All too frequently, the first response is to investigate whether the threat is, in fact, real and, only then, decide how to respond. In a wildfire, this period may be relatively prolonged in that there is a period of time in which people may be aware of a general threat of a wildfire and then a subsequent period when they realize their immediate peril. Numerous studies, particularly in Australia, discuss the problems and conflicts that arise in the initial phase when determining that a wildfire is approaching. This process of decision-making rests heavily on the risk perception for oneself and for loved ones, including pets and livestock.

However, the decision-making in the more immediate situation of a wildfire must often be reconstructed from the location of the remains, as is the case with the Camp Fire. In this context, the remains found in residences tell a picture of how people faced their last moments. Overall, there are three basic directions: (1) fleeing, (2) sheltering, and (3) acceptance. Those who flee are often found in areas near or under their vehicles, in the entry areas of their homes (front or back doors), on porches, or in the garage. In some cases, evidence of packing or other collection of material may be present although most has been consumed by the fire. Most appear to have been caught "midstride" by the inferno that consumes the home. It is possible that, like the people seen continuing to shop or eat, these individuals continued their packing and organizing without realizing the urgency of their situation. In North America, unlike Australia, it is rare to see anyone who was actively fighting a fire, aside from deaths in the fire services. However, it is possible that those who are fleeing in the vicinity of their residence had been attempting to fight the flames. As the Australian experience shows, fighting a wildfire requires considerable preparation in terms of firefighting gear, protective clothing, adequate water supplies, and physical stamina, usually far in excess of those who initially imagine themselves "taking a stand" against the flames (Handmer et al., 2010; McLennan et al., 2013).

A second group are those who have either decided to shelter in place or are unable to leave and are having to attempt to shelter in place. Many of our recent California wildfires have produced anecdotes of those individuals, often males, who have refused to leave, much to the frustration of authorities who are concerned about needing to rescue these people as the danger increases. If rescue is not possible, people tend to move indoors to escape the intense heat from the approaching fire front. In most cases, given the intensity of the recent wildfires, chances of survival within a home that becomes actively involved is minimal, but when the fire hits, such individuals usually resort to the instructions given on how to respond to a structure fire when fire suppression will arrive shortly and where leaving the building is not possible. In that case, a commonly heard set of advice is to go to the bathroom, use wet towels to block the doorway of smoke, and even fill the tub with water and get into it (Thompson et al., 2004). This is not recommended as an alternative to evacuation but has appeared as online advice, particularly when dealing with a fire in a multistory building where exit routes may be blocked. During the California wildfires, a large number of people were found in bathrooms. From the circumstances, it appears that they saw that exiting the building was blocked by the flames and fled to the bathroom to shelter. Unfortunately, bathrooms typically only have one exit and windows, if any, and are often designed to provide privacy by obscuring or distorting the views. The bodies of the victims are often found huddled in the wreckage of the room, their chances of fleeing once the building caught fire impossible. In the Camp Fire, one such victim was found wrapped in a soaking wet comforter in the bathtub. All that remained unburned were the feet that were twisted into the remnants of the damp comforter.

The third group of victims are those who appear to have faced the inevitable. It is as if they reached the stage where they examined the possible protective actions they could take and found none (Kuligowski, 2016). A number of the Camp Fire victims were found sitting together in their recliners in the living room, in one instance, it appeared that they were holding hands, a connection that withstood even the body movement known to occur with burning. Others were found so that it appeared that they were sitting on their beds, feet and lower legs off the mattress springs. Pets are often found nearby. For whatever reason, either inability or reluctance to leave, these people decided to stay and, in their final moments, appear to have chosen to face the reality of their situation. This group of victims who appear to have accepted their fate are the hardest group for the last responders to handle emotionally (see Chapter 22).

One version of this "acceptance" are those who die by suicide rather than burn. Often death is due to a gunshot wound, with the presumed choice being a quick death under the control of the victim themselves as opposed to one by flames. Unfortunately, we have seen instances wherein the individual is found completely unburned and the location may have been survivable had they not chosen to end their lives (see Chapter 15).

The other observation we have seen from the Camp Fire, as well as other wildfires, is that people trapped in the fire will tend to cluster together in their final moments. This has been termed a "convergence cluster" and is often seen in high-rise fires (Kuligowski, 2016, Chapter 20). In wildfire residences, it is unusual to find separate locations for those who have died in one structure. Instead, they are found clustered together, bodies intermingled, sometimes also with pets. It is likely that the more able-bodied individuals stayed to help with one or more people who would need assistance in leaving. Unfortunately, these clusters often result in extensive commingling of the cremated remains (Chapters 12 and 17). Skull fragments and spinal columns may be the only indication of multiple victims in initial observations.

Of the factors identified in the prior literature, it is evident that some will play a role in wildfire deaths. People are usually very familiar with their own homes, the most likely place of death, but they may enter into a longer deliberative period before deciding to act. This period often involves whether they or their family members are able to leave. If moving one person is difficult, it is likely that at least one family member will stay behind rather than abandon the incapacitated person.

9.4 CONCLUSION: IMPACT ON RECOVERY

What can this examination of human behavior in fire tell us about how to enact the search and recovery processes in the aftermath of a wildfire? When confronted with the overwhelming devastation of a community caught in such a fire, how to prioritize the search areas becomes critical. Vehicles are relatively easy to search but structures are much more difficult and the possibilities of significantly damaging and dispersing the remains in the search process is high (Chapter 12 on search protocols). Prioritization of the most likely areas is, therefore, important. Equally important is, in larger buildings, the ability to conduct searches and clear areas in rooms or entries less likely to contain victims so that entry can be gained to those areas where people were more likely to take refuge.

Many homes in the WUI are relatively simple, single-story homes or mobile homes. Room designations are usually identifiable by the remnants of furnishings such as ovens and refrigerators in the kitchen, mattress springs in a bedroom, toilets and bathtubs in the bathroom, and sofa and chair springs in a living or family room. However, there are also larger homes with multiple stories in which upstairs bedrooms have collapsed onto lower floor living spaces. Often an idea of the home construction can be derived from "street view" on maps and help visualize the layout of the home.

Aside from the location of specific rooms, it is also important that searchers be aware that people will likely have formed a group within the structure. Therefore, bodies will tend to be clustered in one location within the house rather than dispersed throughout the structure. Commingled remains will take a long time to retrieve and will require extensive sorting in order to assess how many individuals are present. It is also complicated by having people of shared ancestry among the victims as these individuals often have similar skeletal morphology (see Chapter 17). Commingled remains may also result from someone being with an unrelated caregiver or even a neighbor who stopped to assist.

If a specific person is missing and they are not in their residence or vehicle, it may be helpful, aside from the systematic search of the area, to think how they would react. Searchers should not assume that victims were acting irrationally but that they were seeking some escape. They would be making decisions based on very limited information, limited visibility, and probably little sense of direction. Have they taken shelter in another structure, or did they attempt to reach a perceived safety zone?

When we think about how the victims died, it is inevitable that we have to place ourselves mentally in their shoes. This perspective brings home the terror and anticipation of death that the victims must have experienced.

CASE STUDIES FROM THE CAMP FIRE

Each one of the behaviors and decisions during a wildfire evacuation discussed in this chapter occurred during the Camp Fire with some variations showcasing the complexity of how people react. There were individuals who waited for assistance to evacuate, who were isolated and had no means to evacuate on their own, who tried to shelter in place, who actively tried to defend property from the flames, and who tried to evacuate and were overcome by the flames. There were other individuals who made the decision not to evacuate. For some, this decision was based on past fire threats to the area. The following are some examples seen through the eyes of those who recovered the bodies.

Some of the older couples that were found in their living rooms had been waiting for evacuation assistance from other family members. There were several individuals from the Camp Fire who were older or had a disability that impacted their ability to evacuate safely on their own. Not having access to a vehicle and being socially isolated also impacted whether someone was able to evacuate. Even if they had access to a vehicle did not mean they were able to get out due to the power being out. One of the victims, who was an older female, had a vehicle but was not strong enough to manually open the garage door and a family member that she had been talking to was not able to get to her.

One of the female victims was not willing to evacuate until receiving evacuation orders from a person of authority, even with the environmental cues and social cues of her neighbors evacuating. The victim's adult daughter tried to persuade her to leave and ended up evacuating on her own with their vehicle.

One of the male fatalities from the Camp Fire, who spent years as a volunteer firefighter, spent the day fighting the fire and tried to defend his property and others by cutting a fire break. He later returned home and died that evening when the fire ended up crossing the canyon for a second time. There is another account of someone who tried to defend their property against the fire while his wife was sheltering inside with their animals. The husband ended up being rescued by emergency services, and the wife was unable to be rescued from inside the house.

For the individuals found in association with vehicles, and some that were found outside, many had been trying to actively escape the fire. However, some of the individuals found outside were on their porch or driveway waiting for evacuation assistance. One of the observable impacts of the Camp Fire is how people influence each other and their decisions. One of the wheelchair-bound victims that had been waiting for evacuation assistance on their porch was linked to one of the victims found in the middle of the road, with their dog, under their vehicle. The individual with their vehicle was the stepson and caretaker to the individual who was in the wheelchair on the porch. They did not have cellphones and the landline was down, the stepson would not have been able to evacuate his stepfather by himself. His last-minute evacuation after the realization of having to leave his stepfather behind is thought to have contributed to his own death. Behavior and decision-making during an evacuation event is important to understanding the best way to proceed during recovery efforts after a fire.

REFERENCES

Ahrens, M. (2019). *US fire death rates by state research.* Quincy, MA: National Fire Protection Association (NFPA).

Al-Rousan, T. M., Rubenstein, L. M., & Wallace, R. B. (2014). Preparedness for natural disasters among older US adults: A nationwide survey. *American Journal of Public Health, 104*(3), 506–511.

Bethel, J. W., Foreman, A. N., & Burke, S. C. (2011). Disaster preparedness among medically vulnerable populations. *American Journal of Preventive Medicine, 40*(2), 139–143. https://doi.org/10.1016/j.amepre.2010.10.020

Blanchi, R., Leonard, J., Haynes, K., Opie, K., James, M., & de Oliveira, F. (2014). Environmental circumstances surrounding bushfire fatalities in Australia 1901–2011. *Environmental Science & Policy, 37,* 192–203.

Fahey, E., Lehna, C., Hanchette, C., & Coty, M.-B. (2016). Geographic mapping as a tool for identifying communities at high risk for fires. *Journal of Burn Care & Research, 37*(4), e303–e309. https://doi.org/10.1097/BCR.0000000000000303

Graham, T., & Roberts, D. (2000). Qualitative overview of some important factors affecting the egress of people in hotel fires. *International Journal of Hospitality Management, 19,* 79–87.

Handmer, J., O'Neil, S., & Killalea, D. (2010). *Review of fatalities in the February 7, 2009, bushfires.* Melbourne, Australia: Victorian Bushfires Royal Commission.

Hannon, L., & Shai, D. (2003). The truly disadvantaged and the structural covariates of fire death rates. *Social Science Journal*, *40*(1), 129–136. https://doi.org/10.1016/S0362-3319(02)00263-X

Hayes, L., Straub, A., Bartelink, E., Kendell, A., & Milligan, C. (2020). Training needs for Search and Rescue (SAR) teams during mass-disaster fire scene recovery: Lessons learned from the 2018 California Camp Fire. *American Academy of Forensic Sciences, 556.*

Haynes, K., & Tibbits, A. (2007). Trends in Australian bushfire fatalties over the last 100 years. *Bushfire CRC Research Report.* Victoria, AU: Australian and New Zealand National Council for Fire and Emergency Services.

Haynes, K., Tibbits, A., Coates, L., Ganewatta, G., Handmer, J., & McAneney, J. (2008). 100 years of Australian civilian bushfire fatalities: Exploring the trends in relation to the "stay or go policy". *Bushfire CRC Research Report.* Victoria, AU: Australian and New Zealand National Council for Fire and Emergency Services.

Hilhorst, D., & Bankoff, G. (2004). Introduction: Mapping vulnerability. In G. Bankoff, G. Frerks, & D. Hilhorst (Eds.), *Mapping vulnerability: Disasters, development and people* (pp. 1–9). London: Routledge.

Howle, E. M. (2019). California is not adequately prepared to protect its most vulnerable residents from natural disasters. *Emergency Planning Report, 2019–2103.* Sacramento, CA: California State Auditor.

Kobes, M., Helsloot, I., de Vries, B., & Post, J. (2010). Building safety and human behaviour in fire: A literature review. *Fire Safety Journal*, *45*, 1–11.

Kuligowski, E. (2009). The process of human behavior in fires. *National Institute of Standards and Technology Technical Note 1632* (p. 15). Gaithersburg, MD: National Institute of Standards and Technology.

Kuligowski, E. (2013). Predicting human behavior during fires. *Fire Technology*, *49*, 101–120. https://doi.org/10.1007/s10694-011-0245-6

Kuligowski, E. (2020). Evacuation decision-making and behavior in wildfires: Past research, current challenges and a future research Agenda. *Fire Safety Journal*, 103129. https://doi.org/10.1016/j.firesaf.2020.103129

Kuligowski, E. D. (2016). Human behavior in fire. In *SFPE handbook of fire protection engineering* (pp. 2070–2114). https://doi.org/DOI 10.1007/978-1-4939-2565-0_58

Lehna, C., Speller, A., Hanchette, C., Fahey, E., & Coty, M.-B. (2016). Development of a fire risk model to Identify areas of increased potential for fire cccurrences. *Journal of Burn Care & Research*, *37*(1), 12–19. https://doi.org/10.1097/BCR.0000000000000297

McLennan, J., Elliott, G., Omodei, M., & Whittaker, J. (2013). Householders' safety-related decisions, plans, actions and outcomes during the 7 February 2009 Victorian (Australia) wildfires. *Fire Safety Journal*, *61*, 175–184. https://doi.org/10.1016/j.firesaf.2013.09.003

McLennan, J., Ryan, B., Bearman, C., & Toh, K. (2019). Should we leave now behavioral factors in evacuation under wildfire threat. *Fire Technology*, *55*(2), 487–516. https://doi.org/10.1007/s10694-018-0753-8

Paulsen, R. (1984). Human behavior and fires. *Fire Technology*, *20*(2), 15–27.

Proulx, G. (2003). Playing with fire: Understanding human behavior in burning buildings. *ASHRAE Journal*, *45*(7), 33–35.

Ramachandran, G. (1990). Human behavior in fires—a review of research in the United Kingdom. *Fire Technology*, 149–155.

Sime, J. (1983). Affiliative behaviour during escape to building exits. *Journal of Environmental Psychology*, *3*, 21–41.

Sime, J. (1992). Human behaviour in fires summary report. *Central Fire Brigades Advisory Council for England and Wales, Research Report Number 45*. London, UK: Crown Copyright. https://www.ukfrs.com/sites/default/files/2017-09/Human%20Behaviour%20in%20Fires%20-%20Summary%20Report.pdf

Sime, J. (1995). Crowd psychology and engineering. Safety *Science*, *21*, 1–14.

Smith, K. (2013). *Environmental hazards: Assessing risk and reducing disaster* (6th ed.). London: Taylor and Francis.

Thompson, N., Waterman, M., & Sleet, D. (2004). Using behavioral science to improve fire escape behaviors in response to a smoke alarm. *Journal of Burn Care & Rehabilitation*, *45*, 179–188. https://doi.org/10.1097/01.BCR.0000111767.05553.91

Toledo, T., Marom, I., Grimberg, E., & Bekhor, S. (2018). Analysis of evacuation behavior in a wildfire event. *International Journal of Disaster Risk Reduction*, *31*, 1366–1373. https://doi.org/10.1016/j.ijdrr.2018.03.033

Yang, J., Peek-Asa, C., Allareddy, V., Zwerling, C., & Lundell, J. (2006). Perceived risk of home fire and escape plans in rural households. *American Journal of Preventive Medicine*, *30*(1), 7–12. https://doi.org/doi:10.1016/j.amepre.2005.08.045

CHAPTER 10

How Human Bodies Burn

The Process of Thermal Damage, Body Movement, and Shifting Fuel Loads

Alison Galloway, Chelsey Juarez, and Elayne Pope

In planning and training to recover bodies following a fatal wildfire, knowing what to expect is critical. Search and rescue teams must prepare for a very wide range of events, including mountain rescue, water rescue/recovery, missing individuals with diminished capacity, and collection of evidence. Few have specific training in the recovery of burned remains and especially not those in which the damage to the remains is as extensive as frequently seen in wildfires. Common problems encountered in the search and recovery efforts are (1) the expectation of finding a "full body" so that searches either miss or trample over the fragile remains produced by the fire or (2) the expectation that anybody has been reduced to ash so that any small item that looks vaguely bonelike is assumed to be all that is left of the person. The latter situation results in many "false positives" during the search efforts, each of which must be cleared.

In addition to understanding *how* a body looks after a wildfire, we must also understand that *where* a body will be found will affect how it burns. It is important to understand how bodies are changed by fire, particularly one that results in complete or almost complete cremation of the remains (Bohnert et al., 1998; Pope, 2007; Symes et al., 2014).

There are usually three situations in which bodies are found: (1) outdoors, when the victim was trying to flee on foot, often between the residence and a vehicle or after having left a vehicle blocked on the road, (2) when the victim was still inside a vehicle overtaken by the fire, and (3) where the victim was inside a structure. The condition of the body typically varies by the location, although those in vehicles and structures may be similar in the level of destruction.

10.1 INITIAL CONDITIONS

In wildfires, the victim usually does not die during a slow-burning fire that produces high levels of carbon monoxide, resulting in unconsciousness due to carbon monoxide poisoning. Victims die relatively quickly once the fire descends but may have taken actions in anticipation of the fire, such as fleeing, sheltering, or showing acceptance of the inevitable (see Chapter 9). They may die from the inhalation of hyper-heated air, burning the air passages, or from the massive superficial burning.

DOI: 10.4324/9781003168010-13

Once dead, the body collapses (Figure 10.1). The fire will begin by burning the hair and clothing. Skin surfaces that are exposed to heat will begin to discolor to tan, reddish brown, or brown and then scorch, shrink, and develop blisters (Moritz, 1949; Adelson, 1954). Original skin pigmentation must be taken into consideration when assessing the color changes as darkly pigmented skin will appear dark, tightened, and shrunken without first appearing tan or light brown. The blisters typically form in and around the areas of skin change so that there is a gradation from unburned skin to blistered skin to discolored skin. Blisters are not a sign of vitality unless they are accompanied by inflammation.

Areas of skin that are in direct contact with surfaces remain protected between the body and the ground/floor substrate. These areas will be unburned despite extensive damage in the areas where heat exposure is greater. Similarly, areas that have tight clothing also tend to be somewhat protected, depending on the flammability of the material and position of the body as face up, face down, or lying on their side.

With superficial burning, body movement is minimal. There may be some deformation of facial features that include shrinking of the nose and ears along with retraction of the lips and protrusion of the tongue. Tongue protrusion is a natural heat-related occurrence and does not signify that the person was alive at the time of burning (Bohnert & Hejna, 2016; Madea & Doberentz, 2015 [contra Bernitz et al., 2014]). Some splaying of the fingers and toes (if barefoot) may be apparent but the contraction of the larger muscles to produce larger movement will require more heat. One must also be aware that bodies may be positioned in such a way that thermal damage will be differential even in these early stages. For example, if the body is seated, upper areas may be more heavily damaged. If the person was on an item of furniture such as a bed or chair, that item will begin burning at the same time that the body is affected. Those areas closest to any available combustible fuel source will exhibit more severe burn damage. Body segments that are closest to burning materials can move or lean toward the heat source.

If the fuel load around the body is limited, as is often the case when the body is found in an open space, the damage often terminates at this stage. The body would be

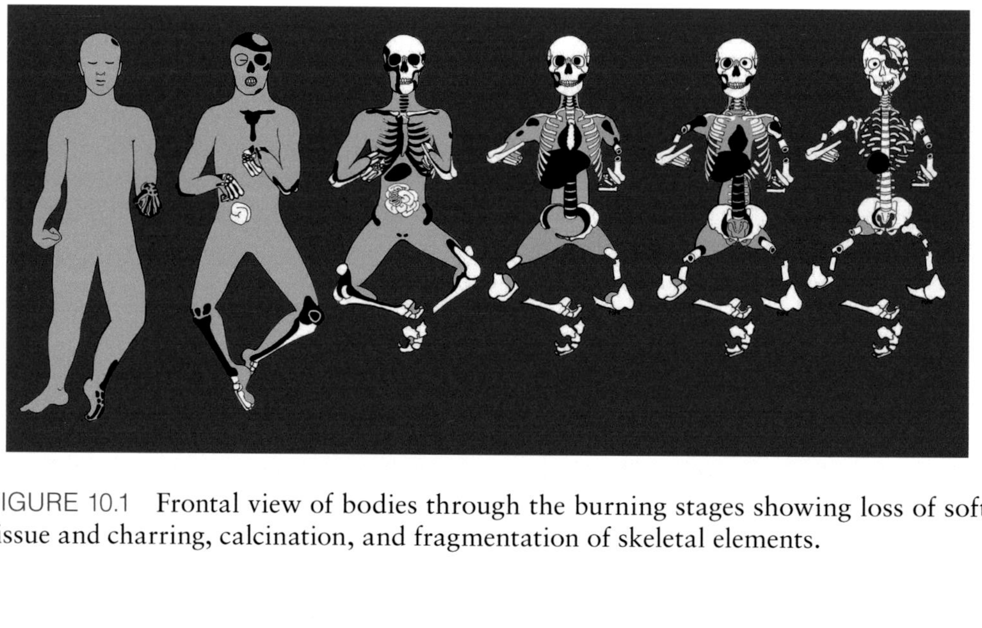

FIGURE 10.1 Frontal view of bodies through the burning stages showing loss of soft tissue and charring, calcination, and fragmentation of skeletal elements.

found intact although much of the clothing may be gone. Synthetic fabrics tend to burn or melt quickly with heat. Natural fabrics, such as cotton and silk, burn quickly but without melting and may self-extinguish, particularly if pressed between the body and another surface. However, the discolored, blistered body with remnants of clothing is the usual result.

10.2 DAMAGE BY SURROUNDING FUEL LOAD

In non-wildfire situations, it is common that fire suppression will arrive relatively early in the burning sequence. Bodies are found intact, as scorched or charred remains. However, in wildfires, fire suppression is usually nonexistent and the burning of a vehicle or structure will continue unchecked. Damage to the body will also continue.

10.2.1 Superficial Changes and Body Movement

If there is still external fuel available, such as furniture, structural elements, or interior of a vehicle, then the damage to the body will also increase as these fuel sources are consumed by the flames. The surface of the skin changes from discoloration to charred. Blistering continues along the margins and the shrinkage of skin will cause splits to occur. These skin splits expose the underlying layers, including subcutaneous fat followed by skeletal muscles.

At this point, there will be noticeable movement of the hands, feet, wrists, and ankles. The fingers will splay apart, and the small flexor muscles begin to contract, causing the fingers to curl inward along with a flexed wrist. This is a normal reaction to the fire and does not indicate any voluntary or pre-fire activity on the part of the deceased. The toes also splay followed by flexion. The arched foot and ankles extend downward as the shrunken Achilles tendon and calf muscles shorten.

Charred skin surfaces and skin splits expand to expose more and more of the underlying tissues, including subcutaneous fat and skeletal muscles. Some of these fats will be liquified by the heat, producing an oily sheen to the surface. These exposed areas are initially not charred, contrasting with the charred skin surrounding the split. However, as the areas of skin are consumed and the underlying tissue also charred, the entire exposed body will be seen simply as a blackened surface. Only closer inspection will show that there is skeletal muscle, fat, and in some cases, bone exposed.

10.2.2 Soft Tissue Loss and Bone Damage

The head will show retraction of the lips, exposing the anterior dentition. The posterior dentition tends to endure longer due to protection by the cheek musculature (Delattre, 2000) but will eventually also succumb to the fire. The heat will cause the highly mineralized dental enamel to fracture (Campbell et al., 2011; Federchook et al., 2018). Enamel and the underlying dentine have differing levels of organic material and therefore shrink at different rates. The enamel, which has low moisture and low organic material, tends to stay the same size but the higher organic content of the dentine causes it to shrink. The dentine then pulls inward as it shrinks and portions of the enamel will eventually sluff away. The dentine crown will shatter if hit with water during fire suppression or by falling debris; otherwise, it will passively fracture and fragment with only the roots found intact remaining within the jaw (molars) or as fragments in the substrate.

The facial features will also continue to deform so that the nose, lips, eyebrows, and ears gradually shrink and burn. The tongue forms a protective plug in the oral cavity as it often protrudes from the mouth due to swelling from heat changes. Eyelids may temporarily shrink, making the eyes appear open but then burn away to leave a charred tissue mass in the orbits.

Areas of the body where the skin is relatively thin and close to the bone, such as on the scalp of the forehead, the shins, and the flexed knuckles are vulnerable to heat damage. The skin will be consumed quickly, exposing the underlying bone. Exposed bone initially appears as fresh and once exposed to heat, it will appear discolored (yellow/white [greasy], then brown [greasy], and then brown/black), then charred. In the final stage of calcination, the bone will appear gray, as the organic materials have burned away leaving only a brittle inorganic bone structure that retains all the features as an unburned skeleton.

Body movement during this burning process accelerates significantly. The neck muscles contract so that the head is tilted backward, and the chin extended anteriorly. The arms begin to reposition into the pugilistic posture with the elbows and wrists flexed with clenched hands and fingers. In the pugilistic stance, the flexed and internally rotated arms and flexed hand, and wrists are to the sides and front of the chest along with partially bent knees, which appear as if the person was fighting (boxer pose), hence the name. As the wrist and forearm area burns, the hand will detach either by heat fractures through distal radius and ulna or as the tendons and ligament are burned through at the wrist. The remaining hand is repositioned proximally with the shrinking forearm muscles, where it will be held by the remaining tendons of the skeletal muscles. The elbows and upper arm will move above the substrate when the body is supine with arms flexed beside and/or over the chest. In some cases, the arms may appear over the head, which results from a combination of proximity to heat sources during the later stages of the fire and contracture of deeper remaining muscles of the shoulder and back, both of which influence the arm's final position.

The legs will also move. As the heat is applied to the larger muscles of the calves and thighs, larger body movement is seen, though delayed in comparison to the movements of the smaller arm muscles of the same body. The Achilles tendon shrinks and calf muscles contract pulling the ankle and foot downward into full extension, so the toes appear pointed. The front of the shin (anterior tibia) is charred bone and fractures above the ankle, causing the foot to detach from the lower leg. The remnants of the foot may either fall to the substrate or remain attached and drawn into the larger calf muscles on the back of the leg. The knees flex, causing the upper legs to spread apart due to the weight of the still-fleshed thighs. The heels or lower parts of the leg are drawn together along the midline, forming a "ballerina" pose. At this time, the adductor muscles at the hip and also pull the thighs wide apart, resulting in a splaying of the thighs that could be incorrectly interpreted as a sexual assault. This positioning of the legs is also attributable to the bulky thigh musculature where its thicker muscle layers take longer to induce the flexion at the hip and knee. Movement of the knee continues until it is in full flexion by which time the distal end of the femur is exposed and burned bone at the knee. The bones around the knee will show heat fractures.

On the torso, the fire will continue to burn through the subcutaneous fat layers and skeletal muscles. If the body is in the supine position (face upward), then portions of the internal organs will typically be exposed in the abdominal area outside of the body and appear to be extruding. Rib surfaces are often exposed along the sides of the body and begin the transition from discoloration to charring to calcination. Charred intercostal muscles of the chest wall leave windows between ribs that show the internal aspects of the chest where the heart and lungs will char into hardened black masses, leaving a partial void inside the ribcage.

10.2.3 Deep Tissue and Bone Loss

As the burning continues, the hands and feet will often appear to be lost "from" the body as these areas have very little flesh to protect the bone and have greater surface area for heat exposure. However, the small bones of these areas are one of the most common intact skeletal elements when the recovery is careful. The foot bones will typically be deposited under the ankle area, possibly close to the torso. Portions of the hand and wrist bones may have fallen into the chest area, or around the body depending on the movement and final position of the arms.

As the hands and feet are detached, other joints also are exposed and exhibit fragmentation. This process is most visible in the areas above the ankle, the knee, the wrist, the elbow, and the shoulder. Bone that has been exposed to heat loses its organic component and becomes exceptionally fragile (Thompson, 2005). Bone itself shrinks like skin splits and result in small superficial heat fractures that can appear as linear, longitudinal and transverse, semicircular curved, and jagged checkered (Buikstra & Swegle, 1989; Heglar, 1984; Herrmann & Bennett, 1999; Mayne Correia, 1997; Shipman et al., 1984; Symes et al., 2014; Walker et al., 2008). Additional fractures during the fire may result from falling debris if, for example, in a structural fire there are falling beams, roofing or lighting fixtures. Alternately, the body itself may fall through the floor(s) producing additional postmortem fracturing. However, even absent these factors, heat fracturing alone will cause eventual fragmentation of the skeletal elements. These fragments are, however, relatively large and retain morphological features that may allow for identification.

Heat-induced fractures can be distinguished from pre-fire fractures due to the differential coloration of the fracture margins and the changes in body movement around long bones. Pre-existing complete fractures in long bones allow "scissoring" of the bones as the broken ends slide past one another within the shrinking muscles. Protected areas such as the base of the skull may retain pre-fire fractures even when there is extensive delamination of the upper vault (Bohnert et al., 1997).

Destruction of the face and cranial vault are also seen. Facial anatomy is complex with a melding of very thin bones around the inner orbit and along the nasal opening with thicker bone along the margins of the face. All the thin bones of the face are vulnerable to fragmentation both during and after the fire. Early in the fire, the lower face is protected by the cheek muscles and the subcutaneous fat. However, as these tissues are consumed, the facial bones become calcined and develop heat fractures.

The vault, the dome of the skull, will develop heat fractures to the outer table in the form of delamination and separation of the outer layer (Pope et al., 2004). The bones of the vault consist of two distinct compact layers separated by spongy bone, called the diploe. Because the outer table of bone is most directly subjected to intense heat, this surface shrinks first due to the loss of organic material. When that occurs, the outer portions of the skull fracture through the diploe and may fall off the vault. The inner table is adjacent to the brain, which has high moisture content and is more resistant to heat, so it will fracture secondarily. When the outer table separates, it leaves a textured surface on the skull formed by the diploe, which lies within the hard outer and inner surfaces. Once the vault is breached by a full-thickness heat fracture, the brain itself will char and shrivel, leaving a mass of black carbonized material in the cranial base of the skull.

As the thicker musculature of the cheeks is lost to the flames, the premolars and molars become exposed and fracture similar to the anterior teeth. Roots for these teeth tend to have more structural adherence to the jaw so may be retained in the bone. That adhesion is particularly true for the upper molars, which have three curved roots.

10.2.4 Alterations to the Pattern of Thermal Damage

While this progression is typical of bodies, some factors will alter the pattern. One of the most significant is the effect of constraints on the body that limit movement. In the wildfire situation, this may come about by the collapse of structures onto the body or the presence of nonflammable units (e.g., sides of the car or dashboard) that may limit some limb movements. For this reason, observations about body position should also note surrounding context with copious photography when possible.

A second reason for changes in the pattern of body movement and, consequently, damage to the remains is the loss of substrate. Initially, this substrate is often the item of furniture upon which the person was sitting or lying. Wooden bed frames collapse, leaving only the metal springs of the mattress. This collapse may be uneven, depending on the progression of the fire and the body may be tipped to one side or even rolled onto the floor from the sagging coil springs. Chairs, sofas, and recliners also show similar loss of integrity, essentially spilling the body onto the floor.

However, one of the biggest disruptions in a wildfire, or any non-suppressed fire, is the loss of the floor itself. Most bodies are found in the foundation area of the structure—in manufactured homes, this will be under the I-beams that supported the home. The intact portions and all the fragments of bone are deposited downward with some resulting additional breakage as well as some displacement as this process is also uneven.

10.3 SELF-SUSTAINED BURN DAMAGE

A common misconception is that the damage to the body is equivalent to the fuel load available in the area surrounding the body. This assumption ignores the fact that the body itself provides an active fuel source that can sustain fire long after the surrounding fuels are consumed (DeHaan et al., 1999; DeHaan & Nurbakhsh, 2001; Hejna et al., 2019). Experimental data show that bodies do not elevate deep internal temperature significantly in structural fires for 60 minutes, indicating that this fuel load is not directly responsible for the full destruction of the remains.

The contribution of the victim's body comes from subcutaneous and deep fats and fuels the fire as it is rendered (DeHaan, 2012). The body will begin to burn using the body fats as an additional fuel source from rendered subcutaneous fat that turns to liquefied grease. The rendering process of subcutaneous fat begins early during the fire from exposure through skin splits that release liquefied grease. As the body is penetrated by heat damage, organ fat and marrow also provide additional fuel sources. Rendered fat is absorbed into the surrounding materials (clothing/fabrics, carpet, wood, carbonized tissues) where it has available wicking materials for sustaining the fire. This liquified grease typically pools around the torso and upper thigh areas. However, where the fats accumulate depends on the substrate materials and topography. Some substrates will allow for absorption of fats, while other substrates are less porous and allow for pooling, such as on wood or concrete floor. The transition from fat as a supplemental fuel to the primary fuel begins several minutes into the fire and can last long after the surrounding fire has self-extinguished. Flames several feet to inches high are visible for many hours and the rendering process continues until suppression or natural self-extinguishment.

In a wildfire situation, most fires are not suppressed. Therefore, bodies will continue to burn for hours or even days smoldering in fire debris, long after the fire has passed and the structure or vehicle has been consumed. It is this self-sustained burn that is responsible for the more advanced destruction of the body in the absence of surrounding combustibles.

Eventually, the flames will have consumed most of the soft tissue and transformed the adjacent bone to calcined skeletal remains. Only organs with a considerable density and high moisture content tend to survive this process. The most typical findings are remnants of the heart and liver, both of which can be useful for the extraction of usable DNA (see Chapter 15).

The result that is common in structural and vehicles in wildfires is that the "body" now consists of something along a spectrum beginning with an articulated charred spine from the base of the skull to the pelvis, possibly with proximal (upper) portions of the thigh bone to only calcined bone fragments in some rough approximation of anatomical order. This would be classified as stage 5–6 (Pope et al., n.d.) or stage 5 (Glassman & Crow, 1996). This is the scenario for most of the search and rescue/recovery operations—highly fragmented and heavily damaged bones.

10.4 TYPICAL APPEARANCE OF WILDFIRE BODIES

To return to the points at the beginning of this section, how will bodies appear in the aftermath of a wildfire. For people caught in the open, where there is little surrounding fuel, the burning will be minimal. Hair will typically be singed, and the skin may appear discolored and slightly shrunken. If there is some light fuel around, there may also be blisters. Radiant heat from nearby structures can also cause these changes even if the flames do not directly contact the body. Such remains are usually quickly recognizable and can be retrieved intact.

Victims in vehicles tend to be largely skeletonized but the skulls may be mainly intact. This effect is due to the positioning of the body within the car seats. During the height of the fire, the head is uppermost and within the most intense heat zones, producing significant changes. However, fuel loads within a vehicle are quickly consumed. By the time the vehicle has largely self-extinguished, the head remains well above the area where body fats are pooling and the remaining soft tissue is being consumed.

While there is considerable calcined bone on the skull, it often remains intact in vehicle fires without fire suppression. The rest of the body will also show recognizable skeletal elements. Rendered fats will often pool in the car seat, but some of that pooling may dissipate as the seat itself is consumed. The metal infrastructure of the seat holds the individual above the rendered fat that pools in the floorboard. What may be confusing in wildfire recovery is that there may be multiple victims, and if there was a crash involved, they may have been dislodged from the seat. Because of skull preservation, an estimate of the number of individuals can be made but may need to be adjusted if there are also infants and young children present, where preservation is lessened. However, the presence of human remains in a burned vehicle is usually very obvious. As noted earlier, the base of the skull, spine, and pelvic areas often provide a good means for estimating the minimum number of individuals.

Victims in structures are most heavily damaged because of the effects of the fire, the consequences of the self-sustained burning process, and the damage produced by the collapsing structure. The body may appear as a blackened spine with expansions at the base of the skull, the midsection where the remaining internal organs sit, and at the pelvic area (stage 5–6 in Pope et al., 2022). In the area surrounding the torso, there will be the fragmented remains of other body parts—portions that may be critical for determining the number of individuals present. In multistory structures, more complete cremation is often seen due to the greater fuel load and possible collapse of more than one level of building.

10.5 BODY LOCATION IN STRUCTURES AND PROBLEMATIC SEARCH TECHNIQUES

Problematic search approaches cause further damage to the remains (see Chapter 12). One approach that has been practiced in fire scene search processes is to "shuffle" through the interior of the house or structure until the body is "uncovered." This is not an effective tactic given the extreme level of destruction of the body and the fragility of the remains. However, as the recommended search protocols in this volume advocate, a visual search of the surface is often very effective. The reason that the bodies may be seen from a visual inspection of the debris surface is linked again to the process of burning.

The body is only partially consumed by the surrounding fuel loads in the actual fire of the structure or vehicle. By the time those fuels are consumed and the structural fire has self-extinguished, the remains usually consist of a sizable torso with portions of the limbs and significant soft tissue on the torso, shoulders, and hips. Debris that has fallen on the body often include burned wooden beams and other partially burned material. Throughout the after-fire period, this charcoal and other matter will be reduced to ash only. In the meantime, the body, over which these materials lay, is still burning slowly. The mass of the body tissue forms an elevated surface and the ash falls to the side, leaving the body on the surface. Hence, the body, or what remains of it, is often located on or very close to the surface.

The exception to this situation is when there is non-combustible roofing material. In wildfire areas, metal roofing, whether on a normal structure or a mobile home, will remain although buckled and warped by the heat. Once removed, the remains are often close to the surface of the remaining structure. More difficult is when there is a tile or slate roof that will collapse as the supporting beams are burned through. The result can be a considerable thickness of roofing material over now largely crushed human remains.

It is also important to remember that the effects of burning will be blended with the decomposition process in wildfire situations since many remains will not be collected quickly. While charring seems to inhibit some decomposition, heat damage and the release of bodily fluids will attract insects quickly, accelerating decomposition in some areas of exposed soft tissue (Avila & Goff, 1998; Gruenthal et al., 2012). In some cases, body location can be aided by observation of increased insect activity in the area of burned remains (McIntosh et al., 2017).

10.6 DIFFERENTIATING WILDFIRE DAMAGE FROM PRE-EXISTING CREMATIONS STORED IN THE HOME

In the extreme, the body will simply be portions of calcined bone, similar to what is produced by a crematorium (Bohnert et al., 1998) before the normal pulverization process that is done to produce the "ash" normally associated with cremation. Bone morphology will be evident on some portions, but there will be large quantities of fragmented long bones and ribs that cannot be identified as to exact location. It is the presence of these larger fragments that allow separation of recent victims from the professionally cremated remains that people often retain in their homes. The latter has been extensively pulverized after cremation to produce a fine-grained material (Warren & Maples, 1997; Warren & Schultz 2002).

10.7 CONCLUSION

There are many assumptions as to what to expect when searching for bodies after a devastating fire. Often people think there will be a charred corpse or that the body has been completely reduced to ash. Instead, the burning process for human bodies is a lengthy and complex process involving both external sources of fuel and consumption of the internal fuels long often long after external sources are depleted.

Understanding how bodies burn allows for refinement of the search process and may help reduce the number of false-positive finds. When the deployment of search personnel requires both effectiveness and efficiency, adjusting expectations will allow for a quick review of areas, using greater critical separation during the search, where bodies should be obvious and a more careful assessment of areas where burning is more complete.

REFERENCES

Adelson, L. (1954). Role of the pathologist in arson investigation. *Journal of Criminal Law, Criminology and Police Science*, *45*, 760–768.

Avila, F. W., & Goff, M. L. (1998). Arthropod succession patterns onto burnt carrion in two contrasting habitats in the Hawaiian Islands. *Journal of Forensic Sciences*, *43*(3), 581–586.

Bernitz, H., van Staden, P., Cronjé, C., & Sutherland, R. (2014). Tongue protrusion as an indicator of vital burning. *International Journal of Legal Medicine*, *128*, 309–312.

Bohnert, M., & Hejna, P. (2016). Tongue protrusion in burned bodies. *International Journal of Legal Medicine*, *130*, 1253–1255.

Bohnert, M., Rost, T., Faller-Marquardt, M., Ropohl, D., & Pollak, S. (1997). Fractures of the base of the skull in charred bodies—post-mortem heat injuries or signs of mechanical traumatization. *Forensic Science International*, *87*, 55–62.

Bohnert, M., Rost, T., & Pollak, S. (1998). The degree of destruction of human bodies in relation to the duration of the fire. *Forensic Science International*, *95*, 11–21.

Buikstra, J. E., & Swegle, M. (1989). Bone modification due to burning: Experimental evidence. In R. Bonnischsen & M. H. Sorg (Eds.), *Bone modification*. Orono, ME: Center for the Study of the First Americans.

Campbell, M. N., Fairgrieve, S. I., & Farigrieve, S. I. (2011). Differentiation of traumatic and heat-induced dental tissue fractures via SEM analysis. *Journal of Forensic Sciences*, *56*(3), 715–719. https://doi.org/10.1111/j.1556-4029.2010.01693.x

DeHaan, J. D. (2012). Sustained combustion of bodies: Some observations. *Journal of Forensic Sciences*, *57*(6), 1578–1584.

DeHaan, J. D., Campbell, S. J., & Nurbakhsh, S. (1999). Combustion of animal fat and its implications for the consumption of human bodies in fires. *Science and Justice*, *39*(1), 27–38.

DeHaan, J. D., & Nurbakhsh, S. (2001). Sustained combustion of an animal carcass and its implications for the consumption of human bodies in fires. *Journal of Forensic Sciences*, *46*(5), 1076–1081.

Delattre, V. F. (2000). Burned beyond recognition: Systematic approach to the dental identification of charred human remains. *Journal of Forensic Sciences*, *45*(3), 589–596.

Federchook, T., Pokines, J., Crowley, K., & Grgicak, C. (2018). Recovery of DNA from teeth exposed to variable temperatures. *Forensic Anthropology*, *2*(3), 143–151.

Glassman, D. M., & Crow, R. M. (1996). Standardization model for describing the extent of burn injury to human remains. *Journal of Forensic Sciences*, *41*(1), 152–154.

Gruenthal, A., Moffatt, C., & Simmons, T. (2012). Differential decomposition patterns in charred versus un-charred remains. *Journal of Forensic Sciences*, *57*(1), 12–18.

Heglar, R. (1984). Burned remains. In R. A. Rathbun & J. E. Buikstra (Eds.), *Human identification: Case studies in forensic anthropology* (pp. 148–158). Springfield, IL: CC Thomas.

Hejna, P., Bohnert, M., & Janík, M. (2019). Unique thermal destruction of the body following suicidal burning. *Forensic Science, Medicine, and Pathology*, *15*(2), 262–266. https://doi.org/10.1007/s12024-018-0076-6

Herrmann, N. P., & Bennett, J. L. (1999). The differentiation of traumatic and heat-related fractures in burned bone. *Journal of Forensic Sciences*, *44*(3), 461–469.

Madea, B., & Doberentz, E. (2015). Protrusion of the tongue in burned bodies as a vital sign? Letter to the editor concerning the paper "Tongue protrusion as an indicator of vital burning "by Bernitz et al. *International Journal of Legal Medicine*, *129*, 313–314.

Mayne Correia, P. (1997). Fire modification of bone: A review of the literature. In W. Haglund & M. Sorg (Eds.), *Forensic taphonomy: The postmortem fate of human remains* (pp. 275–293). Boca Raton, FL: CRC Press.

McIntosh, C., Dadour, I., & Voss, S. (2017). A comparison of carcass decomposition and associated insect succession onto burnt and unburnt pig carcasses. *International Journal of Legal Medicine*, *131*, 835–845.

Moritz, A. (1949). Death due to conflagration. *NEJM*, *240*, 901–902.

Pope, E., Juarez, C., & Galloway, A. (2022). Refined classification system for thermally damaged human remains by body segment. *Forensic Anthropology*, *5*(1), 57–72.

Pope, E. J. (2007). *The effects of fire on human remains: Characteristics of taphonomy and trauma*. Fayetteville, AR: University of Arkansas Press.

Pope, E. J., Smith, O. C., & Huff, T. G. (2004). Exploding skulls and other myths about how the human body burns. *Fire and Arson Investigator*, (4), 23–28.

Shipman, P., Foster, G., & Schoeninger, M. (1984). Burnt bones and teeth: An experimental study of color, morphology, crystal structure and shrinkage. *Journal of Archaeological Science*, *11*, 307–325.

Symes, S., L'Abbe, E., Pokines, J., Yuzwa, T., Messer, D., Stromquist, A., & Keough, N. (2014). Thermal alteration to bone. In J. Pokines & S. Symes (Eds.), *Manual of forensic taphonomy* (pp. 367–402). Boca Raton, FL: CRC Press.

Thompson, T. J. U. (2005). Heat-induced dimensional changes in bone and their consequences for forensic anthropology. *Journal of Forensic Sciences*, *50*(5), 1008–1015. Retrieved from www.ncbi.nlm.nih.gov/pubmed/16225204

Walker, P., Miller, K., & Richman, R. (2008). Time, temperature, and oxygen availability: An experimental study of the effects of environmental conditions on the colour and organic content of cremated bone. In C. Schmidt & S. Symes (Eds.), *The analysis of burned human remains* (pp. 129–135). Amsterdam: Elsevier Academic Press.

Warren, M. W., & Maples, W. R. (1997). The anthropometry of contemporary commercial cremation. *Journal of Forensic Sciences*, *42*(3), 417–423.

Warren, M. W., & Schultz, J. J. (2002). Post-cremation taphonomy and artifact preservation. *Journal of Forensic Sciences*, *47*(3), 656–659.

CHAPTER 11

Deployment Strategies for SAR/USAR Teams

Kyle Wilson, David Bibby, Carla Halford, and Alison Galloway

11.1 INTRODUCTION

In the aftermath of a wildfire, search and rescue (SAR) teams often form the core of the personnel deployed in search and recovery efforts. However, the traditional methodologies utilized in the search for a missing person in the wilderness setting must be adapted to this radically different environment. Understanding the approaches needed, how to maximize the already honed skills of the searchers, and the hazards and obstacles

FIGURE 11.1 SAR teams working in smoke of the Camp Fire 2018.

Source: A. Galloway

DOI: 10.4324/9781003168010-14

they will face is essential in pre-fire training, in the on-the-ground training and the fire scene, and in preparations.

SAR typically focuses on locating and extracting live, even possibly responsive, people who are lost and/or injured. Training emphasizes search tactics, navigation skills, survival training, emergency medicine, and transportation of victims. Conversely, in wildfires, the victims are expected to be deceased with bodies camouflaged by charring or cremation and possibly covered by debris from the structure in which they burned. "Rescue" is no longer relevant in most cases, but there is still urgency to recover victims and alleviate the uncertainty for their families and friends, to allow repopulation of the area, often working in inclement weather that could adversely impact the ability to collect the remains safely and completely.

In megafires such as the 2018 Camp Fire, the potential number of victims may initially be hundreds to thousands, many with only vague information on where they were last known to be. SAR teams perform the unenviable but essential task of locating the remains and also clearing areas where remains are not present (Figure 11.1). In this chapter, we examine how the roles of SAR changes in the wildfire context; specifically, changes to field preparation, deployment strategies, consideration of environmental hazards, and on-the-ground and post-recovery support.

11.2 TYPES OF SEARCH AND RESCUE TEAMS

Contemporary terrestrial SAR practices are derived from the maritime context in which a person or vessel lost at sea could best be located. This is usually seen as a closed system in that the area in which the person or vessel is located is known and the nature of the victim or victims is also known. For example, a fishing vessel may have last been seen off a specific section of coast or a pilot was known to bail out at a certain point. The search grid can be calculated based on how much area is to be searched, the size of the individual or object to be found, and how much of the water surface can be seen from the search vessel or aircraft. The pattern of search calculates how many passes and how far apart the passes should be to achieve a high likelihood of successful detection.

Some of this theoretical framework has been translated to wilderness search and rescue (SAR) and urban search and rescue (USAR), both of which involve primarily terrestrial work. However, often these searches are considered "open" because the victim or object sought may not be present in the search area. While they may have last been reported in a specific area, it is possible that they have since extracted themselves from that location and may now be in the "rest of the world." They may never have been in the area in the first place, may still be lost but in another location, or may even join in search efforts, not realizing that they are the object of the search.

In California, wilderness SAR falls under law enforcement, usually through the county sheriff's offices. Urban SAR falls under the fire branch of the emergency response function framework. Wilderness SAR is designed for the location and retrieval of victims lost in urban, rural, or wildland settings. USAR is designed to confront a wide variety of hazardous situations, such as collapsed buildings or infrastructure, and is managed under the city or county fire departments. Because USAR groups are only formed where there is sufficient need, such as large urban areas prone to earthquakes, tsunamis, or other disasters, such teams are fewer in number than wilderness SAR teams. California currently has SAR teams in all counties. In addition, eight of the

28 national USAR teams are located in California, supported by either city or county fire departments.

Different jurisdictions must anticipate what training will be needed to meet the demands of their area. Specialized teams (Table 11.1) are frequently formed to develop the skills for the terrain in which they operate. For example, an alpine county where avalanches are a relatively common hazard around ski resorts will likely have an alpine team as well as a canine unit trained to locate buried individuals. Rugged mountainous terrain requires climbing and ropes skills that may be less useful in flatter areas. In addition, teams are also assigned to "types" with type 1 requiring the most extensive training and type 4 needing the least.

Training is an ongoing commitment on the part of the volunteers. Most training is handled within the unit, but advanced or specialized training may be provided

TABLE 11.1 Various Types of SAR Teams in California

Team Type	Team Functions
Alpine	Teams trained to work at over 7,000-feet elevation with intense cold and highly variable terrain requiring climbing techniques
Canine	Teams of specially trained dogs with their handlers
Area/air scent	Searches for and detects subjects in wilderness or open spaces
Avalanche	Searches for and detects subjects buried under snow/ice
Cadaver (HRD)	Searches for and detects decomposing human remains
Water	Searches for and detects human remains under water
Disaster	Searches for and detects inaccessible subjects
Trailing	Dogs that locate and follow a human scent trail
Fixed-wing aircraft	Pilots trained to work over varying complexity of terrain from high mountains to urban areas
Ground searcher	Teams trained for searches in varying ruggedness of terrain (Ground search skills are basic for all SAR teams.)
Incident support team	Teams ready for rapid and prolonged deployment to support SAR teams with search management and coordination
Mounted	Teams whose horses can traverse a range of terrains and whose riders possess "ground search" training
Off-highway vehicle (OHV)	Teams trained in the use of four-wheel drive or off-road vehicles
Swift water and flood	Teams trained for rescues in moving water and flooded environments
Technical rope rescue	Teams used to conduct carry-outs or rescues in steep terrain and other environmental challenges
Tracking	Teams trained to follow human tracks in wilderness conditions
Underground	Teams trained to work in man-made and natural underground situations
Underwater	Dive teams working in a range of conditions
SAR/USAR teams	Law enforcement supported teams

Source: California Office of Emergency Services (2023)

by third-party organizations, such as Mountain Rescue Association and National Association for Search and Rescue (NASAR). Statewide training is also utilized.

County SAR teams are all-volunteer groups, supported by the county sheriff's office staff. Oversight and liaison duties are borne by one or more officers from the department. Sheriff offices oversee training and certification, recruiting and vetting volunteers, providing equipment support (level varies), and liability coverage. Team members are also issued a standardized uniform so that they are clearly identifiable and visible in the field. The majority use high visibility orange shirts.

In larger jurisdictions, where there are larger teams and specialized units, SAR is often quasi-independent with sheriff's officers acting as liaison between SAR and the administration. In smaller counties, the sheriff's office often plays a larger role in the organization and maintenance of SAR, considered collateral duty. Some will also have separate non-profit status to allow for additional fund-raising for specialized equipment.

In either case, the quality of the leadership on both the sheriff's and SAR sides is important. Leadership is not only responsible for organizing training and callouts but also keeping team visibility high in the community—leading to a continued pattern of recruitment.

11.3 FUNDAMENTALS OF SAR STRATEGY

All SAR searches attempt to maximize the probability of detection, or POD (Perkins 2013, NASAR 2019). This term refers to the probability that the victim, in the case of a wildfire that means a decedent, will be found within the search area. In developing the strategy for deploying the teams in the field, the search manager needs to understand whether the POD is low, medium, or high. The level will depend on a number of factors including the speed of the search, the duration of the search, the number of searchers available, the size of the area to be searched, the spacing between searchers (critical separation), and the size of the object or person that is the subject of the search.

The other factor that determines success of a search is the probability that the victim is in the area. As noted earlier, terrestrial searches are often open searches because it is not known if the person is even in the area. This factor—is the person within the search area or in the "rest of the world"—is known as probability of area (POA).

The probability of success (POS) is, therefore, the product of POD and POA. When the probability that the person is in the area is high, but the difficulty of the terrain is extreme, the probability of detection will be diminished, lowering the probability of success. When all factors for successful detection are high, but the probability that the person is within the area is low, it is highly possible that no amount of effort will be successful.

Search strategies depend not only on the terrain and number of team members but how they are deployed. Ideally, teams work where each member can see the area between themselves and adjacent team members. For smaller objects, or remains that may be hard to detect, spacing must be closer while objects that are more visible allow for wider spacing between team members. This determination of spacing is therefore essential and will vary by situation. One method to determine this distance is known as the Northumbrian rain dance, after the techniques developed in the Lockerbie aircraft bombing. Team members move away from an object of the approximate size of the search object, then turn and walk back until it becomes visible. The average distance from the members to the object determines the visual horizon and the "critical separation" for the actual search (Perkins 2003, 2008a, 2008b). Once deployed to the search areas, team members space themselves at this critical separation distance and move in line across the search trajectory. However, critical separation has been shown to vary considerably, even in terrain that looks relatively homogeneous (Perkins 2018). Furthermore, the connection between the range at which objects can be detected and the effective sweep width or spacing of searchers has not been fully evaluated (Cooper et al. 2003, Russo 2021).

11.4 SEARCH AND RECOVERY TRAINING AND WILDFIRE TRAINING

Sheriff's personnel assigned to SAR usually receive a week-long direction and control course that covers search management, the resources needed, and the availability of needed resources depending on the location and timing of the search. This training will also include a tabletop map exercise and a mock search. Essentially, it is a crash course in SAR operations. Usually this is taken during the first year of assignment to SAR although it is not a requirement. Enrollment often depends on availability for both space in the course and release from normal duties. In addition, advanced direction and control courses are beginning to be offered and these focus on the software commonly used in search management and on the information that is being derived from data collection using that software. The mapping programs with the overlain GPS data on search patterns and where people or objects are found provides data from which to derive more efficient search methods.

There is little direct training for any wildfire interaction although it is likely, given the frequency of wildfires in the West, that this will change. At the present, the training primarily focuses on survival skills for officers who may be trapped within a wildfire. It provides basic information on where to stop, ditching of unnecessary or hazardous gear, and how to shelter. In California, this is offered through Firescope California, a collaborative effort of the California Office of Emergency Services (CalOES) and the state fire marshal.

SAR team members are all, regardless of the specialty, trained in basic ground searches. This preparation involves basic navigation skills, determination of critical separation, utilization of GPS and radio equipment, basic ropes to secure and transport potential victims, and first aid. These skills are kept fresh by monthly training meetings along with a monthly field training. This training focuses on the location and rescue of live victims along with collection of evidence, another common use of SAR teams.

Most SAR teams, until recently, did not receive specialized training in wildfire searches. Unfortunately, this lack leaves teams unsure of what to expect. Since the dramatic increase in the incidence of wildfires in the West, SAR is also adjusting their training to include information on how human bodies burn in order to know what level of damage to expect during recovery operations. These sessions also include information on common structural elements that will appear "bone-like" after a fire, such as drywall, insulation, and ceramics. The issue of distinguishing human and nonhuman may also be addressed, although referral to the attending anthropologist is recommended since size alone will not be sufficient to identify a pet.

Training also includes how to adjust the search patterns for wildfire situations. Rather than a grid search with critical separation, structures in fire zones need to be searched from the perimeter. Adjustments must be made for larger structures where the interior may not be visible from the perimeter due to intervening walls or simple distance.

Canines and their handlers go through a lengthy process to produce a human remains detection (HRD); these canines are also known as cadaver dogs (CARDA 2023, SWGDOG 2023). Dogs are usually one of the working breeds, although that is not a requirement, but the dog must show the drive and focus needed for SAR work. Training normally begins with a puppy or young dog (less than two years old) and takes about two years to complete. Basic training includes socialization and obedience but also includes agility training to overcome the obstacles normally encountered in a search. Search training itself is very rigorous, usually two to three days (including some nights) per week until the team is ready to pass the certification test. The test involves finding persons or objects within a relatively large area based solely on the dog's ability to locate the search object.

HRD dogs are trained with material with the scent of human remains, either donated body segments, burned tissue, or material soaked in decomposition fluids. There is not widely available exposure to burned remains although HRD dogs seem to quickly alert to burned remains based on their training with unburned material. They tend to focus on the largest and least burned segments, usually the pelvic area.

In addition to the training of the dog, the training of the handler is equally important and extends beyond their ability to read the alerts of their dog. All handlers must be skilled in basic ground search techniques, search navigation and documentation, and communication. They must be capable of providing first aid for their canines, understand how to handle biohazardous material, and understand crime scene protocols and incident command.

In Northern California, Chico State Anthropologists and CalOES have developed a regional training program that will provide wildfire response training to SAR groups and dog handlers six times per year. The training provides lecture-based and on-the-ground training in search protocols and exposure to burned human bone to assist with bone recognition in the field. A similar program of field tests, including a burned scenario, is provided in San Luis Obispo County.

There is also a large financial investment in this volunteer activity. Handlers must buy uniforms and search equipment for themselves and their canines, transport and house their dogs during deployment, and spend numerous hours in training, even after certification. The minimum maintenance training is 16 hours per month. In addition, the team must maintain records of their training and deployment.

11.5 MUTUAL AID FOR SAR/USAR IN THE CASE OF WILDFIRE

In the case of a major disaster, such as a wildfire, the affected jurisdiction will request mutual aid through the Office of Emergency Services, usually starting with neighboring areas unless the need is for specialized personnel and/or equipment. In California, that agency is CalOES. Wildfire resource requests usually entail additional fire personnel and engines, as well as supplemental law enforcement. Law enforcement typically manage roadblocks and patrols, including providing backfill for unaffected areas as local agencies focus on those within the fire zone, and, as imminent danger has diminished, SAR/USAR teams.

SAR teams maintain rosters of certified members, usually online, and will issue a call via email or text for activation when mutual aid is requested. The call to members will specify what type of personnel are needed ("ground pounders," HRD dog teams, drone operators, etc.), the probable length of deployment, and the equipment needed.

Teams normally will travel with at least their 24-to-72-hour backpacks, so multiple days can be handled. Whereas in normal operations, members often have to accommodate work hours, employers are often more lenient during major disasters.

The SAR management will also review the spectrum of those being deployed to ensure there are experienced searchers among the group and that search management is also in place. Because of the continuous training, there is usually considerable trust and cooperation between team members.

The need for mutual aid for a megafire does not negate the incidence of local emergencies. Larger agencies that may have a number of ongoing needs for SAR teams may need to hold some teams in reserve. Smaller agencies usually deploy all available members and find other ways to accommodate any need that arises during the time.

Because mutual aid is going to be ultimately managed by the requesting agencies, it is important that the contributing search teams coordinate with that incident command center. Trying to establish a separate command center for each team will be counterproductive. The solution is to leave a team member or law enforcement team liaison at the incident command post once the teams arrive. The liaison provides the command with a list of resources being contributed and the names of the personnel involved for accountability. The incident command will then inform the liaison where the SAR teams should stage and what areas and structures need to be searched. This information will determine whether grid searches or perimeter searches are needed. The command will also provide the communication lines (e.g., radio frequencies) and what should be done if human remains, or suspected human remains, are found. Typically, information on a find will be relayed back to the command post, and an anthropologist will be dispatched to verify the material. If the remains are clearly human, coroner/anthropology teams will handle the collection.

Assignments for SAR search sectors are provided by search management to the team leaders. Sectors are typically determined using identifiable boundaries, such as roads, waterways, or ridgelines. Search management will determine what resources will be used and the sequence in which they will enter the sector. For example, it may be prudent to allow the dog teams to conduct an initial search of the area, with ground teams to follow afterward. Team leaders will determine the best approach their team will take in a specific area. Partially collapsed structures or those with large metal roofs may need outside services to remove hazardous or concealing material. It is also important to coordinate between ground search and HRD dog teams as to the sequence of searching.

11.6 SEARCH AND RESCUE TEAM DEPLOYMENT IN WILDFIRES

The search strategy in wildfires will vary by the type of terrain and the structure and vehicle distribution. SAR teams are used to working in a variety of wilderness settings, but the fire zone is often one that they have not previously experienced. Surface vegetation, such as grasses and brush, is often absent, yielding increased visibility, but the uniform blackening of almost everything makes differentiating objects extremely difficult even in open spaces.

Most searches begin with a known subject or object and a "last known place." However, in massive fires such as the Camp Fire, the initial search was faced with an open population in which there were well over a thousand reports of people missing and the last known place was often vague. As a consequence, in the Camp Fire all structures and vehicles were searched. In subsequent fires such as the North Complex

Fire and the Almeda Fire in Oregon, law enforcement moved quickly and effectively to narrow the search parameters to those most likely to have perished. It is also possible that those missing have chosen this time to disappear to the "rest of the world" and may no longer be in the area, despite not having contacted family and friends.

Research on successful searches for missing persons has resulted in a body of knowledge on "lost person behavior" (Koester 2008). There is some parallel information on human behavior in fires (see Chapter 9), although it often focuses on behavior in large structures to improve escape exiting. In wildfires, people can be expected to flee in vehicles if possible, but these may be overtaken by the flames. They may flee on foot, trying to outrun the fire front.

Sectors are usually established based on the instructions from the incident command post (Figure 11.2). Typically, searchers will be sent to a specific area in which the suspected missing person was last known to be. At this location, they will need to

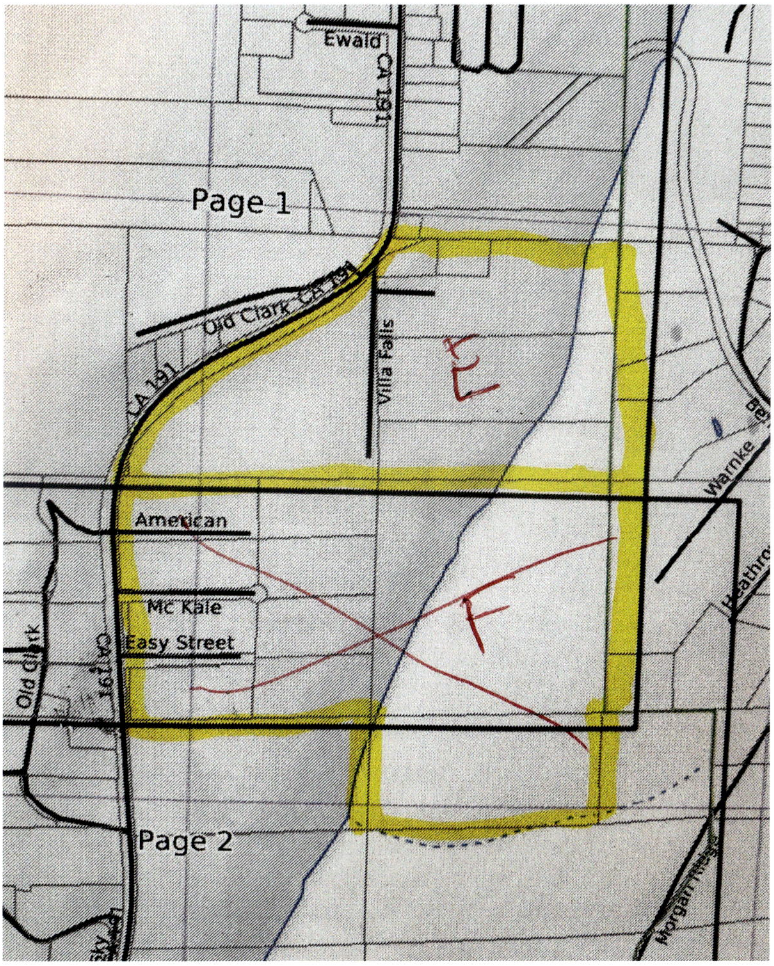

FIGURE 11.2 Map distributed to SAR teams to search specific areas. "X" indicates that the segment has been searched and cleared.

Source: K. Wilson

FIGURE 11.3 Amador County SAR team searching the structure from the periphery.

Source: K. Wilson

search all the structures within the vicinity (Figure 11.3). While the residence may be the most likely location of human remains, people have also been found in outbuildings, vehicles, or even open space. One difficulty with fire zones is that street addresses are largely absent, so even finding the assigned location can be difficult. Fortunately, programs such as SARTopo and GIS allow searchers to locate buildings and mark those that have been searched and cleared.

The initial searches often focus on vehicles and structures. Vehicles are relatively easy to search as adult human remains in such fires are skeletonized but identifiable. However, determining the number of victims can be more difficult as there may be children and pets traveling with the vehicle, and in many cases elements from multiples individuals are commingled. It is also possible that victims may have fled the cars and have perished in the immediate area or be located underneath the car. Victims in open areas tend to be considerably less burned than those inside or underneath a car.

Structural searches require more consideration, based upon the nature of the structure to be searched (Figure 11.4). Normal detached structures, such as single-family homes, typically present as remaining foundation walls, with remnants of bed, sofa, and recliner springs visible, along with kitchen appliances, and chimneys allowing some orientation as to room usage. Such dwellings should be searched from the periphery by ground search teams. HRD teams may be helpful, especially when the home is large or where there are obstructions such as intact walls, overlapping stucco or tile, roofing material, or collapsed chimneys. For example, in one recent fire, dogs alerted to a vent in a larger obstructing wall, telling searchers that there were human remains within the structure that could not be seen by searchers.

FIGURE 11.4 Typical single-family residences after the wildfire: (a) single-story home with foundation and stucco walls; (b) mobile home.

Source: K. Wilson

The other common type of structure in wildfire areas is mobile homes and manufactured homes. After the fire, these present as large I-beams perched on top of fire-cracked cinder blocks. Many have metal roofs that collapsed on top of the wreckage, obscuring the underlying material. In these cases, coordination of the approach is more complex. HRD dog teams may be able to work best with the captured scents under the roof if it is structurally sound enough for the dog to enter safely. Otherwise, removal of the roof will need to occur before the ground search can be conducted from the periphery. Roof removal may be accomplished manually, but often small excavators will be used to lift and place the material to one side. Other material should be left in place.

Use of all-terrain vehicles (ATV) is often relatively limited during the immediate aftermath of a wildfire in terms of actual searches. However, such vehicles may be useful to transport search teams to their assigned areas. Normal road access may be limited by fallen trees and powerlines, and the ATV may be a means of circumventing these obstacles. In open areas, the danger of collapsing root systems and septic systems makes ATV use problematic.

Some SAR teams are equipped with drones to search open areas or areas that are too hazardous for ground searchers to cover. Drone use is limited by several factors in wildfires. Foremost is that drone use will depend on whether air support is still being used in wildfire containment and suppression efforts. If that is the case, then no drones can be used. The second limitation is the visibility in the residual smoke and the ability to identify an object seen as a victim in the overall blackened surface. Drones may prove useful in identifying outlying structures and assessing the structural damage that will need to be cleared prior to SAR search teams gaining access.

Searchers may also be the first to spot other needs during their work. Abandoned pets and livestock are a common problem and information on live animals in need should be forwarded to the command post. If small animals can be easily contained for subsequent rescue, that is appreciated by the animal services and the families. Deceased animals may be noted, but the primary focus of the initial search is on human remains.

Those involved in the wildfire recovery process will face hazards even after the fire front has passed and remaining fires are largely extinguished. SAR members should be advised of and should follow proper safety precautions and have the requisite equipment (see the following section titled "SAR Team Support"). SAR members experience levels vary, all members must work together to ensure everyone's safety.

Wildfire hazards for SAR members are numerous. In most cases, the fire front has moved past the search area and fire containment is focused ahead of the remaining fire. Left behind is a landscape that is almost entirely charred, with a mixture of burned and still intact structures. It is also important to remember that this landscape is often nestled beneath a thick blanket of smoke that can obliterate almost all daylight. In addition to a smoldering or new fire, dangers can be both easily observed or invisible, requiring SAR teams to be extremely cautious and constantly evaluating the situation.

With the power outages due to the loss of power lines, many people in the post-fire area turn to the use of alternative power sources such as gas-powered generators. Heavy equipment may also be in use in the recovery operation. Both of these processes can produce deadly levels of carbon monoxide. Carbon monoxide is an odorless, colorless gas that can cause sudden illness and death if inhaled. SAR teams, therefore, need to be aware not only of their own exposure but also note if others in the area are being lax in their safety measures.

Wildfires deposit ash on outdoor surfaces which can cause irritation of the skin, nose, and throat. Ash and dust, especially from burned buildings, may contain toxic and cancer-causing chemicals as not only have wooden components of the house burned but also furnishings, insulation, wiring, appliances, plastics, and many other unknown materials. In rural areas, the presence of drug manufacturing and agricultural facilities is also a known hazard, with a heavy chemical presence.

Often confined spaces need to be searched for remains. A confined space is characterized by limited entry or exit, air flow is limited, and the space is not intended to be occupied for extended periods of time. Examples of a confined space include pipes, pits, septic tanks, storage tanks, wells, fire shelters, and basements. Confined spaces may contain toxic gases, a lack of oxygen or explosive conditions, all making them potentially deadly areas to work in.

Extremes of heat and cold are common in wildfire areas. Because such fires often occur during the hot, dry season, those arriving at the fire scene are often expecting a continuation of this weather. However, the extreme smoke will create an environment where temperatures are considerably lower than normal. At the same time, there will be hot zones where fires linger in fallen trees, tree stumps, and deeper layers of collapsed structures. The work itself can be rigorous, so body heat will accumulate under the necessary personal protective equipment that must be worn.

There are many physical hazards, such as broken glass, electrical wires, nails, wood, metal, plastics, and other solid objects found in the area of fire damage. These hazards can cause puncture wounds, cuts, and other injuries. Because of the overall charred appearance, these hazards are often not easily seen.

Unstable fire-damaged structures are a common occurrence. These hazards include partially burned flooring, stairways, railings, balconies, roofing, fireplace chimneys, walkways, roadways, and bridges, all which may have structural damage and can be dangerous. Stucco and tiled walls often collapse as they become detached from the supporting structure (Figure 11.5). This collapse can mask other dangers so should be approached cautiously.

After a fire, many trees will be weakened from burning around the base of the trunk. The tree can fall over or blow down without warning. SAR members should be on the lookout for ground hot spots, a possible indication of a burning root system or smoldering stumps and vegetation. Portable temperature monitors can be helpful

FIGURE 11.5 Stucco walls standing around the perimeter of a home that can pose a hazard for searchers.

Source: Chico State University

FIGURE 11.6 Downed power lines and broken power poles are a common post-fire hazard.

Source: A. Galloway and K. Wilson

in identifying such issues and dispatch should be informed so the fire personnel can complete the suppression.

Downed or damaged electrical lines are widespread in the post-fire zone (Figure 11.6). These lines frequently obstruct roads but also will lie in the areas of burned residence that will need to be searched. For obvious reasons, never assume the power lines are de-energized. The incident command post may have further information on whether these are active or not, but caution is wise regardless.

Most rural communities rely on propane as at least one source of power. Many homes will have a propane tank in the range of 125 to 2,000 gallons, depending on their reliance on the fuel for heating or for emergency power. In addition, there may be smaller barbeque-type tanks for specialized usages. These tanks will explode from the heat sending shrapnel flying in the area. The sound of propane tanks exploding can be heard clearly in many videos from the Camp Fire. If searchers smell gas, notice a leaking tank, or see fire in the area of a tank, it should be immediately reported to the command post.

Post-fire SAR includes inspecting damage, clearing debris to expose underlying areas, and securing areas that may be potentially hazardous. Slips, trips, and falls are almost inevitable during this process, but SAR teams can work to minimize the danger by clearing paths into affected areas. This will allow entry without stepping on or over hazardous material. Obviously, areas to be cleared must be thoroughly checked beforehand for human remains. All hazards that cannot be moved should be identified and marked to help others. Ladders used to check over the top of obstructions need to be secured to prevent slippage and must be placed carefully to avoid overhead dangers. A personal fall arrest system, which includes a full body harness, energy absorber, and solid anchor, should be employed when working at height.

Due to the intense heat of the wildfire, underground structures such as culverts and septic tanks may be compromised. Septic systems, in particular, are commonly placed within what will be the search area of a residence. Many such systems have a plastic or even a wooden cover rather than a concrete lid. The covers can partially burn during the fire, leaving a deceptively thin layer covering the pit. In addition, root systems from burned trees will continue burning long after the fire front passes and can also weaken the ground upon which searchers will walk (Figure 11.7). If the search area or walking surface is suspected to be compromised or where there is standing water covering the search area, the ground should be checked or probed before stepping forward.

SAR work in wildfire conditions is tiring, leading to musculoskeletal injuries. SAR members are at risk for developing stress, strain, and injuries to hands, back, knees, and shoulders. This risk may be exacerbated by field camping or other temporary housing conditions.

SAR members should avoid extended work shifts and be allowed sufficient time for rest and recovery. Extended work shifts should not be maintained for more than a few days, especially assignments that require heavy physical or mental awareness. SAR members must be able to recognize the signs and symptoms of potential health effects and signs of fatigue in themselves and others. SAR members will not only be challenged physically but also mentally. The work environment, the hours worked, and witnessing total devastation firsthand can be mentally overwhelming for some.

The California Rescue Dog Association (California Governor's Office of Emergency Services Law Enforcement Branch 2005) provides guidelines for the use of canine search units. Teams are best used where there is visibility is limited by vegetation or other matter, where a hasty search is needed, where the POD is high in smaller areas and in areas inaccessible to human searchers. For the HRD or cadaver dog teams, the times where they are best used are to locate additional remains in areas where a body segment has already been found or to search an area where a body is suspected to be. In the wildfire setting, visibility to ground searchers may be limited

FIGURE 11.7 Large hole left by burned tree trunk and associated root systems.

Source: K. Wilson

by structural debris (Figure 11.8). In some cases, the POD may be high because a missing person has been linked to a location, for example by a 911 call, but searchers have not been able to locate the body. Often these locations are inaccessible to human searchers without significant investment of time to clear entry points and risks damaging the remains.

Certified HRD dog teams utilize the canine's incredible ability to distinguish specific odors associated with human remains along with the dog's training to respond to that odor with an alert indicator. Certification also depends on the handler's ability to recognize the alert from their canine partner and to articulate where the material is located. Similar to the levels of proficiency found in SAR teams, HRD dog teams are categorized by types. Type 1 dogs are used for small areas where there is suspected to be a deceased subject. They will normally work less than five acres in a day's assignment. In contrast, type 3 dogs work in areas where proper foot protection and protective gear is required.

Deployment of the dogs to the field should be coordinated with the command post and utilizing a canine team liaison who can inform the command about the type of dog team best suited for each assignment. For example, if it is suspected that there

FIGURE 11.8 HRD dog team working the interior of a building during the Camp Fire recovery efforts.

Source: C. Halford

may be injured survivors in an unburned area, then area/air scent teams may be needed rather than HRD teams. HRD teams will be focused on areas with suspected deceased individuals.

The liaison can also work with the command post to time the use of the dogs to provide the best conditions for them to be successful. Buildings to be searched should have undergone mop-up operations by the fire service to minimize or eliminate any remaining hot spots. The fire service heavy rescue should also examine the building for stability issues and resolve safety issues prior to SAR entry, including dog teams.

Scent conditions are best when there is moderate wind to widen the scent mark for the dogs, cooler temperatures, higher humidity, and less direct heating from sunlight. Even in a wildfire setting, this means that the dogs will be more effective early in the day rather than in the late afternoon. A good strategy to facilitate this deployment is to pre-position the HRD dog teams so they can begin their work at dawn.

Use of HRD dogs can be useful in separating human and non/human remains in the field. It is part of the certification process to expose the dogs and handlers to non-target odors and distractions. At times after wildfires, large fleshed segments may be located without visible skeletal elements. HRD dogs will typically smell then ignore such remains if they are not human but will concentrate attention to areas where there are human victims, even if the remains have already been collected. This distinction becomes a time-saver for SAR teams.

Commercially cremated remains are a common finding in residential fires as people have retained the ashes of loved ones until they decide on a final resting place. These remains may be a source of false-positive alerts by the dogs in that the dog and handler correctly locate remains, but the task at hand is for recent victims rather than ashes of prior decedents.

As with any search, handlers must also be aware of the hazards to which their canines are exposed. In a wildfire scene, these can be quite different from those seen in normal field searches. Handlers are responsible for the necessary PPE and gear for their canines. This would typically include such items as boots and goggles. Handlers also need to ensure that they have sufficient drinking water and usually have some cooling stations (wading ponds with water) established if the temperatures are warmer. Decontamination facilities should be provided at the end of each shift for the dogs and their handlers. For example, the National Guard provided this service during the Camp Fire.

A review of injuries from the Camp Fire (Gordon and Ho 2020) show that lacerations and abrasions were the most frequently encountered injury to search dogs. About one-third of the dogs also experienced weight loss, lethargy, and fatigue. These dogs, all HRD certified, had been deployed an average of about five and a half days. Handlers also made frequent use of eye flushing to clear the face of accumulated ash. As with human searchers, the sharp objects, such as metal flashing, nails, screws, and broken glass, were hazards for dogs and the use of paw protection may be advisable. Dogs' paws should be checked frequently. At the Camp Fire, such checks allowed dogs to be treated quickly in the field, and most were able to continue working with additional protection.

At some point, a search or searches must be terminated. For many terrains there is information on the probability of detection (POD), although it is acknowledged that this is highly variable (Perkins 2018). Unfortunately, we do not have similar data on the POD for human remains in either open spaces, structures, or vehicles. Typically, vehicles can be examined at close quarters, so the POD is high. Open areas can also be covered effectively with a grid search. It is the structure fires that are more problematic. If there are no visible remains following a perimeter search and the HRD dogs do not alert to the area, the structure can be marked as completed. However, it is possible that if the person or persons remain missing, a more intensive search by an anthropological team may be needed.

The decision to cease SAR operations in the overall fire area is made by the incident command. This is often a balance between the number of residents still missing, the recovery of basic infrastructure, removal of hazards such as partially fallen or seriously weakened trees, and the pressure to allow repopulation of the area.

The additional roles of SAR teams in wildfires and other major disasters can vary. In some cases, they may be used in evacuation but there are some cautions with this assignment. SAR members lack the legal authority to give evacuation orders so if citizens refuse to comply or choose to violate a SAR staffed roadblock, SAR does not have the authority to enforce the order. SAR teams may also be helpful in some evacuations where people need to be extracted from isolated areas either by helicopter or by rope. However, aside from searches, SAR teams are also extremely helpful in providing logistical support, such as running equipment between posts, supporting the shelters, and conducting welfare checks. Overall, they are a valuable and flexible resource that should not be overlooked.

11.7 SAR TEAM SUPPORT

Most SAR teams are not routinely equipped for wildfire deployment in terms of specialized equipment. Some equipment, such as helmets and trekking poles, are readily adapted to the wildfire situation. However, other equipment, such as respirators and temperature monitors, are not normally part of the field kit. For agencies, having stockpiles of such material for both their own personnel as well as the SAR teams becomes a budgetary concern due to both secured storage and renewal requirements for supplies that have expiration dates.

Often, the teams base their supply and expendable stock decisions on the immediate needs of their own jurisdiction. In areas where there are large tracks of forest with little fuel management, the need for supplies will be greater if there is a wildfire. When there is strong fuel reduction, wildfires are most likely allowed to burn with containment within pre-existing or newly constructed lines limiting the impact on residences. In such areas, there is less investment on expendable or specialized equipment.

Under mutual aid, however, it is possible and likely that SAR teams will be deployed from neighboring counties. SAR teams typically arrive with a trailer, truck, or van with equipment and a mobile command post for their team. Most teams do not yet carry specialized equipment and personal protective equipment (PPE) for fire searches, but this is likely to change as the frequency of fires increases.

While SAR teams are trained to navigate with basic equipment such as a map and compasses, increasingly they utilize mapping software. SARTopo provides a GIS approach to ground navigation. However, field use of such maps requires either prior downloading of the appropriate maps or an active connection in the field. Therefore, coordinating and restoring communications links, such as cell service, is critical. This software can pinpoint structures, property lines, and hazardous areas, such as steep slopes or slide areas.

PPE is typically brought with the team in their equipment supplies. Because of the normally chaotic situation into which the teams are sent, having at least a few days' worth of PPE is advisable. Once scheduled for deployment, but prior to actual wildfire cleanup and recovery operations, it is necessary to identify and evaluate hazards in the area to determine what protective measures are needed. If the use of PPE is warranted due to the overall high hazard risk, then search management should determine the type of PPE that will best protect from the identified hazards. That PPE should then be fit to each SAR member and members should receive appropriate training in the necessity, use, maintenance, and limitations of the PPE. Once in the field, this PPE must be worn by all search members, including the handlers of the HRD dog teams.

Protective clothing shall be used when hazard exposure may negatively impact the SAR member's personal health. Appropriate protective clothing selection requires anticipation of contaminants and work conditions. Selection criteria may need to address both chemical and physical protection by preventing skin contact, while maintaining durability and preventing soaking either from sweat or rain, preventing both heat and cold stress, and may need to be adjusted to accommodate specific tasks.

Typically, a disposable Tyvek-type coverall will be worn during the search process. If these are not available, at the very minimum, SAR personnel should wear protective clothing consisting of a long-sleeved work shirt and long pants to protect against injury from abrasive materials commonly found in wildfire cleanup. Coveralls can be adjusted at the wrist and ankles with duct tape to prevent excess material catching on protruding objects. Such adjustment also helps keep the material out of contaminated areas, such as water from fire suppression efforts. However, this may also increase the heat accumulation by lowering the release of body heat. Thinking about cross-contamination is also important. If coveralls are used in the field and then team members drive back to the staging area or to another assignment in this clothing, the vehicle will also be contaminated. Often decontamination processes at the end of a shift will allow the members to resume normal attire—in time to then get back into the now-contaminated vehicles.

Head protection is important during search operations where there is the danger of head injury from flying or falling objects, electrical shock or burns. Frequently, searchers, who are focused on the ground objects, will miss the precariously balanced broken branches that hang directly overhead. The selected head protection must meet the requirements of the American National Standards Institute (ANSI) standard Z891.

Foot injuries are another major concern during wildfire searches. These injuries can originate from electrical hazards, hot/corrosive/poisonous substances, falling objects, and crushing or penetration. For example, it is a common experience to pull multiple nails and screws from the soles of boots at each break period. Safety shoe selection is based on the requirements and specifications in the American Society for Testing and Materials (ASTM) standard F2412–05 and ASTM standard F2413–05.

Appropriate face or eye protection must be worn when SAR personnel may receive eye injuries, such as punctures, abrasions, contusions, or burns, from encountering flying particles, hazardous substances, or projections. Because there are frequently ongoing fires, embers continue to be a persistent problem long after the fire front has passed. In addition, the search process itself will disturb ash and small particles. Protective eyewear should meet the requirements of the ANSI standard Z87.1 for safety eyewear.

Exposure to excessive noise is a distinct possibility due to the use of heavy equipment and power tools both in the clearing of overlying debris that hinders the search and in the work to restore the basic infrastructure to the area. To reduce noise exposure to allowable limits, hearing protection in the form of earplugs or earmuffs shall be worn (OSHA standard 29CFR1910.95).

All SAR personnel need appropriate hand protection when their hands are exposed to wildfire hazards such as absorption of harmful substances, cuts or lacerations, abrasions, punctures, chemical/thermal burns, radioactive materials, and thermal extremes. Unfortunately, in wildfire situations, many of these hazards are not visible or even predictable; therefore, multiple types of gloves may be required. Some gloves are designed to prevents cuts and punctures, a common hazard working with fire debris, while others are designed to protect against chemicals or extreme temperatures. Temperatures even of the soil around burned areas can be sufficient to produce surface burns on the skin.

The atmosphere at the wildfire site may present serious inhalation exposure risk to unknown contaminants that can temporarily or permanently harm SAR personnel. These unknown contaminants may exist in different physical form, such as the following:

- Particulates (such as dust) are fine solid particles suspended in air.
- Mists are small liquid droplets suspended in air.
- Fumes are produced when solid materials are heated, evaporated, and condensed into very fine solids suspended in the air.
- Vapors are substances in the gas phase at a temperature at which the same substance can also exist in a liquid state.
- Gases are the physical state of a material where the molecules move freely and are independent of each other. The other physical states are solid and liquid. Common toxic gases include carbon monoxide (created by internal combustion engines and fires) and hydrogen sulfide (created by rotting materials).

In the aftermath of the fire, the air is dense with smoke and probably consists of multiple forms of contaminants. Studies on firefighters suggest that exposure to such substances can produce chronic and relatively irreversible lung damage (Lee et al. 2022).

When respirators are required in the SAR process, selection will be made to ensure sufficient protection against specific respiratory hazards. Respirators fall into two main categories, each designed to protect against specific respiratory hazards.

- Air-purifying respirators (APRs) remove particulates, mists, fumes, gases, and vapors from the air using filters, cartridges, or canisters.
- Atmosphere-supplying respirators (SAR or SCBA) provide clean breathing air (from air tanks or air compressors) to the user rather than filtering out contaminants from the surrounding air.

To help reduce exposure to ash, soot, and other nuisance-type particles common to the cleanup process an air purifying respirator with N95 or P100 rated particulate filtration are the most commonly used. The "N" designation indicates the respirator is not oil-resistant, while the "P" indicates that the respirator is oil-proof. The numeral "95" refers to particulate filtration efficiency, removing at least 95% of contaminants, and the "100" filtration efficiency indicates the removal of 99.97% of airborne particles. To maintain the designed level of respirator efficiency, the respirator must have two straps to ensure a tight fit against the face.

SAR members who are required to wear a respirator should be medically evaluated, fit tested, and trained per OSHA standard 29CFR1910.134 prior to deployment. Respirators used voluntarily by SAR members must follow OSHA standard 29CFR1910.134 App D. Regardless of the respirator in use, it must be approved by the National Institute for Occupational Safety and Health (NIOSH).

Food and water are essential for the support of all personnel in the fire zone and SAR teams are no exception. Team members usually have one to three days of food in their packs and can survive without additional food. However, at most disaster scenes, local agencies quickly mobilize food supplies for the myriad of workers in the area as there is a need to provide for the many firefighters involved in containing the blaze. Services such as the Red Cross and local suppliers often step in quickly with food trucks for breakfast and bag lunches and bottled water for the field.

Housing can be more difficult. SAR teams are equipped to camp, although that is obviously not recommended within the fire zone due to ongoing hazards and the need to simultaneously work on infrastructure and fire suppression. Most hotel rooms will already be filled to capacity with evacuated residents and other emergency personnel. Sometimes bunking arrangements can be made with local colleges or other larger facilities. However, it is often the case that teams will sleep either in their vehicles or with local hosts known to team members or to the sheriff liaison staff.

Sanitary facilities are usually available at the staging post within the fire zone. Due to the lack of "cover" within search areas due to the destruction of all undergrowth, it is also helpful to provide portable toilets throughout the search areas. Such care is definitely appreciated by search team members.

The strain of this work is also drawing attention to the need for mental health support. Most team members are familiar with finding deceased individuals from prior rescue assignments. In the fire zone it is often not the deaths that are the disturbing factor but the randomness of those deaths. Finding remains in one burned-out home while surrounding houses are untouched can highlight the unpredictability of these disasters.

Finally, there is financial accounting that must be maintained to cover expenses. This may include worker's compensation for injuries suffered by team members on the search. The requesting agency will also likely be eligible for disaster relief and must make a solid accounting of any expenses it incurred through using mutual aid.

11.8 LESSONS LEARNED FROM RECENT WILDFIRES

Strategic deployment of SAR teams is critical in massive fires where there may be many deaths. Their ability to systematically search and locate remains frees other personnel to focus on the many other duties that arise in the aftermath of a wildfire, including maintaining a secure perimeter, facilitating and coordinating the recovery efforts for roads and utilities, preventing looting, and repopulating areas that have been searched and deemed safe.

Understanding the missing population—who is *actually* missing as opposed to those who have not yet contacted all their family and friends—is critical for developing the search strategy. Work by local law enforcement in locating evacuated residents is crucial to limit SAR investment to the higher-priority areas. SAR teams can be utilized for "global" searches, but experience has shown that it is much more effective to be able to target those who are most likely to have perished. This targeting provides answers for desperate friends and families who anxiously await an outcome.

The skills needed in wildfire search and recovery are relatively easily built on existing ground search skills. To that body of knowledge, there needs to be an adaptation of the search strategies to focus on likely areas where remains can be found and training on the identification of burned human remains. Prior preparation as to the hazards of working in such conditions is also important. Understanding that this work can also take a toll on searchers allows for provision of support services, including for mental health.

REFERENCES

California Governor's Office of Emergency Services Law Enforcement Branch. 2005. Mutual aid guidelines search and rescue - Canine. https://carda.org/wp-content/uploads/2022/10/OES-Guidelines-with-Appendices.pdf (Accessed March 2023).

California Office of Emergency Services (CalOES). 2023. Search and rescue mutual aid. www.caloes.ca.gov/office-of-the-director/operations/response-operations/law-enforcement/search-rescue-mutual-aid/ (Accessed March 29, 2023).

California Rescue Dog Association. 2023. Frequently asked questions. https://carda.org/faq/ (Accessed March 27, 2023).

Cooper, D., Frost, J., and Robe R. 2003. *Compatibility of land SAR procedures with search theory.* Potomac Management Group, Alexandria, VA.

Gordon, L. E., and Ho, B. 2020. Injuries and illnesses among human remains detection-certified search-and-rescue dogs deployed to northern California in response to the Camp Fire wildfire of November 2018. *JAVMA* 256(3): 322–332.

Koester, R. J. 2008. *Lost person behavior: A search and rescue guide on where to look—for land, air and water.* dbS Productions, Charlottesville, VA, 398 pp.

Lee, C. T., Ventura, I. B., Phillips, E. K., Leahy, A., Jablonski, R., Montner, S., Chung, J. H., Vij, R., Adegunsoye, A., and Strek, M. E. 2022. Interstitial lung disease in firefighters: An emerging occupational hazard. *Frontiers in Medicine (Lausanne)* 9: 864658.

National Association for Search and Rescue. 2019. *Fundamentals of search and rescue.* 2nd Edition. Jones and Bartlett Learning, Burlington, MA.

Perkins, D. 2003. Chapter 3—searching in a group. In *Field search skills.* Centre for Search Research, Ashington, Northumberland.

Perkins, D. 2008a. *Critical separation and the probability of detection for grid searching by a land SAR field team.* Centre for Search Research, Ashington, Northumberland.

Perkins, D. 2008b. *The critical distance method: Estimating the probability of detection for grid searching by a land SAR field team.* Centre for Search Research, Ashington, Northumberland.

Perkins, D. 2013. *Probability of detection for the search manager.* Centre for Search Research, Ashington, Northumberland.

Perkins, D. 2018. *The variable nature of probability of detection for ground search teams.* Centre for Search Research, Ashington, Northumberland.

Russo, T. 2021. "New" perspectives on ground SAR planning. *Cibola SAR* 9.

Scientific Working Group on Dog and Orthogonal Detector Guidelines (SWGDOG). 2023. SWGDOG SC8—substance detector dogs: Human remains detection (HRD) land and water. www.ojp.gov/pdffiles1/nij/grants/231952.pdf (Accessed March 2023).

CHAPTER 12

Search and Recovery Protocols for Victims of Large-Scale Wildfires

Eric Bartelink, Ashley Kendell, Colleen Milligan, P. Willey, and Alison Galloway

Large-scale wildfires have disrupted the lives of millions of citizens and have resulted in the deaths of more than 2,400 individuals globally over the past two decades (Mizutori and Guha-Sapir 2018). Drought conditions driven by climate change have created favorable conditions for these recent massive fire events, which often cause a large number of fatalities. Within the United States, most large-scale fire events have occurred in the western states. Given these circumstances, forensic anthropologists working within wildfire-prone areas should become familiar with wildfire scene search and recovery protocols that maximize the recovery of highly fragmentary and burned remains. Wildfire contexts are unique in that temperatures and fire duration greatly exceed that found in typical fire scenes (e.g., structure and vehicle fires), resulting in a much greater thermal alteration of remains (Milligan et al. 2023). In addition, victims may be recovered from within structures, vehicles, or outdoor contexts, often several days after the fire event. Because an accurate list of missing persons may not be available for several days or weeks following the fire event, all fire-affected areas should be treated as potentially containing human remains during the search process.

In this chapter, we first provide a history and synopsis of current recovery protocols for fatal fire victims and note their importance especially in cases of suspected homicide. We next discuss a field protocol developed during the recovery of burned human remains from the 2018 Camp Fire in Northern California, the most fatal wildfire event in the state's history. We then compare our wildfire victim recovery protocol with current fatal-fire-victim protocols and provide recommendations for future wildfire events.

12.1 CURRENT PROTOCOLS FOR RECOVERY OF FATAL FIRE VICTIMS

Fatal fire scenes are among the most challenging scene types given that thermally altered remains are usually highly fragmentary and fragile and may be located under layers of

DOI: 10.4324/9781003168010-15

burned debris (Symes et al. 2012). Thermal alteration to building materials, furniture, electronics, and other material complicate the search and identification of fatal fire victims, especially to non-specialists who may not be familiar with the appearance of highly fragmentary, burned remains (Dirkmaat et al. 2012; Fairgrieve 2008). Thus, non-specialists may unknowingly disturb or damage burned human remains during the search process, or may incompletely recover them. Fire suppression efforts, or use of heavy machinery (e.g., overhaul of a fire scene), may also cause damage to burned remains and further disturb the scene context. Because fire is often used by criminals to disguise evidence of a crime (especially homicide), it is imperative that properly trained recovery experts assist with the recovery of fatal fire victims (Symes et al. 2012).

12.1.1 Fatal Fire Search and Recovery Methods

Although fatal fire scenes are common, few published forensic anthropology protocols exist for the search and recovery of fatal fire victims (Cooke and Ide 1985; Dirkmaat 2002; Dirkmaat et al. 2012; King and King 1989; Fairgrieve 2008; Mayne Correia and Beattie 2002; Symes et al. 2012). In an early and influential publication, Bass (1984) opined that fire events cannot completely destroy a body and that systematic recovery methods are critical to properly document a fire scene. Bass (1984) further noted that a proper forensic archaeological recovery can also provide negative findings (i.e., determine the absence of a fire victim). More recently, Dirkmaat (2002) outlined a more detailed approach for processing fire scenes with potential human remains, adopting many of the essential methods used in previous forensic archaeology recovery protocols (Dirkmaat and Adovasio 1997). These protocols emphasize the importance of *in situ* examination of burned remains, including reconstruction of the position and orientation of the body and the association of the remains with other types of physical evidence within the scene (Dirkmaat 2002; Dirkmaat and Cabo 2016; Dirkmaat et al. 2008, 2012). The use of trained forensic archaeologists at the undisturbed fire scene is clearly important for carefully documenting scene context, especially in cases involving possible homicides and where there is the potential of commingling of two or more fire victims.

The goals of a fire scene recovery include the complete *in situ* documentation of the victim's remains and the associational relationships between the victim, physical evidence, and personal effects (Dirkmaat 2002; Dirkmaat et al. 2012). These goals should provide key evidence that aids in personal identification of the fire victim and the circumstances surrounding the death (manner of death as homicide, accident, suicide, etc.). Complete recovery, detailed scene documentation, and careful packaging and transport of the remains are imperative to the integrity of burned remains cases, especially regarding personal identification and assessments of perimortem trauma (Dirkmaat et al. 2012; Mayne Correia and Beattie 2002).

The most comprehensive recovery protocol for recovering fatal fire victims was developed by Symes and colleagues and published in a 2012 US Department of Justice report (NIJ grant No. 2008-DN-BX-K131). Building on earlier work by Dirkmaat and colleagues (2012), this report presents an idealized recovery process especially pertinent for processing homicide scenes, or scenes where homicide is suspected. Due to the fragmentary nature of fire-altered remains, the protocol is designed to fully document the scene context from start to finish and to recognize other potential forensic evidence *in situ*. The protocol was developed using a large-scale mock fire scene in Bridgeville, Pennsylvania, in conjunction with the authors' prior casework experience (Symes et al. 2012; Dirkmaat et al. 2012:123–125). The recovery methods emphasize written and photographic scene documentation throughout the entire recovery process, mapping the overall scene and surrounding landmarks (roads, structures, etc.) with a total station and GPS, and georeferencing the scene using a standard coordinate system (Dirkmaat et al. 2012; Symes et al. 2012). The overall recovery process ideally includes a written narrative team (note takers), a photography and videography team, a provenience team, a search team, a forensic significance team, a mapping team, an excavation team, a screening team, and a remains collection team (Symes et al. 2012).

Following Dirkmaat et al.'s (2012: 123–125) condensed synopsis of this protocol, *phase 1* begins with a large-scale line search of the scene, with searchers lined up shoulder to shoulder and progressing on foot into the structure. The scene is demarcated into either search corridors or grids for each identifiable room within the structure. In addition to the anthropology team members, at least one member is a fire investigator who is knowledgeable about fire origin and fire progression patterns. As the line search progresses through the structure, debris is moved behind the search line, with searchers taking note of stratigraphic profiles of the burned debris piles. *Phase 2* begins once potential human remains are located within the structure. A rapid search is done approximately 1.5–3.0 meters around the remains to demarcate the boundary of the immediate scene, which includes both human remains and associated evidence. At this stage, a trowel is held perpendicularly and used to slice through the debris pile from the top layer to the bottom (i.e., a modified "cake-cutting" method), and debris is moved into buckets and sorted manually on tarps. Once remains are identified on the tarps or *in situ*, the excavation pace slows. In *phase 3*, the debris is carefully removed from the remains and evidence, which is then sifted offsite (using 6 mm mesh screens). Once remains are completely uncovered, the position and orientation of the body is recorded, and the scene is documented extensively using hand-drawn sketches, photography, notes, and coordinates (total station, GPS, etc.). For cremated remains, debris can be collected around the remains to later sift in the laboratory using finer mesh geological sieves. Finally, in *phase 4*, remains are carefully packaged for transport. The protocol recommends that the head, hands, feet, and other fragile structures are wrapped in plastic wrap or aluminum foil to prevent further fragmentation. Once remains are securely packaged, they can be wrapped in white sheets, placed into a body bag that has a stiff board on the bottom for support and then transported to the forensic anthropology laboratory or morgue.

12.2 MODIFIED PROTOCOLS FOR SEARCH AND RECOVERY OF WILDFIRE VICTIMS

12.2.1 Wildfire Fatality Search and Recovery Methods

Search and recovery procedures for large-scale wildfire fatality scenes involve three priorities: (1) locating human remains, (2) scene documentation, and (3) complete recovery of human remains and medical/dental implants for identification purposes. For the 2018 Camp Fire, the forensic anthropology team's priorities were limited to locating and recovering the remains of the majority of the victims, whereas the sheriff-coroner teams oversaw scene documentation, photography, recording death scene locations, and transportation of recovered remains (Bartelink et al. 2020; Milligan et al., 2023). Symes et al. (2012)'s fatal fire scene protocol calls for the simultaneous and sequential work of several teams in the field and is organized into several phases that involve large-scale searches following corridors or room boundaries. When remains are found, the protocol calls for grid excavation and for the remains to be left *in situ* and is designed to take one to three days for the recovery of a fire victim from a burned structure. While the search phases for the Camp Fire victims generally followed a similar pattern, the recovery process itself mainly emphasized screening only the area around the remains and taking a single GPS point for all victims recovered at an address. Because the fire-affected area was identified as a mass fatality incident and not a crime scene, the main objectives were to locate and recover remains in a manner that maximized identification information but not to reconstruct events at each individual scene. The wildfire protocols were developed from past mass wildfire incidents in California and combined objectives from both existing fire scene and mass fatality protocols.

12.2.2 Search Organization

The search for wildfire victims requires coordinating the efforts of multiple organizations. For the Camp Fire, this coordination included sheriff-coroner teams, search and rescue (SAR) teams, CAL FIRE teams, and anthropology teams. The composition of the anthropology team in the Camp Fire varied from day to day, depending on overall team size. In the early days following the disaster, team size was small. Anthropology team members were embedded within SAR teams that were responsible for searching approximately 18,500 burned structures within the disaster zone. However, this organization changed several days into the recovery process as additional team members were added from California and Nevada. The final, and ideal, team configuration was small Anthropology teams embedded with coroner's investigators, along with CAL FIRE personnel available to assist with removal of large debris (appliances, roof material, etc.). In addition, small anthropology teams were also on call at a staging area within the disaster zone for deployment to specific addresses to verify whether flagged items were human, nonhuman, or non-osseous material. To help coordinate search teams in the field, and the data being compiled from the searches, one anthropologist was also stationed in incident command (see Milligan et al., this volume).

Each morning, once teams were organized, excavation gear and personal protective equipment was split among the anthropology-sheriff-coroner teams. Each team received a list of search addresses based on missing persons reports or possible remains callouts compiled the previous day. These targeted searches were complicated when address locations were inaccurate or imprecise (e.g., trailer parks without trailer numbers). Throughout the day, the anthropology-sheriff-coroner teams also received additional callouts from incident command when suspected remains were found during SAR and CAL FIRE searches of residences.

During the course of the Camp Fire response, the following protocol was developed, and it was revised for subsequent fires, such as the 2020 Bear Fire, also in Butte County. For each residence or vehicle associated with a missing person or possible human remains, a small number of team members would conduct a perimeter search

FIGURE 12.1 Typical burned residence that should be first searched using a perimeter approach. Note that some wall and roof material may obstruct view and need removal.

first (Figure 12.1). In most cases, human remains were at least partially visible on the surface (see Galloway et al., this volume). If no remains were located based on the perimeter search, and the address was not associated with a missing person(s) report, the search team would stop and move to the next residence or vehicle of interest. If no remains were located during the perimeter search and the address *was* associated with a missing person(s) report, a small team would enter the structure and conduct a systematic line search on foot. If no remains were located at this point and there was strong evidence for a missing person at the address, a larger team would conduct a more intensive systematic survey of the burned structure using small hand tools. If remains were discovered at any point in the survey, the search was halted. During both the 2018 Camp Fire and the 2020 Bear Fire, CAL FIRE and Urban Search and Rescue teams were responsible for removing large debris items, such as roofs, walls, showers, and large appliances to permit thorough searches.

12.2.3 Recovery Operations

When human remains were identified, a careful excavation was conducted using trowels, dustpans, brushes, and screens (Figure 12.2). For most fire scenes, human remains were heavily charred or calcined and extremely fragmented. All identifiable

FIGURE 12.2 Careful excavation of remains within a structure. Note the area where remains were located is taped by search teams awaiting recovery team excavation.

skull and dental remains, medical implants, and tissue-protected bone fragments were placed in separate paper evidence bags and labeled as potentially important for identification purposes. Separation by body region for collection and transportation was much more difficult for most body segments given the extensive fragmentation of the calcined remains. Although small geological hand or soil sieves were used in some cases, most often remains and debris were screened using 1/8-inch (3.175 mm) mesh (Figure 12.3). Two weeks after the 2018 Camp Fire initial fire event, it began to rain, which resulted in the mixing of remains with wet debris, making recovery efforts a challenge. For these scenes, a wet screening approach was implemented using fire hoses set to trickle water into the screens. Both the dry and wet excavation and screening strategy were effective in recovering heavily fragmented skeletal material, as well as dental appliances, pacemakers, orthopedic devices, and personal effects.

As mentioned previously, coroner investigators were instructed by Butte County Sheriff's Office to conduct scene photography, scene documentation, and transfer of custody of remains and medical devices (Figures 12.4–12.5). Human remains, medical devices, and personal effects were placed into labeled paper bags, which were then transferred to body bags. Remains were then transferred to the Sacramento County Medical Examiner's Office for identification. Finally, a smaller sheriff-coroner team visited each fatality location with a total station to document the location of each fire victim.

Bone identification in the field is an important part of the recovery process as some locations had a mix of nonhuman remains and non-osseous material that mimic bone.

FIGURE 12.3 Screening of all material from the area of the body allows for maximum recovery of fragmented bone and teeth.

FIGURE 12.4 Coroner's office personnel were responsible for documentation of the scene, photography, and assignment of case numbers.

FIGURE 12.5 Once recovery was completed, remains were taken by the coroner's office personnel for transport to the temporary morgue.

Aside from fire victims, anthropology teams received dozens of callouts each day to identify material located by SAR, CAL FIRE, and sheriff-coroner teams during the Camp Fire. Often, these were non-osseous materials, including burned building debris, such as drywall, foam, wood, or melted plastic. Even more common were callouts for human versus nonhuman bone identification. Because the region of Northern California where the Camp Fire took place maintains an avid hunting community, burned trophy mounts, antlers, and deer bones were commonly encountered. Nonhuman remains were also often identified in kitchen areas and included burned remains of turkey, chicken, beef, and pork. Finally, hundreds of pets (mostly dogs and cats) perished in the fire, as residents evacuated quickly or had already left their homes before the fire and were unable to return. In a few instances, non-fire-victim-related materials were located in burned residential structures, including dental molds, an anatomical human skull, and a prehistoric human skull.

12.3 COMPARISON OF PROTOCOLS FOR SEARCH AND RECOVERY OF FATAL FIRE VICTIMS

The Wildfire Mass Fatality Protocol (outlined earlier) and the Comprehensive Fatal Fire Victim Recovery Protocol (outlined in Symes et al. [2012]) show several similarities as well as differences (Table 12.1). Some of the largest differences relate to the size and

TABLE 12.1 Comparison of Symes et al.'s (2012) Fire Victim Scene Recovery Protocol with Wildfire Victim Recovery Protocol

Fatal Fire Scene Protocol (Symes et al. 2012)	Description	Teams	Wildfire Fatal Fire Scene Protocol for Unassociated Addresses	Description	Teams	Wildfire Fatal Fire Scene Protocol for Associated Addresses	Description	Teams
Phase 1	Rapid, systematic large-scale search	Search team, forensic significance team	Phase 1	Perimeter walk around structure and vehicles, small-scale search of surrounding property	Small search team, forensic significance team	Phase 1	Perimeter walk around structure and vehicles, small-scale search of surrounding property	Small search team, forensic significance team
Phase 2	Evidence of human remains found, rapid large-scale excavation	Excavation team, screening team	Phase 2A	No evidence of human remains, *search stops at this phase*		Phase 2A	No evidence of human remains, small team line search	Small search team, forensic significance team
			Phase 2B	Evidence of human remains found, rapid small excavation to determine excavation boundaries and number of victims	Anthropology excavation team	Phase 2B	Evidence of human remains found, rapid small excavation to determine excavation boundaries and number of victims	Anthropology excavation team

(*Continued*)

TABLE 12.1 (Continued)

Fatal Fire Scene Protocol (Symes et al. 2012)	**Description**	**Teams**	**Wildfire Fatal Fire Scene Protocol for Unassociated Addresses**	**Description**	**Teams**	**Wildfire Fatal Fire Scene Protocol for Associated Addresses**	**Description**	**Teams**
Phase 3	Fine, detailed excavation in the immediate vicinity of human remains	Mapping team, excavation team, screening team	Phase 3	Fine, detailed excavation in the immediate vicinity of human remains	Anthropology excavation/ screening team; coroner mapping/ documentation team	Phase 3	Fine, detailed excavation in the immediate vicinity of human remains	Anthropology excavation/ screening team; coroner mapping/ documentation team
Phase 4	After comprehensive documentation and collection: removal and transport	Evidence-bagging team	Phase 4	Collection: removal and transport	Anthropology/ coroner teams	Phase 4	Collection: removal and transport	Anthropology/ coroner Teams

scale of the fire scene and the differences in investigative goals. Wildfires are measured by destructiveness (total count of structures lost) and fatalities (number of victims associated with the fire). This means that a single fatal wildfire event creates many potential recovery scenes. Early in the law enforcement recovery phase, information on potential missing persons is collected and disseminated to search teams. However, all structures or properties affected by the wildfire may require searching to recover known victims and unknown, unreported victims. For wildfire protocols, this necessitates procedures for "unassociated" addresses (addresses not connected to known missing persons reports at the time of the search) and "associated" addresses (addresses linked to a known missing persons report). Victim recovery from wildfires centers on the successful closure of the missing persons list through systematic property searches and the positive identification of recovered victims. While many recent wildfires in the western United States have included criminal investigations into the cause and origin of the fires, the individual recovery sites of victims are not treated as a traditional crime scene.

Phases 1 and *2* of traditional and wildfire recovery protocols emphasize the use of teams to carefully and systematically investigate a burned structure to locate human remains. However, for wildfire scenes, a perimeter search is a more effective starting point given that most structures are completely burned to ground level and human remains are often clearly visible on the surface. In addition, *phase 1* of wildfire protocols also accounts for perimeter searches of vehicles and the surrounding property of a residence (including water features such as ponds or pools). *Phase 2* protocols also need to be expanded to accommodate both associated and unassociated property searches.

For unassociated property searches in wildfires, the search should stop at a perimeter search of the residence if no remains are seen. This would be *phase 2A* for unassociated sites. In the absence of known missing persons data at the address, stopping the search after a negative perimeter search preserves the integrity of the scene and the possibility for complete collection of the remains if the property is later found to be associated with a missing person or persons. Unless remains are seen, line searches or more extensive excavation within the footprint of a residence or vehicle risks unintentional damage or destruction of the remains. During searches of unassociated sites, the search team is simply gathering preliminary information on the potential for any obvious victims at the site.

Phase 2A for associated sites has the additional step of a small team line searching within the footprint of a residence. For associated sites, this additional step is necessary because investigative information suggests that a victim might be on the property. The priority for associated sites is locating the remains and eliminating the potential for missed remains. For both unassociated and associated sites, *phase 2B* commences if remains are located during the earlier phases. *Phase 2B* includes a small-scale excavation to determine the boundary area around the human remains and the number of victims at the site.

In *Phase 3*, Symes et al.'s (2012) protocol emphasizes detailed mapping, reconstruction of the location, position, and orientation of the body, and documentation of relevant physical evidence during excavation and screening. In contrast, *phase 3* in the wildfire protocol focuses mainly on complete recovery of remains through excavation and screening, with mapping limited to the recordation of a single data point with a total station by sheriff-coroner teams. As discussed earlier, individual property sites in wildfire scenes are not treated as crime scenes and the goal is complete recovery of remains and not reconstruction of the scene. This also results in an expedited search and recovery process, usually taking three to four hours per scene instead of one to three days. Rapid but complete recovery was critical in the Camp Fire event because (1) there were hundreds of addresses listed as priority searches (i.e., associated with either missing persons cases or probable sighted remains), (2) approximately 18,500 structures needed to be searched, and (3) statewide resources, such as sheriff-coroner teams, SAR teams, National Guard, and CAL FIRE, were only available for a finite period. Even with the fast pace of search and recovery, the search efforts lasted 21 consecutive days, resulting in the recovery of all fatal fire victims.

Finally, for *phase 4* in the wildfire protocol, cranial and dental remains and medical devices are bagged separately for identification purposes. In only a few cases during the 2018 Camp Fire, human remains were intact enough to clearly discern specific body regions to bag separately (beyond the skull and dentition). Finally, it should be noted that all scene photography, documentation, mapping with a total station, and transfer of custody are all typically handled by the coroner's investigators, not by the anthropology teams.

12.4 CONCLUSION: LESSONS LEARNED FROM THE 2018 CAMP FIRE RECOVERY EFFORT AND SUBSEQUENT FIRES

There were several lessons learned from the 21-day recovery effort of the Camp Fire disaster area. These lessons can be addressed in the following four areas: team composition, search operations, recovery of remains, and health and safety concerns. Team members varied from professional forensic anthropologists to undergraduate interns. It was critical that more experienced team members were paired with less experienced team members. Professional forensic anthropologists, highly trained graduate students, and undergraduate interns were key to the success of the victim recovery effort. Success also required flexibility because team size varied substantially from day to day. Having anthropology teams paired with sheriff-coroner teams was recognized as the most effective strategy for completing all phases of the search and recovery protocol.

In general, SAR teams were uncomfortable in their ability to recognize human remains in the field. Although SAR members often have experience locating human skeletal remains, few had ever worked in a wildfire mass fatality context or identified burned remains. In the second week of the recovery effort, anthropology teams began to provide onsite training to SAR teams and now provide strategic regular training to SAR members throughout the state and a "just in time" training guide for future mass fire scenes.

In some of the first fatal-fire-victim scenes, sheriff-coroner teams recovered remains without an anthropology team. Many of these scenes had to be revisited because remains had not been completely recovered, and in some instances, this second recovery resulted in confusion over whether there were two fire victims or one. In subsequent wildfire responses, particularly those in 2020, anthropology teams have standardized search strategies using the priority search pattern developed in our wildfire protocol.

Although anthropology teams rarely work directly with human remains detection canine teams, they are often included in recovery efforts. For body detection following wildfires, the dogs used should be specifically trained as human remains detection (HRD) dogs rather than dogs trained as "live find" rescue. A greater problem is that the FEMA alert standard for HRD dogs is that they should find the greatest concentration of the scent pool, lie down at that point, and bark. This technique works well for bodies buried in building rubble or mudslides but is not appropriate for wildfires. Unfortunately, the dogs focus on the largest remaining segment, such as the pelvis, and lie down on top of other body parts, possibly fragmenting and commingling remains further.

During the Camp Fire, many of the callouts to dog alerts were where canines had alerted on an area of interest. In almost all cases, these hits were negative for human remains or represented nonhuman animal remains. The data indicate that hits, where the canine team located remains before human searchers, were only associated with two of the fatal fire scenes. For dogs that are trained for HRD, there will be some confusing scents when it comes to victims of the fire because these dogs can also detect cremated remains that may have been housed in the burned structure. The "twice burned" are important for later recovery efforts but usually are not first priority. Fire scenes are also particularly dangerous environments for working dogs with nails, broken glass and ceramics, and structural metal that can cause permanent paw injuries. In addition, poor air quality and presence of toxic chemicals and particulate matter are extreme hazards for HRD dogs. Based on the available information, it is unclear how effective search canines are for large-scale wildfire scenes given the enormous search area and the extent of thermal destruction.

Another area that needs improvement for future wildfire scenes is to develop consistent scene documentation methods between sheriff-coroner teams. Because coroner investigators derived from almost every county in the state, documentation methods varied widely. Completeness of body collection should be a major priority, and all scenes should include an anthropology team onsite prior to excavation of human remains.

Finally, search teams encountered several potential hazards in the field. These included poor air quality from smoke and particulate matter, sharp metal glass, smoldering trees, downed power lines, uneven terrain, hazardous waste, unstable trees, flash flooding, and potentially unexploded ordinance, firearms, and ammunition. In future wildfire recoveries, it would be beneficial to have a hazardous materials expert onsite to address safety concerns.

The 2018 Camp Fire and subsequent wildfires have tested the available protocols for recovery of burned human remains. While the general format is appropriate, the goals in a wildfire are for complete victim recovery and positive identification. Use of perimeter searches for structures and vehicles, a focus on addresses or locations involving missing persons reports, and a multidisciplinary team approach are all key to successful victim recovery and identification in wildfire recovery scenes.

REFERENCES

Bartelink, E.J., Kendell, A.E., Galimany Skupham, J., Gardner, K.S., Hayes, L., Hegel, C., Reeves, V.C., Straub, A., Timmons, M. and Tray, L. (2020). Search and recovery protocols for fatal fire victims of the 2018 California Camp Fire. *Proceedings of the Annual Meetings of the American Academy of Forensic Sciences*, Anaheim, CA.

Bass, W.M. (1984). Is it possible to consume a body completely in a fire? In: T.A. Rathbun and J.E. Buikstra (eds.), *Human Identification: Case Studies in Forensic Anthropology*. (pp. 159–167). Charles C. Thomas, Springfield, IL.

Cooke, R.A. and Ide, R.H. (1985). *Principles of Fire Investigation*. Institution of Fire Engineers, Leicester.

Dirkmaat, D.C. (2002). Recovery and interpretation of the fatal fire victim: The role of forensic anthropology. In: W.D. Haglund and M.H. Sorg (eds.), *Advances in Forensic Taphonomy: Method, Theory, and Archaeological Perspectives* (pp. 451–472). CRC Press, Salem, MA.

Dirkmaat, D.C. and Adovasio, J.M. (1997). The role of archaeology in the recovery and interpretation of human remains from an outdoor forensic setting. In: W.D. Haglund and M.H. Sorg (eds.), *Forensic Taphonomy: The Postmortem Fate of Human Remains* (pp. 39–64). CRC Press, Boca Raton, FL.

Dirkmaat, D.C. and Cabo, L.L. (2016). Forensic archaeology and forensic taphonomy: Basic considerations on how to properly process and interpret the outdoor forensic scene. *Academic Forensic Pathology* 6(3): 439–454.

Dirkmaat, D.C., Cabo, L.L., Ousley, S.D. and Symes, S.A. (2008). New perspectives in forensic anthropology. *American Journal of Physical Anthropology* (S47): 33–52.

Dirkmaat, D.C., Olson, G.O., Klales, A.R. and Getz, S. (2012). The role of forensic anthropology in the recovery and interpretation of the fatal-fire victim. In: D.C. Dirkmaat (ed.), *A Companion to Forensic Anthropology* (pp. 113–135). Blackwell Publishing Ltd., West Sussex.

Fairgrieve, S. (2008). *Forensic Cremation: Recovery and Analysis*. CRC Press, Boca Raton, FL.

King, C.G. and King, S. (1989). The archaeology of fire investigation. *Fire Engineering* 142(6): 70–74.

Mayne Correia, P.M. and Beattie, O. (2002). A critical look at methods for recovering, evaluating, and interpreting cremated human remains. In: W.D. Haglund and M.H. Sorg (eds.), *Advances in Forensic Taphonomy: Method, Theory, and Archaeological Perspectives* (pp. 435–450). CRC Press, Salem, MA.

Milligan, C., Galloway, A., Kendell, A., Zephro, L., Willey, P. and Bartelink, E.J. (2023). Recovery and identification of fatal fire victims from the 2018 northern California Camp Fire Disaster. In: S. Ellingham, J. Adserias Garriga, S.C. Zapico and D.H. Ubelaker (eds.), *The Forensic Evaluation of Burnt Human Remains*. Wiley-Blackwell, Chichester.

Mizutori, M. and Guha-Sapir, D. (2018). Centre for Research on the Epidemiology of Disasters International Disaster Database (CRED) and United Nations Office for Disaster Risk Reduction (UNISDR). Economic losses, poverty & disasters: 1998–2017. www.preventionweb.net/files/61119_credeconomiclosses.pdf

Symes, S.A., Dirkmaat, D.C., Ousley, S., Chapman, E. and Cabo. L. (2012). *Recovery and interpretation of burned human remains* (Report No: 237966, Award No: 2008-DN-BX-K131). National Institute of Justice, Washington, DC.

CHAPTER 13

To Be Ready
Preparations for Fatal Wildfire Recovery Operations

Alison Galloway, Eric Bartelink, Tim Gocha, and Marin A. Pilloud

Recovery operations for wildfire scenes will vary considerably, depending upon the number of missing persons or suspected fatalities, the condition of the scene, and the size of the recovery operations. Often the recovery is complicated by the presence of multiple simultaneous fires that require staffing at each location. In these cases, the recovery teams are often smaller and the duration of the search longer. Whatever the case, there are some steps that potential recovery teams can take before deployment to mitigate the situation once their services are requested.

As much as possible, it is useful to know at what stage of an operation the team will be entering. Equipment needed for search operations differs from what is needed for recovery and from what is needed for analysis. As access to the scene may be restricted, transporting large amounts of equipment that is not needed can be problematic, particularly when also transporting personnel.

13.1 IDENTIFICATION OF STAFFING POSSIBILITIES

Those who are associated with forensic laboratories or coroner's units already know the size of the team to be dispatched to a wildfire recovery effort. Many anthropologists are not directly affiliated with a medical examiner or coroner's office but, instead, are affiliated with a university. The advantage is that they may have access to undergraduate and graduate students who can assist with recovery operations. In addition, alumni of the programs may also be available to help, which increases the number of higher skilled team members. A contact list of possible candidates or social media may be useful to contact potential team members, but this raises the potential of contacting interested but unqualified individuals. It is essential that potential team members are vetted to ensure they are qualified and able to conduct complex and potentially physically and mentally demanding searches.

In large part, those who participate in this recovery activity do so on a volunteer basis unless payment for services has been pre-authorized by a local or state entity. The

DOI: 10.4324/9781003168010-16

lead agency will often supply reimbursement for out-of-pocket expenses, such as fuel for vehicles. They also will supply food in the field either directly or through volunteer services such as the Red Cross or Salvation Army.

Some anthropologists may be affiliated with specific governmental responses, such as the Disaster Mortuary Operational Response Team (DMORT), meaning that they work as temporary government employees for the duration of deployment. An assignment with DMORT requires an extensive application and background checks and training exercises. It is not something that can be implemented in order to participate in an ongoing disaster. DMORT is not routinely dispatched and must be requested by the lead agency or state. Further, DMORT will only deploy team members when local assets are unavailable or unable to assist.

One significant concern for those who bring teams of volunteers is the hazards of such work (discussed further here). For those dispatched by an agency or employed by an academic institution, such as a university, worker's compensation will typically cover any injury incurred in this service. Students who participate may also have to sign waivers through the university's risk management department to release the institution of liability in case of injury. For those self-employed or retired, however, worker's compensation is not in place and their services are often rejected because the liability for the lead agency is too great.

To accommodate these concerns, self-employed or retired recovery workers need to gain some governmental affiliation that would allow them, in California, to be designated as a disaster service worker. In California, this status is distributed through the county of residence and must be arranged well ahead of any deployment. In other states, there may be means to provide services through national organizations that provide disaster services.

One problem that has proven harder to surmount is the difficulty in linking into the law enforcement and fire service network, especially in the midst of a disaster. Unfortunately, lead agencies are inundated with volunteers, some excellent, some barely qualified, and some fraudulent. Without time to check on the qualifications and reputation of every volunteer, agencies, understandably, go with those with whom they have worked previously or who come recommended by colleagues from whom they may be receiving mutual aid. Having pre-existing links is, therefore, essential. Medical examiners and coroners in one's home region may help facilitate work under a mutual aid agreement.

At times, natural disasters, including wildfires, can be so destructive that resources in the state where the disaster occurred are quickly exhausted or spread too thin, necessitating assistance from out-of-state experts. The ability for these out-of-state individuals to respond varies, especially in what preparations can be made beforehand, largely based on whether they work at an academic institution or government agency. To illustrate this, the out-of-state response to the 2018 California Camp Fire is considered in the following.

On the evening of November 10, 2018, anthropologists from California State University, Chico, recognized the need for additional anthropologists to aid search and recovery efforts and reached out to colleagues in northern and southern Nevada to ask for assistance. The team from northern Nevada came from an academic institution, specifically the University of Nevada, Reno (UNR), and consisted of two faculty members, 14 current graduate students, and one alumna of their graduate program. The team from southern Nevada consisted of four individuals, all of whom were affiliated with both an academic institution, the University of Nevada, Las Vegas (UNLV), and a government agency, the Clark County Office of the Coroner/Medical Examiner (CCOCME). At UNLV, the southern Nevada team represented one adjunct faculty member and three graduate students, while at the CCOCME, they were in the roles of a forensic supervisor, a part-time death investigator, a part-time forensic technician, and a forensic anthropology intern.

Although one does not typically think of a university, with its bureaucratic layers, as allowing for a rapid response, in the case of the California Camp Fire, the team from UNR was able to respond much more swiftly than the team from southern Nevada. In part, this was due to geography (Reno, NV is ~171 miles from Chico, California) but also due to being from an academic institution. All students already had all of their paperwork to volunteer in recovery efforts completed with the university; therefore, the team was able to respond the very next day and the following two weekends. In total, they assisted November 11–12, 16–18, and 24–25 of 2018. All efforts by the UNR team were initially self-funded; however, students and faculty were eventually reimbursed for gasoline and some food expenses through UNR, using funds received from local anthropological casework. The rapid response from the UNR team was undoubtedly a boon for resources on the ground in California. However, as the university considers the students as volunteers and not employees, the university does not consider itself liable for any injury incurred during recovery efforts.

The team from southern Nevada was not able to respond as quickly as those from UNR, in part due to geography (Las Vegas, Nevada, is ~600 miles from Chico, California) but also due to being employees of a local government agency. While the faculty and administration at UNLV gave swift and open-ended approval for the faculty member and graduate students to miss teaching and coursework responsibilities, permissions through government channels were not quite as fast. The coroner and assistant coroner at the CCOCME gave tentative approval for the team to respond but instructed them to wait until an Emergency Management Assistant Compact (EMAC) agreement could be established between California and Nevada. EMAC is a national mutual aid agreement that allows for sharing resources across state lines during governor-declared states of emergency, including natural disasters. EMAC was first introduced in 1993, was ratified by Congress in 1996, and to date has been enacted in all 50 US states, the District of Columbia, the US Virgin Islands, Guam, and the Northern Mariana Islands (Kapucu et al. 2009, emacweb.org). Importantly, EMAC includes provisions for reimbursement of out-of-state personnel, as well as liability and workers compensation insurance coverage (Kapucu et al. 2009).

In order for proper permissions to be in place for CCOCME team to deploy, the anthropologists at CSU-Chico would need to ask Butte County Sheriff's Office (the lead agency on the Camp Fire) to make a request for out-of-state resources through the California Office of Emergency Services/California EMAC coordinator, who would then take that request to the California Governor's office. The California governor then would work with the governor of Nevada, who in turn would work with the Nevada EMAC coordinator and then down the chain of command to the Clark County (Nevada) county manager and eventually to CCOCME. Perhaps not surprisingly, permissions through this system moved slower than through a university administration and by the morning of November 11, no agreement was yet in place. To try and expedite departure, the southern Nevada team then offered to deploy as academic anthropologists under the umbrella of UNLV rather than government employees from the

CCOCME. This request was denied by the CCOCME because without an EMAC agreement, the team would not have liability coverage while in the field.

Because an EMAC agreement was not yet in place by November 11, and due to the ten hours of drive time between Las Vegas and Chico, the CCOCME coroner relented and permitted the team to deploy that day. In total, the CCOCME team was deployed November 11–17, although the EMAC was not fully set up until the team was already in place. All expenditures by the CCOCME team were originally self-funded, although the team was later reimbursed by Clark County, who in turn was reimbursed by the state of California. Importantly, this not only included gasoline and meals but also salary and hourly pay for all employees.

In order to prepare for assisting with an out-of-state mass fatality, responders from government agencies should familiarize themselves with the basic mechanisms of EMAC agreements so they know what to expect when one is being set up. The established protocols for establishing EMAC mutual aid agreements simplify the preparation process for government employees, though they might not allow for as rapid of a response for government employees as those from academic institutions. For responders from academic institutions, however, there are multiple steps that can be taken to help prepare for out-of-state emergency response. Academic practitioners should inquire with their university administration to see if protocols can be developed for expedited travel applications to allow faculty and students to have liability and possibly workers' compensation coverage while on out-of-state responses. Additionally, although EMAC does not have established provisions for academics *per se*, if academics are employed by a public university, there should be accommodations that should be made. Therefore, it is recommended that forensic anthropologists who work in academia should contact their state EMAC coordinator to begin establishing a framework that would allow them to deploy to out-of-state emergencies with the same liability, worker's compensation, and reimbursement coverage afforded to government employees. If such a framework cannot be established to allow academics at public institutions to be covered by an EMAC agreement, anthropologists should identify funding sources to cover out of pocket expenses, such as gas and meals, incurred by student participants.

13.2 DEPLOYMENT EXPECTATIONS

Given the extended recovery operations at specific disaster sites such as the 2001 terrorist attacks at the World Trade Center in New York City or the 2021 Florida condominium collapse, one might expect that the recovery crews in wildfires would typically work extremely long shifts. However, wildfire recovery is multipronged, and it is common that recovery teams will retreat during the evening and night hours in order to allow the fire crews, utility repair crews, and road repair teams to do their work unimpeded. Fire crews and those hired specifically for the work need to fell large but weakened trees and bring down snags along roadways. Power lines need to be cleared and new poles placed into position and wires restrung. Cell service, often managed by mobile towers, needs to be stabilized or replaced. Road signs and crash barriers have often been destroyed and need replacement before the area can be repopulated. Whole sections of roads, including bridges and overpasses, may need to be replaced. These services are essential both to support the overall recovery operations but also make it ready for evacuated families to return.

This activity means that housing must be arranged for any personnel who are coming with the recovery team. Often there are contacts in the area willing to provide accommodations, but it may be necessary to make use of barrack situations. Hotels and other normal accommodations are often already fully booked with those who have evacuated, news reporters, and government-employed disaster workers.

13.3 HAZARDS EXPECTED IN THE FIELD

Preparation requires that those anticipating deployment have some idea of the types of hazards that they will face. Wildfire scenes are extremely chaotic, particularly in the early stages due to the issues of disrupted communication, obstructed roads, ongoing fire issues, difficulties with coordinating operations across multiple agencies, and staff availability. The ongoing effects of the fire will be constant and unpredictable, especially during the first few days following the fire event.

In the immediate aftermath of a wildfire in a wildland-urban interface, smoke and the ensuing darkness will be one of the most difficult situations encountered. Even at noon, visibility can be compromised to the point that it looks closer to midnight. Buildings and vehicles have to be searched by flashlight. Even days later, lingering smoke will obscure the sunlight, necessitating additional illumination to inspect enclosed areas. These light sources need to be able to run on batteries since electricity may be unavailable, and there may be continuing fire issues that preclude use of gasoline-powered generators.

Smoke is especially dense in the fire scene and contains hazardous particles that can produce permanent damage to the airways. This smoke is particularly hazardous for those with heart or lung disease (including asthma), people with diabetes, older individuals, and women who are pregnant.

Wildfire smoke also travels considerable distances and can accumulate in areas far away from the fire where wind patterns and natural topography, such as depressions or mountain ranges allow for concentration of smoke. Consequently, the need for masks may also extend to the off-duty hours.

The ongoing fire also generates a diversity of issues. Fires will continue to burn in the trunks and root systems of trees making footing difficult. Smoke and sometimes flames in trees or collapsed buildings are a common sight until the firefighters are able to conduct a thorough mop-up operation. Even if the flames are not present, the burned areas can retain considerable heat and use of a portable heat sensor may be helpful to ensure that no one is burned by hot metal or soil.

One of the deadliest situations in the aftermath of a fire is unstable trees. While the tree may be standing, there may be internal fire that is weakening the core of the tree. The tree can fall once the core is too weak to support the trunk. In addition to full trees, large branches are often caught on other trees and may come crashing down at any point. Because recovery crews are typically dispatched prior to the completion of fire crew mop-up activities, these trees are still a major concern. It is made more problematic as recovery teams typically are "ground-focused" in that they tend to only look down.

The burned structures and vehicles also contain a large number of sharp edges, ranging from exposed nails and screws to jagged metal edges from a variety of building materials and car frames. Some of these are clearly visible but many are hidden in the debris mass. In addition, there is a lack of stability in many structural elements. For example, mobile homes are reduced to the large I-beams held up on fire-cracked cinder blocks. Interspersed beneath these are the remains of the house contents, including broken glassware and china, along with construction debris.

Many rural areas depend on propane and septic systems, both of which produce working hazards during a search. Propane systems may explode even after the passage of the fire front. These systems include larger household tanks up to 1,000-gallon capacity as well as the smaller five-gallon barbeque-type tanks. Septic systems may have a concrete lid that will usually withstand the fire. However, many systems have plastic lids that will melt or a wooden lid that will burn. Neither may be visible on the surface. While not deep enough to cause drowning, few recovery personnel are willing to risk falling into a septic tank.

Unfortunately, aside from the possible exposed septic systems, restroom facilities are often nonexistent in the field. Portable toilet facilities may be present at the staging area, but rarely are they distributed to the field. For those personnel who need facilities, the usual approach of "find a tree or bush" is no longer an option as those have all been burned out. There may also be search teams, repair crews, and media persons interspersed around the landscape, making calls to nature more problematic. Despite the possible lack of restroom facilities, it is still important to ensure that team members stay hydrated throughout the day.

Recovery work can be physically and mentally taxing so team members should be prepared. Mobility is limited in recovery situations and the physical work of lifting and removing debris, hauling buckets to screening stations, and moving equipment within the scene places stress on the body. Individuals with impaired health will need to adjust their pace to accommodate the work, as well as wear their protective gear. They should also bring any needed medication with them during deployment.

Recovery work can be taxing on mental health (see Chapter 22). Finding people as they were positioned as they died and the enormity of the destruction can trigger adverse reactions, including vicarious trauma, in those involved with the recovery work. Vicarious trauma involves the traumatization of those who are not directly experiencing a traumatic event or crisis (e.g., injury, loss of a loved one, loss of property due to a fire) but instead interact with individuals who are experiencing direct trauma or respond to the aftermath of a traumatic event (Love and Langley 2020, Goldstein and Alesbury 2021). This phenomenon was originally recognized in mental health professionals, and more recently it has been recognized in first responders including forensic practitioners. For forensic practitioners, vicarious trauma could result from handling a sensitive case (abuse victim, child death) or working on a mass fatality incident. The psychological association to victims of trauma can manifest in mental stress, fatigue, burnout, and feelings of ineffectiveness (Love and Langley 2020, Goldstein and Alesbury 2021). It is important for team members to have ready access to counseling during and after a stressful experience, such as recovery operations in a wildfire event.

13.4 EQUIPMENT AND PERSONAL SUPPLIES

Because the first days of a wildfire recovery are chaotic, even in the best of circumstances, it is important that the trained human remains recovery teams have sufficient

FIGURE 13.1 Range of equipment showing from upper left, soil screen, garden rake, quarter-inch standing screen, plastic bucket, mason's trowel, dustpan, tiler's pad.

material on hand to begin the recovery process. Often the consumables used during this time can be replaced (with permission) as the lead agency is able to get new material to the field. However, there are basics of personal protective equipment, recovery equipment, and transportation equipment (Figure 13.1, Table 13.1) that the recovery teams need to be able to bring to the field. A five-to-seven-day supply is often sufficient to clear the possible delays.

Team members should be able to bring heavy work pants, long-sleeved shirts, and work boots with thick soles. Temperatures can vary in the recovery area. While there may still be active fires, the heavy smoke often reduces temperature by blocking sunlight. At times, work can be sufficiently physical to increase body temperature so flexibility in clothing layers is helpful.

13.5 REGIONAL PREPARATION

Regional agencies can also make significant preparations for the possibility of a mass fatality event, in addition to their emergency preparedness protocols. Specific to wildfires, the recovery teams note that there are four areas where regional preparation is helpful. First is the management of the missing persons list so that there are clear guidelines for prioritization that have been rehearsed and that there are also clear and timely instructions on removal of names because they have been found alive or a body at the suspected location has been recovered.

Second, many of the areas affected by wildfires are more rural or marginal. They may include large encampments of individuals experiencing homelessness, campsites, recreational vehicle sites, mobile home parks, and hybrid residential areas where there is a mixture of a permanent and transient population. These areas are often completely devastated by wildfire as the close proximity of the housing units allow the flames to pass from one structure to the next. Often the only building left is the community center, often separated from the homes by a large parking area and a swimming pool. While camping sites are often controlled by online registration that allows identification of potential campers, homeless encampments and transient homes are much more fluid in occupation and with fewer registration formalities. In these situations, the local park manager or spokesperson may be able to assist in initiating a cellphone check that can reveal if any residents are unaccounted. However, such individuals must trust the agencies making contact as there will be suspicions that such checks are really a guise for serving warrants, deporting, or arresting those who have evacuated.

Third, regional agencies can also help in areas, particularly RV and mobile home parks where identifying markers have been destroyed. Planning departments have files of the unit maps for such locations, and these can be accessed. Then the unit number can be spray-painted on the road in front of each unit. This allows the recovery team to focus on a single area when asked to look for a missing person associated with one unit and when the team is faced with a large park of destroyed homes without identifying numbers.

Fourth, there is often a rush to "get into" buildings that will impede recovery efforts (see Chapters 11 and 12). However, many rural structures also have metal roofing that obscures the underlying debris. Small excavators can be used to lift these panels and place them in a cleared area for later removal. However, dog handlers often prefer to run their human remains detection dogs around or through a structure before the roof is lifted as the metal concentrates the odors. Anthropologists need roof panels removed before they can begin their perimeter and detailed searches. Excavators often want to lift not only the roof but also appliances, water tanks, and any other visible metal once they are located to eliminate return visits. However, this often includes mattress springs and springs from sofas and chairs. These are prime locations for finding remains and thus need to be retained *in situ* so that remains do not get dispersed. Furthermore, removal of appliances often makes interpretation of room identity difficult. Clear protocols established prior to a disaster are extremely helpful so that recovery crews and dog handlers are not left arguing with the excavator operators.

13.6 CONCLUSION

Wildfire recovery of fatalities requires intensive effort built upon readiness to perform the tasks. While we often think that this preparation focuses on stockpiling equipment and providing adequate training, our experience with wildfires also highlights preparation for what will be encountered. Deployments are unpredictable, often lengthy, physically grueling, and emotionally taxing. Preparation of equipment and training and being informed about what is expected are critical.

REFERENCES

EMACweb. Retrieved December 1, 2021, from emacweb.org.

Goldstein, J. Z., & Alesbury, H. S. (2021). Self-reported levels of occupational stress and wellness in forensic practitioners: Implications for the education and training of the forensic workforce. *Journal of Forensic Sciences*, *66*(4), 1307–1315.

Kapucu, N., Augustin, M.-E., & Garayev, V. (2009). Interstate partnerships in emergency management: Emergency management assistance compact in response to catastrophic disasters. *Public Administration Review*, *69*(2), 297–313.

Love, J. C., & Langley, N. R. (2020). Exploring educational needs beyond technical competency: Laboratory management, court testimony, and vicarious trauma. *Forensic Anthropology*, *3*(2), 82–90.

SECTION IV

Post-Recovery Processes Following a Mass Fatality

Section IV of this volume focuses on post-recovery processes following a mass fatality event. The first five chapters (Chapters 14–18) provide a review of post-recovery analyses from the perspective of the coroner, pathologist, odontologist, morgue anthropologist, and DNA analyst, respectively. The final chapter, while not focused specifically on wildfire response, presents an overview of the disaster victim identification process following the international Grenfell Tower Disaster that occurred in London in 2017. This chapter provides a point of comparison for the international response and the US response in the case of a mass fatality incident.

Chapter 14 opens with a discussion of advance preparation in the event of a mass fatality event. The authors state that writing a mass fatality plan is imperative, and this plan must be flexible and amenable to modification, such as including new technology (e.g., integration of Rapid DNA technology in the aftermath of the Camp Fire). Chapter 14 goes on to outline the morgue facility needs following a mass fatality incident, including supplies, technology, and personnel. In addition to the general facility needs, designated stations must be established for the efficient processing/identification of remains. A flow chart is provided to illustrate the sequence of stations from admitting to pathology. Throughout this discussion the importance of documentation is emphasized, and difficulties associated with wildfire victim identification is highlighted. The author closes by stressing the importance of teamwork in the identification process.

Chapter 15 reflects on the role played by the forensic pathologist in establishing cause and manner of death in fatal fire victims. While the questions posed during the postmortem examination of a fire victim are similar to those posed in any other death investigation, there are a number of challenges specific to fire deaths, including time of death. In addition to the question of cause and manner, pathologists are thoroughly trained in differentiating trauma sustained during a fire, from that occurring before a fire or after, during recovery of the remains. Additionally, as was mentioned in the previous chapter, identifications are frequently more difficult in fire deaths than in other circumstances and the pathologist can help to facilitate identification through the appropriate and most efficient means.

DOI: 10.4324/9781003168010-17

Chapter 16 discusses the role of forensic odontology in wildfire victim identification. Following the 2018 Camp Fire, forensic odontology was used as one method of identification for fire victims. This chapter examines how the odontological identification process worked, including the reconstruction of postmortem dentition, the location of antemortem records, and the comparison of the two for positive identification. Throughout, the authors discuss some of the major challenges encountered in wildfire victim identification and the chapter closes with suggestions for future mass fatality response.

Chapter 17 provides an in-depth discussion of the role of the anthropologist in post-recovery analysis of human remains. The chapter is written from the perspective of an anthropologist stationed in the morgue and examples are drawn upon from the Camp Fire. The chapter begins by outlining how burned remains are systematically assessed in the morgue setting, including a discussion of some of the most frequently encountered challenges. Drawing upon lessons learned from previous fire victim analyses, the authors provide guiding principles for future analytic work and discuss areas in which additional research would prove beneficial.

Chapter 18 provides an introduction to Rapid DNA identification and its application to disaster victim identification. The first use of Rapid DNA at a major mass casualty event was during the 2018 Camp Fire, and the authors use lessons learned from this disaster as the exemplar for the overview of Rapid DNA technology provided here. The chapter presents the standard protocols by which unidentified human remains were processed using Rapid DNA technology. A total of 69 sets of remains were subjected to Rapid DNA identification using the ANDE system. Of these, 62 (89.9%) generated DNA IDs that were utilized for familial searching. All DNA IDs were produced within hours, in stark contrast to traditional DNA methods that can take months to years to receive results. In total, 58 victims of the Camp Fire were identified using Rapid DNA technology, compared to 22 victims identified using other more conventional modalities.

The final chapter of this section, Chapter 19, presents an overview of the disaster victim identification process following the international Grenfell Tower Disaster, which occurred in London in 2017. The chapter outlines the INTERPOL Disaster Victim Identification Guide and the standard mortuary processes utilized following this mass fatality event. While not written from the perspective of a wildfire event, the chapter provides a point of comparison for the international response and the US response in the case of a mass fatality incident. The chapter also highlights the similarities in the level of destruction, the degree of commingling, and the complexities of recovery between deaths due to wildfires and those in multistory residential buildings.

CHAPTER 14

Morgue Operations during a Mass Fatality Event

Kim Gin

When a mass fatality event occurs, morgue operations are an integral part of the successful handling of that event. The proper identification, examination, and ultimately, quick release of the victims for final arrangements by the family are the main goals for any agency routinely, and during a mass fatality event, these goals remain the same, just on an elevated level. There are many moving parts to these seemingly simple goals. This chapter focuses on these topics and provides important information that will aid in the preparation and management of any mass fatality event but also specifically address the issues that arise from handling victims of wildfires which are often the hardest victims to identify. The most important thing to understand from the very beginning of any mass fatality incident is that this will be an intense time of flux and change within the operations of a morgue. No two events will be the same, and the issues that come with these events will require flexibility for successful morgue operation.

14.1 PREPARATION

Preparation for mass fatality incidents is a must; however, being completely prepared for every possible incident type or issue is nearly impossible, no matter the time spent on planning. Even though it seems contradictory, it is extremely important to prepare written plans before a mass disaster occurs. Having a plan in place is important as that plan can be changed and molded to fit the needs that arise during an incident. Practice the written plans and scenarios as much as possible until everyone involved in a potential event feels comfortable with the necessary steps.

Of equal importance is keeping the mass fatality plan updated. This step becomes even more important after an event has occurred. This is the time to make real-world changes to your written plan. Look for issues that came up during the incident and make those needed changes. One example of an issue faced at the Sacramento County Morgue when working on the Camp Fire victims in 2018 that was not properly addressed in the mass fatality plan was the need for experts in anthropology to assist with two different steps: timely identification and release of victims. Anthropologists were needed from the time remains were found and in the majority of the cases before the remains could be released to rule out commingling of remains. The various experts needed during an event was mentioned in the written mass fatality plan, but there was no detail outlined

DOI: 10.4324/9781003168010-18

regarding the extreme need for these experts. This turned out to be a very important multi-step process that required coordination and a definite update to the plan.

The plan also had to be updated to accommodate for the inclusion of Rapid DNA. The Sacramento County Coroner's Office was the first office to use this identification method during a mass fatality event and the need to incorporate it into an updated plan was very necessary. The turnaround time for Rapid DNA results was significantly reduced over traditional methods, which affected other aspects ranging from identification to releases and even more important as it turns out, death certification. During the actual event, the plan was changed in practice to accommodate Rapid DNA into the order of identification, but the plan had to be updated to reflect this change.

Once updates are made, keep staff apprised of changes remembering to also immediately include newly hired employees. Incorporate partners into the plan by meeting and exercising the plan when there is no actual event to work. Accurately managing a morgue during an event is dependent on partners outside of the organization. Teamwork is key and working on these partnerships routinely is very important. Outside pathologists, other death investigation agencies, DNA specialists, and professionals such as anthropologists and odontologists will be part of the morgue operations team and should be able to seamlessly work in the morgue during an event. That is not possible if the work is not put into these partnerships outside of a mass fatality event.

Another focus should be on securing equipment that would be needed in a mass fatality event. If acquiring this equipment is a budgetary issue, acquiring grants or partnering with other jurisdictions that can assist with needed equipment is a good way to solve this problem, keeping in mind that the best time to do this is well before the equipment is needed. Once the preparation is complete, bear in mind that despite all the training and planning, each incident is different and quickly resolving issues is the key to successfully handling a mass disaster.

14.2 TEMPORARY VERSUS PERMANENT MORGUE SITES

After any incident, it will be necessary to assess whether or not a temporary morgue, either fully or partially functional, should be set up. This decision will depend on the event itself. If a fire burns the morgue, the permanent morgue site is no longer an option. A fully functional temporary morgue would address all aspects of identification, examination, and final release of victims and should be chosen carefully. The temporary site should have an adequate water supply, existing drainage, and good sanitation. Pre-existing sanitation is preferable. The site should also have access to standard household current at 110–120 volts and 220 voltage to accommodate trucks and semi-trailers. When choosing a fully functional temporary site, keep in mind that the flooring should be non-porous, preferably concrete floors that can be decontaminated easily. There should be plenty of room for various stations, exam rooms, X-ray rooms, and administrative needs. Avoid attaching any type of family assistance center to the morgue no matter the type of incident, but having it close by is optimal for staff to easily access the center.

If the actual morgue can be used (Figure 14.1), it may be necessary to set up a temporary morgue or holding station as victims are located at the site. This can be something as simple as a refrigerated secured truck where victims can be stored until they can be transported to the morgue. During the Camp Fire, a small refrigerated box truck was used at the incident site for refrigerated storage and at the end of the day the wildfire victims were transported to the Sacramento County Morgue (Figure 14.2).

FIGURE 14.1 Entry bay at a permanent morgue with entry cleared to accommodate transfer of multiple victims.

Source: Sacramento County Coroner

FIGURE 14.2 Refrigerated box truck for transportation of remains from incident site to morgue facility.

Source: Sacramento County Coroner

14.3 ROUTINE WORK DURING AN EVENT

During an event, the routine, everyday work does not stop. Every effort should be made to maintain normal day-to-day operations while simultaneously handling the mass fatality event. Separating the two aspects of mass fatality casework versus normal operations case work is necessary to ensure that decedents not involved in the event are properly handled. Assigning staff to mass fatality versus routine casework may be necessary. It also may be necessary to request mutual aid from other agencies (volunteers or a Disaster Mortuary Operational Response Team, commonly known as DMORT, which is operated through the US Department of Health and Human Services) to bolster your staffing. "DMORT members provide technical assistance and consultation on fatality management and mortuary affairs" (U.S. Department of Health and Human Services, 2017). Assess the needs at the time of the event and the response time for assistance as the event progresses. Asking for assistance through the various avenues or even a combination may be needed to adequately cover routine work and mass fatality operations.

Staffing will be stretched during this time, so reaching out to other agencies that investigate deaths is a good idea. It may be necessary to request mutual aid for pathologists, autopsy assistants, and death investigators, to name a few. The Sacramento County Coroner's Office looked to the Sacramento Office of Emergency Services for assistance with acquiring specialized medical volunteers during the Camp Fire response. Volunteers from the Sacramento Medical Reserve Corps worked in the morgue taking X-rays, moving remains from station to station and sweeping the floors clean of burnt ash during the event. These volunteers are trained medical personnel that can tolerate the kind of work that occurs in a morgue and are very valuable after an event. Prior to the wildfire, members of the Corps toured the facility and discussed ways the volunteers could support line staff which proved to be invaluable when the fire started (Sacramento County Office of Emergency Services, n.d.).

Taking care of all staff is very important while working an event. Taking care of volunteers is even more important as they often will be traveling from outside the area. Make sure that lodging is secured and that volunteers are routinely fed. Schedule breaks and mealtimes for them and encourage them to use that time to rest and recharge. Bring in or cater food for the volunteers and be careful what is ordered for meals and snacks. For example, ordering barbeque for staff working on fire victims would be a huge mistake.

14.4 WHAT ARE THE MORGUE FACILITY NEEDS DURING AN EVENT?

The first problem that arises in an incident no matter the size of the morgue is the need for more storage space for decedents. Having a secondary source on hand or through mutual aid such as a refrigerated trailer is a very important resource. (Figure 14.3) The one used for the Camp Fire was a 52-foot trailer that was moved to the secure employee parking lot of the Coroner's Office and was purchased ten years before the event occurred and could easily hold approximately 100 of the wildfire victims. There are some regulations surrounding the use of these refrigerated trailers, so renting one when an event occurs may not be a viable option.

FIGURE 14.3 Refrigerated semi-trailer.

Source: Sacramento County Coroner

There are a lot of different choices out there for extra storage if a semi-trailer truck would not work. A refrigerated Conex unit (Figure 14.4) can be purchased in various sizes and placed in a stationary area or moved to where it is needed, although it would require a specialized move. There are also other smaller options on the market that can be utilized for storage of bodies on a much smaller scale (Figure 14.5) and can be stationed easily in a smaller space. Whatever is purchased or obtained through a mutual aid request, it is important to make sure that the electrical needs are addressed in the area it will be used or that it can run off of a generator or other power source. Sacramento County had refrigerated space already on hand with the refrigerated 52-foot semi-trailer, so space was not a big problem after the Camp Fire, but that did not mean there were no problems with storage. The issue quickly became the lack of racking and tables for the racks (Figure 14.6). Stacking decedents is not an acceptable practice, especially in the fragile condition of many burn victims, so good use of the available space was the major problem. To remedy this issue, backboards borrowed from the local fire department and specialty remains boxes used by mortuaries were obtained and used until more racks could be obtained (Figures 14.7 and 14.8).

Some morgues have X-ray machines, but some do not. Specialized equipment, such as X-ray machines or dental X-ray machines, are good purchases prior to an event. If

FIGURE 14.4 Refrigerated Conex box.

Source: Sacramento County Coroner

the morgue does not have either of these at the time of the event, they can be rented for use during the event. Make sure to also include safeguards for obtaining X-rays if the morgue is not equipped for that or if the morgue is mobile. There are plenty of options for equipment that can be purchased or rented that allows for obtaining safe X-rays in the morgue or field.

Morgue operations, after a mass fatality event, is ideally split into administration and identification/examination. The names of the sections may vary from agency to agency, but the responsibilities will be the same. The responsibilities of the identification/examination section revolve around the identification and examination processes. The typical responsibilities for the administration are highlighted here:

1. Monitoring staffing and managing volunteers, security, supplies, and any equipment needs
2. Documenting labor and purchases, as well as making purchases

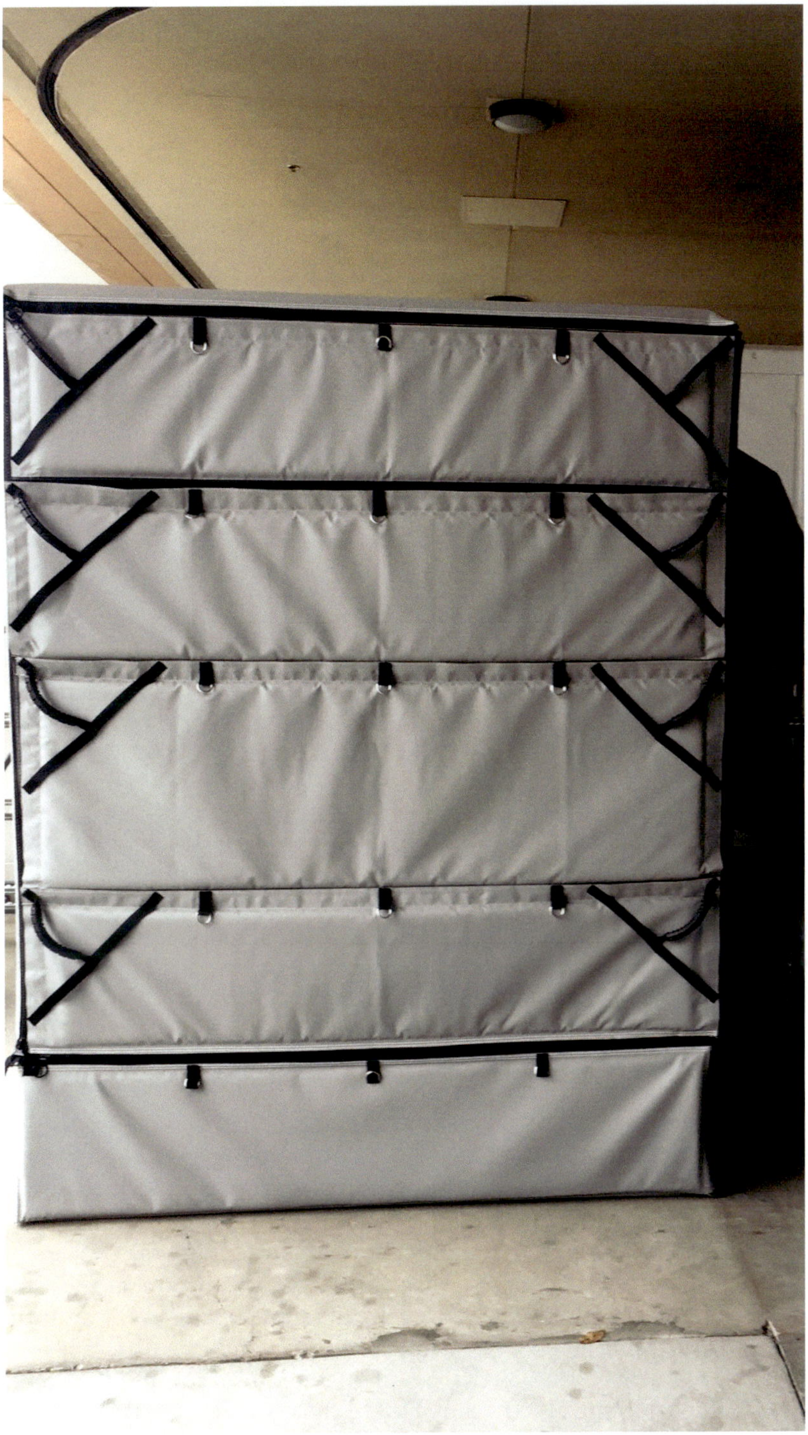

FIGURE 14.5 ResponStor morgue storage unit.

Source: Sacramento County Coroner

FIGURE 14.6 Storage racks commonly used for storage of human remains.

Source: Sacramento County Coroner

3. Death certification and completing any necessary disaster victim packets
4. Approving identifications, maintaining logs and paperwork/documentation
5. Inputting any electronic data into systems
6. Maintaining security and confidentiality both at the site and on paper
7. Managing specialists/mutual aid
8. Anything else needed regarding administration specific to the event

Identification and examination covers the various specialty fields that have a hand in both identification and examination of the victims and the support staff. This can include volunteers, even though they are also listed under administration. Large-scale disasters will necessitate more specialists within the field of pathology, odontology, and anthropology that will need to work as a team to quickly examine and identify decedents.

When processing a significant number of decedents from a single event, workstations and designated work rooms should be set up to streamline the processing, examination, and identification of remains. There are some variations on the workstations that can be set up in the configuration that works best for the event and the location of the morgue. If the morgue is in the field, the setup would be different from a setup at the morgue itself where the natural setting of the morgue might factor into the procedures. The most natural flow no matter the location would likely start with the admitting station and end with either the final release station or after care station. The decision on final release versus after care depends on how overwhelmed the system is from the incident and if embalming or cremation has to be included in morgue operations for public safety reasons.

FIGURE 14.7 Mortuary boxes ready for remains.

Source: Sacramento County Coroner

FIGURE 14.8 Backboards borrowed from local fire departments.

Source: Sacramento County Coroner

There are some variations in the literature regarding stations, but the most common flow is admission of the remains, scanning of the remains, examination by pathology (including DNA sampling), examination by a specialist (such as an odontologist or anthropologist), and documentation, identification, and final storage or release of remains (Leditschke et al., 2011, p. 12). These stations or rooms can be created with material on hand (Figure 14.9) or can be purchased (Figure 14.10) or even possibly obtained through mutual aid in some jurisdictions.

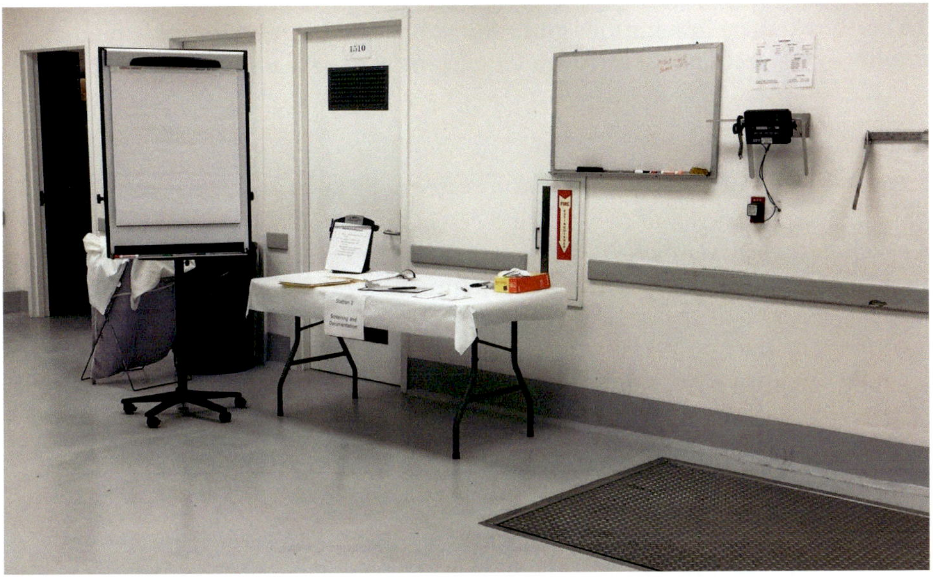

FIGURE 14.9 Impromptu station.

Source: Sacramento County Coroner

FIGURE 14.10 Purchased station.

Source: Sacramento County Coroner

There are quite a few stations and rooms that can be set up for mass fatality events. The following is a comprehensive list of stations with explanations for each one.

14.4.1 Admitting Station

At this station, remains and personal effects are admitted and assigned reference numbers, such as a case number. In big events, escorts or trackers can be assigned at this station to accompany the remains until examination/identification is completed and to ensure the security of the case file or documents. In addition, the tracker will ensure that proper documentation is complete, signed, and attached at each station. This station can be set up as one permanent station or as a temporary station at the event site.

14.4.2 Receiving Station

The receiving station is where the decedent remains and property/evidence are documented and the chain of custody is initiated. The receiving station is a must, but it is particularly necessary if the admitting station is set up at the incident site and decedents/property/evidence are transported to a stationary morgue.

14.4.3 Screening/Triage

At this station, remains, personal effects, evidence, and debris delivered from the incident site in the body bag are screened and triaged. This entails the following:

- Take radiographs of bags prior to screening/triage; separate diagnostic human tissue from material evidence, debris, and personal effects
- Take photographs prior to disturbing clothing, property, and foreign objects
- Complete anatomic charting if applicable at this stage
- Document any personal effects or evidence
- Complete chain-of-custody forms for evidence removed
- Determine path for remains based on protocol
- Bag any human tissue/remains having potential for identification
- Store any tissue that does not have potential for ID
- Store unassociated personal effects
- Flag any personal effects or dangerous material items (e.g., bomb fragments) that could not be removed without possible damage or could be dangerous

If remains are determined, at any later station, to be unrelated, they should be separated and returned to screening/triage for assessment and direction.

14.4.4 Documentation Station

At this station, remains, personal effects, and evidence are photographed and documented in detail and with the following in mind:

- Take photographs prior to disturbing clothing, property, and foreign objects
- Place proper documentation in the photo, including a scale, when applicable
- Take standard autopsy-type photographs (anatomical position) for complete bodies
- Take full-face photographs if applicable, keeping in mind that many wildfire victims are often the most degraded due to fire and may be reduced to just bones

14.4.5 Print Station

This station should be equipped to take finger/foot/palm prints of remains or body parts using paper and ink or digital printing. This station should also be equipped to make castings if necessary.

14.4.6 Pathology Station/Room

This station can be set up in the autopsy area or, if at a mobile morgue, set up near the area where examinations are conducted or as the entire area where exams are conducted. DNA samples can be taken with other sampling in this area while autopsies are conducted. Bones should not be sampled if the body is not intact, or an anthropology exam has not been conducted. Bones are easily consumed in DNA testing, and the inclusion of Rapid DNA into the mass fatality identification response makes it necessary to wait until after the anthropology and/or odontology exam is completed.

14.4.7 Anthropology Station/Room

This station or room should be set up for the anthropologists to examine the bodies/remains. The anthropologist's role is significant from beginning to end when it comes to wildfire victims, and having a room or large area to sort remains can be very beneficial for identification of wildfire victims.

14.4.8 Odontology Station

This station or room should be set up for the odontologists to conduct exams on any decedent, which would include taking X-rays, reviewing X-rays, reviewing antemortem records, and examining remains. More and more dentists are using digital X-rays that can be emailed quickly for identification purposes. If the antemortem X-rays are digital, have a computer set up to view them or an X-ray light box if the X-rays are on actual film. In a large-scale event, this station can become separate sections, divided into a dental postmortem section, where the actual dental examination of the remains occurs; the dental antemortem section, which might work closely with the family assistance center or designated investigators working on obtaining antemortem records; and the comparison section, which compares the antemortem and postmortem records for the purpose of identification.

14.4.9 DNA Station

This station or room should be set up for staff working on obtaining and running samples. It should be located near the exam room(s). When factoring in Rapid DNA, a room should be set up for actually running samples onsite.

14.4.10 Final Holding Station

This station is usually a refrigerated area where processed remains are held until release. All human remains (identified, unidentified, and common tissue) should always be stored with complete dignity with remains covered and without stacking. The holding areas for processed victims and for common tissue should be separated from remains that have not been processed and from where specimens (e.g., for DNA, histology, and toxicology) are stored while awaiting transfer to the lab for analysis. Remains should be held until the victim can be released for final disposition. Identified decedents should always be assessed in final identification review for release. Unidentified decedents should be sent to refrigerated holding while identification is still pending.

14.4.11 Final Identification Review

When remains are ready to be released, the supervisor or assigned personnel and forensic specialists involved in the identification should do the following:

- Conduct a final review of the methods of identification used for the remains
- Physically examine the remains to ensure that the biological attributes of the deceased (based on the ante mortem information) match the identification modality
- Ensure that the numbers (case numbers) associated with the remains are accurate
- Documentation should include signing and dating the forms
- Ensure death certification has been initiated/completed for all remains that have been identified

If the next of kin/legal authority has authorized after care and the after care is provided at the incident morgue, the identified remains can be routed to an after care station.

14.4.12 After Care Station

It may be necessary to set up this station if the funeral homes and crematories are so overwhelmed that final disposition cannot be carried out within a reasonable timeframe, creating a public safety hazard. This station would include embalming, cremation, and casketing to ensure remains of victims are cared for properly.

14.4.13 Final Release Station

Upon completion of the final identification, human remains and associated personal effects that are not deemed evidence should be released according to the standard operating procedure of the Office.

An information resource center (IRC) can be set up for records compilation. The IRC can be set up as a station, but more likely will require more room than a singular station. The IRC is the central repository for collecting, recording, and storing antemortem and postmortem information, including the following:

- Keeping the information systems used in the morgue and all records secure
- Matching of antemortem and postmortem files at all stages
- Receiving electronic antemortem data from the family assistance center or medical personnel directly and ensuring the data is added to the flow for identification
- Electronically logging antemortem and postmortem data into all systems
- Death certification
- Written identification summaries as remains are identified

All records and data must be kept secure and confidential in accordance with the Health Insurance Portability and Accountability Act (HIPAA) and any local laws.

14.5 CASE STUDY: MORGUE STATIONS FOR THE CAMP FIRE VICTIMS

In the Camp Fire, the following workstations/work rooms were set up to accurately process, examine, and identify the remains located in the aftermath of the wildfire (Figure 14.11):

1. **Admitting Station:** This station was set up using a refrigerated box truck in Butte County. The remains were assigned a case number for tracking purposes, and all pertinent information that could aid in identification was included with the remains. Documentation at this stage was information located in the field, case number assigned, and other relevant information like diagrams, photographs, and so on.
2. **Admitting and Receiving Station:** This station was set up in the stationary morgue entrance. The facility was designed to accommodate processing mass fatality remains with the stations outside the morgue entrance, but the smoke from the wildfires was so heavy that the stations had to be moved indoors, thereby limiting the number of stations.
   At this station, the decedents (in body bags) were delivered from the incident site. The remains admitted here were given a second tracking number, and pertinent information was entered into the existing case management system using

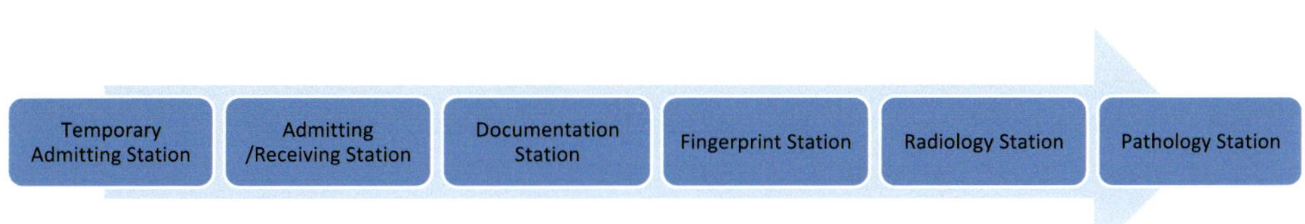

FIGURE 14.11 Sequence of stations from admitting through pathology.

an identifier in the case number just for the wildfire victims. All incoming body and property bags were documented, and the chain of custody was initiated. This same information was listed on a large sheet of paper where handwritten notes could be made by all staff then updated in the case management system daily. This was set up in this manner because it soon became apparent that mutual aid would be requested from other counties. Those personnel would not be familiar or have access to the case management system. It was easier to assign one staff member to make the updates electronically.

As part of the intake process, staff assigned a plastic sleeve with an escort tracking form (see Figure 14.12), pathology exam form and a blank anthropology exam form. This established the chain of custody and was retained with the decedent at all times. Other forms were added in the sleeve as appropriate to keep everything together. The tracking document was placed on the top in the sleeve for easy viewing and fastened to the outside of the bag or container.

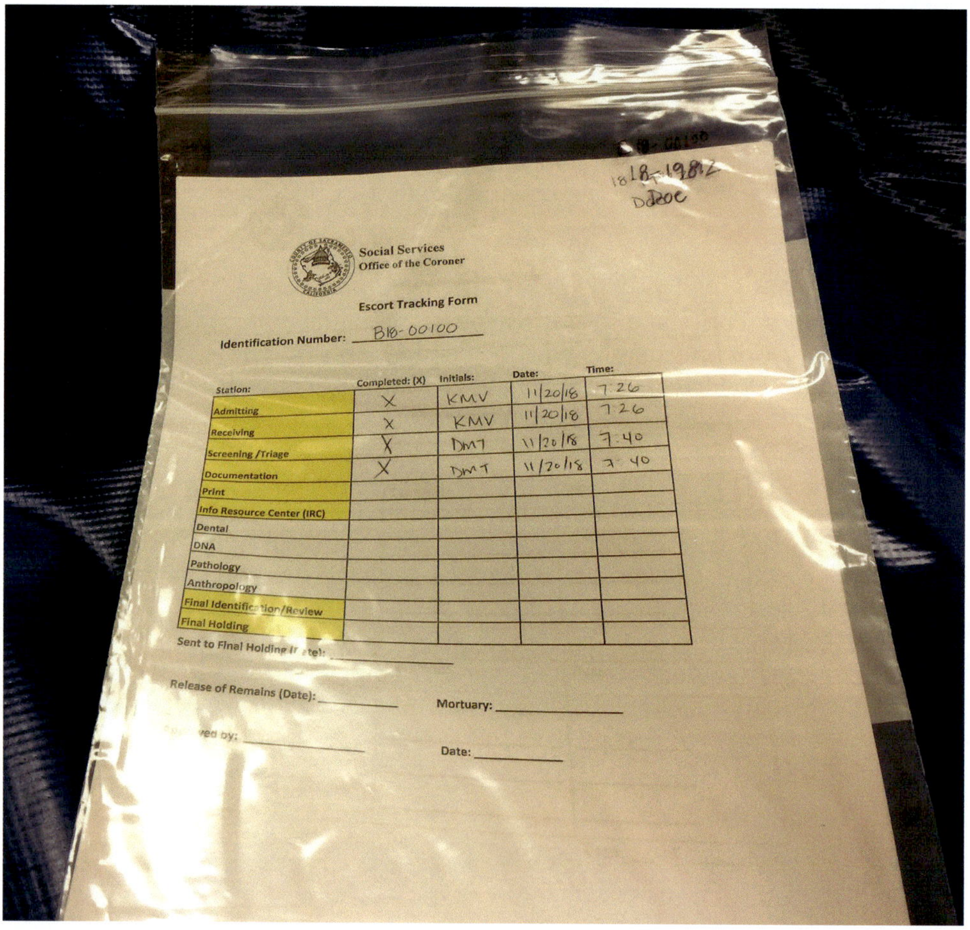

FIGURE 14.12 Sample escort tracking form.

Source: Sacramento County Coroner

3. **Documentation Station:** Because of the limited space in the morgue, this station was set up to take photographs and process property and evidence that came in with the remains.
4. **Fingerprint Station:** This station will likely not get much use when it comes to wildfire victims, but it is one of the necessary stations in a mass event. This station was set up for obtaining digital prints, paper, and ink processing and for casting.
5. **Radiology Station:** This station was set up for X-rays of bags/boxes, decedents, and taking dental X-rays. All body bags were radiographed to facilitate safe handling of collected remains. The pathologist or anthropologist read the radiographs to assess the contents of the bag for effective sorting and locating hazardous substances. In some morgues, this station might include a CT scan. Use of portable radiographs in the field should also be anticipated and could be incorporated into this station.
6. **Pathology Station:** This station was set up in the autopsy area itself. With the inclusion of Rapid DNA, sampling was completed at exam if fluid or tissue samples were available. For bones and/or teeth only, the DNA sampling was conducted after exams were conducted by an anthropologist and/or an odontologist (Figure 14.13).
7. **Anthropology Station:** This station was set up in the autopsy suite so the pathologists and anthropologists could work together on cases. For a large-scale event like this one, the anthropologists need some room to sort bones. Unfortunately, space was limited so this station was set up in two autopsy bays instead of a whole room, which would have been the ideal scenario.
8. **Odontology Station:** The odontology station was set up near the X-ray area in the morgue. It was adjacent to an office that had a light box and a computer and had room for examining remains.
9. **DNA Station:** The DNA station historically with wildfires has been one of the last stations the remains will go through. With the inclusion of Rapid DNA in the Camp Fire identification process, this station became a room next to the autopsy suite. This change was made because fluid or tissue samples were taken at autopsy if fluids or tissue were available so that samples could be run while the examination was being conducted. If bone was needed, the bone was taken only after the anthropologists and odontologists had conducted their exams. This affected the flow and was based on samples available. Having the DNA station in the actual morgue allowed for quicker testing times.

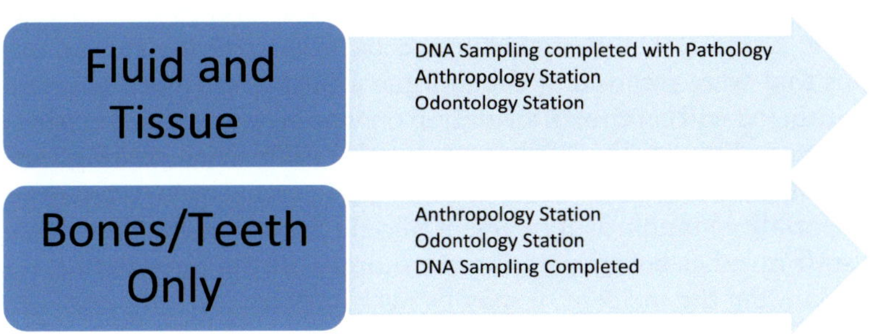

FIGURE 14.13 Sequence of stations after Pathology, dependent upon state of remains.

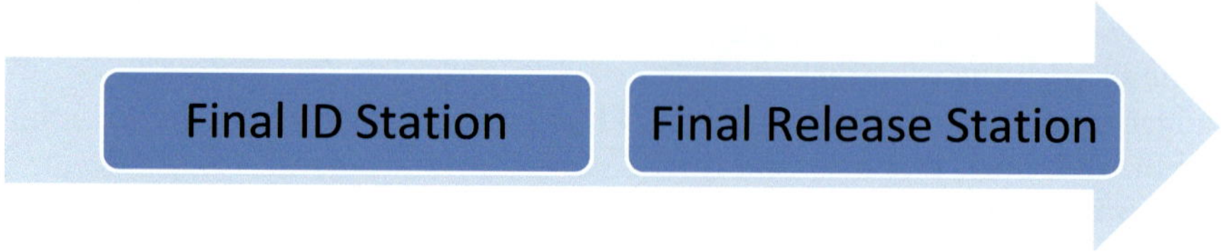

FIGURE 14.14 Final sequence from final identification to release.

10. **Final Identification Station:** This station was set up to have a supervisor check that everything was completed for the victim identification, a death certificate was completed, and all necessary documentation was completed (Figure 14.14). Final identification review was conducted by a supervisor as part of the tasks for this station.
11. **Final Release Station:** At this station, the remains were either approved for release to the designated funeral home or designated to be held until the family could make final arrangements.

An information resource center was set up in a nearby meeting room. Even though the case management system was all electronic, paper files were put in place for each case, by case number, to hold any documents needed for identification and release of the remains. This room also had a white board that was updated every day with identification numbers and releases. Having this constant change of information clearly displayed made reporting of statistics for the event a manageable task.

14.6 DOCUMENTATION

The best way to ensure everything is handled appropriately is to maintain logs and update documentation throughout the process and before remains are released (Figure 14.15). Logs should be maintained at each station to document what has been completed on each decedent. Examples of logs include but are not limited to photography logs, fingerprint logs, radiology logs, and personal effects/evidence logs. Each station should also be equipped with directions as to what should be documented at that particular station.

In addition to station specific logs, there are other types of logs that should be available in the morgue. The morgue site reception control log can be used to document remains that were received at the morgue and the transport driver information. A morgue sign-in log will capture information on who is entering and exiting the morgue and at what times. This can be used for documentation when seeking reimbursement for staff time and volunteer hours and also maintains security in the morgue.

A confidentiality standards agreement should be signed by anyone that is not a permanent staff member before entering the morgue. If the information is highly confidential surrounding the incident, it may be necessary to have all permanent staff sign the form as well. The form should include information on photography and recordings while onsite and not using any photographs or recordings of the site; the remains or

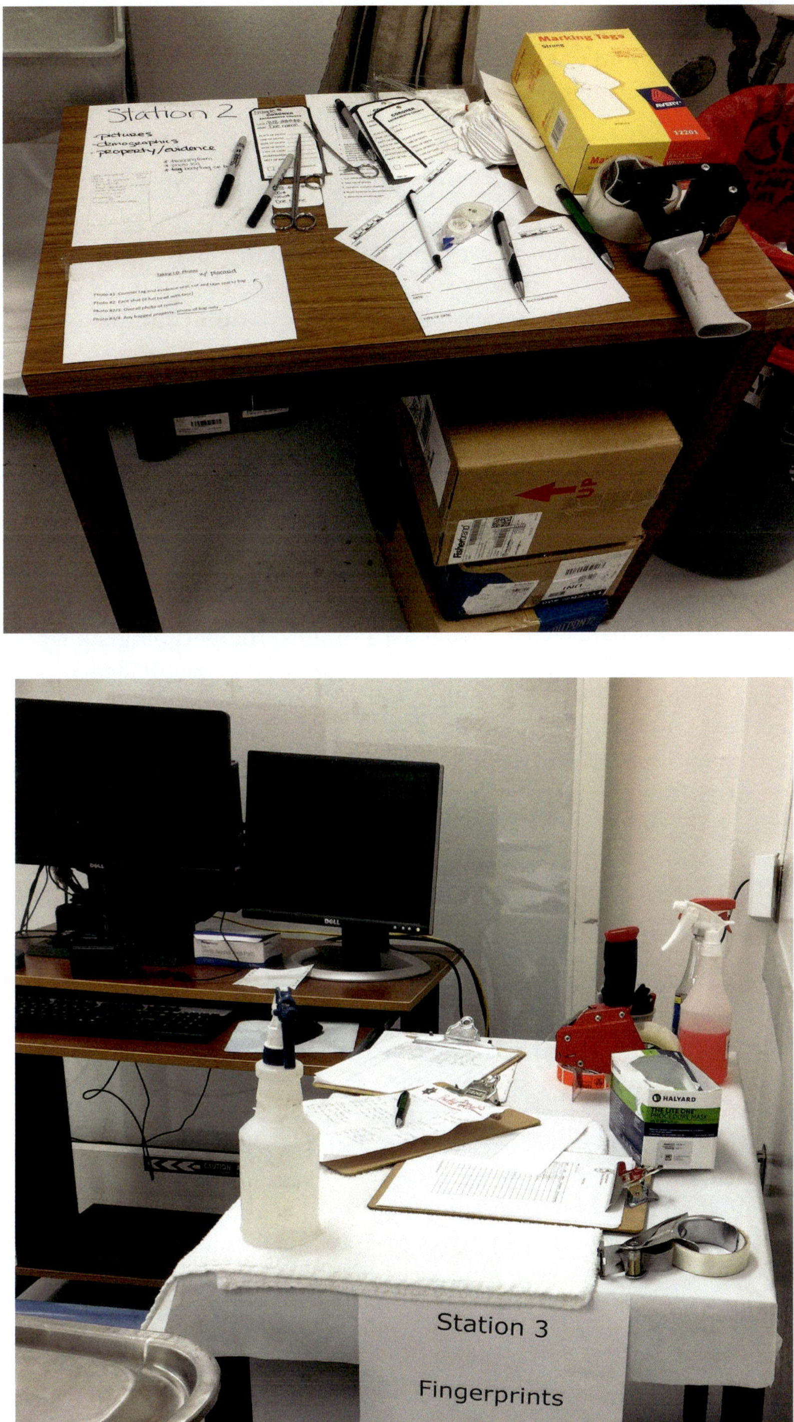

FIGURE 14.15 Station logs and station directions.

Source: Sacramento County Coroner

anything else designated as off-limits. It should be stressed on the agreement that the volunteer/employee should not take any photographs or make any recordings with their own devices without permission.

14.7 ISSUES SPECIFIC TO WILDFIRE DEATHS

Identification of wildfire victims is very difficult especially in an open event that covers a wide area. The remains are typically so highly degraded that making quick identifications with fingerprints is nearly impossible. Of the 84 victims examined after the Camp Fire, only five victims could be identified by fingerprints.

The bulk of the identifications from this event were made using Rapid DNA. Because this new procedure yielded results so fast, the identifications were often made before the cause and manner of death was determined, especially if the pathologist had ordered toxicology to assist with the process. This meant that families could make arrangements for their loved one, but the death certificate listed pending as the cause and manner. This created problems for families attempting to obtain aid through the Federal Emergency Management Agency, or FEMA (U.S. Department of Homeland Security, 2020). FEMA requires a death certificate with a final cause and manner of death when processing paperwork. To assist families, the pathologists who examined the decedents devised a flow plan for quickly issuing a cause of death so manner of death could be established and a completed death certificate could be issued.

As mentioned earlier, introducing Rapid DNA into the identification process required that the flow of work in the morgue changed. What that meant for planning purposes was that the remains had to be handled in two different ways. If a fluid or tissue sample could be taken at autopsy for Rapid DNA testing, it was taken. If the remains were bone only, the sampling had to wait until a forensic anthropologist could come into the morgue and make sure there were no issues of commingling and that the remains were properly photographed and documented. If the sample included teeth, an odontologist had to examine the tooth prior to testing. Only after the necessary exams were completed could a bone or tooth be sampled for testing purposes.

There was a huge need for forensic anthropologists in the field and in the morgue in order to expedite testing and release of victims to mortuaries. The anthropologists were in the field to recover remains, but once they were sent to the morgue, they were needed again to further examine the bones. Forensic anthropologists from all over California and Nevada worked tirelessly to assist on scene and in the morgue, but because of the limited number of these professionals, remains were often held until the morgue examination could be completed. Having this extra step in the morgue simply required coordination between all parties to maximize their time. Whenever possible, they were given an assistant in the morgue to help them, and they often worked in tandem to expedite cases.

14.7.1 Media

The media can be very helpful after a mass fatality event occurs. They can assist with getting information to the public especially when samples are needed for testing. It is helpful to have a public information officer (PIO) who can work with the media and free up staff to work on actual caseload. If a PIO is not available, it will more than likely be necessary to assign a staff member to work with the media requests that come in. It is likely they will want photos so having a supply of photos taken onsite by a designated staff member can help with this type of request. Every effort should be made to pick a staff person who understands the inner workings of the office and morgue and can readily answer questions without having to look for staff to answer questions posed by the media.

The media will also request statistical information. They will usually want information often on body counts, identification counts, mode of identifications, and so on, so having those numbers available every day, even multiple times a day will be helpful. Setting a time to release that information to the media and notifying them of such can save an immense amount of staff time. Make sure the times are honored and the information is released when it is promised. The reporters need this information to make their deadlines and will be more likely to help with getting information out the public if they get information in a timely manner.

14.7.2 The Standard for Identification

The standard for investigating, examining, identifying, and releasing decedents should be as close to the normal process for an office as feasibly possible. Some offices might decide not to autopsy victims if the cause and manner is clear and the incident is not a crime. Even if it is a crime, it may be that the suspect is known and may also be deceased, so conducting autopsies on multiple victims may not be needed. The decision on type of examination should be made once all the information is known.

The standard for identification should be rigorous. DNA identifications should be made using high probability percentages. If the percentage is low, identification should not be made by DNA alone. Dental identifications should only be made if the odontologist examines the antemortem and postmortem records and makes the match. Hardware identifications can be made via information from medical records on identifying numbers. Just knowing that the individual had medical hardware is not enough to make an identification. It is acceptable to make identifications on a number of factors when one modality alone is not enough. Circumstantial identifications are acceptable if enough of the modalities point to a probability of identification and it has been established that the person is truly missing.

The standard for releasing identified decedents should absolutely be that the decedent should be identified first. The remains should be examined to eliminate issues of commingling. All the documentation should be completed, and the death certification done before release.

14.7.3 Dignity

This is a time when everything is rushed. A mass fatality event amplifies workloads while not offering a reprieve on getting exams, identifications, and releases at a leisurely pace. Even though this is all happening so fast, take a step back and remember to honor the victims and their families by treating them with respect and dignity. If there is a way to honor religious beliefs, take the time to do so. Treat all the victims as you would want your family treated.

14.7.4 Teamwork

The field of death investigation is a very exclusive field that is generally woefully understaffed. It is always important to work together in any death investigation, and during a mass event, it is even more important. Not many people can just step in and start working in this field, so the different offices and professionals will have to come together to work with each other. Many people will want to volunteer once an incident occurs, but unless they are trained in this field, it will be hard to accept help as it will cost more time to get them prepared. Start working together as a team before an incident occurs. Make connections and plan together, so if an incident occurs, it can be managed properly for the victims and their families.

14.8 CONCLUSIONS

Staffing and organizing a morgue facility to accommodate a mass disaster, in addition to normal daily operations requires planning and preparation. It requires teamwork and flexibility but with an adherence to a high standard of performance and respect for the dignity of the deceased. Knowing what stations are needed and where additional resources can be spent are critical to a successful completion of the identification process and returning remains to their families and communities.

REFERENCES

Leditschke, J., Collett, S., & Ellen, R. (2011). Mortuary operations in the aftermath of the 2009 Victorian bushfires. *Forensic Science International*, *205*(1–3), 8–14. https://doi.org/10.1016/j.forsciint.2010.11.002

Sacramento County Office of Emergency Services. (n.d.). *Sacramento medical reserve corps*. Retrieved December 28, 2020, from https://sacoes.saccounty.net/SacramentoMedicalReserveCorps/Pages/default.aspx

U.S. Department of Health and Human Services. (2017, September 9). Disaster mortuary operational response teams. *Public Health Emergency*. www.phe.gov/Preparedness/responders/ndms/ndms-teams/Pages/dmort.aspx

U.S. Department of Homeland Security. (2020, September 20). Help after a disaster: FEMA individual assistance can help you recover. *FEMA.gov*. https://www.Fema.Gov/Fact-Sheet/4562/Help-after-Disaster-Fema-Individual-Assistance-Can-Help-You-Recover; www.fema.gov/fact-sheet/4562/help-after-disaster-fema-individual-assistance-can-help-you-recover

CHAPTER 15

Role of the Forensic Pathologist in the Wake of a Fatal Wildfire

Deirde Amaro, MD

15.1 INTRODUCTION: ROLE OF THE FORENSIC PATHOLOGIST

The majority of fire-related deaths should fall under the purview of a board-certified forensic pathologist for determination of the cause of death. Responsibility for determining the manner of death will depend on the jurisdiction of the case. The United States has a hodgepodge of different medicolegal death investigation systems, with different standards and requirements that vary from jurisdiction to jurisdiction. Though uniformity of medicolegal death investigation systems and a push toward nationwide medical examiner systems has been strongly proposed (National Research Council, 2009), the United States is still a long way from achieving that goal. In brief, in a medical examiner jurisdiction, the forensic pathologist is responsible for determining both *cause* and *manner* of death; in a coroner or sheriff-coroner jurisdiction, the *manner* of death determination often rests with the coroner and his/her deputies. Regardless, since most fire-related deaths are non-natural OR at least not clearly natural from the scene investigation, it is difficult to imagine a scenario where a fire-related death is not tasked to the forensic pathologist, the physician subspecialist specifically trained in identifying and understanding disease processes and trauma that result in human death, for determination of the cause of death.

Most commonly, fire-related deaths are associated with a manner of death assignation of accident since, in most locales, the majority of deaths encountered are of those unfortunate individuals or families caught in housefires. Secondarily, the house fire might be the result of an individual who suffered a *natural* event, leading to their inability to douse the fire source. One classic example is an older cigarette smoking adult with a bad habit of smoking in bed, despite likely exposure to repeated education on the dangers of such habits. Suicide in fire-related deaths (self-immolation) is notably rare, particularly in developed countries (Mohammadi, 2020), not surprising perhaps because of the widespread general understanding of the intense pain and suffering associated with that mode of demise. The viscerally horrifying approach of a wildfire, however, may indirectly lead to a suicidal death. In one such instance, an elderly man was found completely unburnt, lying on an outdoor patio porch swing. His death was due to a gunshot that entered the mouth and exited the top of his head. He had no documented history of suicidality, but his residence was in the path of a rapidly approaching wildfire. Let us not forget, however, that the terrifyingly destructive nature of fires

DOI: 10.4324/9781003168010-19

can be perversely appealing to the homicidal offender seeking to hide his/her carnal crimes. For example, the badly burned remains of a homicide victim was found on the backseat of a burnt-out car that had been left in a remote, isolated area. Despite extensive charring, close examination of the skull revealed a gunshot wound (Figure 15.1). Furthermore, fire-related deaths due to an arsonist's actions would most likely be classified as *homicide* by the majority of forensic pathologists. The cause of death in these instances would likely be indistinguishable from that of the aforementioned classic housefire death, and the appropriate assignation of manner of death would rely heavily on the scene investigative findings (Figure 15. 2).

FIGURE 15.1 The body of an initially unidentified male was found in the charred remnants of a vehicle in a very remote area (left photo). Environmental issues hindered examination at the scene, but postmortem examination revealed a gunshot wound of his skull (right photo, courtesy Chico State Human Identification Lab)

FIGURE 15.2 This 86 year-old woman died in a housefire that was started by an arsonist.

The question of *natural* versus *accidental* death becomes particularly critical in deaths involving vehicle (e.g., car or plane) crashes followed by conflagration where the bodies are of course subjected to blunt force trauma in addition to burns (Figure 15.3). In this example, the smoldering remains of a semi-truck that crashed into a hillside and burst into flames contained the charred body of the driver and sole occupant. At autopsy, no soot was located in his airway, and his carboxyhemoglobin saturation was minimal. The cause of death was found to be related to his significant underlying natural disease, and though non-lethal blunt trauma was identified, the manner of death was ultimately determined to be natural.

The same discussion can be extended to the calamitous scenario of the wildfire. Again, the majority of manner of death assignations will likely be *accident*, followed by *natural*, then *homicide*, then *suicide*. Let us also remember that the determiner of manner of death holds a fifth card still: that of *undetermined*. A key difference between the house fire death and the wildfire death, generally speaking, is the extent of burn injuries with the latter tending toward more complete charring and obliteration of the flesh (Figure 15.4). Human remains from the typical wildfire tend to consist of a badly charred body, often with a calcined skull, calcined and charred torso with large areas no longer intact, and truncated limbs. In a housefire, burned bodies tend to be more complete and often with the preservation of many of the internal organs (Figure 15.4).

FIGURE 15.3 The smoldering remains of a semi-truck that crashed into a hillside and burst into flames (left photo). The charred driver and sole occupant of the semi-truck that crashed into a hillside (right photo).

FIGURE 15.4 Charred remains left in the rubble from a wildfire, compared to the charred remains in a "standard" house fire in Figure 6 (left photo). Relatively preserved intestines are visible protruding from the abdomen of a victim of a house fire (right photo).

15.2 MAJOR QUESTIONS ADDRESSED BY THE FORENSIC PATHOLOGIST: SPECIFIC CHALLENGES WITH CONFLAGRATION

The major questions tasked to the forensic pathologist with a fire-related death are not much different from any other death. There are, however, extra challenges that arise with conflagration.

Fire-related trauma can range from barely discernible inhalational injury to a body barely recognizable as human. What may come as a surprise to the novice, though, is how relatively preserved the viscera may be despite widespread thermal alterations (Figure 15.5), even resulting in obliteration of facial features particularly if the victim was found face down or with the anterior torso (chest and abdomen) pressed up against something that was not burning.

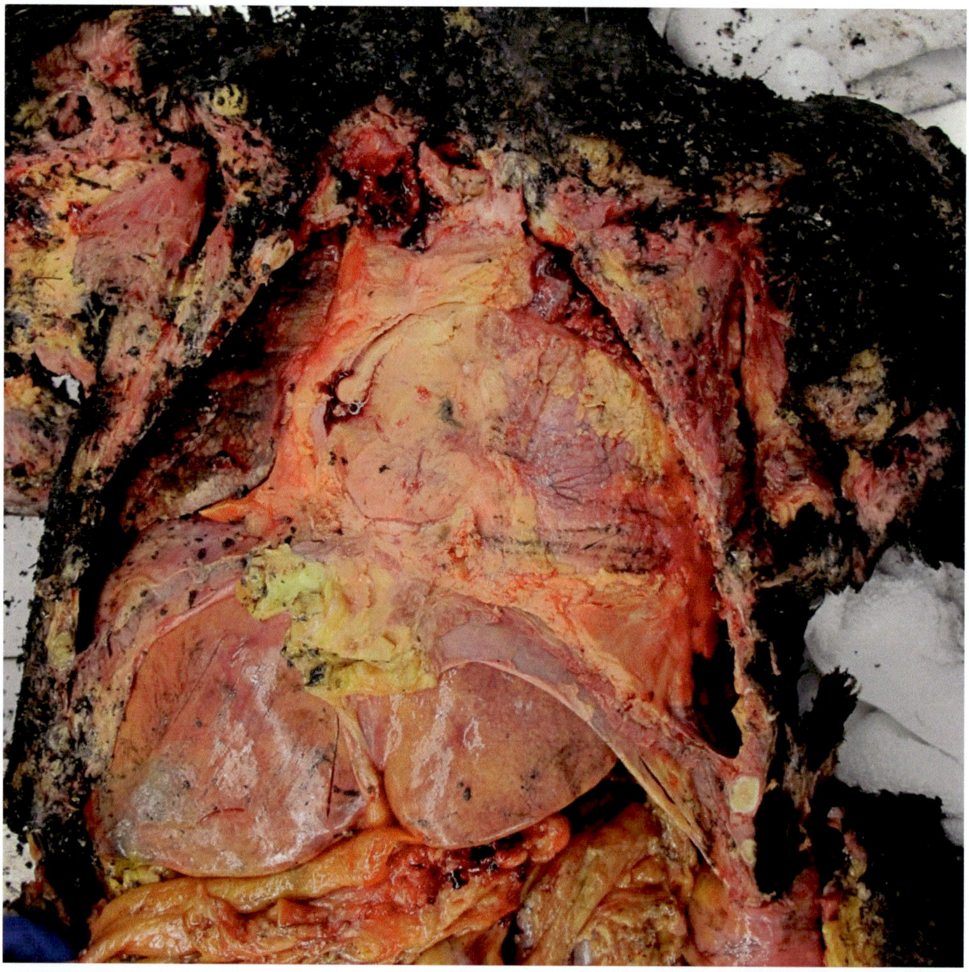

FIGURE 15.5 Driver of the semi-truck from Figure 15.3. Despite widespread charring with obliteration of facial features, etc., the viscera were still relatively preserved and easily examined for indications of natural disease processes and trauma.

Regardless, one of the initial challenges presented by conflagration is often the most basic question of *who*—who was overcome by the lethal flames? There will be a further discussion of this under the "Identification" section, but briefly, circumstantial evidence can provide a clue but usually is inadequate for the rigors of modern medico legal death investigation systems.

The *what* from the perspective of the forensic pathologist is the cause of death. Did the person die from smoke inhalation? From being burned alive? From blunt trauma sustained during a frantic, desperate attempt to escape the fire via motor vehicle that ended in a crash? From a natural disease process (e.g., heart attack) that preceded the fire? Or from a lethal injury inflicted by someone else that preceded the fire? Multiple bodies at a scene involving fire does not guarantee the same causes of death are appropriate for each. In one case, an elderly couple was involved in a solo motor vehicle accident where the crash was quickly followed by fiery consumption of the vehicle and its occupants, including a small dog (Figure 15.6). The elderly driver had soot deposited in the airways, indicating he was alive at the time of the fire; the elderly passenger did not show soot deposition, but there was lethal blunt trauma, indicating she had died from the crash itself, not the fiery conflagration that followed.

Definitively teasing apart trauma sustained during a fire, after a fire (i.e., during rough recovery), or prior to a fire is often challenging, the level of which is usually directly proportional to the extent of fire damage. Fire itself introduces some well-known artifacts that may be confusing to the novice. This includes the formation of the

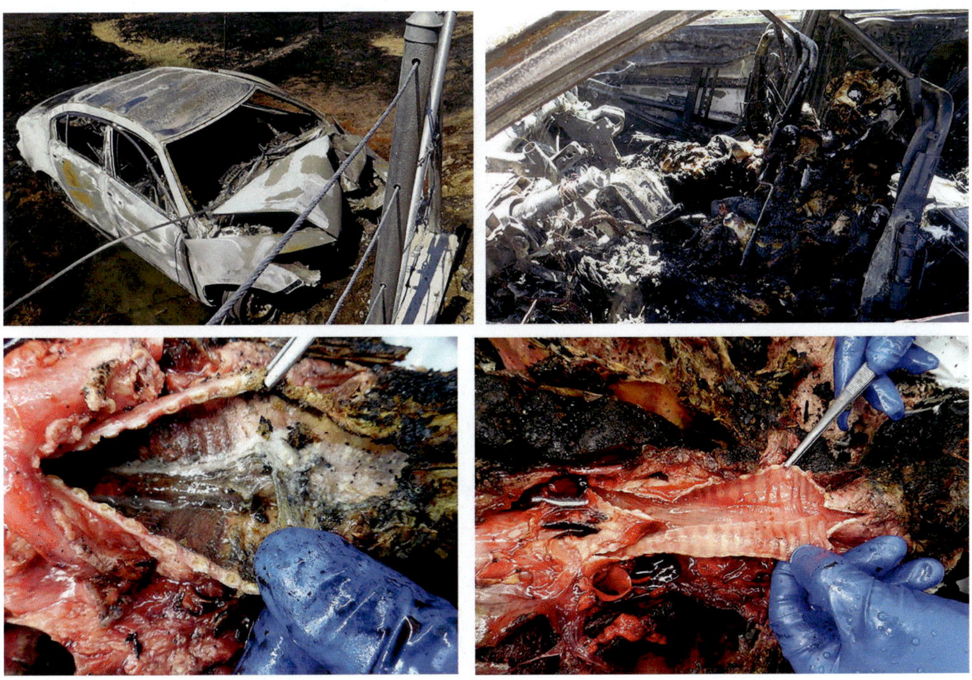

FIGURE 15.6 The burnt, crashed car carrying two elderly passengers (top left). Two charred bodies, later determined to the elderly driver and his elderly female passenger (top right). Soot deposition of the driver (bottom left). Lack of soot deposition of the passenger (bottom right).

"thermal epidural" or epidural blood in the skull of a fire victim (Figure 15.7). Epidural hemorrhages, when not due to heat, are almost always traumatic in nature, classically due to a skull fracture involving the temporal bone, which damages the temporal artery, resulting in the often lethal accumulation of blood in what would otherwise be essentially a liquid free space. The consistency of a thermal epidural is often described as "spongy" and does not usually fool the trained practitioner. Furthermore, the presence of liquid or "cooked"/chalky-appearing blood around the nose and mouth may be initially alarming, suggesting a more nefarious cause; however, this is recognized as a heat-related artifact.

Tied in with the *what* question is the one the forensic pathologist is most often asked by investigating law enforcement officials and family members: was the decedent alive at the time of the fire? This will be delved into further in the next section. The answer has potentially far-reaching implications, extending to the courtroom and attempts at monetarily quantifying the extent of emotional suffering of those left behind by the decedent.

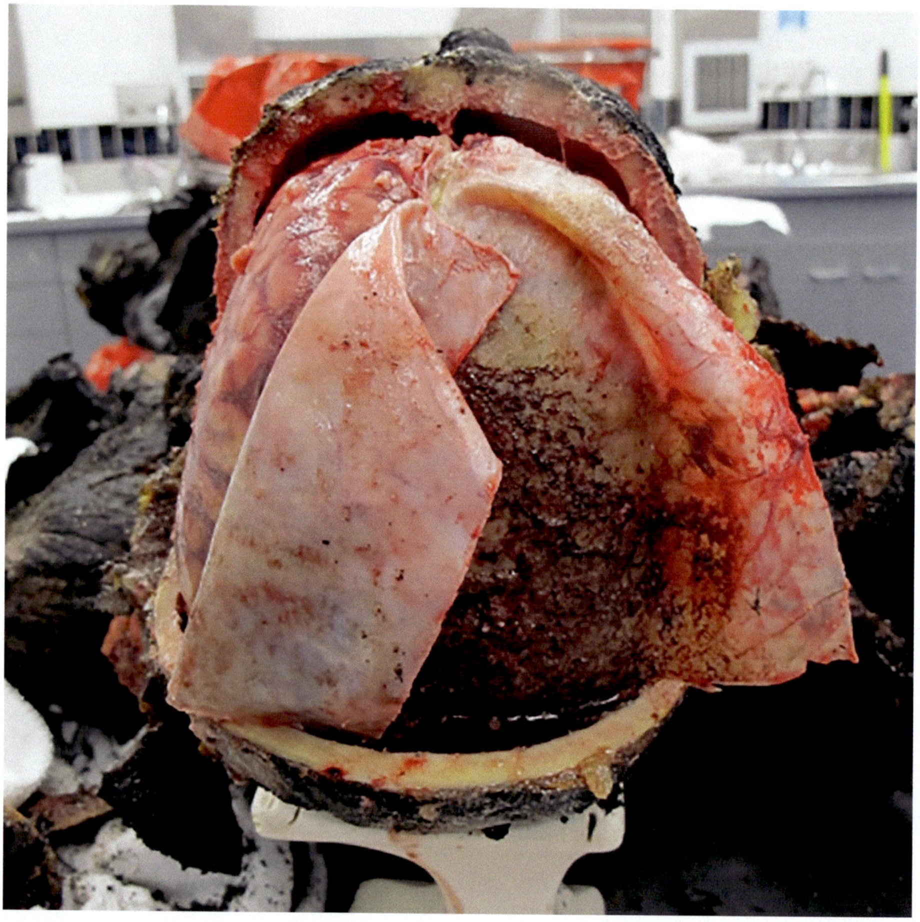

FIGURE 15.7 Driver of the semi-truck from Figure 15.3 displayed artifactual bleeding in the epidural space, so-called thermal epidural.

And it should be remembered that at the end of the day, the cause-of-death determination, like any other medical diagnosis, is essentially a highly educated guess, contrary to what is depicted in television shows and movies.

15.3 BASIC AUTOPSY PROCEDURES

Autopsy procedures related to the processing of burnt remains may vary depending on the extent of the thermal injuries. According to the NAME Forensic Autopsy Standards, all charred remains require radiographic examination (Peterson, 2015). Generally speaking, the process begins with the careful, meticulous documentation and collection of human remains from the site of the fire. This aspect is covered more extensively and expertly in other chapters and utilization of forensic anthropologists may be critical to the optimal success of that mission, with particular emphasis on the accurate separation of commingled remains. Once brought to the morgue facility, the examination of charred or burnt remains usually begins with full body radiographs. This may be of a single body bag or body bag plus all additional containers that we used to collect a single suspected decedent. The purpose of the radiographs is essentially twofold: (1) to identify potential features (e.g., remote trauma, medical hardware, jewelry) that may aid in identification and (2) to help rule out the presence of radio-opaque material suggestive of missiles or weapon fragments that may suggest a more nefarious scenario behind the decedent's presence in a fire.

Prior to putting scalpel to skin, or whatever charred fleshy remnants are recovered, it may be prudent to meticulously check the remains and collect potential trace evidence (e.g., fragments of charred clothing). As is commonplace for the trained forensic pathologist, recognizing and subsequently documenting the *pattern* of the injuries is important. Is there sparing of the back, indicating the victim was pressed up against something less flammable? Is there an irregular pattern suggestive of accelerant use? Contrary to what may be reported by the general media, recovering a charred body with a "pugilistic" posture (i.e., the arms and knees are flexed) does *not* indicate the person was alive at the time of the fire and trying to "fight off the flames." This is merely the response of the tissue to the thermal stress. Larger muscles (biceps > triceps; quadriceps > hamstrings) tend to thermally contract harder, resulting in the classic posturing that is unrelated to antemortem activities.

Arguably, one of the most important anatomic regions for forensic examination at autopsy is the neck, which houses the trachea (proximal airway) and may afford the quickest answer to the question of whether or not the victim as alive at the time of the fire. Since burned bodies tend to have a lot of carbonaceous debris that gets scattered and smeared with manipulation of the body (and is a challenge to clean after autopsy!), it is best to open the airway *in situ* – that is, as it sits in the neck in order to minimize the artifactual introduction of soot. Sometimes, however, there is no trachea left due to the extent of thermal damage to the body; there might still be evidence in the lower airways in the chest.

As always, the autopsy provides the one—and hopefully only, barring exhumation—opportunity to collect samples for potential testing, and it is prudent to maximize this opportunity. Minimum specimens taken at autopsy for laboratory testing, per NAME standards, include vitreous (eye) fluid, urine, and blood (Peterson, 2015). With bodies subjected to thermal damage, the forensic pathologist may count themselves fortunate to be able to access even one of those sources. Forensic toxicologists, fortunately, have devised multiple ways to analyze different samples, including tissue and cooked/chalky blood. In severely charred remains, a conversation with your friendly forensic toxicologist may help to optimize success in terms of adequate sample procurement, including sample source and specimen requirements. Toxicology results may be critical in helping to determine whether or not the victim was alive at the time of the fire.

15.4 SPECIFIC CHALLENGES MORE IN DEPTH—IDENTIFICATION

One of the basic, foremost responsibilities of the medicolegal death investigator and forensic pathologist is to determine the identity of the deceased; conflagration frequently complicates this critical determination and to an extent proportional to the extent of the fire damage. It is essential also to remember that the process of identification begins with the scene and prompt involvement of trained professional in medicolegal death investigation is crucial (Carroll, 2017).

While victims of housefires may have relevant preservation of their facial features and/or fingers (for fingerprints), thus affording visual identification or fingerprint identification, with wildfires, there is rarely this kind of sparing due to the overwhelmingly destructive nature. Identifications may also be made based on unique tattoos, again requiring a comparison from a known, satisfactorily identified individual. Identification via dental comparisons becomes more commonplace. If an adequate radiographic technology is available at the ME/C office, then dental radiographs can be taken in house and used for comparison with antemortem (before death) radiographs. Unfortunately, this requires there to already be a good suspicion of the likely identity along with available antemortem records. Not uncommonly, particularly in rural areas where wildfires are more prone to happen, routine dental care may not be pursued, and old records may have already been destroyed or lost. Interestingly, even without remaining teeth, radiographic identification is possible based on unique jaw or other skeletal anatomy. However, with more subtle variations, a forensic radiologist, odontologist, or anthropologist may need to be consulted. Also regrettably, many ME/C offices are not adequately equipped (National Research Council, 2009), and it may be necessary to utilize the office of the local forensic odontologist, one who usually spends the majority of their time treating living patients. To minimize clinical disruption, rather than transport the entire charred body to the local dentist, the upper and lower jaws may be removed after autopsy examination and taken for radiographic comparison. (NB: this office, lacking in house radiography, traditionally removes the jaws and transports them in a standard Tupperware container; see Figure 15.8).

Another potential route of identification relies on the recognition of medical or surgical hardware which usually contain unique serial numbers. Pre-autopsy radiographs may alert the forensic pathologist to the potential viability of this route of identification; alternatively, or coincidentally, the suspected victim's medical history, uncovered as part of the investigation, may suggest this avenue (see Figure 15.9). Orthopedic hardware usually survives even the worst fires, but it can be technically challenging to locate and reveal the serial number on the prosthetic in severely charred victims. While confirmation of presumptive identification with the serial number tends to be straightforward and relatively expedient, with a bit more legwork, medical hardware can assist in identifying a complete J. Doe (i.e., one for whom not even a presumptive identification has been made). If the implant manufacturer can be identified, based on logo markings or other characteristic features, the manufacturer may be able to provide

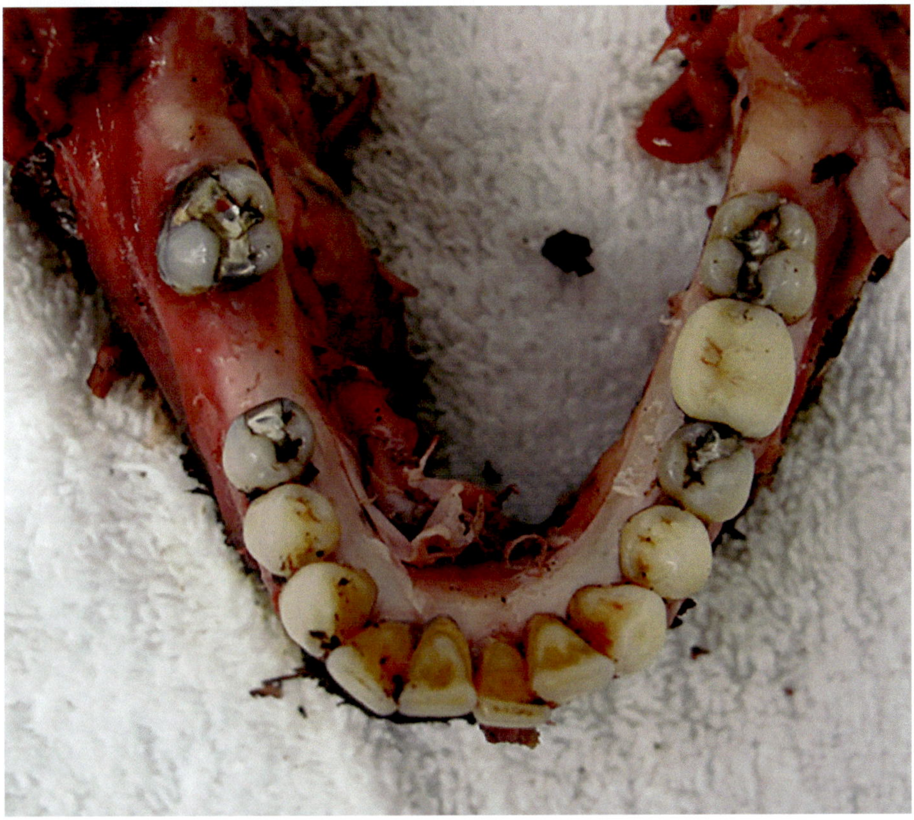

FIGURE 15.8 Lower jaw (mandible) removed to aid in definitive identification via forensic odontology.

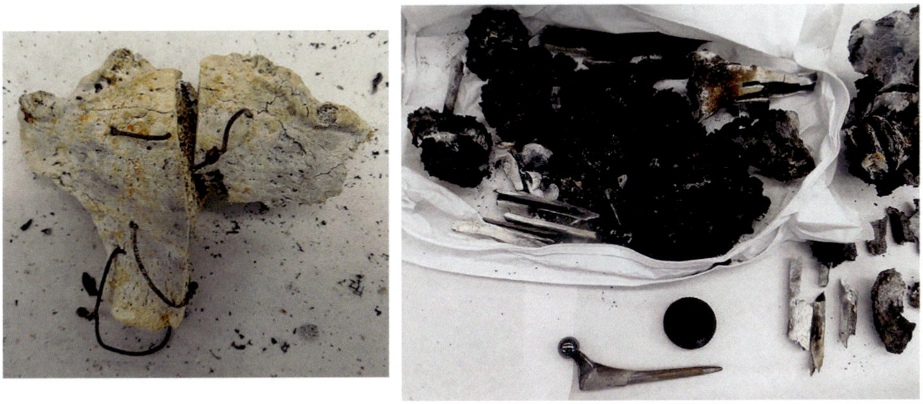

FIGURE 15.9 Manubrium with surgical wire in a decedent known to have had open-heart surgery (left photo). Charred remains of a wildfire victim. At the bottom center of the image are components of orthopedic hardware (hip replacement). Comparison with suspected victim's medical records showed matching serial numbers on the medical hardware, confirming his identity (right photo).

either patient-specific information or geographic areas/facilities that received that particular batch of devices, thus providing a workable lead (Blessing, 2018).

Perhaps the least used method of identification is DNA, but again this requires comparison with the suspected person or relative thereof and may not be possible with a complete John or Jane Doe. Discussion of DNA techniques, particularly ones that are of use in a mass fatality, however, is beyond the scope of this chapter (see Chapter 18).

If the circumstantial evidence is strong enough, and there is a strong suspicion of the decedent's identity, as is often the case with wildfires that tear through a person's home or vehicle or house fires, autopsy can be used as an adjunct to the circumstantial evidence to rule out inconsistencies in the identity. For example, in Figure 15.10, an elderly male was found dead in a residential fire. Only one person was known to reside at that residence, and his vehicle was still there. He had never been fingerprinted, so even though two fingers were printable, there was no comparison available. Outdated dental records showed dentition that was not *inconsistent* with those remaining at the time of his death. Autopsy revealed no medical/surgical hardware, but there was the absence of the appendix; appendectomy (surgical removal of the appendix) was his only documented surgical history. Furthermore, his car remained at the residence, nothing was stolen, and his banking accounts showed no activity after the fire. Thus, identification was confirmed based on the overwhelming totality of the circumstantial evidence and the lack of inconsistencies found at autopsy

FIGURE 15.10 Charred human remains in a structure fire. The solo inhabitant presented an identification challenge that was eventually resolved via the totality of the circumstances.

15.5 SPECIFIC CHALLENGES MORE IN DEPTH—ALIVE AT THE TIME OF THE FIRE?

As mentioned previously, a critical question that one aims to answer with an autopsy is the question of whether or not the person was alive at the time of the fire. This is relevant not only for answering the cause of death question but also extends past the medicolegal death investigation arena into the arena of prosecution and charges brought against suspects. Death by fire is generally understood by even the general populace to be a particularly, excruciatingly painful way to die. Thus, being alive at the time of the fire may raise the specter of a "torture enhancement" being brought to bear with adjudication.

Forensic pathologists have essentially two, generally complementary means of investigating this avenue. One is provided at autopsy with the gross (i.e., macroscopic) examination of the airways for evidence of soot deposition, seen as black deposits on the interior of the trachea (Figure 15.11). The second is afforded post autopsy with, at a minimum, a specific toxicological assay for carboxyhemoglobin saturation. The carboxyhemoglobin saturation is a reflection of the antemortem exposure to carbon monoxide, which is one of

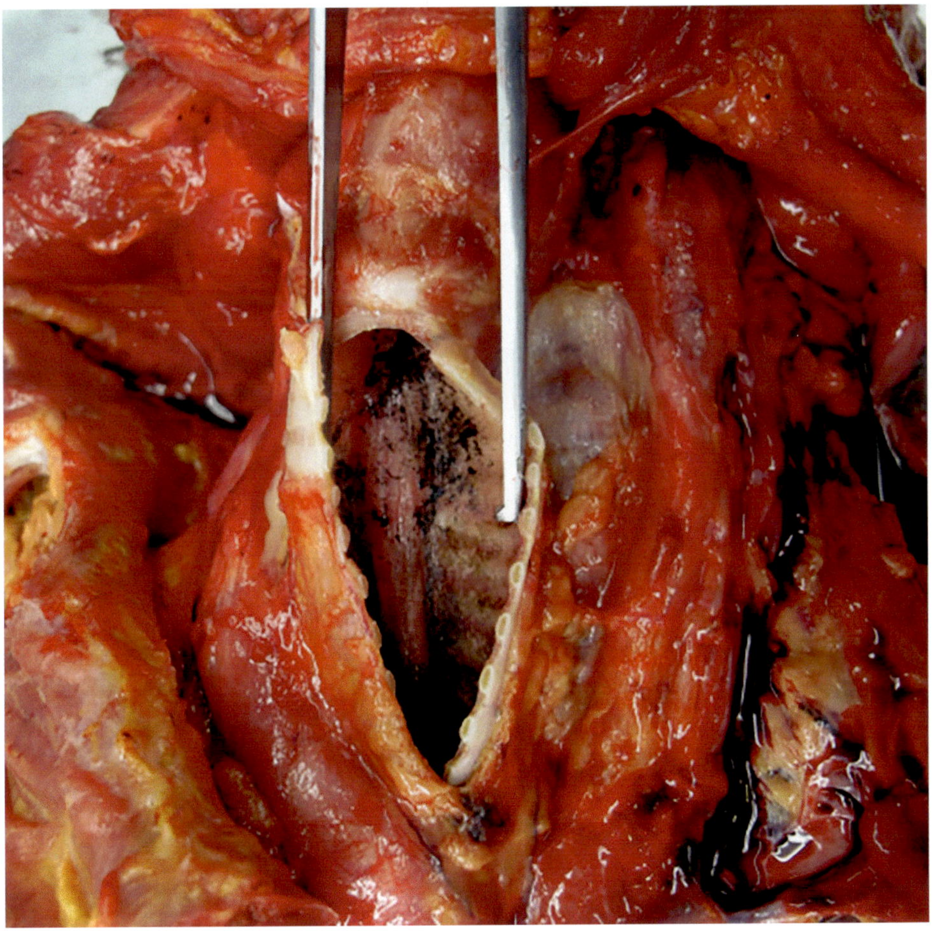

FIGURE 15.11 In situ opening of the trachea, revealing soot deposition in a house fire victim.

the products of combustion. The binding of carbon monoxide to hemoglobin, the oxygen-carrying protein in the blood, interferes with the body's ability to transport oxygen, therefore causing a chemical asphyxia. With the burning of structures, particularly homes with polymers and synthetic materials, other toxic gases are released including hydrogen cyanide, which causes a chemical asphyxia via a different mechanism; thus, carbon monoxide exposure coupled with hydrogen cyanide exposure is thought to have a synergistic effect and deaths attributed to smoke inhalation with lower-than-expected carboxyhemoglobin levels are often thought to be due to the presence of other, untested toxins. Though this sounds relatively straightforward, challenges may arise in the pre-analysis phase with the procurement of samples for testing, as well as in the post-analysis phase with interpretation of the results. Ideally, blood would be able to be collected at autopsy and sent for toxicologic analysis. Unfortunately, with fires, all the liquid blood may have been cooked off, leaving dried chalky remnants. This can still be collected and analyzed, though it is less ideal. "Fresh" muscle or other organ/tissue is another less preferred alternative, and it might be wise to consult with a forensic toxicologist to help determine the best samples to collect.

15.6 FINAL WORDS

Wildfires wreak devastating havoc across communities. The first and *last* responders (medicolegal death investigators, forensic anthropologists, forensic pathologists, etc.) may be faced with an unprecedented assault on their physical capabilities, in terms of

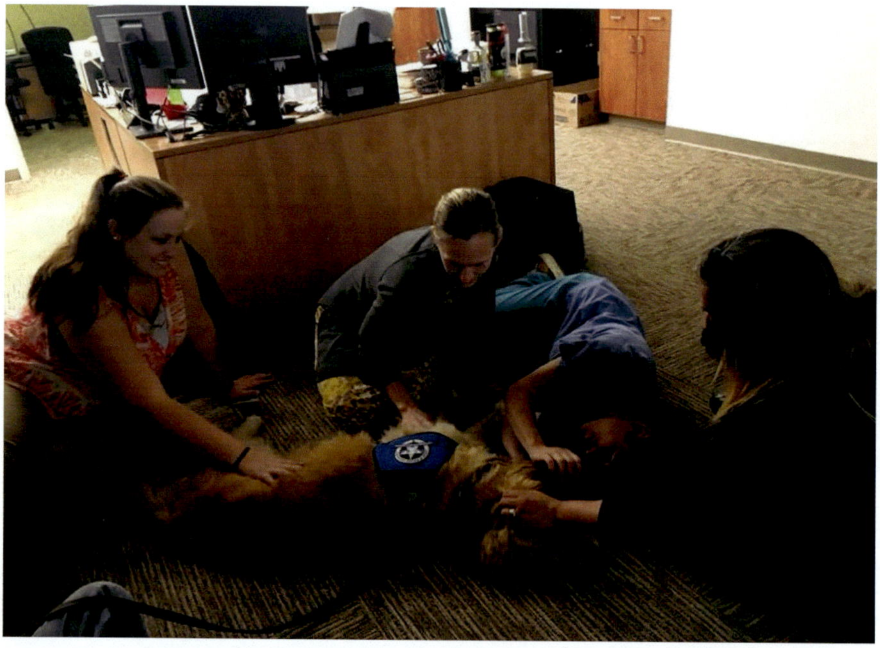

FIGURE 15.12 Comfort dog visiting the ME/C office during the aftermath of a devastating wildfire, providing much needed therapy to the last responders.

Source: Photo courtesy of Lutheran Church Charities K-9 Comfort Dog Ministry

the logistics of handling such a complicated mass fatality, and the majority of forensic pathologists likely never encountered such situations during their (many) years of training. Fortunately, the skills and knowledge regarding fire-related deaths relevant to the "common" house fire or motor vehicle that burst into flames serve well with regards to the wildfire-related death. Conflagration, whatever the cause, results in similar autopsy challenges but those that can be successfully navigated. Unfortunately, it is not just the assault on the physical capabilities that must be considered. With mass fatalities including wildfires, the forensic pathologist and their dedicated team of medicolegal death investigators may also be confronted with a potentially overwhelming *emotional* toll. ME/C offices work closely with allied agencies, the same agencies tasked to step in to help fight wildfires and mitigate their destruction. This of course puts those first responders at risk of suffering a fire- and/or other job-related injury or death. If it is the latter, it is the responsibility of that community's last responders to investigate the death, with all that that entails. This invisible trauma must also be recognized and addressed, and some agencies take direct action in the form of providing access to chaplains, counselors, and canine comfort therapy for the last responders (Figure 15.12)

REFERENCES

Blessing, M. L. (2018). Identification of Bodies by Unique Serial Numbers on Implanted Medical Devices. *Journal of Forensic Sciences*, 740–744.

Carroll, E. J. (2017). Trends in United States Mass Fatality Incidents and Recommendations for Medical Examiners and Coroners. *Academic Forensic Pathology*, 318–329.

Mohammadi, A. K. (2020). Suicide by Self-Immolation in Southern Iran: An Epidemiological Study. *BMC Public Health*, 1646.

National Research Council. (2009). Strengthening Forensic Science in the United States: A Path Foward. National Academy of Sciences.

Peterson, G. (2015). *Forensic Autopsy Performance Standards*. National Association of Medical Examiners.

CHAPTER 16

Forensic Odontology in the Identification of Wildfire Victims

James D. Wood

Forensic odontology is a valuable tool in the identification of fire victims since teeth survive fire better than most other parts of the body. Tooth enamel is the hardest substance in the body and many dental restorations are harder and more resistant to fire than the teeth themselves. However, the severe burning seen in some fires presents a challenge in resolving an identification.

Wildfires have ravaged many parts of the state of California since 2015, consuming millions of acres of land, destroying thousands of homes and businesses and taking many people's lives. In the areas of Northern California, odontologists were called to respond to a series of fatal wildfires, including the fires in Lake County in 2015 and those in Sonoma, Napa, and Mendocino Counties in 2017. These fires built on the experience from their normal practice, which, in this area, generally produces about ten cases of thermally altered dentition per year.

In early November 2018, a wind-whipped wildfire tore through a suite of communities in Butte County, California. People were trapped in their homes, their cars and in open spaces with nowhere to go. Eighty-five people perished in the deadliest wildfire disaster in the history of California. The fire was labeled the "Camp Fire" by the Department of Forestry and Fire Protection (CAL FIRE) based on its origin off Camp Creek Road.

The identification process for the victims of the Camp Fire required the coordinated efforts of many thousands of people. For the forensic odontologists, it presented a test of how to position the use of dentition in the identification process in the face of a changing landscape of identification, including rapid DNA. In addition, the role of dentistry was necessarily smaller due to the very fragmented and degraded condition of the remains. To examine how this component of the process worked, this chapter looks at the work on the reconstruction of postmortem dentition, the location of antemortem records, and the comparison of the two for positive identification. The chapter concludes with some lessons learned from the Camp Fire and other Northern California fires and how odontology should continue to be involved in identification of wildfire victims.

16.1 FORENSIC ODONTOLOGY AND THE CAMP FIRE: DEALING WITH DISASTER

The Camp Fire represented what an enormous challenge it can be to identify victims of a mass disaster that is spread over a large landmass with near total destruction. The

DOI: 10.4324/9781003168010-20

initial challenge was actually locating potential victims. The coordinated search and recovery efforts by law enforcement and volunteers can be a painstaking and lengthy process. In the case of the Camp Fire, recovery efforts began as soon as areas were safe to enter. Victims were located over a two-and-a-half-week period as thousands of acres of burned land, thousands of homes and hundreds of cars and trucks were individually searched. Further, the challenge of pending inclement weather can and did complicate the process and increase the urgency of conducting detailed searches.

When the remains were recovered, they were transported to the morgue facility in Sacramento (Chapter 14). Here they were assessed by various specialists in order to establish positive identification, if possible, or match circumstantial evidence to known missing persons. It was into this process that the forensic odontologists played an important role.

For the Camp Fire, the services of two forensic odontologists were requested, including the author. In addition, two other experienced forensic odontologists volunteered to assist for a few days. All had prior wildfire experience and so were accustomed to handling burned remains. All also were familiar with the morgue setting that often requires specialists to work in unusual circumstances and with unfamiliar equipment. As they had other responsibilities, like the anthropologists (see Chapter 17), they worked hours into their schedules to try to meet both the needs of the identification process as well as competing interests. None held a dedicated position as a full-time forensic services provider. The forensic odontologists volunteered their services and charged nothing for their work on the identification efforts for Camp Fire victims.

16.1.1 Postmortem Dentition

Identification efforts were coordinated with systematic examinations by pathology, anthropology, dental, and DNA collection and analysis. In many cases, dental evidence was isolated during recovery (see Chapter 12); in others, remains were meticulously scrutinized for any dental evidence in the morgue by either the pathologists (Chapter 15) or anthropologists (Chapter 17). Odontologists were able to work alongside the pathologists when scheduling allowed, in order to extract dentition from the remains. In some instances, additional material was retrieved after the odontologists had reviewed a case, requiring additional attention.

Wildfire victims are often very badly burned with very significant thermal damage to the bones and teeth (Chapter 10). In the Camp Fire, most of the victims were found in their cars or their homes. These settings and the bodies within them mostly burned for many hours without suppression, significantly consuming soft tissue and fragmenting bones and teeth. What was ultimately recovered was extremely fragile. For the most part, only victims found outside of homes and cars actually had more intact remains, possibly due to a lower fuel load associated with their bodies. Most remains ranged from severely burned heads and torsos to fragments of bones and teeth.

Recovered remains examined by the forensic odontologists consisted of some complete and intact dentitions but mostly tooth root fragments, fragments of the upper and lower jaw bones (maxillae and mandibles), and dental restorations. Evidence that survived relatively well included metallic dental restorations, such as metal frameworks for removable partial dentures, metal posts within teeth that had been endodontically treated, silver amalgam fillings, metal substructures for porcelain fused to metal crowns, entire porcelain fused to metal crowns, all ceramic crowns, and root canal filling material (gutta-percha) within some endodontically treated teeth. Such items are of value in their own right for identification but can also provide clues as to the age of treatment, the techniques used and even, in some cases, whether this is domestic or foreign work. The level of preservation of these restorations, given the poor quality of the actual dentition, was somewhat surprising and certainly welcome. It stands as testimony that attention to the odontological record in wildfire recovery should be sustained.

Dentures do not survive extreme fires well and may not have been worn by the decedent at the time of death, depending on the timing of arrival of the fire front. California state law requires that a full denture have identification incorporated within it; however, patients can decline this addition and many dentists do not place identification in dentures.

All of the available dental portions for each individual case number were collected and examined by the odontological team. With detailed knowledge of dental anatomy, some roots can be sorted by tooth class, upper or lower arcade, and side. This information allowed some portions of roots to be repositioned in the appropriate root sockets of the respective bone. However, the experience can be likened to trying to complete a jigsaw puzzle with little idea of the final picture and with half or more of the parts missing. Sorting, rearrangement, and reconstruction of the cases with minimal remains helped to ensure that each set of remains was indeed a single individual.

The reconstruction process is further complicated due to the shrinkage of both bone and dental elements. As noted in Chapter 10, the enamel, with its lower organic component, shrinks less but is sloughed off as the underlying dentine shrinks. With a hollow interior for the root canal and pulp chamber, the dentine will typically shatter, leaving only the root section intact. Furthermore, the alveolar bone in which the teeth normally reside also shrinks and can warp somewhat in response to the heat.

While dental enamel is the hardest substance in the body, in the Camp Fire victims only a small number of cases permitted any enamel recovery. In the majority of those cases, with the exception of the intact bodies, the enamel recovered was in the form of a shell with no associated dentin or root structures. The extreme fire temperatures and the length of burn time badly degraded the dental structures present. In many cases, individual isolated roots of teeth were the only evidence recovered making dental identifications nearly impossible in those cases.

Reconstruction of fragmented remains is extremely challenging. In cases where alveolar bone is present it can be possible to re-associate root fragments to their origin. This is verified radiographically, and if the odontologists agree, the roots or teeth can be glued together with cyanoacrylate. Associating roots with alveolar bone is extremely helpful as in some cases the unique character of the bone and positions of teeth will lead to an identification. Another way to stabilize badly burned fragile remains from further disintegration is with aerosol hairspray—the old sticky kind. Without coronal tooth structure, identifications can be very challenging but not impossible. Experience and an excellent working knowledge of dental anatomy is critical in the aftermath of extreme fire events.

When a calvarium, mandible or individual teeth were recovered and reconstructed to the extent possible, a forensic dental examination was conducted, digital radiographs (X-rays) and digital photographs were made of the dental remains for a future opportunity to make a comparison to antemortem dental records. Because many of the victims were represented by fragments of bone and portions of the tooth roots only, films were made to focus on unusual dental features such as restorations, crowns, or root canals along with overall dental and bone morphology.

Sixty sets of remains were examined by the dental team, and in 35 of those cases, dental evidence was recovered. Unfortunately, due to the demographic distribution of the victims, many were totally or partially edentulous. Notable features were recorded on paperwork to accompany the victim and retained at the morgue. Odontological examination was noted as completed on the morgue sequence forms.

16.1.2 Antemortem Records

Dental identification relies on the procurement of antemortem records, preferably with radiographs (periapical, panoramic radiographs, etc.) and digital photographs. The more recent the records, the better the possibility that there will be fewer changes in the dentition due to additional tooth loss, restorations that may have changed the profile of earlier work and growth changes in the upper and lower arcade. However, dental radiographs of any age are extremely valuable and should be collected.

In considering how to locate dental records for a wildfire, it is important to understand the population of victims. Fortunately, in the Camp Fire we did not have any juvenile victims who often do not have any significant dental restorations and also have rapidly changing dentitions. For such a group, it is essential to find very recent antemortem records. Other adults may not have significant restorations if they are on the younger side but may have available radiographs. Many older individuals may have significant dental work, including replacement of teeth lost well before death in the form of full or partial dentures and bridges. Some of these devices will survive the fire, as noted, and be useful in the identification process. From the odontological perspective, populations living at the wildland-urban interface, such as the Sierra Nevada foothills, often include many for whom dental care is infrequent due to financial reasons, aversion to dentists, or complications of other health issues. This group presents a very difficult situation as they often have substantial antemortem tooth loss and antemortem records may be difficult to locate. Some have had significant dental work performed at some point in the past but when and where is difficult to track.

For the Camp Fire, coroners' investigators and sheriff's deputies initially compiled lists of missing persons (see Chapter 6) and worked through those lists, focusing on homes where the decedents may have lived and on cars abandoned and badly burned in their search for human remains. Eliminating survivors from the list of the "missing" is a critical step, given the complexity of retrieving antemortem records. This process reduced the missing list, which at one time surpassed 1,400 names, to a number below 100 individuals.

While there were a few young to middle-aged adults among the Camp Fire victims, most were older to elderly. The time depth of these records could be quite extensive but more obscure to track. Even when there is a suspected name for a decedent based on the location of the find, it can be a difficult task to actually locate the dental practice involved and then actually obtain the antemortem dental records. The Camp Fire situation illustrates a number of issues with this process. Only eight of the eighteen dental offices in the fire area survived the fire. Some dentists who lost their practices had cloud-based backups of digital records, some had backups on portable offsite storage devices, and some were operating with traditional dental X-rays films in their records. Some dentists who had digital records were not consistent or regular in the backup of their records and as such some records were not completely current. Those who were still using traditional methods with onsite storage were unable, for obvious reasons, to help. Even if their practice had not been totally destroyed, the entire fire area was secured due to safety concerns.

Because the area of the Camp Fire was attractive to those in retirement, many were relatively new arrivals in the area. Therefore, some victims had been seen outside the area and investigators had to backtrack with families to find out the name of the prior dentist. Not all families will know the dentist's name, and in some cases, they may only know the prior area of residence. At such times, tapping into dental networks, insurance coverage and other sources may allow for identification of the prior dentist(s). In the Camp Fire, the Northern California Dental Society was a critical resource. When people were receiving some form of public assistance, such as MediCal health coverage, then the California Department of Justice (DOJ) was able to work through its insurance provider to locate and obtain antemortem records. DOJ was also able to assist in locating antemortem records. Since time had elapsed since their last examination, there is also the possibility that the dentist has moved or retired. It was found that, in some cases, the attending dentists had purged the records due to the amount of time that had passed since their last appointment. In other cases, individual periapical films were available for a possible victim, however, the films depicted a part of the dentition that was destroyed or not recovered. High-quality antemortem dental records, offsite storage of digital images, and retention of records all contribute to the ability of a forensic odontologist to make comparisons in a disaster scenario.

16.1.3 Comparison of Postmortem and Antemortem Records

When dental identifications were possible, they were based upon a unique dental restoration or an associated metal restoration. Considering the extreme thermal damage to the dental remains and in many cases a lack of antemortem dental records, the dental team was only able to positively identify 15 victims of the Camp Fire. However, in situations where other means of positive identification were precluded by the thermal destruction of the body, such identification may be crucial. Without a positive identification, many legal matters are held in abeyance until all possible avenues for identification are exhausted and the identification must be called on circumstantial evidence. This delay imposes additional burdens, financial and emotional, on the surviving family members.

16.2 LESSONS LEARNED

Each time we face a disaster, new things occur, old lessons are reinforced, and adaptations made to fit the circumstances. The Camp Fire and subsequent fires are no exception. Therefore, it is important that we reflect upon what went well and what did not in a disaster and learn and plan for the future.

One of the most critical things, as a forensic odontologist, is to establish a good working relationship with law enforcement and the coroner/medical examiner community early in the disaster. This relationship is important for two reasons. Law enforcement must be aware of the contributions that can be made by a forensic odontologist, particularly in situations such as the Camp Fire, where the destruction of remains is so severe that dentition may be the only available means of identification. While DNA analysis is becoming increasingly important (see Chapter 18), the level of damage in a number of cases of wildfire fatalities means that there may be no retrievable DNA. The forensic odontologist can be the last possible professional to provide the critical date necessary to make an identification.

The other reason that the relationship between the forensic odontologist and law enforcement is important is that the work of the odontologist must be matched by the investigative skills of the law enforcement community to retrieve antemortem data, narrow the possible parameters for comparison, and explore other avenues whereby dentition can be matched with postmortem records. In order for that to happen, the odontologist must be able to communicate what is needed, what level of identification different approaches can take, and what is feasible given the condition of the remains. The networks for dental healthcare providers are often more apparent to the odontologist and may allow the investigators to advance more quickly in their pursuit of antemortem information. The odontologist also needs to have access to the missing persons lists and information on where those people may have been. When there are multiple victims at one location, selecting the most likely candidate among a group for being the person with a retrieved dentition may be essential for a timely identification.

Due to the minute nature of the remains with which the odontologist works, where their work comes in the sequence of identification is important. When there are readily available antemortem dental records, then a dental identification may be the easiest way to proceed. However, with the highly damaged remains, a different strategy may be important. Odontological identification is best oriented to those remains (1) where DNA analysis is least likely to be effective and (2) where there are identifiable dental elements, especially with dental restorations. As additional dental elements were recovered during examination by other specialists, the ideal sequence should place the odontological examination after all dental material has been separated. Frankly, in wildfire identifications, the ideal sequence must fall prey to the difficulty of scheduling and decision-making and flexibility in working as a team is essential. Communication among the team members, either directly or through written documents is important so that all can make the best of what is, in any description, a bad situation.

Creativity is required in locating dental records, and the odontologist may be best positioned to utilize both traditional and less apparent networks to retrieve records. Many victims have made a series of moves prior to their final residence, leaving a scattered and disjointed history of dental care. Local dental organizations may be important to distribute member alerts to their links. This approach may be important when a prior residence is only known in general, and the identification of a dental care provider is no longer known. For example, during the Wine Country fires of 2017, one victim had lived out of state for many years and was relatively new to the area. Locating their records was a challenge. Ultimately, working with coroners' investigators, a map of the large urban area where the decedent had lived was used. A five-mile diameter circle was drawn on the map with the previous residence as the center point. The detective then located all of the dental offices within that area and called them. Ultimately, this simple approach located dental records, and we were able to identify the decedent.

Many state agencies also have access to dental information through their publicly assisted healthcare programs. These records may be critical when the disaster strikes a community where many residents require various forms of government assistance. This access may provide additional leads as to where dental records may be available as the governmental support program will have been responsible for compensating for care.

Beyond these steps that are significant in the immediate aftermath and identification process, there are also broader adjustments by dental care providers that would be helpful. For one, dentists should seriously consider retaining all digital records indefinitely. Whereas in the past, storage required expensive space for paper records and radiographic films, most practices have switched primarily to digital formats. Storage space in the digital world is now incredibly abundant and inexpensive. While digitizing prior records and saving these for future use would be ideal, at a minimum all digital records should be retained indefinitely or to some agreed longer duration since care. Among these radiographs and images will be most important.

While keeping records is important, archiving them requires additional effort. As we probably all know, records can be destroyed. If these records have been backed up recently to a cloud-based or offsite location, then the span of deleted/destroyed material is kept to a minimum. However, a regular and consistent schedule of backup is critical. As seen in the Camp Fire, there was one case where the most recent backup of information was more than a year old.

16.3 THE PATH FORWARD

The role of the forensic odontologist is evolving in the face of disasters such as wildfires. Their skills may be the only means for making a positive identification when remains are burned beyond the point of retrievable DNA, and there are no other identifying features such as orthopedic implants or medical devices. The excellent preservation of dental restorations combined with careful recovery of the victims remains from the scene make identifications possible. The efforts of the forensic odontologist are based on a commanding knowledge of dental anatomy but also their ability to help locate antemortem records and make a comparison utilizing the available information.

While it is increasingly more tempting for law enforcement to try to use DNA analysis first, I would argue against that. First of all, if significant dental remains are available and there are antemortem dental records, an identification can be completed very quickly. This is important to family members waiting to find out what may have happened to a loved one. Second, forensic odontology is a small fraction of the cost of a DNA analysis. Rapid DNA is showing remarkable results; however, costs remain high, and as we saw in some cases, dental evidence survived in a meaningful way when DNA analysis was not possible. The California Department of Justice Missing/Unidentified Persons unit requires that a dental examination of remains is performed before submission of tissue to the state DNA lab for the creation of a profile. I would argue that a forensic dental examination be performed, if possible, prior to cases being submitted for DNA analysis in a mass disaster.

CHAPTER 17

Anthropological Responsibilities in Post-Recovery Analysis

Lauren Zephro and Alison Galloway

The work to identify the deceased victims of a wildfire is not limited to recovering the remains from the fire scene. The anthropological analysis must continue into the morgue setting in order to maximize information obtained from each set of remains. In the morgue, the anthropologist serves as a critical member of a larger analytical team consisting of the pathologists, odontologists, DNA analysts, fingerprint experts, and those who work with obtaining and matching the postmortem and antemortem data.

This chapter lays out the role of the anthropologist in the post-recovery analysis, the issues that are most frequently encountered, some of the guiding principles for future analytic work, and areas in which additional research would prove beneficial. While much of this chapter derives from work on the victims of the Camp Fire, it is also informed by analysis of other burned material and experimental work on the burning process.

17.1 CIRCUMSTANCES OF THE CAMP FIRE MORGUE ANALYSIS

Recent fatal wildfires in the US West often occur at the interface of forested and more recently urbanized areas. Frequently, these disasters occur in relatively rural counties with a relatively small population base and sparse county facilities. The local morgue facilities are often insufficient to handle the number of fatalities, the scale of the teams involved in the post-recovery analysis, and the issue of proximity to families who want closure and the press coverage. Arrangements for moving remains to larger facilities in neighboring counties or to temporary morgue units mean that the anthropological teams must be split between the field and the morgue functions. For example, in the Camp Fire, the collected remains were taken to the morgue facilities of Sacramento County Coroner's Office, approximately two hours south of the Butte County seat of Chico. Consequently, the field teams were unable to participate in both arenas and additional members were needed to be located or portions of the existing team diverted to the morgue.

Delegation to "morgue work" may appear less attractive to the practicing anthropologist. Often, we want to be "part of the action." So, in part, we hope this chapter will focus on the critical importance of this aspect of the recovery process. Without the anthropological input, determination of the number of recovered individuals would be unclear and valuable time lost in searching for bodies already recovered or establishing identity from fragmentary remains when the body had already been identified from

DOI: 10.4324/9781003168010-21

other material collected separately. Anthropologists are also essential when the remains are so badly burned that the possibility of DNA analysis is excluded, and circumstantial evidence may be the only means of including or excluding an identity.

17.2 MORGUE PROCESSING OF WILDFIRE DECEDENTS

Remains recovered following a wildfire vary from barely singed to those that approach the level of destruction seen with a commercial cremation. In addition, many remains will be further fragmented by falling structures, recovery efforts and transportation to the morgue facilities. Remains often arrive with considerable non-osseous material also included in the collection. Often this material has been included because the bone is embedded in the molten glass or metal, or so wrapped in wire that field extraction is impossible.

Field removal of nonhuman osseous material is common but often small portions of such material is included with the human remains collected. People have often gathered their pets around them prior to being overcome by the fire. In rural areas where many fires are found, there will also be hunting trophies or collected skeletal elements. In a number of fires, anatomical human specimens have also been included in the recovered "victims."

Aside from the burned remains, there may also be individuals who died of natural causes during or after the fire and those who committed suicide in anticipation of the arrival of the flames. These remains may be burned as badly as those who perished due to the direct action of the fire or may be entirely unburned. All are considered victims of the natural disaster.

Bodies vary from intact remains showing only superficial singeing, to those whose remains are more seriously damaged. The majority of remains from fires, such as the Camp Fire are in more advanced stages. These remains are typically composed of a badly charred torso, often reduced to the base of the skull, spine, and pelvic area. When the body has also been exposed to various building collapse or larger amounts of fuel, the body may only be large pieces of calcined bone.

Bodies are transported to the morgue in a variety of containers, which affects the integrity of the remains when presented for post-recovery analysis. Those individuals whose bodies are largely intact are often brought in body bags. This process, however, often results in crushing of smaller bones that may have become detached from the main body in the process as bags are moved, strapped in place, and emptied. Often these small bones filter to the corners of the bags where they are more vulnerable to damage. Use of an internal sheet with which to wrap the body may improve preservation. More fragmented remains arrive in paper bags, metal containers or plastic lidded buckets. Limiting the movement of material within the container diminishes the fragmentation of remains during transportation, but using multiple containers may increase damage as containers are repeatedly opened and emptied at the various stations. While no specific treatment is considered superior, the care in which material is confined within the container is critical. However, packing material should not cling to the bones, as is the case with cotton wool or a loosely woven fabric. Instead, it is better to brace the inner container or upper surfaces with non-clinging material (inflated air bags, wadded paper, tightly woven cloths, etc.) to prevent undue movement.

Standard morgue proceedings on the handling of remains should apply, with some modifications, in wildfire deaths (see Chapter 14). The body bags or containers of remains are photographed, numbered, and tagged. If computed tomography is available, this is also a good way to document the status of the material upon arrival. CT scans can also be used to make some skeletal assessments, such as age based on epiphyseal fusion or appearance of degenerative conditions, without directly accessing the remains (Blau & Briggs, 2011).

Paperwork for the processing is generated to include a cover sheet with the types of analyses anticipated. All paperwork is placed in a plastic sealable envelope and attached to the container. The remains are then passed through a series of stations, covering the range of analyses that will be conducted on the bodies. At each station, the paperwork generated at that station is added to the envelope and the cover sheet completed to show the status, personnel, date, and time of work.

However, as we experienced in the Camp Fire, not all experts may be available throughout the processing so there may be differences in the order in which analyses are conducted. In many cases, it will take time to mobilize the various experts and their availability may also fluctuate. In many cases, individuals will have to travel into the area to assist and even basic needs such as accommodations may be difficult.

The rapidity with which remains arrive at the morgue varies by the recovery efforts themselves. In many wildfire situations, most of the remains are found relatively soon after it is possible to enter the area and begin searching. Transportation must also be arranged from the recovery site to the morgue facilities. These processes often mean that there will be an accumulation of remains at the beginning of the work period and gradual reduction as missing persons lists are resolved. Constant morgue attendance by all the experts would include considerable "downtime" waiting for new material and additional expense for the recovery efforts.

It is usually helpful for anthropological analysis to occur early in the sequence of analyses. Anthropologists can separate out those items that provide information such as dental elements, indicators of age and sex, and any identifying elements, such as healed fractures, anomalies, pathological conditions, and the more obvious implants and sutures. Elements that could contain viable DNA can also be set aside in this initial sorting process. Unfortunately, if the material is opened up repeatedly, there is increasing fragmentation, often rendering further anthropological analysis more difficult.

Anthropological analyses consisted of removing all the available material from a case and sorting what material can be assigned to element and side. Because of the extreme fragmentation, identification of side is often problematic. The bone may be identifiable as to element, such as a portion of the humeral head but not to side. Unfortunately, most protocols utilize an anatomically correct layout that may be inappropriate for the highly fragmented bones found from wildfire scenarios. Instead, a large piece of paper covering the surface of a gurney can be marked with the following body segments (Figure 17.1):

- Head
  - Teeth
- Spine
- Ribs
- Upper limb
  - Pectoral girdle
  - Arm (humerus) and forearm
  - Hand
- Lower limb
  - Pelvic girdle
  - Thigh and leg bones
  - Foot
- Unsortable bone

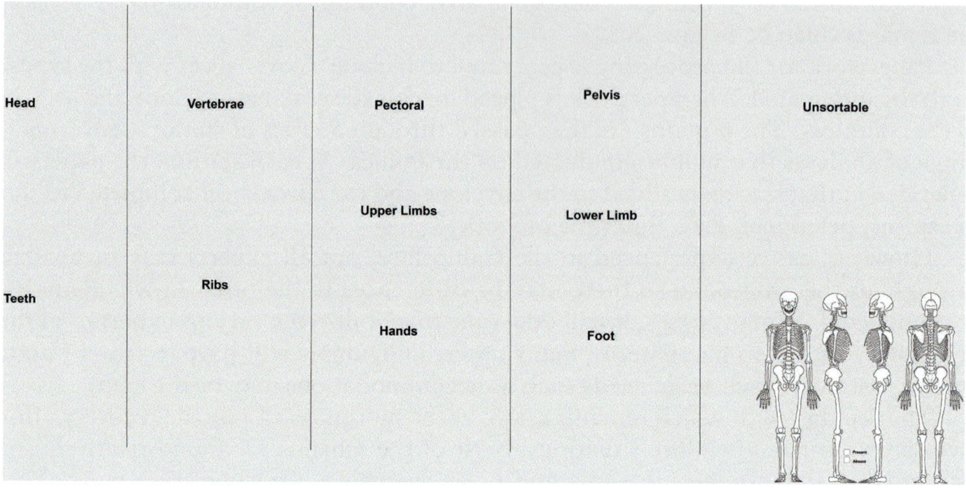

FIGURE 17.1 Schematic for sorting remains compared to anatomical approach (lower right). Schematic may be written on a large piece of butcher paper laid over an autopsy or other table. Analysts can quickly sort through material and assess completeness of field recovery and identify the possibility of repeating elements or difference in morphology/size suggesting additional individuals may be present.

Utilizing this format allows for the anthropologist to see if all body segments are present, to assess whether both sides are present, even when some identifiable skeletal fragments are not attributable to right or left side, to address consistency in morphology and age/sex characteristics, and to identify when there are more elements than may be warranted by a single individual.

Based on this assessment, it is then possible to make notes of when interpretations as to sex, age, and identifying features have been found. Recording forms should be used (see Appendix A) that allow for conclusions and some descriptions of the basis of that determination. Anatomical charts, such as the INTERPOL DVI Postmortem (pink) form (INTERPOL, 2018), are often not particularly useful. By working in teams, anthropologists can also provide onsite peer review of the forms, documented by a countersignature.

Once all analyses have been completed (see Chapter 15), remains are stored until identification is established. The coroner's office oversees the coordination of the analyses and identification processes.

17.3 ANTHROPOLOGICAL CONSIDERATIONS

In any forensic anthropological analysis, the scope of the work must be defined prior to the initiation of analyses. Working with the victims of a wildfire is no different in this need but the scope itself does not fully overlap with that of a forensic investigation. Whereas in most forensic work, there is less focus on the biological profile and more on trauma and time since death, in wildfires, identification of the remains is usually the primary goal and discussion of postmortem interval and taphonomic events is less important.

The responsibilities of the anthropologist include separation of any nonhuman or non-osseous material, identification of bones by element and side if possible, and identification of completeness of recovery and potential for multiple victims per identification number. Some elements of the biological profile may be possible to assess, including some indicators of sex and age. In our experience with the Camp Fire victims, ancestry identification is rarely possible due to the extreme fragmentation of the remains and the fragility of the bones that preclude removal of overlying charred soft tissue. If skulls were actually intact, it generally meant that the body itself was only lightly burned. With Rapid DNA analysis readily available, defleshing remains for cranial measurements is not appropriate or productive. Stature estimation is difficult due to fragmentation of long bones and significant bone shrinkage. There are, however, important contributions from anthropology. The following are specific considerations gleaned from the analysis of Camp Fire victims.

17.3.1 Human/Nonhuman/Non-osseous Material

Because people often died in their homes, their remains could also be commingled with those of their pets, food items, skeletal collections, or even the already cremated remains of their loved ones. As much as possible, these items were removed from the remains in the field and set aside for the families to collect (especially cremains or pets) or were disposed of in order to prevent future alerts about found skeletal material.

Despite this care, small- to medium-sized pieces of nonhuman skeletal material was often intermingled with the remains. Assignment of these bones to domestic animals, such as cats or dogs, as opposed to those assigned to cuts of meat was important, and families could then decide on how to handle the material from the household pets.

In addition, there was a large amount of non-osseous material included with the bodies that were more extensively cremated. The most common material was burned drywall and could be separated quickly. However, melted glass and metal were also common and had to be assessed for whether or not this material contained any skeletal elements. Finding bones encased in melted glass or aluminum was not uncommon. Additionally, some elements were firmly fixed to metal objects and could not be safely separated. Inevitably, non-osseous material had to be retained with the remains.

17.3.2 Material for Positive Identification

The larger items, such as prosthetic devices (e.g., hip, knee, and shoulder replacement material), were often located and bagged separately at the time of recovery as these are useful for positive identification. Some smaller items, such as sternal wires, pacemaker wires, surgical sutures, and cranial fracture hardware were also among the remains as these were less likely to be separated. The presence of these items may be useful for supporting a circumstantial identification even if they no longer can be compared radiographically.

Because of the reliance on DNA analysis, identification of body segments that represent better reservoirs of viable samples assists in processing. These segments include portions of the spinal column, pelvis and hip joints, charred liver or heart samples, and occasionally other portions of the body. Differential burning can occur in structural fires particularly when portions of the house, such as tiling or dry wall, fall over a part of the body.

17.3.3 Incomplete Recovery

The most common problem with recovered remains is that major portions of the body may not be present. This problem is more likely to occur in the beginning of recovery efforts before the anthropological teams are fully mobilized and integrated into the recovery efforts. However, the circumstances of the fire, including multiple story structures, can distribute remains of a single individual over a wider than anticipated area.

Identifying when recovery is incomplete and communicating that to the field teams is important to prevent the remaining sections from being assigned to an additional individual. Increasingly, coroners and medical examiners try to ensure that all skeletal material is collected prior to families being allowed back to their homes. This recovery completeness is an effort to limit the trauma that the families face on return to their devastated homes and shows respect for the victims whose lives were lost.

17.3.4 Split Recovery

Because of the movement of bodies within the buildings as they burned (see Chapter 10), as well as movement of the bodies as the furniture and floors disintegrated, some remains were split into different units and recovered some distance apart. In other instances, initial recoveries were bagged, and later recovery teams also found material, and these were not immediately associated with the prior number. In these cases, remains from a single individual arrived at the morgue with multiple identifying numbers. Obviously, this situation results in an additional "victim" and the possibility of considerable time spent looking for the identity of a second person who may have died at that location.

Using the information on body elements represented allows for fairly rapid assessment of incomplete recovery and then bags could be compared when matched by the address of recovery. If there appeared to be a match, then all bags were examined on adjacent tables to see if these matched morphologically.

17.3.5 Commingled Recovery

The most difficult situation is that of commingled remains. Often victims cluster together as they try to escape or realize that their chances of survival are gone. As a result, victims die closely entwined and subsequent burning reduces all to a single mass of burned bone. The victim who may be larger in body size or more protected by the presence of others may be the only one where there is any remaining tissue with viable DNA.

Determining the number of the victims and some clues as to their identity is important for the recovery process as unnecessary effort may be expended in trying to locate people who have already been recovered. In many cases the victims are family members, increasing the distress for those who have survived.

However, in the wildfire situation, this is an extremely difficult task. In situations like this, the bodies are often extremely fragmented as there has been enough body mass with the combined victims to ensure that the bodies burned for a long period after the surrounding fuel (see Chapter 11). That process, combined with structural collapse of the house, reduces bones to an assemblage of fragments. As a result, anthropological analysis will be essential to see if there are multiple instances of a single element that will document the number of individuals.

17.4 LESSONS LEARNED

Processing remains from the Camp Fire required approximately 13 days of work between two anthropologists. Initial work was conducted approximately one week after the initiation of recovery efforts. Subsequent visits occurred over the next two extended weekends. One anthropologist (AG) had also spent four days in the recovery efforts in Paradise and Magalia prior to the morgue work, which helped provide some context to the morgue analyses. A final visit from the larger team occurred approximately two months later to review a few cases where positive identification had not yet been possible on commingled material.

Although both anthropologists were experienced in forensic analysis, the Camp Fire analysis required a steep learning curve to adjust to the demands and limitations of the material. In the following sections, we try to outline the major ways in which we realigned our work to the situation.

17.4.1 Pace of Analysis

The pace of analysis is fast—usually eight to ten remains were analyzed per person per day. The routine consisted of opening the body bag or other container, laying out the remains by body segment, assessing the available information, completing paperwork, and providing peer evaluation when staffing levels permitted. Typically, two to three gurneys were in use during periods of analysis, representing two stations and a floating table to use as needed.

The pace of work was determined, in part, by pressure to complete the work so that other segments of the team could gain access to the material. Additionally, it was obvious that the material itself would not provide significantly more information by further examination. Working through every bone fragment and attempting to identify elements was not necessary as it did not provide any additional forensically useful information. On top of all these considerations, families who were displaced or were looking for those who were missing applied considerable pressure on the coroner's office to release remains.

The balance between providing sufficient time to work on the burned remains while not delaying the overall process is a difficult one. Because many remains provide only limited information, they can be processed easily. Other cases may be fully fleshed and anthropological examination may be largely pointless. In contrast, some cases, especially those involving commingling, will take considerably more time. In one case, both anthropologists worked four hours just to establish proof of the minimum number of victims—three instances of a right scaphoid and three instances of a left calcaneus (one highly fragmented).

17.4.2 Importance of Locations

When the remains arrive at the morgue, they are given identification numbers by which they are referred until a positive identification is made. Unfortunately, this numbering system also implants an expectation that the remains associated with each number consist of one, complete individual. As more than one pathologist is working to evaluate the remains, often one number is given to one pathologist, while the next number, from the same location, is given to another pathologist. Both can document what they see but comparison of material does not occur.

As the anthropological team began its work, the coroner's unit asked that we assess specific cases where commingling or incompleteness were suspected. This determination was usually based on whether or not another person was still listed as missing from a location. However, it became apparent that all cases needed to be evaluated based on the location of the find with the anthropologists looking between the bagged remains to evaluate the material. Data sheets with addresses of recovery were located and all remains from the same address were subsequently analyzed simultaneously. One difficulty was the number of mobile home parks with a single address and no remaining unit identification. Consequently, many remains could be assigned to a single "address" but actually have been retrieved from completely different homes.

17.4.3 Limitations of Available Information

When initially assigned to the morgue, both anthropologists anticipated being able to lay out the remains in anatomical position. As noted earlier, this process would be typical of that seen in the INTERPOL disaster victim identification protocols (INTERPOL, 2018). It quickly became apparent that the destruction was far too extensive to permit such detailed identification. Instead, we had to adapt to the situation with a simplified layout system. The use of paper also limited the contamination possible by allowing a simple replacement of a new sheet with each case.

We had also expected to be able to say much more about each individual. However, in many cases the bones were so fragmented that even sex was not easy to assign. Size could have been useful but the degree of bone shrinkage—often differential within a single body—made even this less useful. Not uncommonly, a portion of the pubic bones or the sciatic notch would be located. Other indicators were portions of the frontal bone showing the supra-orbital area. Often overall gracility/robusticity allowed for a weighting given to male or female.

Age assessments are much broader than commonly provided by skeletal analysis. Essentially, in this adult series from the Camp Fire, we could assign individuals as young adult (ongoing or recent epiphyseal fusion), middle adult (full fusion but no degenerative conditions), and older/elderly adults (those with degenerative conditions). Age indicators in terms of degenerative conditions, particularly of the spine with visible osteophyte development, collapse of vertebrae, and osteoarthritic changes to the facets, were noted, but as most individuals who died were older to elderly (see Chapter 20), this was not particularly helpful.

17.4.4 Separation of Commingled Remains

When remains were identified as commingled, there was the expectation on the part of the coroners and pathologists that the anthropologists would then be able to separate all the remains into the two or more individuals. Often this is simply not possible, and the bulk of the material is unsortable. Typically, a few fragments could be pulled from the cremated mass and attributed to a large individual while others could be attributable to a small individual. Occasionally, indicators of sex or age could also be found.

Explaining the problem of commingling was difficult, even within the coroner's unit. There is the desire to return individual victims to the families as a single unit, and there is also a cognitive bias inherent with the numbering system. Despite the proof that two bags of remains each contain more than one individual, the desire to track elements by "body number" means that there is pressure to always be able to return an element to its "correct bag"—even when the bag number is irrelevant to individual identity.

Anthropologists often play a critical role in explaining that the families should be informed of the situation and given a range of options as to the treatment of the remains. They may wish to have the small number of identified remains separated and agree to different treatment of the unsortable material. They may wish to keep all the material together and manage a joint internment or disposal or they may wish to make an arbitrary division of the material into "individuals." Obviously, this is not the decision of the anthropologists or the coroners, but it is one where anthropologists must communicate the ramifications of the commingling to those who have contact with the family.

17.4.5 Value of Small Bones

Initial recovery often involves personnel who are not trained in recovery of burned bodies. Large charred segments of the torso and bigger pieces of calcined bone may be collected but smaller bones, often that have filtered down into the debris, are left behind. Small bones of the hands and feet often are well-preserved despite calcination and are extremely helpful in determining the number of individuals. Not only may they not be collected by the untrained recovery team, but the movement of team members around the visible remains often destroys these critical elements.

17.4.6 Importance of Teamwork and Preparation

While we often recognize the contributions of the pathologists, odontologists, and DNA specialists, there are many support personnel whose work may be underacknowledged. One group in particular was critical for the success of our efforts and that was the autopsy technicians who provided assistance. They anticipated the pace of our work so that cases were available once one set had been completed. They uploaded photographs from cameras, organized images with case numbers, and provided the placards and scales needed for documentation. They also protected the workspace, consisting of double gurneys and a reference skeleton.

The other lesson was the importance of experience and training. Both anthropologists had prior experience working with burned human remains. Despite that, there was a steep learning curve in adapting this knowledge to the wildfire situation. If an anthropologist without such prior experience is tasked with this work, it becomes much more difficult, and they cannot also dispel any incorrect assumptions about how bodies burn, thermal fracturing, or shrinkage/warping of bone.

17.5 AREAS FOR FUTURE RESEARCH

As the need for anthropology to be applied to wildfires increases, so does the requirement for a research paradigm and protocols that incorporate the specific needs of this area of inquiry. Previous burned bone research, based on experimentation and case-based observations (see, for example, Schmidt & Symes, 2015, and Fairgrieve, 2008, for summaries), has been conducted to speak to the forensic or archaeological context and is ripe for expansion in order to be applicable in a wildfire setting.

As evidenced by our work, expanding on previous burned bone research, such bone shrinkage and the tolerance of differential shrinkage within a single individual, is crucial. Since the fundamental question we are answering in a wildfire context is the minimum number of individuals and we are dealing with incomplete, fragmentary recoveries, more experimental research that explores individual variation due to burning is fundamental to our ability to accurately determine if there is more than one individual represented when repeating bones are not available. For example, analysis of one case indicated solely on element size and morphology that at least two individuals were present. The distal portion of the femur was notably larger in epicondylar breadth than the breadth of the proximal portion of the tibia that showed cortical bone along the margins of the tibial plateau. All elements were calcined, and DNA extraction was unsuccessful on the elements in question, and since the bones were consumed for DNA extraction, they were destroyed. No other contextual information indicated that there was more than one individual at the residence, thus, the possibility of a second individual is still unresolved. Research exploring shrinkage must take into account more fundamental research questions into the differences in burning among fresh, decomposed, and skeletonized bone. Research into the effects on burning must also consider the temperature and duration of burning in an experimental setting. Other factors, like age relating to the proportion of mineral versus organic material in bone and sex differences related to bone density and morphology, should also be considered as possible variables.

In addition to research that specifically addresses nuances related to burning bone and its interpretation, research should also address logistics and successful case management in the wildfire environment, to include standardized protocols for the rapid and thorough processing of remains in a morgue setting with multiple analytical stages. Lastly, osteology is more challenging in a wildfire situation. Hands-on training for anthropologists with burned bone is needed to support the professional development of anthropologists working in the field.

REFERENCES

Blau, S., & Briggs, C. (2011). The role of forensic anthropology in Disaster Victim Identification (DVI). *Forensic Science International*, *205*, 29–35.

Fairgrieve, S. (2008). *Forensic cremation: Recovery and analysis*. Boca Raton, FL: CRC Press.

INTERPOL. (2018). *Post mortem (pink) form for unidentified human remains*. https://www.interpol.int/content/download/5325/file/PostMortem

Schmidt, C., & Symes, S. (2015). *The analysis of burned human remains* (2nd ed.). Amsterdam: Academic Press.

APPENDIX A

Anthropology Worksheet for Burned Remains*

Date: ________________ Coroner case number: ________________
Time: ________________ Agency case number: ________________
Anthropologist: ________________ Signature: ________________ Peer: _____
Photos: ________________ Archived: ________________

Anthro sex:	***Based on:***
Anthro age:	***Based on:***
Anthro ancestry:	***Based on:***
Anthro stature:	***Based on:***

Body parts present:
Condition of remains/comments:
Sample for DNA:
Minimum number of individuals:
Recommendations:

NOTES:

CHAPTER 18

A Practical Guide for Implementation of Rapid DNA Identification in Mass Fatality Events

Lessons Learned from the 2018 Camp Fire

Richard F. Selden, Rosemary Turingan Witkowski, and Eugene Tan

18.1 INTRODUCTION

Rapid DNA identification is beginning to revolutionize disaster victim identification (DVI). After two decades of technology and product development, individuals without backgrounds in forensic DNA analysis and genetics can now perform Rapid DNA analysis outside the laboratory, dramatically accelerating victim identification. The application of Rapid DNA to DVI samples is based on more than two decades of development of foundational laboratory methodologies. These advances have led to victim identification from a wide range of mass casualty events, including wars (Alonso et al. 2001), terrorist attacks (Holland et al. 2003), plane crashes (Hsu et al. 1999; Leclair et al. 2001), and natural phenomena, such as typhoons (Deng et al. 2005) and hurricanes (Donkervoort et al. 2008). Yet forensic laboratories are faced with capacity issues and backlogs on a daily basis and are not, in general, well-equipped to process quickly the large numbers of samples, including degraded samples and difficult samples, such as bone and teeth, required to identify disaster victims.

Rapid DNA provides a powerful alternative to conventional laboratory DNA processing. The rationale for utilizing Rapid DNA to process DVI and family reference samples and to perform kinship analysis near the mass casualty site includes the following:

- Elimination of the interval between victim recovery and receipt of samples by a laboratory.
- Minimization of the requirement for storage of victim remains (they may be released to the family by the appropriate jurisdictional authority).

DOI: 10.4324/9781003168010-22

- Reduction in the deterioration of sample quality (the more time elapsed between time of death and time of sample processing, the greater the potential for DNA degradation).
- Improved results. By generating results rapidly in the field, it is possible to provide immediate feedback to sample collectors. For example, if an initial analysis is unsuccessful, obtaining an additional sample (from the same or different tissue type and quantity) increases the potential for generating useful genetic information.
- The ability to process challenging samples, including degraded bone and tissue, with data quality that is at least as good as and often superior to those generated by conventional laboratory methodologies.
- The ability to utilize nontechnical operators. Even a small mass casualty event can overwhelm local and regional laboratories. Rapid DNA enables a dramatic increase in throughput by matching the number of operators to the magnitude of the disaster.
- The ability to integrate DNA workflow with that from forensic anthropology, odontology, radiology, taphonomy, and other critical disciplines. Traditionally, DNA data was generated long after the disaster, and real-time integration with these disciplines was not possible.
- The ability to process samples locally, within the borders of a given nation. In many cases, processing of victim samples must, by law or by custom, occur within the country that experienced the mass casualty event. By performing analysis locally, Rapid DNA empowers nations to perform DVI effectively.
- Increased throughput with decreased time to result.

Taken together, these advantages allow more samples to be processed with improved outcomes using Rapid DNA. Most importantly, the Rapid DNA identification system can bring timely closure to grieving family members.

Most jurisdictions have not experienced mass casualty events, and the application of Rapid DNA to DVI is quite recent. Accordingly, the goal of this report is to provide a practical guide to the implementation of Rapid DNA in DVI to allow advance preparations for such events or to provide a concise overview to authorities facing their first mass casualty. The first use of Rapid DNA at a major mass casualty event was during the 2018 Camp Fire, the deadliest wildfire in California history, and we will use lessons learned from this disaster as the exemplar for this overview. However, it cannot be emphasized enough that every disaster is unique and presents concomitantly unique identification challenges that require flexible thinking and tailor-made strategies and protocols. Nevertheless, certain fundamental and unifying concepts will be discussed.

18.2 INTRODUCTION TO RAPID DNA IDENTIFICATION

Rapid DNA identification (Carney et al. 2019; Della Manna et al. 2016; Grover et al. 2017; Moreno et al. 2017; Palmbach et al. 2014; Tan et al. 2013; Turingan et al. 2016, 2019) is defined as the fully automated process of generating a DNA ID (also referred to as a short tandem repeat [STR] profile or DNA profile) from a forensic sample, typically performed outside the laboratory by nontechnical operators, and with results available in less than two hours. The DNA Identification Act of 1994 established the

FBI's authority to build the National DNA Index System (NDIS), but as a result, DNA testing has been limited to approximately 200 accredited forensic labs. The unintended consequences of the lab-centric approach to DNA testing (both in the US and worldwide) have been delays in evidence processing and the development of substantial evidentiary backlogs. The problem can best be summarized as follows: the CODIS (Combined DNA Index System, the FBI's program of support for criminal justice DNA databases as well as the software used to run these databases) has assisted more than 528,887 investigations (between 1998 and 2020), but well over 250 million crimes have occurred during this period—meaning DNA data has an impact of only approximately 0.2% of US crimes. Laboratory methods for evidentiary and DVI sample analysis are slow and cumbersome, requiring both highly trained scientists, sophisticated laboratory equipment, and a highly controlled laboratory environment. With forensic laboratories overburdened with the day-to-day workload of evidentiary samples, their capacity to process a sudden influx of DVI samples is quite limited. By enabling DNA analysis to be performed outside the lab by nontechnical operators, Rapid DNA has the capability of dramatically accelerating DNA processing of DVI samples.

The ANDE Rapid DNA identification system consists of five major components:

- The instrument (see Figure 18.1, Carney et al. 2019) is ruggedized and can be operated by nontechnical users outside the laboratory.
- The chip (see Figure 18.2, Turingan et al. 2020) is a single-use consumable that integrates all steps performed in DNA identification, including DNA

FIGURE 18.1 The ANDE instrument. Ruggedized and certified to US MIL STD 810G for shock and vibration, the instrument can be transported to a disaster site and operated outside the laboratory by nontechnical users.

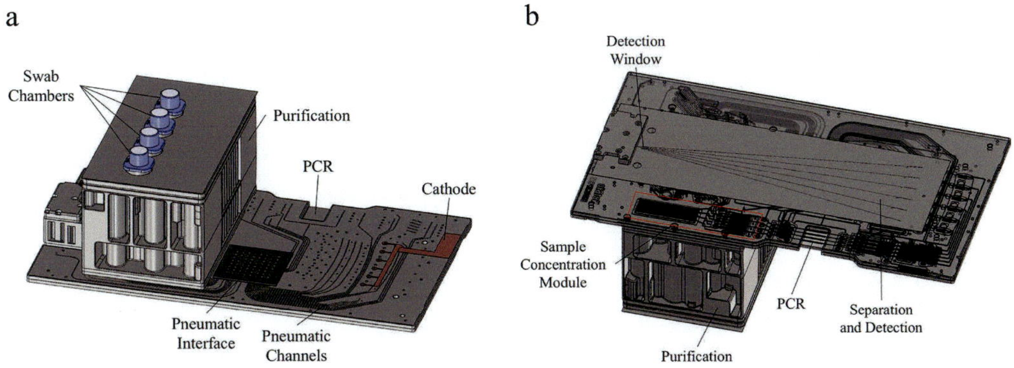

FIGURE 18.2 The ANDE I-Chip (a—top view; b—bottom view). The single-use plastic consumable chip (dimensions: 295 mm × 165 mm × 93 mm) processes up to four DVI samples per run. Each I-Chip processes four samples and each A-Chip processes five buccal swabs per run. All reagents are present within the chips—the operator simply inserts the sample into the swab chambers and then inserts the chip into the instrument. All sample processing steps occur automatically within the closed chip and the resulting data is also processed automatically. The DNA IDs may be stored on the instrument until exported to the FAIRS DNA database for kinship or matching analysis.

purification, STR amplification, and electrophoretic separation and detection. The chips are stable at room temperature for six months, and two types are available: the A-Chip for buccal swabs (whether from unidentified human remains or from family reference samples) and the I-Chip for all other sample types, including DVI samples.

- The swab cap contains an embedded RFID chip, critical for maintaining evidence chain of custody and minimizing sample mix-up.
- Expert system software automatically performs data processing and analysis to generate a DNA ID.
- FAIRS, an integrated package of analytical software, including database generation and management, search and match, and kinship determination functionalities.

The ANDE system utilizes a multiplexed assay that interrogates 27 STR loci simultaneously (23 autosomal, 3 Y-chromosomal, and amelogenin). Termed FlexPlex27 (Figure 18.3), the assay contains all expanded CODIS, UK, INTERPOL, European Standard, German, and Australian core loci, and D6S1043, an important STR marker broadly used in China. Accuracy, concordance, precision, resolution, peak height ratio, sensitivity, species specificity, and all other relevant measures meet or exceed required metrics (Grover et al. 2017). Use of an STR assay that includes all commonly used STR loci is important as it allows data generated in different countries to be compared effectively. Finally, the ANDE system has received NDIS approval from the FBI (Carney et al. 2019) and approval from the US Department of Defense and is readily validated in field- or laboratory-based settings.

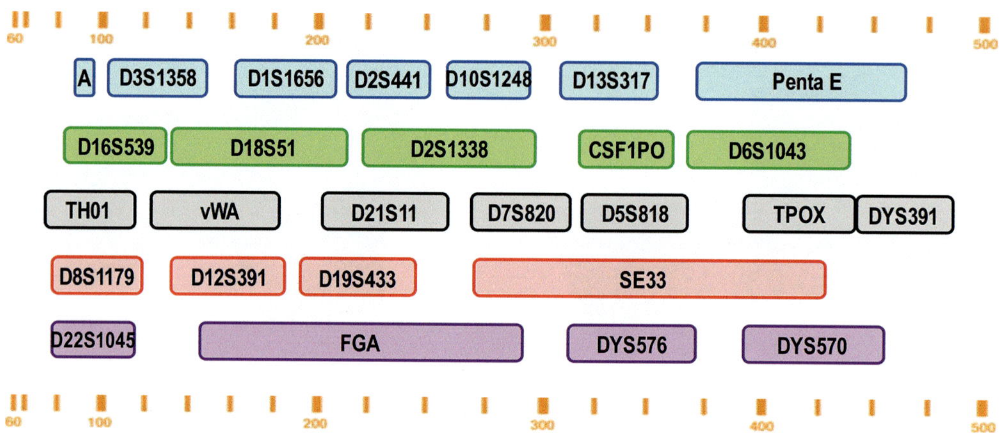

FIGURE 18.3 Configuration of the FlexPlex STR assay. FlexPlex is a 6-Color assay (including an Internal Lane Standard) that interrogates 23 autosomal STR loci, three Y-chromosomal loci, and amelogenin (for determination of biological gender). FlexPlex generates data compatible with databases around the world, including the CODIS core 20 loci, ENFSI/EDNAP Expanded European Standard Set, Australia's National Criminal Investigation DNA Database, Canada's National DNA Data Bank, China's National DNA Database, Germany's DNA-Analyze-Datei, New Zealand's National DNA Profile Databank, and United Kingdom's National DNA Database. Each STR locus generates alleles based on a defined size range and color (i.e., the type of fluorescent dye with which the amplified fragment is labelled). Further details on the FlexPlex assay can be found in Carney et al. (2019).

18.3 INTRODUCTION TO THE 2018 CAMP FIRE

In November 2018, Butte County, California, was decimated by the Camp Fire, the deadliest and most destructive wildfire in state history. Over 150,000 acres were destroyed, and at its peak, the fire consumed 80 acres per minute. On the day the Camp Fire started (CAL Fire 2019; Washington Post 2018), emergency systems in the State of California were already severely strained by a mass fatality shooting in Ventura (VC Star 2018) and the Woolsey Fire in Southern California (US National Park Service 2018). The Camp Fire response was coordinated by the Butte County Sheriff's Office and involved collaboration with California's Office of Emergency Services, CAL FIRE, the National Guard, California Highway Patrol, and sheriff-coroners' investigators and search and rescue teams from throughout the state. In addition, Butte County Sheriff's Office requested the assistance of forensic anthropology teams from California and Nevada.

The Sacramento County Coroner's Office was tasked with determining cause of death and identifying Camp Fire victims. Unidentified human remains (UHRs) were transported daily from the fire impacted area to the Sacramento County Morgue. UHR intake typically consisted of cataloging personal items found with remains, photographing remains and the items found, fingerprinting if possible, documentation of information on the decedent, full X-rays, and examination by one or more forensic anthropologists, pathologists, and odontologists.

Although California has suffered frequent wildfires, it soon became clear that the death and destruction caused by the Camp Fire was far beyond that previously experienced in the region. As the number of reported missing climbed, first to hundreds and then to thousands, Butte County Sheriff Kory Honea decided to include Rapid DNA analysis in the victim identification effort. On November 12, four days after the Camp Fire started and two weeks before it was contained, ANDE Corporation presented a proposed approach to incorporating Rapid DNA into identification activities. By November 14, a small team consisting of two Rapid DNA scientists and two operators were onsite at the Sacramento County Morgue.

The details of morgue operations are presented elsewhere in this volume, but several observations will be made here. Most importantly, the Sacramento County Coroner Kim Gin immediately realized that simple, fast, and yet effective methods of interdisciplinary communication would be critical. To meet this challenge, she employed the decidedly low-tech method of posting large (two-by-three-foot) pieces of paper for each set of unidentified human remains. Each discipline summarized their ongoing findings on each sheet, and when cases were closed, the sheets corresponding to the identified victims were moved to a separate area. Despite the myriad number of laboratory information management systems that are available, when large numbers of individuals from outside a given institution arrive to work together, a simple piece of paper is sometimes the most effective means of collating information and promoting communication. In addition, the coroner ensured that every individual working on identification, regardless of discipline, was made aware of overall process flow from UHR intake on, including the set of identification modalities being employed and the individuals responsible for each modality. These initial organizational decisions were critical to the ultimate success of the work. Although they may seem simple, identification efforts in mass casualties are often hampered by lack of communication, lack of information sharing, and unnecessary bureaucracy.

18.4 RAPID DNA PROCESSING OF UNIDENTIFIED HUMAN REMAINS DURING THE CAMP FIRE

During the early hours of ANDE's involvement, it was far from clear that Rapid DNA would play a major role in the identification process. After all, Rapid DNA had never before been used in a mass disaster, although the approach had proven useful and successful in both government-sponsored disaster exercises and small-scale real-world applications. Just as importantly, the remains of the Camp Fire victims were severely degraded and the ability of Rapid DNA to process severely burned and calcined remains had not been tested. To develop a strategy for Rapid DNA implementation when confronted with a mass casualty event, it is important to perform an initial assessment of the remains, which will vary based on the following:

- Location of remains (e.g., exposed, buried, submerged in fresh or salt water).
- Environmental conditions (e.g., temperature, humidity). Temperature, moisture, and oxygen levels in the depositional environment, soil composition, and pH affect the ability to obtain analyzable DNA from biological specimens (Latham and Miller 2019).
- Approximate age of remains (days vs. weeks vs. longer periods).

- Type of remains, amount of material available, and sample accessibility. Determine if there is sufficient material present to perform repeat analyses if necessary and what types of tools are needed for collecting samples.
- Nature of insult (e.g., burns, chemical or radioactive exposure, gunshot, explosion, crushing, insect infestation).

The practical application of these considerations is to allow a first responder to determine which sample types should be collected when one or many sets of exposed human remains are encountered. This determination is based on two related criteria: first, the sample types that are most likely to generate useful DNA IDs using the ANDE system and second, the sample types that are easiest to collect. It is emphasized that there is no single order of priorities for sample selection, and the following is simply a starting point for consideration. In the early days following a mass disaster or when a newly deceased body is found, buccal swabs are typically the Rapid DNA sample of choice, and these should be obtained for as long as possible (typically several days of environmental exposure or months in a refrigerated morgue). The advantage of buccal swabs is that they are simple to obtain (including by non-technical users) and simple to process.

Under certain circumstances, buccal swabs cannot be collected due to insect infestation, burned or decapitated remains, or other reasons. Buccal swabs, generally the simplest sample type to collect, illustrates the importance of the initial assessment described earlier. For example, a plane crash in a temperate climate may lead to insect infestation within several days, whereas one in a polar zone (or a continental zone in winter) may allow infestation-free buccal samples to be recovered for weeks. Anticipating such conditions will allow for more effective strategic, tactical, and logistical planning in the hours or days prior to arrival onsite. It cannot be overemphasized that the response to a mass casualty begins the moment that the identification professional is alerted to the event—gathering information and formulating a response plan (knowing that it will evolve) is critical. In addition to developing a sample collection strategy in advance, it is imperative to assess each set of remains onsite to determine the optimal types of samples to process (Hartman et al. 2011; Calacal et al. 2015). Diligent advanced planning offsite improves the response but cannot replace exposure to the conditions onsite.

When buccal swabs are inaccessible or otherwise problematic, cardiac blood (liquid or clotted) and muscle (swabs or tissue fragments) are typically reasonable to collect for up to five days of exposure. When severe degradation and prolonged aging beyond several days are present, DNA contained within bone and teeth is protected (Amory et al. 2012; Davoren et al. 2007; Lee et al. 2010; Loreille et al. 2007; Pajnič 2016; Parsons et al. 2018; Vanek et al. 2017) and typically persists for much longer than in soft tissues. The type of bone being analyzed also plays a role in DNA typing success, with denser and more compact bones yielding more DNA than non-weight-bearing structures (Mundorff et al. 2009; Mundorff and Davoren 2014). The results of our previous work evaluating the utility of various sample types taken from exposed remains over one year are consistent with and expand upon these previous studies and established that these principles can be applied to generating DNA IDs in the field using Rapid DNA identification technology (Turingan et al. 2019).

With respect to the Camp Fire, the initial assessment of human remains was based on photographs sent as the ANDE team travelled by air to Sacramento. The majority of fire victims were recovered from residences, with the remaining recovered from vehicles or outside. The vast majority of victims showed extensive thermal destruction, consisting mainly of burned bones ranging from single bones to partial skeletons, most of which were calcined. Occasionally, bodies with heads, torsos, and extremities with variable amounts of burned soft tissues and organs were recovered. Fragments of jaws and loose teeth were present with some of the remains. The condition of most individuals was analogous to remains that are commercially cremated (prior to their pulverization into ash), reflecting the immense heat and long duration of thermal exposure.

Based on this assessment, it was clear that buccal swabs were unlikely to be useful, that bones and teeth would play a major role in the identification efforts, and that cardiac blood, muscle swabs and fragments, and other tissue types, if available, should be considered. Furthermore, the excessive temperatures generated by the fire led to the possibility that it may not be possible to generate DNA IDs from some or even all of the victims (whether by Rapid DNA analysis or conventional laboratory methodologies).

To process these highly degraded samples, two ANDE Rapid DNA instruments were utilized, with the instruments placed in a recreational vehicle (RV) located outside the Sacramento County Coroner's Office. One individual worked with the coroner's staff to collect and then process the samples, and a second individual performed the Rapid DNA runs in the RV. Logistical challenges that were important in establishing the Rapid DNA process workflow included the need to do the following:

- Document and photograph every sample prior to and following processing and link this information to case IDs and sample IDs. A case ID was generated by Butte County during the victim recovery process and a second by the Sacramento County Coroner's Office on intake (these were both prominently displayed on the wall charts noted earlier). ANDE generated a case ID for each set of remains and linked these to the Rapid DNA swab barcodes for each sample within the set. For each sample, the identical swab barcode was associated with the sample intake form. All of this metadata was entered into a spreadsheet.
- Document and photograph swabs that are collected and those processed in the ANDE system. We developed a simple sample intake form for UHR that included the Butte County, Sacramento County Coroner's Office, and ANDE case IDs; the sample barcode; photographs of the sample; a brief description of the methods implemented to collect and process the samples; and any other relevant notes. A similar intake form was created for FRS (which also included identifying information for the donor and the missing relative and kinship information). The UHR and FRS intake forms were intentionally kept simple, incorporating only critical information in order to allow them to be completed quickly.
- Create a log sheet for all ANDE runs (both FRS and UHR), associated case and sample IDs, and a brief summary of results output by the ANDE instrument (whether or not the sample generated a useful DNA ID and, if so, the number of FlexPlex loci detected). The DNA ID itself is exported to the kinship analysis software, but this simple summary in the log sheet allows the user to quickly let others on the team know which samples need recollection or reprocessing.
- Ensure convenient access from the designated site for sample collection to the RV where the ANDE systems were located. This involves stations for changing

and removal of personal protective equipment (PPE) at specific entry and exit locations. In some disasters, UHR sample collection and Rapid DNA processing may be co-located, but UHR and FRS sample collection and processing must not be co-located in respect to family members.

Ensuring efficient sample documentation and process workflow is critical early in the response. Not only does this minimize the time required during sample documentation, processing, and data collation, but this also expedites analysis of results. Optimizing productivity also minimized the need to relocate and resample the remains once they had been sealed and stored either in a refrigerated van, in an onsite refrigerated morgue, or in temporarily locations in designated laboratory areas—all of which were accessible only by certain personnel. In conventional laboratory processing, generating results can requires months or years and these logistical considerations do not apply; with Rapid DNA onsite, they become of paramount importance.

A total of 69 sets of remains were subjected to Rapid DNA identification using the ANDE system. Of these, 62 (89.9%) generated DNA IDs that were utilized for familial searching, and essentially all these DNA IDs were produced within hours of sample receipt. One measure of the effectiveness of Rapid DNA identification is the relative number of samples yielding full DNA IDs (i.e. those containing all 20 of the STR loci selected by the FBI for human identification—also known as the CODIS core loci (US FBI n.d.) and partial DNA IDs (those containing less than 20 of the CODIS loci). Of the DNA IDs, 95.2% contained 20 or 19 CODIS loci, a remarkably high percentage, particularly considering the degraded state of the remains.

Samples from seven sets of remains did not generate DNA IDs. Bones from these cases were subjected to manual DNA processing and picogram quantities of DNA were generated for all samples. The average fragment size was typically approximately 100 base pairs, explaining the samples' inability to generate DNA IDs; most STR alleles are between 100 and 500 base pairs.

With respect to the 62 samples generating useful DNA IDs, 37 samples were blood (typically obtained via cardiac puncture) or fragments of clotted blood. Tissue fragments (muscle [five cases], liver [seven cases], brain [one case], and unidentified soft tissue [two cases]) generated useful data in 15 cases. The tissue fragments had one feature in common—a slight degree of color that distinguished them from the surrounding charred, black remains. Samples identified using muscle, liver, or tissues typically were obtained from remains consisting of small portions of the torso (Figure 18.4), while samples using bone were obtained from small bags of bones isolated from surrounding building debris (Figure 18.5). Figure 18.6a shows the DNA ID generated from processing the flesh associated with the torso in Figure 18.4. Figure 18.6b shows the DNA ID generated from processing select non-calcined fragment from sorted human bones in Figure 18.5. Finally, ten cases were resolved using bone fragments. In these cases, only a small number of charred bones and bone fragments were available (Figure 18.7).

In severely degraded remains, bone is the sample type of choice for DNA analysis. Genomic DNA from soft tissue degrades soon after death due to autolysis, microbial contamination, and environmental insult, but DNA present within bone (particularly dense cortical bone) and teeth may remain relatively intact for years, decades, or millennia (Green et al. 2006; Latham and Madonna 2013). Over the past 20 years, DNA typing in forensic laboratories has become a standard tool for DVI following mass casualty events including the World Trade Center and other terrorist attacks (Brenner

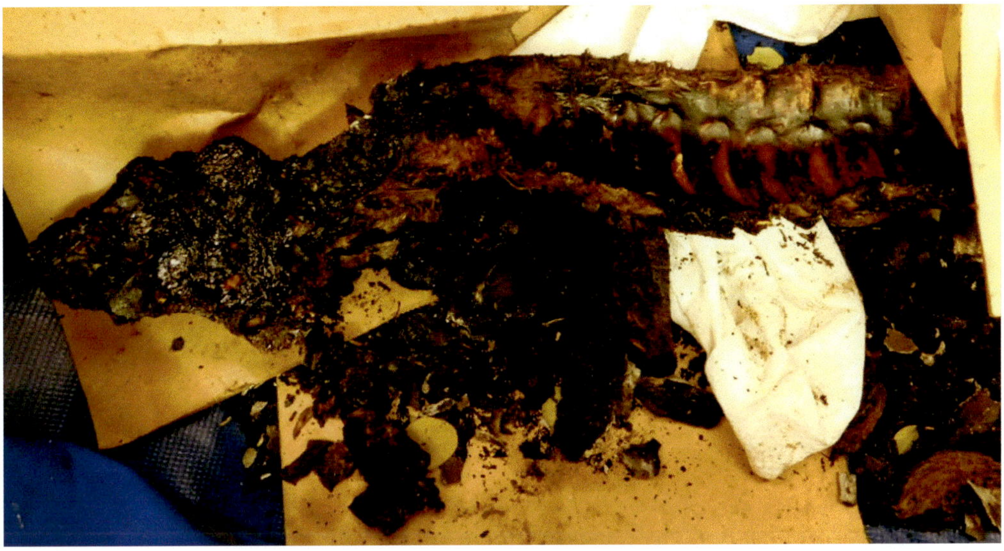

FIGURE 18.4 Photograph of burned remains with visible tissues for collection and analysis.

FIGURE 18.5 Photograph of fragmented bones found with building debris.

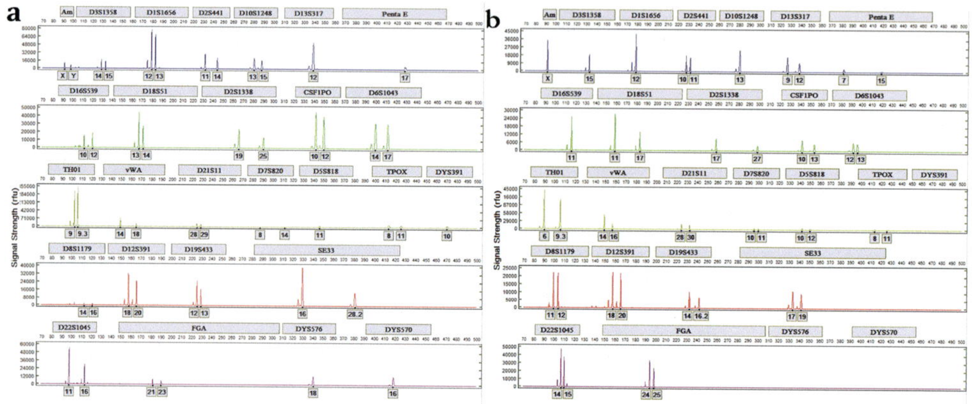

FIGURE 18.6 Rapid DNA IDs generated from burned remains; (a) from slivers of soft tissue scraped from a burned torso of a male victim and (b) from a select non-calcined bone fragment (approximately 500 mg pulverized with a hammer).

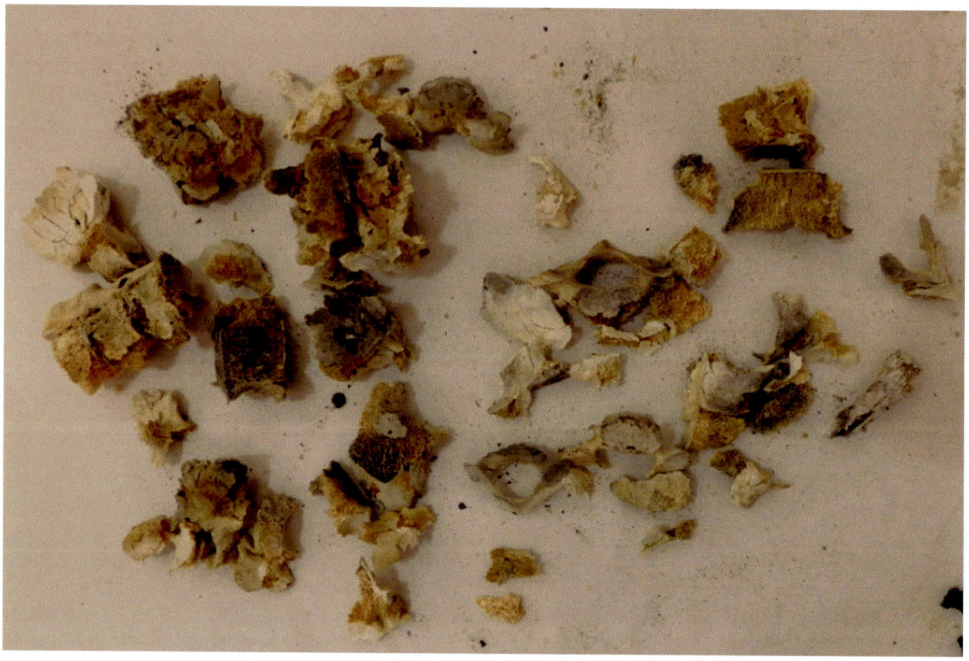

FIGURE 18.7 Photograph of fragmented human remains as identified by anthropology.

and Weir 2003; Biesecker et al 2005; Sudoyo et al 2008), natural phenomena (Deng et al. 2005; Donkervoort et al. 2008; Hartman et al. 2011; McEntire et al. 2012), and plane crashes (Hsu et al. 1999; Leclair et al. 2001). In the conventional lab, DNA analysis of bone and teeth is even more complex and time-consuming than blood, buccal swabs, and soft tissue—which means that although bone and teeth are the best candidates to generate useful DNA information, they are the least likely to be processed in DVI. There are a small number of labs that specialize in forensic DNA analysis of bone, and many forensic labs transfer their bone and tooth samples to these specialist labs—which then become overwhelmed with samples. The solution to this problem is straightforward. We have simplified bone and tooth DNA processing with Rapid DNA and laboratory-quality results or better can be obtained outside the lab in at least two hours (Turingan et al. 2019, 2020; Turingan Witkowski et al. 2021). The Camp Fire was the first mass casualty event in which this technology was obtained in the field (Gin et al. 2020; ISHI Report 2019), and the ANDE Rapid DNA System has since been used following Hurricane Maria (NAAG & ASCLD 2019), the Conception Dive Boat Fire (ISHI Report 2019; ISHI Blog 2020), the Calabasas California Helicopter crash (ISHI Report 2019), and a number of other disasters.

18.5 VICTIM IDENTIFICATION BASED ON RAPID DNA RESULTS

Once DNA data from unidentified human remains become available, they must be compared to other DNA data in order to make a positive identification of the victims. There are two basic approaches to this comparison. First and most commonly, DNA IDs from the remains are compared to those from potential family members. Ideally, family reference samples (FRS) are obtained from first degree relatives (parents, children, or siblings) from each of the victims, and the DNA IDs generated from the FRS are placed into a database for comparison. FRS from second degree relatives (e.g., grandparents, grandchildren, half-siblings, aunts, uncles, nephews, nieces) may also be useful, particularly when first degree samples are not available. (A general rule for FRS collection is to collect buccal swabs from any and all family members who are willing to provide them—in some cases, the DNA obtained from even distant family members can aid the identification effort.) Although STR data from second degree (and more distant) relatives may lead to a positive identification, other DNA-based modalities, such as single-nucleotide polymorphism (SNP) and genome sequence analysis are, in general, better-suited to identification of non-primary relatives. Finally, some victims have no known blood relatives and cannot be identified based on an STR comparison. These victims can be identified using forensic genealogy techniques (Katsanis 2020; Ge and Budowle 2020).

The second approach is to perform a "self" comparison of a victim's DNA ID. DNA IDs can be generated from personal items belonging to missing individuals—toothbrushes and hairbrushes are particularly useful in this regard. In the Camp Fire, tissue blocks from prior surgical procedures were utilized to generate DNA IDs in two cases. In certain settings, the DNA ID from a given missing person may have been generated previously and, if accessible, may be utilized as well. Regardless of source, the set of self DNA IDs is then placed into the FRS database for comparison.

The fact that mass disasters often claim the lives of multiple members of the same family must also be considered; once one set of remains is positively identified, that DNA ID can then be utilized to identify related victims. Furthermore, there are potential complicating factors in performing kinship analyses: for example, adopted children cannot be identified using the DNA of adopted parents and identical twins cannot be distinguished by STR analysis. Although these and other complex familial relationships do occur, the vast majority of familial relationships in a mass casualty event are straightforward and routinely can be made using Rapid DNA. A reasonable goal is to identify the standard relationships essentially immediately. The relatively uncommon complex cases can be resolved by finding additional family members or by performing additional DNA studies (e.g., SNPs and genomic sequencing) in the lab—these steps will likely require months or more to complete.

Collecting FRS can be challenging during and in the aftermath of a mass casualty event. The initial goal in the response is to save as many lives as possible, and in a dangerous and chaotic setting, collating the list of missing persons may not be prioritized. The number of missing persons reported may far exceed the actual number of victims, in part because the underlying event may displace large numbers of individuals. Family members may not be aware that a relative is missing or may be aware but located too far from the FRS collection sites. Family assistance centers (FACs) may be set up near the site to allow relatives to obtain information on family members and to provide information and FRS samples for DNA testing. In the Camp Fire, we set up a small FAC in a commercial building in Chico, California. One ANDE Rapid DNA system was deployed at the FAC for FRS buccal swab processing, with one operator responsible for performing runs.

The immediate availability of DNA IDs from UHR led to an aggressive law enforcement effort to collect FRS. The Butte County sheriff used daily press briefings and organized a program to enable donors to provide buccal swabs across the nation. DNA IDs from a total of 255 FRS were placed into the 2018 Camp Fire DNA database. Of these, 219 were processed in the ANDE Rapid DNA System using A-Chips, with the vast majority processed at the FAC. Thirty-six samples were generated by conventional laboratory processing, and the results were forwarded to the Sacramento County Coroner's Office for database searching.

To perform kinship analysis, database searching was performed using the FAIRS software (ANDE Corporation). The FAIRS software package imports and decrypts run data from the Rapid DNA instrument, creates UHR and FRS databases, and performs all kinship analyses. FAIRS allows nontechnical users to perform the following types of familial searches: (1) search for references attempts to match valid references in the database to the selected victim, (2) search for victim attempts to match valid victims in the database to the selected reference, and (3) comprehensive search that allows any victim or a reference to be searched against all samples in the database. The third approach is useful in a number of circumstances, including, for example, when it is suspected that multiple victims are biologically related.

The following was calculated for each victim-reference pair:

- The number of matched loci: A matching locus is defined as one in which at least one allele is shared between the victim and the reference.
- Combined relationship index (CRI): The CRI is the likelihood of the tested relationship for the victim-reference relative to that of two unrelated individuals. This is determined by calculating the likelihood ratio (LR) at each locus and then determining the CRI by multiplying the LR for each locus (32). ANDE FlexPlex27 includes two sets of loci that are genetically linked—(1) loci SE33 and D6S1043 and (2) D12S391 and vWA. The LR from one of the linked loci is included in the CRI. The kinship algorithms utilized by FAIRS meet the guidelines set by the American Association of Blood Banks (Sozer et al. 2010).

When performing kinship analysis, the references with the highest CRI (and above a preselected threshold) are presented to the user. For victim searches, the victims with the highest CRI (above the threshold) are presented. Finally, the probability of relationship is calculated and is based on the CRI and an assigned prior probability. An operational prior probability of 0.2% was used early in the analysis when the number of victims was thought to be approximately 500. The prior probability was gradually increased to 5% as the number of missing diminished.

Remains from 58 individuals were identified by searching against the 255 DNA IDs in the FRS database. As the number of samples in the UHR and FRS databases quickly increased, we performed searches at least twice daily. The initial Rapid DNA identifications were made on the fourth day of the fire (the day Rapid DNA systems were deployed), and most identifications were made within two weeks (by which time the vast majority of remains and FRS were received by the morgue), well before the fire was brought under control.

Remains from four individuals with Rapid DNA results did not generate familial matches in the FRS database. DNA samples from these remains were then subjected to whole genome sequencing, a process that required several months in the laboratory. Comparisons of these whole genome sequence results to those from a small number of potential family members led to two additional identifications. A third identification was made by comparing genomic sequence data to that obtained from an antemortem slide from the victim (determined to have no known next of kin), and a fourth identification was made using genetic genealogy.

A total of 22 identifications were made by conventional modalities. Radiographic features, such as fractures, could not be identified due to the state of the remains, but two identifications were made based on co-recovered hardware. Dental evidence was present in 35 of 60 sets of remains examined by the dental team but the combination of extensive sample degradation and absence of dental records (in many cases due to dental office destruction by the fire) led to only 15 identifications being made by forensic odontology. Five identifications were made by fingerprint and thumbprint analysis. Personal effects for 29 of the victims recovered were transported to the morgue to assist with identification. Only two such effects, in both cases military dog tags, supported identification.

Taken together, 58 identifications were made by Rapid DNA, 4 by genomic sequencing, and 22 by conventional modalities. Nine of the 58 Rapid DNA identifications were confirmed by identifications made using other modalities (eight by odontology and one by fingerprints). This result is consistent with our subsequent experiences with Rapid DNA for DVI—approximately 50 Rapid DNA identifications have been confirmed by other modalities. In 100% of cases for which data from other modalities was available, the data validated the Rapid DNA result.

18.6 INTEGRATION OF RAPID DNA ANALYSIS WITH CONVENTIONAL IDENTIFICATION MODALITIES

Despite its simplicity and ease of use, Rapid DNA cannot and should not utilized in isolation for DVI. A basic approach to sample type selection has been outlined earlier, and there is enormous value is working with forensic anthropologists to ensure that optimal samples are selected. Along with the determination of victim age, sex, and stature, it is critical for anthropologists to determine when comingled remains are present. In the Camp Fire, three cases included two or three sets of commingled human remains. Two cases also included a set of human and one or two sets of animal remains, likely household pets. Commingling of human remains is a common occurrence in mass fatality scenes given that multiple fire victims often live or work together. These cases are complex for fire scenes, as human remains have been reduced to small, calcined bone fragments, making it difficult to recognize skeletal duplication (i.e., evidence of the remains of more than one individual). Similarly, fragmentation of remains is commonly encountered, and anthropologists can assess remains to attempt reassociation—Rapid DNA was utilized to accomplish reassociation in two Camp Fire cases. The remarkable efforts of the forensic anthropology team (coordinated by California State University, Chico) were essential for Rapid DNA identification of the severely degraded UHRs.

In addition to selecting the optimal sample type for Rapid DNA analysis, the timing of sample collection is also of practical importance. As Rapid DNA processing is destructive, certain samples should be evaluated by other disciplines prior to this processing. For example, in a case with a single tooth, odontological evaluation should precede Rapid DNA analysis. More broadly, establishing and maintaining intradisciplinary communication (including anthropology, pathology, radiography, odontology, and fingerprint and Rapid DNA analyses) improves the overall speed and efficiency of DVI. When an identification was made by Rapid DNA, alerting the odontology team members would allow them to reassign resources accordingly (especially helpful in challenging odontological cases). As noted, the coroner's establishment of a centralized site for case updates was an important tool for intradisciplinary communication.

18.7 CONCLUSIONS

Unlike previous disasters for which DNA identification may have required months to years (ICRC 2009), the ability to generate DNA results quickly had a major impact on process flow in the Sacramento County Morgue during the Camp Fire. When DNA IDs were generated on particularly degraded remains, odontologists and pathologists were able to focus their efforts on other cases with potentially better outcomes. In many disasters, governments do not permit samples to be shipped to foreign laboratories, and Rapid DNA equipment can be employed locally, near the disaster site, by non-technical operators. Most importantly, the technology enables rapid identification, critical to providing support to family members. In previous disasters, family members have often waited years for identifications; the pain of losing a family member need no longer be amplified by the pain of waiting for a definitive identification. The first successful deployment of Rapid DNA Identification at a mass disaster augurs well for continued expansions of the use of the technology in mass casualty events and, more broadly, in law enforcement (US Congress 2017) and human trafficking applications (Washington Post 2019).

Implementation of Rapid DNA for DVI is straightforward. Non-technical operators can be trained to use the system in less than an hour; kinship analysis and databasing software is easy to use and purpose-built for use with the ANDE system. From a logistics perspective, the most important issues are to (1) locate the Rapid DNA instruments proximal to the sites for anthropology, radiographic, and odontological evaluations; (2) locate the Rapid DNA instruments within the FAC to allow efficient processing of FRS; (3) establish nomenclature rules for handling FRS and UHR samples and protocols for entering Rapid DNA results into DNA databases for kinship analysis; and (4) ensure all useful FRS data generated in conventional labs is incorporated in the FRS DNA database maintained at our near the disaster site. For professionals not accustomed to receiving DNA data during their identification work or thereafter, the availability of that data essentially immediately may seem shocking—but over time, Rapid DNA will be seen as a routinely used tool in the identification armamentarium, much to the benefit of the families of the victims.

The incorporation of Rapid DNA identification during and immediately following mass casualty events is a dramatic improvement in DVI. Rapid DNA identification was successfully integrated into real-time victim identification during the 2018 Camp Fire. Due to the extensive degradation of the remains, DNA analysis was typically the only effective modality. In approximately 90% of cases, Rapid DNA identification generated DNA IDs and was the primary identification modality of the Camp Fire, with 58 victims identified (as compared to 22 by conventional modalities). As the remains in the Camp Fire were at the extremes of degradation, it is expected that in other disasters (e.g., earthquakes, tsunamis, terrorist attacks), remains will be less degraded, and Rapid DNA identification will be readily applicable to these mass casualty events.

REFERENCES

Alonso, A., et al., 2001. DNA typing from skeletal remains: Evaluation of multiplex and megaplex STR systems on DNA isolated from bone and teeth samples. Croat Med J. 42(3): 260–266.

Amory, S., et al., 2012. Automatable full demineralization DNA extraction procedure from degraded skeletal remains. Forensic Sci Int Genet. 6(3): 398–406.

Biesecker, L.G., et al., 2005. DNA identifications after the 9/11 World Trade Center attack. Science 310(5751): 1122–1123.

Brenner, C.H., and B. Weir, 2003. Issues and strategies in the DNA Identification of World Trade Center victims. Theoretical Population Biology 63(3): 173–178.

Calacal, G.C., et al., 2015. Comparing different post-mortem human samples as DNA sources for downstream genotyping and identification. Forensic Sci Int Genet. 19: 212–220.

CAL FIRE, 2019. Top 20 deadliest California wildfires—2019. https://fire.ca.gov/media/5512/top20_deadliest.pdf (accessed September 27, 2019).

Carney, C., et al., 2019. Developmental validation of the ANDE™ rapid DNA system with FlexPlex™ assay for arrestee and reference buccal swab processing and database searching. Forensic Sci Int Genet. 40: 120–130.

Davoren, J., et al., 2007. Highly effective DNA extraction method for nuclear short tandem repeat testing of skeletal remains from mass graves. Croat Med J. 48(4): 478–485.

Della Manna, A., et al., 2016. Developmental validation of the DNAscan™ rapid DNA analysis instrument and expert system for reference sample processing. Forensic Sci Int 25: 145–156.

Deng, Y.-J., et al., 2005. Preliminary DNA identification for the tsunami victims in Thailand. Genomics Proteomics Bioinformatics. 3(3): 143–157.

Donkervoort, S., et al., 2008. Enhancing accurate data collection in mass fatality kinship identifications: Lessons learned from Hurricane Katrina. Forensic Sci Intl Genet. 2(4): 354–362.

Ge, J., and B. Budowle, 2020. Forensic investigation approaches of searching relatives in DNA databases. J Forensic Sci. 66: 5989.

Gin, K., et al., 2020. The 2018 California wildfires: Integration of rapid DNA to dramatically accelerate victim identification. J Forensic Sci. 65(3): 791–799.

Green, R.E., et al., 2006. Analysis of one million base pairs of Neanderthal DNA. Nature. 444(7117): 330.

Grover, R., et al., 2017. FlexPlex27—highly multiplexed rapid DNA identification for law enforcement, kinship, and military applications. Int J Legal Med. 131(6): 1–13.

Hartman, D., et al., 2011. The contribution of DNA to disaster victim identification (DVI) effort. Forensic Sci Int. 205(1): 52–58.

Holland, M.M., et al., 2003. Deveopment of a quality, high throughput DNA analysis procedure for skeletal samples to assist with the identification of victims from the World Trade Center attacks. Croat Med J. 44(3): 264–272.

Hsu, C., et al., 1999. Identification of victims of the 1998 Taoyuan Airbus crash accident using DNA analysis. Int J Legal Med. 113(1): 43–46.

International Committee of the Red Cross (ICRC)., 2009. Missing people, DNA analysis and identification of human remains—a guide to best practice in armed conflicts and other situations of armed violence. 2nd ed. pp. 19–25. www.icr.org/en/doc/assets/files/other/icrc_002)4010.pdf (accessed November 2009).

ISHI Blog., 2020. Rapid DNA identification: Conception boat fire—2020. www.ishinews.com/questions-for-rapid-dna-identification-conception-boat-fire/ (accessed October 19, 2020).

ISHI Report: How the Santa Barbara Sheriff's Office Is Utilizing Rapid DNA., 2019. https://promega.foleon.com/theishireport/november-2020/answers-now-how-the-santa-barbara-sheriffs-office-is-utilizing-rapid-dna/

Katsanis, S.H., 2020. Pedigrees and perpetrators: Uses of DNA and genealogy in forensic investigations. Annu Rev Genomics Hum Genet. 21(1): 535–564.

Latham, K.E., and M.E. Madonna, 2013. DNA survivability in skeletal remains *In* Manual of Forensic Taphonomy. J Pokines and SA Symes, eds. Taylor and Francis Group. Pp. 385–407.

Latham, K.E., and J.J. Miller, 2019. DNA recovery and analysis from skeletal material in modern forensic contexts. Forensic Sci Res. 4(1): 51–59.

Leclair, B., et al., 2001. Enhanced kinship analysis and STR-based DNA typing for human identification in mass fatality incidents: The Swissair flight 111 disaster. J Forensic Sci. 49(5): JFS2003311– JFS2003315.

Lee, H.Y., et al., 2010. Simple and highly effective DNA extraction methods from old skeletal remains using silica columns. Forensic Sci Int Genet. 4(5): 275–280.

Loreille, O.M., et al., 2007. High efficiency DNA extraction from bone by total demineralization. Forensic Sci Int Genet. 1(2): 191–195.

McEntire, D.A., A.-A. Sadiz, and K. Gupta., 2012. Unidentified bodies and mass-fatality management in Haiti: A case study of the January 2010 earthquake with a cross-cultural comparison. Int J Mass Emerg Disasters. 30(1): 301–327.

Moreno, L.I., A.L. Brown, and TF Callaghan 2017. Internal valication of the DNAscan/ANDE™ rapid DNA Analysis™ platform and its association PowerPlex® 16 high content DNA biochip cassette for use as an expert system with reference buccal swabs. Forensic Sci Int Genet. 25: 100–108.

Mundorff, A., and J.M. Davoren, 2014. Examination of DNA yield rates for different skeletal elements at increasing post mortem intervals. Forensic Sci Int Genet. 8(1): 55–63.

Mundorff, A.Z., E.J. Bartelink, and E. Mar-Cash, 2009. DNA preservation in skeletal elements from the World Trade Center disaster: Recommendations for mass fatality management. J Forensic Sci. 54(4): 739–745.

NAAG & ASCLD, 2019. Partner to assist Puerto Rico Forensic Science Laboratory—2019. www.naag.org/crimina-law/press-releases/naag-ascld-partner-to-assist-puerto-rico-forensic-science-laboratory/ (accessed January 14, 2019).

Pajnič, I.Z., 2016. Extraction of DNA from human skeletal material. *In* Forensic DNA Typing Protocols. Springer. Pp. 89–108.

Palmbach, T., et al., 2014. Utilizing DNA analysis to combat the world wide plague of present day slavery-trafficking in persons. Croat Med J. 55(1): 3–9.

Parsons, TJ et al., 2018. Large scale SNA identification: The ICMP experience. Forensic Sci Int: Genetics.

Sozer, A, et al., 2010. Guidelines for Mass Fatality DNA Identification Operations. American Association of Blood Banks.

Sudoyo, H., et al., 2008. DNA analysis in perpetrator identification of terrorism-related disaster: Suicide bombing of the Australian Embassy in Jakarta 2004. Forensic Sci Int Genet. 2(3): 231–237.

Tan, E., et al., 2013. Fully integrated, fully automated generation of short tandem repeat profiles. Investig Genet. 4(1): 1–15.

Turingan, R.S., et al., 2016. Rapid DNA analysis for automated processing and interpretation of low DNA content samples. Investig Genet. 7(1): 1

Turingan, R.S., et al., 2019. Identification of human remains using Rapid DNA analysis. Int J Legal Med: 1–10.

Turingan, R.S., et al., 2020. Developmental validation of the ANDE 6C System for rapid DNA analysis of forensic casework and DVI samples. J Forensic Sci. 65: 1056–1071. https://doi.org/10.1111/1556-4029.14286

Turingan Witkowski, R., et al., 2021. Rapid DNA identification of human skeletal remains. *In* Forensic Genetic Approaches for the Identification of Human Skeletal Remains. A Ambers, ed. Elsevier. Pp.325–350.

US Congress., 2017. Congress.gov H.R. 510—rapid DNA act of 2017. www.congress.gov/bill/115th-congress/house-bill/510 (accessed August 18, 2017).

US Federal Bureau of Investigation (FBI)., n.d. Frequently asked questions on CODIS and NDIS. www.fbi.gov/services/laboratory/biometic-analysis/codis/codis-and-ndis-factsheet

US National Park Service (NPS)., 2018. 2018 Woolsey Fire. www.nps.gov/samo/learn/management/2018-woolsey-fire.htm (accessed July 18, 2019).

Vanek, D., et al., 2017. Results of a collaborative study on DNA identification of aged bone samples. Croat Med J. 58(3): 203–213.

VC Star—Part of the USA Today Network., 2018. Thousand Oaks shooting: 13, including officer, killed at Borderline Bar and Grill—2018. www.vcstar.com/story/news/2018/11/07/multiple-victims-reported-shooting-to-bar/1927732002/ (accessed November 7, 2018).

Washington Post., 2018. Explosive and destructive 'Camp Fire' in Northern California is burning 80 acres per minute—2018. www.washingtonpost.com/weather/2018/11/08/explosive-destructuve-camp-fire-northern-california-is-burning-acres-per-minute/?nondirect=on (accessed November 8, 2019).
Washington Post., 2019. Homeland security to test DNA of families at border in cases of suspected fraud. www.washingtonpost.com/immigration/homeland-security-to-test-dna-of-families-at-border-in-cases-of-suspected-fraud/2019/05/01/8e8c042a-6c46–11e9-a66d-a82d3fd96d5_story.html?utm_term=.b4611915101f (accessed May 1, 2019).

CHAPTER 19

Operation Northleigh—the Grenfell Tower Disaster Victim Identification Process

Gaille MacKinnon and Gillian Fowler

Wildfires occur in forested areas, brushlands, or grasslands, but the devastation we see in such fires can also occur in residential units. This chapter provides an international perspective on a disastrous fire within a high-rise residential unit in the United Kingdom using the disaster victim identification (DVI) process of the INTERPOL (International Criminal Police Organization). It includes international approaches where such protocols would be applied to many WUI fires as well.

19.1 DESCRIPTION OF THE INCIDENT

Given the ongoing nature of the police investigation and the Grenfell Tower Public Inquiry, a brief overview of the DVI process has been provided by Detective Chief Inspector Andrew Chalmers, Metropolitan Police Service (MPS),[1] Deputy Senior Investigating Officer and Senior Identification Manager for Operation Northleigh.[2]

> *On Wednesday 14th June 2017 at 0055hrs the London Fire Brigade was called to a large fire at Grenfell Tower, a twenty-three floor block of predominantly public housing in North Kensington, London, United Kingdom. The fire, originating in a 4th floor flat, rapidly spread throughout the entire structure. The conflagration developed into a full facade fire with multiple breaches of fire compartmentation throughout the building structure. This included the single central stairwell being compromised by dense smoke and heat.*
>
> *Many residents remained within their flats in accordance with the extant fire safety instructions or, unable to escape, migrated upwards in a vain attempt to escape the fire.*
>
> *Seventy people lost their lives as a result of the fire and one mother-to-be escaped, but subsequently lost her unborn child, as a direct consequence of her involvement. In many cases parents and children died alongside each other, and in many cases gathered together with neighbours and friends.*
>
> *The fire destruction within the tower was extensive with temperatures in excess of 1000°C (1830°F) being experienced for a protracted period in many parts of the building. In the higher levels, all combustible material and internal structures within the concrete framework of the tower were effectively destroyed. The degree of physical damage*

DOI: 10.4324/9781003168010-23

to the bodies of those trapped within or who jumped from a height was similarly devastating. The rescue phase of the emergency response was concluded at 2000 hrs on 14th June 2017 when it was determined that no one remained alive within Grenfell Tower.

The Metropolitan Police Service immediately opened a criminal investigation into these deaths and a Full Public Inquiry was ordered by the Prime Minister. The Police investigation and the parallel Grenfell Tower Inquiry continue to explore criminal causation for and the public safety implications of this tragedy.

At the termination of the fire, the Disaster Victim Identification operation, the process of recovering and identifying the remains of those who died, commenced. Ante mortem data was gathered for those reported missing and believed to have died; remains were recovered within the tower using, in many cases, archaeological methodology; and an anthropology-led forensic mortuary process evolved to overcome the degree of physical damage caused by the fire. The Disaster Victim Identification Response remained an "open" incident with the total number of fatalities remaining unconfirmed until 15th November 2017 when the Coroner confirmed the formal identification of the 70th and last fatality. At this point, the Coroner and the Metropolitan Police Service could assert with absolute confidence that every person who died as a result of the Grenfell Tower Fire had been identified. In every single case, identified remains have been repatriated to their respective bereaved families.

19.2 THE INTERPOL DISASTER VICTIM IDENTIFICATION GUIDE

The forensic anthropological examination of the victims from the Grenfell Tower incident was conducted within the multidisciplinary framework of the INTERPOL disaster victim identification (DVI) and postmortem (PM) data collection and documentation systems (Interpol, 2018b). These internationally recognized documentation systems were used in conjunction with the forensic anthropology protocols and working practices that were developed by the Grenfell Tower forensic anthropology team in order to assist the victim identification process of the victims of this incident.

The INTERPOL is a nongovernmental global police organization that provides a range of expertise and services to 194 member countries, and supports national efforts in combating crimes across three global areas: terrorism, cybercrime, and organized and emerging crime. In 1984, INTERPOL produced the first Guide to Disaster Victim Identification. This guide is updated every five years and is advised by a number of scientific working groups who are routinely involved in DVI incidents, including pathology/anthropology, odontology, fingerprints, and molecular biology (*www.interpol.int/en/How-we-work/Forensics/Disaster-Victim-Identification-DVI*).

The purpose of the INTERPOL DVI Guide is to provide baseline standards and guidelines for conducting a DVI operation and facilitating the identification of victims from disaster incidents. It can also be used to assist in establishing DVI teams and in the management of DVI operations by those countries that either do not currently have a DVI capacity or have never been confronted with such operational situations. The guide has been designed to inform a number of separate audiences: national and local authorities, emergency contingency managers and planners, law enforcement, and operational and forensic practitioners. The documents also provide sufficiently flexible guidelines and structures that accommodate differences and variations in jurisdictional legal systems, policies, and practices and is revised over subsequent years (Interpol, 2018a).

Part A of the Guide contains high level reference material in respect to the conduct of DVI operations. Further extensive detailed information can be accessed through linked annexures in Part B. These annexures outline operational and procedural information designed to inform the main technical aspects of conducting a DVI operation. They can also provide standardized approaches for practitioners, although the content remains sufficiently broad enough to allow for varying international practices or circumstances (*ibid.*).

The INTERPOL DVI Unique Reference Number (URN) classification system was used for each of the deceased victims recovered and examined from Grenfell Tower (Interpol, 2018b). This system is briefly described here in order to provide an understanding of its utilization within this incident.

The INTERPOL DVI Guide provides best practice advice and guidelines in the recovery and identification of deceased disaster victims. Within this system, each deceased disaster victim's body or any separate body part is allocated a unique reference number at the scene. This number stays with the remains and any related personal property that can be clearly attributed to the deceased victim and is used on all documentation and samples from the deceased victim throughout the DVI operation.

The format for an INTERPOL DVI number **(PM 44 0000 A)**, as demonstrated in this example, is as follows:

"PM" (postmortem) precedes the number that refers to the remains of a deceased disaster victim.

"44" refers to the telephone country code indicating the country dealing with the DVI operation (in this case, "44" denotes the telephone country code for the United Kingdom).

"0000" is the unique reference number (URN) allocated to the deceased disaster victim.

"A" is the letter allocated to identify a scene or, in the case of this incident, a designated zone within a flat or communal space (*ibid.*, 99).

19.3 OVERVIEW OF THE OPERATION NORTHLEIGH MORTUARY PROCESS

A brief overview of the Operation Northleigh DVI mortuary flow and examination process of human remains recovered from Grenfell Tower is provided in Figure 19.1.

The recovery of the human remains from the individual flats and communal spaces at Grenfell Tower was undertaken by dedicated teams of forensic archaeologists and DVI- and search-trained police officers from MPS and other police forces around the United Kingdom. Following the recovery of human remains from Grenfell Tower and prior to the postmortem examination, postmortem computed tomography (PMCT) was conducted on each URN-labelled body bag. The PMCT team of forensic pathologists, radiologists, and an anthropologist was led by the chief forensic pathologist Professor Guy Rutty of the East Midlands Forensic Pathology Unit, Leicester Royal Infirmary, Leicester (UK).

A preliminary assessment of the human remains, and any associated clothing or personal effects was then undertaken and, depending on the case, included initial

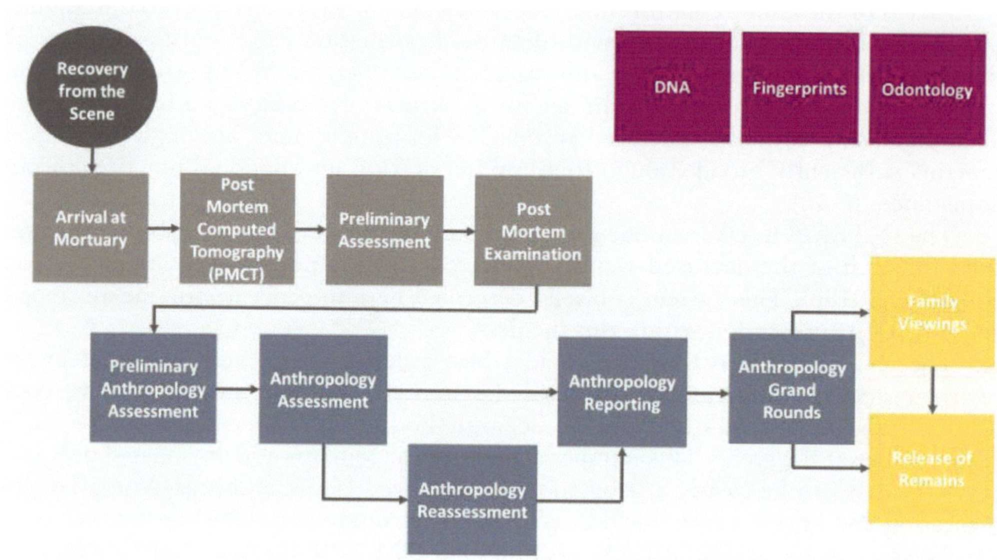

FIGURE 19.1

examinations by forensic pathologists, odontologists, anthropologists, fingerprint experts, and DVI police officers. The postmortem examination of each URN containing human remains was conducted by Home Office[3] forensic pathologists and, depending on the case, also included forensic anthropology and odontology examinations. Forensic anthropologists were asked to attend the postmortem examination of cases where a preliminary anthropological assessment or "triage" of skeletonized human remains or multiple, commingled skeletal remains was required.

Following the initial postmortem examination, extensive forensic anthropological examinations were then undertaken in a dedicated temporary DVI facility adjacent to the Westminster Public Mortuary in central London. Each examination of human remains was conducted on a flat-by-flat or communal space basis for the 17 separate recovery locations within Grenfell Tower where human remains were found. The human remains that were recovered from each of these locations were examined at the same time by forensic anthropologists to ensure that all of the remains from a particular flat or communal space could—where possible—be physically reassociated.

The INTERPOL DVI annexures for the forensic anthropology examinations were completed by DVI-trained police officers from the MPS utilizing the postmortem "supporting information" documents and data collection systems. The forensic anthropology recording forms, protocols, and working practices together with the anthropology examination record information systems that were created specifically for utilization within the Grenfell Tower DVI incident, were completed and managed by members of the forensic anthropology team. All photography and image capture undertaken for the forensic anthropological examinations, together with the management of the photographic record information and database systems, was undertaken by MPS police photographers.

The overall management of the DVI and forensic anthropological examination process was overseen on a day-to-day basis by officers and civilian staff from the MPS, the City of London Police, and the British Transport Police, who variously undertook the roles of mortuary senior identification managers (SIMs), postmortem coordinators (PMOCs), and forensic operations managers (FOMs) for the incident. Further assistance, advice, and support to the Operation Northleigh DVI operation was provided by the office of Her Majesty's (HM) Senior Coroner for Inner West London, Dr. Fiona Wilcox, and the management and staff of the Westminster Public Mortuary, London.

In some cases, this process became dependent on receiving confirmation from the authorities at Grenfell Tower that the comprehensive forensic archaeological and DVI recovery, sieving, quality assurance and clearance procedures undertaken within each flat or communal space had been completed before the examination and reconciliation of human remains could be undertaken with the DVI temporary mortuary.

On completion of the forensic anthropology and odontology examinations for each victim recovered from a specific flat or communal space, the human remains and all associated recovery and mortuary examination and documentation case files were reviewed in a process called anthropology grand rounds. This process was led by the senior coroner, the MPS deputy senior investigating officer and incident senior identification manager, the postmortem coordinator, the forensic operations manager, and the lead anthropologists and odontologists.

In cases where the deceased victim was recovered from a multiple victim recovery flat or communal space within the building, the human remains and the case file documentation and photography for all the deceased victims from the flat or communal space were collectively reviewed. This review included the confirmation of the minimum number of victims, the context and recovery position of the human remains from each flat or communal space, the nature and extent of the commingling of human remains identified at that particular location, and any additional information that may be pertinent to the particular flat or communal space under examination. The anthropological information provided and reviewed during anthropology grand rounds was subsequently used to inform the deliberations of the incident's Identification Commission, which was conducted under the direction of the senior coroner.

Following the completion of the formal identification process of a victim, or victims in the cases where multiple individuals or multiple family members had died, a number of bereaved families requested permission to view the remains of deceased family members. Care and consideration for the bereaved families was a particular concern to the forensic anthropologists of this incident and was an important and necessary focus of our work. With the permission and support of the senior coroner, bereaved families were given the opportunity to meet the lead anthropologists to receive information regarding the condition of the remains of their loved one(s).

If the family requested to view the remains, the lead anthropologists were present at the viewing to answer any questions that the family may have had with regards to the anthropology and reconciliation examinations that had taken place. These viewings were carefully managed by the coroner's officers, police family liaison officers (FLOs), police DVI mortuary officers, and anthropologists, who collectively offered support and assistance to bereaved families during the viewing of the remains of their loved one(s). This process provided families with the opportunity to understand the process of the anthropological examination and the DVI identification process—and, importantly, provided the families with reassurance that although often protracted scientific analyses were necessarily being undertaken by the authorities, respect, dignity, and a duty of care for the deceased were at the forefront of the Operation Northleigh DVI process.

19.4 OPERATION NORTHLEIGH FORENSIC ANTHROPOLOGY PROTOCOLS

Forensic anthropologists and archaeologists are routinely deployed to mass fatality disasters, particularly when the condition of the bodies of deceased victims may be severely compromised by commingling with the bodies of other deceased victims or be affected by varying states of preservation or decomposition, trauma, disruption, fragmentation, thermal damage, cremation, or differential body conditions that display a range of these characteristics (de Boer *et al.*, 2020; Fowler, 2019; MacKinnon, 2018; Harrison and Ryder, 2018; Dutch Safety Board, 2015; Adams and Byrd, 2014; Indriati, 2014; Mundorff, 2012; Blau and Briggs, 2011; Leditschke et al., 2011; Sledzik *et al.*, 2009; Adams and Byrd, 2008; Mundorff, 2008).

There were seven flats within Grenfell Tower that contained the remains of a single deceased victim, nine flats where the remains of multiple deceased victims who had died together were recovered, and one communal space within the building where two individuals who had died together were recovered. DVI recovery and forensic archaeological teams worked together within Grenfell Tower to locate, record, and recover the bodies of each deceased victim who had died in the incident, with careful excavation and removal of the structural debris within each flat and communal space within the building to ensure that the remains of each deceased victim were recovered (Harrison and Ryder, 2018).

Given the catastrophic effect that the fire caused to the bodies of the deceased victims, forensic anthropologists examined those cases where the deceased victims had been affected by thermal damage, skeletonization, extensive fragmentation, cremation, and commingling. Commingling refers to an assemblage of human remains that contains more than one individual and often also comprised multiple, incomplete, or fragmentary skeletal elements or body parts.

The devastation wrought to the flats and the communal space where multiple individuals died together inevitably resulted in the commingling of the victims' bodies. This phenomenon has previously been described as disaster-induced commingling, where human remains may initially appear to belong to a single individual, but closer examination reveals that the remains of one or more individuals are embedded or mixed together with one another (Mundorff, 2012).

The nature and the extent of the commingling from this incident required that the anthropological examination of victims be done on a flat by flat or a communal space basis. This approach ensured that all human remains recovered from a particular location were examined in tandem and in conjunction with one another so that the entirety of the remains of each deceased victim were collectively examined and assessed. Where the commingling of human remains was identified, each individual was examined to ensure that the remains were reconciled—where possible—to the individual to whom they belonged.

The anthropological and odontological examination of multiple deceased victims from a single recovery location initially presented a number of operational challenges.

1. Information was gathered by the police and the fire service call center from phone calls made by individuals trapped in the building, providing authorities with an initial indication of where people were and how they moved between floors and flats during the fire. However, in a number of flats, remains of

unknown individuals were found who did not fit the profile of people who were believed to be in the flat at the time.

2. Due to structural issues and health and safety concerns associated with work in the building, there could be a considerable time delay between initial body recovery operations within an individual flat and completion of the recovery operation. These delays, while unavoidable, would then affect the time needed for all of the anthropology examinations of human remains from the flat to be completed and, therefore, victim identification.
3. As all of the anthropology examinations needed to be conducted on a flat-by-flat basis, all human remains recovered from a single flat needed to be examined at the same time and in the same space. This required a large examination and working space area with multiple examination tables. The establishment of a temporary DVI mortuary facility resolved this challenge, with a facility erected adjacent to the Westminster Public Mortuary and subsequently used for the duration of the incident. The erection of the physical infrastructure of the temporary DVI mortuary facility, the provision of the physical security arrangements, and the supply of portable refrigeration storage, material resources, and logistical support were overseen by the Office of HM Senior Coroner and the MPS.
4. Anthropology protocols needed to be flexible in order to accommodate unexpected problems and challenges.
5. DNA analysis was not appropriate for the majority of the victims as the catastrophic nature of the fire had caused severe calcination and cremation of the bodies. Therefore, detailed anthropological examinations of the often extensively commingled human remains needed to separate the remains of one victim from another before odontology examinations could be undertaken.

19.5 FORENSIC ANTHROPOLOGY UNIQUE REFERENCE NUMBER (URN) CLASSIFICATION SYSTEM

The anthropological examination of the human remains within each URN recovered from Grenfell Tower was classified as either a primary or secondary URN. A primary URN generally contained the remains of one distinct individual. This classification was used to encompass almost complete or partially complete fleshed human remains and/or body parts. A highly fragmented skeleton may also be classified as a primary URN if, at the point, it was deemed to represent one distinct individual.

The classification of a secondary URN could encompass either a single or a small assemblage (less than 12) of skeletal elements, a single body part, or multiple, fragmented skeletal human remains. There were a number of circumstances where remains may be designated as a secondary URN by the forensic anthropology team, and this term was generally used when an URN did not contain the remains of one distinct individual. For example, where there were no fleshed human remains, or a distinct, highly fragmented skeleton, assessed to be present within the URN.

The use of the secondary URN system and the number of URNs designated under this classification from an individual flat or communal space was also necessarily influenced by the level of destruction to the internal structure and/or contents. For example, in a number of cases, extensive destruction of the structure and contents further contributed to the disarticulation, extensive fragmentation, commingling, and dispersal of the bodies of deceased victims, with the result that human remains may not be specifically attributed to any one victim at the point of recovery.

During the DVI recovery process at Grenfell Tower, a number of flats within the building were deemed to be unsafe for the recovery teams. The removal of a DVI and forensic archaeology recovery team from a flat necessarily interrupted the process of recovery of human remains and often resulted in multiple revisits to the flat to ensure that all human remains had been recovered. Any human remains that were found during subsequent revisits to that space were classified as a secondary URN. This classification was also applied to multiple, fragmented skeletal human remains that were recovered during the various stages of the clearance, sieving, and quality assurance processes undertaken within each flat and communal space to ensure that complete recovery of human remains had taken place.

19.6 FORENSIC ANTHROPOLOGY STANDARD OPERATING PROTOCOLS

Standard operating procedures were developed and necessarily evolved throughout the Operation Northleigh DVI process in order to encompass and overcome the challenges that were encountered during the forensic anthropology examination of the human remains from Grenfell Tower.

19.7 PRELIMINARY ANTHROPOLOGY ASSESSMENT

If required, a preliminary anthropology assessment took place during the postmortem examination in which one URN was examined at a time and generally encompassed the following procedures:

1. Complete a schematic human skeleton diagram (if possible) to assist later association of remains after the postmortem examination.
2. Provide assistance to the forensic pathologist with the separation of osseous (bone) and non-osseous material and charred soft tissue.
3. Separate the osseous and non-osseous material and charred tissue into separate storage bags.
4. Identify and separate the human remains into skeletal regions (cranial, dental, post-cranial, vertebrae, long bones, etc.).
5. Provide a general description of the contents of the evidence bags contained within each URN and ensure recording and photography of seals/bag numbers.
6. Provide anthropological advice to the pathologist/odontologist/biologist as required, such as information on biological profile, minimum number of individuals (MNI), and sampling of skeletal elements for DNA analysis.

Following the preliminary anthropology assessment, the remains were returned to a refrigerated storage facility and were subsequently examined on a flat-by-flat or a communal space basis, whereupon a complete anthropology assessment of the human remains was conducted.

19.8 CASE DOCUMENT REVIEW

The following documents were reviewed prior to anthropology examination:

1. Forensic archaeology context/recovery notes for the recovery location
2. INTERPOL DVI Recovery Booklet
3. Scene photographs of the recovery location and the *in situ* context of the skeletal elements/body parts/remains
4. PMCT of the skeletal elements/body parts/remains human remains present
5. INTERPOL DVI Post-Mortem Booklet
6. Preliminary anthropology assessment notes (if undertaken)

19.9 INTERPOL DVI APPENDICES

The following INTERPOL DVI PM Booklet documents (pink) were completed for each URN:

1. Form 835 (Appendix 2)—Appendix Body Sketch for soft tissue remains/body parts (combination of 835 and 840 were used where required)
2. Form 840 (Appendix 3)—Appendix Skeleton Sketch for skeletal remains (see previous note)
3. Form 700—Supporting Information Form
4. Additional recording forms were used where required (e.g., juvenile and adult skeletal diagrams)

Draft copies of Forms 835/840 and 700 were initially used to record each URN. When the case had been completed, the forms were given to the DVI mortuary police officer who transcribed the information into the master DVI Post-Mortem Booklet of the URN under examination.

19.10 FORENSIC ANTHROPOLOGY EXAMINATION

The forensic anthropology examination of the human skeletal elements/remains generally encompassed the following procedures, which were also utilized if a forensic anthropology reassessment occurred:

1. Identify and sort the remains into anatomical regions, and reconstruct fragmented bones (where possible).
2. Place the remains in anatomical position, and complete the skeletal map/body part illustration.
3. Record the human remains with the appropriate scribed document template to include (points "h" to "n" are further documented here):
   a. Flat/Communal Space Location and Floor
   b. URN
   c. Name of Lead Anthropologist

   d. Name of Anthropology Assistant
   e. Date
   f. Time Started
   g. Time Finished
   h. Inventory of Skeletal Elements/Body Parts/Remains
   i. Condition of Remains
   j. Biological Profile
   k. Skeletal Variation and Individuating Features
   l. Reassociated Material
   m. Disassociated Material
   n. Unattributed Material

4. Identification of the remains present within the URN.
5. Reconstruct the fragmented remains present within the URN. Note that this may involve the reconstruction and reattachment of skeletal elements to body parts/human remains.
6. Complete an inventory of remains present within the URN.
7. Provide a statement on the condition of the remains present within the URN.
8. Construct a biological profile of the remains present within the URN.
9. If necessary, request additional PMCT images of particular anatomical structures and/or surfaces to assist with the construction of a biological profile.
10. Identify commingling of human remains—where present—within the URN. Where possible, assess and place the commingled remains within the URN into the following categories: (a) reassociated, (b) disassociated, and (c) unattributed.
11. Where possible, establish where the reassociated and/or disassociated remains within each URN should be reconciled.
12. Identify the minimum number of individuals (MNI) within each flat/communal space.
13. Ensure that a photographic record is maintained throughout the anthropology examination.
14. Complete examination of all URNs in the flat/communal space prior to any reassociation/disassociation of remains.
15. Document, illustrate, and photograph all reassociations/disassociations of remains.
16. Following all reassociations/disassociations of human remains, finalize and complete the MNI calculation for the deceased victim(s) from within the flat/communal space.
17. Repackage all human remains according to attribution scale, prior to the resealing of the body bag/s.
18. Liaise with pathologists, odontologists, biologists, PMCT team, the Office of the Coroner, the DVI reconciliation officers, police officers, and staff as required.
19. Provide "Request to Retain," "Request to Rescind," and "Interim Anthropology Reports" to assist and support the identification process of each deceased victim.
20. Liaise with the Office of HM Senior Coroner, the FLOs, the PMOC(s), the FMOs, and the DVI mortuary police officers, in order to assist with family interviews and the viewing of the remains of deceased victims.

19.11 BIOLOGICAL PROFILE

The assessment of the biological profile was considered if the particular skeletal elements/body parts/human remains were available. These methods are internationally recognized standards and widely accepted by the scientific community. However, it must be noted that a number of these methods derive from population reference samples which may not be representative of the geographical, chronological, and genetic background or lifestyle of the deceased victim. For example, most standards used for the estimation of age and sex have been established using modern European and American skeletal series, which have been shown to not apply equally to populations in other parts of the world (Işcan and Steyn, 2013). There is variation within single populations in the rate of skeletal maturation for age-at-death estimation and also significant variation between populations (White *et al.*, 2012). Where possible multiple methods were used in assessing each aspect of the biological profile.

19.12 AGE-AT-DEATH

Methods used to estimate age-at-death included examination skeletal maturity in juveniles (Cunningham *et al.*, 2016; Schaefer *et al.*, 2009). Skeletal maturity in adults was estimated by the examination of the pattern and texture of the pubic symphysis (Brooks and Suchey, 1990) and the auricular surface of the pelvis (Osborne *et al.*, 2004; Lovejoy *et al.*, 1985). Morphology of the sternal end of the right fourth rib was examined where possible (Işcan and Loth 1985; Işcan *et al.*, 1984, 1985, 1987). If the right fourth rib was not present or intact, the sternal end of one of the surrounding ribs was used. Where possible, multiple methods of age estimation were utilized in order to provide an age-at-death or age range category.

The presence or absence of degenerative joint disease (Hardcastle *et al.*, 2014; Waldron, 2009; Mann and Hunt, 2005; Aufderheide and Rodríguez-Martin, 1998; Rogers and Waldron, 1995), cranial suture closure (Meindl and Lovejoy, 1985), and alveolar resorption (Hillson, 1996, 2008) was also noted. However, in the majority of cases, these methods were considered as complementary to the previously mentioned methods used in the assessment of skeletal maturation and degeneration.

Where possible, the estimated age-at-death range for an individual was placed into one of five designated categories: *juvenile*, *adolescent*, *young adult*, *adult*, and *older adult* (Cunningham *et al.*, 2016; Waldron, 2009). If the age-at-death range fell across multiple categories, the lowest end of the estimated range was used. If an estimated age-at-death range was not possible, the most suitable category based on skeletal maturity or degeneration was used.

The five designated categories of *juvenile*, *adolescent*, *young adult*, *adult*, and *older adult* are described in the following:

Juvenile Estimated age range between birth and 9 years and includes individuals who are likely to have not yet begun puberty. "Juvenile" has also been used as an umbrella term to describe any skeletal element(s) that has not reached full skeletal maturity.

Adolescent Estimated age range between 10 and 16 years. This stage begins with puberty at about 10–13 years in girls and 12–16 years in boys and includes the adolescent growth spurt.

Young Adult	Estimated age range between 17 and 25 years. This stage begins with the ending of puberty until the time at which all the epiphyses, except for the medial end of the clavicle, have completed fusion.
Adult	Estimated age range between 26 and 40 years. This stage begins from the end of the growth spurt, the attainment of adult stature, the completion of dental maturity, and the achievement of full reproductive maturity.
Older Adult	Estimated age range over the age of 40 years based on degenerative processes observable on the skeleton.

19.13 SEX

In accordance with Bass (2005) and Buikstra and Ubelaker (1994), biological sex was based on cranial and pelvic morphology, relying on differences of sexual dimorphism in the human skeleton. Due to the nature and the function of childbirth, the morphology of the pelvic girdle presents the most variation between male and female physiology (White *et al.*, 2012). The female pelvic girdle tends to be wider and larger to compensate and accommodate the birth canal, compared to the male pelvic girdle, which is narrower and higher (Bass, 2005; Buikstra and Ubelaker, 1994).

In the skull, female crania and mandibles tend to be more gracile with slighter smaller features, whilst male crania and mandibles present as more robust with heavier and larger features (White *et al.*, 2012). There is an overlap between male and female cranial form and sex estimation is not always possible. In such cases, other categories of possible/probable male or female are generally used or, when these features cannot be assessed, the estimation of sex must necessarily remain undetermined (Bass, 2005; Buikstra and Ubelaker, 1994). There are currently no reliable methods for estimating sex in juvenile remains, as the skeletal features and morphology that are used in the estimation of sex only manifest after puberty when certain bones of the body completely fuse (Cunningham *et al.*, 2016).

19.14 ANCESTRY

The morphological estimation of ancestry was only possible in a small number of cases due to the catastrophic effects that the fire on the majority of the victims. Estimation of ancestry was based on cranial morphology with reference to the non-metric traits described by Hefner (2009) and Rhine (1990). Morphological characteristics of the cranium appear more frequently in some population groups than others. The general consensus within forensic and physical anthropology with regards to ancestry estimation is that there is more variation within population groups than between them, and as a result, "race" does not exist (Işcan and Steyn, 2013).

It is accepted, however, that human populations are broadly aligned via biological traits to geographical regions or continents and comprise African, Asian (including the Americas, Southeast Asia, the Pacific Islands, and Oceania), and European (including the Middle East and South Asia) (Brace, 1995). Therefore, when assessing ancestry, it is acceptable to use specified cranial traits to determine which ancestry these traits are most consistent with (Işcan and Steyn, 2013).

19.15 STATURE

Due to the shrinkage caused by thermal damage, the lack of long bone fragments that could be measured, and the absence of antemortem information on individual victims' stature, stature could only be estimated for one individual.

19.16 SKELETAL VARIATION AND INDIVIDUATING FEATURES

Individuating features are features or variations in features within the human skeleton and can include the identification of pathological processes, antemortem trauma, and the presence of non-metric traits. Individuating features within the human remains examined were identified with the assistance of a number of pertinent references, including Lewis, 2017; Koudela *et al.*, 2015; Hardcastle *et al.*, 2014; White *et al.*, 2012; García-García *et al.*, 2010; Walker *et al.*, 2009; Waldron, 2009; Mann and Hunt, 2005; Devriendt *et al.*, 2005; Aufderheide and Rodríguez-Martin, 1998; Rogers and Waldron, 1995; and Barnes, 1994.

19.17 THERMAL DAMAGE

Given the catastrophic nature and the subsequent effects of the heat and fire on the bodies of the deceased victims from Grenfell Tower, forensic anthropologists were asked to examine those cases where the remains of deceased victims had been affected by thermal damage, skeletonization, extensive fragmentation, cremation, and commingling. A brief overview of the changes that occur to human remains exposed to heat and fire is provided in Chapter 10. Here we include how these changes challenge the anthropological examination within a DVI incident.

Thermal damage to bone often makes attempts to construct a biological profile of human remains very difficult. There were a number of different population groups represented in those who died in this incident, which, together with the very high temperatures and duration of the fire, often limited construction of individual biological profiles of human remains.

In addition, the heat-induced fracturing, the internal collapse of structures, and the challenges associated with body recovery operations resulted in highly fragmented skeletal elements. Where possible, individual skeletal elements were meticulously reconstructed to allow for the maximum amount of information to be recovered from each element and, where possible, to reconcile the skeletal element back to the individual to whom it belonged. This was particularly challenging in the cases where commingling of human remains had occurred.

Given that the remit of the Operation Northleigh forensic anthropology team was to assist in the DVI identification process, the patterned thermal destruction of the bones of the deceased victims was not specifically charted nor interpreted further than was necessary to provide a general description of the condition and, where possible, a biological profile of the human remains.

19.18 ATTRIBUTION OF HUMAN REMAINS

Attribution of remains to an individual was based on six categories, and these were generally made in reference to a main body part and/or identified dental or skeletal remains. These categories are outlined here in a descending order of confidence of attribution.

1. **"Physical and/or mechanical fit"** referred to two bone fragments originate from the same bone and that could be physically reconstructed and/or reunited back together. "Mechanical fit" referred to an anatomical articulation that was congruent with two joint surfaces (i.e., where two bones meet to form a joint).
2. **"Most likely associated"** referred to remains that could be confidently associated to a main and/or identified body part and/or skeletal elements but could not be physically or mechanically fitted back together. This attribution could be based upon the biological profile of the remains, visual pair matching of the skeletal elements (e.g., size, morphology, pathology), color/degree of calcination, and anatomical position of remains at the scene. This designation was also used where there are no repeated elements for the anatomical region under examination.
3. **"Consistent with"** referred to remains that were consistent with the identified body part/skeletal element (e.g., adult/juvenile, male/female, gracile/robust) but where it was not possible to associate the body part/skeletal element according to the "Most likely associated" description provided in category 2.
4. **"Exclusion"** was used when a bone was disassociated from one URN and could only be attributed to another individual by the process of elimination.
5. **"Unattributed"** in a primary URN referred to skeletal elements/fragments that could not be directly or confidently attributed to the individual. For a secondary URN, "unattributed" referred to skeletal elements/fragments that could not be directly or confidently attributed to any of the individuals recovered from a flat or communal space.

   Following anthropological examination, skeletal elements that were designated as "unattributed" were separated from the identified and reassociated remains. This unattributed material remained within the same URN but was designated with the letter "U" (e.g., unattributed bone from *PM 44 0000* became *PM 44 0000 U*). The unattributed material within an URN was reviewed during the anthropology grand rounds process to determine whether the unattributed skeletal elements could ultimately be released (in cases where only the remains of a single family were present) or retained (in cases where multiple unrelated victims were present).
6. **"Disassociated"** referred to remains not associated with the individual. However, as these skeletal elements have been recovered with the remains, following anthropological examination, they are separated from the remains and stay within the same URN but are designated with the letter "D" (e.g., disassociated bone from *PM 44 0000* becomes *PM 44 0000 D*) to await coronial review at the anthropology grand rounds. The disassociated material within a URN is reviewed to determine whether the material can ultimately be released or retained by the senior coroner.

19.19 DISASSOCIATION OF HUMAN REMAINS

Each individual URN was inventoried and laid out in anatomical position (where possible). Any remains that were not considered to belong to that individual were recorded as "additional bones" under that URN number before any reassociation process could take place. Additional bones were recorded in the following instances:

1. There was a clear recognition of a repeated skeletal element (e.g., two proximal right tibiae).
2. The size and shape of a skeletal element were considered to be morphologically different.
3. There was a difference in the biological profile, such as the presence of adult remains commingled with a juvenile skeletal element or age/sex differences.
4. Recovery position of the remains after a review of the scene photographs.

19.20 REASSOCIATION OF HUMAN REMAINS

Where possible, the disassociated skeletal elements were reassociated to the relevant individual within the flat or communal space. A decision to reassociate an element was based upon the following:

1. Physical fit/mechanical fit
2. Visual pair matching
3. Biological profile
4. Pathological characteristics or disease processes that were evident upon the skeleton
5. Exclusion (by process of elimination)
6. Information provided by other forensic disciplines, such as odontology or DNA analysis
7. Recovery position of the individual and consideration of the association or commingling of other individuals from the flat/communal recovery space.
8. Miscellaneous anthropological observations

19.21 CALCULATION OF MINIMUM NUMBER OF INDIVIDUALS (MNI)

Once all examinations and reassociations had been completed for a flat or communal space, a total MNI was estimated. In some DVI incidents, the MNI may underestimate the true number of individuals as it is only based on the recovered skeletal elements (Adams and Byrd, 2014; Mundorff, 2012). However, given the nature of this particular disaster, in that the deceased victims were recovered from particular locations within flats/communal spaces and each location was comprehensively excavated and examined, the MNI for each flat/communal space could be confidently ascribed.

1. The MNI count was based on the most repeated element/anatomical landmark, taking into account any age and sex differences. For example, four right adult femora provide a MNI count of four individuals. However, if another bone (e.g., a tibia) was that of a juvenile, the MNI in this flat/communal space would become five individuals.
2. Photography and recording of the most repeated element/anatomical landmark in the flat/communal space (e.g., eight right mastoid processes). Any other bones that could increase the MNI count due to age or sex differences were also photographed.
3. Completion of the MNI form and explanation of the MNI calculation.
4. Repeated elements used in the MNI calculation were returned to their original URN.

The information generated from these examinations was entered into the Operation Northleigh electronic case and database information systems, whilst hard copies were filed within the individual URN case folder. The URN folders associated with each flat or communal space were then collated and filed on a flat-by-flat/communal space basis. If required, "Request to Retain" forms were completed and sent to the senior coroner for approval. These forms were issued in cases where the examination of remains had not yet been completed and therefore the remains needed to be retained. Following the deliberations of the Identification Commission and the confirmation of the identification of a deceased victim, a "Request to Rescind" form was completed and sent to the senior coroner for consideration. Upon receipt of coronial approval, and in coordination with the FLOs, coroner's officers and mortuary staff, and the deceased victim's family, the remains were released.

19.22 REPATRIATION

Forensic anthropologists recognize that due to the complex nature of their work related to the identification of victims of mass fatalities, it is sometimes necessary to include social anthropological techniques, including interviewing the victim's relatives. The essence of social anthropology can be applied to the antemortem investigation within a DVI context. Information meticulously gathered from people, as well as from official civil registries, medical records, and official records of events, may provide further insights into the disaster and those who are missing.

The complexity originates from working with memory and suffering and the high emotional and psychological burden of families searching for a loved one in a mass fatality incident (Rosenblatt, 2015; Wagner and Kešetović, 2016). This "trauma" must then become the subject of a forensic investigation, and those carrying out the investigation must be sensitive to the fact that the family are already in mourning even though the missing person has yet to be located and positively identified (Fowler, 2019).

In the case of the Grenfell Tower incident, this work was undertaken by FLOs of the MPS in consultation with the forensic anthropologists working in the mortuary. Family care was a distinctive strategy of the forensic anthropologists working in the mortuary and was the necessary focus of their work (Drawdy and Katzmarzyk, 2016). This care gave the families the opportunity to be involved in the process by meeting the mortuary team and receiving information regarding the condition of the remains of their loved ones. This process avoided speculation around the truth behind the death of their loved one, and viewing the remains with an anthropologist gently explaining the circumstances provides irrefutable proof that their loved one has died. The viewings were carefully managed by the anthropologists who offered support throughout, and families were given all the time they needed. The remains were laid out in the viewing room at the mortuary on a white shroud in relative anatomical position, including charred body parts and multiple fragmented skeletal remains. This helped the family members understand the challenges the DVI teams faced and reassured them that the remains were being treated with the utmost consideration and respect.

The desired end result of all concerned in the DVI process is the release of the victim's remains for burial once they have been positively identified. In a small number of cases, the remains were identified via secondary indicators where there were no dental remains or records, or the remains were too degraded to yield a DNA profile. In these instances, a more detailed social and osteo-biological profile of the victim was required to match the skeletal characteristics recorded in the remains of the victim. FLOs would interview the family members in their homes due to the nature of the material to be discussed, creating an informal, not an authoritative, setting. The FLOs were advised by the anthropologists as to the type of questions to ask in relation to questions regarding activity/occupation patterns, antemortem skeletal trauma, and medical/hospital records. This was particularly important in cases where the victim had sustained antemortem skeletal injuries prior to moving to the UK, and as a consequence, such injuries may not have been noted in their UK medical records. Information can be revealed about medical conditions by listening to the family member describe the person and how they lived. This antemortem information, when taken directly from interviews with family members, can help to build a unique profile of the victim, be used to support an identification, and also—importantly—be considered against the archaeological and contextual relationships of the human remains as noted at the time of recovery (Wagner and Kešetović, 2016).

19.23 CULTURAL AND RELIGIOUS CONSIDERATIONS

The profile of the victims of the Grenfell Tower fire was very complex as there were diverse population groups that were further divided according to culture, language, and religion. During meetings with families and viewings, the anthropologists took time to reassure the families that their remains were being treated according to their beliefs and customs. Death rituals are very specific to the community and their belief system. This is observed in funerary rites, such as how to dress the deceased and prepare them for leaving the mortuary (Pinzón González, 2016). When these traditions have been disrupted due to the protracted nature of a DVI incident, it is important for the families to recover some of these rituals with support from the anthropologists. Members of the mortuary team liaised with religious leaders who conducted ceremonies at HM Coroner's Office. Not only are these rituals for the dead, but they also give their blessing to the mortuary team who are carrying out this work (Fowler, 2019).

Keeping the families of victims away from the process and completing the analyses in closed laboratories is counterproductive and can lead to rumors and conspiracy theories about what is being done to the remains of the dead. Showing the families the respect and meticulous detail attributed to the remains by the mortuary team reassures them that although scientific analysis is being undertaken, respect and dignity for the victim lies at the heart of this process (Rosenblatt, 2015).

19.24 CONCLUSION

The Grenfell Tower disaster presented the attending forensic archaeologists and anthropologists with a unique set of challenges that had not been encountered before in a mass fatality incident in the United Kingdom. The victims of this incident were for some time deemed to be an "open population" in that the number of people who had died and their potential identities was not known for some time. In addition, whilst the authorities knew who lived in each flat within Grenfell Tower, information received from emergency calls placed by people in the building during the fire revealed that some individuals were leaving their own flats and moving up and down through the building in an attempt to either escape the fire or to find and be with friends and family members. Therefore, the initial number of people known to usually be resident in a particular flat did not necessarily match the number of victims that were subsequently identified within that flat and, in some cases, were entirely unrelated to the residents of that flat. Given the extensive destruction of both the tower and the flats within it, the identification of the number of victims within a single flat could also often be difficult to ascertain, whilst the degree of commingling of victims from some flats made separation of each person's remains at the point of body recovery very challenging.

The structure of Grenfell Tower was also constantly monitored to ensure the safety of recovery operations teams and personnel. In a number of cases, the recovery of human remains from a flat was halted until safety and remedial works were undertaken to make it safe for teams to return to the flat to complete the search and recovery of human remains. These works necessarily could cause delays of many days or weeks whilst the flat was made safe and therefore affected the scheduling of anthropological examinations for the victims from that particular flat. These delays were often very difficult for the victims' families to accept and required sensitive handling, transparency, and ongoing discussion between the families and the Office of HM Senior Coroner and the MPS.

There were also additional health and safety challenges associated with working in the building, which included working at great height; restricted access into and out of the building via a single narrow concrete stairway; the destruction of the windows and doors of flats, which left the spaces open to the weather and the elements (particularly the wind and the rain); and high-level personal protective equipment, which oftentimes made communication and recording and recovery activities difficult.

It was certainly also the case that during the first week of operations undertaken in the main mortuary space of the Westminster Mortuary, it became clear that individual anthropological examinations of remains could not be conducted in isolation but rather that all of the human remains recovered from a single flat should be laid out and examined together. The extensive level of commingling and the number of reassociations and disassociations of skeletal elements from one victim to another was quickly recognized and therefore required the original forensic anthropology protocols to be rapidly adapted.

The subsequent erection of a dedicated temporary mortuary facility for the forensic anthropology team provided us with a very large examination space and multiple examination tables to undertake the examination of each victim on a flat-by-flat basis with, essentially, each flat being treated as a separate fatal fire scene. Both the temporary mortuary and the main mortuary were provided with a 24-hour scene guard and an outer and inner cordon that ensured that only personnel with the relevant permissions could enter particular spaces.

In terms of the recruitment of anthropologists, the lead anthropologists for this incident were all highly experienced in international casework encompassing war crimes, crimes against humanity and genocide, and national and international DVI incidents. They were able to draw on both graduate students and early career practitioners with PhDs to work in the mortuary as anthropology assistants who provided assistance to each anthropology examination and also maintained the database and physical case folder systems.

It is important to ensure that forensic archaeologists and anthropologists are involved from the outset in the planning phase for the recovery and identification process of victims from mass fatality incidents, ideally working in close collaboration with the police, the office of the coroner or medical examiner, emergency responders, and DVI-trained officers and personnel so that the most appropriate and comprehensive recovery and identification strategies and methodologies can be formulated and implemented—and importantly, with the knowledge that these recovery, examination, and identification methodologies and protocols may need to be changed during the incident based on new information or challenges that are encountered.

In the United Kingdom, the Home Office has discipline-specific DVI response teams (who work under the aegis of UK DVI) who can be deployed to a mass fatality incident in the UK or abroad. It is essential that an ongoing DVI recruitment and training program for both experienced and early career forensic archaeologists and anthropologists is in place to ensure that if they are deployed to a mass fatality incident, they will be cognizant of their collective and individual roles and responsibilities.

Mock DVI exercises are staged on an annual or every two year basis by the Home Office for the police, fire service, urban search and rescue, and other emergency responders that include practitioners from a variety of forensic disciplines (anthropology, archaeology, forensic biology, odontology, pathology, radiology). These exercises encompass a mass fatality scenario usually run over a weekend or several days, which requires all DVI-trained officers from the emergency services, government agencies, and forensic disciplines to attend and participate. It is only by providing the opportunity for continuing professional development and education in mock DVI deployments that the emergency services, government agencies, and practitioners within the forensic discipline-specific cadres can become acquainted and familiar with DVI operations.

In our experience, each DVI incident presents the judicial and government authorities, emergency responders, forensic practitioners, and operational and logistics personnel with diverse and unique challenges. These challenges require integrated, multidisciplinary approaches and solutions in order to recover and identify the victims of mass fatality incidents in a scientifically rigorous and timely manner. In addition, the authorities must maintain complete transparency and engagement with victims' families, allow the viewing of the body of their loved one, and actively facilitate funerary rites or rituals prior to the release of the body to their family, friends, and community.

NOTES

1. The Metropolitan Police Service is the territorial police force responsible for law enforcement in the Metropolitan Police District (MPD) of London, United Kingdom. The MPD covers 620 square miles and serves over eight million people within the 32 boroughs of Greater London (excluding the Square Mile of the City of London).
2. Please note that this incident was given the operational name "Operation Northleigh" by the Metropolitan Police Service.
3. The Home Office is a ministerial department of the government of the United Kingdom, and it is responsible for immigration, security, policing, and law and order.

REFERENCES

Adams, B. and Byrd, J. (2008) *Recovery, Analysis, and Identification of Commingled Human Remains*. Academic Press: Oxford.

Adams, B. and Byrd, J. (2014) *Commingled Human Remains: Methods in Recovery, Analysis, and Identification*. Academic Press: Oxford.

Aufderheide, A.C. and Rodríguez-Martin, C. (1998) *The Cambridge Encyclopaedia of Human Paleopathology*. Cambridge University Press: Cambridge.

Barnes, E. (1994) *Developmental Defects of the Axial Skeleton in Paleopathology*. University Press of Colorado: Niwot.

Bass, W.M. (2005) *Human Osteology: A Laboratory and Field Manual*. 5th edition. Missouri Archaeological Society: Springfield.

Blau, S. and Briggs, C. (2011) The role of forensic anthropology in Disaster Victim Identification (DVI). *Forensic Science International*, 205 (1–3): 29–35.

Brace, C.L. (1995) Region does mean race: Reality and convention in forensic anthropology. *Journal of Forensic Sciences*, 5 (40): 171–175.

Brooks, S. and Suchey, J.M. (1990) Skeletal age determination based on the os pubis: A comparison of Acsádi-Nemeskéri and Suchey-Brooks methods. *Human Evolution*, 5 (3): 227–238.

Buikstra, J.E. and Ubelaker, D.H. (1994) Standards for data collection from human skeletal remains. *Proceedings of a seminar at the Field Museum of Natural History. Arkansas Archaeological Survey Research Series*, 44.

Cunningham, C., Scheuer, L. and Black, S. (2016) *Developmental Juvenile Osteology*. Academic Press: London.

de Boer, H.H., Roberts, J., Delabarde, T., Mundorff, A.Z. and Blau, S. (2020) Disaster victim identification operations with fragmented, burnt, or commingled remains: Experience-based recommendations. *Forensic Sciences Research*, 5 (3): 191–201.

Devriendt, W., Piercecchi-Marti, Adalian, P., Sanvoisin, A., Dutour, O. and Leonetti, G. (2005) Hyperostosis frontalis interna: Forensic issues. *Journal of Forensic Sciences*, 50 (1): 1–4.

Drawdy, S.M. and Katzmarzyk, C. (2016) The missing files: The experience of the international committee of the red cross In: Congram, D. (ed.), *Missing Persons: Multidisciplinary Perspectives on the Disappeared*. Canadian Scholars' Press: Toronto, 60–73.

Dutch Safety Board. (2015) Crash of Malaysia Airlines Flight MH17. Available from: www.onderzoeksraad.nl/en/page/3546/crash-mh17-17-july-2014

Fowler, G.M. (2019) *Forensic Anthropology and Truth-Seeking in Guatemala* (Doctoral thesis in preparation, University of Lincoln).

García-García, A.S., Martínez González, J.M., Gómez Font, R., Soto Rivadeneira, A. and Oviedo Roldán, L. (2010) Current status of the torus palatinus and torus mandibularis. *Medicina Oral, Patología Oral y Cirugía Bucal. Ed. inglesa*, 15 (2): 12.

Hardcastle, S.A., Dieppe, P., Gregson, C.L., Arden, N.K., Spector, T.D., Hart, D.J., Edwards, M.H., Dennison, E.M., Cooper, C., Williams, M. and Davey Smith, G. (2014) Osteophytes, enthesophytes, and high bone mass: A bone forming triad with potential relevance in Osteoarthritis. *Arthritis and Rheumatology*, 66 (9): 2429–2439.

Harrison, K. and Ryder, D. (2018) Operation Northleigh archaeology reports. Unpublished report.

Hefner, J.T. (2009) Cranial nonmetric variation and estimating ancestry. *Journal of Forensic Sciences*, 54 (5): 985–995.

Hillson, S. (1996) *Dental Anthropology*. Cambridge University Press: Cambridge.

Hillson, S. (2008) *Dental Anthropology*. Cambridge University Press: Cambridge.

Indriati, E. (2014) Forensic anthropological roles in disaster victim identification of two Jakarta Hotels bomb blasts. *Damianus Journal of Medicine*, 13: 148–157.

Interpol. (2018a) Disaster victim identification guide. Available from: https://interpol.int/content/download/589/file/18Y1344 E DVI_Guide.pdf

Interpol. (2018b) Annexure 13: INTERPOL guidance: Numbering in disaster victim identification operations. Available from: https://www.interpol.int/content/download/5760/file/21Y2169 E DVI_Guide2018_Annexure13.pdf

Işcan, M.Y. and Loth, S.R. (1985) Determination of age from the sternal rib in White Females: A test of the phase method. *Journal of Forensic Sciences*, 31 (3): 990–999.

Işcan, M.Y., Loth, S.R. and Wright, R.K. (1984) Age estimation from the rib by phase analysis: White males. *Journal of Forensic Sciences*, 29 (4): 1094–1104.

Işcan, M.Y., Loth, S.R. and Wright, R.K. (1985) Age estimation from the rib by phase analysis: White females. *Journal of Forensic Sciences*, 30 (3): 853–863.

Işcan, M.Y., Loth, S.R. and Wright, R.K. (1987) Racial variation in the sternal extremity of the rib and its effect on age determination. *Journal of Forensic Science*, 32 (2): 452–466.

Işcan, M.Y. and Steyn, M. (2013) *The Human Skeleton in Forensic Medicine*. 3rd edition. Charles C. Thomas: Springfield.

Koudela, K., Koudelová, J. and Zeman, P. (2015) Concave impressio ligamenti costoclavicularis ("rhomboid fossa") and its prevalence and relevance to clinical practice. *Surgical and Radiologic Anatomy*, 37 (3): 239–245.

Leditschke, J., Collett, S. and Ellen, R. (2011) Mortuary operations in the aftermath of the 2009 Victorian bushfires. *Forensic Science International*, 205: 8–14.

Lewis, M. (2017) *Palaeopathology of Children: Identification of Pathological Conditions in the Human Skeletal Remains of Non-Adults*. Academic Press: London.

Lovejoy, C.O., Meindl, R.S., Pryzbeck, T.R. and Mensforth, R.P. (1985) Chronological metamorphosis of the auricular surface of the ilium: A new method for the determination of adult skeletal age at death. *American Journal of Physical Anthropology*, 68 (1): 15–28.

MacKinnon, G. (2018) Operation Northleigh anthropology reports. Unpublished report.

Mann, R.W. and Hunt, D.R. (2005) *Photographic Regional Atlas of Bone Disease: A Guide to Pathologic and Normal Variation in the Human Skeleton*. Charles C Thomas: Springfield.

Meindl, R.S. and Lovejoy, C.O. (1985) Ectocranial suture closure: A revised method for the determination of skeletal age at death based on the lateral-anterior suture. *American Journal of Physical Anthropology*, 68 (57–66).

Mundorff, A. (2008) Anthropologist-directed triage: Three distinct mass fatality events involving fragmentation of human remains. In: Adams, B. and Byrd, J. (eds.), *Recovery, Analysis, and Identification of Commingled Human Remains*. Academic Press: Oxford, 123–144.

Mundorff, A. (2012) Integrating forensic anthropology into Disaster Victim Identification. *Forensic, Science, Medicine, and Pathology*, 8 (2): 131–139.

Osborne, D.L., Simmons, T.L. and Nawrocki, S.P. (2004) Reconsidering the auricular surface as an indicator of age at death. *Journal of Forensic Sciences*, 49 (5): 905–911.

Pinzón González, M. E. (2016) Psychosocial perspectives on the enforced disappearance of Indigenous peoples in guatemala. In: Congram, D. (ed.), *Missing Persons: Multidisciplinary Perspectives on the Disappeared*. Canadian Scholars' Press: Toronto, 102–118.

Rhine, S. (1990) Nonmetric skull racing. In Gill, G.W. and Rhine, R. (eds.), *Skeletal Attribution of Race: Methods for Forensic Anthropology (4)*. Maxwell Museum of Anthropology: Albuquerque.

Rogers, J. and Waldron, T. (1995) *A Field Guide to Joint Disease in Archaeology*. John Wiley: Chichester.

Rosenblatt, A. (2015) *Digging for the Disappeared: Forensic Science after Atrocity*. Stanford University Press: Stanford.

Schaefer, M., Black, S. and Scheuer, L. (2009) *Juvenile Osteology: A Laboratory and Field Manual*. Academic Press: London.

Sledzik, P., Dirkmaat, D., Mann, R., Holland, T., Mundorff, A., Adams, B., Crowder, C. and DePaolo, F. (2009) Disaster victim recovery and identification: Forensic anthropology in the aftermath of September 11th. In: Steadman, D.W. (ed.), *Hard Evidence: Cased Studies in Forensic Anthropology*. 2nd edition. Prentice Hall: Upper Saddle River, 289–302.

Wagner, S. and Kešetović, R. (2016) Absent bodies, absent knowledge: The forensic work of identifying Srebrenica's missing and the social experience of families In: Congram, D. (ed.), *Missing Persons: Multidisciplinary Perspectives on the Disappeared*. Canadian Scholars' Press: Toronto, 42–59.

Waldron, T. (2009). *Palaeopathology*. Cambridge University Press: Cambridge.

Walker, P.L., Bathurst, R.R., Richman, R., Gjerdrum, T. and Andrushko, V.A. (2009) The causes of porotic hyperostosis and cribra orbitalia: A reappraisal of the iron deficiency-anemia hypothesis. *American Journal of Physical Anthropology*, 139 (2): 109–125.

White, T.D., Black, M.T. and Folkens, P.A. (2012) *Human Osteology*. 3rd edition. Elsevier: Oxford.

SECTION V

The Impact of Wildfires

The final chapters of this volume take a broader perspective to the wildfire damage, addressing both the populational impacts and the psychological ones. Chapters 20 and 21 provide a data driven approach to identifying victim vulnerabilities to wildfire, including factors such as social and geographic isolation and population demographics. The authors conclude that agencies should work to identify and protect the most vulnerable groups prior to a mass fatality incident. The final chapter closes with a discussion of the psychological impact of mass disasters on first responders, stating that destigmatizing psychological impacts and prioritizing responder psychoemotional health should be an essential piece of every mass disaster response.

Chapter 20 presents a geographic perspective on the victims of the Camp Fire, describing the distribution of fatalities and examining the possibility that social and geographic isolation played a role in these fatalities. The chapter begins with a discussion of the development of wildland-urban interface (WUI) communities and how living in these communities comes with inherent risk of fire death. The chapter then turns to a discussion of risk factors for wildfire death from the level of the population to that of the individual, again keeping the focus on the variable of isolation. Using qualitative data from news items, remembrances, and other published sources on a sample of the victims, the authors describe the spatial and social networks that selected individuals attempted to utilize after learning of the fire.

Chapter 21 provides a demographic comparison of fire deaths drawing on data from early California wildfires and comparing this data to more recent Australian bushfire fatalities. The authors find that fire victim vulnerability is variable and changes through time, with different demographic subsets being more adversely affected in different temporal periods. Spatial differences were also noted, as populations continue to expand into the WUI both nationally and internationally. The authors conclude that in order to identify and protect the most vulnerable groups, responding agencies must consider this time-space continuum and its relationship to the demographic makeup of impacted populations.

Chapter 22 discusses the psychological impact of mass disasters on first responders. The chapter begins with an introduction to the role first responders play in mass disaster response and discusses how the definition of "first responder" must be expanded to include individuals from many sectors in the professional, non-professional, and

DOI: 10.4324/9781003168010-24

volunteer realm. Regardless of the title/responsibilities of the first responder, the psychological impacts of disaster response are immense and must be recognized and appropriately addressed. The author states that destigmatizing psychological impacts and prioritizing responder psychoemotional health should be an essential piece of every mass disaster response.

The final chapter of this volume, Chapter 23, provides some concluding thoughts on (1) the need for preparation at many levels prior to any incident in order to facilitate an effective and efficient response, (2) collaboration and the formation of multidisciplinary teams, making for smoother recovery and increase the chances of making positive identifications of fatalities, and (3) open lines of communication in all directions.

CHAPTER 20

Demographics and Locational Analyses of Wildfire Victims

Casey Hegel, Samuel Mijal, Jacquelyn Chase, and Peter Hansen

20.1 INTRODUCTION

This chapter presents a detailed geographic perspective on the fatalities in the Camp Fire. We describe the distribution of fatalities and examine the possibility that social and geographic isolation played a role in these fatalities. This chapter begins with information on the development of wildland-urban interface communities and the risk inherent in building and living in these areas. We next turn to the geography of fatalities in the fire with a map of where remains were found, with some demographic information accompanying each location and summarized for the whole group. This analysis includes data on the distance to nearest neighbor to further examine the hypothesis of isolation. Next, using qualitative data from news items, remembrances, and other published sources on a sample of the victims, we describe the spatial and social networks that selected individuals attempted to draw upon as the fire closed in. We have found nothing that suggests that most victims were overwhelmingly either socially or geographically isolated, but the inability by many of the victims to evacuate on their own was certainly a factor in their deaths.

20.2 THE RISK OF WUI RESIDENTIAL DEVELOPMENT

What does it mean to be vulnerable to wildfire in the wildland-urban interface (WUI)? The WUI is where human settlements approximate flammable wildland vegetation. By definition these areas and everyone who lives in them are vulnerable to wildfire, but risk is not spread equally among WUI populations. This chapter looks at vulnerability to wildfire in the WUI through a socio-geographic examination of fatalities in the Camp Fire.

In the United States WUI is an official designation that allows firefighters, planners, insurance companies, residents and civilian organizations, such as fire safe councils, to plan for wildfires. This planning is greatly needed. Whether it is because these areas are highly desirable or whether they are affordable, across the United States WUIs are growing faster than any other kind of settlement (Berube et al. 2006; Beebe and Wheeler 2012) and already account for one-third of all housing units in the United States (Kramer et al. 2019). In the United States, 80% of acreage used for new housing has been outside of urban areas in recent years (Mann et al. 2014). Of all buildings lost

DOI: 10.4324/9781003168010-25

to wildfire in the US, 69% are in WUI areas, whereas in California, this percentage is 75% (Mann et al. 2014). Researchers have shown that the rush to rebuild after a fire often outweighs calls for cautious planning (Mockrin et al. 2018).

While some people advocate for a moratorium on development, it is certain that growth will continue in areas that are at high risk for fire and ill-prepared for evacuations. Most of this growth occurs in areas where road networks are already in place. It is rare for improvements such as widening roads or creating more opportunities for egress to keep up with housing development (Cova 2005). Roads are often restricted by the presence of ridges and slopes, and by the preference by residents for privacy and quiet (Cova 2005). These decades of growth in the WUI have coincided with decades of record propagation of flammable vegetation as well (Cova 2005).

In part due to the human presence in wildland areas, fires themselves are becoming more frequent (Balch et al. 2017; Kramer et al. 2019), while climate change is making them more explosive and less responsive to suppression. Stories of megafires around the world recount how search and rescue, not to mention fire suppression, completely broke down and people had to figure out, alone or in groups, how to save their own lives.

A WUI designation is based on three spatial criteria: distance, density, and contiguity (Bento-Gonçalves and Vieira 2020). A settlement could be a WUI if it is sufficiently densely populated (to distinguish it from a rural settlement) and is located within a certain distance (approximately 1.5 miles) from the edge of wildland vegetation. This vegetation must also be sufficiently contiguous and dense to qualify as a wildland (as opposed to a park, for example). WUIs exist in many different kinds of terrain, biome, and settlement. Towns, suburbs, or large lot estates can be WUIs, which can abut or be intermixed with flat grasslands, mountainous pine forests, or rolling oak woodlands (Beebe and Wheeler 2012).

WUIs are socially, demographically, and economically diverse as well (Edgeley and Paveglio 2019). Some WUIs are high-income suburban enclaves, close to services and population centers; others are economically depressed semi-rural remnants of bygone extractive economies. Many WUIs are recreational destinations where second homes can outnumber year-round residences. Others, like Paradise, are made up of a mix of retirees (many of them low income) and workers who commute to regional cities. Paradise, and many other small towns in the Sierra Nevada foothills, is a long-established town linked to a number of booms and to ongoing settlement trends, including the search for affordable housing by retirees and young families. Many people also choose WUIs to live in because they offer a sense of independence and privacy. The unincorporated areas of Butte County that also suffered heavy losses in the Camp Fire were mostly sparsely populated communities known for their independence and relative isolation. It is this diversity that allows us to ask the question about vulnerability without being redundant. All WUIs are by definition at risk for wildfire, but their diversity warrants further research into how different people and communities adapt to and ultimately survive fires.

Once the trend toward WUI growth became noticeable in the United States, as well as in Australia and Canada, there was a shift in responsibility to residents of WUIs to manage wildfire and prepare evacuation strategies, with the understanding that rescue operations may not be possible. This transfer of risk has become more explicit as fires have been classified increasingly as extreme events (Tedim et al. 2018). Ironically, preventive burning and landscape modification programs that do exist in the United States tend not to be in WUI zones, possibly because of the difficulties in conducting prescribed burns and other fuel maintenance in areas largely made up of private ownership

(Bento-Gonçalves and Vieira 2020). Research on evacuations has shown that even under the best of circumstances where a national policy created clear directives to help people prepare for fire, such as Australia's shelter in place program, many people have no plan and in a firestorm end up sheltering passively (Whittaker et al. 2013; Folk et al. 2019).

Given each fire's uniqueness (time of day, time of year, terrain, speed, direction), it is difficult to predict how people will react. Research across several megafires is beginning to reveal some patterns, keeping in mind the huge variation in how and why people die in wildfire. Besides noting people's individual vulnerabilities, there is interest in their behavior during a fire. This behavior is of course contextualized not only by socio-demographic characteristics (age, gender, income, homeownership) but also by social and geographic networks and the presence of authorities before and during fires.

The perception of risk often affects how people end up reacting to a disaster (Hilhorst and Bankoff 2004). But perceived risk is often not just based on a person's thoughts to their own life but also includes perceptions about property loss (from destruction or looting) and about risk to other people and to animals (Lazarus 2014). Reviews of many fires show that people in WUIs tend to leave more readily than those in rural (more remote) settings, and that people alone (especially men) tend to refuse to evacuate more often than do women (McLennan et al. 2019). The source of information about a fire event can also contribute to whether someone chooses to evacuate or stay (McLennan et al. 2019). Research shows that people respond more to warnings by neighbors, family, and friends than to those by the authorities, perhaps due to "warning fatigue" in fire-prone areas. McLennan et al. (2019) also note that evacuation warnings are often not geographically specific enough for residents to take them seriously. Instead, individuals often have relied on more personalized information as noted earlier and by their own visual cues (smoke and fire) that speak more to their immediate surroundings.

While the literature on evacuation mentions communication with family members, friends, and neighbors before fires to discuss evacuation plans, there is little about geographic and social isolation in WUI areas and whether isolation factors into survival during an evacuation. The settlement patterns of WUIs, along with networks of families, friends, and neighbors within this geography, are likely important variables to understand the outcomes for people who are confronted at a moment's notice with the need to save themselves (and animals and belongings) from a wildfire but who have no means to escape on their own (Cova 2005). Understanding these networks is in line with the desire among hazards researchers to see vulnerability as socially and geographically contextualized (Brenkert-Smith 2011; Paveglio et al. 2009).

We can assume that social and geographic isolation can be deadly in an emergency situation, especially for the most vulnerable. Similarly, it is likely that personal vulnerabilities can be offset by networks of support—friends, neighbors, family, authorities, and organizations that can communicate with and reach vulnerable people during a catastrophe. A contextual perspective also requires a look at the broader challenges facing everyone who lives in fire-prone areas such as evacuation congestion, lack of information, and warning fatigue that might cause people to doubt or ignore information. Official communications and rescue operations were overwhelmed during the Camp Fire and most people and organizations responsible for others (hospitals, nursing homes, schools) were on their own, and it is astounding that so many people (including many vulnerable individuals) survived the fire. A notable feature of survival during the Camp Fire is that only one person died who lived in a collective setting (in this case an assisted living complex). Many others evacuated successfully in groups with caretakers or guardians.

Individual and contextual factors all contributed to whether people delayed evacuation during the Camp Fire. The wide range of possibilities can be seen in some of the behaviors and decisions during the first day of the fire according to accounts from family and friends of the victims. Behaviors ranged from attempting to escape the fire, waiting for evacuation, refusing to leave, thinking it would be safe to stay, or staying behind to save their property or pets. We recount some of these stories further here.

20.2.1 Demographics and Geographic Distribution of the Fatalities

A large majority of the fatalities were in the town of Paradise (65), followed by the unincorporated communities of Magalia (9), Concow (10), and Butte Creek Canyon (1). Figure 20.1 provides an overview of the fatalities within the footprint of the Camp Fire and illustrates the presence of the WUI in this area.

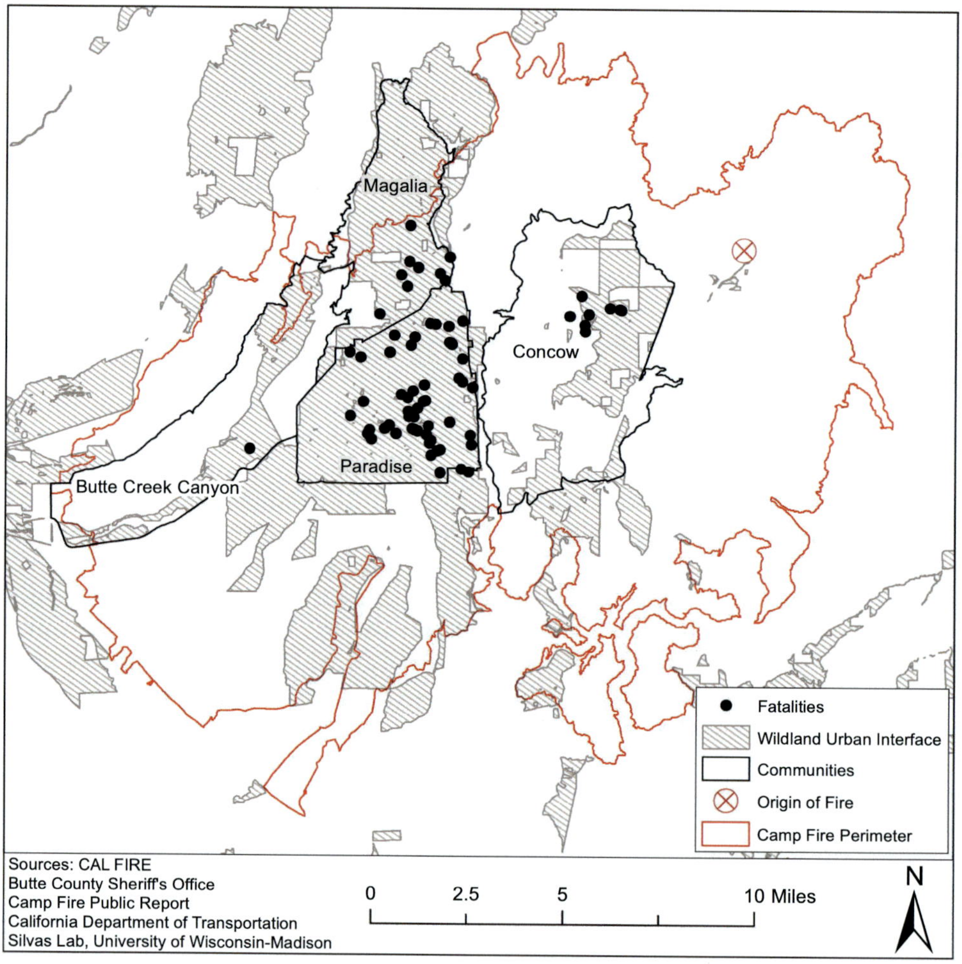

FIGURE 20.1 Map of the Camp Fire burn zone indicating locations of fatalities.

The following map (Figure 20.2) indicates whether the fatalities occurred in the home, outside the home, or in a car. It is clear that few of the deceased were attempting to evacuate, unlike other recent catastrophic fires such as the Black Saturday Fire in Australia in 2009 (Whittaker et al. 2013) and the Pedrógão Grande Fire in Portugal in 2017 (Assembléia da República and Comissão Técnica Independente 2017), where most people died in vehicles after having delayed evacuations. As noted elsewhere in this volume, the majority of individuals were found in a residence, with 59 being found inside their residence and 16 individuals outside of their residence. Ten individuals were found in association with their vehicles, eight inside and two located directly outside of their vehicle. Out of the individuals outside, 13 were found on their porches or in their driveways, suggesting they were either trying to flee or they were waiting for help for evacuation.

Previous examinations of Camp Fire community demographics highlight two significant attributes among the deceased. First, older persons are overrepresented in the

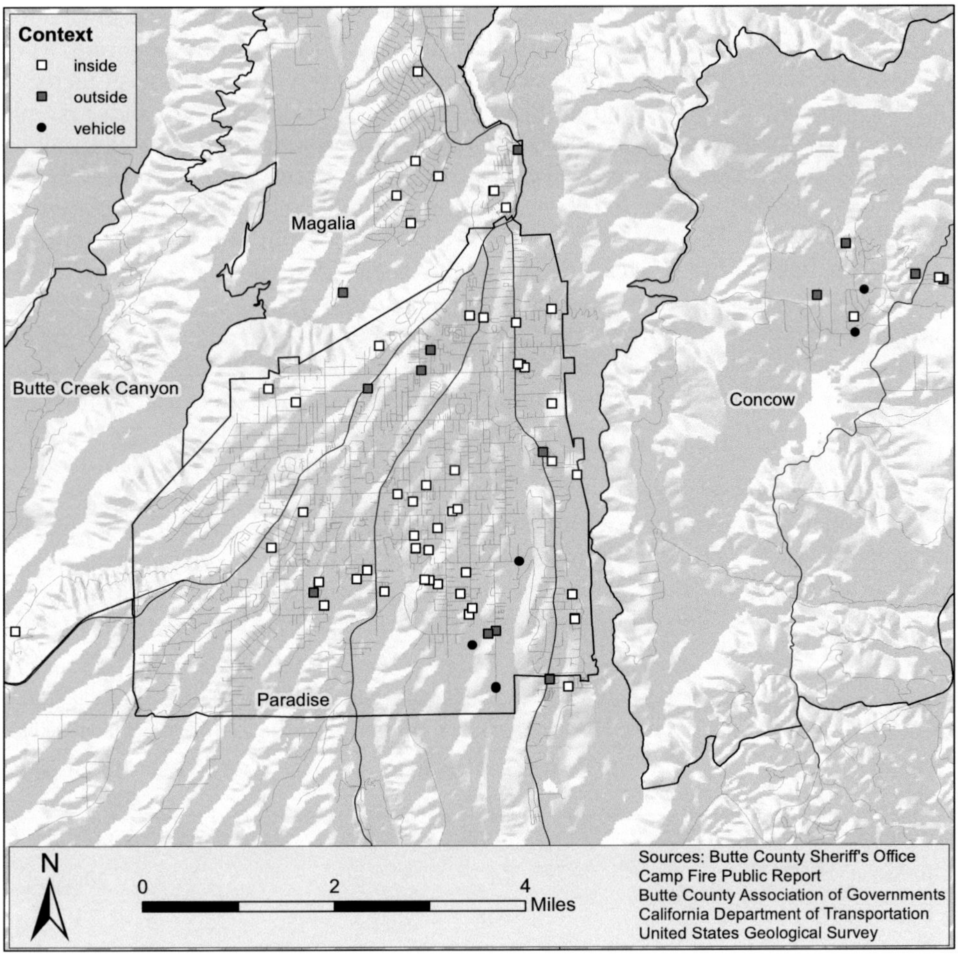

FIGURE 20.2 Camp Fire deaths in Concow, Paradise, and Magalia by location of remains (indoors, outdoors, vehicle).

Camp Fire fatalities when compared to estimates from the 2010 US Census for the three Camp Fire communities (United States Census 2018). Camp Fire fatalities average 72.0 years old at death versus an average age of 49.8 years old for the communities (Mijal and Willey 2020). Around 80% of the deceased were over 65 years old. Table 20.1 summarizes age and gender demographics.

Second, Camp Fire fatalities exhibit mobility disabilities at a substantially higher rate than the Camp Fire communities represented in data from the 2017 American Community Survey (United States Census 2018). Survey information estimated that in the year prior to the fire 14% of the Camp Fire communities reported ambulatory disabilities, in contrast to at least 28% (n = 24) of the Camp Fire victims (Mijal and Willey 2020). At least 46% (n = 39) had disabilities that may have impacted their ability to evacuate either on foot or in a car. It is common for disabled individuals to depend on others to drive them places. Even if a car was onsite, if the person who typically drove the car was not available, it could not be mobilized for an evacuation by a disabled individual. Another factor that possibly influenced the ability for people to escape, and that is related to income and other factors of vulnerability, was access to a working vehicle.

Many survivors actually had to abandon cars in the process of evacuating, as they ran out of gas, their cars broke down or they crashed or ran off the roads. A factor that affects all residents in WUIs but could be particularly treacherous for older people is the state of the roadways (Cova 2005). Unmaintained private roads, for example, can be a deathtrap for inexperienced drivers during a fire. Even well-maintained arterials can become overwhelmed during an evacuation of a relatively densely populated WUI such as Paradise. The Town of Paradise had created evacuation zones to reduce pressure on the roads, but the fire proceeded with such ferocity that the roads became clogged immediately. Traffic jams prevented people from turning from residential streets onto main evacuation channels during the Camp Fire. Many people ended up leaving their cars to escape on foot. The evacuation was harrowing for all, but older individuals with mobility problems especially suffered during that chaotic morning. Many people tried to go back into that area to save someone but were turned away by roadblocks and authorities, which some acknowledged probably ended up saving them from also ending up as a victim of the fire.

The higher-than-expected representation of older age groups and disabled individuals in the Camp Fire fatalities suggests these were factors contributing to their deaths, although many others with similar characteristics did escape the fire. Because older adults are more likely to be alone, it is important to consider how this may have

TABLE 20.1 Camp Fire Fatality Demographics Compared to the California Census Data

Demographic Variable	Percent in Fatalities Data	Percent in Census Data (2013–17)
Age over 65	80.9	24.8
Age between 45–65	14.3	30
Age between 18–44	4.8	27.3
Age under 18	0	17.8
Male	48	47.8
Female	52	52.5

factored into outcomes. The following map (Figure 20.3) shows fatalities by information on whether each person died alone or in the company of others who either survived or died as well.

This map indicates that the vast majority of all deaths occurred in areas of relative high population concentration and road network. There was no clear evacuation zone where people could have headed locally, a fact that perhaps contributed to the feeling of helplessness that overwhelmed some of those who chose not to evacuate their homes despite the fact these homes themselves (at least in Paradise) were physically isolated. A nearest neighbor analysis of the locations of homes where people were deceased shows that the minimum distance to the closest neighbor was 2.68 meters (8.8 feet) and the maximum distance is 210.48 meters (690.5 feet). The mean is 43.36 meters (142.2 feet) and the median is 28.79 meters (94.5 feet).

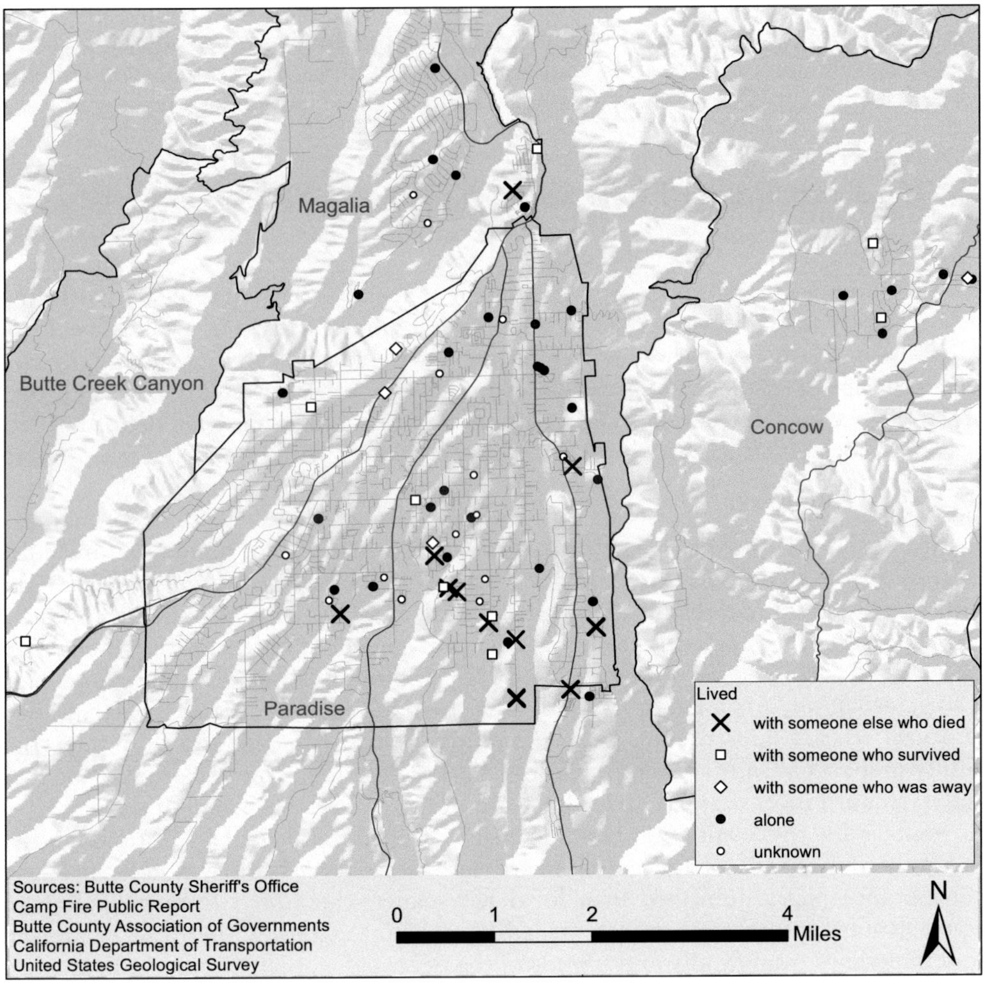

FIGURE 20.3 Camp Fire deaths in Concow, Paradise, and Magalia by social network (alone, with others who died, others who survived, or others who were away from home).

TABLE 20.2 Camp Fire Fatalities by Type of Housing

Type of Housing of Victim	Number of Victims
Single-family home	33 (38%)
Mobile/manufactured home	29 (34%)
Multi-family home	9 (10%)
Apartment or residential home	4 (4.7%)
Unknown	10 (11.7%)
Total	85

Table 20.2 presents the distribution of fatalities by type of housing, for those where this information was available. The Census Community Survey data for housing shows that in Paradise, 69% of the population were living in single family homes, and 17% lived in mobile homes, suggesting that among the fatalities residents of mobile homes were overrepresented while those of single-family homes were underrepresented.

20.3 SOCIAL NETWORKS AND CONNECTIONS OF CAMP FIRE VICTIMS

Every community represents a complex system of social and geographic networks that are constantly being constructed and maintained. Social networks are deployed dramatically in disaster scenarios. Individuals in each community are differentially connected to aspects of these social networks, as communities have marginalized groups who live in various degrees of social isolation. Social isolation has been defined as "the absence of social interactions, contacts, and relationships with family and friends, with neighbors on an individual level, and with 'society at large' on a broader level" (Berg and Cassells 1992). Socially isolated individuals are not able to make new or maintain existing social relationships. The causes of social isolation are numerous, including depression, illness, disability, and domestic violence. In interface areas, people may also choose to live alone. Adults over the age of 65 are more likely to be impacted by social isolation, with one study estimating that over one-quarter of independently living older adults are socially isolated (Cudjoe et al. 2020). Although living alone does not equate to social isolation, it is a factor in conditions surrounding evacuations. Understanding the social relationships present in a community helps to understand how that community prepares for and reacts to wildfire. This section looks more closely at the individual circumstances that led up to the death of this vulnerable group of people.

Sources for this evaluation come primarily from interviews and testimony given by family and friends of the deceased to various sources. Data was collected from remembrance pages published in a local newspaper, the *Chico Enterprise Record*. Supplementary information was provided by the Butte County Sheriff's Department from interviews from family and friends of the deceased, gathered to assist in identifying remains. Videotaped legal testimony given during the Camp Fire Investigation and reported on in the Camp Fire Public Report was also used (Ramsey et al. 2020). Some additional information was gathered from *Fire in Paradise: An American Tragedy* in which the authors conducted interviews with family and friends of the deceased (Gee and Anguiano 2020). Together these data provide insights into the lives of the Camp

Fire victims' social context. This data may support comparative analyses between fires as communities grapple with the risk of living in fire-prone areas.

Based on these diverse sources, we reconstructed indicators of all of the victims' social connections. First, data was collected on household makeup. Individuals were identified as either living alone, living with others, or unknown. Individuals who lived with other people were sorted into five groups based on who they lived with: significant other, child (including stepchildren), parent (including stepparents and in-laws), sibling (including stepsiblings), and roommate. Next, community relationships were scored, first as present or absent. Then the present scores were sorted into eight groups: significant other, child (including stepchildren), parent (including stepparents and in-laws), sibling (including stepsiblings), friend, roommate, organization (church, fraternal order, etc.), and other. When one individual fell into multiple groups, the presence of a significant other took precedence, followed by children, then parents, siblings, friends, roommates, organizations, and finally others.

Of the 85 Camp Fire fatalities with available information, 33 (38.82%) were reported to have lived alone, while 38 (44.71%) lived with at least one other person. Of those that lived with other people, the majority (21, 55.26%) lived with a significant other. Child was the next common category (9, 23.68%), followed by parent and roommate (3, 7.89% each), and then sibling (2, 5.26%). An independent samples t-test was conducted to compare mean ages between individuals who lived alone (mean = 76.36 years) and those who lived with at least one other person (mean = 67.08 years) and showed that there was a statistically significant difference between the two groups ($t = 2.770$, $df = 69$, $p = 0.007$). Older individuals were therefore more likely to be living alone. This could be due to several factors, including the death of a significant other and adult children moving out of the household.

Based on this assessment of social relationships of victims, we concluded that 8 (9.41%) of the 85 fatalities were noted as having no significant ties to others in the community while 59 (69.41%) had at least one relationship with someone else in the community. Of the 59 with community relationships, significant other was the most common relationship (35.59%), followed by child (23.73%), sibling (11.86%), friend (5, 8.47%), parent and organization (4, 6.78% each), roommate (3, 5.08%), and other (1, 1.69%).

A qualitative analysis of social relationships provides additional insight into how people become victims of disasters. Social interactions provide a safety net when more formal security plans such as planned evacuations and automated emergency alerts fail. This is especially important for vulnerable portions of the population who may lack resources, such as a vehicle to evacuate in or a phone to receive an emergency alert.

Outlining the contribution of social connections in evacuation from a catastrophic wildfire are multifaceted and often best represented in a narrative format. This next section outlines the situation of 11 people who perished in the Camp Fire. These cases are meant to illustrate the complex relationship between unique vulnerabilities and failures in social systems that likely contributed to these victims' deaths. This narrative description starts with cases of people who were more isolated and follows with examples of people who were clearly in daily contact with relatives or friends.

20.3.1 Case Studies from the Camp Fire

The starkest example of social isolation is the case of the unknown male individual who perished in the fire. The body of an adult male (Victim #1) was found commingled with the remains of an older woman (Victim #2) at the residence she shared with her husband (Gee and Anguiano 2020). Forensic anthropologists estimated that Victim #1 is an older male with dental work and crowns. Nothing else is known about this individual, and there are no outstanding missing persons. Victim #2's husband speculated that the unknown male could have been working on an illegal pot grown in the area and may have tried to help his wife escape when the fire overtook them (Gee and Anguiano 2020). Regardless, this individual had no clear connection to the town of Paradise or the surrounding communities. This lack of social connections likely limited his options during the evacuation and ultimately ended in his death inside a stranger's home.

Another example of a person who lived in isolation was Victim #3, who died in the outskirts of Magalia. Victim #3 was described as a "quiet man who liked to live alone" (Chico Enterprise Record 2019). He preferred living in a remote area. He had no postal address, no phone, and no vehicle. He did have a neighbor for whom he would occasionally do yard work. In the chaos of the fire, the neighbor did not remember about Victim #3's situation until after evacuation, leaving Victim #3 without any way to escape.

Another example of isolation is that of Victim #4, who lived in a manufactured home hidden by substantial tree growth (Chico Enterprise Record 2019). While records show that he had lived in Paradise since at least 2014, very little is known about him outside of interactions with law enforcement. Tellingly, no comments from community members were available in remembrance articles. Since no vehicle was found on Victim #4's property, it was assumed that he had no transportation to escape the fire (Ramsey et al. 2020). His existence on the margins of Paradise, without transportation and presumably without mobilized social networks, limited his ability to escape the fire.

Victims #5 and #6 lived in a single-family home in Paradise. Victim #5 was an elderly female and was a breast cancer survivor who also suffered from diabetes (Chico Enterprise Record 2019). Both she and her husband, Victim #6, utilized oxygen tanks and walkers. They had no children. While Victim #5 mostly stayed inside the house, Victim #6 occasionally worked on his lawn and struck up a relationship with his closest neighbor, who would sometimes help them with the trash or bring them food (Gee and Anguiano 2020). The only other source of information about these victims was from a social worker who visited them monthly. When the fire swept through the community, their neighbors fled. It had not occurred to anyone in the community to warn them. It is not known if either victim had attempted to call anyone to assist them in evacuating.

Victim #7, another elderly female, lived alone in her Paradise apartment (Chico Enterprise Record 2019). The area was closed off to public access and difficult to approach (Superior Court of Butte County 2020; Ramsey et al. 2020). While she had been a teacher in her past, she had fallen into poor mental and physical health more recently and rarely left her home. She had no spouse or children and was estranged from her family, although she had begun communicating with her sister. There is no information about her maintaining any social relationships in the community. At the time of the fire, she was recovering from a recent hospitalization and was receiving at-home care. Caregivers could not access the area around her residence to give her any warning. A search and rescue team located her remains in her unburned apartment two weeks after the fire (Superior Court of Butte County 2020; Ramsey et al. 2020).

People may have chosen a solitary life, but most of them who died were not without friends, family members, or neighbors, many of whom left a record of these connections in published remembrances. One example was Victim #8, an older male, of Concow, who was described by family as “a hermit” and “a nice guy” (Chico Enterprise Record 2019). At the time of the fire, he had been living in a camper van on his friend’s property (Gee and Anguiano 2020). The friend was woken up before 7:00 a.m. by another person living in a trailer on her property. All three evacuated the property with Victim #8 taking his friend’s vehicle with two dogs. Victim #8 collided with a tree a mile and a half from the property. His body, along with the dogs, were located in the cargo area of the vehicle (Ramsey et al. 2020).

Victim #9, an older female, lived with her sister, Victim #10, who was a few years younger, at the time of the fire in Paradise. Victim #10 was a devoted Pentecostal Christian (Chico Enterprise Record 2019). Victim #9 was in close contact with her children and grandchildren, while Victim #9 was active in her church community. The description of final moments shows both sisters in contact with others. Family members spoke with Victim #10 on the morning of the fire, who said she and her sister had no intention of leaving. In another call to a family friend, she said God told her “it would be safe to stay” (Gee and Anguiano 2020). Later in the morning, firefighters drove down the street, sirens blaring, to alert residents to evacuate. Family members wonder if the sisters changed their mind at the last minute but could not get their car started. The remains of both sisters were found within their home.

Victim #11 lived with his adult daughter. He was an energetic octogenarian, holding a full-time job, teaching Sunday school, and volunteering as a docent at a local museum (Ramsey et al. 2020). He had considered retiring and was writing a book, subsequently lost in the fire. He woke his daughter on the morning of the 8th, warning her of a fire on the ridge and insisting she evacuate (Gee and Anguiano 2020). As a former firefighter, he was no stranger to wildfires (Ramsey et al. 2020). Victim #11 stayed behind to aid neighbors in preparing for the fire. He also assisted firefighters in reconnoitering the fire perimeter. At 5:30 p.m. he parted ways with the firefighters to assist neighbors in defending landmark buildings. He spoke with his daughter again at 10:30 p.m. He was last seen headed back to his home. He was confident that the fire would not be able to jump the Feather River, though it had already done so earlier in the day. Spot fires would have made it nearly impossible to leave his home when the fire jumped the canyon for a second time (Gee and Anguiano 2020). Victim #11’s remains were found on the front porch of his residence (Ramsey et al. 2020).

20.4 CONCLUSION

Recognition of vulnerability in WUI communities is crucial to wildfire preparedness and emergency response. Some research is already using census data on economics and indicators of ethnicity and immigration status to identify which WUI communities would be most vulnerable in a wildfire (Paveglio et al. 2016). Communities that are at higher risk need to have updated and current plans for future disasters (e.g., planned evacuation routes) that keep the needs of vulnerable citizens in mind. At the individual and neighborhood community level, having an evacuation plan and knowing people in the area can also influence successful evacuation (Paveglio et al. 2018; Méndez et al. 2020).

Given the large number of older and single individuals in the population of those who lived in the burn scar area of the Camp Fire (and especially among those who died), and knowing that WUI populations will likely continue to age at even a faster rate than the general population, it is important to explore age-related vulnerabilities. The deceased did not overwhelmingly appear to be socially or physically isolated, although they did present characteristics of vulnerability, such as the presence of physical disabilities that made it hard or impossible to self-evacuate. Learning that vulnerable people could not reach their loved ones because of failed communications and that they could not be evacuated due to traffic congestion could lead to solutions that are relevant to a less mobile population. Even though there is no evidence that people died *because* of isolation, it is important to remember that only one person in a collective situation (an assisted living) was left behind during evacuations and therefore died.

Rebuilding efforts could take social isolation and physical mobility into account. Multifamily housing may not just be more affordable; it may save people's lives who otherwise could be forgotten or left behind during an evacuation. Clustered development has also been shown to reduce the likelihood of losing residences during wildfires in California (Mann et al. 2014), and it can avoid sprawl into wildlands.

REFERENCES

Assembléia da República and Comissão Técnica Independente. 2017. "Relatório: Análise e apuramento dos factos relativos aos incêndios que ocorreram em Pedrógão Grande, Castanheira de Pera, Ansião, Alvaiázere, Figuero dos Vinhos, Arganil, Gois, Penela, Pampilhosa da Serra, Oleiros e Serta, entre 17 e 24 de junho de 2017." Lisbon, Portugal.

Balch, Jennifer, Bethany Bradley, John Abatzoglou, Chelsea Nagy, Emily Fusco, and Adam Mahood. 2017. "Human-Started Wildfires Expand the Fire Niche across the United States." *PNSAS* 114 (11): 2946–2951.

Beebe, Craig W., and Stephen Wheeler. 2012. "Gold Country: The Politics of Landscape in Exurban El Dorado County, California." *Journal of Political Ecology* 19: 1–16.

Bento-Gonçalves, A., and A. Vieira. 2020. "Wildfires in the Wildland-Urban Interface: Key Concepts and Evaluation Methodologies." *Science of the Total Environment* 707.

Berg, Robert, and Joseph S. Cassells. 1992. Social Isolation among Older Individuals: The Relationship to Mortality and Morbidity. In *The Second Fifty Years: Promoting Health and Preventing Disability*. Robert L. Berg and Joseph Cassells, eds. Pp. 243–262. Washington, DC: National Academies Press (US).

Berube, A., A. Singer, J. Wilson, and W. Frey. 2006. "*Finding Exurbia: America's Fast-Growing Communities at the Metropolitan Fringe." Metropolitan Policy Program*. Washington, DC: Brookings Institution.

Brenkert-Smith, Hannah. 2011. "Homeowners' Perspectives on the Parcel Approach to Wildand Fire Mitigation: The Role of Community Context in Two Colorado Communities." *Journal of Forestry* 109 (4): 193–200.

Chico Enterprise Record. 2019. "85 Lives, 85 Stories: These Are the Lives That Ended in California's Deadliest Wildfire." *Chico Enterprise-Record*, November 7. https://extras.chicoer.com/campfireremembrances/

Cova, Thomas. 2005. "Public Safety in the Urban-Wildland Interface: Should Fire-Prone Communities Have a Maximum Occupancy?" *Natural Hazards Review*, 99–108.

Cudjoe, Thomas K.M., David L. Roth, Sarah L. Szanton, Jennifer L. Wolff, Cynthia M. Boyd, and Roland J. Thorpe Jr. 2020. "The Epidemiology of Social Isolation: National Health and Aging Trends Study." *The Journals of Gerontology: Series B*. https://doi.org/10.1093/geronb/gby037

Edgeley, Catrin, and Travis Paveglio. 2019. "Exploring Influences on Intended Evacuation Behaviors during Wildfire: What Roles for Pre-Fire Actions and Event-Based Cues?" *International Journal of Disaster Risk Reduction: IJDRR* 37: 101182.

Folk, Lauren, Erica Kuligowski, Steven Gwynne, and John Gales. 2019. "A Provisional Conceptual Model of Human Behavior in Response to Wildland-Urban Interface Fires." *Fire Technology* 55: 1619–47.

Gee, Alistair, and Dani Anguiano. 2020. *Fire in Paradise: An American Tragedy*. New York: W.W. Norton and Company.

Hilhorst, Dorothea, and Greg Bankoff. 2004. Introduction: Mapping Vulnerability. In *Mapping Vulnerability: Disasters, Development and People*. Greg Bankoff, Georg Frerks, and Dorothea Hilhorst, eds. Pp. 1–9. London: Routledge.

Kramer, H. Anu, Miranda H. Mockrin, Patricia M. Alexandre, and Volker C. Radeloff. 2019. "High Wildfire Damage in Interface Communities in California." *International Journal of Wildland Fire*. https://doi.org/10.1071/WF18108.

Lazarus, Naomi W. 2014. "Re-Specifying Disaster Risk: Concepts, Methods, and Models." *GeoJournal* 79 (5): 635–648.

Mann, Michael, Peter Berck, Max Moritz, Enric Batllori, James Baldwin, Conor Gately, and Richard Cameron. 2014. "Modeling Residential Development in California from 2000 to 2050: Integrating Wildfire Risk, Wildland and Agricultural Encroachment." *Land Use Policy* 41: 438–452.

McLennan, Jim, Barbara Ryan, Chris Bearman, and Keith Toh. 2019. "Should We Leave Now? Behavioral Factors in Evacuation Under Wildfire Threat." *Fire Technology* 55 (2): 487–516.

Méndez, Michael, Genevieve Flores-Haro, and Lucas Zucker. 2020. "The (in)Visible Victims of Disaster: Understanding the Vulnerability of Undocumented Latino/a and Indigenous Immigrants." *Geoforum* 116: 50–62.

Mijal, Samuel, and P. Willey. 2020. "Demography of the Camp Fire Fatalities." *Proceedings of the American Academy of Forensic Sciences*, February 20, p. 83.

Mockrin, Miranda H., Hillary Fishler, and Susan Stewart. 2018. "Does Wildfire Open a Policy Window? Local Government and Community Adaptation After Fire in the United States." *Environmental Management* 62: 210–228.

Paveglio, Travis, Jesse Abrams, and Autumn Ellison. 2016. "Developing Fire Adapted Communities: The Importance of Interactions among Elements of Local Context." *Society and Natural Resources* 29 (10): 1246–1261.

Paveglio, Travis, Pamela J. Jakes, Matthew Carroll, and Daniel R. Williams. 2009. "Understanding Social Complexity within the Wildland—Urban Interface: A New Species of Human Habitation?" *Environmental Management* 43: 1085–1095.

Paveglio, Travis B., Catrin M. Edgeley, and Amanda M. Stasiewicz. 2018. "Assessing Influences on Social Vulnerability to Wildfire Using Surveys, Spatial Data and Wildfire Simulations." *Journal of Environmental Management* 213: 425–439.

Ramsey, Michael L., Mark Murphy, and Juan Diaz. 2020. "The Camp Fire Public Report." *Butte County District Attorney*. www.buttecounty.net/Portals/30/CFReport/PGE-THE-CAMP-FIRE-PUBLIC-REPORT.pdf?ver=2020-06-15-190515-977

Superior Court of Butte County. 2020. "People of the State of California v. Pacific Gas & Electric." Case No. 20CF01422.

Tedim, Fantina, Vittorio Leone, Malik Amraoui, Christophe Bouillon, Michael Coughlan, Giuseppe Delogu, Paulo Fernandes, et al. 2018. "Defining Extreme Wildfire Events: Difficulties, Challenges, and Impacts." *Fire* 1. doi:10.3390/fire1010009.

United States Census. 2018. "American Community Survey. U.S. Census Bureau's American Community Survey Office." http://factfinder2.census.gov

Whittaker, Joshua, Katharine Haynes, John Handmer, and Jim McLennan. 2013. "Community Safety during the 2009 Australian 'Black Saturday' Bushfires: An Analysis of Household Preparedness and Response." *International Journal of Wildland Fire* 22: 841–849.

CHAPTER 21

Demographic Vulnerabilities and Wildfire Fatalities

P. Willey (with Samuel Mijal)

21.1 INTRODUCTION

As all disasters, wildfires are severe events that disrupt the environment, social networks, communities, and lives. Although wildfires have long-lasting, persistent impacts, among the most immediate concerns is the loss of human life. Identifying the demographic patterns of wildfire fatalities spotlights the groups most at risk and offers hope that they may be better protected and spared from future infernos.

Natural disasters are such overwhelmingly disruptive events that some authorities claim that all groups of people are equally at risk (Bocquet-Appel and Arsuaga 1999, Keckler 1997, Paine 2000, Chamberlain 2006). As a consequence, people in disasters should die equally whatever their demographic parameters. Variously called mass, crisis, disaster, and "living" mortality, deaths during disastrous conditions result in a mortality distribution that should resemble the entire population's age and sex census frequencies when the event occurred. A living population's age and sex distributions result from differences in fertility and mortality.

Under most everyday circumstances, however, common patterns of fertility and attritional mortality occur. They produce a predictable age and sex population profile, whose forms are broadly known and have been modeled (Brass 1971, Coale and Demeny 1983). By age, attritional mortality impacts the young and old more than the intervening age groups. When that mortality frequency is displayed graphically, the result is a U-shaped curve, with deaths of the young and old filling the two ends of the distribution. Although much of longevity is due to environmental constraints and behavioral patterns, heritable factors are also influential (e.g., Cohen et al. 2020, Timmers et al. 2020).

By sex, attritional mortality is greater among males than females. That difference begins in utero (McMillen 1979, Chahnazarian 1988, Rettaroli and Scalone 2021) and continues throughout life. Although typically outnumbering females at birth, greater male mortality happens at birth (Jakobovits et al. 1987) and persists unabated through childhood (Costa et al. 2021; Zarulli et al. 2021). Sustained higher male mortality occurs during adolescence (Costa and Victora 2021; see Perner et al. 2022 for a contrary example). In late adolescence and young adulthood, both sexes experience

DOI: 10.4324/9781003168010-26

increased mortality (Masquelier et al. 2021), largely from risk taking (Bozick 2022) with males in much greater peril than females. Higher probability of death continues to dog males as middle-aged adults. Then especially in old age (>65 years), males fail (Zarulli et al. 2021; Hägg and Jylhävä 2021). With such persistent male mortality throughout the life span, older cohorts have proportionally fewer males than females (Ritchie and Roser 2019).

In a nutshell, attritional mortality frequencies differ both by age and sex. Under normal circumstances, attritional mortality is greater in the young and old and in males. In classical catastrophic mortality, the resulting age and sex distributions resemble the living or census profile of the population. In a disaster, it is argued, all groups are equally represented among the dead.

The universality of this assertion about disaster demography has been questioned, however. As counterexamples, cholera deaths in Russian (1830–1912) disproportionately struck 20-to-59-year-olds (Hoch 1998); the elderly suffered more in a hurricane (Friedsam 1962), tornado (Glass 1980), and cyclone (Sommer and Mosley 1972); and males were impacted more than females in floods (Jonkman and Kelman 2005) and landslides (Pereira et al. 2016).

By identifying what groups suffer fatalities most frequently, this work considers whether wildfires result in catastrophic or attritional mortality profiles. More than just a hypothetical exercise, the results have important implications for understanding disasters and the accompanying mortalities. With that demographic foundation and groups most at-risk established, we can better plan, educate and anticipate, and implement practices that will improve survival in disasters. Revealing such generalities requires temporal and geographic comparisons. This chapter describes and compares the demography of recent California wildfire fatalities with earlier California wildfire victims and recent Australian bushfire deaths.

21.2 MATERIALS AND METHODS

Demographic mortality data come from recent and earlier California wildfires and the 2009 Australian bushfires. Missing data are also considered. As much as possible, these data consist of all fatalities, including those who are not identified after a fire or who are identified but lacking some demographic information.

21.2.1 Pre- and Post-1990 Fatal California Wildfires

To identify the California wildfires with the greatest numbers of fatalities, the 20 deadliest California fires through 2020 are employed (Figure 21.1, Table 21.1; California Department of Forestry and Fire Protection 2020; also see "Introduction," this volume, Table 3.1). For those fatal fires, online sources were searched for the victims' ages and sexes. (See Table 21.1 for principal sources). Statistics were calculated using SPSS. Comparative national and state demographic data come from the 2010 US Census (United States Census Bureau 2010).

For a historical comparison, we divide California wildfire victims by the date when the incident occurred, using 1990 to separate earlier from more recent fires. That date is selected because it includes the largest time gap between fatal fires: 23 years

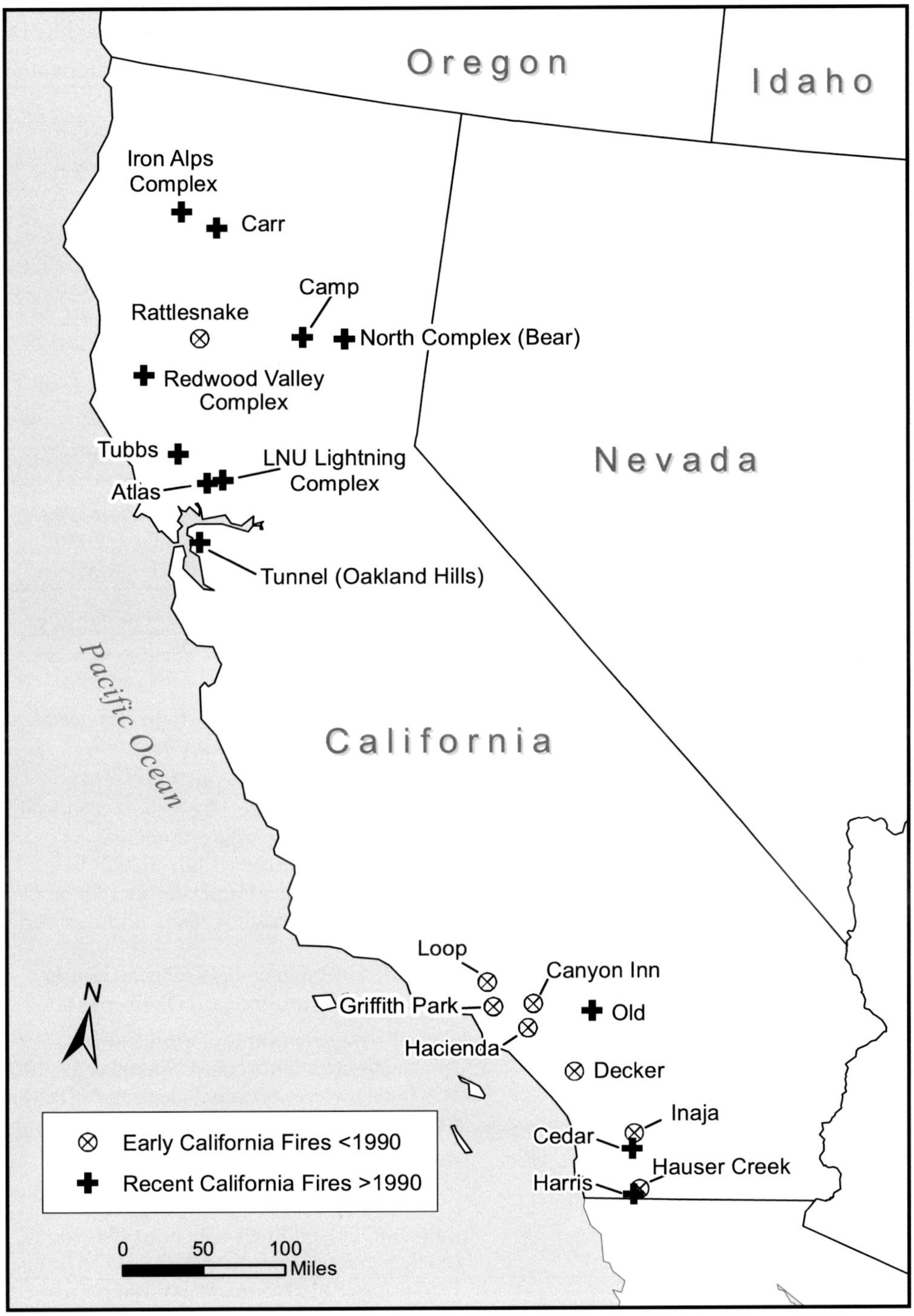

FIGURE 21.1 Map showing locations of deadliest recent (1990–2020) and early (1933–1989).

Source: Map drawn by Judy Stolen

TABLE 21.1 California Wildfires with the Greatest Number of Fatalities Arranged by Date

Fire	County	Date	Deaths	Principal Sources of Demographic Information
Older California Fatal Fires (<1990)				
Griffith Park	Los Angeles	1933	29	www.gendisasters.com/california/8214/los-angeles-ca-griffith-park-fire-oct-1933; accessed November 18, 2020
Hauser Creek	San Diego	1943	11	www.wlfalwaysremember.org/incident-lists/169-hauser-creek.html; accessed July 5, 2020 Ages from www.findagrave.com/virtual-cemetery/691656?page=1#sr-161149537; accessed July 5, 2020
Rattlesnake	Glenn	1953	15	https://wlfalwaysremember.org/incident-lists/481-rattlesnake-fire.html; accessed July 5, 2020
Hacienda	Los Angeles	1955	6	November 17.2020 www.findagrave.com/virtual-cemetery/691567?page=1#sr-161134067
Inaja	San Diego	1956	11	www.wlfalwaysremember.org/incident-lists/166-inaja-fire.html; accessed July 5, 2020 www.wildfirelessons.net/HigherLogic/System/DownloadDocumentFile.ashx?DocumentFileKey=bbdf2228-820f-e5ec-c0f7-6101290a03d3&forceDialog=0; accessed July 5, 2020
Decker	Riverside	1959	6	November 17, 2020, www.wlfalwaysremember.org/incident-lists/175-decker-fire.html.
Loop	Los Angeles	1966	12	www.pasadenastarnews.com/2016/11/01/its-been-50-years-since-12-hotshots-died-in-the-loop-fire-heres-how-family-survivors-remember-them; accessed July 5, 2020 file:///C:/Users/pwilley/AppData/Local/Temp/loop_fire_investigation_1966–1.pdf; accessed July 5, 2020 https://wlfalwaysremember.org/incident-lists/174-loop-fire.html, accessed October 6, 2020
Canyon	Los Angeles	1968	8	www.wlfalwaysremember.org/incident-lists/269-canyon-inn-fire.html; accessed November 17, 2020. www.findagrave.com/virtual-cemetery/691648; accessed November 17, 2020
			98	Total
Recent California Fatal Fires (>1990)				
Tunnel (Oakland Hills)	Alameda	1991	25	localwiki/Oakland/Firestorm. https://books.google.com/books?id=IeNGDQAAQBAJ&pg=PT167&lpg=PT167&dq=aina+turjanis&source=bl&ots=DBUgYYq4aG&sig=ACfU3U2znbdt4Kc_svQzABZUKnKgrpfMxA&hl=en&sa=X&ved=2ahUKEwjo1_Wdp7nqAhXSsJ4KHQeLD_EQ6AEwAHoECAoQAQ#v=onepage&q=aina%20turjanis&f=false

(*Continued*)

TABLE 21.1 (Continued)

Fire	County	Date	Deaths	Principal Sources of Demographic Information
Cedar	San Diego	2003	15	www.cbsnews.com/elements/2003/10/30/in_depth_nature/whoswho580954_0_1_pers. http://lakesidehistory.org/cedar-fire; accessed July 5, 2020
Old	San Bernadino	2003	6	https://web.archive.org/web/20100621034216/http://rimoftheworld.net/columns/neufeld/old_fire
Harris	San Diego	2007	8	www.latimes.com/archives/la-xpm-2007-nov-08-me-burn8-story.html https://voiceofsandiego.org/2007/10/23/additional-fatalities/
Iron Alps Complex	Trinity	2008	10	www.cbsnews.com/elements/2003/10/30/in_depth_nature/whoswho580954_0_1_pers
Tubbs	Napa, Sonoma	2017	22	www.kqed.org/news/11626796/north-bay-fires-fatalities-victims-list
Redwood Valley Complex	Mendocino	2017	9	https://mendovoice.com/2017/10/names-of-deceased-redwood-fire; accessed 7/14/2020
Atlas	Napa, Solano	2017	6	localwiki/Oakland/Firestorm
Camp	Butte	2018	85	Mijal and Willey in press
Carr	Shasta, Trinity	2018	8	https://en.wikipedia.org/wiki/Carr_Fire
LNU Complex	Colusa, Lake, Napa, Sonoma, Solano, Yolo	2020	6	www.dailyrepublic.com/all-dr-news/solano-news/fairfield/cal-fire-reports-lnu-complex-fire-33-percent-contained/ Accessed November 17, 2020. www.timesheraldonline.com/2020/09/02/three-fatalities-from-lnu-complex-fire-identified; accessed November 17, 2020 www.timesheraldonline.com/2020/09/02/three-fatalities-from-lnu-complex-fire-identified/
North Complex/ Bear	Plumas, Butte	2020	15 or 16	www.actionnewsnow.com/content/news/Bear-Fire-List-of-identified-victims-572406441.html
			215	Total

Source: California Department of Forestry and Fire Protection (2020)

from the 1968 Canyon Fire until the 1991 Oakland Tunnel/Hills Fire. That date occurs about midway in the time span and separates the top 20 deadliest wildfires into roughly equal halves. Finally, the natures of California fatal wildfires differ dramatically before and after 1990, with urban-wildland interface fires predominating in the more recent period.

21.2.2 Australian Black Saturday Bushfires Fatalities

For comparison, the February 7, 2009, Australian Black Saturday Bushfires fatalities provide an international perspective. These fires in Victoria, Australia (Figure 21.2), constitute the natural disaster with the most fatalities in recent Australian history. Extreme heat, low humidity, and strong winds resulted in several major fires spotted across southeastern Australia. The fast-moving flames consumed 1.1 million acres, destroyed over 3,500 buildings, and killed 173 people. (See Xanthopoulos and Galloway, this volume, for more details). Bushfire fatality demographic information comes from the Victorian Bushfire Royal Commission Final Report (2010), supplemented by other documents that the commission produced.

21.2.3 Missing Data

As a major challenge, some wildfire victims remain unidentified while some others are identified but lack specific demographic information. These omissions and absences require analytical compromises. Consequently, in these analyses, I use what information

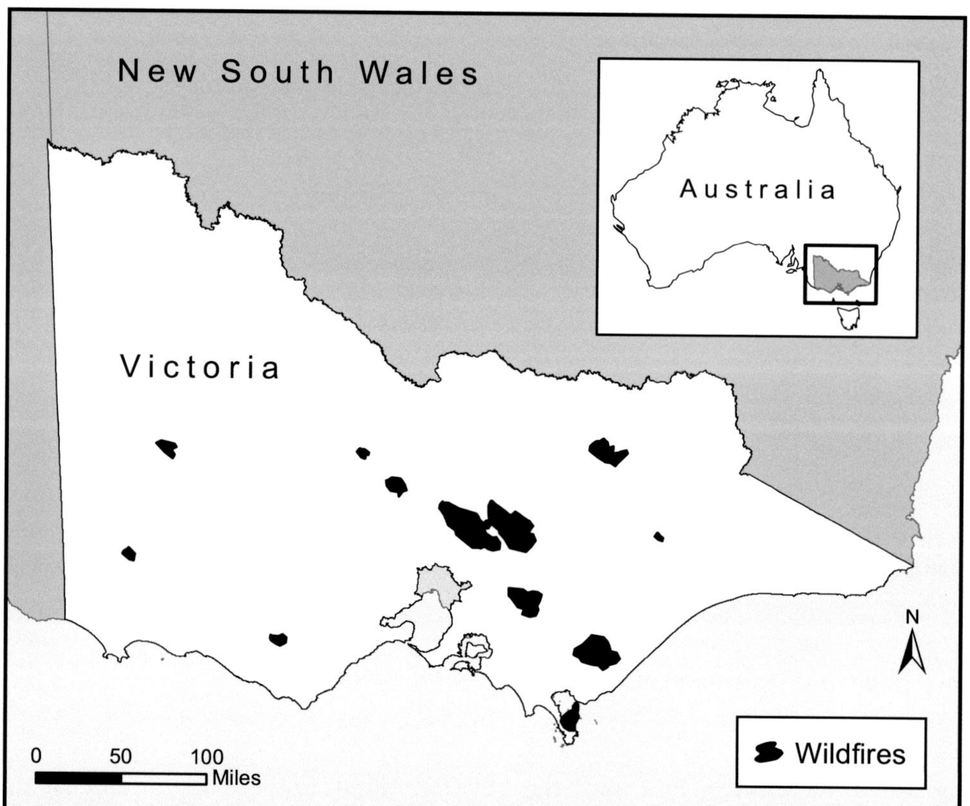

FIGURE 21.2 Map showing location of 2009 Australian Black Saturday Bushfires.

Source: Map drawn by Judy Stolen

is present, available, and appropriate for the questions at hand. Number of fatalities include all persons, whether they were identified or not. Assessments involving sex include all fatalities with established sex, whether age was known or not. Age considerations employ the documented number of completed years that the decedent lived. As a consequence of these compromises, the counts for the various parameters (number of fatalities, known sex, known age) differ depending on the demographic information available. The discussion section of this chapter considers additional limitations.

21.3 RESULTS

21.3.1 Recent (1990–2020) California Wildfire Fatalities

From 1990 to 2020, 215 Californians died in 12 wildfires. Of that number, 213 (99.1%) have been identified, and age and sex information are available.

The ages of the recent California fire fatalities vary from 4 to 101 years (Figure 21.3), with a mean of 63.62 years. No infants, and few children and adolescents died in the blazes. Tragic exceptions include two children ages 4 and 5 years who succumbed in the 2018 Carr Fire and adolescents in the 2003 Cedar, 2017 Redwood Valley and 2020 Bear fires. Adolescents (12 to 18 years), account for 4.2% (n = 9) of the identified fatalities. The few young adult deaths mostly occur among firefighters (e.g., 2008 Iron Alps). At the other end of the age spectrum, older adults represent a large proportion of the victims. Nearly half (46.0%, n = 98) of identified recent California fire fatalities were 70 years or older. A statistically significant difference between ages in the 2010 census and California wildfire fatalities exists (Kolmogorov-Smirnov test), with older individuals overrepresented in the fatalities.

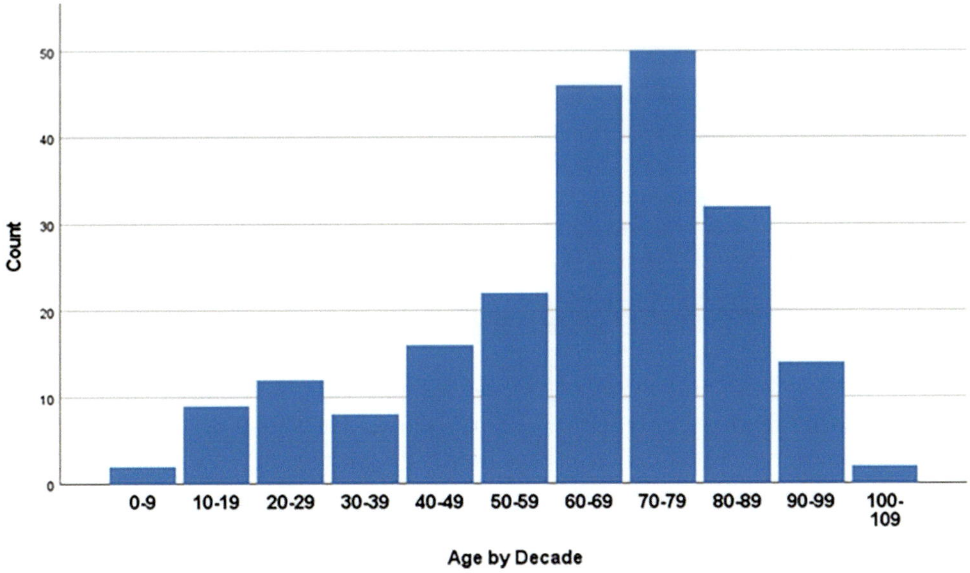

FIGURE 21.3 Ages of recent California wildfire fatalities by decade. Note that most fatalities occur in the older age intervals.

By sex, recent California female fatalities account for 46.2% of the total and male fatalities the other 53.7%. The 2010 US Census indicates the percentage of female Californians as 50.3% and male Californians as 49.7%, resulting in a statistical difference between the overall California population and recent wildfire fatalities ($\chi^2 = 41.3841$, df = 1, P = ~0.000). Males more frequently perish in recent California wildfires than their numbers in the general population would suggest.

21.3.2 Early (1933–89) and Recent California Wildfire Fatalities

In the overall California wildfire fatalities including both recent and early periods (1933 to 2020), a total 313 people died in the 20 deadliest wildfires. Marked differences occurred among the deadliest California wildfires depending on the period. Spanning 56 years, the early fires caused 98 deaths while, in the last 30 years, 215 individuals perished. That difference represents a quadrupling in the annual average number from 1.75 fatalities per year in the early period to 7.2 deaths per year in the recent period.

In addition to the increasing average annual fatalities, geographic differences exist between the two periods (Figure 21.1). All of the 20 deadliest California wildfires occurred either in Northern or Southern California, none in Central California. A less distinctive time separation also occurs. In Northern California, all but one of the fatal fires (1953 Rattlesnake Fire) occurred recently, while in Southern California all but three fires (2003 Cedar, 2003 Old, and 2007 Harris Fires) occurred during the early period. This distribution suggests that life-threatening fires have shifted from the chemise and chaparral-chocked Southern California northward into the forested foothills of Northern California.

Of the 98 fatalities in the early California wildfires, 74 (75.5%) have identities and at least some demographic information. Almost all of those 24 unknown persons come from the 1933 Griffith Park Fire (n = 23). The ages of the identified early California wildfire fatalities vary from 16 to 45 years, with a mean of 26.34 years (n = 68; Figure 21.4). No infants or children died in the early blazes. In early California fires, however, the most vulnerable groups proved to be young adults, most of whom served as firefighters. Particularly tragic, adolescents from nearby probation camps (1968 Canyon and 1955 Hacienda Fires) were thrown into fight fires and suffered the ultimate penalties. (See discussion this chapter and Chapter 1, "Introduction," in this volume for more details on firefighter losses.)

The ages of early California wildfire fatalities differ markedly from those of recent California wildfire victims ($t = 24.025$, df = 268.399, $P < 0.001$). Early wildfire victims averaged 37.23 years younger than their more recent counterparts. Even when comparing early wildfire fatalities only with recent California male fatalities (excluding recent female fatalities), the statistical difference holds ($t = 14.994$, df = 160.270, $p < 0.001$). That difference doubtlessly derives from the early period's young adult firefighter fatalities.

Considering sex, all early California wildfire fatalities were male. Not a single female perished. The absence of female fatalities is likely due to gender roles during early times and the risks associated with firefighting.

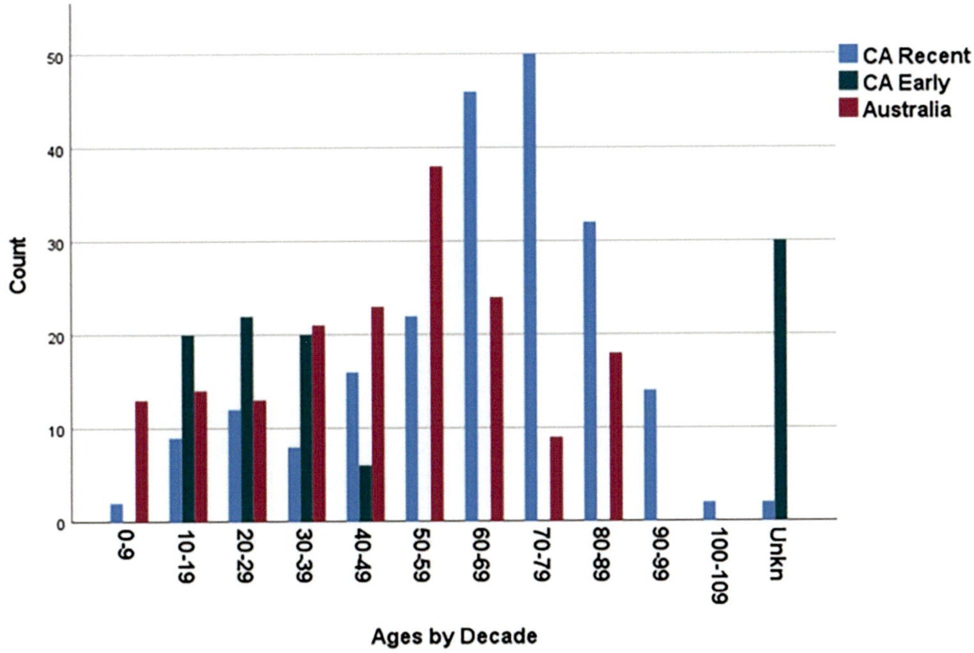

FIGURE 21.4 Ages of wildfire fatalities compared. CA Recent = recent (>1990) California wildfire fatalities, CA Early = early (<1990) California wildfire fatalities, Australia = 2009 Black Saturday Bushfire fatalities, Unkn = fatalities with unknown ages. Note large numbers of older fatalities in recent California wildfires, large numbers of adolescents/young adult and unidentified fatalities in early California wildfires, and large numbers of middle-aged adults in Australia bushfires.

21.3.3 Australian Black Saturday Bushfires and Recent California Wildfire Fatalities

Among the 173 Australian Black Saturday fatalities, all have been identified and have demographic data. They vary in age from 22 months to 88 years (Figure 21.4), with a mean of 47.21 years. A comparison of fatality ages with census information from the 2009 fire-affected area indicates two major differences. First, children and teenagers are underrepresented in the bushfire fatalities; they make up only 15.5% of the fatalities but constitute 31% of the population in the fire-affected area.[1] Second, middle-aged and older adults (>50 years) are overrepresented in the bushfire fatalities; they make up 51.1% of the fatalities but only constitute 31% of the population in the fire-affected area. Greater fatalities in that adult age group is attributed to able-bodied, middle-aged adults staying in the fire zone to defend property (Handmer et al. 2010). Older adults (>70 years) suffered the most. They amounted to almost twice as many fatalities (15.5%) as that age group constitutes in the fire-affected area census (8%). Greater fatalities in that older adult age group resulted from older individuals having challenges in mobility, stamina, and decision-making capacity (Handmer et al. 2010).

The Australian fatalities' ages are younger than the recent California wildfire fatalities ($t = 7.323$, $df = 384$, $P < 0.001$). The mean age of the Australian fatalities

(47.21 years) is more than a decade and a half younger than the recent California mean age (63.62 years).

Moving from age to sex, more males than females perished in the Black Saturday Bushfires. A total of 73 females (42.2%) and 100 males (57.8%) succumbed. In contrast, in the fire-affected area, the population was 49.2% females and 50.8% male, a significant difference from the bushfire fatalities ($\chi^2 = 10.4489$, df = 1, P = 0.001227). In particular, fatalities in age group 50–59 years showed an exaggerated sex discrepancy: 24 (63.2%) males and 14 (36.8%) females (Handmer et al. 2010:27). Comparing these Australian sex results to recent California fire fatalities, the sex distributions are similar ($\chi^2 = 0.640$, df = 1, P = 0.424).

These disproportional numbers of Australian male fatalities are attributed to more adult males remaining in the area to defend property and pursue other risky pursuits while females chose to evacuate (Handmer et al. 2010:8; Eriksen 2014a, 2014b; Whittaker et al. 2016). Males' reluctance to evacuate early and inability to defend homes in an overwhelming megafire caused their disproportionate deaths.

Decisions to remain behind had been influenced by Australia's "stay and defend or leave early" policy. That policy was established following the 1984 Australian Ash Wednesday Bushfires. Last-minute evacuations and resulting traffic jams caused as many as a third of those attempting to escape to die in their vehicles or while fleeing on foot (Haynes et al. 2008). Those losses were supplemented by evidence that actively protected houses stood ten times more likely to survive as well as their defenders (Ramsay et al. 1996). Following the 2009 Black Saturday tragedy, however, the policy was revised to a more open-ended "prepare, act, and survive" (Victorian Bushfire Royal Commission 2010).

21.4 DISCUSSION, COMPARISONS, AND LIMITATIONS

This section compares fatalities in California wildfires and Australian bushfires with those in other locations. Deaths by age, sex, disability, social factors, and occupation are considered. The final portion of this section presents limitations of this analysis.

21.4.1 Age

The age of wildfire-related fatalities has a different distribution than the censuses. Proceeding from young to old, relatively few subadult fatalities occur compared with their proportion in the population. Supporting the present work, infants and children fare well in all kinds of recent US fires (US Fire Administration 2019). Adolescents become more vulnerable but still are underrepresented among overall wildfire fatalities. As tragic as they are when they happen, relatively few subadult (<18 years) deaths occur, presumably because their caretakers make early decisions and take prudent steps to safeguard their charges. Youth are kept out of harm's way.

Notable exceptions to safety among adolescents do occur. Institutional youths served as firefighters and died in two early California fires. In the 1955 Hacienda Fire, five members of the Los Angeles County Youth Probation Forestry Camp Crew 5–1 and a fire captain attempting to rescue them died. A similar disaster occurred again in 1968, when seven "juvenile delinquents" on probation and their foreman from the Los

Angeles County Youth Probation Forestry Camp Crew 4–4 died in the Canyon Fire. Following these fatalities, the Los Angeles County Fire Department discontinued using probationary youth to battle wildfires.

At the other end of the age spectrum from subadults, disproportionately large numbers of elderly wildfire fatalities occur in both recent groups. In addition, the 1983 Ash Wednesday Bushfire (Haynes et al. 2008, cited in Handmer et al. 2010) killed disproportionate numbers of elderly. Also in the Mediterranean region, elderly prove vulnerable in wildfires. They are more likely to die in Greece during the 2000 Haraugi Fire (Xanthopoulos 2007, 2015) and in a Greek historical survey (1977–2013; Diakakis et al. 2016). More broadly in the Mediterranean region, a historical survey (1945–2006) of southern Europe (Greece, Italy, Spain, and Portugal) finds elderly civilians over-represented among the fatalities (Molina-Terrén et al. 2019).

More generally the elderly have proven vulnerable in dire circumstances other than wildfires. Their numbers are over-represented among fatalities in all kinds of recent US fires (US Fire Administration 2015, 2019). Powell et al. (2009) found the elderly one of the most impacted groups in natural disasters and conflicts. And elderly suffer more in other catastrophic events, such as hurricanes and cyclones (Friedsam 1962, Rappaport 2000, Sommer and Mosley 1972), tornados (Glass 1980), and flooding (Ashley and Ashley 2008).

21.4.2 Sex

The trends in vulnerability by sex are even clearer than those by age. Male fatalities in wildfires almost always exceed female fatalities. This statement is true in all three of our study groups, with the early California wildfires displaying absolutely no female fatalities—none at all.

Looking farther afield, bushfires preceding the Australian Black Saturday find similar sex distortion among earlier fatalities (Handmer et al. 2010:27; Haynes et al. 2008, Blanchi et al. 2014). Considering all kinds of US fire-related deaths, a recent survey shows male fatalities exceed females (US Fire Administration 2019).

In the Mediterranean region, a Greek historical summary (1977–2013) finds more males dying in wildfires; the observation remains true even when excluding the predominantly male firefighters and considering civilians alone (Diakakis et al. 2016). Civilian males are also more at-risk in a longer (1945–2006), broader geographic (Greece, Italy, Spain, and Portugal) survey. When firefighter fatalities are included with that assessment of civilians, the sex discrepancy jumps (Molina-Terrén et al. 2019). With firefighters added to the calculation, male fatalities exceed 80% (males 83.4%, female 16.6).

An exception to this frail male trend occurs. In the 2018 Camp Fire, female wildfire fatalities outnumber male fatalities, 44 to 41. Perhaps this observation is due to the fatalities' older ages, into which few males survive (see Hegel et al., "Demographics and Locational Analyses of Wildfire Victims," this volume; Mijal and Willey 2022).

21.4.3 Societal Disability and Physical Impairment

Although difficult to assess with the present data sets, disability or impairment is often associated with vulnerabilities and increased death frequencies in disasters. The disabled suffer more in many kinds of disasters (Fjord and Manderson 2009, Alexander et al. 2012), such as earthquakes (Chou et al. 2004), hurricanes (McGuire et al. 2007), and floods (Jonkman and Kelman 2005)—and of course wildfires.

Using a subset of this wildfire base sample in an earlier work, we found the impaired at particular risk (Mijal and Willey 2022). During the 2018 Camp Fire in California, more than 40% of the fatalities appeared to have suffered disability. Most frequently they had ambulatory issues, followed by cognitive problems, and difficulties living unaided.

In the US, considering all fire-related fatalities (2008–17), the disabled were found to be more vulnerable (US Fire Administration 2019). In addition, fire deaths are greater in US areas with larger proportions of disability (Ahrens 2019).

In the Australian Black Saturday Bushfires, nearly a quarter of the victims had chronic health problems and an additional 5% suffered acute disability (Handmer et al. 2010). Taken together about 30% of the fatalities had disabilities that limited their abilities to make decisions and to escape the flames.

In Greece, the mobility-impaired and their caretakers are at risk (Xanthopoulos 2007). There, as well as elsewhere, those with ambulatory issues require assistance evacuating and make them vulnerable (Fahey et al. 2016).

Often disability is not a sole, independent factor. Being elderly and having a disability increase vulnerability in many different natural disasters (McGuire et al. 2007). Older adults tend to be more frequently impaired, both through the normal wear and tear associated with aging as well as from disabilities that tend to accumulate toward the end of life.

Curiously, though, the most severely disabled are at reduced risk in disasters. They often live in hospitals or other care facilities that have plans for evacuations and move their charges to safer locations in timely manners (Saliba et al. 2004, Robin 2000). Those older adults who live relatively independent lives, are housebound with mobility challenges, have disabilities and illnesses, need special medical equipment, and require assistance to evacuate are more at risk than these people living under direct medical care and supervision (Fernandez et al. 2002, Morrow 1999).

21.4.4 Some Social Factors

This work has emphasized demographic and physical attributes contributing to wildfire fatalities. On the other hand, it is clear that many wildfire risk factors occur from cultural/social aspects, such as socioeconomic status, housing, escape routes, information availability, transportation, support mechanisms, and social networks. Many other studies have considered socio-cultural vulnerabilities to wildfire (Charnley et al. 2015, Kolden and Henson. 2019, Wigtil, et al. 2016), as well as disasters more generally (Barrios 2017, Oliver-Smith 1999, Oliver-Smith and Hoffman. 2002). Social aspects prove pivotal, especially social networks and occupations.

Social networks are important. Families, familiars, and friends provide information, are relied upon in stressful times, give assistance, and make collective decisions. Along those lines, we have already considered children and caretakers' roles in the US and Australian bushfires. So when group decisions are made, members of the group tend to survive or die together. As a tragic example of the latter, among the 2018 Camp Fire victims were the three Hefferns. They consisted of the grandmother/mother, the daughter/mother, and the granddaughter/daughter. The three failed to evacuate and their remains were found commingled in a bathtub (Ramsey 2020).

For the most part, however, individuals lacking developed social networks are particularly at risk during wildfires. They tend to be isolated, have less information, and make poorer decisions in catastrophic events. Concerning the Black Saturday Australian victims, Handmer et al. (2010:8) conclude, "A small number of fatalities appear to have been at least somewhat reclusive; with only very occasional communication with family, neighbours or the community." Compounding risk, the elderly in particular tend to have fewer social contacts (Berg and Cassells 1992, Cudjoe et al. 2020, National Academies of Sciences, Engineering, and Medicine. 2020).

21.4.5 Firefighters

In addition to social networks, some professions involve greater exposure to wildfire danger, in particular the people mobilized to fight fires. Early California fatalities show an overwhelmingly disproportionate number of firefighter deaths. Fortunately, both the more recent California wildfire and Australian bushfire fatalities have proportionally fewer firefighter fatalities than in earlier times (Haynes et al. 2010, Blanchi et al. 2014). Despite the decrease in firefighter deaths in both recent California and Australia, firefighters remain at risk. As examples, in the California 1991 Oakland Tunnel Fire, a fireman and police officer died; in the 2008 Iron Alps Fire, a helicopter crash and falling tree killed ten firefighters.

Firefighters in other parts of the world have fared worse. Recent (1945–2016) Mediterranean region fatalities (Molina-Terrén et al. 2019: 92, table 5) show almost half of those fatalities involved people who were combating fire (firefighters, volunteers, plane crews, forest service officials). Firefighting was and remains a dangerous occupation (Mangan 2007).

Firefighter fatalities tend to be male. Before and through much of the 20th century, firefighting was stereotyped as "man's work," so few opportunities for female firefighters existed. In the US, the California Department of Forestry formed the earliest all-woman wildland firefighting crew in 1942 (Women in Fire n.d.), but their numbers were few and no wildfire fatalities have occurred in either the earlier or more recent periods.

21.4.6 Limitations

As all projects, challenges plague this research. They include inadequate identifications, number of deaths, and differences in defining fatalities.

Lack of identifications occurred, especially among the early California wildfire victims. As an extreme example, the 1933 Griffith Park Fire stands out. Of the 29 dead in the Griffith Park, only six (20.7%) were identified by name, and only five of those six individuals had associated ages. The other 23 (79.3%) lacked identification and all associated demographic information. Working on the Griffith Park Reconstruction Finance Corporation project when the fire ignited, those unidentified individuals probably tended to be younger, less socially established males. Had their demographic data been available, it probably would have shown even more forcefully the vulnerability of adolescent and young adult males in early California wildfires. Even in later times with much improved identification techniques, locating demographic information proved challenging. As an example, in the 1968 Canyon Fire the dead totaled eight, but only three of them were associated with exact ages, another two with approximate ages, and three with no ages at all. Recent California fires also have missing age data but to a much lesser extent than that earlier fire.

The number of dead in some fires remains uncertain. As an example, again the 1933 Griffith Park Fire is notable. The District Attorney's Office established the official number of dead as 29. However, the chair of the International Labor Defense League's investigating committee set the number of deaths at 58—double the official count (Eberts 1993).

The recent 2018 Camp Fire serves as another example of clashing body counts. Beyond the 85 persons who officially died in the blaze, an additional 50 deaths have been attributed to the fire. These additional deaths occurred following the victims' escape from the inferno (Associated Press 2020). As an example, the claim mentions a 95-year-old woman who was recuperating in the area following surgery when the fire occurred. She evacuated to a safe facility, where she caught norovirus and died. The death certificate indicates cerebrovascular hypertension as the cause of death. Although not officially included in the Camp Fire death count, these drastically different definitions reflect disparities in what constitutes wildfire fatalities.

So what is a wildfire fatality? Most wildfire fatalities result from direct thermal exposure and/or smoke inhalation. Some other wildfire deaths occur from fire-related activities (e.g., firefighters in 2008 Iron Alps helicopter crash). Other fire-related deaths prove even more indirect. As an example, several of the 2003 Old Fire fatalities died of heart attacks, which were considered triggered by the fire and stress related to evacuation.

Some of the Australian bushfire fatalities are attributed to heart attack, vehicle accident drowning, and electrocution (Handmer et al. 2010, Haynes et al. 2010). In Spain about one-third of those wildfire-related fatalities involve aircraft and accidents (Cardil and Molina 2015).

Among the most tangential fire-related fatalities, one 2007 Harris Fire fatality (Suzanne Elizabeth Casey; Voice of San Diego 2007) had safely evacuated from the fire zone and was staying in a hotel, but she fell when leaving a restaurant and died from the resulting head injury. Authorities included her as one of the fire victims.

Lack of identifications, missing demographic information, number of deaths, and differences in defining wildfire fatalities constitute challenges to this work. How counts are established and who is a wildfire fatality have important ramifications for comparability among data sets and the conclusions that rely on uniformity among data sets.

21.5 SUMMARY AND CONCLUSIONS

Returning to the central questions of this work, who constitute the most vulnerable groups in wildfires and how are their deaths demographically distributed? Do those fatalities follow an attritional or a catastrophic pattern?

To review, recent California wildfire and Australian bushfire fatalities prove to be disproportionately elderly adults, while early California wildfires disproportionately killed adolescents and young adults. Over the intervening decades, firefighting approaches and protection of firefighters have improved, making firefighters safer, at least in some countries. The recent rise in elderly fatalities suggests that greater numbers of older inhabitants have moved into wildland-urban interfaces, thereby increasing their exposure to wildfires. In addition to old age, elderly persons are more prone to mobility and cognitive difficulties as well as social isolation, compounding their vulnerability and making them more likely to become wildfire victims.

Considering sex, almost universally across time and space, males fare more poorly in wildfires than females. They should be labeled as "frail males." In recent years there has been decreased male vulnerability, but they still remain proportionally more at risk than females.

Using that summary as a foundation, we return to the central issue of whether the wildfire deaths represent a catastrophic or attritional mortality pattern. The findings show that wildfire fatalities' demography is neither entirely classically catastrophic nor entirely attritional. Examining ages of wildfire fatalities, subadults (<18 years) usually fare well, yielding fewer fatalities than either model would predict. On the contrary, the elderly are over-represented in wildfire fatalities. An attritional model predicts that the old and young would die in greater numbers, but instead of a U-shaped mortality curve, wildfire fatality age distribution forms a modified reversed L-shaped distribution. Youngsters are under-represented and elderly over-represented. The classical catastrophic model predicts that all ages die in the proportions that they occur in the census. Clearly that is not the case, either.

Considering wildfire fatalities' sex distribution, more males die in wildfires than females. While broadly in keeping with the attritional model, males die in exaggerated numbers, not typical of attrition. In a classical catastrophic model, both sexes should experience losses equally. Clearly that is not the case either. So neither attritional nor catastrophic models reflect wildfire fatalities' age or sex distributions. Wildfire mortality is nuanced and variable.

To identify and protect the most vulnerable demographic groups, we need to consider predictions and forecasts. Vulnerability changes. Recent decades in areas with Mediterranean climates show an increasing number of wildfire fatalities. This trend is likely to accelerate. Exacerbating factors include an environment continuing to dry, more short-term periodic droughts, lengthening of the fire season, seasonally high winds, expansion of the urban-wildland interface into fire-prone foothills and mountain, and increasing numbers of elderly and impaired. A flexible approach is required to identifying what demographic groups are at risk, as well as in planning, educating, training, and executing evacuations.

ACKNOWLEDGMENTS

I welcomed Ashley Kendell. Alison Galloway, and Colleen Milligan's invitation to contribute this chapter for their volume, and I appreciate Alison and Ashley's edits. Initially, Samuel Mijal collaborated on the effort, but his life took a turn and he followed a different path. When he was unable to continue contributing, he relinquished and graciously stepped down. While active, Sam collected the Australian demographic data, calculated preliminary statistics, and outlined many of the paper's principal points. This project continued to be fun without him, but it would have been even better with him. Judy Stolen drew the maps. I take full responsibility for any errors, omissions or sins.

NOTE

1. For a contrary claim indicating children (<12 years) were at greater risk in the Australian Black Saturday Fire, see Handmer et al. (2010:16). Although listing children among the most vulnerable population segments, their table shows the opposite. Those numbers indicate half the child fatalities expected based on the fire-affected area's census (Handmer et al. 2010:28–29). Our data support this revised conclusion.

REFERENCES

Ahrens, Marty. (2019). *US Fire Death Rates by State*. Quincy, MA: National Fire Protection Association.

Alexander, D., J.C. Gaillard, and B. Wisner. (2012). Disability and Disaster. In *Routledge Handbook. Hazards Disaster Risk Reduction*, edited by B. Wisner, J. Gaillard, and I. Kelman, 413–423. New York: Routledge.

Ashley S.T., and W.S. Ashley. (2008). Flood Casualties in the United States. *Journal of Applied Meteorology and Climatology* 47: 805–818. doi:10.1175/2007JAMC1611.

Associated Press. (2020). Death Toll Camp Fire Likely Includes 50 More People: Report, February 12. www.nbcbayarea.com/news/local/death-toll-in-camp-fire-likely-includes-50-more-people-report/2232783/.

Barrios, R.E. (2017). What Does Catastrophe Reveal for Whom? The Anthropology of Crises and Disasters at the Onset of the Anthropocene. *Annual Review of Anthropology* 46: 151–166.

Berg, Robert, and Joseph S. Cassells. (1992). Social Isolation among Older Individuals: The Relationship to Mortality and Morbidity. In *The Second Fifty Years: Promoting Health and Preventing Disability*, edited by Robert L. Berg and Joseph Cassells, 243–262. Washington, DC: National Academies Press.

Blanchi, R., J. Leonard, K. Haynes, K. Opie, M. James, and F.D. de Oliveira. (2014). Environmental Circumstances Surrounding Bushfire Fatalities in Australia 1901–2011. *Environmental Science & Policy* 37: 192–203.

Bocquet-Appel, J.P. and J.L. Arsuaga. (1999). Age Distributions of Hominid Samples at Atapuerca (SH) and Krapina Could Indicate Accumulation by Catastrophe. *Journal of Archaeological Science* 26(3): 327–338.

Bozick, R. (2022). Ambient Air Temperature, Air Quality and the Timing of Excess Mortality among Young Men in the United States. *Human Ecology* 50(2): 373–383.

Brass, W. (1971). On the Scale of Mortality. In *Biological Aspects of Demography*, edited by W. Brass, 69–110. London: Taylor and Francis.

California Department of Forestry and Fire Protection. (2020). Top 20 Deadliest California Wildfires. www.fire.ca.gov/media/5512/top20_deadliest.pdf (accessed October 5, 2020).

Cardil, A., and D.M. Molina. (2015). Factors Causing Victims of Wildland Fires in Spain (1980–2010). *Human and Ecological Risk Assessment: An International Journal* 21: 67–80. doi:10.1080/10807039.2013.871995

Chahnazarian, A. (1988). Determinants of the Sex Ratio at Birth: Review of Recent Literature. *Social Biology* 35(3–4): 214–235.

Chamberlain, Andrew. (2006). *Demography in Archaeology*. Cambridge: Cambridge University Press.

Charnley, S., M.R. Poe, A.A. Ager, T.A. Spies, E.K. Platt, and K.A. Olsen. (2015). A Burning Problem: Social Dynamics of Disaster Risk Reduction through Wildfire Mitigation. *Human Organization* 74(4): 329–340.
Chou, Y.J., N. Huang, C.H. Lee, S.L. Tsai, L.S. Chen, and H.J. Chang. (2004). Who Is at Risk of Death in an Earthquake? *American Journal of Epidemiology* 160(7): 688–695.
Coale, A.J., and P. Demeny. (1983). *Regional Model Life Tables and Stable Populations*. 2nd edition. Orlando: Academic Press.
Cohen, A.A., B.K. Kennedy, U. Anglas, A.M. Bronikowski, J. Deelen, F. Dufour, G. Ferbeyre, L. Ferrucci, C. Franceschi, D. Frasca, and B. Friguet. (2020). Lack of Consensus on an Aging Biology Paradigm? A Global Survey Reveals an Agreement to Disagree, and the Need for an Interdisciplinary Framework. *Mechanisms of Ageing and Development* 191: 111316.
Costa, J.C., A.M. Weber, S. Abdalla, G.L. Darmstadt, and C.G. Victora. (2021). Levels and Potential Drivers of Under-five Mortality Sex Ratios in Low- and Middle-income Countries. *Paediatric and Perinatal Epidemiology* 35(5): 549–556.
Costa, J.C., and C.G. Victora. (2021). A Scoping Review of Methods for Assessment of Sex Differentials in Early Childhood Mortality. *BMC Pediatrics* 21(1): 1–17.
Cudjoe, Thomas K.M., David L. Roth, Sarah L. Szanton, Jennifer L. Wolff, Cynthia M. Boyd, and Roland J. Thorpe, Jr. (2020). The Epidemiology of Social Isolation: National Health and Aging Trends Study. *Journals of Gerontology: Social Sciences Series B* 75(1): 107–113.
Diakakis, M., G. Xanthopoulos, and L. Gregos. (2016). Analysis of Forest Fire Fatalities in Greece: 1977–2013. *International Journal of Wildland Fire* 25(7): 797–809.
Eberts, Mike. (1993). The Fire of '33. http://lafire.com/famous_fires/MajorIncident-index.htm (Accessed November 19, 2020); file:///C:/Users/pwilley/AppData/Local/Temp/1933_Griffith_Park_Fire_Story_Eberts_1993.pdf
Eriksen, C. (2014a). *Gender and Wildfire: Landscapes of Uncertainty*. New York: Routledge.
Eriksen, C. (2014b). Gendered Risk Engagement: Challenging the Embedded Vulnerability, Social Norms and Power Relations in Conventional Australian Bushfire Education. *Geographical Research* 52: 23–33.
Fahey, E, C. Lehna, C. Hanchette, and M.B. Coty. (2016). Geographic Mapping as a Tool for Identifying Communities at High Risk for Fires. *Journal of Burn Care & Research* 37(4): e303–e309. https://doi.org/10.1097/BCR.0000000000000303
Fernandez, L.S., D. Byard, C.C. Lin, S. Benson and J.A. Barbera. (2002). Frail Elderly as Disaster Victims: Emergency Management Strategies. *Prehospital and Disaster Medicine* 17(2): 67–74.
Fjord, L., and L. Manderson. (2009). Anthropological Perspectives on Disasters and Disability: An Introduction. *Human Organization* 68(1): 64–72.
Friedsam, H.J. (1962). Older Persons in Disaster. In *Man and Society in Disaster*, edited by G.W. Baker and D.W. Chapman, 151–184. New York: Basic Books.
Glass, R.I. (1980). Injuries from the Wichita Falls Tornado: Implications for Prevention. *Science* 207: 734–738.
Hägg, S., and J. Jylhävä. (2021). Sex Differences in Biological Aging with a Focus on Human Studies. *Elife* 10: e63425.
Handmer, John, Saffron O'Neil, and Damien Killalea. (2010). *Review of Fatalities in the February 7, 2009, Bushfires*. Centre for Risk and Community Safety, Bushfire Cooperative Research Centre, Royal Melbourne Institute of Technology University. www.bushfirecrc.com/sites/default/files/managed/resource/review-fatalities-february-7.pdf (accessed December 24, 2020).

Haynes, K., J. Handmer, J. McAneney, A. Tibbits, and L. Coates. (2010). Australian Bushfire Fatalities 1900–2008: Exploring Trends in Relation to the Prepare, Stay and Defend or Leave Early "Policy." *Environmental Science & Policy* 13(3): 185–194.

Haynes, K., A. Tibbits, L. Coates, G. Ganewatta, J. Handmer, and J. McAneney. (2008). 100 Years of Australian Civilian Bushfire Fatalities: Exploring the Trends in Relation to the "Stay or Go Policy." Report for the Bushfire Centre for Risk and Community. https://www.researchgate.net/publication/242556183_100_years_of_Australian_civilian_bushfire_fatalities_exploring_the_trends_in_relation_to_the_'stay_or_go_policy' (accessed October 2022).

Hoch, Steven L. (1998). Famine, Disease, and Mortality Patterns in the Parish of Borshevka, Russia, 1830–1912. *Population Studies* 52(3): 357–368.

Jakobovits, A., Á.A. Jakobovits, and A. Viski. (1987). Sex Ratio of the Stillborn Fetuses and Neonates Dying in the First Week. *Early Human Development* 15(3): 131–135.

Jonkman, Sebastiaan N., and Ilan Kelman. (2005). An Analysis of the Causes and Circumstances of Flood Disaster Deaths. *Disasters* 29(1): 75–97. doi:10.1111/j.0361-3666.2005.00275.x

Keckler, C.N.W. (1997). Catastrophic Mortality in Simulations of Forager Age-at-Death: Where Did All the Humans Go? In *Integrating Archaeological Demography: Multidisciplinary Approaches to Prehistoric Populations* (Occasional Paper No. 24), edited by R.R. Paine, 205–228. Carbondale: Center for Archaeological Investigations, Southern Illinois University.

Kolden, C.A., and C. Henson. (2019). A Socio-Ecological Approach to Mitigating Wildfire Vulnerability in the Wildland Urban Interface: A Case Study from the 2017 Thomas Fire. *Fire* 2(1): 1–19.

Mangan, R. (2007). *Wildland Firefighter Fatalities in the United States: 1990–2006*. Missoula, MT: National Wildfire Coordinating Group, Safety and Health Working Team, National Interagency Fire Center, US Forest Service, Missoula Technology and Development Center.

Masquelier, Bruno, Lucia Hug, David Sharrow, Danzhen You, Colin Mathers, Patrick Gerland, Leontine Alkema, and UN Inter-agency Group for Child. (2021). Global, Regional, and National Mortality Trends in Youth Aged 15–24 Years between 1990 and 2019: A Systematic Analysis. *The Lancet Global Health* 9(4): e409–e417.

McGuire, L.C., E.S. Ford, and C.A. Okoro. (2007). Natural Disasters and Older US Adults with Disabilities: Implications for Evacuation. *Disasters* 31(1): 49–56. doi:10.1111/J.1467-7717.2007.00339.X.

McMillen, M.M. (1979). Differential Mortality by Sex in Fetal and Neonatal Deaths. *Science* 204(4388): 89–91.

Mijal, Samuel, and P. Willey. (2022). Disability, Disaster, Demography, and the Camp Fire Fatalities. In *The Marginalized in Death: A Forensic Anthropology of Intersectional Identity in the Modern Era*, edited by Jennifer Byrnes and Iván Sandoval-Cervantes, 151–174. Lanham, MD: Lexington Books.

Molina-Terrén, D.M., G. Xanthopoulos, M. Diakakis, L. Ribeiro, D. Caballero, G.M. Delogu, D.X. Viegas, C.A. Silva, and A. Cardil. (2019). Analysis of Forest Fire Fatalities in Southern Europe: Spain, Portugal, Greece and Sardinia (Italy). *International Journal of Wildland Fire* 28(2): 85–98.

Morrow, B.H. (1999) Identifying and Mapping Community Vulnerability. *Disasters* 23(1): 1–18.

National Academies of Sciences, Engineering, and Medicine. (2020). *Social Isolation and Loneliness in Older Adults: Opportunities for the Health Care System.* Washington, DC: National Academies Press. https://doi.org/10.17226/25663.

Oliver-Smith, A. (1999). What Is a Disaster? Anthropological Perspectives on a Persistent Question. In *The Angry Earth: Disaster in Anthropological Perspective*, edited by Anthony Oliver-Smith and Susanna M. Hoffman, 18–34. Milton Park: Routledge.

Oliver-Smith, A., and S.M. Hoffman. (2002). Introduction: Why Anthropologists Should Study Disasters. In *Catastrophe and Culture: The Anthropology of Disaster*, edited by S.M. Hoffman and A. Oliver-Smith, 3–22. Santa Fe, NM: School of American Research Press.

Paine, R.R. (2000). If a Population Crashes in Prehistory, and There Is No Paleodemographer There to Hear It, Does It Make a Sound? *American Journal of Physical Anthropology* 112: 181–190.

Pereira, S., J.L. Zêzere, I. Quaresma, P.P. Santos, and M. Santos. (2016). Mortality Patterns of Hydro-Geomorphologic Disasters. *Risk Analysis* 36(6): 1188–1210. doi:10.1111/risa.12516.

Perner, M.L., A.K. Mortensen, H. Castenbrandt, A. Løkke, and B.A. Revuelta-Eugercios. (2022). Gendered Mortality of Children and Adolescents in Nineteenth-century Denmark. Exploring Patterns of Sex Ratios and Mortality Rates. *The History of the Family* 12: 1–23.

Powell, S., L. Plouffe, and P. Gorr. (2009). When Ageing and Disasters Collide: Lessons from 16 International Case Studies. *Radiation Protection Dosimetry* 134(3–4): 202–206.

Ramsay, G.C., N.A. McArthur, and V.P. Dowling. (1996). Building in a Fire—prone Environment: Research on Building Survival in Two Major Bushfires. Proceedings of the Linnaeus Society of New South Wales—Sydney 1995.

Ramsey, Michael L. (2020). The Camp Fire Public Report: A Summary of the Camp Fire Investigation, June 16. Oroville, CA: Butte County District Attorney's Office. PGE-the-CAMP-FIRE-PUBLIC-REPORT.pdf (accessed August 17, 2022).

Rappaport, E.N. (2000). Loss of Life in the United States Associated with Recent Atlantic Tropical Cyclones. *Bulletin of the American Meteorological Society* 81: 2065–2073. doi:10.1175/1520-0477(2000)081,2065: LOLITU.2.3.CO;2

Rettaroli, R., and F. Scalone. (2021). The Human Sex Ratio at Birth and Late Fetal Mortality: The Italian Case. *Biodemography and Social Biology* 66(2): 172–190.

Ritchie, Hannah, and Max Roser. (2019). Gender Ratio. https://ourworldindata.org/gender-ratio (accessed August 16, 2022).

Robin, D.W. (2000). Preparing Long-term Care Facilities for Natural Disasters. *Annals of Longterm Care.* www.annalsoflongtermcare.com/article/950.

Saliba, D., J. Buchanan, and R.S. Kington. (2004). Function and Response of Nursing Facilities During Community Disaster. *American Journal of Public Health* 94(8): 1436–1441.

Sommer, A., and W.H. Mosley. (1972). The East Bengal Cyclone of November 1970: Epidemiological Approach to Disaster Assessment. *Lancet* 1: 1029–1036.

Timmers, P.R., J.F. Wilson, P.K. Joshi, and J. Deelen. (2020). Multivariate Genomic Scan Implicates Novel Loci and Haem Metabolism in Human Ageing. *Nature Communications* 11(1): 3570. doi:10.1038/s41467-020-17312-3.

United States Census Bureau. (2010). United States Census/American FactFinder. http://factfinder2.census.gov (accessed January 8, 2021).

United States Fire Administration. (2015). *US Fire Statistics*. Emmitsburg, MD: US Fire Administration. www.usfa.fema.gov/data/statistics

United States Fire Administration. (2019). Fire in the United States 2008–2017. www.usfa.fema.gov/data/statistics/reports/fius_2008-2017.html (accessed November 12, 2020).

Victorian Bushfire Royal Commission. (2010). The 2009 Victorian Bushfires Royal Commission Final Report. http://royalcommission.vic.gov.au/Commission-Reports/Final-Report.html (accessed December 24, 2020).

Voice of San Diego. (2007). Additional Fatalities, October 23. https://voiceofsandiego.org/2007/10/23/additional-fatalities/

Whittaker, J., C. Eriksen, and K. Haynes. (2016). Gendered Responses to the 2009 Black Saturday Bushfires in Victoria, Australia. *Geographical Research* 54(2): 203–215.

Wigtil, G., R.B. Hammer, J.D. Kline, M.H. Mockrin, S.I. Stewart, D. Roper, and V.C. Radeloff. (2016). Places Where Wildfire Potential and Social Vulnerability Coincide in the Coterminous United States. *International Journal of Wildland Fire* 25: 896–908.

Women in Fire. (n.d.). History of Women in Firefighting. www.womeninfire.org/firefighters/history-of-women-in-firefighting/ (accessed November 20, 2020).

Xanthopoulos, G. (2007). Forest Fire Related Deaths in Greece: Confirming What We Already Know. *Wildfire 2007: IV International Wildland Fire Conference*, 12.

Xanthopoulos, G. (2015). Forest Fires in Greece: Past, Present and Future. In *Wildland Fires: A Worldwide Reality*, edited by A. Gonçalves and A. Vieira, 141–151. Hauppauge, NY: NOVA Science.

Zarulli, V., I. Kashnitsky, and J.W. Vaupel. (2021). Death Rates at Specific Life Stages Mold the Sex Gap in Life Expectancy. *Proceedings of the National Academy of Sciences* 118(20): e2010588118.

CHAPTER 22

Psychological Effects of Mass Disasters on First Responders

Carolyn G. La Jeunesse

22.1 INTRODUCTION: FIRST RESPONDERS AND MASS DISASTERS

> *There is a cost to caring. Professionals who listen to clients' stories of fear, pain and suffering may feel similar fear, pain and suffering because they care.*
>
> (Charles Figley, 1995)

While this chapter specifically references the *psychological* impacts of mass disasters on first responders, it is important to emphasize that disasters are traumatic events where "mind, body, spirit and relationships with others can be wounded" (Walsh, 2007, p. 207). Mind, body, spirit, and social interactions all are linked inextricably through various neurohormonal, physiologic, behavioral, cognitive, and psychoemotional processes (Courtois & Ford, 2016). Fortunately, professional, non-professional, and volunteer responders and relief workers also can experience satisfaction, a sense of accomplishment, deeper understanding of life and relationships, and personal growth through their actions working collaboratively to help others. A comprehensive focus on disaster mental and behavioral health for responders considers and incorporates attention to the risks and the very real possibility for maintaining health and wellness even in the face of serving in some of the most difficult settings and circumstances.

Disasters pose greater risks to the mental, behavioral, and physical health of first responders compared to the risks they encounter in the course of their usual daily work (Lainie et al., 2011). Also, in mass disasters, first responders and their loved ones and communities are often directly impacted by the disaster. Impacts that intersect life domains and roles add additional layers of stress as responders attempt to balance both personal and professional obligations in circumstances where all manner of response resources are inadequate. These risks and impacts are influenced by factors such as the following:

- The scale, scope, intensity, complexity, and duration of the "human, material, and economic or environmental losses" (ICRC, 2021; Payne & McManus, 2020) encountered by responders
- The cause of the disaster (whether it was a natural disaster or human-caused)
- If human-caused, whether it was accidental or intentional

DOI: 10.4324/9781003168010-27

- If accidental, whether it was preventable or not
- Response resource limitations (time, skills, knowledge, expertise, human capacity, institutional/organizational capacity, physical resources, etc.)
- Disruptions in social, peer, and organizational support for responder well-being both before, during and in the aftermath of the event.

Empathy is necessary for working effectively with people who are in distress. However, empathy is a double-edged sword that also puts helping professionals at greater risk for compassion stress and compassion fatigue (Figley, 2002). And, as Cristea et al. (2014) suggest, different aspects of empathy ("empathic concern" and "personal distress") also may differentially impact effectiveness, satisfaction, resilience, and recovery in the face of disaster-related work. Just as the human mind, physiology, and interpersonal interactions are complex, so, too, are the myriad ways individuals are impacted when working in disaster settings.

The International Disaster Database (EM-DAT) (CRED, 2021) "contains essential core data on the occurrence and effects of more than 21,000 disasters in the world, from 1900 to present." Housed at the Center for Research on Epidemiology of duration of disasters and humanitarian emergencies, this data reflects the "global disaster burden" and highlights the variety, size, geographic distribution, and severity of disasters. These data highlight the enormous effort, expertise and resources needed for preparedness and response. Indirectly, these data can serve as a reminder of the vast human resource capacity required to respond to the scope and scale of disasters. Given the characteristics of mass disasters, it is unrealistic to expect that responders will always be fully prepared or resourced for the work they must do, much less how they will be impacted. However, overtly stating this reality to responders can serve as "expectation management" that can alleviate some distress when working in large-scale crises.

Mass disasters also may directly impact first responders, their families, and the communities in which responders live and work (Tracy et al., 2011). When this occurs, responders and their families suffer additional burdens that can compound psychological impacts of disaster work (Bonanno & Mancini, 2012). Responders and their families can benefit when made aware and prepare for this potential confluence of direct and indirect impacts.

Disasters are traumatic events that impact responders in predictable ways. If responders personally experience trauma related to the disaster or their disaster-related work, there is concern about primary traumatic stress (PTS), post-traumatic stress disorder (PTSD), anxiety, depression, substance misuse, and self-harm or suicide. If responders are witness to or hear stories of injuries, death, and suffering of others, there is concern about secondary traumatic stress (STS), vicarious traumatization, compassion stress, and compassion fatigue.

The variety and accumulation of stressors can result in harm to individuals and institutions, compromise individual and group efficacy, and compromise the ethical decision-making fundamental to optimal disaster response activities. The stress of witnessing large-scale destruction, injuries, death and suffering can be compounded by the stress of establishing and coordinating work across disciplines and sectors, often in austere or physically difficult settings, and in agencies or with other workers with whom responders are unfamiliar. Despite "the best" forward planning and preparation, it is stressful to coordinate response activities, stage, deploy and access resources, and establish and navigate communications and teams. This operational and organizational "stress" contributes an additional burden of psychological risks to responders.

Optimal disaster preparedness, response and recovery must consider and attempt to address the confluence and complexity of these stressors; doing so contributes to responsible stewardship of precious and often limited financial, human, and institutional resources and "hard" disaster assets. All of these impacts on human experience and relationships, as well as related reactions and coping responses and strategies, must be considered in order to holistically address responders' psychological well-being.

22.2 WHO ARE THE FIRST RESPONDERS IN LARGE-SCALE DISASTERS?

Traditionally, the term "first responder" refers to law enforcement, fire service, emergency medical, emergency service dispatch, and search and rescue professionals. They are the first and principal front-line defense in the face of disasters. In mass casualty events "resulting in a number of victims large enough to disrupt the normal course of emergency and health care services" (PAHO, 2019), impacts are vast, overwhelm response and recovery capacity, and most often involve first responders from outside those categories of traditional first responders. Some mass disasters (e.g., the COVID-19 pandemic, large-scale 21st-century wildland fires, and massive extreme weather events) have such scope, scale, intensity, duration, and/or geographic distribution that there simply never will be adequate resources for optimal response and recovery.

In large-scale disasters, improved response and recovery efforts heavily depend on expanded ranks of first responders, and the definition of "first responder" expands to include a larger number of both professional, non-professional, and volunteer disaster-response and relief workers across sectors and disciplines (Alexander & Klein, 2009). This workforce "surge capacity" is critical to more comprehensive, effective, and efficient disaster response and recovery. Individuals and teams from the private sector, academia, civil society, government, and non-profit organizations contribute specialized knowledge, expertise, skills and resources that enhance disaster responses. For instance, the Security Surge Capacity Force (US Department of Homeland managed through the Federal Emergency Management Agency) is one such US governmental mechanism that can be activated to draw from the larger federal workforce "to augment the federal response to a catastrophic disaster" (US DHS Surge Capacity Force, 2021).

These additional responders can include forensics scientists, social scientists, anthropologists, criminologists, global and public health professionals, human and animal health professionals, clergy and spiritual care providers, mental and behavioral health specialists, coroners and medical examiners, mortuary workers, community-based emergency response team members, enlisted and reserve military personnel, humanitarian aid workers (Macpherson & Burkle, 2021), utilities workers, and technical and communications specialists.

With such heterogeneity among responders comes high variability in how they are prepared for psychological impacts of disaster work and the resources available to them to manage stressors leading up to, during, and following deployments. Macpherson and Burkle (2021) specifically note that professional humanitarian aid workers (approximately 450,000 worldwide) "experience an industry-wide failure to adequately address psychological health issues." As well, Mao et al. (2018) identified that "unaffiliated volunteers were most susceptible to negative psychological consequences" (p. 602).

Tim Gocha:

I know one of my most difficult moments in the Camp Fire recovery was a scene with several pets around the foot of a recliner that a decedent was sitting in when they passed. The legs of the decedent were clearly comingled with faunal elements and so to separate as quickly as I could I decided to define the cranial-caudal extent of the dog, so I could remove that and focus on recovery of the decedent. At the caudal end of the dog, I found the cranial end of another dog, quickly defined that only to find at their caudal end was a cat. It appeared they were all huddled around "their person" at the time of passing.

Of course, some of the scenes of human decedents were somewhat triggering, but this situation hit me the hardest. FACTS recently had an Army Mortuary Affairs Unit visit for a workshop, and with them were two psychologists who study mental health issues in those exposed to death, in particular mass fatalities. They asked a question about what were some of the most difficult moments, and I relayed the early anecdote. One of them astutely observed that maybe because it was an unexpected experience finding pets in a way that seemed familiar, rather than the human decedents and general destruction I knew to expect. I know this is very anecdotal, but thought it worth mentioning how unexpected finds can be even more triggering than those we expect (albeit still difficult).

Alison Galloway:

So many of those we found seemed to have faced the fire with courage. Like Tim, the scene with the people, who also appeared to be holding hands, and their pets was hard to process. Another couple was also found in their matching chairs in the living room, small portions of a burned Bible still floating in the air. Others died alone, sitting on their beds, waiting to be engulfed by the flames.

What is equally hard is the longer-term changes. This is particularly true of those of us who do this work and live in fire-prone areas ourselves. While we can work to protect our own property, have our evacuation plans and boxes at the ready, and know all the phone numbers to call for getting help with livestock, I still drive around the neighborhood and subconsciously note which homes will almost definitely burn, which may burn, and which have a chance of surviving. Like many of us, I am "on-edge" from mid-spring until late fall, torn between the possible need to be deployed to a wildfire fatality and needing to evacuate myself.

All those responding to disasters will be impacted psychologically by what they experience and encounter in the course of that work. In their 2018 review paper, Mao et al. examined 55 articles on disaster work-related psychological impacts. Those "identified in the literature included firefighters, police officers, military personnel/soldiers, healthcare professionals, and volunteers" suffering from "acute stress disorder (ASD), anxiety and depression, post-traumatic stress disorder (PTSD), and other psychological disorders" (p. 602). When their own or adjacent communities are impacted, community members often serve as volunteer responders or relief workers. Without the prior experience, specific skills, and clarity about roles and responsibilities, volunteers are at comparatively higher risk for untoward psychological outcomes (Thormar et al., 2010). Because of this, as well as the unpredictable nature of disasters, household and community preparedness are becoming increasingly important for the entire response effort.

22.3 OVERVIEW OF PSYCHOLOGICAL IMPACTS OF DISASTERS ON FIRST RESPONDERS

> *First responders are always at the forefront of each incident or disaster, and they ensure the safety and well-being of the population. . . . This constitutes a great risk for the behavioral health of first responders, putting them at risk for stress, PTSD, depression, substance use, and suicide ideation and attempts.*
>
> (SAMHSA, 2018, p. 12)

> *Studies of traumatic event experience have shown that most people who experience an event do not develop psychopathology (9, 53). Having the capacity to continue functioning after a traumatic event is common and characteristic of normal coping and adaptation (5, 6). This phenomenon has become known as "resilience" and is an emerging concept in the disaster mental health literature.*

The very nature of mass disasters results in greater numbers of and relatively more intense stressors than those which first responders encounter in the course of their daily work. The enormity of suffering, injury, death, property damage/loss, disruption of economies, and environmental damage, as well as the complexity and size of operations, can overwhelm even well-trained and resourced responders. Awareness of these risks, education and training, support and interventions, and ongoing iteration of wellness resourcing become both more important and also potentially more difficult to provide during mass disasters. These investments in responder well-being are essential to maximizing efficacy and efficiency of disaster responses, safeguarding and stewarding precious human and organizational resources, maintaining operational competency of teams, and abiding by ethical mandates to protect responders placed in harm's way by virtue of their work as public protectors.

All those responding to disasters will be impacted psychologically (Benedek et al., 2007) by what they encounter in the course of that work. There is tremendous exposure to troubling sensory input. The smells, sounds, visions, physical sensations, and even tastes associated with disaster scenes can impact responders both consciously and subconsciously. Furthermore, sensory input after an event can trigger future disturbing memories and sensations, and senses can be activated by recalling disaster-related memories or experiences (Baranowsky & Gentry, 2015, p. 18). From death, serious injuries and property and environmental damage to interactions with distressed or traumatized co-workers or disaster survivors, there is tremendous exposure to destruction of property and the environment and to the suffering of others. Each responder's experience of and how they react to and cope with these stressful exposures is highly individual. At the same time, there are predictable reactions and responses, risks and protective factors, and both beneficial and harmful ways that individual responders cope with difficult disaster-related experiences (Marmar et al., 2006; SAMHSA 2018; Thormar et al., 2010). Any one individual's risk, psychoemotional injury, coping, recovery, and resilience are influenced by many factors (Brooks et al, 2015, 2016). These factors include but are not limited to the following:

- Cultural influences
- Prior experiences with trauma
- Social supports (Prati & Pietrantoni, 2010)
- Experience and preparation for disaster work

- Influences and cultures of the hierarchies and organizations in which responders work
- The ways they find or make meaning of what they experience or witness (Matthews & Marwit, 2006; Neimeyer, 2000; Erikson, 1976)
- Prior experiences with death, loss, and bereavement (Walsh, 2007)
- An individual's grieving style (Doka & Martin, 2011)
- Pre-existing or comorbid behavioral or mental health issues (Javidi & Yadollahie, 2012; Rutkow et al., 2011).

It is well-established (Stamm, 2016; Greinacher et al., 2019) that helping professionals (including first responders and relief workers) experience compounded mental and behavioral health risks through exposures to traumatic and stressful circumstances encountered in the course of their usual daily work. These exposures and risks increase during disaster-response work, and the ill-effects are often cumulative (Marmar et al., 2006). As noted in the SAMHSA Supplemental Research Bulletin (2018, p. 12), some of these professionals may try to cope with these stressors "by trying to disregard their reactions or using other maladaptive techniques such as substance misuse." This knowledge better informs and can be used to develop more impactful policy and programs directed specifically at needs outlined in the SAMHSA Bulletin (2018). It is promising to see that legislative bodies increasingly are addressing this need through formalized recommendations (Texas, 2018), laws (Commonwealth of Massachusetts, 2018), and proposed legislation (U.S. Congress, 2019–2020) to assess, study, and develop interventions to support first responder mental and behavioral health.

22.4 HOW DISASTER RESPONSE WORK IMPACTS FIRST RESPONDERS

Each responder will uniquely experience, react to, and cope with different encounters in the course of their disaster-related work. The following two statements serve as "bookend" reminders of the risk and impacts, the beneficial possibilities, and the need for assessment and care to enhance health, recovery, and resilience in the face of disasters:

> *The human health consequences of natural and/or manmade disasters can be widespread, profound, and long lasting. Health surveillance and treatment programs are critical for the appropriate management of the health conditions among affected responders and residents in the aftermath of disasters, irrespective of their industrial, natural or terror origin.*
>
> (Lucchini et al., 2017, p. 10)

> *It must be acknowledged that disaster response personnel often remain psychologically healthy throughout their careers. The trajectory of trauma is complex; while individuals may experience emotional and physical distress in the course of their work and following a disaster event, many do not develop psychopathology.*
>
> (Thompson et al., 2017, p. 63)

When discussing the psychological impacts of disaster work on both professional and civilian first responders, it is particularly important to remember and emphasize that staying psychologically healthy is an achievable ongoing process that requires awareness, support, and both collective and individual effort. For purposes of advancing knowledge, practices, and interventions, it is important to identify gaps in understanding how responders are impacted and to iterate practices, policies, and interventions over time.

There is a large body of research and literature related to the psychological impacts of disasters on first responders. This literature is often stratified by category of responder (e.g., medical services, humanitarian groups, law enforcement, fires services, emergency operations center operations, relief workers, search and rescue/ recovery) that elucidates detailed specifics for these and other categories of workers. This section will include a brief overview of the most common impacts categorized by aspects of psychological experience. However, as mentioned in the introduction to this chapter, it is critical to consider these psychological impacts together with physical, social and spiritual/existential impacts. Psychological impacts of disaster work can include:

- Stress
- Depression
- Anxiety
- Post-traumatic stress (PTS)
- Post-traumatic stress disorder (PTSD)
- Compassion stress (secondary traumatic stress; vicarious traumatization)
- Compassion fatigue (secondary traumatic stress disorder)
- Burnout
- Suicide/suicide ideation
- Substance misuse
- Ethical exhaustion

22.5 AWARENESS

> *Professional quality of life (ProQOL) is the quality one feels in relation to their work as a helper. Both the positive and negative aspects of doing your work influence your professional quality of life.*
>
> The ProQOL introduction https://proqol.org/Home_Page.php

Mass disasters can overwhelm or severely challenge responders' professional abilities, efficacy, and stamina. Additionally, such events can overwhelm their ability to cope with the personal impacts of witnessing (and often experiencing) associated suffering, loss, and destruction. As "caregiving professionals," the "cost of caring" (Figley, 1995, p. 1) can be enormous, and the negative consequences can extend to impact families and communities and the lives of individual responders. On the other hand, what is done to support responders' health and well-being and to build hardiness and resilience has positive impacts across life roles and domains (Dumas & Sanchez-Burks, 2017; Alexander & Klein, 2009; Delongis et al., 1989).

Creating awareness is the first step in helping first responders effectively prepare for, navigate, recover from, and even grow in the face of work-associated stressors (Thompson et al., 2017; Figley, 1995). This is particularly important with regards to the psychoemotional impacts of disaster work since that stigma associated with seeking help can compromise access to care (Keenan & Royle, 2008).

Leaders deploying personnel to disaster responses can contribute to improved mental, behavioral, and physical health outcomes. Responder self-care hinges on awareness of the risks, the ways they may be impacted, and resources and supports available. The impacts on the physical health of responders generally are more accepted as a "given" and comparatively less stigmatized than psychological impacts. Those physical impacts "make logical sense" when considering long work hours, poor working conditions, intense physical demands, disruptions to sleeping and eating, and inadequate "recovery" time between crisis responses. However, there is still considerable stigma attached to the mental and behavioral health consequences associated with disaster- and crisis-related work (SAMHSA, 2018; Kranke et al., 2017a).

Individuals benefit from being made aware that their own previous experiences of trauma and loss impact their perceptions and approaches to work. The same factors influence how they will be impacted by, respond to, and recover (or even grow) in the face of disaster-related psychoemotional or spiritual/existential injuries. Similarly, each responder's "grief style," personality attributes, cultures, prior experiences of death and loss, and "accepted" gender-related norms will influence how they grieve, mourn, and find or make meaning in their experiences of disaster-related losses (Doka & Martin, 2011).

Disaster "causation" also influences psychological impacts of disasters. How people process their reactions to and what they understand about traumatic events are influenced by the actual or perceived nature of the disaster (Pearlman et al., 2014):

- Natural versus human-caused or exacerbated (e.g., floods, wildland fires, landslides)
- Preventable versus unavoidable
- Preponderance of deaths "out-of-the-natural order" (e.g., involving deaths of children or youth)
- Real or perceived discrimination or bias in preparedness, pre-event warnings and notifications, and/or deployment of response "assets"
- Components of violence (e.g., mass shootings, genocide)

Attending to responder well-being starts with leadership that provides comprehensive individual and team preparedness, resourcing, and support for the commonly encountered experiences and predictable risks. Support for responder well-being and resilience starts with creating awareness that all aspects of responders' lives will be impacted during disaster response work. At a minimum, this "awareness development" does the following:

- Underscores the ethical mandate for self-care to improve both work competency and the ethical decision-making required in the course of deployments
- Stresses the need for "a range of deployment cycle mental health and well-being support processes" (McCormack, 2017, p. S175) and behavioral health assessments (Williams et al., 2008) to support responders from pre-deployment through post-deployment periods.
- Elucidates the range of burdens responders face when trying to do their work as well as manage personal, family, and community impacts
- Provides training, education, intervention, resources, and supports to maximize responder health and well-being

- Destigmatizes recognition of and help-seeking for the mental, emotional, spiritual, cognitive, social, and behavioral impacts of the work
- Normalizes, encourages, and rewards self-assessment, self-care, and help-seeking behaviors for responders
- Helps individual responders understand their personal risks related to personality attributes, coping styles, prior exposure to and experiences of trauma (their own or others), and underlying mental and behavioral health issues
- Overtly states that organizational and operational aspects of disaster responses can pose additional mental health risks that are largely outside the responder's locus of control
- Is respectful of demands on responders' time, addresses training and resourcing gaps, and minimizes redundancies in training requirements.
- Ensures equitable access to responders regardless of race, ethnicity, national origin, religious affiliation, gender, sexual preference, age, or disability
- Identifies those at particular risk for untoward outcomes or who may experience increased barriers to training, support or resources, and seeks to remedy those risks and eliminate those barriers
- Emphasizes that the help they provide to those they serve can provide a sense of purpose, satisfaction, self-worth, and even joy that can be potent counterbalances to "negative stressors" encountered when witnessing, and then working to address the suffering of others (Stamm, 2002; Kranke et al., 2017b)
- Highlights the psychological benefits of social support (Prati & Pietrantoni, 2010; Brooks et al., 2015, 2016) and peer support (Kranke et al., 2017b; Feuer, 2021; Jahnke et al., 2014)

22.5.1 Ethical and Legal and Considerations

First, do no harm. Do good. Honor autonomy. Be just. These tenets of biomedical ethics (Beauchamp & Childress, 2001) are basic standards that can be used to guide optimal disaster responses. These ethical standards are guides to minimize harm, maximize outcomes for the most people, equitably distribute burdens and benefits, and honor individuals' rights to self-determine. During mass disasters, balancing these tenets can be particularly challenging. Biomedical principles can be used to guide responder preparedness policies and programs to maximize outcomes for those impacted by disasters, as well as to safeguard the health and well-being of responders.

First responders deployed to the front lines of disasters arguably are the most valuable assets (Brown et al., 2015) tasked with the "protection and preservation of life, property, and the environment" (Prati & Pietrantoni, 2010, p. 403). Policy-makers, decision-makers, and disaster management and response leaders have a mandate to responsibly steward disaster response resources, including human capital (US Department of Emergency Management, 2019). This mandate extends well beyond economic considerations; perhaps most important is the duty of care to the well-being and protection of personnel on the front lines of disasters who risk the most to serve communities (Rutkow et al., 2011). Mental health supports should extend from the pre-disaster *through* post-deployment periods in order to provide the comprehensive care necessary to address the range of risks to mental health that may predictably impact workers well beyond their deployments.

The impetus to support psychological health of first responders is twofold. The first relates to these ethical principles as well as legal obligations and considerations (Benedek et al., 2007). These efforts aim to prepare, protect, and support those who are placed in harm's way by virtue of their work defending people, other animals, property, and the environment.

Second is the "duty to inform" responders of the specific risks they may encounter and provide them the resources necessary to minimize and mitigate personal harm and suffering related to their work (Figley, 1995). Both of these mandates also relate to the mission-efficacy imperative to optimize operations and outcomes. Responders can attend better to their work and remain better invested if they are adequately prepared, if they are resourced, and if they believe they are supported and that they and their families will be cared for should they be harmed, disabled, or killed in the course of their work.

Additional considerations derive from ethics of care,[1] wherein particular attention is paid to protecting particularly vulnerable persons and communities, those who are disenfranchised or marginalized, or those who predictably are at greater risk in disasters. In disasters, this can include individuals and groups such as the homeless/houseless (Gin et al., 2016); the elderly; those with mental, developmental or physical disabilities; children; historically marginalized or disenfranchised groups; those with substance misuse issues; hospitalized patients; and those in tertiary care facilities (Parmar, 2019). In addition to being the ethically and operationally correct thing to do as part of disaster planning, preparedness, and response, adequate protections for the most vulnerable can alleviate an additional burden of stress for responders.

22.6 HOW FIRST RESPONDERS ARE IMPACTED BY THE STRESS OF DISASTER WORK

22.6.1 The Compassion Fatigue Continuum

> *[R]esilience does not indicate the complete absence of any psychological symptoms after traumatic event exposure; rather, it describes the ability to "bounce back."*
>
> (Goldmann & Galea, 2014 p. 171)

As "helping professionals," first responders are vulnerable to the stressors related to their roles as societal caregivers. This acute or accumulated "secondary traumatic stress" (Figley, 1995, p. 7) occurs when responders witness (either directly or indirectly) the suffering of those they aim to help. If unaddressed, or if exposure is intense, this stress can negatively impact responders' personal health and well-being (DeWolfe, 2000). Additionally (and of particular importance from the standpoint of disaster-related policy-making, training, resourcing, and interventions), these stressors can compromise professional competence and safety of operations and impair ethical decision-making (Lachman, 2016), all particularly critical components of disaster-related work.

During disasters, in addition to these natural, expected and unavoidable "secondary traumatic stresses" (Figley, 1995), first responders may directly experience trauma ("primary traumatic stress") or losses. So aspects of grief, loss and trauma can complicate responder experiences. According to Figley (2002, 2003), compassion fatigue is a natural consequence of working with clients who have experienced distressing events, which develops both because of this exposure and because of the caregiver's empathy.

As Figley illustrates in the compassion fatigue model (2001), the ability to cope with and recover from stressors is dependent on many factors, including an individual's prior memories of trauma, their level of empathic concern and empathic activity, the intensity and length of exposure to the suffering of others, other aspects of life that they must manage, and their ability to discern how to help without harming themselves in the process. In their empathic discernment model, Radey and Figley (2007) illustrate how this compassion stress and compassion fatigue can be minimized and mitigated through modulating one's personal affect, discerning personal limits and boundaries in work, and seeking and utilizing organizational support resources. Discernment ahead of and during exposure can reduce accumulated compassion stress, potentially avert development of compassion fatigue, and improve the satisfaction derived from the work of helping others who are suffering.

22.6.2 Stress Encountered from Work Conditions: Burnout

> *Burnout is a psychological syndrome emerging as a prolonged response to chronic interpersonal stressors on the job. The three key dimensions of this response are an overwhelming exhaustion, feelings of cynicism and detachment from the job, and a sense of ineffectiveness and lack of accomplishment.*
>
> Maslach and Lieter (2016, p. 103)

For purposes of this chapter, burnout will be considered more related to organizational and occupational circumstances often beyond the control of the worker. Kahill (1988) identified five general categories of burnout related symptoms—physical, emotional, work-related, behavioral, and interpersonal—which differ from those encountered in compassion fatigue and includes components of physical, emotional, and mental exhaustion. Unlike compassion fatigue, which can develop rapidly and is a more a condition and state of being, burnout is the result of a process that develops over time.

In addition to the aforementioned stressors related to their interactions with those they serve and care for, responders inevitably encounter stress related to institutional, organizational, hierarchical, leadership, management, situational, environmental, and operational aspects of work over which they may have little influence or control. This latter type of stress can lead to responder "burnout" and contribute to attrition, disability, and decreased investment or efficacy in the work (Regehr & Millar, 2007). Edelwich and Brodsky (1980) describe burnout as "a progressive loss of idealism, energy and purpose experienced by people in the helping professions as a result of their work conditions" (p. 166). Symptoms of burnout are different from those of compassion fatigue and contribute more to a sense of frustration and disillusionment than those seen in compassion fatigue. Maslach and Leiter (2016) describe burnout as including "overwhelming exhaustion, feelings of cynicism and detachment from the job, and a sense of ineffectiveness and lack of accomplishment" (p. 103).

There is a large body of work examining the mental, behavioral, and cognitive health impacts of disasters on those in the helping professions, including first responders and relief workers. Synopses (SAMHSA, 2021; Stamm, 2016; Alexander & Klein,

2009; Thormar et al., 2010) provide particularly thorough and concise reviews of the research and literature related to risks, protective factors, and both adverse and positive impacts. Much of that research and literature references adverse consequences, such as anxiety, depression, substance misuse, and primary and secondary traumatic stress. However, there is increasing interest in and research on positive psychoemotional outcomes, such as post-traumatic growth, compassion satisfaction, and resilience. In preparing and supporting disaster response and relief workers, it is important to present a balanced view of the potential risks and rewards of this work. Witnessing death, injury, destruction, and suffering can be very distressing and even overwhelming. On the other hand, responders can derive great satisfaction and experience personal growth and increased appreciation for life through the process of helping others and their contributions to decreasing that suffering and loss. Just as those who are most empathic are at greatest risk for compassion stress, so, too, do they have greater potential for deriving satisfaction, personal and relational growth, and developing resilience.

As mentioned in the introduction to this chapter, disaster responders are impacted in a "global" sense (all aspects of their lives and experiences). Yassen (1995, p. 184) categorizes the "personal impact of secondary traumatic stress," such as those encountered by first responders and relief workers into five categories: cognitive, emotional, behavioral, spiritual, interpersonal, and physical. In this same table, Yassen elucidates prominent characteristics of this secondary traumatic stress, ranging from difficulty concentrating and self-doubt to anger, depression, and anxiety, and a sense of overwhelm. Physical symptoms include elevated heart rate, aches and pains, and other somatic manifestations, as well as immune system dysfunction. In the spiritual and relational realm, Yassen notes people may question the meaning of life, or develop a sense of hopelessness or weariness, or even question closely held religious convictions. The outward expression of this stress can manifest in behaviors such as hypervigilance, irritability, changes in appetite and sleep, substance misuse, excessive risk-taking or self-harm, and withdrawal from families and social circles.

22.6.3 Minimum Standards for Preparing Responders

> *If responders are unaware of the need to monitor their physical, emotional, and spiritual needs, they may begin to experience difficulties in their work and personal lives.*
> SAMHSA Disaster Responder Stress Management, 2021

Policymakers and decisionmakers benefit from understanding the myriad ways first responders are impacted by disaster response and recovery work. Such understanding better informs resourcing, funding, research, policy, and response and recovery operations that prioritize caring for those on the front lines. Prioritizing first responders' well-being is critical, *especially* in mass disasters. In such scenarios, resources (including human capital) are predictably inadequate to meet all response and recovery needs. Therefore, each responder is relatively more pivotal to "best" response and recovery efforts. Fully competent and optimally functioning responders become even more important since people are the only "asset" capable of assessing and navigating fluctuating operational needs and adjusting to shifting gaps and barriers in response capacities. That full competence and functioning is possible only when responders are physically and psychologically fit and healthy.

In addition, it is essential that volunteers and non-professional responders and relief workers also are trained in the basics of disaster mental- and behavioral health. Properly trained, these additional responders are valuable contributors to disaster response operations, bolstering response capacity beyond what can or should be provided by professional first responders. These volunteers and non-professional responders hail from the private sector, non-profit and professional organizations, community- and faith-based organizations, and academic institutions. They provide critical support as disaster response "force multipliers" and "resource optimizers" by doing the following:

- Providing special expertise, skills, and/or subject matter knowledge
- Contributing, operating, and/or setting up "hard assets"
- Performing highly skilled (leadership, technical, communications, medical, biosecurity, public health, environmental protection, etc.) and general response work to expand the response "work force"
- Stepping into professional roles within official incident commands, associated working groups, and various field operations
- Taking over temporarily to provide respite and recovery time for professional first responders who are overly taxed by the intensity, demands, and duration of responses.
- Supporting and coordinating activities between volunteer groups and lightening the additional responsibility of cross-sector coordination normally assigned to professional responders

However, even among professional first responders, training and support for health and well-being in general, and mental and behavioral health in particular, vary greatly. Many individuals are inadequately prepared for how they will be impacted by what they will encounter in the course of their daily work, much less in the face of disaster-related work. This is particularly concerning for volunteers, where, "regardless of the type of disaster, volunteering may lead to mental and physical morbidity," principally PTSD, and "vary from considerable to high levels of mental health complaints" (Thormar et al., 2010, p. 534). Thormar et al. also posit that in addition to lack of training, volunteers may have a number of particular risks for "post-disaster psychopathology" and PTSD, including inexperience, youth, and insufficient "social or organizational support" (Thormar et al., 2010 p. 530). Disaster-related risks identified in this review range from issues of identification with victims and degree of social support to personality and organizational and operational aspects of disaster work.

The Supplemental Bulletin provides a concise overview of "risk and protective factors for behavioral health in first responders" (SAMHSA, 2018). The Bulletin serves as an excellent synopsis to guide training, resourcing and support for first responders. While the risks for professional first responders may differ greatly from that of other responders, inevitably there will be overlap especially during large-scale disasters when massive numbers of individuals with a range of lived experiences show up to help.

22.6.4 Special Considerations for Volunteer Responders

In disasters, volunteers and professionals from a variety of occupations often are exposed to and affected by the same risks and stressors as career first responders.

But unlike law enforcement, fire service, emergency medical, and search and rescue professionals, many volunteers have little or no basic education or training in fundamentals of disaster response work, much less personal risk or self-care. This results in increased threats to overall well-being and resilience. Additionally, lack of training and practical skills can compromise overall response efforts when properly trained responders must divert time and energy to "managing" those who are not properly trained.

In his article on his experiences working the World Trade Center Attack response, paramedic Louis Cook (2001) gives a glimpse into these problems in the aptly named section, "Problems created by good intentions":

> *Early on in the incident, we saw many well-intentioned medical professionals involving themselves in situations for which they were unprepared, untrained, and unequipped. Several lone physicians, dressed in scrubs and running shoes, where found in the collapse zone providing medical intervention to potentially trapped victims. In some cases, impromptu medical clinics had been established. Once identified, these physicians were politely but firmly escorted out of the area because they created problems, such as medical oversight and accountability, liability, patient tracking, and safety to name but a few.*

The same ethical mandate for proper training in both disaster response and self-care extends to volunteers. In this same section, Cook further notes that

> *in the collapse zone, in heavily damaged buildings and covered in dust, well-intentioned people offered food to the rescuers. However, given the disruption to water and gas, the lack of handwashing, unrefrigerated food, poorly cooked food, and dust-contaminated food all presented the potential to cause illness among the already worn-down rescuers. Public health officials and the police eventually eliminated these "chow lines," and a more organized system of mass feeding was organized.*

Untrained, these individuals contribute to the following:

- Increased risk of harm to themselves and other workers
- Complicating disaster response operations when those volunteers become potential or actual victims who then require professional disaster response resources
- Burdening of professional or properly trained responders who must divert time, energy and physical resources to manage and protect these untrained volunteers
- An additional burden of unnecessary work and frustration for professional responders

Proper training, prior experience, and support throughout the disaster-response cycle can insulate workers from some psychological impacts and can improve well-being and resilience. Kranke et al. (2017b) posit that, as noted with some former military members volunteering with Team Rubicon,[2] proper training, prior work in chaotic and dangerous settings, education on how to deal with disaster-impacted civilians, peer support, and a sense of purpose gained from helping others can limit disaster-work related stress and improve "mental health and self-esteem" (p. 506).

Thormar et al. (2010) elucidate some of the particular risks for volunteers:

> *Unlike professional workers, volunteers are often quickly selected based on an urgent need caused by a disaster. This may result in volunteers lacking experience, appropriate preparedness, and training. Yet their role exposes them to the same difficult tasks professionals take on . . . Volunteers come from different professions and do not belong to a workplace with a structured support network like those that may exist within, for example, police and fire service organizations.*
>
> (p. 530)

22.6.5 Barriers to Obtaining Help for Psychological Impacts of Disaster Work

Barriers to psychological self-care abound in the helping professions. Despite the known risks and calls for action (SAMHSA, 2018) to address this, several impediments to help-seeking remain. Those include the following:

- Lack of priority to mental and behavioral health in training, education, resourcing, and support for responders and their families
- Ongoing stigma, shame and guilt associated with mental and behavioral health problems
- Institutional cultures which support maladaptive coping strategies
- Overall societal access to mental healthcare
- Penalization of affected workers by organizations, agencies, or leaders
- Insufficient self-assessment and assessment by organizations to identify and remedy coexisting mental and behavioral health burdens that increase risk when responding to disasters.

Stigma around mental and emotional health challenges and barriers to care remain particularly troublesome phenomena among first responders (Keenan et al., 2009, Haugen et al., 2017). Of these, stigma is one of the greatest barriers to self-care (Lanza et al., 2018).

In addition, there is great variability in the quality, quantity, accessibility, and efficacy of training, resources, preparation, interventions, and support provided to both professional and volunteer responders. Even when adequate training and resourcing are available, responders benefit from regular reminders about the benefits of accessing and utilizing those resources. This is especially true when new recruits encounter self-care materials during initial training; there may be little that is relatable until responders work in the field and encounter the stressors mentioned in that training (La Jeunesse, personal interviews with responders, 2012–21). It is important that responders receive regular reminders of training, professional and peer support, organizational resources, personal assessments and self-care strategies, and instructions for easy access. These regular reminders from both leaders and peers help "normalize" and destigmatize experiences of work-related psychological and emotional distress. Reducing stigma and normalizing experiences can lower the barrier to seeking help and engaging beneficial coping strategies and resources.

Policymakers can contribute to improving the health and well-being of responders by collaborating with disaster mental health specialists and subject matter experts. Thoughtful policy supports improved mental health safeguards without overly burdening organizations and individuals with redundant or irrelevant education and training requirements. Policymakers can offer further support by supporting their constituents with the legislative, administrative, and regulatory frameworks that facilitate identifying and filling gaps in training, education, resourcing, and support throughout the disaster management cycle (from pre- to post-deployment).

Ongoing research and monitoring and evaluation are critical components to assess and improve existing and future programs aimed at responder well-being. This research requires funding but, importantly, also some policy innovation that will allow for longer funding periods on research and program awards so that the long-term, as well as the near-term efficacy of these efforts can be adequately assessed.

With increased media coverage and social media comes increased pressure on policymakers to "fix" the myriad problems associated with disaster-related suffering and reduce risk and harm to those responding. The pressure from constituents can be intense, yet it is imperative that policy aimed at enhancing safeguards for responders does not inadvertently cause harm or detract from the considerable workload already demanded of professional responders. The best interventions are likely to come from an identified need, with enough preliminary data about impact and scope so that proposed programs, rules, and regulations can be assessed over time to ensure the efforts are accomplishing the original intent for any given policy intervention.

22.7 ONGOING AND FUTURE OPPORTUNITIES

1. Use scientific evidence and data to address gaps and redundancies (Tol & van Ommeren, 2012).
2. Increase the emphasis on normalizing and destigmatizing psychological impacts of disasters on responders and relief workers.
3. Prioritize responder psychoemotional health.
4. Consider responder well-being as an essential component of improved safety of operations (using high-reliability organizational principles for high-risk operations/enterprises).
5. Factor in decompression periods post-deployment prior to responders returning home.
6. Improve pre-deployment assessments (both self-assessments and assessments of individual responders by people in their sponsoring organizations/agencies).
7. Continually evaluate and iterate disaster mental and behavioral health protections and outcomes as part of disaster "lessons learned" and post-event after-action reviews and reports.
8. Improve guidelines and assurance of personnel preparedness for inexperienced volunteer or non-professional responders so that the overall disaster response is not hampered or so that these personnel do not suffer unnecessary harm.
9. Increase research around impacts of gender shifts within the ranks of disaster responders.
10. Encourage key actors in agencies to continually remind responders about support (education, training, interventions, peer support, resourcing) available to them.
11. Determine which agencies, departments, and organizations may need increased resources for fundamental education, training, resourcing, and support, then direct resources there to more evenly prepare responders across jurisdictions.

12. Properly steward disaster preparedness and response resources by utilizing what is already in place within agencies: remind responders of available resources more regularly; review resources for effectiveness and accessibility across the ranks of responders; revise over time with input from end-users.
13. Dedicate additional resources to traditionally marginalized or disenfranchised responders (based on gender, race, religion, age, national origin, sexual preference, ethnic origin, ability, etc.), those who experience discrimination, or those who are expected to be impacted by implicit bias either within organizational cultures or the communities in which they serve.

22.8 CONCLUSION

With increasing global population, climate change, biodiversity degradation, and violent conflicts, it is expected that mass disasters and humanitarian crises will continue to take an enormous toll on disaster response capacity worldwide. People remain the cornerstone of planning, preparedness, response, and recovery. An emotional toll will be exacted anywhere people come together to help during crises. On the other hand, with support and self-care, responders can find in those acts of service ongoing or renewed purpose, increased professional satisfaction, appreciation for life and relationships, improved resilience, and greater appreciation for the strength and hardiness of humanity as together, they rise to challenges and find ways to not just survive, but thrive, in the face of crises (Bonanno, 2004; Tedeschi & Calhoun, 1996).

REFERENCES

Alexander, D. A., & Klein, S. (2009). First responders after disasters: A review of stress reactions, at-risk, vulnerability, and resilience factors. *Prehospital and Disaster Medicine*, *24*(2), 87–94.

Baranowsky, A. B., & Gentry, J. E. (2015). *Foundations of the trauma practice model in trauma practice: Tools for stabilization and recovery.* Boston, MA: Hogrefe Publishing Corporation.

Beauchamp & Childress (2001). *Principles of biomedical ethics* (5th ed.). New York: Oxford University Press.

Benedek, D. M., Fullerton, C., & Ursano, R. J. (2007). First responders: Mental health consequences of natural and human-made disasters for public health and public safety workers. *Annual Review of Public Health*, *28*, 55–68. https://doi.org/10.1146/annurev.publhealth.28.021406.144037

Bonanno, G. (2004). Loss, trauma, and human resilience: Have we underestimated the human capacity to thrive after extremely aversive events? *American Psychologist*, (59), 20–28.

Bonanno, G. A., & Mancini, A. D. (2012). Beyond resilience and PTSD: Mapping the heterogeneity of responses to potential trauma. *Psychological Trauma*, *4*(1), 74–83. https://doi.org/10.1037/a0017829

Brooks, S. K., Dunn, R., Amlot, R., Greenberg, N., & Rubin, G. J. (2016). Social and occupational factors associated with psychological distress and disorder among disaster responders: A systematic review. *BMC Psychology*, *4*, 18. https://doi.org/10.1186/s40359-016-0120-9

Brooks, S. K., Dunn, R., Sage, C. A., Amlot, R., Greenberg, N., & Rubin, G. J. (2015). Risk and resilience factors affecting the psychological wellbeing of individuals deployed in humanitarian relief roles after a disaster. *Journal of Mental Health, 24*(6), 385–413. https://doi.org/10.3109/09638237.2015.1057334

Brown, J. T. (Coordinator) et al. (2015, May 13). *Deployable federal assets supporting domestic disaster response operations: Summary and considerations for congress*. CRS Report R43560. Washington, DC: Congressional Research Services. https://sgp.fas.org/crs/homesec/R43560.pdf

Centre for Research on the Epidemiology of Disasters (CRED). (2021). *International Disaster Database (EM-DAT)*. www.emdat.be/

Commonwealth of Massachusetts. (2018). *An Act relative to critical incident intervention by emergency service providers. S.2663, The 190th General Court (2017–2018)*. Retrieved April 4, 2021, from https://malegislature.gov/Bills/190/S2633/BillHistory

Cook, L. (2001). The World Trade Center attack: The paramedic response: An insider's view. *Critical Care, 5*(6), 1–3.

Courtois, C. A., & Ford, J. D. (2016). *Treatment of complex trauma: A sequence, relationship-based approach*. New York: Guildford Press.

Cristea, I. A., Legge, E., Prosperi, M., Guazzelli, M., David, D., Gentili, C. (2014). Moderating effects of empathic concern and personal distress on the emotional reactions of disaster volunteers. *Disasters, 38*(4), 740–752. https://doi.org/10.1111/disa.12075

Delongis, B., Kessler, R., & Wethington, E. (1989). The contagion of stress across multiple roles. *Journal of Marriage & Family, 51*(1), 175–183. https://doi.org/10.2307/352378

DeWolfe, D. J. (2000). *Training manual for mental health and human service workers in major disasters* (2nd ed.). Rockville, MD: US Department of Health and Human Services, Center for Mental Health Services.

Doka, K. J., & Martin, T. L. (2011). Grieving styles: Gender and grief. *Grief Matters, 14*(2), 42–45.

Dumas, T., & Sanchez-Burks, J. (2017, October 31). The professional, the personal, and the ideal worker: Pressures and objectives shaping the boundary between life domains. *Academy of Management Annals, 9*(1). https://doi.org/10.5465/19416520.2015.1028810

Edelwich, J., & Brodsky, A. (1980). *Burn-out—stages of disillusionment in the helping professions*. New York: Human Sciences Press.

Erikson, K. (1976). *Everything in its path: Destruction of a community in the Buffalo Creek flood*. New York: Simon & Schuster.

Feuer, B. (2021). First responder peer support: An evidence-informed approach. *Journal of Police and Criminal Psychology*. https://doi.org/10.1007/s11896-020-09420-z

Figley, C. R. (1995). *Compassion fatigue: Coping with secondary traumatic stress disorder in those who treat the traumatized*. New York: Brunner/Mazel.

Figley, C. R. (2001). *Gift from within—PTSD resources for survivors and caregivers*. Retrieved May 26, 2021, from www.giftfromwithin.org/html/What-isCompassion-Fatigue-Dr-Charles-Figley.html

Figley, C. R. (Ed.). (2002). *Treating compassion fatigue*. Philadelphia, PA: Brunner/Routledge.

Figley, C. R. (2003). Fishing lessons for treating the traumatized: History of the traumatology certification program. *Traumatology, 9*(4), 187–192.

Gin, J. L., Kranke, D., Saia, R., & Dobalian, A. (2016). Disaster preparedness in homeless residential organizations in Los Angeles County: Identifying needs, assessing gaps. *Natural Hazards Review*, *17*(1), 04015022.

Goldmann, E., & Galea, S. (2014). Mental health consequences of disasters. *Annual Review of Public Health*, *35*, 169–183. https://doi.org/10.1146/annurev-publhealth-032013-182435

Greinacher, A., Derezza-Greeven, C., Herzog, W., & Nikendei, C. (2019). Secondary traumatization in first responders: A systematic review. *European Journal of Psychotraumatology*, *10*(1). https://doi.org/10.1080/20008198.2018.1562840

Haugen, P., McCrillis, A., Smid, G., & Nijdam, M. (2017). Mental health stigma and barriers to mental health care for first responders: A systematic review and meta-analysis. *Journal of Psychiatric Research*, *94*, 218–229.

International Federation of Red Cross and Red Crescent Societies (ICRC). (2021). *What is a disaster*? Retrieved February 16, 2021, from www.ifrc.org/en/what-we-do/disaster-management/about-disasters/what-is-a-disaster/

Jahnke, S. A., Gist, R., Poston, W. S. C., & Haddock, C. K. (2014). Behavioral health interventions in the fire service: Stories from the firehouse. *Journal of Workplace Behavioral Health*, *29*(2), 113–126.

Javidi, H., & Yadollahie, M. (2012). Post-traumatic stress disorder. *Journal of Occupational and Environmental Medicine*, *3*(1), 2–9.

Kahill, S. (1988). Symptoms of professional burnout: A review of the empirical evidence. *Canadian Psychology*, *29*(3), 284–297. https://doi.org/10.1037/h0079772.

Keenan, P., & Royle, E. (2008). Vicarious trauma and first responders: A case study utilising Eye Movement Desensitisation and Reprocessing (EMDR) as the primary treatment modality. *International Journal of Emergency Mental Health*, *9*(4), 291–298.

Keenan, P., Royle, L., & Farrell, D. (2009). Issues of stigma for first responders accessing support for post traumatic stress. *International Journal of Emergency Mental Health*, *11*(2), 1–7.

Kranke, D., Weiss, E. L., Gin, J., Der-Martirosan, C., Constantine Brown, J. L., Saia, R., & Dobalian, A. (2017a). A "culture of compassionate bad asses"": A qualitative study of combat veterans engaging in peer-led disaster relief and utilizing cognitive restructuring to mitigate mental health stigma. *Best Practices in Mental Health*, *13*(1), 20–33.

Kranke, D., Weiss, E. L., Heslin, K. C., & Dobalian, A. (2017b) "We are disaster response experts": A qualitative study on the mental health impact of volunteering in disaster settings among combat veterans. *Social Work in Public Health*, *32*(8), 500–509. doi:10.1080/19371918.2017.1365033

Lachman, V. (2016). Compassion fatigue as a threat to ethical practice: Identification, personal and workplace prevention/management strategies. *MedSurg Nursing*, *25*(4), 275–278.

Lainie, R., Gable, L., & Links, J. M. (2011). Protecting the mental health of first responders: Legal and ethical considerations. *Journal of Law, Medicine and Ethics*, *39*(s1), 56–59. https://doi.org/10.1111/j.1748-720X.2011.00567.x

Lanza, A., Roysircar, G., & Rodgers, S. (2018). First responder mental healthcare: Evidence-based prevention, postvention, and treatment. *Professional Psychology: Research and Practice*, *49*(3), 193–204.

Lucchini, R. G., Hashim, D., Acquilla, S., Basanets, A., Bertazzi, P. A., Bushmanov, A., . . . Todd, A. C. (2017). A comparative assessment of major international disasters: The need for exposure assessment, systematic emergency preparedness, and lifetime health care. *BMC Public Health*, *17*(1), 1–12.

Macpherson, R. I. S., & Burkle, F. M. (2021). Humanitarian aid workers: The forgotten first responders. *Prehospital and Disaster Medicine*, *36*(1), 111–114. https://doi.org/10.1017/S1049023X20001326

Mao, X., Fung, O. W. M., Hu, X., & Loke, A. Y. (2018). Psychological impacts of disaster on rescue workers: A review of the literature. *International Journal of Disaster Risk Reduction*, *27*, 602–617.

Marmar, C. R., McCaslin, S. E., Metzler, T. J., Best, S., Weiss, D. S., Fagan, J., . . . Neylan, T. (2006). Predictors of posttraumatic stress in police and other first responders. *Annals of the New York Academy of Sciences*, *1071*, 1–18. https://doi.org/10.1196/annals.1364.001

Maslach, C., & Leiter, M. P. (2016). Understanding the burnout experience: Recent research and its implications for psychiatry. *World Psychiatry*, *15*(2), 103–111.

Matthews, L. T., & Marwit, S. J. (2006). Meaning reconstruction in the context of religious coping: Rebuilding the shattered assumptive world. *OMEGA-Journal of Death and Dying*, *53*(1), 87–104.

McCormack, L. (2017). Psychological wellbeing as a priority throughout the deployment cycle. *Prehospital and Disaster Medicine*, *32*(S1), S175. https://doi.org/10.1017/S1049023X1700468X

Neimeyer, R. (2000). Narrative disruptions in the construction of the self. In R. A. Neimeyer & J. D. Raskin (Eds.), *Constructions of disorder: Meaning-making frameworks for psychotherapy* (pp. 207–242). Washington, DC: American Psychological Association.

Pan American Health Organization. (2019). *Mass casualty management system. Course manual*. Washington, DC: PAHO.

Parmar, A. (2019). Ethics of emergency preparedness. Issues in planning for patient care during disasters. *Harvard Medical School Center for Bioethics*. Retrieved May 31, 2021, from https://bioethics.hms.harvard.edu/journal/ethics-disaster-healthcare

Payne, A., & McManus, J. G. (2020). Psychological consequences: Responders and community. In *Operational and medical management of explosive and blast incidents* (pp. 611–622). Cham: Springer.

Pearlman, L., Wortman, C., Feuer, C., Farber, C., & Rando, T. (2014). Sudden, traumatic death, and traumatic bereavement. In *Treating traumatic bereavement: A practitioner's guide* (pp. 3–17). New York: Guillford Press.

Prati, G., & Pietrantoni, L. (2010). The relation of perceived and received social support to mental health among first responders: A meta-analytic review. *Journal of Community Psychology*, *38*(3), 403–417.

ProQOL Introduction. Retrieved May 18, 2021, from https://proqol.org/Home_Page.php

Radey, M., & Figley, C. R. (2007). The social psychology of compassion. *Clinical Social Work Journal*, *35*, 207–214. https://doi.org/10.1007/s10615-007-0087-3

Regehr, C., & Millar, D. (2007). Situation critical: High demand, low control, and low support in paramedic organizations. *Traumatology*, *13*(1), 49–58. https://doi.org/10.1177/1534765607299912

Rutkow, L., Gable, L., & Links, J. (2011). Protecting the mental health of first responders: Legal and ethical considerations. *Journal of Law, Medicine & Ethics*, *39*(S1), 56–59. https://doi.org/10.1111/j.1748-720X.2011.00567.x

Sander-Staudt, M. Ethics of care. *Internet Encyclopedia of Philosophy*. Retrieved May 31, 2021, from https://iep.utm.edu/care-eth/

Stamm, B. H. (2002). Measuring compassion satisfaction as well as fatigue: Developmental history of the compassion satisfaction and fatigue test. In C. R. Figley (Ed.), *Treating compassion fatigue* (pp. 107–119). Brunner-Routledge. www.researchgate.net/publication/232476002_Measuring_compassion_satisfaction_as_well_as_fatigue_Developmental_history_of_the_Compassion_Satisfaction_and_Fatigue_Test

Stamm, B. H. (2016, January 16). *The secondary effects of helping others: A comprehensive bibliography of 2,017 scholarly publications using the terms compassion fatigue, compassion satisfaction, secondary traumatic stress, vicarious traumatization, vicarious transformation and ProQOL*. https://proqol.org/uploads/CF-CS-VT-ProQOL_Term_References_Posted_1-16-2016.pdf

Substance Abuse and Mental Health Services Administration (SAMHSA). (2018). SAMHSA first responders: Behavioral health concerns, emergency response, and trauma. *Disaster Technical Assistance Center Supplemental Research Bulletin*. Rockville, MD. https://www.samhsa.gov/sites/default/files/dtac/supplementalresearchbulletin-firstresponders-may2018.pdf

Substance Abuse and Mental Health Services Administration (SAMHSA). (2021). *Disaster responder stress management*. www.samhsa.gov/dtac/disaster-response-template-toolkit/disaster-responder-stress-management#:~:text=This%20podcast%20by%20SAMHSA%20DTAC,structures%20and%20self%2Dcare%20practices.

Tedeschi, R. G., & Calhoun, L. G. (1996). The posttraumatic growth inventory: Measuring the positive legacy of trauma. *Journal of Traumatic Stress*, *9*, 455–471. https://doi.org/10.1007/BF02103658

Thompson, A., Vaughan, A., & Pearce, L. (2017). Perceptions of psychosocial on behavioural responses in emergency operations centres. *International Journal of Mass Emergencies and Disasters*, *35*(1), 61–83.

Thormar, S. B., Gersons, B. P. R., Juen, B., Marschang, A., Djakababa, M. N., & Olff, M. (2010). The mental health impact of volunteering in a disaster setting: A review. *The Journal of Nervous and Mental Disease*, *198*(8), 529–538.

Tol, W. A., & van Ommeren, M. (2012). Evidence-based mental health and psychosocial support in humanitarian settings: Gaps and opportunities. *Evidence-Based Mental Health*, *15*, 25–26.

Tracy, M., Norris, F. H., & Galea, S. (2011). Differences in the determinants of posttraumatic stress disorder and depression after a mass traumatic event. *Depression and Anxiety*, *28*(8), 666–675.

US Congress (116th-2019-2020). *H.R. 1646 Helping Emergency Responders Overcome Act (HERO Act)*. www.congress.gov/bill/116th-congress/house-bill/1646

US Department of Emergency Management. (2019). *Emergency management program policy, responsibilities, and requirements. Departmental Manual, Emergency Management Program, Series 900*. Washington, DC: United States Department of the Interior.

US Department of Homeland Security. (2021, January). *Surge capacity force*. Retrieved April 4, 2021, from www.dhs.gov/surge-capacity-force

Walsh, F. (2007). Traumatic loss and major disasters: Strengthening family and community resilience. *Family Process*, *46*(2), 207–227. https://doi.org/10.1111/j.1545-5300.2007.00205.x

Williams, J., Nocera, M., & Casteel, C. (2008). The effectiveness of disaster training for health care workers: A systematic review. *Annals of Emergency Medicine*, *52*(3), 211–222.

Yassen, J. (1995). Prevention of secondary traumatic stress in individuals. In *Compassion fatigue: Secondary traumatic stress disorder from treating the traumatized*. New York: Brunner/Mazel.

NOTES

1. "The moral theory known as 'the ethics of care' implies that there is moral significance in the fundamental elements of relationships and dependencies in human life" (Sander-Staudt, 2021).
2. "[A] disaster relief social service organization with the mission of uniting the skills and experiences of military Veterans with first responders to rapidly deploy emergency response teams" (Kranke et al., 2017b).

CHAPTER 23

Concluding Thoughts and Lessons Learned

In compiling the chapters in this book, the editors sought to bring advice from people who have all worked in wildfire situations. From these perspectives, we felt that there are three areas that we would like to highlight in our concluding remarks. These areas are (1) the need for preparation at many levels prior to any incident in order to facilitate an effective and efficient response, (2) collaboration and the formation of multidisciplinary teams make for smoother recovery and increase the chances of making positive identifications of fatalities, and (3) open lines of communication in many directions are essential. All three areas interdigitate, so they cannot be tackled separately.

The ultimate goal of any wildfire recovery where there have been fatalities is to prevent information from being lost through inappropriate actions. Such will delay the resolution of the identification, and instead of a positive identification, we may be left with basing the determination simply on circumstantial evidence—possibly generating unsettling questions for the family and friends.

In this section, we would like to present our thoughts on these three areas and then add some of our own reflections on the impact of wildfires on those who work on them. This volume involved both first and last responders—yet it is unlikely any will say that working on such fires has not changed the way they see their communities, their families, their homes, and their lives.

23.1 PREPARATION

A recurring theme throughout this volume is the need for preparation. Wildfires are such truly devastating and disruptive events that trying to marshal resources while dealing with the total chaos of evacuations and fire containment is exceptionally difficult. Emergency plans should be reviewed and the eventuality of a wildfire added into the possible causes of that emergency. The impact of that fire should not be underestimated, from the massive need for fire crews, air support, access to remote areas, and hard decisions on what is savable and what can be lost to how to safely evacuate thousands or even hundreds of thousands of people along with their pets and livestock and maintain that evacuation until sufficient recovery has occurred that they can begin to return is no minor undertaking.

While both law enforcement and fire crews often have sufficient equipment and well-developed master mutual aid programs to acquire more if needed, the same may not hold true for other groups. Are the search and rescue teams trained to recognize human remains? Do they have the training on how to approach a search? Do they have

DOI: 10.4324/9781003168010-28

protective gear to deal with search areas that are still smoldering and scattered with dangerous material? Do the recovery teams have enough screens, and are they of the correct mesh size to recover the small fragments found in the aftermath of a fire? What will be expected of the coroner teams, and do they have the recording equipment? Can the command center monitor and track the location of all these units that may be operating outside of normal law enforcement or fire channels? Clearly preparation in this area is not simply an intra-agency function but one that also requires meetings with cooperating agencies and individuals to get the broad spectrum of needs.

It is also highly recommended that specialized resources, such as anthropologists, odontologists, DNA specialists, and SAR/USAR teams trained in burned material be identified and linked into the emergency plans. While the SAR/USAR teams work within an established network for mutual aid, many of the others do not. Some work as private practitioners, while others may have a university or college affiliation. As such, their access to "disaster service worker" status is questionable, and it is that status that provides the coverage of worker's compensation. In other words, the lead agency may have exactly the right type of trained professionals identified but be unable to deploy them due to liability concerns. It is also essential to know if those who "volunteer" have the skills to complete the work and the temperament to face the rigors of the task.

For this volume's core case study of the Camp Fire, it is clear how the prior relationships were critical to a smooth transition. Butte County had to deal with a massive fire that required the inclusion of a number of agencies. Subsequent fires also expanded across county lines and even, in some cases, state lines. Preparing for this possibility makes these developments less daunting.

Butte County had a historic relationship with the anthropological team of Chico State University, which allowed for a quick mobilization of recovery teams. However, accessing additional anthropologists required rapid development of an EMAC agreement with Nevada. Advance preparation allows the lead agency to approach the difficult task of body recovery thoughtfully. Moving into this activity without having the properly trained search teams and recovery teams has the potential of destroying vital information.

23.2 COLLABORATION

Almost every chapter in this book reiterates the importance of collaboration. This concept is essential in the administration of the response from fire, law enforcement, emergency management, and investigations. Each agency has its responsibility and knows how to "stay in one's lane" while contributing to the shared vision. Wildfires are particularly dynamic, requiring a flow of leadership to match the flow of the events.

In a fatal wildfire, collaboration improves efficiency of recovery and the identification process, maximizing the number and quality of the human remains retrieved and also including potentially identifying artifacts, such as surgical sutures, pacemaker wires, and orthopedic implants. However, these teams need significant support in terms of dispatch coordination, coroner's documentation, and local agencies to help with navigation and access. In fact, their work would be immensely harder without this support and the identification process would also bear an impact.

While many are willing to pitch in to help, it is critical to know when to reach out to others for help. There is a tendency in such events to want to hold on to control, but we must be realistic about our own limitations. Wildfires are not short-term events and even the initial phases of containment, mop-up, and repopulation will take weeks—without considering the impact of fatalities. How much can personnel in the field handle before the toll becomes too much? There are others willing to help, and if the preparations are in place, then they will come with the needed resources and trust.

Listening to different voices also sets the stage for forward thinking. This point has been stressed in all aspects from disaster management to post-recovery analysis. Because recovery is itself a destructive process, what is done at one step will have an impact on all subsequent steps. For that reason, understanding what will be needed by later stages is essential for a smooth operation. This "forward thinking" approach prevents information from being lost and is well worth the small amount of additional time it takes to do in the first place.

23.3 OPEN LINES OF COMMUNICATION

Careful attention to maintaining open lines of communication is essential. While providing solid information in a communication takes time, like collaboration and forward-thinking, it pays in the long term. In the management of the incident, it is important for all team members to be on the same page and communicate that outward to all the response operations and also to the public.

For the public, it is reassuring to see that the response is a coordinated message in which each function is being capably performed. As members of the public who live in fire zones, the editors can attest to the value of the daily press conferences. These efforts reassure the public that they are being informed, where to find the maps, what to expect in the short term, and what steps need to happen before evacuated but unaffected areas can be repopulated. The public does not often have a clear image of (1) the devastation that occurs in a wildfire and (2) how much work must be done to make it safe for repopulation. Let them know what it takes, and they will be more accepting of the time lag.

The open lines of communication also relate to the retention and transfer of knowledge during the course of the response. To some extent, in the initial phase, this continuity comes because the same people are usually in place. However, this is not a sustainable practice so communication between shifts is important. Within the ICS system, this is built-in. For those whose involvement may be less formally structured, documenting what has been done, what has worked, where there are problems, and how to care for the team is often information that is lost as one crew leaves and another arrives. Where possible, documentation of decisions is highly recommended

One phenomenon that was especially apparent with the Camp Fire was the enormous number of people who were reported missing. In the initial days, these reports were being filed with many agencies until the Sheriff's Office amalgamated all the inquiries. This combined list was so large, well over a thousand people, that there was considerable shock. However, clear communication that this included people—who likely had evacuated, who had left the area long ago, who may have never lived within the area of the fire's footprint, or who were simply duplications of other inquiries—helped calm not only the public but also the agencies involved.

Finally, we strongly encourage those involved in wildfires, or any type of mass disaster, to publish their approaches. We do not need to keep reinventing the wheel with each event. Let us build upon what is learned each time.

23.4 CHANGING WORLDVIEW OF FIRST AND LAST RESPONDER

We would like to close with a brief discussion of how wildfires have affected those involved long after the event. In such disasters, searchers and recovery teams see a landscape where most indications of life have been obliterated. Occasionally there will be a house, or a shed, or a carport that is untouched but usually there is only a pile of charcoal and ash, a chimney, a foundation, and the remnants of burned appliances. We become attuned to that expectation so deeply that returning to unburned areas is often disturbing. It is as if the unburned area is the abnormal place rather than the fire zone.

Because of this distortion of worldview, we recognize that awareness of your own mental health is important. We enter the fire zone with a set of expectations that often fail to match the reality. This discord can lead to a situation where you can make poor decisions in the field. It can also have lasting impacts. Debriefings and subsequent care should be more of an expectation rather than being seen as trivial or a failure of character.

For those of us who are directly involved in recovery of human remains, people worry about how such gruesome work will affect us. For the most part, burned remains are significantly less unpleasant than many of the decomposing remains upon which we often work. However, in wildfires, we do see how people face final moments. We can imagine their terror, even when they had accepted their fate. We can see ourselves in such circumstances, and that is the disturbing part.

As we return to our normal lives, wildfire has changed how we see our own homes and our communities. If we live in more WUI areas, we automatically classify neighboring houses as to which are likely to survive. As we drive around, we assess the escapability of roads, where people are likely to be trapped due to limited egress, and wonder where people can flee when fires move quickly. We assume that most homes will be completely destroyed. We see how even those who try to prepare their homes for that event greatly underestimate the power of a wildfire. We try to convey that but the immensity is hard to depict.

For all those involved, we face the annual and lengthening fire season with a different kind of dread. It is not just that there will be the inconvenience of smoke or evacuation or even the fear that we will lose our own homes but that people can die and we will be picking up their remains—yet again seeing how they chose to face their deaths.

Index

Note: Page locators in **bold** indicate a table. Page locators in *italics* indicate a figure.

For Product Safety Concerns and Information please contact our EU representative GPSR@taylorandfrancis.com Taylor & Francis Verlag GmbH, Kaufingerstraße 24, 80331 München, Germany